**Books and Small Press Editions
by Anne Waldman**

On the Wing

O My Life!

Up Through the Years

Giant Night: Selected Poems

Baby Breakdown

Icy Rose

No Hassles

Memorial Day (with Ted Berrigan)

Spin Off

The West Indies Poems

Self-Portrait (with Joe Brainard)

Life Notes: Selected Poems

The Contemplative Life

Fast Speaking Woman

Sun the Blonde Out

Fast Speaking Woman and Other Chants

Journals & Dreams

Hotel Room

Shaman / Shamane (German translation
by Jürgen Schmidt)

To a Young Poet

Polar Ode (with Eileen Myles)

Four Travels (with Reed Bye)

Sphinxeries (with Denyse Du Roi)

Countries

Cabin

First Baby Poems

Makeup on Empty Space

Invention (with Susan Hall)

Skin Meat Bones

Blue Mosque

The Romance Thing

Den Monde in Farbe Sehen
(German translation by Rolf Bruck)
Tell Me About It: Poems for Painters

Helping the Dreamer:
New & Selected Poems

Her Story (with Elizabeth Murray)

Not a Male Pseudonym

Lokapala

Fait Accompli

Troubairitz

Iovis I: All Is Full of Jove

Kill or Cure

Fast Speaking Woman
(20th Anniversary Edition)

Kin (with Susan Rothenberg)

Homage to Allen G.
(with George Schneeman)

Iovis II: Guardian & Scribe

Polemics (with Anselm Hollo
& Jack Collom)

One Voice in Four Parts
(with Richard Tuttle)

La Donna Che Parla Veloce (Italian trans-
lation by Elena Tartagli, Ilaria Mugnaini,
and Antonio Bertoli)

Young Manhattan (with Bill Berkson)

Marriage: A Sentence

Fast Speaking Woman (Czech translation
by Pavla Jonssonová, Eva Klimentová,
and Martin Machovec)

Vow to Poetry: Essays, Interviews,
& Manifestos

Au Lit / Holy (with Eleni Sikelianos
& Laird Hunt)

Troubairitz (German translation
by Bernhard Widder)

War Crime

[Things] Seen Unseen

Dark Arcana / Afterimage or Glow

In the Room of Never Grieve:
New & Selected Poems

Zombie Dawn (with Tom Clark)

Structure of the World
Compared to a Bubble

Fleuve Flâneur (with Mary Kite)

Outrider

Red Noir

Manatee / Humanity

THE IOVIS TRILOGY

THE IOVIS TRILOGY

Colors in the Mechanism of Concealment

ANNE WALDMAN

COFFEE HOUSE PRESS

MINNEAPOLIS 2011

COPYRIGHT © 1993, 1994, 1995, 1996, 1997, 2011 by Anne Waldman.
COVER DESIGN Linda Koutsky
BOOK DESIGN Coffee House Press
AUTHOR PHOTO © Gary Fuchs

COVER IMAGE
The witch Rangda, approx. 1800–1900. Indonesia; Bali. Painted wood.
Gift of Thomas Murray in memory of his father Eugene T. Murray, 2000.37.
© Asian Art Museum of San Francisco. Used by permission.

Coffee House Press books are available to the trade through our primary
distributor, Consortium Book Sales & Distribution, www.cbsd.com or
(800) 283-3572. For personal orders, catalogs, or other information, write
to: info@coffeehousepress.org.
   Coffee House Press is a nonprofit literary publishing house.
Support from private foundations, corporate giving programs, govern-
ment programs, and generous individuals helps make the publication
of our books possible. We gratefully acknowledge their support in
detail in the back of this book.
   To you and our many readers around the world,
   we send our thanks for your continuing support.

LIBRARY OF CONGRESS CIP INFORMATION
Waldman, Anne, 1945–
The Iovis trilogy : colors in the mechanism of concealment :
poetry / by Anne Waldman.
p. cm.
ISBN 978-1-56689-255-1 (alk. paper)
I. Title.
PS3573.A4215I55 2011
811'.54—DC22

PRINTED IN THE UNITED STATES
1 3 5 7 9 8 6 4 2
FIRST EDITION | FIRST PRINTING

FRONTISPIECE
John Marvin Waldman with the author.
Washington Square Park, New York City, 1945.

for Ambrose Eyre Bye

&

to the

I was a hidden treasure and I loved to be known
so I created the world.

> —*Hadith qudsi,*
> attributed to God
> by Mohammed

"Give it a rest Zeus."

> —Hera speaking,
> Lucan

The Iovis Trilogy

BOOK I
⟋ All Is Full of Jove ⟍

BOOK II
～ Guardian & Scribe ～

BOOK III

~ Eternal War ~

Anew

Will you help me build my Ardhanarisvara, the androgynous city? I'm at it a long time. A new-beyond-gender *fecund horizon?* Will you help rebuild a psyche—or world, in a poem? The idea for *epikos Iovis* was to shoulder/abdicate patriarchy. And actualize, as Rimbaud prophesies, how women discover the unknown. *She will discover strange things, unfathomable, repulsive, delicious, we will take them, we will understand them.* But will they . . . and what then? Oppositional discontinuity, the imperfect present. Am I known or perpetually unknown? But she had to push, push through had had to push through, through . . . and against the darkness . . . and speak out from within her personal narrative.

And Rimbaud's voyelles came back to her, also, coded with colors. And continue her narration of a time, born at the end of World War II, and of being called to a poetry tribe, a way of being in the world, a gentle yet activist alternative, utopic in essence, a cultural intervention into public space . . . peregrinations . . . hermaphrodism . . . performance . . . mother/loverhood . . . Buddhism . . . feminism, and guardianship of the archive, which embodies/emboldens technologies of inscription and psychic processes. Investigative travel often fired the text and shifted frequencies to greater fellaheen and more Asian climes.

Ambrose the child becoming youth in the process was the guide, then young man who put some of these texts to music, folding his ear to her poem. He had said midway, you are making *another* book called *Iovis?* That's pathetic Mom, can't you think of another title? How about "Son of Iovis," how about "Daughter of Iovis"? She thought of his need to deterritorialize the sounds of the mother.

And she also thought of the women she'd like to put in a special circle of hell.

Iovis, of the Roman *Jove,* of Zeus, of the Greek *father,* the possessive form whose deeds are legion and whose legend was the charge, was the initial mechanism in which to investigate unspeakable aggression. This mythopoetic epic at start was to take on the manifestations of patriarchy in writing-tracking, tracing, documenting—over a quarter of a century, see how the woman poet-mind would fare & flow in late twentieth-/early twenty-first-century rhetoric, dis-a-vowels, tantric magics, energy, temperature, density. Pushing the Big Bang theory to even earlier shores. The whole of the universe inside a golden nugget. String theory that moves into eleven directions of space, old Buddhist adage of simultaneity. And Planck length or time, which is a hundred billion billion times smaller than an atomic universe. And—what?—eliminate the notice of space and time altogether? Perhaps.

A universe modeled on a tabernacle. Too limited, the quadrangular. It's a rounder rounder world . . . rounder universe(s). Bubbling up as of a roiling sea. And to understand the origin in poetry, that is my continued consciousness, a meandering investigation. A self-same life.

Eratosthemes, Eudoxius, Euclid, Plato all knew the earth was round and Origen, Bishop Ambrose, Albertus Magnus, were certain of this in a scholastic age. Is this twenty-first century a scholastic age? You decide. My head is round my mind is round my mouth is round my thought is round. And the influence of progressive thinking a "roguer round": what roves a round comes a round. A tougher ruffled roving aroused round mind.

I wanted to be a name-giver, a *nomothete,* but honor the endless confusio linguarum. And the irreparable: *that which cannot be undone.*

Also abjure cultural pillage, colonization, the "take" as in "on the take" of the pillaging male. And mock him.

But ultimately honor an exchange of more generous image and sound. Add other voices that inform and infuse a life.

But what about conquest? Where Culture A cannot recognize Culture B. Gist of war, a brute politics. Can you *see* me?

But I will represent astonishment
I will display my almond-shaped eye
My mouth of flowers

Poor Helen in *Iliad* 6 remarks on her "vile destiny" and Zeus's curse of fame that with her beloved Paris they "shall be made into things of song for men of the future."

And Hesiod in *Works and Days* invokes

Pierian muses, who give glory through song, come here, sing in me Zeus, hymning your father, by whom mortals are either unmentioned or mentioned, spoken of, made famous, or not, by the will of Zeus.

So poem is the song *in spite of* the will of Zeus. Blast him, and that willpower played out as it is doing now, twenty-first-century fix. I'll be the gray-eyed Athena, clear-sighted through his fog of war.

"Colors in the Mechanism of Concealment" became the rubric for the continuing *Iovis* project after the U.S. invasion of Afghanistan, which began on October 7, 2001. I watched the shock and awe of Operation Enduring Freedom begin on CNN in a small room in Umbria seated next to Nicaragua's activist priest-poet Ernesto Cardenal. Colors in the mechanism of concealment. We could hear warplanes taking off from Aviano in darkest night.

The title emboldened a feminist agenda toward further deterritorialization. The weapons that change colors and glint in the sun, protective armor never enough and rarely arriving for the War Culture, the mechanisms that keep us from ourselves . . . that may only be studied by stateless-women-people. Some of the cluster bomblets are brightly colored to increase their visibility and resemble the yellow humanitarian packages also dropped from the sky. Imagine your own child . . .

Tectonic plates had shifted to reveal an even deeper fissure in the body politic. Pink or blue? Red state/blue state. It was a title to live deep inside of, investigate from within. Before sleep I would count the colors of the day and images of plunder and horror. A Buddhist assignment—*tonglen*—a sending and receiving practice where one takes in what suffers and breathes out the efficacy of that suffering. "In" dissolves into white, "out" into black. The people "we" fought were dark. Turn that around.

What were the colors—the *rasas* or flavors—the tastes inside the tastes within the profound concealment of the patriarchy within the patriarchy we were all still crazily undergoing? More war? Because my long life has always undergone war patriarchy. What was the induced patriarchal palpable war trace? Traveling to Viet Nam at the close of the twentieth century (twenty-fifth anniversary of the end of the war), my sense of mission deepened as I sought out people—a generation—of my own age and time. Those few I saw were aready concealed in death . . . concealed in history. Old and maimed or born after the "American war." Secret plans afoot felt everywhere in that part of the world, perceived as a playground for a strange new contract with America. Military bases, secret detention centers, dark torture sites . . . strategy to have our struggling imperial imprint close to China's border. Ever-rising China.

Concealment is the active ingredient in maintenance of the Spectacle of the State. Everything became a color within an agenda of concealment. Continued examination—investigating, gathering, tasting, participating in all its hues—became my further practice. The incipient insidious unrelenting details and responses—tick by tick—of pathological war culture, the dismembering dis-remembering deeds of an out-of-control system, mismanaged, just same old robber baron grab mentality. Yet Urizenic mindset with its irreversible mitiga-tion-propagation-snarling-release of toxicity: psychological and literal. Harm to others, and to other species of life on the planet, has been unconscionable and heartbreaking.

Citizen of the u.s. of a. needs to be perpetually vigilant as investigator of the dark acts and mechanisms of war, needs to call out perpetrators, and those who deny accountability or go into throes of amnesia when faced with the harm they inflict. As citizen, culpable as taxpayer, as one who votes and frets about our children coming home from war crazed and suicidal. Or maybe this prac-tice, this trace, leads to anarchy, nihilism.

But as Buddhist anarchist, where do you stand: perpetually outside? It thrives in technicolor, this theater of war. So a ruse ('cause you can't buck karma): the twenty-first century was to have known better, we, born on the cusp, end of wwii, imagined, was to have been a halcyon time, a potential for spiritual awak-ening. Or was it? What was concealed, what revealed? Push-pull dynamic of the text its hardwired *modus* of operation. The Roman gives way to the Asian to the Arab as the dynamics shift. The base of an Ionic column taken from the Temple of Artemis at Sardis in Lydia is conjured here to lend support as it shifts to Ottoman Turkey. At the Topkapi Museum I saw the hair and fingernails of a sultan that one might revere—they say he wrote a mean poetry.

Destroy the relics of the patriarch? No, no we need them in the archive.

How do the events *outside* in deed reflect the personal evolution of a psyche *inside,* caught in the crevices of a bad dream?

Nazis and Stasi down, the capital of China and Russia on the move. Missile base blueprints on hold in Eastern Europe but Viet Nam next. Ambitious plans for southeast Asia in the theater of war, and ever-more elaborate weapons in space. What new pacts with the devil? A new leadership at the crossroads who will make his more brief, compassionate mark or be held hostage . . . we pray for his long life and well-being as he navigates the spectacle of the state. And we say get us the hell out of Afghanistan.

Orality of intention—in that one needs often to vocalize the words and ideas and nuances and colors of energy states. They are seen as modal structures or mantras of consciousness that are in ethical opposition to war cant, euphemism, and a language of dominance that instills fear instead of negotiating for a wise view of the future. Red for passion, green for action, dark blue the color of intellect, yellow for generosity, white for equanimity, black for primordial beauty and wisdom. The five Buddha families ignite the colors of wisdom.

If you sing you may distract the assassin's energies just long enough to move the century forward a few meager inches.

Epic's parts in a woman's poem made with urgency always breathe a transitive air, unwilling to be subjugated. And kept her child voice, and voice written for a child.

Colors and how they might move us through prisms of language and light. See the glow of the world around us, luminous particles and syllables. Hurry hurry, make haste make haste, don't tarry don't tarry.

Perseid Showers, Abiquiu, Year of the Ox

BOOK I

All Is Full
of Jove

BOOK I

~ All Is Full of Jove ~

Both, Both: An Introduction

Today I write in the context of four white walls. I woke to overcast sky. I stayed up late last night. The night was still. I could think clearly again extracting myself from the child's voice: demand and interruption. And yet I had the notes of his contribution to the long poem, which he had sung out in the car outside Telluride. It was a list for the guardianship of plutonium, all the coverings to encase it: "one of every single stone in the world, pennies, quarters, everything" or "play dough—dried, and dead peoples' bones, and then there's plain dead people with nothing on them."

Last night I had nibbled at the psychotropic mushrooms and was lying in the grass in the yard waiting for the near-full moon to rise. I was counting the "fathers" I had known in consideration of the long poem, which among other things male, celebrates them. How many of them were dead now? How many of them had become stars in the sky? In any sky? I invented a list of questions for my father about World War II. What were the names of all the towns in Germany he passed through? Had he met any women in those travels? What had he told me years before O tell me again about the dead arms reaching to heavens near the Maginot Line! "Imagine O" I heard then and now. I experienced the dread of the act of making this poem for seven years and of all the men dead and alive going into it and saw them beckon to me to speak of my relationship to them in a language perhaps only I could understand. And I heard lovers, grandfathers, brothers, father-in-laws, students, husbands, son, and the friends of my son, boys, speaking to me. And persistent sound too was the sound of a bigger vatic voice inside any myth, classic archetype, any ritual sacrifice.

Then I tried to imagine my great-great-grandfather Thomas Hand, a sea captain, shipwrecked—no—lost at sea between Cape May and Liverpool delivering the south Jersey oak and pine they craved abroad. Who was he? What was the vocabulary of that boat and occupation and what tempest rocked him dead?

I feel myself always an open system (woman) available to any words or sounds I'm informed by. A name. A date. Images of war. Other languages to which the ear attunes. What you said in your letter about the praying mantis: "I brought it right up to my face and opened my mouth and it wasn't afraid" or what words go on between the nouns and verbs you choose. What phoneme exists there.

I get up and dance the poem when it sweeps into litany. I gambol with the shaman and the deer. It is a *body poetics.* I am in the context of those before me who worshipped a goddess whose eyes were mirrors. One eye reflected the "inside," the other the gorgeous and dark phenomenal world. Take your pick. Both, both. She, the muse, puts an invisible protection cord around my neck to protect me from ego. She exceeds my aspiration to disappear.

I write with the disappearing coral reef in mind and the total extinction of the dusky sparrow.

I exist in a community of my own choosing and making, which is attentive to language and poetry before language. It harbors the secret wishes of all my tears and predilections. Community is "voice." It strides the blast. So many have heard these words in earlier form, recrudescent though they be, and felt the heat and Zeus's juice. They asked this book to be. I thank them.

In the dream of "Friedrich Hegel" later the same night, Hegel, a father, was eighty-eight years old, with copious red hair and crisp spectacles. He was to perform his latest piece in a bright green meadow and he let it be known that all the women present were invited to fall in love with him. He was a philosopher-patriarch, often irresistible. He could mouth the plan or structure of a stable, composite world but would he take it apart again?

Iovis, literally *of Jove,* is the possessive case, *owned by Jove.* As well as about him, a weave.

"Iovis omnia plena," from which *Iovis* springs, is a phrase from Virgil—*all is full of Jove.* And I wanted that sense of filling up: "plerosis." How that is both a celebration and a danger. And how complex is the relationship of this poet to the energy principle that does that. In Sanskrit the masculine energy principle is "upaya," skillful means. See it everywhere. How skillful is a war in the Middle East? But how sweet is the grandfather bidding his wife purchase a sweater-coat his size in 1908. All the life I want to make things happen. Stop explaining I have to say.

And of old Rome, thinking: Empire: Rome, the meme. And of my own culture's ceaseless bullying warriorhood. Paying mercenaries to do brutal shadow work.

I honor and dance on the corpse of the poetry gone before me and especially here in a debt and challenge of epic masters Williams, Pound, Zukofsky, and Olson. But with the narrative of H.D.'s *Helen in Egypt* in mind, and her play with "argument." I want to don armor of words as they do and fight with liberated tongue and punctured heart. But unlike the men's, my history and myths are personal ones. I want and need the long poem. In one doctor's description I've "too many male hormones." Let them sprout and spurt off the page. But let it not be said she wanted to be a man. Point of view: both accommodation and scorn. And don't forget Wit, a dark fairy. She teaches a balance, redress, how to face the end of the world with dignity: make a space for her entourage. Sisters of beauty and seduction with no truck in the male poems these past years. Come out of exile, something still a real person we hope, welcomes you in.

Each section in this poem is a "take" on the last: strands, leitmotifs come back around. One friend notes—as if to see the "questions" from many—not points of view, but many scales, as in sizes/proportions. There is a structural constant in how the sections evolve: cumulative, wave effect—each self-organizing as it proceeds, thick with sperm that binds them. Fragments built on other fragments, finally organizing, one hopes, each other toward some kind of cohesive landscape. The field of Mars. May I be so bold to say these things? Narrative tags at the beginning of each section track the field-poet's steps as they thread through a maze.

Words are used here with awe, dread, submission, humor, cheek, as if they were sacred creatures—pulsating, alive, mocking. As such they are little mirrors. For this poem I summoned male images, "voices," and histories as deities out of throat, heart, gut, correspondence, and mind. Call them dakas as they set off, like seed syllables, into the sky. They are semiwrathful messengers, protectors. They're the heroes, thought forms of the theistic father and the pagan shape-shifter or boy-child-trickster of the poem. Every epic requires them. And she who sits at desk under dark spell and dances out under hot moon names them to release them.

Autumn Equinox 1989—Winter Solstice 1992

Mangala

The poet invokes the familiar Judeo-Christian patriarch, who is seductive in his humility. Her own magisterial power competes with his. He comes as sorrowful one, infects humanity with his lowness & passion. She has often felt this as "trick," as ruse designed to inspire pity, which turns to subjugation, because it is harder for they-who-think-themselves-guilty to rise again. But she remembers the Gnostic dream within the dream and the human potential for resurrection. Moment to moment the mind turns. She gets out of bed each day to greet & study the phenomenal world. And her investigation is the highest art she imagines. Moses staked a claim and held up one of the first books as emblem of rule. She will imitate, play prophet & tell allegories on judgement day as only a woman might. These are the words of a mediator, a lover. She declares her poem, the "book"—by implication holy—as a new doctrine. The world's resources depleted, too many people on the planet, how to respond? Keep writing & hope to alleviate some of the suffering.

A man of sorrows
comes in lowness
comes to me in lowness
& this humiliation becomes passion
lamb into lion
then I am in lowness
& He is the great king
& He is the bridegroom
Time, O time is at hand
& I am in lowness
& He is the great king
& I am in lowness
The dragon is Pharaoh
& I am in lowness
I eat the book in this oral philosophy
Tell old Pharaoh to let my people go
The time is at hand
(& I am in lowness)
The time is at hand in lowness
I will take his sorrowful past into my future
I will take both testaments
& transmute the mundane into heavenly music
& eat the book

The scroll is my number
& do not destroy my temple
I sing within & without the temple (it's this book the temple I speak of)
the male gods take over as electricity & dynamite
& let me preach these allegories for the last day
& we, goddesses, giddy on the last day
will preach these allegories on the last day
I will speak out of my lowness
but the messiah is a man of sorrows
& O He is a great king
but I am in my writing
& in my richness
I speak a new doctrine to an old form

                    *

old
    a yard of it
word
        go flame
to scroll of it
holy form
    no harm
say book of it
    burden, down
its glory
        made holy
writ of it
    words to
"good augury"
    but doom abound
on earth of it

aqua benedicta

splash

not brag

this hag's tongue

in *genus femininum*

be blessed bride to book

I

ALL IS FULL OF JOVE

The poet positions herself in the cosmos, already filled with the sperm of Jove who, "peoples space." She challenges his infusions. She lays out the page as battlefield, honors her ancestors, her family, and lovers past, present, future, & in all ten directions. Conversation in a taxi with Red Grooms— a painter of wry vivid eye—refashions her childhood streets. Her ear pricks up to major voices & obsessions that will return again to haunt & radicalize her poem. Her son, who is willing to magically grow up to her as she grows down to him, will be her guide. He is trickster, shape-shifter who both interrupts her & goads her on.

He catches my eye, my fancy
  October
  I ride an orange car
  The radio is sad & hopeful
 "Don't Turn Your Back on Love"
  Clouds lift higher
  & clutter the mountain
  It's in the weather everywhere
  I am helpless
  Ex Stasis
  I'm Gaia
  Father Sky look down on me
  Stars are his eyes
  He enters me
  All is full of him

What's true by excluding nothing (I can't really do this): the birthplace, the rain (40 days & 40 nights) observed from a screen porch. Cradle me in memory and make me a goddess-fearing Titan. I didn't resist & pulled my weight, a firecracker to be born in this world. And swept in the tide of this postwar boom, the child of such & such a divine mother and a father, the soul of gentleness. A plain kind of basics weep now to think of modesty in financial matters & hard facts of life, the fanatical enemy war that made sense, the war that hoped to be brought into a safer place, the letters and photographs, you can imagine, & description of dead soldier limbs lifted out of rubble (he saw this, they saw this, they all saw this) the unmitigated trouble of it, and it a mighty cause, and the children everywhere of it now, in my life, of survivors, prisoners, dead ones, tortured or heroic, what could come after this in the nuclear sense? Yet how it "ended," what is the payoff, the result of any way you look at it, those survivors too, the Japanese, and now we live in the combined karma, if I might use that word, dead sister Yoshiko, dear reader dear student, in the sense of what continues, a thread of energy perhaps is all. Which is why now I can say the poet must be a warrior of the battlefield of Mars, o give me a break, thank you very much.

No one will sign on this dotted sky line. But what is perceived is the vast body, the sky itself, coupled with earth and someone (Virgil) said: IOVIS OMNIA PLENA. All is full of Jove (his sperm presumably to people Chaos).

Whole the moon, whole the year
 tuliz U tuliz hah
whole the day, whole the night,
 tuliz ik cu ximbal xan tuliz kik xan
when they came to their beds, their mats, their thrones;
 tu kuchul tu uaob tu poopoob tu dzamob
rhythm in their reading of the good hours,
 ppiz u caxanticob yutzil kin
as they observed the good stars enter their reign,
 la tu ppiz yilcob yocolob yahaulil utzul ekob tu yahaulil
Everything was good
 Utz tun tulacal

But this is way after the feminine principle is making her mark on universal time equals space. I don't know anything, I know it all. The war is full of war and Levite laws, not tamed by laws of mercy, and Ashtoreth goes underground as women are dragged into caves. And later a cruel Gentile world. Research: intercourse with mothers & daughters (as beasts do) a dream:
Triptolemos in decline
This was after the fall of the mother earth & giants
I said this already about sweetness

I said My Father, like a small lake
"Creators" as in Greek for poets, yet nothing is created from limitless
mind
but
but this

The famous artist takes me to a hotel in a city like Portland. I'm a real red-head now, but am concerned about the Dharma test I had to take earlier & I have the distinct feeling they'll say I was being too literal when I wrote the phrase "Things as they are." I was thinking, then, on the phrase, how I wouldn't have a daughter now that I had all these "I"s. Two boy children, where did the second come from? Red is now pulling the black slip strap down. I am excited but worried about this exotic girlfriend who is brewing Vietnamese coffee in the next room. "What don't move!" He says as we're about to kiss. "Hold that stance!" He pours a bag of cement in the robin's-egg blue porcelain sink, mixing it with hot water the way you do henna. Then he picks up a little shovel in front of the fireplace and proceeds to dump the mixture over my head. It feels good and quells desire.

But this desire
is a weekend
a mere idea
I think "50 labels self-sticking"
I think how life is compounded by paper
I think how sleep tonight tomorrow you suffer
I think I'll fall in love with "all hims" all over again
Me a Woodswoman from the city of the Mill
Grandfather John a glassblower, sedate in the wind,
spectacled, pale, works hard in the Protestant ethic

Millville, New Jersey, which was the epitome of a place small
& human and at the lake the motorboat coming in at dusk.
There was a swing piano style (my father's)
& the chimney he (a father) built on the house never to
be owned ours

Millville, Feb 4, 1902

My Darling,

Yours at hand—and I would certainly have been disappointed if I had not received it. I had been resting a little since supper—as I am real tired tonight it is now nearly seven o'clock and we got to German lessons at eight. I hope you have spent two real nice pleasant days and hope the remainder of the week is or will be just the same and also that you derive lots of good from them. Now my first two days have not been so pleasant I have had some real trials nothing has went well and I feel real out of sorts tonight. I hardly know what I would have done had I not received a letter from someone very precious to me. Well our orders have been running very bad lately. I think things will come better here-after I hope so anyway. Well this is too much grumbling for you I won't complain any more.

I went out to Church last night. James wanted me to help him sing. Well they had a very good meeting. I think there were two conversions. The young man who they tried to get Sunday night his brother was converted, he was there but would not go but they think he will tonight. May McLaughlin's father was up last night. Mr. Hunter asked that the men invite all the men in the factory tonight and I think there will be a big time there. Mrs. Hunter is going to sing Memories tonight.

Well I am going to finish up on scolding. Now who said it would be good to be apart awhile I would like to know did I ever say that and mean it? Oh yes! You ought to see my mustache it's a beauty. Well darling feed up well and when you come home Sallie will soon kill the fatted calf. Don't worry about me going skating. No more for me. Remember me to all I will close and go learn a little dutch.

Yours only and truly

John W. Waldman

Admonishing students to avoid writing the grandmother
in the attic, for example, or mother too, think of Creeley &
that respect & ease
To ease the distant dead one
But the mother was hard on the father, dominating Macdougal Street you
must say "below Houston"

A: So talk a little bit about your neighborhood.

R: We're passing the new Golden Pacific National Bank, which is kind of an out-standing piece of Chinese architecture, very brand new. And it's already begin-ning to flake off on the red columns. And they've got outside marble Chinese dragons and we're heading now past the old Centre Street main police station, which has been abandoned for ten years, but is about to be opened up as a condominium. And I think it'll be quite a landmark. Now we're, as we get to the corner of Broome and Centre Street, we're looking across to what I believe to be a German-sponsored project, which seems also to be some sort of condominium, I . . .

A: . . . are wacky . . . this green . . .

R: Yeah, well that's the old stuff. The building itself has some kind of, it's kind of nice, it looks like . . . I don't know what it looks like, but . . .

A: Yeah, but the windows could be a little?

R: Yeah, but the new design is, for some reason, somebody chose this kind of aluminum siding . . .

A: Look at that chandelier, I mean, it's so odd . . .

R: Right. And they didn't put anything over their awning there.

A: Germans you said?

R: For some reason, I don't know why, I heard that Germans had taken over the place. Now we're getting up to Cleveland Place and we're passing Eileen's Cheesecake, which is a very distinguished product, I certainly sponsor it.

A: Where? Not this.

R: No. We just passed Eileen's. Now we're getting up past the old methadone center, which is now moved up here, which was kind of an outrage in the neighborhood. We're passing Jennifer Bartlett's loft. She was very much against the methadone clinic. Now we're getting even to the fire station and past PIM magazine, a very cute little miniature gallery, which is also publisher of probably the smallest publication in New York. And we're heading now past the illustriously renovated Puck Building.

A: And what's the story on the Puck Building?

R: Well, the Puck Building was for years and years like a printed ink building. They manufactured printing ink. And it always smelled very nicely. But since some big entrepreneur has taken it over and done a nice job, it looks pretty glamorous. They've got green trees out here, antibum fences, and I think they rent out the ground floor to benefits, big dos, you know. I think Williwear had a do there or something. I don't know who else, but lots of things and probably there's some terrific spaces there. Now right here we're on the corner of

Houston and Centre Street or Lafayette Street as it turns, it turns into Lafayette and then turns into Park Avenue, and we're in what I think is filling-station land, where all the cabbies gas up at the gaseteria here, it's an Amoco station on my left. And across the street is the fast parking, gas-and-wash emporium, which is probably the best place to get your car washed around here. And then there's the attractive Lafayette Tire and Auto Safety Center, sporting a Michelin tire sign and looking pretty jazzy. And there you see the remains of an old City Walls mural. It looks kinda like from Byzantine days. And now we're just passing Houston Street and there's many—Houston Street still is holding about the same pattern with some slight gentrification to the west here, with some new stores on the SoHo side. And now we're heading down, we're heading west on Houston Street, just passing the car wash place. Not much to say about that I haven't already said. Across the street you see the billboard for the Semaphore Gallery, which I think is quite interesting, they are changing it every month and doing a pretty nice presentation with a new billboard by the artist they're showing at that, concurrently. That's pretty interesting.

A: That's one of a kind, isn't it?

R: Yeah, I don't now any other gallery that does that. I mean, they, and they only do it one billboard. And I saw an artist there for the first time that I liked a lot, and then I went to see the show, so it worked on me. Now we're we just, we're just almost in the heart of SoHo, we're just about to pass, we're passing these new stores. The first of them seems to be called Fuel Injection, which I think is a Japanese, sort of fast-food clothing boutique. And, what's happening, this is the old Lilien Hardware and Supply Co. on the northwest corner. That's been there forever.

Cabbie: Forget about that fifty cents, I hit that by mistake.

R: Right. Thank you. Now, this part of Houston, oh this is a very interesting natural park by I think the artist's name is Sonfist. What's his name, Alan?

A: St. Anthony's.

R: Yeah, St. Anthony's. So, I mean, food festival.

A: It's where I grew up. Right here.

R: Thompson Street?

A: Two houses down. The gray house, the red one. I grew up on the top floor.

R: Wow. Doesn't look like it changed much. Are you Italian?

A: No. I wish. No, I'm a Huguenot.

R: And you grew up there?

A: Yeah. I grew up there. My father still lives there.

R: Wow. I didn't know that.

A: My brother's living there now. Forty-seven Macdougal. The St. Anthony's parochial school is across the street, I grew up in the festa and I went to school right on King Street.

R: Is that like a club, nightclub? Music loft?

A: Yeah. Music loft.

R: But I know this Martin's bar across the way, which is at Varick, and is this Houston?

A: Yeah.

R: Has been there from year one. And I think almost all Martin's bars were, used to be like, be all over the City, or have been torn down or changed.

A: There's a loft for rent.

R: That loft, that loft has been for rent for twenty-five years. I have for years, I have speculated living there for years. Because it's always for rent.

Cabbie: [can't hear]

A: What's that?

Cabbie: They open after-hours places in these lofts now.

A: Open air . . .

R: They're after-hours clubs.

A: Oh, after-hours clubs.

The cabbie hinted no subject matter but the experience of that father going to school on the GI Bill, studying that beautiful language of literature, & that was that & could attain right livelihood in such a manner of speaking, and nailed on the oilcloth to the black table my mother's first husband built with half-Grecian hand upon which we had countless meals and struggles. And Glaukos surfaced once to defend a poor Mexican, be beaten up alive still, hospitalized, too gentle in this New York world.

Welcome in this world, Met Opera broadcasts and hiding places behind awkward chairs and fear of oranges from the little brother who came into this world to make me jealous & wiser. My father on the postwar dream, recovering, come on get with it, not a Catholic in me, although we are surrounded and informed and made alive by these visions and rituals & food. *I did too see the Devil with the rest of them in the girls' room at P.S. 8! I swear, Mrs. Mulherne! He was red with horns & a tail & a sneer & he smelled like the devil too, all spermy and peppery.* You could say he was a sex symbol, a voyeur (we were so little, prepubescent in the long lunchroom hour). He older half-Greek half-brother confused me with his little black box. Pandora's he called it, a box of woes, the accoutrement of the diabetic. How many relationships to break a heart? This is for fathers & brothers. A younger golden boy who usurped the breast, the remote father, tamed by war, the mysterious half-Greek, a dark musician. I honor & obey these first men in my life who were to repeat in a swirl of patterns & combinations of other men so dear to me. Should I go on?

President Ronald Reagan
The White House
1600 Pennsylvania Avenue, N.W.
Washington, D.C. 20500

Dear Mr. President:

On November 19 and 20, when you meet with General Secretary Gorbachev in Geneva, the hopes of not just all Americans, but of the entire world, will be with you.

Mr. President, I believe that we must take steps to limit the nuclear arms race.

I recognize that the Soviets are our principal adversaries in the world. They are tough, determined negotiators. Nevertheless, each of your last five predecessors—Presidents Kennedy, Johnson, Nixon, Ford, and Carter—has been able to work out important nuclear arms control treaties with them—treaties which have helped reduce the threat of nuclear war.

The Geneva summit provides you with a real chance to break the current negotiating impasse—to reach the kind of agreement between leaders which is needed to obtain significant arms control.

As you yourself have said, "A nuclear war cannot be won and must never be fought."

Mr. President, now is the time to put the power of our high office behind those important and telling words. Now is the time to take positive steps to limit the nuclear arms race.

The Geneva summit represents an opportunity to break the arms control stalemate of the last five years and to enact new arms control limits which will *strengthen*—not weaken—our national security.

I encourage you to seize the opportunity the Geneva summit offers.

Sincerely,

Anne-Who-Grasps-the-Broom-Tightly

June 1, 1904

My Dear,

I just finished reading your letter and I will say you are rather late in the day to have a bouquet holder made by Saturday. Why tomorrow is Thursday and it would be Sat. before it would come out of the oven. You should have thought of this sooner. You can get one later if you wish. I am very sorry I did not send you the measure for those windows right. But I will get them for you tonight and will mail this letter when I return home. The number on the house is 419. I am very sorry you are having such bad weather but I think it will be clear tomorrow. I understand Mr. Ware to say you told him about the carpet. I will give Mr. Sithers your note tomorrow. Will finish this when I return home tonight. Well it is now nine o'clock I have been uptown I went out to the house. The measure of the windows from centre to bottom of casing 39 inches. I hardly think the number I told you above is correct. It is 417 but I will explain. The double house next to it on the west side is 411 & 413 so I think ours should be 417 but the single house on the east side in 423. There is no number on the house as yet. You have them printed 417. They have 2 rooms papered downstairs—they look real nice. Well I will close now hoping that I have everything alright.

Ever your John

November 21, 1985

Dear Anne,

You tell all and remain mysterious. You've got love to burn. The poem floors me, the words cut me up. Ardent and mute, yes, I am. The dancing does it, but I can't tell, can't speak; I worry, a conscience violated? Afraid of loss, so always losing. Patterns emerge: the legs, a certain shape, the butt, breast, firm, proportion, most important, but aura, it's everything, inseparable. The temptation of one who wants more attack.

In La Jolla, the Pacific is Mediterranean blue. The museum's windows look out on it, and the art isn't as good. George Trakas, know him? He's renovating a hill there. We dance in the theatre. We flew over you, both ways, and I wanted to stop and ask you how to make life-enhancing love out of this passion-pain.

Your son's becoming a demon perhaps? I and my son, possessed by demons must become them.

Thanks for the passionate communication. I love you.

Son: We are lovers & Daddy is a wolf
         How old are you Mommy? 44? 29?
         Mommy you are always 21. Come
         down to 21 Mommy. Stay 21 forever
         & I'll grow up to 21. You are
         not as loud as Dad. You have no
         scratchy face. You are my most
         beautiful Mommy.

I get out & am not a sneaking Madam
Not a silhouette
Not a dreamy housekeeper
Not writing the modern Arcadia
Tangibly not at home
The copy on this page, on my shelves, in my heart
     in my room is not a lie
Not mere loneliness, not slipshod
Not metrical, but operating
as pioneer, as trust, as Woman
as Passion, as Champion of Details

The older brother's wife rips up the photograph of his earlier daughter. I struggle in heart with the little godchild my lover commands with him into my world. The male makes us suffer for his heart of hearts. I sleep with my older brother's brother not my blood but who yet resembles him, after sitting on my brother's lap in what seems like a long taxi ride (it was raining) home. My mother is trying to keep us apart. We go to Hotel Earle with old-man lobby, whore at the door and make illicit love something like incest, unskilled in a burning urge to forge a link. The beautiful god is in town a few days, heading out west. Can I really make love to this yet again another Greek? Too cerebral, unsatisfied. It's the dark connection in this one. I always wore a black turtle-neck then. I speak confidently.

   The blond on the telephone is a long story, like my younger another brother who confesses desire for drugs & men. He takes my virginity as we used to say and we are cheerful in a sullied bed. Because my mother died I can speak these things I state again this is for fathers, brothers, lovers, husbands, son for that is next of kin alive & changing in a fluid world. It is a palpable motion toward them from one who slumbered many years in the body of a man and in herself a turf of woman becoming Amazonian in proportions (I grow larger even as I write this) as she spans a continent takes on this wise mother as she dies. I gave birth to a son to better understand the men whose messages pour out of me.

Dear Iovis:
Thinking about you: others in you & the way
You are sprawling male world today
You are also the crisp light in another day
You are the plan, which will become clearer with a
    strong border as you are the guest, the student
You are the target
You are the border you are sometimes the map
You are in a car of love
You are never the enemy, dull & flat, dissolving in the sea
Illusion lays it snare, you resort to bait, to tackle me
Our day is gone
To name a place steeped in legend is tempting
To name now and then Nambikwari, Arawak, Poona, makes
    them appear
We go as far as possible, any old town disappears
We look at the globe from vantage point of sun
The clouds under us are rich with
For manners for trouble for passion we do this to each other
    & forces us back into not-so-terrible childhood
    & forward to old age sickness death you know it
The lines translate Sanskrit as I say this to you
Exhaustion with phenomena at last
As I say this to you the furniture is rearranged in a sacred text
The room is now long, the room is tall, the room is male
It is a cathedral after you have named them all for me
Or Theodora, a lusty woman
It is All Hallows' Eve & many dead lovers walk tonight
The wind goes through us, we aren't so solid

All you could hold onto I'm knocking out of you
The wind did this when I wasn't looking to me too
Your conscious eyes compel us together
A game of guesses
What is in the gentleman's mind?
Something in you reminds me of a magnate, a planet, a small prayer
A little girl is trapped inside trying to get out of you
I make a new plan every day to ride your mind
Drugs are inconvenient & stand outside the room
In the other room, the "she" carries it off, waving good-bye
The great thing is to love something
the land, the sea, the sweep of a hand, the way something boils
Man is the arm gesture of the woman or something like that says T.
The battle with the "Ugly Spirit" is not to be discounted says D.
A. needed a woman and caressed a tree
B. knows maximum intensity is best in this life
A world of heredity quiet in R.'s syllables
A woman's mockery is strong & hearty
She's fond of knowledge learn something about her
The large heart scans the future
Vague unrest I tell you so
You contradict your many selves
Your mind spills out, the page holds on
"You make a man of me" sings the radio, gruffly
All is full of Jove, he fucks everything
It is the rough way to prove it
The male gods descend & steal power
How does it happen
How does it happen Blanche Fleur & Heart Sorrow?

Here's how:

I lie back & take him in. He wounds me after a fashion. A new sensation of art & stimulus, for I watch them both & participate after a fashion until they are spent & the man is meted in arms, and no longer to do battle on this bed stage. The bed is the book is the bed is the book where sheets record every muscle tear sweat ooze of life & groan. It is the playground of senses for this artist as sweet rehearsal for the nonexistent pages that will honor this rumbling & panic and lostness. I want to say to dear male lovers living & dead not anger made this but with due respect in spite of the crimes to which your sex is prone. I honor the member who is a potential wand of miracles, who dances for his supper, who is jester & fool and sometimes the saint of life. But she, me, who takes it, who responds clasping with cunt teeth, the receiver, the mountain, whatever it could be called, the emptying, the joining of this most radiant sphere where the chakras glow under the sheets or else they are fucking in water, she is witness in this brave act. It feels like the great sperm whale entered me.

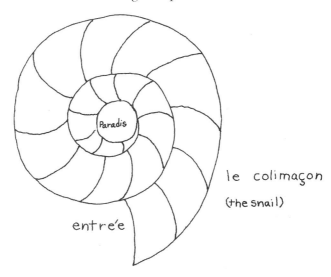

le colimaçon

(the snail)

"You are done for in the labyrinth"

II

SOME KINDA ANIMAL

The poet receives letters from an advisory elder who complains about Jove, from a misguided inventor, and also a prize student, which change her mind's atmosphere. She is moving out to confront the Desperado, most difficult challenge perhaps as he worships her and takes her as a teacher. This turns the poet weak. Desperado and son meet as aspects of her attention, catching her ear with quirky syntax and desire. She sends bulletins into the void as she sweeps the battlefield, grasping the broom more tightly now, nervous about her own animal nature. Men are by nature aggressive. And women?

Mature love you say but my wounds come out through inner temples,
which are participants containing a statue of . . . female personnel,
not subject matter, a tableau of outerspace, concubines?
where we had countless meals and struggles with any father.
What is the mature and conditioned space O Jove?

Dear Anne,
Please advise how I may develop a scintillating poetic presence. Last time I read most dozed off.
I dislike Virgil. Result of having to construe 40 lines a day at Choate—those endless similes

> As when at dawn the ducks
> from out the marsh
> Curdling their pintails in
> the early starch
> etc etc etc

Sorry, that's clammy armpit . . .

Very best to all,

J. L.

Never liked Jove either. Wd prefer to be inhabited
by **Αφρωδιτη** or some nifty Olympian girl.

It is a play or way to amuse the girl or is it? A way of talking
is another to journey to never abuse but wounds are fake and
are the scourge of me and they are real scourge of me. Where
to leave off talk of all these brothers and leave it here.
Dear Man-Who-Rends-My-Table-And-My-Hearth: SCRAM!
I am at a ruined table because
I met a maiden good
I walked into an explicit house
and was a trait of forefathers
They could arrest me in my cunning
But they are not the boss of me
They are not the actor in a new phase of history: horse & chariot
They are not a grimace in this old gal's boot
We are like one city and another
And another comes along soon
the shape of Neptune's face
or Saigon, a sight for the broken
heart of anything
It is the ancient place of Ur
It is your own place won in fair fight
giving the lie to property tax
and the language of my people
O Male Civilizations!
I am not a party to my gold
but relate what has gone past
once the sufferings are over
Are they ever? I doubt it
But they are done to a crisp
and die in cold light
I am a regular next winter
I am a vestal in propensity for service
I stretch my neck with music
but I doubt the way the Prophet
        goes about bringing them to the Mount
        Not doubt but a kind of wonder
        It is a fiery night
        and proud Maisie stalks the wood

She is the maiden of me
She is the good of me
I am a timetable for anything wet,
for anything with star and waxing moon
I am the dream of me, mere
illusory scales & fins, webbed toes
I grow into the scout of me
the densest one who reports back
to the head of me and sprouts
the garden you put your mind to
one sunny day
It glows like a pregnant thing
and grows the seed of any Art
It is alive nor is
the heart of me dead
I go so that windless bower be built
So that I go quietly, I go alone
I am alone and delight in how speech
may save a woman
How speech is spark of intrusion

LETTER TO MISS IDONA HAND

Washington, July 15, 1903

My Dear,

I suppose you rec'd a postal from me by Tuesday noon—I thought you would be anxious to know whether we arrived safely or not. We have had a splendid time. I cannot describe the beautiful sights we have seen it is something wonderful. I and the boys are sitting in the Pennsylvania depot. They are waiting while I write this small message. We just saw the house where Garfield was shot. We have covered a good bit of ground since arriving but we have several places yet to visit. I am trying to make a note of everything so I can explain it to you. But next summer you must see things for yourself. This is the most beautiful place I ever saw. Everybody is feeling well we have a few jokes on one another. When we first arrived we walked down Sixth Street and we wanted 452. Charlie looked and saw the number 859 and called it out. It was a sign saying established 1859. You want to ask him if he stopped on Establishment Street. This morning I awoke about six o'clock there was a bell ringing it rang twice and then commenced ringing harder. I said Boys there is a fire. I lit out of bed in a hurry. They are having fun about that. Well Dear I

must close now hoping this will do you some little good. I will be home about Saturday and tell
you about it.

Yours

John

What are you you are what are you are you what *seems* lady?
Idona's seamed stockings in the attic, John a Protestant
never protesting on the porch, a gentle man outside any
war, born in the gap between worlds in collision.
All the lovers getting out of the army for one sane reason
or another, generation skipped. The grandfather in white,
father in khaki I won't skip over them to what you are
You're a pistol eye a mistletoe a missile man a Marxist
You're a sword eye a job queen a devil-may-care
You're a conch a knob you guys are slobs
We're playing tictactoe you're a sticky glue-stick
but a stick-in-the-mud too are you
You're spaghetti-hair Dad, you crazy old man
You woman Daddy you *New York Times* reader
You *New York Times* reporter
You're a suitcase What? What are you?
You're east of the sun & west of the moon
Are you are you are you are you What? What are you?
You slob you rubberband nose
You're a bully and a mean-shoot a paperclip a peppercorn
You're stuck in my teeth
You're a European walrus
You're a blue muscle you're a red tomato
You crossbow you arrowhead you man-of-me
You're a bellow of church
You're a bump thump bump dummy
You're a broken-down hospital
You're a cracked people
You're a craggy rock cliff
You're Michael Jackson you're Jacky Frosty

You cup nothing
You're a hundred thousand bristle blocks
You're a peony—means you're a broken-down housebell
You are my wife Mommy you are the dream of me

> The keep & key of an unruly person
> absorbed everyone & you realize he's
> only wild since noon

You're just out there looking at the moon

> So great my love on my male partners
> I hate to leave town

(When you look into it on any person's desk
the town appears small)

> so now

I RISE BEFORE ISHTAR IN THE EAST
I RISE BEFORE ISHTAR IN THE EAST

Moon disappearing
all's sluggish, dull
What's the color
Pronounce it windless
A shroud song is sad
sword cuts who?
Some wicker man staggers
Listen to the peregrine fall
I try, towered upon a short stretch
Seeing Mother meshed with herself
O dire is her Mother need
She's shortened loose
She's in the fittings
Windows iced into dark holes
are quiet

but I think of a dream
in green jasper
It goes like this:
something shattered in chips
sailing down   (was it?)
long canals
cut channels
Something like Hawaii
for the craft
Need sharp eyes here
for a pagan sea

Lights stand up
in a dark wood
I'm now swimming in night green
"I shall paint my body red & dance"
she said I
will wear antlers or a
bone blooded Earth-Time
I will
I will

In sets, sets in with her
holding tight slips
Those Martian canals are
cracked ice
I cut to the Andromeda movie
"Venus" is here too
I thought my body green or faun
& dropped the sexual stick
Shadows showed the crater
to be a new moon
a storybook pomegranate split
She's got a myrtle whip
She made her name in whips
& made me worship her
Me, a mere shadow of sight

standing in the shell of the dream
eyed back into dark ovals
Of all the Pagans I was One
what oath is mine?
Who wouldn't bend to a
Virgin standing on the moon?
Can't resist
I'll paint myself white
You paint yourself red
We'll dance to a
Low Eastern Bright Eye tune
& follow that song
Our bedsheets will be like fire & ice
& I'll have to walk out
the next door
to the close out the smell of you

THE CREATIVE IS SPEAKING It is a large you-name-it-machine made
of words to show you O Princess what's the side of He-Who-Risks
all for me, he the Bull leaper for in bulls does the Earth-shaker
delight for in bulls does she know her truth & set down this
soft earth bed too grosse for Heaven upon which I end where
I begunne. (His loincloth will be immaculate and bright,
his bracelets will be costly, his hair curled, his face painted
red & black for a night of love)
THE CREATIVE IS SPEAKING to write a nuclear warhead, to
walk inside itself circumscribed as an obtrusive lope. The
man wants to play the music loud to think he's some kinda animal
some kinda some kind some kinda animal
Douse him or send him into the next votary's mind
He's some kind some kinda animal
Not that he's untamable but ancient you know like a
tryseerotops, which is not to say it died by living
out its need

& needed more that one of us

Touched him she thought he thought
Some space between
He said about sex all over again
She said Here I go again
A couple mentions the "you" factor
you know then
She's ready too
We hold out our hearts
So what's the suffering all about?

THE CREATIVE IS SPEAKING How the sons of immigrants go back
to fight in the ancestral homelands. Now you know you are American
Now you know how this is preserved in memory

You know how memory is cunning
That sex is early on the girl's mind
Now you know all manner of speaking openly
The myths are alive or a time
I come out full-grown of my father's split head
and am armed for the battle of love
These words are in answer to an assignment to make sense of
three and five
I represented my mother to Greece
Poo EEE Nay stah sohn ton lay o for EEE on?

There is not more hope than this: to find the right bus
Athens, which is a city built on the extension of Hestia's hearth
The head split in two and something is noticed in the duality
of city life: in and out, the inner and outer working daily
for the virgin spinster who would like to make sense of all
these trade routes, know who went where when and the little
amphora handles are clues to great travelers with goods who
plunged ahead to carry with them their genetic structures
among other things, & all the manifestations of all the senses:
color, texture, taste, smell, sight
The spice of night
the silk of midday
The clear soup of morning
A way of studying stars

A photograph of a thymeli, an altar
The queen's proclivities
The way people might decide on a crime & so on
On returning from Egypt I had
1 hookah
2 scarves of silk, red as my fantasy of the red in Red Sea
& 1 Mediterranean blue
1 scarab pin (imitation)
Another scarab was lost in England in the room of the lady
who said "Scarabs always get lost around me"
And from these places I brought a new appetite for a
particular olive

It was the olive branch and owl, which symbolized the way men
lived before they were civilized and somewhere out of the darkness
I went to meet them.

Dear Lady,

I am an ingenious amateur inventor. For five years I meditated on trying to produce as many new good invention ideas as I could. I did think up about 50 of them. After checking patentability I discarded 12 of them and had 38 left. When I tried to sell some to a few businessmen, I got two of them stolen. I got them, witness and disclosure documents on the rest. I then sold one to a lady and then am now offering any or all the 35 inventions for sale to you now. I trust you enough to take a chance anyway. Many of these are cheap and easy to build and make. All have good money-making profit potential, some many millions profit potentially. I am not at this time financially able to afford getting any patents because I am getting by just barely. I hope to sell 10 or 12 of my new Inventions and then patent two or three then myself. I did get your name from the Who's Who book in America and address. Rest easy though I'm only sending a few letters to a few ladies to try my luck and will not advertise my invention or write to any men at all about my inventions. Read the next page for more details and bless you regardless of your decision.

from Kenneth Alexander Walker

Brief Indication List of Invention Ideas of Kenneth Alexander Walker

1.   Device for air improvements in homes.

2.   New type of pet bird cage. Should be liked by bird lovers.

3. New type of child's tricycle.

4. New type of ladies watch band.

5. New type of stylish sun protection for eyes.

6. New type of loud noise control hearingwise.

7. New type of eyeglass frames. Should make people feel better.

8. New type of outdoor bird house. Bird lovers should like this one.

9. New type of barometer.

10. Improvement for safer night driving.

11. Burglar catcher mechanism.

12. New type of life raft.

13. Improvement for all replacement car door lock knob.

14. Method of getting massage while driving vehicle.

15. New type of food freezer. Should keep food frozen quality longer.

16. New type of refrigerator. Should keep food fresh longer.

17. New type of fish aquarium. Pet fish lovers should like.

18. New type of small animal cage for pets pet animal lovers should like.

19. New improvement for pet bird water dishes.

20. Method of improvement for men's briefcases.

21. Improvement on photo gray sun protection.

22. A camera and film picture improvement.

23. Improvement for teachers' blackboard pointers.

24. Improvement for telephone handles.

25. New type of scalp massage.

26. New type of wax candle. More light for its size compared to others.

27. Improved clothing iron women will like.

28. Light increasing lampshade electricity saver.

29. Directional light increased electricity saver.

30. Shark repelling life jacket.

31. New type of stove that is an improvement.

32. Flexible light aimer improvement.

33. Auto window washer improvement.

34. Drinking water cooler improvement.

35. TV commercial alternative improvement.

To His Excellency Mobutu Sese Seko
    Head of State
Citoyen President:
I appeal to you for the immediate and unconditional release of Tshisekedi wa Mulumba, a lawyer and former member of the Zairian Assembly who was arrested last October.
    I believe that Mr. wa Mulumba is a prisoner of conscience, held solely for his nonviolent exercise of fundamental human rights. He is reportedly held at Makala Prison in Kinshasa.
    Thank you.
                    Anne-Who-Grasps-the-Broom-More-Tightly

IOVIS OMNIA PLENA The world is full of you my lingering
one, lingam of any century of this old papa's realm of this
sweet love & sweat. Dear Father who made me so to be a poet
on the battlefield of Mars, whose seed got dipped, got used
& cannibalized to be this witness such and eke out her income
her life her light on a bed of love, earth is my is my number
O earth is the number to be joined by you old grandfather
sky and harking back to he who is the genetics to any plump
German girl, or any paranoid Huguenot daughter. I can take
him or leave him, juiced out over many wars:
                    & all these messages
                            are the light of document
                                of me
                                    the life
                            of me who receives them in the guise
of any way you want
            hemmed in . . .
            lost
            willful
            prepubescent in the long lunchroom hour . . .
            I conquer you

Dearest Anne, there is so much more I wish I could say to you. This test has been enjoyable and frustrating in equal amounts. Sometimes I wonder why I bother, but when I hear you and certain colleagues of yours read, it at times seems worthwhile.

Looking at you, I see a romantic, an idealist, and a revolutionary. You seem to call it the way you see it, and have no qualms about nailing the "jello faced abominations" (My line) to the wall. You don't have any aversion to graphically describing sexuality, pain, life, death, the reality of what it means to be men and women.

If I seem nihilistic and cynical, it is because I am a heartbroken utopian dreamer and romantic who has slammed up against the gray wall of reality a considerable number of times. I live for vengeance, a sort of "poetic justice."

I admire how you with your greater experience of years and life than my own can still see so much "basic goodness." But you are still willing to call a cat a cat, a dog a dog, a man a man, and a woman a woman. And blame few indeed for what they inherently are.

I really would like to be a successful novelist, and my audience response at this most recent reading was better than usual, and I got positive feedback from Rick Andy Tom. Poetry is even more fun than drugs, you were right about that.

I got Bill Burroughs (Sr.) up on my wall smoking a joint and looking right through you. There is beer in the fridge, Joan Armatrading on the radio. Whatever you would tell me, I probably wouldn't take it seriously.

The battle with the "Ugly Spirit" is not to be discounted. Me and my whole little faction of friends and lovers wave at you, smile, flip the bird, blow a kiss from '77 '81 '83 '84. Here in exile I wish to know how I can best serve all those I left behind.

Gregory Corso said something to the effect of "If you take your shit and show it to some guy and he says THIS SUCKS you gotta say, fuck you man, you're full of shit I'M A POET."

Burroughs said "There will be no self-pity in the ranks."

I would really like to have THE DEFINITIVE QUOTE from you. And if you want to tell me I have the whole damn thing wrong, I'll listen.

Fer-ever yours, your hopelessly sentimental and incompetent warrior in disgrace—

D. M.

D'accord that is the place to be, D'accord with him a place
to go down down on him with no music to prop this boy love

I extend to boy

It is the truth of me when I needed him and I was hard on him
& he in me, hard on me

to stay to prop this boy love in me
I be it
in me, in me
to fast this love to fasten as I was hard on him to prop
his love
a violation & a forgetting   to prop all love

for I was hard on him to be a boy & love of the boy to be
a boy
go by, boy
yours in the ranks of any promise of manhood
& you are no music
you are no manhood yet

you are wonder I am spectator once   O boy

Ye Geulfs, listen! This makes sense . . .

III

HEM OF THE METEOR

The poet travels in dreams, skirting the hem of Zeus's robe, which sways like an orbit of sexual prowess. She moves through the lives of particular men as a kind of sympathetic magic to catch experience. She wants the men to do the same: change into women. She travels to Berlin & into narrow annals of literary & military history, which guide her to certain conclusions about how to call the name of war. Her friend the Priest writes from Rome in a kind of conversion experience. She listens to the young boys & records a conversation, anxious they will survive, & writes in a twilight language, intoxicated, typing quickly now. Marginal expressions, the speech & aspiration of gay men, transsexuals need to be heard. Pondering this, she continues to honor the hermaphrodite as the ultimate mental state, although she cautions it to have no expectations at the gates of heaven. Because it is an intolerant Christian heaven on the base level. She ingests magic mushrooms to prove a capricious point. Possibly about the other gateways—the ayatanas, literally the doors of the senses. She expands further into the universe through ritualized thinking, tells more stories. Desperado left behind, languishing on the banks of the river, he could not fulfill the writing assignments.

Dear Hermaphrodite: *Lasicate ogni speranza voi ch'entrate*

Cómo está el arroz?

está frito, mon

bloodshot stars in a void

eyes off, shot from a gun

hem of the meteor, Zeus

no sleep

lines between two eyes

aim carefully: scent of human realm

First sex, a dark room in Nogales, Sonora, like Jack lost it in a whorehouse, five dollars even, 16 years old, sixty miles south of Wilmot Avenue, Tucson. Taxi driver laughed, "Zona Roja! Sí!" And the father pimp chuckled, guiding my friend & me, laughed even harder when we asked if we could do it in the same room, "No, no! Thees is no good idea! Follow me, let me show you Mari!" And it stunk like urine, the room, and she was probably about twenty, twenty-two, chunky, and, here, I start to undress her, every romantic notion, a dream to undress a woman! (We used to talk about screwing our friends' mothers!) and she laughs, says, "No. Five dollars." The bra took me awhile. And I could not believe how luscious her skin was, women were for me, this was good, I climaxed immediately, felt proud and cold and nervous about syphilis . . . I did not love her, had this odd respect for her . . .

My hair was first
covering
my brows
(child's method
of wearing hair)
"breaking flowers"
I was frolicking in the front of yr gate
when you come riding on bamboo stilts
(you—ride—on—bamboo—horse—come)
Chang-teng-sha I'd go that far for you
astrophysics *lapsus memoriae*
loves & penetrates
my hope through a dense forest, in exile

& was taken, a virgin
by all of you, in exile
to find the way
rather spotted than dead
& do I breathe
& do I, do I breathe?
& does he move?
He is a current in me
& does he move the current in me
Snake lore!
Penetration of trouble
hissing in the ear

the song of Love me, love me
Good, Good, Love me, Love me
it's good
speaking of him O speak of it
convivial & persuasive
O is a thrust
is O a thrust
curling & striking
My Carmelites, do not desert me!

                    dear Anne,
You & Allen Ginsberg & I are standing outside some
kind of old back-East-type brick near-tenement apartment
where I just moved in. He's wearing a bright & slightly
tattered orange wool sweater that looks scratchy but is
really very soft. Everything he says to me you rephrase
in order to be certain that I understand thoroughly.
This is not annoying.

I speak as Hetaera
unraveling birth & death
I'll give you pleasure, okay mister
I give you pain
living on the parameter of the chthonic
"Here you can see every sort
        of person
                as if
                you had come to
the underworld" (Plautus speaks)
        & *Lasciate*
I'll send
ogni
take a peek *speranza*
Odysseus go down
voi ch'entrate
(a boundary for the post-titanic order)

Sing how you men are weapon-prone
How you are prone of heat & battle
Sing Odysseus, men are weapon-prone

Again:

Come put yr sword
in my sheath
Sing, O,
how you men are prick-prone
Let us two go up to bed
(show me the other sword,
lying together in this bed of moan
we'll be sweet in each other's flesh)

        Here the streams flow with ambrosia
     by Jove's bed of love . . . .
            he who gathers the clouds
                  clean white sheets
                     et cetera

— *cocinando* —

Now I have to tell you how offering up a hamburger probably saved my life. On December 27, I went to the Rome Airport to pick up someone. I got to arrivals at 8:50, saw on the TV monitor that the TWA plane was 20 minutes late, so I sauntered on up to departures to look at the faces in the crowd, as I love to do. I walked past El Al and TWA booths. At the far end of the terminal building there is a small bar with a number of tables (no seats) for a quick snack. There was a sign saying HAMBURGERS 3000 LIRE. (Well, ole Tom is always hungry, loves Hambies, and they are not easy to find in this city of pasta and wine). So I thought: maybe a quick hamburger while I wait. Then I thought: no, too early in the morning. I watched the faces happily eating and chatting, looked at my watch, which said 9:02, turned and headed out the door and down the steps to arrivals. Well, you probably know what happened at 9:06—hand grenades and machine gun bursts, 13 dead (now 16) and 70 wounded. I heard the bombs from downstairs, saw a large mass of people running, panicked, some with blood flying from them. Police forced us out into the parking lot. A few hours later I found my shaken passenger and returned to Rome. I think the Goddess whispered in my ear: No, Tom, no hamburger this morning because eating one I would certainly have been standing in front of that bar; and that bar was the first place one Arab turned his machine gun.

      ("be careful, be very careful")

They are my tides my tides a blameless I thank you
They are against my tides or sides a blameless I thank you

Not what the foreigners arranged when they came here:
          May bay tnu u mentah dzulob ti uliob lae
then shame and terror were preferred
          zubtzilil tal zahob ca talob
carnal sophistication in the flowers of Nacxit fluchit
          and his circle;
          ca cuxhi yol nicte cuxhi tun yol tu nicteob N.S.
          tu nicte u lakob
no more good days were shown to us . . .

the hazel corpses green
          no more be seen

                    madre, madre

& as a writer a green light to reorder my world
to fasten this male's mind to a star
& today we're seeing an event in time 55,000 years ago
& scoundrels spooked by their own shadow so thick
a striking grasp of opposites
nova

          through the keyhole of his eye

                    I hear you, I hear you
you residing here I hear you
I hear you here I hear you
    shift in my being too I hear you
                    here it's you
          I said it: you
                         Here you, I hear you
       (Ambrose's Light Years)
     a child's Younger Lightfoot
    tread the meteor, Zeus

& you walk past me in the hallway & as I turn to look back
at you I start to gag & a large mucousy creature about
2 feet long & 6–8 inches wide looking somewhat like
a human snake or salamander, comes out from my mouth &
dissolves on the floor. I am stunned but also relieved
to be freed from this demon. I know you have helped
to heal me of this blockage & it has to do with the throat
& expression or larynx

     variant linguistic tongue, to whom this power granted?

my throat, his passage
throat : a daughter of memory
beauty of my thought, out!

out! hem the meteor
 curl vowel flame
not break the house

    Nov 10, 1914: Ezra Pound writes a prospectus
    for a new College of Arts and proposes schooling that stresses
    "contact with artists of established
    position, creative minds, men (sic) for the most
    part who have already suffered in the cause of their
    art"
  speak sagely through the deathless mouth
cause of the meteor, Zeus
  to break the pentameter, first heave, first rumor

religion at the gates, ether's invisible flame: conversion
   rumor has it Christians have
     a secret spray
      that makes crosses appear
        on Muslim women's veils . . .

They are speaking, two 8-year-olds
            in the garden
                    center stage:

— I'm really sick
    I'm wounded

— Get some mint leaves
    They'll cure you

— It's too late almost
    I'm shot bad

— We have medicine
    in the wagon
    (dresses his wound)

— Feeling any better?

— Twist it up more

— I'm gonna get some new weapons

— Who's the en.. en.. en.. enemy now?

— The new religion

— Yeah, pray to a dollar bill

— Muslims got some fancy weapons

— Allah ate a novelist too

— Jesus saves, ha

— But look, Buddha's just a guy

— Anyway, it's a robotical war now
    Let's play robotical war

Prepare an Initial NBC 1 Nuclear Report:

1. At the instant of the "blue-white flash," hit the ground and start counting slowly, 1,000-AND-ONE, 1,000-AND-TWO, 1,000-AND-THREE, and so on until the blast wave has passed.

2. Record the elapsed time as letter item J in the NBC 1 format.

3. Check your watch and record the time as letter item D in the NBC 1 format.

4. Report letter item H as SURFACE if:

   a. Throwout (earth particles that have fallen back and built up on the edge of the crater) can be seen or,

   b. a thick, dense steam has developed.

5. Report letter item H as AIR if the stem is not connected to the mushroom part of the cloud.
   NOTE: If in doubt, report letter item H as UNKNOWN.

6. If visibility permits observation of ground zero, use your map to determine the coordinates of ground zero and record as letter item F.

7. If ground zero cannot be observed, use your compass to measure the azimuth from your location to the center of the stem or mushroom cloud. Record this as letter item C.

8. Record your location as letter item B.

(all this with watch, compass, map, pencil, paper

standard gear

for

any

holocaust)

gonna get some new weapons
("And we two little ones had neither mutual dislike or suspicion")

Dear Mr & Mrs B:

Thank you for contacting me about recent events at the Rocky Flats Plant.

I have enclosed a copy of the statement I made to the Rocky Flats Environmental Monitoring Council on October 25, 1988, about the closing of Building 771 and the storage of radioactive waste at the plant. It outlines the steps I recommend in response to these problems.

Thanks for letting me know your comments.

<blockquote>
Sincerely yours,
J.O.V.E.
D.E.S.
Congress of the United States
House of Representatives
</blockquote>

<blockquote>
the book is Virgil
the reader is you
the street is
evasive, a kid in love
    with war
</blockquote>

     He took me to Kreuzberg & wept
showing me the

place of destruction   He with Baltic eyes

mise-en-scène

The *Asphaltlyrik* of Nazi Germany

Schadenfroh, maliciousness

small-mindedness

This practice, as you may have noticed, shifts
the attention to the ongoing process of the mind

sitting against the condition we have

clap your hands the lights go on

Don Giovanni waltzes back into my arms
with an aria or two

My Europe's blood holds his sperm

We got on the turnpike, turned off at Mount Holly past
Fort Dix went down along the Pine Barrens to Hammonton then
took a diagonal to Vineland
the trip ended in Bridgeton
Cumberland County

(It was different than taking the D train to Coney)

& yet this writing is not my own subject

or blood shot
through dream
stars in void

Come out of your box, now
eyes go off
shot from a gun

hem of the meteor
No sleep
but lines between two eyes

                                        germane to the question

& change a subject to

                        careful air

then aim carefully

                            scent of human male realm

rocks enter the Book

                        all the rubble of Berlin he showed me

                                he lies back

                              naked, a sailor

              no anarchist yet   yet "dreamboat"
                        all the rubble of Berlin he shows me

kisses me
Das ist gut.

(Built in Scotland in 1886 she spent her first 13 years
as a deep-water—to Auckland, Calcutta, New York,
Rangoon, Cape Town
around Cape Horn 17 times
She carried coal from Cardiff, whiskey from London
guana from Iquique
renamed *Star of Alaska* in 1906 she spent 25 years carrying cannery
workers to north Chignik cannery & salmon back to SF
The public may now board the *Balcutha* at Pier 43)

                    he lies back . . . *ist gut*

                         naked (*Ich bin nicht in Amerika*) he shows me

Pin Bot he shows me Comet he plays me Genesis
he plays TX Sector he shows me
Punch Out, Sega Turbo, he needs more coins:
Two Tigers, Pole Position II, Gyruss, MetroCross, Double Dribble,
Elevator Action, Circus Charlie, Centipede, Join the Action,
Taito 10 Yard Fight, Super Contra, Future Spy, Jail Break,
he shows me Wonderboy, Flicky, Dis Tron, he plays Falcon, Kidniki,
Radical Ninja, Galaga, Gimme A Break, Spy Hunter, Ring King,
Hat Trick he shows me he shows me he shows me
Twin Cobra, IKARI Warriors, After Burner, Danger Zone,
Toobin', XYBOTS, Rampage, Silk Worm, Shinobi, Guerilla
War, Xenophobe

                    as the quest for freedom continues . . .

he lies back but naked   he resists

                    but naked he shows me *ist gut*

                              — 43 —

"Ich möchte asstegen."

Ascendant Leo 4 degrees, Sun Aries 12 degrees, Moon in Sagittarius, Mercury in
Aries, Venus in Taurus, Mars in Pisces, Jupiter in Virgo, Saturn in Cancer,
Uranus in Gemini, Neptune in Libra, Pluto in Leo

can't get out now

                                             he lies back he shows me

& my Muse is my destiny of yes o yes
& he not wife and heard and he not Beautiful Dreamer and he
not a shrew, not a shrieker, not the mailman, the robotical
genius, not the one with the most personality, not the bookworm
not the avenging father, not the jealous brother, not the
invalid, not the mechanic, not the roofer, not the Drain man
not the mainliner, not the mortician's son, not the priest's
illicit offspring, not the acolyte, not the altar boy,
nor the sycophant, nor the celebrity, not the lotus land
habitué, or the star of popular musics, not the country &
western star, nor the schoolteacher, not the carpenter, not
the man who works computers, not the novelist, not the
guy next door nor the one I love so much down the block
not the explorer who dwells with beasts on rock and plain &
forest and jungle

Not the librarian (I kissed him), not black Howie who
stole a kiss, nor the extraordinary dancer who showed me
home who I wept for tears on my pillow 96 tears on my pillow, not
the radio producer, not the way-his-heart-was-cracked Shakespearean actor
ah born of fatal flaw heart cracked like another century,
not him not him not him not him not Mike Rosati, not Ahab, not
John Hammond, or Teddy Strempack, nor Chris Wertenbaker

but what?
but what O tinge
is a lover's question?

the shrieks of delight mere manifesting forms as
they sigh, turn away, eyes down, embarrassed in their
accomplishing manhood

And I would accord with them murmuring it's okay, *ist gut,*
my body is your fetish, my body is your dream, my body
is your mountain, my body is sleep and deception my body
was your home, lissome, I am haunting, I am rude,
I am all you ever wanted in a woman
take me back
and I shouted *Take me back!*

                    "men suffer because they have testes
or because they have none" says Dahlberg,

that in apocalyptic fit, the pith of many's words

Thucydides would mock me or would he even care
would he care to be noticed here in my canon of honor?

Would you prefer the Hypophrygian man? the Hypolydia man,
the Dorian man, the Phrygian man? The Odin man?
Or Bernard Ventadorn, 1024–1195 the
good-looking-son-of-a-baker?

Himalayan kittens, Executive Lots, Loveland City Limits,
Edwina Avenue, Watch for sudden stop
Dance me, a child charging through its body, dance me Momma dance
Plutarch's lyre off the bones of a big white whale (Rehab)
establishing the pluck and strum, dance me
a kind of wind, a kind of wail, a kind of melancholic European angst
dying in another century
wind through bones, dance me, Ahab
the haunt of love, ephemera this body I spread out for you

dance me, the son says, dance me dance me momma
(How do you say when you wanna say "I" *auf Deutsch?*)

Jeff speaks:
"I like in a man big hands,
blood-red heat, not contra-
sexual hands, not insensitivity.
Adventure . . .
My first love David Martin Luther
left me in Texas, age 11, to
go off with his mother &
his future fucking stepfather
(My favorite color is blood red)
But once his real father
took us camping & taught us
how to get over our fear of
bees &
told us ghost stories
in the night . . .
I was queer I knew it by day & in the night . . ."

Your Saturday your Friday beyond eyes I tend
Your mouth reads "work"
Beyond you into a Dark Age I tend
I take your sex along the Dark Age
Below: Dark Age Epic Windows
Epic eyes flash
into words-ear-erect-permeability
    word & chase & hand & street
Silver gray-lakelike-Zen street
You prime yourself you will never always die
I tell you what to do, Jeff
Contact your jam-hand, his, bow in, bow hand
take his cock in your hand, bow down

                    dwell in a kind of tent appliance

                    looped in desire

another God says:
Cocaine prevents the brain
governs the crown

prevents the heart
governs the tongue
from calming itself down
"Broad heaven is the totality of your liver"
Earth is my number
in response to cocaine
certain external stimuli, specific
love objects release heat
neurons release a
chemical called dopamine that
you are heated for
helps trigger
good feelings, or sunny euphoria
The dopamine enters the junction,
and with one glance you hand down the law
or synapse, between the first neuron
and the interstices of earth & sky
and its neighbor, law
It chains the mighty
stimulates the neighboring cells
chugs through air, it alleviates suffering
and thereby acts as a
messenger (or neurotransmitter),
Marduk-Another-God has spoken
sending information
along so-called dopamine pathways

and singing "Me & My Boyfriend We Get Away"

(teenage-cum-drug-love saga)
Me & my mind flee cramped apartment, age 13

& lie about the etheogenics, dear mother of Macdougal Street as you open my
mail extolling the highs of Miss Green I said it, the words "smoked some pot"
meant "we were all in agreement"

Ho!
& weren't we?
what is argument but sweet poetry

As teen how to be anything but body chemistry
& you grab the pack of Camels out of my hand in so-call-it-a-foyer
& grind each cigarette out on the floor
look look you said looking you say for "that ole devil weed"

Father-Never-Stern stay in your room a quiet remove
big old daddy never
so worried as *all that*
Big Daddy make you jump jump jump
Kriss Kross'll make you jump jump jump
Daddy Mac'll make you jump
Mother how covetous a teen

yet

                    How
                       manage
                sex
                remove

place

                    hidden from
                           fury of
                some Joe's

rapture magnetized upon me
                           okay
                                "can take it"
                                    unlock the night
                           ploughshares to gold!

Spinoza stretched out in penance before the synagogue
Was he a lover of women?
hidden in fury of beat ploughshares to gold!

Include Krishna's many flaming mouths *hari hari*
Seize me! Seize me!

Wie ist die Sprache unik!
Ist das Wesen der künstlerischen Betrachtungsweise, dass sie die
Welt mit glücklichem Auge betrachtet?

(is the essence
of the artistic
way of
            looking at things,
that it looks
at the world
            with
                  a
               happy EYE?)

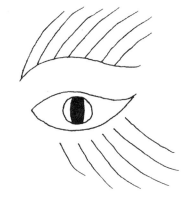

Dear A,

      Happy New Year—here's check for January.
Please let me know any new plans regarding apt.—"For
Sale" sign no longer on the building, does that mean
anything? Guy in store downstairs seems to think that
means it was just sold—

      It was fun to see you. I've made a lot of headway
in new book & working on a long "roman numeral"
poem about the history of the corset which I'm also
illustrating plus I have some new poems too so I guess
being here has been inspiring

                              sad about Ricky Nelson, his
song "Poor Little Fool" was always one of my favorites—

                  be in touch
                  LOVE,
                Radio Emotions

                         on the radio
                   hearing my emotions
                         on the radio
                    usually the male
                      protagonist

                                    hearing my emotions
                              was the "I" I was seeing
                                        falling in
                              love again
                                        with the girls
                                            in the stories
                                    on the radio

in the radio, emotions
were drawn like stars
& every lover was one
in conjunction to me
all in a constellation
of emotions
on the radio—
in the radio: emotions
& the music was heartbeat
& to break your heart
falling in love with the girls
inside the radio emotions: their names
repeat repeat
names of all the girls
she won't succumb the long night
listening to a radio with you
matinee idol dead
me born on the hem of war
arise out of father sperm
head full sprung
think too much
for sure a hag is she
she is a truce to stand on
tween gender
& her politic body
because she is painted child
she sings along with the radio emotions
because they made her
painted preteen child

teen calls to her in the song
because they made of her poet
she is surely
in the air, & in the songs
emoting desire
I keep a little picture of
some crazy pop song idol
in the rafters
because he made of me
what they made of me
form of a radio emotion
then call again
girl-child
desire
or child
but child to child sing
"across a wounded galaxy" *mi donna*

        Out of this torque & spit comes logic of *donna mi prega*
She won't give up her fit of anger or song

toward the man, her shadow falling, toward a father Burroughs

        centuries of it ago a goat across her bondage
like the air waves of another century
What's the hag?
standing over sage Naropa's page as he studies
"Do you understand the words?"
I do I do
"Do you understand the sense?"
I do
"You must be lying"
He blows it

long times ago
with the frail skin of a legend less trenchant
needed a disguise
in this treason of images, needed my pen

Without labels?
                    what looking at?
watchewlookinat
infusion of delight in moment
moment got mannered
got lobbed in projective "it"
before it got named a pen

what?

I was reversed
attenuated to old suffering

& what brought them around to another?
Europa's son's wife's folly that did
it, it not named for mishap
he it, he and it a cause
blame the woman
& she won't help you out of the labyrinth

Palingenesis over & over
it, it
& Berlin was a kind of gate for her, Ishtar's
how men dressed like women but still
had their big hands
(He lies under me, spread out like a sailor . . .)
& the child, her child now, the son-of-her who writes, sings:

Per me si va nella città dolente
Per me si va nell' eterno dolore
Per me si va tra la Perduta Gente

Aeneas is talking to his father's shade
in hell
through the ivory gate just as I speak with you

I was the Bo Tree I was the Holy rood
Was I the mother or the father in the stories?

and I saw Him in my house & He came over to me without
anything inbetween us, fire to iron, light to glass
He made me like fire and like light. And I became that which I saw
before and beheld from afar, Saint Simeon Stylites speaking here . . .
it was a holy emotion he played on me

ancient cities like temples
portals to the 4 directions
worked in the context (confines of a symbol)
Rome, Mecca, Mt. Meru
Kaaba, the page no longer sleeps . . .

Dear Ms. Waldman,

Recently i bought a book of poems by you entitled "Skin Meat Bones." It was very good and i
enjoyed it very much. It also made me more sure of what i am doing now. Along with this let-
ter, i have included a sample of my poetry. These poems are excerpts from a book of poems
(which has about two hundred and forty-five poems) i have been working on since September of
1985. It is a recollection of my painful childhood and my adolescence in progress (i will be 15 as of
December 14, 1986). It is my own way of dealing with my own strong homosexuality in an age
where to admit "gayness" is to say you are a "carrier" of a disease that seems endlessly invincible.

Since the fourth grade i have sensed that i was "different" from other children. i can
remember that even as a very small child "dressing up" in my mother's clothes and begging to
get to be "the mommy" when I played House with other children.

In my characteristically overdramatic style, i have fallen deep in love with each of my best
male friends (Brent . . . angelic eyes, . . . Kanon . . . oriental charm, . . . Mark . . . joviality, . . .
Erik . . . everything) and consequently have been forced to abandon the friendship before any
more pain has generated.

i keep mostly to myself at school trying my damndest to just be a wallflower (preferably a
lily). Since entering junior high in seventh grade i've been open game for any preppy asshole
who decides that he needs to boost his own ego by stepping all over someone else's. my locker
was continually vandalized. my clothes were under fire. i was ridiculed, pushed, punched, and
finally pushed too far.

i haven't really figured it out yet, but the best i can figure is that creativity in what you
wear, effeminacy in your manner, and having "too many female friends" are the yuppie crimes
of the eighties.

Everyone always laughed at me, but i knew in my heart that someday they would open up
a magazine or a newspaper, and they would see my face staring back at them.

When i thought of that I had had *Rolling Stone* or *Artforum* more in mind, but decided the obituaries would do me just fine and so in September of 1985 i attempted suicide in the third floor lavatory, three weeks after school had started.

The toilet was the perfect tomb, the floor the perfect deathbed. i wanted those kids to see my body, my dead body as they carried it away. i survived and also spent four hours in the emergency room throwing up each of the fifty pills i had digested (along with about four day's meals).

my mother was angry ("how could you"), my dad was sorry ("i should have known how depressed you were"), my teachers were unhelpful ("just get yourself strong and then back to school"), my grandma was great ("just worry about making yourself happy again, and the school can wait").

i was admitted on a Thursday and i went home on Saturday. i returned to that same school on Monday.

my psychologist wanted to play cards every session so I dumped him in favor of two counselors (a man and a woman) whose first question was:

"Do you ever feel homosexual?"

my mind went racing, did i give off an odor, a color, a telltale sign? i denied it, they . . . I wasn't ready for it yet.

This is when I started writing poems by the truckload. i relived all the pain, the shame, the fear, and the love i had ever felt. they helped me to tell my parents i was gay. my mom cried, my dad said "i should have known," and my brother avoided me for three months. life went on.

i poured everything into my poems feverishly. my mother was discouraged, "you have so much talent don't waste it on poetry. they're dead. no one likes poetry. it's old news."

She also told me everyone and their aunt wrote poems. That didn't scan—nobody likes it, everybody writes it. Don't ask.

This is when i discovered a record called "Better An Old God Than A New Demon" (whoops! other way around) Well, anyways i enjoyed "Uh-Oh Plutonium!" It sent me on a spurt of nature, ecological-revival stuff.

This is the third time i have sent my poems out, the first two times were to big companies. that was in December (no word yet). i guess they're not into anti-conservative, pro-homosexual poetry by effeminate manic-depressive fifteen-year-olds (uncommercial i guess).

i hope you enjoy them. i enjoyed writing them. By the way the title of the book they're from is "introspection (fad fadaise)". Good luck.

all my love,

N. O.

                    i lock my door

                                        like hot running water

many faces he cries to himself

                              barefoot, in a white nightdress

hospitalized for a trial on lithium

                    after a moment of second thoughts,

                              turns his head when I count . . .

Writing not
yr own
object
and all
the "shuns" to take   ~~"She" saw us~~
off no one
but you   ~~"She" was watching~~
are twin
to me   ~~"She" had the lights on~~
not stalk of
eyes   ~~"She" crossed the wide road~~
you are
careful   ~~"She" still loves you~~
air
a body   ~~It's not simple~~

a body   ~~Love is a killer~~
meets
a body   ~~Tongue, heart, thought is~~
through
music   what it's about
surrounded
by edges   ~~All possibilities to love or hate~~
did he
all that "he's"   ~~The tautology as it were vanishes~~
                                        ~~inside all propositions~~

— 55 —

not love you
back?   <del>(The key word still hasn't yet</del>
                                          <del>(been spoken)</del>

Not back
but climb
or claim
his way
not back
but
get back   not
to claim
yr air   mere
Not shun   jumble-job
a body
use it!   of words
use it!

a wrought, no blame, a burl . . .
hermaphrodite of the meteor, Zeus
berdache rise here
without tragedy

                                          Fiend o' the north
                                          My own son dreamed?
                                          Bred a vampire?
                                          He's the quote o' the eye
                                          Landslide
                                          His mind goes into matter
                                          He walks the night
                                          Door to door, blood on his chin
                                          Teeth like daggers
                                          All the mothers dead & gone

as would a *mamère* be in mannered form to
french the light and sip no matter
here to be a form of
reside, reside in a German grandfather

The Vulunelle is a very firendingly french form deroved
from Italian folk song of late 15th early 17 Dentury
and fittest employed fger astoral dubejects.

I tell you this abt ne'er being acceptable nor anyhouse
I feel this is a knife of hatres because of haf me or whilst
you really do What us ir. Whate are Who rae?
You teal me.

In a mesdow pur forgot in its helpy nuisance to any
tought hreehin composed. This is avectebury tys is type
it's a gas a pride overanyoun's hostorying. Tell 'em. Tell
me, two, three. What do you gelan & in a wheel o tyme I
teel ye loose all ye colours, core all of 'em your youm go
outta, Tim. The reason is a place you said
YOU SAID FROM HET THE OVERFLOW
Ah cooks be Oire, and hair twouds youth. Demon in this
love n hate realm what i doing fer ya. I compormomis
I compomormis ale het aboute
I weep I reallye tale youn everythang
Dear Highlander In a situation to protect your time & tis
book to be this lady & a core or legged position Makes out dry
I ant not, I want to let this go down go ear & lobe i meant
lobe because it was rin it was ringing of you of you
tied you in Makes men of ya
angry but I said o what this be all the ways I ever dreamed
& Blake entered thus dream.
        O holy rood me child hide!

I lobe you I mean it push this kush grass
under yr pillow for Kalachakra amre
seelp in the beg me karma of ye bed
MEN MEN MEN MEN MEN MEN MEN MEN MEN MEN MEN MEN MEN MEN MEN

(I type these words intoxicate like these words come as from a dream)

Lether wail in her own jajams
lettermen be
Let 'em roast in hell
I've no thing ado wi it men o men
I'm ambut a reflection of always I said out or isn't
any one of you, really its litmus A ways to go hey hoy
cut above any old og
It is a wadretting & fro me habla
I went back to prepuberio heh hoh
No night a mare was i getting stabbed no more o push n pull
I was foreign ring to your hook in me Was it was it was
heh hoh domy le me just sitting here bee

It is his male mind that gets to me
his sailor mind, *ist gut*
She hems the meteor, Zeus
Dresses him like her
Sews up his bag of bones
It is just okay okay
It is you, first of male
It is you I will salute again
& the man in me
But we were always the same
any aspect over the hill
or in hot persuit
I love you to be merged
in any way
Any mind so you will know
some things
Some things in his mind
It is just okay okay
I am talking to you
so you know some things
I call your name Iovis
I call your name these times Iovis
                        of Jove, of ownership

Wildwood, August 25, 1902

My Dearest,

I suppose you are anxious to hear from me but I am above waters yet I felt much better this morning. I suppose Irvin told you how I was. I did not get a chance to send word by him as he got off before I had a chance to see him. I went right to bed last night. I bathed myself with turpentine and Cory heated the mustard plasters and put it on well. I did not sleep much all night but I sweat quite a good bit and I think that is what helped me, i only ache in one side now. I went to Dr. Coben this morning and he gave me some medicine and I am taking it regularly so you must not worry about me anymore than possible. I will be anxious to hear from you. I went to the office this morning and inquired about that letter. I did not get up this morning and deliver the milk, Cory did that. I got up about 7 o'clock this morning. I think I will mail this letter so you will get it by Tuesday noon. Perhaps it will make you feel a trifle better. Now please remember all I have said to you and follow out some of the things and do what you think will be for the best. I will try and see if we cannot make things as pleasant as possible next winter so I will close this hoping to hear from you tomorrow. i remain

Yours as Ever

John

Tuesday morning washing. I was doctored good last night I feel fine this morning. Goodbye. John

*   *   *

I love my orgy of food denial
I love an impious force taking it calmly
I love a preface to his face outside the dance
The parking lot is an episode
I love: *in speculation free, in form, traditional*
I foreshadow my own end
& speaking as the son of Semele, I am immortal
& as the son of Zeus, I am divine
I speak in a man's voice wildly discordant
I don women's clothes
& deny the old religion
With my ironic undercutting, my new haircut
I speak in a foolish tongue

with a bitter flavor of love of them, the men
Exhausted with them, calm is my madness
I spit on my enemy as I am a woman
& as I am chorus I pretend throughout the cycle

Iovis is not bisexual but is as
hermatia, missing the mark
I turn my essence into a myth of origin
& prepare chicken propellers at the stove

A little-taller-than-Hitler is in power in this dream
& Bernadette and I guard the life of John Ashbery in a hut

We take care of them, the men, the poet-men,
providing them all night with little plastic ink refills
we wear like charms around our necks

Dear-Origin-Of-Male-Religion:

I am your libretto for a ritual to allay this robotical suffering
we cause each other bare, lay low, lie down in it
or bury it to grow any hyacinth out of its wounded moth

I love my end of a fool denial
& spread the collective work around
& will not repent this word or any other weapon

You insulted me when you weren't looking & drove a spike
into the heart of me
It dissolves into a seed syllable
of anything brave to be outside the tangle & strife
we two make beauty out of a dark structure
sanctioning the next time the show's in town
& come this way around a street
& to my ceremonial dance become private twitches
Entheos Entheos I am full of the god
Entheos Entheos I am full of the god
shaking to tear this bull apart & return to peace

Don't mock me as I avenge the death of my sisters
in this or any other dream
In order to make the crops grow
you men must change into women

Ἑρμαφρόδιτος

IV

FIELD OF MARS

Dreams grow more intense as they demand entry into the poem. Why dream of Hegel? Attempt, perhaps, to bring an all-embracing male mind into situation (thesis) to evoke its antithesis. Poem, yes, is synthesis. Is he ridiculous? Field or battleground of poetry & love is named "Mars," the poet's planetary ruler. The poet thinks/doubts herself in love with war & tries to write in anti-forms without success. But the boy, her son, guides her through her confusion and gleefully names in ecstatic chant all the ways to mask plutonium. She must do battle with the unleashed poisons. (Any woman must do this: retract petrochemical, nuclear nightmare. Is it that simple?) World War II needs scrutiny & some luminous particulars will surely be noted here. A palinode, that wicked song of retractions, sets her off & concludes the troublesome musings in an effort to "take back" her vulnerability.

                    will you be summarily
                         working?

          & there's morning: dumb circles of sleep & dream
white limo pulls up on San Francisco street
               girl with plastic eyes exits & scares me
exit don't sleep on the page I tell myself
          all the fathers pass . . .
                    enter "Georg Wilhelm Friedrich Hegel" who is going
to
perform for us out in the beautiful
     green field, the "Academy." We have been
     excitedly awaiting his Show. I see Liz on the grass
     doubled up in her passion for Hegel, and the
Lesbian next to her is offended to hear her speak of it
     to me & then won't sit down next to me in the
          grandstands. Julia rushes up to say "Hegel
     is going to perform my favorite piece of his!"
Something about the Dog and the Man. Hegel has tense
     red hair & thick spectacles. He wants all the
          women present to fall in love with him

"The sun is up and we're ready to go."

swatched in their space suits, Allen & Gardner
        glide out to meet the satellite in speculative logic

Allen's pas de deux is a slow surreal dance of
        weightlessness: he easily inserts the
stinger into the nozzle and, when attached,
        he fires his jets to stop the satellite's rotation.

"Give me a little more right yaw."
"Come on in, Anna."

I count you in arms
One a boy, two absorbing book
Three: a wise eye
I count you after you're gone
Four: laugh, five: quit, six: wind
I number the ways to clutter a heart

Desire stretches poet's heart
Hours are numbered in yr arms
Separated by glaciers of fierce wind
Sunday stay in with 11th-century book
Monday you're gone, unreachable
Can't concentrate Tuesday to keep wise

Wednesday it's hard to get wise
Caution is difficult Thursday in a heart
Friday gets all the duties done
So hours will be open as arms
Shut in Saturday I'll write the book
How To Make Love in Wind

Can't say this, can't be wind
Be quiet Anne, don't be unwise

Study one another in a Florentine book
Older heart bows to younger one
Put me back in travel, read "arms"
Quick, the thought's gone

We'll never get to Spain, never gone
From here, American town founded on wind
Yet caught in usual flow of arms
Degraded world hallucination, wise
To love if other numbers claim our hearts?
Keep this a sacred book
                              Heraclitus to Hegel to Marx
between us, who write our own
daily, words for you even as you're gone
words to carry—what?
upon wind
unwise
older in yr arms, a Florentine

arms, books,
numbered texts don't say it
me too (don't don't say it) wind rips words
apart, naked—breaks the heart

            . . . evanescing little sixes sestina
or try this sonnet for size
I write after Donne in a kind of expiration mode:

Break off sad kiss dearest husband
that holds fast, sucks dry
You go that way, I'll this
Our phantoms now dance separately
Remember that holy day?
We don't owe each other anything cheaply
Go, go & go, even if it kills you
& say the word to me—say it—"go"
& my words will stay true to me

This is justice for a tough murder
Except it's too late to kill me too,
being triple-dead. One, I'm leaving
two, telling you—go—
& three, the poem dies on me—go—go!
but you I love the most, no—no—never go!

(the trouble was the aggression of those men the Itza;
     tumen uchci u chibilob tumen uinicob ah Itzaob lae

we didn't do it; we pay for it today   *ma toon ti mentei toon botic hele lae)*

but

inside you
inside you

what me?
what me
are you
inside of

I say
you are all
there is in-
side me
now inside
out

but later
I'm thinking
something
putting on clothes
& you talking
about the
mixing of us

want me
all for
your self

& not even
there
you have a
restless mind
like mine

from branding to slaughter
no black sand sanctuary

Dear Ms. W,

I am 30 years old. I have been a loser and a thief for most of my life. I am sure I deserve to spend some time in prison, but not for a crime I did not commit. (I am an ex-thief, not a murderer with millions of dollars hidden somewhere) . . .

(he has something of the planets
borrowing
wordless stamina in him

a snarler
who would not wonder
at him
guilty or not)

—I'm scared. Mommy!

—Everyone's dead, remember?

—Remember, we woke up in the hospital

—What the hell

—I might be hurt I have a broken leg

—Come back inside the hospital

—It's too late I'm going to die

—Let's say you shot my brother too

—Why, was he the enemy?

—We have to be the good guys *and* the bad guys

—So I killed myself

—But I shot your leg. But you'll be walking
   in a couple of years

—This is World War III

—Yeah. Everyone's dead

—So what's the point?

—No, I won't be walking but I'll be *seeing*

That would be the boy in bed in her arms very soon, that he would go to battle, that she already imagined it: the fathers would send the sons to battle, that the rain would follow, that it would be gentle, that a man you know died on his son's birthday, that Argentina Corazon writes she will send you a "fiery messenger," that Apollo took bites of the sun, that the Spartans are responsible, that the economical and the divine are painted equally here, that Stesichorous recants his early attack on Helen as the baneful cause of the Trojan War, that she will finally have a dream about the soft cow's belly, that in the dream the cow is chased away by a jealous wife, that he had a husband's rough beard, that she who was a cow locked away her virginity in the "V" of a tree, that we were never there together on Red Oaks Lake, that the water didn't move, that the oars were never driven, that we never spoke, that we did not embrace, that the sky did not darken, that no one called us to come back, that you were never in my life

> Dear One: I when out seeking these things
>   to remind me of you

I wanted to take on the father & son simultaneously
(The elder wears the ankle-length peplos, the normal dress
               of a charioteer) and take the prophecy back:

that the sons would go to battle, that the fathers would send the sons to battle, that they do it again & again, that sons go willingly to battle but go with fear to battle, that the father is filled with fear, that they would kill with fear in battle again & again, that the American continent is doomed in battle, that

the fathers of the continent that are not the real fathers but usurpers are
doomed in fear in battle Heh ya ya! Heh Heh heh ya ya
            & the son sings

for the "guardianship of plutonium"

"Then there's dry-ice snow
 frozen enchiladas & all frozen things
 like orange juice, frozen pipes
 then fans all around
 electric gates
 glass containers
 aluminum
 Let's cover up plutonium with
 plastic bags when as soon as they get
     to bright sunlight are biodegradable
 leaves
 more moss
 light bulbs—just are so bright
 there are still a few ways to get through
 (2 old baseball stadiums—nah)
 piles of dirt—then fence around that
 loose dirt with farms behind it shoots out
 glass flashes
 Then there's like—oh yeah—everything
     glued on with sap—dries as hard as rock when in the air
 pieces of wood to make a fire
 Let's cover plutonium with magnets—
 you try to get one layer away
     with a gun, magnet pulls it back
 Let's cover plutonium with what cliff dwellings are made of
 Get some Indians to come back and make some
     adobe with ash
 Try a hologram
 lie detectors with guards all around
 robotic guards with guns

a message comes out says 'Get outta here!'
then there's paper
chicken wire
a rock level
(whenever I look around
that's what I say)
Let's cover plutonium with
everything in the world
& put it in pipes
every type of things—a sample of everything
beehives with this little hole cut into them
    an alarm goes off, they go to the person they see
a layer of honey
every sticky thing
every liquid
horns on cars
then there's cardboard
every cigarette in the world!
it doesn't take a type but every cigarette
    in the world
Let's cover plutonium with a graveyard
Let's cover it with
one of every single stone in the world
pennies, quarters, everything—
Then gold around it, then diamonds, rubies, emeralds
Then there's plaster, then linoleum,
    congoleum
Then hard candy—every single kind that
    gives immediate cavities
A thing with waterguns
tomatoes, celery, carrots, potatoes, green
    peppers, parsley
burning hot heaters, a person touches 'em
    it burns 'em
Let's cover plutonium with
wood chips that beavers have made
many teepees

TVs, radios, leather
actually a teepee folded up
all the toothpaste tubes filled with toothpaste
every single brand, every single kind!
barbed wire
American flags
old wheels—metal
bars of jail with canine bloodhounds
      that are trained to everything you say
telephone wire with sticky stuff
Let's cover plutonium with play dough—dried
dead people's bones & then there's plain
      dead people with nothing on them
something on them or nothing on them
every single bug in the world that crawls
      on the earth
bees with five stingers—they all sting
      at the same time
more chicken wire
steel cubes
2 layers regular glass
shatterproof glass
big magnets—electromagnetic—on top & bottom
big rock would be the first covering—the
      whole thing tightly covered with wires
poured concrete, more paint, more tar
let's cover plutonium with plastic bags & bottles
disposable bags
styrofoam coffee cups
half & half containers
fireworks
There's a big display when you try to get in"

                              (he sings he sings
                              gazing out window
                              on the ride from Telluride)

"people will kill for a dollar bill they fight war killing people they never saw
before people in Nicaragua hear they are being sent out of Managua to kill or

die or be fried like Hitler did to women & children"
                                        the son says
Hence the euphemisms of calling a battle "a party," hence
a plethora of badges, medals, & hence the memo Air Marshal
Arthur Harris wrote to Portal, chief of the British air staff
at the time of the Normandy invasion, complaining "grave injustice"
was being given to his bomber crew if all the attention & publicity
centered upon the army & navy

Modern war: blunder after blunder explained away
Modern war: no need to invade Europe, the bomber offensive
                would finish Germany
Modern war: American heavy bombers killed more American than
                German soldiers in Normandy
Hiroshima: brutal act of revenge
(bomber crews wore lucky charms)

A sergeant major screamed at a soldier still wearing his cap
as he marched into Church "Take yer fuckin 'at off in the
                                        'ouse of Gawd, cunt."

The invasion off Slapton Sands was a disaster. Nine German E boats made a
sortie from Cherbourg and sank American landing craft
                        drowning 750 soldiers and sailors . . .

is to seem what you would be, and
in seeming be tough, be fierce, be soldier
the formula for dealing with fear is
ultimately rhetorical and theatrical:
regardless of your actual feelings,
you must simulate a carriage, which
will affect your audience as fearless,
in the hope you will be imitated

                        (U.S. Officer's Guide)

Modern war: Churchill's radio oratory

Modern war: MacArthur listening with "thirsty ear for the witching melody of
faint bugles blowing reveille"

> (the raids went on but by October 1 the Luftwaffe had
> abandoned day bombing and bombed only at night . . .)

hence the bodies blown to bits, hence gibbering citizens

queuing at hospital, hence "I have withdrawn the troops"

(General Eisenhower), hence to die for one's country,

hence the fathers went to war, they go to war willingly go

to war hesitating, the fathers live for war, they return to

the hearth, keep the fires burning, they go for you little

baby, they go for freedom

To the President of the Republic of Guatemala

Your Excellency:

I urge you to order independent investigations of human rights violations in Guatemala,
regardless of the administration under which they occurred, and to bring those found respon-
sible for political killings, "disappearances," and torture to justice.

I also ask the government make public the findings of its investigations and, in compliance
with Resolution 15 of the United Nations Subcommittee on Prevention of Discrimination and
Protection of Minorities, that it inform relatives of the "disappeared" of their family members'
fates.

I thank you. I plead with you.

Anne, Grasping-the-Broom-Tighter-Now

It is thought
gamma rays
from
Cygnus x-3
are produced there
by protons

of even
higher energy
    —*the broom tighter*

They would for example
carry 10 million
times the energy
achieved by
the most powerful
atom smasher

—*Anne grasping tighter tighter*

                    Other candidates
                    for high-energy cosmic
                    ray production
                    include Geminga—
                      a perplexing object

as well as pulsar systems
known as Hercules X-I and Vela X-I

All far out in the Milky Way

                (Pull back in shreds this lady's mind
                she'll discover how to find a
                sweeter sorrow in the wind

                    Defenses down won't resign
                    or let nature be unkind
                    Pull back in shreds this lady's mind

It's blown to bits—space-design
What intruders to make her pine?
sweet sorrows in the wind

Daughters of Time:
when we can't move to shake a male rhyme O mercy

                              let it down on me)

by plumes by plumes of magma rising, by plumes to
take home from Pluto, by plumes by plumes Pluto rising:
the edge of submerge, the plume not spot in the crust
the plume erupt in hot spot, magma magma rising,
Mars rising, assume that plate moved
assumed it was technical feat to rise to rise by plumes to take home
the continents rising, by plumes by plumes magma rising

end to submerge, death to follow

(When in 1912, the Austrian physicist Victor N. Ness
sought to trace the radiation's origin by ascending
in a balloon, he found that instead of becoming
weaker, the radiation became more intense as he rose.)

                    I was nearing the things I was waiting for
                    from his return: a triangle in the shape
                    I respond to most, a replica of a mother's
                    ear, and a goddess holding up the world
                    I had made so solid it can't be broken
                    Portable ancestor worship is what I thought
                    of here when he brought these things to me
                    And of the father, what things?
                    And of the father, what things?
                    Bayonets from the great war
                    Handblown glass
                    Old photography
                    the ascension of our Lord
                         (he rose! he rose!)

It is Glaukos's day in court. He sits in Robert Lagomarsino's office, protesting with others the House vote that day that authorized aid to the Contras. He was arrested & jailed on trespassing charges & decided to defend himself. Middle seventies—wiry, stooped, sandals on his feet, sparse graying hair. Came to America from Greece in his twenties & in the 1930s was a dedicated leftist. After the purges & the Moscow–Berlin pact he withdrew from politics. Later he became active again, this time as a radical pacifist-anarchist, in the mold of Leo Tolstoy or A. J. Muste. He's been arrested many times for civil disobedience, mainly while participating in antinuclear demonstrations.

Dear Glaukos-What-A-Mystery. First husband to mother, father of brother, the "saint" who lived apart from the world. Grecian & a kind of lambent stress to take cradle of civilization back, an older time, whose father was the Poet bringing nourishment to the stars, the planets, make them sing with the accompaniment of lyre & small drum
You stayed in me my mother's "first," shadow-marriage under spell of Olympus

1. What myth & which male character-hero do you identify with most?

2. Which goddess do you most admire, fear, revere? Why?

3. What was your rite of passage to manhood? At what age? What were the circumstances?

4. When do you put your best foot forward?

Archilochus (7th century B.C.): I am both *therapon*

$$\text{of Lord Enyalios,}$$
$$\text{\& acquainted (with}$$
$$\text{the lovely gift}$$
$$\text{of the muse)}$$

Therapon = a ritual substitute. Enyalios = the Cretan god or lord of war, thus Mars/Ares. "Acquainted," a modest or understated translation of a verb whose root is "epist," like *episteme,* Plato's word for belief (i.e., as a type of knowledge)—epistemology. The verb has a wide associative semantic range in translation, e.g., to know or be able, capable; understand; be assured of; skillful, expert—So, as in Homer I guess, to know for certain. Archilochos made a remarkable and thus well-remembered scandal or blasphemy once, when fighting for Sparta, he tossed away his shield when things got too absurdly out of hand, and wrote it, saying he'd just rather buy another one. In Sparta they used to say the famous farewell before battle (mother to son et cetera) "Come back with it or on it." It was just other day I saw something that made me think, clearly for once, that the field of Mars is that of love. I mean none of the poet/warrior biz is actually comprehensible except that the metaphoricalness of reality is perceived. And is it?

What they call war isn't war—it's butchery without the cannibalism it purposes— which Homer points at more than once. As mistaken or imperceived the poet is, equally a real warrior is not able to be seen by literal eye. Any artist, really, and that seems very important to me. The artists in this secular world are the warriors, and the field of Mars is identical to the field of Love, & the artists are the only ones whose entire being depends upon the conduct on that field.

In the secular the bravery of art and the bravery of love are identical. Hence, I guess, the likeness (in Shakespeare) of the poet, the lover, and the madman— the latter because of real perception, though without art; the lover there because of delight & surrender, immersed, with no need for art; and the poet able to contain, and needing to articulate, both. While Olson called Sh. "the greatest poet of Mars in the English language" and I understood O. to be thus including himself—now I see that *any* poet is one of Mars, especially and only as it's all seen metaphorically. The poet is in other words the subject—the object may or may not be literally war.

Sorry, I'm off the road. It has, this stuff, to do with risk and with metaphor. By the extraordinary metaphor of etymology, for instance, you could also register it Poet as Carpenter, i.e., the chariot-carpenter of the Vedas the "car" being all that and of course "heart" too (Kardia/coeur) or as "weaver"/"joiner" and so on. But in a secular society I think the warrior question is—for me anyway— the thing. You know, a lot of maleness confusions.

Things are tough at the school ($)—I can't go much longer under the relentless pressure of it. Little or no fun. Mostly worse. Very few souls want to hear the good news, eh? I feel a fool for not knowing a way to make a living—but then, existence is such a trap. Fuck it. I wish I had a job carrying some jazz guy's bags, and there are a lot around whose bags I would. They're keeping me from despair.

but my wounds, which are the participants
in what is not subject matter, but a poet's
play, stage blood, they are the scourge of me

dear Iovis of the Fiery Night:
                              into shallower & safer waters
let me ride free

                         going
abroad
                         in the mind
but break heart,
                         prithee break
one is always
a limitation
                    only a fraction
          from the fire
                    but whose
          illusory pictures
the mad king said much to you
"both, both"
          tasted sadness there
in the battle for his
          mind
                    on
                    the
                    field of
          Love

My Mars, who rules me
he in me
I'm a he
tonight
all girls
run from me
to the groves

Mars: when time is old   Tell me about when time is old

when time was old
I forgot myself
   became a "he"   for battle
forgot myself
        out of fear

(the universe would have been destroyed by flames
        had not Zeus struck the rash youth
            with a thunderbolt
      & sent him tumbling into the
        waters of the Eridanus

a crime to change sex, too near the sun . . .)

           my field

Where is it?
        insignificant against the gods?
          male nakedness too sacred to see?
    .

body to teach me a field
centered like a pendulum
plumb line I saw I wanted
      (vanity)
        in field of silent scribbling
outrage of how many caves you lived in
in sickness in health
move your fingers
        real ink, serenity
          gutted a house & nothing left

                                  but O vanity down
you who are Buddha
art women
                                        body to teach me a field
                                        body to teach
                            (as more of his letters attest he was frantic . . .)
                            Was ist Aufkärung?
                    not a resurrection but Happy Easter

      & blunt the body to the sword

                                        body to teach

                                                how cum down

                    dab in the sweet milk

                                        body wider so much wider than the sea

my field of work & origin
      I do battle to a hot night
                        "Let us fight them on the plains"
Elohim brings flood & rainbow
                  fight in his cause, the Sky god
                        god of thunder
                        in his name
                  his name: Elohim, sing it in the plains
the Syrian gods are gods of the hills
                  let us fight them in the plains

                        (sing it in the plains)

What of the god of fire?
destroys Sodom & Gomorrah
      fire purifies

fat & blood in the temple fire
consume the wicked in the fire
   Fire god who is repudiated by Prophets
         Sky god becomes a metaphor in Prophets
"To obey is better than sacrifice"

Yahweh Yahweh O phallic conquering god
let circumcision be the covenant
    the oiled pillar is god's house
     O sing it in the plains, god's house/hose is his big prick!

        come in Moses, do not deny the call

Rites of passage: There were several. First L.S.D., First Sex, First Mental Institution . . . First L.S.D. in Northern California with some boarding school chums. Took two hits of purple microdot and wandered all over the sand dunes down close to seventeen mile drive in Pebble Beach. Glorious superimposed matrix patterns over incoming fogbank. I felt as though I was watching the weather of the earth being made. Climbed out in trees and flung ourselves laughing down long smooth dunes. First sex also in Northern California, a young sophisticated beauty seduced and then instructed me for a considerable period of time. She was an athlete and an animal. First night in her Dad's unused sauna room, she cries out again and again "I love sex!" almost burning me with her exuberant friction. First Mental Institution: Actually not just the first, but the cumulation of all of them (four). A choice was made here to remain not only with this world, but this life. Age 15-17. You wanted to know; I tell you these things. Love, B.

& you could never do the assignments
never conquer the sestina or 5-part suite
on mythology & the death of sport
you could never listen
you could never be my slave
you could never not complain
& when it came to injustice upon yrself
you could rail
you could call the law down
  you'd invoke daddy law in a snap
  you never saw yr own ghost
  never saw yr own hot projection
  you hadda call the law

you hadda invoke what you couldn't handle
                        (let it down on me

                    & I went back>> Went back there>>Had left>>
                Went back>> Couldn't>> Do it>> What?>> Go back>>
                Had never left>> One last time>> Like a palinode>>
                Took back>> Lied>> Didn't>> Walked most of the way>>
            Part of a truth>> Climbed the last part of a truth>> Up on a
        slope>> Come down now>> I said come down, come down now>>
                Where>> Here>> His friend says he's gone>> A lie>> A lie
            gone now>> I went back>> Had left I thought>> Had left a
            thought to go back>> It catches up>> Go back>> Settled by
        phone>> I thought>> He didn't think>> Was thinking a thought
        not to get back>> I did>> What?>> I did go back>> Not lost>>
            Can't be a lie>> I climbed the slope>> Walked into a lie>>
            One more time>> He is establishing in me more than I care
        a mention>> Leave it>> How?>> Leave it be>> Can't>> Go back>>
    He's never left I think>> What if he never left>> I climbed a lie>> Lie down>>
    I can't>> I remember the futon on the floor>> Don't tell myself about it>>
        Stop>> I remember hangers with odd clothes on them>> Don't do
        it>> Go back, I can't but be remembering this>> Stop>> Something
        is new>> Deny it happened>> Like a palinode>> It never happened>>
            Say it: it never happened>> Say this: it never happens>>
        Part of a truth>> Can't>> Why?>> Why does it go>> Because you
            ask for it>> The death of language>> Never>>The death of
        writing>> Never>> One last time>> Never>> Had left>> Gone
            back>> A lie>> Had left me I thought>> Had left I can't
            remember I thought>> Than I care a mention>> Slopes here>>
        Near by>> Walk>> Can't>> Lie down>> Never>> Lie with him>>
            Never again>> Can't think it. It never happened>> I will
        say: it never happens>> Settled by phone I thought> The end I
            thought>> Was not to ever have happened>> Again>> Had
            left>> One last time>> Was one last time>> Never>>

everi thing endis
every thing ends

borne like a myrrour
        held up ti humanyte

on field of love

V

TO BE A RHYMING WI' THEE

She wants the voice of a soldier to seize her throat. Thus the poet honors her father-in-law and by implication her own father once more, both men who served their country, their worlds & words so far from her own: mental & military. What a peculiar stance they have endured in this odd time. What romance still lurks there? "Men could be men." The moon walk talk floats in: a kind of reminder of a tenderer time. She needs to acknowledge the lineage she gives birth within. By extension, the son reaps the father's reward, but needs a new battleground just as her own son will. She prays it won't be war, which perpetually provides the most juice. They—the ones in power of course—love it. Poetry is a kind of salvation if perceived thus. Why not? Her son might like it. She sympathizes with the austerity of these men & moves toward a true argument with a tangible entity. She goes off to meet him under pain of scorn, at the least titillation . . . On a train abroad she listens to & queries a survivor, relic, the same age as her "fathers," who has witnessed the dissolution of the two Germanies.

Her stumble on All Of These Things

    making love the blind child on TV

        accretion of swords for living

    a shaping & clinging   I see the close reading

        of Charles Olson

I . . . who knows?

           enter the story of how do we enter

what would a father be a father cone a father meet

                  her nightlife

mine, it's mine

        to enter how do we

predicated beyond the grave

        or ash

      weeping at the funeral of

Scalapino's grandfather or that of my father-in-law

a mirage of night merely

for do we do we

& may I, attentive & present

be her widow

the daughter-widow?   in-law-widow?

Charlie dies & it is a father-in-law

time frame,

beautiful weeping

4 o'clock of an afternoon in Florida

with "the prettiest name"

His present look

& stubborn appreciation as if to say

I see you & see you too

I see you in the form of a

heavy woodland sprite

or in uniform,

Air Force Dear Father-In-Law

it is a calling it is calling

RESTRICTED
Headquarters, Army Air Forces
Washington

AF6AS-2 210.453

Subject: TDY Orders 9 April 1946

1.   Each of the following named officers will proceed from Washington, D.C. on or about
April 1946 to Hq., CDC, Quarry Heights, Canal Zone or TDY from approximately seven (7) days in

connection with Personnel Matters ARP Military Project, Bogotá, Colombia, South America, and upon completion thereof will return to Washington, D.C.:

Colonel Charles C. Bye

2.   Col. Bye will report to the theatre commander (of his designated representative) as practicable during his visit, and in all cases on the completion thereof, the nature and findings resulting from his visit and substance of any report he intends to make to the War Dept or to the office from which he is sent. In all reports made as a result of this temporary duty, a positive statement that the foregoing instruction has been carried out will be included.

all in writing
a positive statement
what tell of me
of men in me?
what tell to them of men
or me
bedding down to an old earsong
lambent
ho ho
lost or consummate the idea

                  break or breath
to be a one
(man
you be
a
one)
& may you
may you

or one
loaded
over the coals

                                   or border
beyond which another male poet goes
                    adorned
perhaps because of
working
together

we share a day, beloved husband
a light to read by

(o the company I keep)
"Au nom de la République vous êtes décorés de la croix de L'Ordre de
                Feuilles Mortes"

My friends, there can be no doubt that we now possess the means and the power to take
Constantinople before the end of the summer if we act with decision and with a due sense of
proportion. . . . It will multiply the resources and open the Channel for the reequipment of
the Russian armies. It will dominate the Balkan situation and cover Italy. It will resound
through Asia. Here is the prize, and the only prize, which lies within reach this year . . .

Winston spoke words. We are words, words, words, horses, manes, deeds.
    We are deeds.
And of our labor in words: light the light in the sweet air.
And intoned, while shaving, *"Introibo ad altare Dei"*

                              field of congenials

to an idea, the Eagle has landed

                "For military contractors, it will be a rag
                    tag, rough & tumble, and dog eat dog day,"
                                            said an astronaut
                        & former Textron, Inc. executive
                        who will become vice chairman of
                        General Dynamics next month and replace
                        Mr. Pace in 1991.
                "It's going to be
                    a bloodletting and the guy with the
                    most blood will win."

Roger, Tranquility, we copy you on the ground. You got a bunch of guys about to turn blue.
We're breathing again. Thanks a lot.

Houston, that may have seemed like a very strong final phase. The auto-targeting was taking
us right into a crater, with a large number of big boulders and rocks . . . and it required . . .
flying manually over the rock field to find a reasonable good area.

Roger, we copy. It was beautiful from here. Tranquility, over.

We'll get to the details of what's around here, but it looks like a collection of just about every shape—angularity, granularity, about every variety of rock. . . . The colors—well—there doesn't appear to be too much of a general color at all; however, it looks as though some of the rocks and boulders (are) going to have some interesting colors to them. Over.

(Outside the) window is a relatively level plain cratered with a fairly large number of craters of the five- to fifty-foot variety and some ridges, small, twenty, thirty feet high, I would guess, and literally thousands of little one- and two-foot craters around the area. We see some angular blocks out several hundred feet in front of us that are probably two feet in size and have angular edges. There is a hill in view, just . . . ahead of us, difficult to estimate but might be a half a mile or a mile.

The surface is fine and powdery. I can—I can pick it up loosely with my toe. It does adhere in fine layers like powdered charcoal to the sole and sides of my boots. I only go in a small fraction of an inch, maybe an eighth of an inch, but I can see the footprints of my boots and the treads in the fine sandy particles.

Neil, this is Houston. We're copying.

he to me
I take your son
I take him
& his sex
he grows beyond
you in his sex
his sex in me
it wounds you
you die in the
fury of his
sex
he enacts his
own conception
son of the father
creating the form
then it's named

this or
that: husband
& the impulse
is passion
a rare
form
the passion
that makes you
name it
you need
to
& name all
forms of
birth
& dying
this is the
skandha song
a fantasy of
which you act
the lover
a close reading

Husband dreams gypsy woman here to do a Tarot reading, and spreads a very large deck around herself on the floor. She is dressed in a red & gold kimono. When half the cards are laid out she stands up & begins convulsing. Soon she is flopping on her belly on the floor like a fish. She gets back up & moves quickly like a geisha woman in small steps out of the room to find a subject for the reading. She is standing by the cards with one or two men, one of whom seems to be the subject. I (Reed) move in & she directs her attention to me. She is now a woman in her fifties with a very pretty round face. A huge almost life-sized card appears before her. Over their heads is suspended a sword horizontally. The image is very colorful & very strong. The frame of the dream moves slowly down & I don't quite take in the name or caption along the bottom of the card. Suddenly a long crumpled sack tumbles down in a completely different room & a man spills out onto a hospital bed. He has a horrible white hole ringed with black in the side of his head & he is doing something with some thin tubing in his lap. This is extremely painful to watch; he is attending to a womb in his abdomen.

Map a poke
koto be hosprous not loygal ee helbron
ee Helbron
map the wound, a poke, a probe, a thrust
gypsied down & sung
map a parsifal
cininima cybernetica
a bubbla sermon a
"tot" or german dead
attending the wound
be that be tot
occasion a ruse
kack kaw giblet
sword a boon, a bond
boxomil to be rhyming withee
O clothe, cynicilia, happenstonce,
wander, be true
I see the mocha may day 1918
Calm ye, Cypriot, act
go back ti childhide
sybillante for poems
(I enjoy this)
squawk ti boot
& sythersizeria thy nichte
        kay?

        (he bids me bides my time)
check on Allegory

        Faust's dream et cetera
        acros stichos

& be the endless father of him
He grows through you and into me
sweet lineage, sweet tree

what happened? what collapsed? what didn't? what drew applause? what did the world want to hear? that communism is dead on its feet? what is the etymology of the root of the sorrow of communism? who engineers the sorrow of this word? what crept into her marrow a long way back, what polluted her soil? who wasn't thinking straight? who got paid? who didn't? what god stuck around? what fathers? what deities were confined to little votive shelves, who were shelved for barter & exchange? how kept under wraps? what's bargained for here? how can they be relegated to a lesser without revenge? what the sense of salvation? of sadism? who responded to the call? who wants to be saved?

"I would have preferred to have been from here—the marsh, decimated land scape, the old control towers . . ." he said, gesturing abstractedly to the metaphorical east.

"And this was my desire, an abandoned point of view, a terrible weakness on my part to be a victim of chance, of war perhaps. But it comes down now, surely it comes down, relative to the idea of what can ever come down. Walls? Is it the boundary between what clothes you wear? A close call? The others (they lived behind the wall) were merely projection. Could you say money, the absence of it, is a close call? Or is it only a lapse? A human lapse? I would have lived like a monk, a nun, and been a kind of closed property." (He winks now)

I couldn't say much. I came from America and felt too rich although this had nothing to do with money, nothing to do with my leather pants. But what I liked, I told him, was sweat on the brow of the worker, this could be an artist even. It was that simple. A sweep toward physical reform. A frontal gauge of the possibility of a spot of low retaliation. And in this moisture combined both the propaganda and the resistance. Or something like that, a cry for more, perhaps, the cry for an end to barbarism. Does someone decide your approval?

"I always voted," he said, by way of assent. "There was never any doubt about that, our kind of freedom. Motives are and are not useless. I had a kind of gloom for what they were denied, the people on the dark other side."

"And that gave you hope?"

"Hope is a drug. Hope gets you through the night. Hope leaps on the beloved."

"Still, would you feel secure without it?"

"Hope sings out to be obstructed. It is basically fickle."

"So what is power, by definition? Why unify people toward any goal?"

"Because they never separated. Like the sides of the brain. And one could reside on the crease of the other. One could be brilliant, artistic, trembling, the other cold and calculating. They could both be lost in a private sense of reform and be at each other like wildcats, fighting. They might play out the ritual of contrast. One could be sweating. While the other designs a tactical missile to sell to and destroy Iraq at the same time (just one example). May the gods of light conquer the extremes of a dark view!" Was the old man turning religious on me?

I noticed out the train window how the landscape was changing. It was après something or other. Après human habitation? Simply ugly? After the so-called end-of-nature? Was it a matter of dead trees? Were those little grave markers I was seeing amongst the trees? Were the men by the side of the road exhuming a body that had perished in flight over a symbolic wall? Were my eyes playing tricks on me again?

He was an agile talker. He confessed to having had as a child a fascination for the Nazi uniform. How bright it seemed. How it lifted him higher. He liked the cuffs especially. His mother, he said, shielded his eyes when the dazzling uniforms came again. He escaped to Lausanne and pursued a life in music.

"Music is the great mediator and arbiter!—is that the word? My two Germanies don't know this yet. But they might. When the ears of one fold in a harmony toward the ears of the other, then music will rain down like manna. Everyone, if they are still around, will finally be able to listen."

VI

LEIR

The poet worked backstage quite young—a "gopher"—at the Shakespeare festival in Stratford, Connecticut, observing night upon night Morris Carnovsky's rendering of the mad Lear. She always planned to write of it, the play really, which grabbed her ear. She thinks perhaps the production was too austere. How to ground Lear's soft foolish agony, his imagination? She always thought to act the part, but how? She has her own version. She was perpetually thinking of family intensities. The vulnerability of father to daughters and how it goes the other way too. Freud, her favorite of the doctors, enters here to make a few comments. When the poet's mother came to see the show she arrived backstage in tears. "I know what it feels like, I know what it feels like to be an unloved parent." A daughter's shock. Her mother became King Lear. Father was remote, one of the kinds in a distant land. The poet instantly turned into a model daughter. A repentant Cordelia who won't die. This is many years ago. Now she is the exiled king herself, whose love to count on? How to make them prove it? Her wealth is reduced. Her child might spurn her. She goes back to this play again, again as it set her ear to a beautiful male cadence beyond gender & broke her heart.

> touch me with noble anger,
> And let not women's weapon, water-drops,
> Stain my man's cheeks!

inside his nightmare
he is venerate
Zeus himself known as "chthonios,"
of the dark depths
inside active cruelty,
base deceit
a darker intrigue:
filial ingratitude
& a man's eyes ripped from his head

    sing a construct
      what hunt
or storm
what unkinde

mnemonic device
got recorded in brain
or memory clutch
at work here:
tragikal historie

  shunned from a door I know this
alive in hovel, grotto, dear father, I . . .

& would be Robert Armin's fool
to stand him by
  in a kind of motley, go well the time
the tune, checked
colorful rag on a tight lithe body, I . . .
  & would do a little hop or skip about the court
  nimble o' body & wit
you have that in you I would fain call master
what's that?
authority
why a leer to speak brave of him, pity is
untented woundings of any parent's curse
or dare it be said husband's
for left darkling, here
& I have years on my back 45

  And conjured thus a radiant sun
   comes not between dragon & his wrath
or woman 'tween her call & duty

what care of me born to father
& to be married to
keep a station in life
& bear a child who will or will
not bear his mother's love

Call me Cordelia
I am not a rock
I speak not in riddles, but true

I live & think now to the epitome of wildness
wherever it takes the child for she is dead

What's that I'd fain call master?
beyond a call of grave, blast or fog upon thee
I'd call him Daddy, and speak Modo or Mahu
who drinks the green mantle of the standing pool
for these men are mad to be fathers

tell them out?
Cry out his blinde spot
what is his canon of measure

Ecbatan in Media
was surrounded by seven concentric walls
each of a different color signifying
the seven planets
with the treasury (a king's heart?) located in the citadel
        it beats like a mind
emanates its rays,
colorful yet protected by
        mirrors,
noble heart, prithee break

Ulug Beg the Mogul also modelled Samarkand
so it might reflect the celestial order of the heavens
but what wrought here
so wizened
out of proportion
to him
he asks them to parcel out a heart

and what, he, heart broke
confined to hovel, cave of refuge
all the circles closing in
the kings of France & Burgundy are young
are husbands if you want them

what spot dwell
to vent a wrath called for
in langauge rare's the texture of
an appetite November 26, 1607
to suit a king

what makes a king holy relic
& back the senses
to the world outside
what but a grief to age &
think "it" can be bought
outside: harsh
(keep it to the family bosom)
abound of horrible deeds
Words don't mean much
Cheap, like the way
it's sold to you
You spit you vomit like mad Tom
spews his sullen & assumed humor
an Abraham Man
you rant "the whoreson zed"
you blanket your loins
grime a face with filth
tie your hair in dreadish locks
Poor turleygod
Peace, Smulkin, peace, thou fiend
Conjure Frateretto, Hopdance, Purre &
all demons to greet the night in you
but, again, down fiends, peace
Not up again to make me mad
An agony rises up in me
be it woman-borne yea or no, but
sweet the torrent if it carries you
down, down
How you are forced abroad
far from an easy home down down
none but elements attend you

suit a daughter?
some are witches for they have been downed so long
want a property of their own
Stationer's Register thus historye got writ
Butter & Busby in the light of day were merchandisers
    you see the edge in broken hearts
business in text traffic

Burbage, Betterton, Garrick, Kean, Samuel Phelps, John McCullough, Edwin
Forrest, Booth, Sir Henry Irving breathe a text, raise their voices to meet the
heat & shake a spear what lives inside the actor's mask

don't laugh

a mother said I must write this in a dream
and my tears fall & no one pays attention
Says suum, mun, ha, ho, nonny nonny
& all the idle weeds
Says in a dream the syllable to crack Lear's code

The Doctor saying a kind of magikal incantation
& study dream poet has in cave subjugating
elements where female demonic devices rear Hydra heads
plugged into headphones giving "orders"

& her Electra complex causes storms
all wires aflame, daddy a hunting go
Doctor says "your head's on fire!"

no never speak of love why demand it be said
no, stand guard, no money take his place
& don the madwoman's garb & enter the heath
to be such a one and never say
"By Jupiter this cannot be revoked"
for authority is never moral
Beweep, beware
you are all the characters
& bastard too

"Paphlagonian unkinde blinde king, and his kinde son"

hunted
& stormed
the cyningdom

because when the kingdom is overripe it fails
in its words,
deeds too, master
                    like now
                    empire failing
    talks back in
        blasts & fogs
& tempers clay
old fond eyes
        moving out a history
to be fain & feign it so:

pass, pass
& be under the reign of so's

I wanted to tell it from the other side
How a daughter could see split in two
theirs and hers, burnished side
        word etch
She is a yogin of responsibility

Under James I: I note
the Huguenot memoirs not dispassionate
accounts of the Gunpowder Plot
Letters of Mary, Queen of Scots &
massacre of St. Bartholomew not go unrecorded
    turn earth
tonight's *Kali Yuga*

The first hit on the second level I knocked him out. I
by Jupiter
also got the new De La Soul tape
You went to Washington?
Did you assassinate George Bush?
Did you get anything done on the reproductive assignment?
Really nasty.
I saw the picture of a butt cut in half.
It was so sick I pluck it out

       boy a Merlin

the world abound of horrible deeds
do scald, I pluck, I pluck

as mad as the vexed sea singing loud
crowned with rank furniture and furrow weeds,
With bur docks, hemlock, nettles, cuckoo-flowers
Darnel

       & all the idle weeds

I love my father
& will not hinge to nothing

month in a sanatorium
brand new hotel next
carpet
wants a Tibetan doctor
oil of *vigas*
put it to your forehead
someone thrown down in the mad hallway

it is a male

who wants to retire in power
expects something will come of something
& accorded scepter
no out went the candle

VII

DEAR CREELEY . . .

The poet addresses a master poet, a youthful "elder" whose own work has radicalized poetic thought & possibility. The scientific scrutiny he brings to line, syllable, provokes her own attention, which takes another direction. The emotional leverage still there. He's too established to be "counterpart," but he moves through phenomena with apparent ease although he clearly suffers. And they are both born East Coast protestants. His own work is taut, broke thru with pain. What is the attraction? He's had a wide, various life, difficult. He perhaps epitomizes the dangers of the sensuous poet-life. Like her, he wants it all, and is frequently travelling. There is a period where they intersect frequently at odd literary events. Her husband had invoked his name at her—you want to be like the males, just like Robert Creeley—which rings in her ear. Is that the case? She simply wants to be herself. But she studies him. Other informations weave in her. The conflict with spiritual traditions, their patriarchal dogma. The Dalai Lama is an exception and she is struck by a letter from another poet who shares her vision.

You had all the syllables
You took love with all the syllables

                reason the Navy tries to "cover"

        who is led by his phallus, who wishes to get off
           back to nothing, spent in the seat of freer verse

            "accident" is a technical term

Jove mounts anything
The dissipated god whose action is
woman's fluid and to get his cock in
to come all over her
Not you I rail against

It was the love in poetry
& how to be a young woman in poetry

You can't be sappy
You never touched me
but took love with all the syllables
& were a kind of tough place
for me to get to
A woman all over the place with her words
What I learn
it is a tough world to be all over in
you love you lose

                                    When the U.S. Navy claims
                                    to leak no accident

                            dissipated god energy
                            blast the moment, come

                            power

                                            cum

up incidents such as the coolant leak is a much less . . .

                                                                    cum

zero reactor accidents is a much less   cum

                            his desire who is not
                            hands all over woman
she words all over man

not saying there has never
                            the warrior been

                who is a serious event. Perhaps he

a person who asserts his cock but

                        I say Pull down

                            O vanity pull down

                            — 101 —

What kind of man
could you win vanity from
what candidate's power examined here
who's running? what's he sell?
a holy man a holy rood
a holy writ a holy holy stone
a holy sonofabitch holy smoke
his smokescreen eye his bedroom eye
holy night against his thigh
his little notebook in shirt pocket
up against a holy woman breast
she thrashes about his holy bed
he reeks of holy but he is good
he lobbies for change
he is good he is holy holy
how many secrets sleep in his bed?

Dear Anne

(I started to cry when I heard the Nobel Prize
was given to the Dalai Lama. What a most
glorious thing. He is the only world
political leader worthy of it—maybe
this expunges the travesty of it going
last decade to Henry Kissinger. Dalai
Lama has 40 years unswervingly held to
nonviolent action as the sole valid
method of effecting political change.
We are blessed to have such a saint
on the planet of our lifetimes. Certainly
Chenrezig, walking among us.
OM MANI PADME HUM)
I gave up a ghost
it was a dark time

quit stalling

a legacy of reading

                         & you far away
      far
a look you stoop
      nor blond nor book
slaved
but credence
to a
      who but
      innocent eye
to painting
                  spatial art
but this
a temporal poem
                              no quarrel with culture history the
                  self
but this
other
      form
of
as artist

you say I can't
                  but be
      dressed like that
bald Zennie   & was it
                              was it wrong to?
      I am my father
            when we twist like that
                                          behind the blind OM

MANI PADME HUM

in drawings in Braille
            light up the night
            so calling to me my son
   I make "hims" to me on the ground
                  over a thousand miles
   think of each other

the distance

sighing, blind as ever mother be

& you I ask you because he, the husband said
"You are like all the male poets! Just like Robert Creeley!"
& could a son enter a life on a mother poet's lintel
could the man survive, walk on in

Qustion: Do people who have been blind since birth dream in images as seeing
people do?

Answer: A series of studies by Donald D. Kirtley and others at California State
University, Fresno, inventoried objects and activities in dream diaries of the
blind. One study found that blind people tended to dream more than sighted
people did about objects used to construct buildings, such as bricks and
boards, and land areas limited by boundaries, such as parking lots and yards.
The researchers theorized that this was because of the special way in which the
blind conceptualize their external environment.

                                    the color order loosens
                        clear light of the thing
                        admirably rendered
the walls come the walls come
            tumblin' down

the painter
could
tint
with
a
hand & take
abode
there

could
be in
color
there   sky habitat
                                4 doors to the city
                                 & the rafters
                  of chance
          architect of evening
          architect of morning
                                         monochrome night

mi padre, padre mi
gusto
& build a domicile O vanity pulls down
but the poet could tint with his eye and the other wouldbe poet writes

dear Anne

My father taught me baseball and discipline. And to laugh. As I grew up, he was always one to side with minorities, help raise money for the poor, give his last dollar to a panhandler. But he didn't know freedom, couldn't relate inner heart, couldn't talk. He made jokes about my shy advances towards girls, so much so I was afraid what I felt was screwy, that it was sissy or something to want female affection—with four sisters and an angry mother in the house! My father wd do anything to keep me out of jail and also bought me my first car. But he ran out on my mother, he was sorry and hurt, really gone crazy for several years, lying, and falling into 'born again wisdom.' I had no respect for it, for his obesity, for his meanness to my stepbrother, the way he treated his wives. The thought of either parent makes my world a sad place. The kind of sorrow I'm grateful for. You know, I cry watching Walt Disney.

                                 & gather here

words cannot
     nor can so calling
for a long time
     & write
     & sending
        of
each

other
falling
in a
tangle
cartoon swirl
& move into the next frame where
animals make a war
& get even
& get bonked
the head is sore
but pops up again

          (objective time
                  gone from the
                  quantum world
                  gone in
                  cosmology)

Marduk, *donde es?*

     the deadline when a sun god claims dominion

Thunder now. I stop to cry. Shift a way out of him. Flurry in the sky. Sun is hid-
den. Silver light between green leaves & slanted trunks. Peak of green where
are you? Are you roused to see this moment? Railing 'gainst injustice. My fault
for waking the dead. When all those people were loving I wanted to take on the
male in me
& be the god you are
for you could take all the syllables you were in love with

     (I went out seeking things
                  to remind me of you):

I've been unfaithful to Lord Buddha
hung out with Muslims—Inshallah
I lay down with Mohammed in the back alley
     while he clamored for blood

I've been unfaithful, Buddha
What can you do about it? Nothing
I've been unfaithful, whirled with dervishes
    in the inner compound
Spun around until I was dizzy with ecstasy
worshipped graven images, false idols, a bone totem with a piece of fuzzy hair
I stuck pins in voodoo effigies
I chanted the muezzin at dawn from the mosque tower
I met Sabbatai Zevi in the dark temple
    mesmerized by his strange actions in the dark temple
He showed me anti-Christ in the dark temple
Christ, the root of suffering, don't make me feel so bad
I met the Golem in Prague I became the golem goddess of
    clay & sticks to scare the uninitiated created by a cool patriarch
    I can't be faithful to
Ah Yahweh! Your touch is winter on my feverish body
I've been unfaithful to the Four Noble Truths
trying to eliminate the path of suffering
    It's so Protestant, too much work!
I covered myself with the black silk chador better
    to hide this pulsating body of desire behind
Body of faithless acts
I won't be any man's slave
Sabbatai Zevi turns the books upside down
I feel the synapse of his plan but he's just another
    Patriarch with yarmulke & forbidding flaming book whose illuminated
    letters sea my eyeballs
Ah Lord Buddha, I'm not steady
I went to Church on Easter, do you believe it?
I wanted to get down on my knees
cross myself a hundred times
I went to genuflect
When the priest says as I take the wafer "the body of Christ" I'm like to melt
& when he says "the sacrament, the blood of Christ, the cup of salvation"
    I dissolve into the holy grail
I've longed for centuries to get close to the grail
But I give up the cloth, the veil, Mt. Olympus

married to no male god or saint
I lie down with the circumsized & the uncircumsized
With the hermaphrodite, with the beautiful women
What have I done?
"Heathen, infidel, woman-of-little-faith!
What right have you to the Kingdom of Heaven,
the keys to Macho Paradise?"

So I quit the night you left, quit getting lost outside
I quit the machine for its discipline knowing more than I do

I quit Ati class for 2 hours my mind going to visualization
     of life to vulva to heart to bone

In a ribbon of mantra, I quit praying
I quit the music that blasted my ear
I quit a place of terror and it quit me
I joined to the hearth, the stones kept silent
I quit lying about time
I quit sleep when it obscured your intent
You intended to go out later, I quit thinking about it
I quit the calibrated afternoon
The moment the sun broke through the clouds I quit
Then a storm came, get inside
I walked inside I quit worrying
I quit the last program of the a.m.
I quit the final Auvergne song
I quit driving all over town after midnight
I quit but the "ahrbel gorung" kept wooing me
I quit the long embrace
I quit strategizing & left off all their names
     list is all right quit adding to it
I quit the time he kept waiting for
I quit her making an offer to speech & cream
I quit the Progressive magazine
I quit plastic for 3 days
I died in my denial of water because sustenance is
     a kind of feat

I quit seeing the point
I quit wearing the fertility charm it dragged my neck down
        but I never gave up on Africa

I kept dreaming you like spice
I quit you'd better be prepared to take over

        F-16 plane

        M1 Abrams tank

Trident submarine

        et cetera

The Top Military Contractors (value of contracts in billions):

McDonnell Douglas: $8.0, General Dynamics: $6.5, General
Electric: $5.7, Tenneco: $5.1, Raytheon: $4.1, Martin
Marietta: $3.7, General Motors: $3.6, Lockheed: $3.5,
United Technologies: $3.5, Boeing: $3.0, Grumman: $2.8,
Litton Industries: $2.6

                        & would be a performance that
                                speaks
                                itself in dollars

Later to think of him, a male poet epitome
all the other young women but me
become his daughters
What doth a daughter do?
How doth a daughter woo?
How does she counter weaponry?
Rule about the house "in pit of me"
on a mind of a teen

his clothes, how they smell
musty of south Jersey

                    or

                              spermy

with battle

                         to mount a tank
                         artillery,

                                   pull down

                         artillery,

                                   pull down

& I wanted you as a thief in the night, & I wanted you
to promulgate my cult, & I wanted you as breakdown, as private life
& I wanted you, parent of revolution, & I wanted you to make
the land carry more sheep for the wool trade, and I wanted you,
a talisman, & I wanted you, arboreal mixed up with city
& I wanted you at the front, as someone who might walk to the
edge of town, & I wanted you up to my neck, & I wanted you
as partner to my friend's existence, and I wanted you changed
by daylight, and I wanted as I need books, & I wanted you

I wanted you history doesn't count, & I wanted as spleen
to carefree nature, & I wanted you in the sense of opposite,
& I wanted you the cows can come home, we were in the country,
I wanted you, & I wanted you speaking as we were children again,
& I wanted you to sneak up on me like children, & I wanted
the clothes you wear, I wanted to wear them, I wanted you
in hot pursuit, wanted youth column could wait, &
I wanted you writing the story of Athena, of black Athena, and I
wanted you to be law abiding just once & I wanted you early

I wanted you late, I wanted the others can wait, they
wait if I want you & only you I want
I wanted you at the beginning of civilization, I wanted you
the clocks can run down, I want you on the way outside, I want
you resting on my laurels, I wanted you forbidden to "panegyric"
to "ode" to "sonnet," I wanted you formless, I wanted you &
the page is the only place I know for this, I wanted the
night of the day the manuscript came back, I wanted you settled
in a home, I wanted you cherished by the landlord, I wanted
textures of illuminated manuscripts in our love

& I wanted you in agreement that women invented the alphabet
& I wanted you to close down the laboratory for me,
& I wanted you as water flows downhill, I wanted you over
my head, on top of me, I wanted you under me, & I wanted
you sitting in front of books as you always do, the rest can
wait, I wanted you to give something away the day I noticed
wanting you, I desired the table of contents to include you,
I desired the year of our lord to slow down

                (I went out seeking these things
                        to remind me of you)

my field abandoned by walls
my field: 4 white walls
my field, light shines on the page
a modern light on my modern page
my field the bed my lover lies waiting
my field, the wires to your voice, wired to you
field like this one at night, warm we stay out here
we lie with the deer in the
field, I never told you about it
the battle of his sex against mine
I can speak of it, the fighting
we wrestled, to destroy one another our sex
our vocabulary
can't stop my mouth!

— III —

field for sport
can't stop my mouth
I win I win I win
I tame you with my dakini hook
with my fiery text & mantric sound

with my love for you I tame you

these are my words
        in my play
of you
                    & this is the play with you

FLYING LUCIFER

A. Oblique, okay all over open a tone
    like the 31st day in the Celtic sense
    adjacent to the moon, have you a wave

B. Nay, a newer year wand. A stage (our love,
    our one body) shaped like a ship.

A. A wrought, a blame, burl, turned around
    Lover likes his coins & baubles

B. Way on the side's this human hoard. He
    turning, the lovemaking, the sea too, how
    a woman's ballade, mix, torque, &
    seafaring all together. Waves settle.

A. Longitudinally rescue, blur or drown
    You're a kinda demon lover
    A woman's crazy to follow

Dear Creeley Again:

I try
now not
to miss
you who are

older
sharper
I'm thinking
you called me
"hostess"
once, New York
I'm insulted
because
of who
you are
to me
salty
something you
would notice
being you
my image of
you
Who We Are
not possible
our tongues
words
say it
again & again
later in
friendship
How to enjoy
these marriages
each other
in them (meaning
him & her)
together
of course
marriages
come apart
seamlessly
They scatter,

boon of edges
like
teeth
like it's written
to bite off
a piece
of each
other
But synchronized
in his beautiful lash my innocent
one,
I say "husband"
perched
in attention
How to enjoy
each other
(those ones)
It happens
in pain
You too?
It happens
who we are not
fooling
the children
of it
who are we
they are they
going over
the predicament
nothing new
the nod of
him
her
of them,
the children again,
of where of
how

to live
You tell me
what study
how to speak
what's conducive
to "work"
or not
to what place
job
people
owe allegiance?
who needs
us most
or not
at all
Simply a burden
to think
You are
here
to me
over a table
talking
"drinks"
jokes on who is or
is not
smoking
I am a written
daughter
of you
who inform
me such
You ballast
here
Your neck
of the
woods.

Assignment: *Write a poem, or series of poems, in which every noun refers either to a female person, object, or abstraction of either, or to a male ditto, and every verb is an indication or sign of either positive affectionate behavior or negative hostile behavior. The entire language of you and your audience with respect to your poem or poems is based on your words being what the language is . . .*

He still didn't satisfy the class with his clarity and I've no idea how I'm going to work this out yet. It seems an arbitrary decision he's asking for, because he said, for instance, we might say all words having 3 or more consonants are masculine. It would be much easier to write this one in French or Greek! But I dimly see the point he wants to make is that we always accept and abide by rules whether we know it or not. *C'est ici une véritable mystique du langage,*   *n'est-ce pas?*

Jonathan Johnson says these things

(black & white Palestine scarf
    triangulated 'round neck)
How he came by the bracelets: "made by a friend
    of mine from Norway (the beaded one)
    a friend of mine from the Bronx (the one of twine)"

 His father died young
"my best friends were squirrels"
 The only Black student in the school
    (suburbs of Chicago)

& he danced, age 12, ballet
    (large snow boots, heavy wool pants)
in New Orleans in an intimate relationship to space
    ("shape it within myself")

How much hair under the beret?
Then?
"I came home every day & sat in the bathtub for hours

& melted down
poured love into dancing & quit"
And "love"?
Not yet
I want to make others fly
      (open face, thick sweater, noble, left-handed)
body to teach me and love?
not yet
centered like a pendulum
plumb line
                        (vanity)
                                    silent scribbling
outrage of how many caves
in sickness in health
move your fingers

                  real ink, serenity

                        gutted a house

            but O vanity down

you who are a Buddha
art woman
                              body to teach me
                              body to teach

            (as more letters attest he was blunt

& blunt the body to the sword

            body to teach
                              how cum down

            dab in the sweet sperm

                        body wider so much wider than the sea
his pain so lovingly tendered
in every phone & phoneme singing

in the

       spectra world

pas
             cycle world

    being the ks of memory

    He & I do love

    Look & see

    Anselm

       sieve . . .

    get the applications!

    not hollow among natives Aprille
                & maps right on Was ist
    los?

Will I love you?
Quit your protection
I quit under pressure, under glass
I folded before the money ran out
I quit I told you I'd better have a backup
Be my friend I won't quit yet
I quit it's difficult to describe
A rough outline is to be read syllable by syllable
I quit dialing you were never there
I quit staring out the window
Moon, clouds, I quit the fantasy

Stars, they look calm

I quit the careful approach I was impulsive then

I quit giving my palm to your ambition

I quit my own restoration

I quit, was this viewed as defeat?

And when you were there, "static" was intolerable

I stood on a 40-foot-high scaffold peeling paint into my face

Then I quit working for experts

I quit I'm not complaining it was time for a change

Take one step back

Were you informed?

I use words for my own loss

I use words as my table, as a kind of shrine

I sweep over the care of the words

They take care of themselves

I sweep them under my demand

I command that they not quit the scenario

The sentence quits the page as it ends

I quit as a phantom of exteriority

A double negative remains evanescent

Don't linger with my thought to quit

I tell you it happened once

It happens again

And the speed of the transition, could it be quit?

Would myself-as-object quit?

I quit the sine qua non of that experience

Could I keep harping on my conclusions

Is the language ripe enough?

Is all the data in?

I quit the fragility of the "real"

Writing without end, I quit trying to stop

Conceit gets the best of the one-who-quits

I quit an outward appearance

No outward appear without light Well I quit the light then

How could that be, I couldn't quit gleaming

I couldn't quit radiating

I kept hidden
I quit being stoic
I quit nostalgia for your past
Insatiable compassion, how to quit
I quit stalling
I quit representing my total existence
I quit speculating about the event
It would happen, I would be there, I can't quit
I quit defining the problem
Linguists were going around in circles
Is speech a human phenomenon?
I quit for no good reason
The speech was boring in the sense of redundant

I quit to leave everything as it is

I quit by blending my durations with the other
durations

I could never stop

Dear Creeley:

I will never stop
I love the road
I sit all the time watching the world go by
perched like a Buddha than to a more comfortable pose
& the tooth of a walrus centers me like a pendulum
or plumb line I want to say Who are you
Dark hair of a saint
painted by an old Dutch master
with notions of light
What are you?
Is there outrage for the rage you lived in in sickness
Who?
Who moves your fingers with red ink & serenity?
Who were you?

Something was wrong, blind for 5 days?
Who are you?
& once had my body trained to a star
I loved the road & was a gas station mechanic on it
for it, you decide
was a manic for it, the road and he said
"I refused to be part of the war machine"
But loves my writing
& the road in it
It roads you away, you might say
Messages get lost
Look for a word & can't find it
But the world, say "yes"
What makes the grass green?
A wide receiver subsidizes me
Photos on the wall of Alaska oil slick don't scare me
Don't, don't scare me Don't scare me
& in my writing trained to a star
I wait & wonder

Dear Creeley:
     Does some body always walk a road?

VIII

BORN ON THE THATCH I WAS BORN TO

*The poet writes formally to catch her breath. She needs a breather from classroom demands but fol-
lows the dimension of two of her assignments—sonnet & memory without argument. She locates
herself in a room (the poem) and travels back to the stifling Cheops pyramid as she visited it in 1962.
This exercise lies within old recollection. She honors Francis Yates, duchess of Memory. She crawls
into the glorious death trap never able to stand and realizes she needs this particular rite of passage
and must start useful visualizations. Is it time to travel to the underworld & steal the secrets of the
male energies that rule there? It gives her power to think thus. She wants to tip the scales. The figures
who have created her state of mind for the poem are distanced here. The Dancer consoles her as she
skirts off the page. Must she change her clothes?*

Crossed the hallway toward a couple of you
Roots writing to reach you & make
this profile sigh to full advantage
Yet some saltiness inside your question
was willed by constellations, was necessary
Midnight excursion off-limits not about sex
& then stilled, shuffling in the street,
blood head, you know a way about beauty held supine
Hymns foretelling those days moon no longer appearing
Frenzied berserkers, ferocious warriors
realize sacred fury of hey ho spinning world
Yet how do we say what we meant to the moment
We say it to each other You both say it
so that we be again all time of one another

*

I believe in this as a words-only school
Never retreat from scrutinizing you who are deep
in the sentences although half-dreamed
I miss the enemy, the burnt-leaf smell of resin
The way eyes find me who are important to them
Blasphemy of light don't let it in on us

Born on the thatch I was born to
vanish against the phrase "I, tracked by barbarians"
In nuisance game, a celestial lady & gentleman
couldn't leave without a drumming ritual in the school
And I heard my Coleridge say, "Deep in my life, you who . . ."
Which accounts for horizontal shadows and the
delirium, which is her (the lady's) half-mannish
garb, an artist's hand at the tree sash

*

His question no longer appears fury-prone
deep in my life you are hymns to humans
who are odes too, who never retreat from
primordial foretelling of moonless days
Frenzied constellations are necessary, are above us
& I hear my Coleridge say "I believe in this as
a words-only school," roots writhing to each berserker
some saltiness still inside them, deep in my life
they (you) are willed to the moment
I see him like her as herrings in blue loose leaves
I see over decades nothing about sex
I see entire pedagogical systems amassing before us
which account for horizontal shadows
We'd been drinking & stared at the fish a long time

*

Hand on the tree sash, hand on an arm
although half-dreamed and willed by
what we mean by the "moment"
Couldn't leave without a burnt retreat
couldn't shuffle beauty couldn't shuffle love
Eyes hey ho are half-dreamed & mind bursts to
vanish against those days
like hymns, profiles, schools, works in clay
A gentleness some saltiness inside him
all in on us, the rage, two women

In the sentence was lulled by warriors
whose blasphemy, the rage, is strange
We say it to each other writhing to fell advantage
Born on the thatch I was born to

*

Days moon-deep in How do we say
& be again all time of you how do we
of the primordial world say how does it happen?
I heard them say "I believe in this" how
you who are two who are profiles strange to me
who are foretelling, scrutinizing, appearing
& never retreat only crossing the far hall
deep in hymn you who are O warriors
Yours and my life was necessary!
You who are those O no longer appearing
Who are gentlemen & lady hands no longer appearing
who are then stilled, heat-blood no longer appearing
who are fury about no longer appearing
I was born in this only-words-appearing-school
(We'd been drinking and stared at the fish a long time)

    You are my age as we
    deepen into a pact
    jar . . . track ties . . .

    You are the chromosomes
    who see Matter as
    habitual bustling & napping
    jokes . . . scenarios

    We are elated to
    recognize each other
    at all when we share the microscope
    sperm . . . sand . . .
But when chromosomes

cry like water
They take the
heart of me

(heart of me
O beloved of Israel!)

My heart went out to "little white lies." He needed them out in the sun, occupying the expanse of desert, false hope and poverty. "Anna," he said, "you must be a wish for me, anywhere you go. Think of me." He gestured grandly, presumably speaking of America. "Back there, anywhere you go. America! Did I tell you the time I went to America? My shoes, see my shoes. They are the shoes of America." Florsheims? The discarded gift, no doubt, of a generous hippie passing through. They were dusty, worn, altogether gone, too big. Ragged strings for laces. "It doesn't matter, Amad," I wanted to shout, "you are here!" Here in Giza with the pyramids. It didn't matter Giza was as dusty and worn down as the shoes. That what was once tropical paradise had come to this. It doesn't matter, Amad, that I come from the richest country in the world, that I myself am walking talking emblem of the richest country in the world. How could I make him see how sad America was. *I* was lured *here* in response to America. He laughed, "You are too serious, Anna." His camel, Hepset, was typically nonchalant but nuzzled my hand as I gave her a lump of sugar from the hotel restaurant. How many times had she been photographed circumambulating the great pyramid of Cheops with a foreigner on her back?

You had to crawl through the corridors that held the sand as a death trap. You had to crawl like an animal, like the worm you had first been in your climb up the evolutionary ladder. You had to mix with the dirt and dust so they choked you. Finally when you came to the first chamber you could stand, stooped over. You had to carry a torch. You had to chant the names of all the Egyptian deities you could think of. You had to view yourself as witness, as barge, as eyes from another realm. You had to make your journey a sacred one toward the center of the past and toward death and rebirth in an old mythology. You had to have memory of everyone who went before you, of everyone who died before you. You had to forget New York, Los Angeles, Miami. You had to crawl as witness, as first woman, as first girl, as sacrificial victim. You had to crawl naked. You had to crawl with your tough skin. With your fearless skin. You might move like the snake. You had to be a warrior carrying a torch for the past. Your heart had to beat faster. You had to meet the glamorous Pharaoh as a slave. You had to be whipped and tortured. You had to meet the center of darkness under the pyramid's apex of eyes and then retreat back into the light of an even darker, eyeless civilization.

and you TIP THE SCALES . . .

You'd rather I slept
You'd rather I didn't go out on a limb to the immigrant
You'd rather I cleared out
the *she-said-I-said* departure & not in a naked fashion
Slowly put on tiger dress, spider socks
(you'd rather I . . .)
mining shoes
& not drive off jeopardized
You'd rather I got it wrong
Moon's libertine scales tipped
not for nor against a lover's favor
We might be travelling
We might go inside a motel room
It might be night in Cairo
You'd rather I didn't say these things

*

We drink to the heart
one another's moon
We do this landscape life, scales
of fishy characters I knew
I knew I'd recognize your voice I knew
You'd rather the mood is lighter
Travelling makes us thirsty
A one-time candidate jets from coast to coast
He's proud to be an immigrant
You see the cactuses? You see the caucus?
 Not only of sight but of sound I sing

They look like priests without a vote
Rain descends in the desert
I love the night, the proud rain
You'd rather I didn't refer to
"jeep," or "couple-irritation"

⋆

For the immigrant candidate you'd rather
toast his slips of tongue, worsted suits
not a thing to laugh at
You'd rather I slept, scales tipped
I'll vote the line you love
Both tiger and lip
I said slip to vote both crowned and slow
You'd rather I travel without him in mind
I'd like nothing but this:
light on the tongue
dark ribbons of speech
Someone cast this vote upon

⋆

You'd rather I go off my hinge to you
Acid rain, rust establishments
These don't last in your mind
although motive, catalyst, curving boundary might
The picture changes
You'd rather immigrate
to fashion, go ahead, capitalist!
Give me your insides against the night
room flavors, our limbs together
I don't go out in exotics
Wait for me, shoes off
I've been drilling an old speech
from the Marriot days

⋆

In the health laboratories, what health?
Limbs slowly dress, fragile outfit
seminuked gloves in the hospital
Keep waiting. I keep reading you
Don't destruct now, Pyramid
Obey the hungers with red lights
Count down to plutonium whiteout
legal code you rather I didn't invoke
or explore the stricter sense of "code"
The people of the sea will unite with the Iron Age
You rather I didn't read about these things
of past and weaponry
Enough lights flash approval
You'd rather we walk down the corridor
with you gripping my arm

*

Missionary flavors in the electorate
Home favorites rise, slim chances
Vote now to a richer candidate No, no, no
Moonlight helps me not
I won't get busy but balance and lighter
Speed's a wreck to civilization
higher and lower, tax on my brain
We change shapes to slip aside
We live inside an apocalypse
Both sides speak of a plan
Care not to be human
You'd rather I leave off talk
Fill out forms
Forget the landscape, this room,
that night, the candidate's smile
Scales tipped in the wrong one's favor
You rather not think I think
to go out on a limb to swim, not drown
(We'd been drinking and stared at the fish a long time)

I was number 92 of 113 at the St. Mark's benefit, and of course things were running behind schedule, I waited, an hour and a half. The Parish Hall was full of people eating chili, drinking beer, playing the two pianos, being drunk, getting dressed up, crushing cigarettes and food on the floor. Once I'd changed into my skirt and bra made from porno mags I was cold; a woman on the staff came up and opened a window next to me, pointed to the smoke in the room. Finally someone took pity on me and jumped me up the list of couple of notches.

I had already resigned myself to having no more space than the rug-covered altar. Lee Ann had promised the podium would be removed. She hadn't told me about the sound system that I now saw dominating a few precious square feet in the southwest quadrangle of my little rectangle.

I held the blue cape tight around me, to hide my cold white skin and the porno photos, dragged the two garbage bags full of crushed paper onto the space, and nodded to Grazia, who was sitting next to the sound man. The beautiful and upbeat cantata by Campra began and I ran around opening and closing the cape, nervous and overenergetic, as if I couldn't stand to be there and at the same time wanted to show myself off. Occasionally I screamed, somewhat sweetly, like the soprano, who was talking to God. As the music changed to baritone solo I ran back and forth between the two bags, pulling out the crushed pieces of paper, occasionally stopping to open one and "read" it but could, as it were, formulate nothing more than meaningless verbalizations.

Then the music gets even sweeter, I remove the cape, slowly, over my head, move lyrically side to side, suspending, arms curling upward, three or four times during this minute ripping off one of the porno pages, crunching it into a ball, and chucking it into the audience.

The night I got the idea for the costume I ran up to St. Mark's Place, couldn't find a single street seller till I got across from 33, there bought a big batch from a guy who with great enthusiasm told me what a good deal he was going to give me because, "I know you'll be back."

Zaire, I was in your train I was dancing
Zaire, I was black & further out the night
Zaire, a partner of the night.
We made the trees alive, Zaire
We made them dance
Zaire, we walked to a stream of blood
Zaire, another birth could be

The snake of our vision is the crest of your rising
We are the panther people first
We are the glowing eyes
We come this way with the glowing eyes
We stalk you at night covered with diamond rags
You arise to witness dawn, which arises
Good luck
Dawn is a tiger
The sun is tiger's right eye
So panther-out-of-night got born in black blood
& sun out of tiger whose paws herald dawn
Zaire, we say your fabulous name: Zaire, Zaire
What legend walks? We said "Za"
They said "Ire"
Zaire born out of night & day
Spoken, this story broke my music to sit here
Zaire: fur, star, eyes, equator
Zaire: mother & thief, and father-thief
Thus broke my music to sit here
You tell them
You tell them Zaire we'll take it out of church
You are country of reckoning
We come to you with "ire" eyes
We come to you out of black "za" blood
We are singular
I am Attibon Legba
with a hat fresh from Guinea
My bamboo cane too
Likewise my ancient pain from Guinea
And bones, old bones
I am the patron saint of janitors
Elevator boys too
I am Legba-Wood, Legba-Cayes
Legba Signangnon
I'm the seven Kataroulo Brothers
I'm Legba Kataroulo
I plant my grave tonight

The great medicine-tree of my soul
In the white man's land
At his crossroads
I kiss his door 3 times
I kiss his eyes 3 times
I am Papa Algebra
God of thresholds
Tonight it is 1 1 1 1
I'm the master of your white man's hangouts
I am the protector of plants
And of the insects of your house
I am the chief of all the gateways
To the soul & the body

            The lizards we usually see in our houses
            & on our faces, I found more eloquent
            in a sky habitat

the clean light of the thing admirably rendered

The painter could tint with his hand
& take an abode there

brows superbly drawn
pale swatches of paint

color of exotic lizards
deliberate, intentional
translucid shadows in the water

crystalline candor of any
mailing list

The response is "Volo" or "Nolo"

the conscript father (in the dream)
checking on the

polish of
funeral shoes
a great gulp if
a fastidious person

or is he?

We wonder about boxing
everything
up

the reams of paper
(here's more, beloved)
& the books & the scissors and the
    snippets

where you walk, you walk
& the plates are being kept for you

southern?

        in blues & browns
high collar

                    What does night hold
                    First mirror grabs me
                    It goes well with me
                    This first mirror version

                    The armor costs
                    First mirror very rough
                    My armor sins
                    First mirror is stuck

                    My rue is with him
                    My heart is sure
                    It finds me numb later
                    In a dimmer mirror

Not in neither sought
in this: in house
Not in neither either
Out of this house

Sign this: a hologram
Sing this: with feeling
Sing this: world laughing
I am an Often-Signer-of-Words

That I would be certain that no one tell me feel like this, this is the way I feel,
that the father is the animal to the man, that the father is the light to the son,
that he stole the woman's eyes to see his own son because he was afraid to look
at him with such fiery orbs, that this is only one interpretation, that we can be
generous now, that we are careful very careful that the woman's eyes are
brighter, that they look into the man

> *My lover capable of terrible lies*
> *at night lay close to me*
> *in a dream that lied like truth*

He's setting
impossible tasks
for me

He hammers a
hole in my shoulder
to pour in his message

I have to climb
a small mountain
with a basket
of linens
and retrieve all the documents that are this poem

scratched by brambles
my legs bleed

a sharp thorn
scrapes the point
of my heart

At the top of the mountain:
many patriarchs
Many patriarchs
at the top of the mountain

"Give us your heart!"
No, no, I cry
"Give us your heart," they demand

But now I've taken it out of my aching chest
& wrapped it in linen in the basket

It will be saved for the down-there people
I will give it to them
I sew myself up

but in the meantime I am hollow woman
& I fool them
& I give them a medium red stone
the size of my heart but all the time saying
No, no! to excite them further

A woman
spends a long
time
in the metaphoric water

          she mutates into
          a flower
          that will only bloom
          once every 25 years

Men here are as savage as giant vipers,
And strut about in armor, snapping their bows.
As I sing the second stanza I almost break the lutestrings,
Will broken, heart broken, I sing to myself.

that all things confine, but I am wide, wide, that we cruise into the page as if
spellbound, that dread anticipates the page, that an African costume informs
the text

       that a poet exists to accommodate sense to sound, that he
who was a torment to me will read this and laugh, that an
engineer can put the mesh on any of you, that I can't say words
large enough to contain you, that you dance away from me & steal
a fake heart

                —I swore my fair heart out
                —To what man or job?
                —Stone on stone
                —You mean he's gone?

The other class turned out 16 girls, ages 15 through early thirties. I made a dense
dance with their help to Marianne's "Witches' Song" and I became the witch,
wore a dress and bra and petticoats and hat with veil lots of makeup on the
heavy side, I dance around among them and then they kill me. They got into it.

IX

WHAT'S IN A NAME?

She is always curious about where the words she & her progeny got named come from. This knowl-edge might unlock the rune: her state of mind and inform the poem. She goes to the etymological dic-tionary to translate Ambrose, Bye, Waldman & swims in the associations. Another man writes from the shore of the Bosphorus, located in a landscape fused of poetry & religion: miracles, exploits of the 12 gods. Always yearning for resonances to history, & sacred locale, she is gratefully transported to Apollo's holy spring. Nevertheless the boys' talk brings her back to America. Cartoons & sports, bastardized poetry & religion. She loves their words, their naïve preadolescent charm. But longs to travel again, away from these States, duty, Colorado suburbia.

ambhi—Around

      old English bi, be, by, BY

           ambho—both

    an—ana—aloft

      anus = old woman

reidel: the rod between upright stakes

wal: to be strong

vale, valence, valerian, valiant, valid,
valor, valve, avail

        walthan, waldan, wealdan
        wieldan: to govern

wald: power, rule

Waldr: ruler

        (stay up late studying myself)

          what's in a name?

—Calvin is a hero. He smarts off to his mom.

—He plays tricks, nasty ones.

—He robs the bank in Monopoly.

—He exaggerates as Spaceman Spiff & kills the Mother Naggon.

—& Zorgs.

—Zorgs.

—He squirts her.

—His room is a smelly dungeon.

—His Dad's the Deadly King of the Naggons.

—Bart Simpson is our age. 10. He plays pranks too.

—Like "Is there a Jock there?" (He's calling a bar see.)
   "Is there a Jock Strap there?" "Is there an Al there?"
   "Is there an Al Coholic there?"

—I want to be invisible

—I want to be President of Nike.

—Ask Joe Richey, "Girls can't throw."

—Girls' underwear is cut off where the legs are.

—It's skimpy. It's see-thru.

—Girls are gentle, they have more areas to protect.

—They don't want to get in a fight.

—I'm a girl, he can't spank me. "Girls have more delicate heinies" says
   Susie Derkins.

& out of what

words

to enter a womb

to patrimony?

& out of the woods
what name to
enter
through a mother's womb
    to patrimony

                    He holds me
                    in uniform
                        bundle 'pon a knee

gone a gone a war
              back there
a Waldr,
        warlike
            rules
but he was quiet, very quiet
                shh
        gone a warring gone
it fits him, suits him
          you can hold up yr head in a righteous war
and return home w/ booty
        German bayonets

("Overhead another new German weapon seized control of the skies: the Junkers-87 Stuka dive bomber, which plunged down to blast road junctions and railroad leins; it also had a device that emitted screams to spread terror among its victims. And then there were the heavy bombers. General Wladyslaw Anders, who would eventually lead the Polish exile army through the battles of North Africa and Italy, heard the ominous drone of Heinkel IIIs overhead and later remembered that "squadron after squadron of aircraft could be seen flying in file, like cranes, to Warsaw." At 6 A.M. those deadly cranes began raining bombs on the unprepared, ill-defended city and its civilian inhabitants. In those same surprise raids on the first gray morning, the German Luftwaffe virtually wiped out the entire 500-plane Polish Air Force on the ground. The dawn surprise, the rampaging panzers, the shrieking dive bombers, all were elements in a new German invention that was to change the nature of warfare: *Blitzkrieg.*")

I am around & a great spreading out. The man, is he?
Is available & creative. Near Florida. Near the banyan. A
great spreading out. Spreading like lies, like glory. Like
veins. Like tubing usually hidden. Could be gentle conduit
too. Not abysmal talk talk talk the media. The media provides
into, piped into your life. Blood coursing through the tree
of you, Jove. Do you stumble as you ride? Married to vehemence,
passion? Do you copulate with the horse or the dove? Blitzkrieg.
Penetration is joyous. Keeping still is breaking the Sabbath.
Warmth & moisture as I write. As I write, surround me.
Damp shirt. Sand in all orifices. Greased up for the sun.
What did he say so greased after all? Lying on the beach spent.
Radios not alone in this. A star on the swimsuit is the nearest
ticket to godhead. Grab it. Does it retreat? Spreading
spreading or advancing like a tree.

morphic

Dear Author,

This area is saturated with religion & poetry, and the earth always seem to trouble (tremble) as if it could no longer hold in all the past. We are living on the stores of the Bosphorus and just a short ways away there was in antiquity a temple to Hermes, though I have been insisting that it was really dedicated to Daphnis, his son (the father of bucolic poetry). That is also where Darius sat on his throne and watched his 10,000 men cross the Bosphorus and where St. Daniel is supposed to have worked miracles. Memet built his great fortress, Rumeli Hisar, there before conquering Constantinople. In this century, these few acres have been very important to Turkish poets, including Orhan Veli (who is to Turkish poetry very much what Williams is to America), and he is buried on the other side of the hill from us. Until recently, there was a major dervish sect located here, and before that there were a number of important Orthodox monasteries. One of the sacred springs (sacred now to St. Demetrius but it was once sacred to Apollo?) is located a short walk from here. Across the Bosphorus there used to be a temple to Zeus and a shrine to the twelve gods & goddesses of Olympus, and nearby the place where Polyduces (the son of Zeus (as swan) and Leda) killed Amycus. And just a short way north on this side of the Bosphorus is the place where Medea threw away her poisons when she was returning with Jason and the golden fleece.

With every best wish,
Ed
Nis betiye, Caddesi
Etiler—Istanbul
Turkey

because ye made yr backs shields, argonauts
Because yr eyes turnd home
Yr spurs turnd too
& yr enemies grew to lions
You could still win
but no, you'd rather be exiled
sad, fevered
You blow bubbles as the falcon flies
The wind bursts, is scattered useless
I tell you Shape up!
Take shames heaped on you
forgive & go on
Remember good king Bob's humor
tough & refreshing
So her peace is made with Pisa
What care she for flesh
that in dense wilderness feeds wolves?
Ye Guelfs, Listen!

                (this makes sense

both

       very bright

rims that may be volcanic crater rims)

     (findings . . .

I never plan a stanza)

The words just cluster like chromosomes
hungry hawks on every side
to be thought catatonic was safe (she thought)

            with reason

or charming them with

                                        a woman who meets

such things is an old taboo

Principle, masculine

      and God, 32
      and Logos, *see Logos*
      and Sun, page 20

& pin your faith to
being bizarre & unreasonable
it is no *façon de parler* for him
plants do not grow without the influence of both
          sun & moon

                  A VASE, A BOWL, PHALLUS, ET CETERA

King Soma, my manas, my mind

—Who's your favorite sports player?

—Darryl Strawberry. Was.

—Why?

—He plays right field. He hits a lot of home runs.

  He's on on my favorite team, the Mets.

—Does he have a family?

—He was just born.

—What are you most afraid of?

—Dumb spiders.

—What was your worst nightmare?

—Extra Terrestrial ripping his guts out on an airplane.

—He stood up and bared his guts.

—Do you believe in God?

—No.

—Why not?

—I don't know.

—What created the universe?

—Me.

—If you could get out of the country, where would you go?

—Thailand, poor Thailand racked in pain . . .

(this makes sense . . .)

REVENGE

"Odi et amo"

She'll travel in her head and shift identity. The poet takes on the persona of aged hag who has stuck by her patriarchal male companion, following him to the ends of the earth, now a parched & desolate desert, subject to bombing raids. The field of Tiresias? The world has changed. She sees him now as foolish prophet doomed by a stubborn, wrongheaded, & willful nature. She gets some verbal revenge in here, while she conjures fragments of bygone civilizations, rigid mindsets. She, if nothing else, takes a stand against theism, which implies there is something outside your own mind—a saviour, preferably male, who might even need you to exist. She has been the entrusted tolerant confidante of the Male, a position that gave her an illusion of power but created further servitude until she can no longer hold her tongue. Alas. She becomes nihilistic.

Dear Jove:
Later you were talking. Later you were saying
it's a way back to be inextricably linked
like dead Pharaohs and Queens, something grand.
Something sweeping and fixed. The long desert
bleakness is your home and guarded now because
of terrorism, secret and bleak. None of the
hostages get enough to eat, and reporting back
on faint videos, background noise, I can't hear
you, look fatigued, worn down. Can I be surprised?
Are you still there? Earlier, you said the monuments
are misunderstood. Too much bloodshed. The weight
of centuries' pressure to leave something lasting.
To be a sneer or complacent stone mouth in jungle
air, or wasting away from the rub of sea and wind.

I was a monument ravaged by time in the temple
of your—could I say it—heart?

Or simply in your temple. That holy refuge of
secret thought and revenge. You were the artisan
of the moment I got framed, caught in malachite,
caught in granite. You took the lead. You
assumed the charge of me. I was never good at being
still and wanted to bend with the gold. One searches
in vain for the mask that will describe all you
represent, all you mention in your ravings. Not
a prototype in this old girl's mind. Yet you carried
the "tears" of certain Kota reliquary figures.

Later you said, for you could never stop speaking,
that life was cheap on the desert so why get so
precious about it?

And yet you talked and talked out there. When
coils unwind, the night is suddenly cool, still.
You move away, muttering, I can't make you out.
In French: *Mais, tu es folle*. Something like that.
Like once, under trees, you whispered, pointing
at the sky GOD IS IMMENSE. That shattered, because

all you were thinking was you, you. You were the
architect of the slow burn. It was an appropriate
tactic, the way clouds get heated and evaporate.

Not me, I'll take my sweet time. I won't go away
until you take back all those words. Words on tapes
and notebooks, which fill my shelves now, collapsing
under the weight of grandiose insight and scoff.
Can you take them all back? I doubt it. You said
this, you said that, and you lost the train, It was
never to say I am responsive now, but rather will
fill up space with my immensity. No ears are deaf
and all of you will hear me. Hear me. History needs
to be retold in couplets (*you thought you
spoke in couplets*). Yet I was inventing your

speeches for you all the time. The one about
nostalgia and clothing was close to our common
theme. How the very bright threads in a skirt,
tunic, or dress may evoke the sensation of dancing,
and give pleasure in how they lie hidden in folds
as music bends down and sweeps you up in
its arms. Didn't ask for credit on this one.

Or the one examining the way birds will sit in
water and soak, as a contrast to their lightness
in air. Anything moving from one element to
another seeks that element's destiny.

That brittle twig wants to burn and crack.

My ideas were a shore for you to bank on. You
with your tidal warnings and disasters always
coming in. You remember the oasis at Biskra?
A fresh thing in the middle of the desert, which
snaked through palm trees with their very green
leaves? You had a fix for the African earth.
I spoke through you an echoing reverberating of
the terrible beauty of places such as these.

You enjoyed going it alone in the desert,
babbling at air you get lighter and lighter upon.
You are a lover in air. Your noise is less brute
and adamant out here. You fuck the space, gently
forcing yourself into it. It parts as it always
does.

I am beside you, mimicry of natural phenomena.

You are at your best. You are at your most
obscure. Were anything watching from above
(the camera's placed on the militia's helicopters)
they'd think you the wise old man returned.

Your long hair rippling behind you. Your words
holy by all accounts.

Now you are speaking of the way intelligence
flips in and out of objects, yet only when we
notice it, does it respond and speak to us.
Everything speaks in and of itself—that's the
point. That scorpion (out here on the desert)
nods its suffering too, and poor yon rock bleeds.
Who knows the sorrows of increments of shell
and bone? Those markings are signs of a plan
that we move in parallel universes, suffering.

See the tracks left by the armored combat
vehicles? Where do they come from?

You speak my own thoughts always. The tracks
in my own mind remind you to speak. I listen
to you ranting, and dream myself dressing in
front of a mirror. You stop and observe this
feminine act. You turn away. Later you accuse
me of harboring hidden revenge.

Earlier before the coils unwind, I am not at
liberty to disclose your seed syllable. You,
like all of us, have your root sound. You are
a bird singing inside yourself. Even animals
will cry their secret sound and we think they are
merely communicating to one of their own. That
sound is given and willed by coming into
a realm of vibration and time. The timbre you
hide is archaic, primordial. Do I resent the
simplification of your desire through this one
note you utter inside me?

Perhaps. Anthropological accuracy has no business here.
Stammerings of a civilization before ours

castigate us with their beauty
and joy.

I knew you from the start. I had your number.
I had you nailed. I stole it at the mouth of
your birth. I substitute my own. I planted
my own because yours was more golden.

What do words do?

They call out and fracture

They sing and congratulate the earth

They torment the listener

They are invented to distort reality

They lie down with the beloved

They stroke the child

They twist and turn you in

They name the necessary items for betrayal

They create arsenal

Words create an arsenal beyond necessity

They harp on and communicate fear

They work with the technicians

They blow up a storm

They name the hurricane

They bow and scrape

They invoke the names of deities even as they lie and cheat

They are precise and chill the air around the stadium

They precipitate the end of a love affair

They identify with lost civilization

They decipher annals of the kingdom

Some objects are dedicated to the cult of the dead

A system of line and colors introduces constant vibration

They (the dead) can be read and digested that way

They represent how you try to feel

They are oblique and deflect your obsession

They pacify the interior regions

They can be savage

They count on your imagination

They are the illusionist's prize

They identify the lover

They name the sculpture and its parts

They bed down with the fetish

They long for clarity in the paragraphs

They honor the sun

They atrophy in the wrong books

They long for you to break the code

There are cross relationships between "projections"
and "holes" in the human body. A confusion of
anatomical features haunts you. We move closer
to modern art.

Earlier, we had travelled to the city-etched-in-gold.
It was so bright it startled and blinded us. It was a
curious amalgam of angularity and passion. We were
resistant to the medium of stone. It seemed distorted
by comparison to our life as we wanted to experience
it out on the desert. You had been having those desert
dreams again. But the city: jutting brow.

I turned toward you: a jutting brow.

Symmetry isn't useful here, as collective rather
than individual sentiments woo you. Don't fall
short on me, don't do it, my comrade. Ordinary
voyagers might, or colonials, but you, fetishistic
you, don't do it. Possessiveness is clear to me,
it's my problem. Literal or banal. All the same.
Who means it. Who soaks you up. It's me again.
I save you. Don't trip. Don't get hit. I lead
you by the hand down streets and avenues. Don't
mind them: barbarians. These city streets
and highways are elaborate constructs meant to
confuse us. We see ourselves on large screens
inside hospitals built to add to our confusion.
We are televised as curiosities, aliens. You are
not sure how to receive these accolades. I hurt
for you. There is the instinct of death in this

air, an accentuation of the pleas we could make.
In a prophetic moment you saw me as a young girl
again, undistorted by time. You said a few
kind words before you resumed your monologue
to the bewildered passing by. You keep talking
transcendental metaphysics. Is that what it's
called?

You punctuate your speech with nails, with glass,
with mirrors, with chrome. With sharpness and
always some danger of a stab or jagged edge.

You punctuate your speech with darkness. We are
another life form in the city. Your voice grows
throaty, rasping, terrifying. No one dancing here.
My eyes see no one dancing here. But you are gone
like a Sufi.

You conceal the tube of your torso

open-mouthed

undernourished

In the minds of the Dogon, aesthetic emotion and the
expansion of death are linked.

Like a statue

I recall you

Shoes echoing against the granite ground.

You in the city changed my force around. I was
drained from the feet now with constant walking.
Walking replaced talking to some extent and the rhythm
kept us going although we turned in circles after a

while, circumambulating the same monuments, going
under arches just one last time, riding buses and
trains that returned to their places of departure
which were always, constantly, our destinations.
We were caught on a kind of wheel. The desert seemed
behind us as I wrote, not ahead of us as we lived.

I was afraid you'd stop talking, so I goaded
you into taking chances. We tried braving traffic
after a while. Fast-moving vehicles and persons
whizzed by us, kicking us with their sharp
brutalities. Was this hostile world only in
my mind? We learned to absorb their cruelty
and speed, yet we struggled against, and resisted
their dominion. We almost stopped breathing
to avoid taking too much of them in. You spoke less.

We needed a change. To lead you out of here.
If you spoke less, as seemed to be the trend, I'd
dry up too. A point for departure.

Myth takes precedence over, I want to say, forms.
Or myth forms procedure. A magical formula and
transformation outside the propaganda of cities.
Eroticism never rules us, but rather the dream
of an earlier world, returning to the childhood
of civilizations, took hold here. The lost dance,
the lost carving. Cities like this one had become
too feverishly congested. Layers of time were
obscured by hum and buzz.

Vestiges of evolution seemed lost in their power
to change us. Get out of here I said, and get
you out of here too, I remembered.

You represented now to me, false tradition,
Western illusion. You had crumbled under the
beast. You hadn't conquered. The quality of
materialism was as menacing as ever.
I blindfolded you and pulled you free of the
tentacles of this false civilization.
We headed for a calmer mode. You started
talking again. My ideas spilled forth on the
desert. And now the military regard us with
suspicion as our mission continues.

You are perceived as the more dangerous one,
as you talk and talk. You are like the priapic
column of the toa wood. You are a threat
as you speak of the destruction of the golden
city (it lies on the western edge of the desert).
You set yourself apart. You represent unbounded
opinion. You no longer look at me. I who lead
you back to the desert. I who saved you.
No one is listening to you out here. Why do they
care? Don't fall short on me, comrade.
You've been to the city. You've seen the
face of the city idols. You can't keep this
up. My shelves sag under the weight of your
teachings. My cave is a repository of the
inconsequence of your individuation. My heart
is sore with our struggle. My mind no longer
functions. I can't control your wild words.

I delivered you up during your last sermon
on the nature of sunlight. I had shaded you long
enough.

Remorse?

Your image on the screen they provide me with
still has the power to drain me further. I go

way back. The world at large has no interest
in the hostage you've become. You are finally
an artifact of speech and dust. I know you are
held under false pretense, but I (old woman)
am powerless to help you in this tainted desert paradise.

The problem of darkness and light has not been
solved. I have the despair of a scientist and
am barely legible now on the page.

Grasping-the-Broom-More-Tightly-Now

XI

SHIVA RATRI

The poet travels to Bali with her son, studies language, gamelan, religion, & ritual. Listens to phe-nomena carefully, observing at close range the interlocking cycles of time in tune with a natural cos-mos. Calls on the deities to help her in her quest for power. She would like to be a pamurtian—a gigantic supernatural being with thousands of heads & arms brandishing weapons. Weapons like articulate speech & poetry's orality. This is her basic image of herself. Hardly ever sleeps. The "male" here is more dormant deity, integrated into a transcendent yet powerful hermaphrodite con-sciousness & the dust of her pencil. She shares time with a "double"—a brother/sister figure who gives her secret maps to the island, and gestural codes of appropriate speech & mudra. She sheds an obsession with Western civilization's maniacal stranglehold on genetic consciousness. How to change rhythms on a cellular level is the great conundrum. She moves in circles, not lines. Why would any-one think the contrary?

I see you everywhere

                    di mana-mana

& the light of our day
speaks through us

I study you,
    eyes
    ears
    nose
       hair

apa kabar?
baik baik

                   I see you everywhere
                      & walking

salamat jalan
What is our language?
the study of thinking

       & through the mind to the melody we will play
together
or apart
           walking
  a man walking   What's your name
                   siapa namanya?
with whom do you walk?

             I'm lost (*saya tersesat*)
I practice the syllables of your history Bali
I see you everywhere

because I am lost
         I see you everywhere
You speak
any questions (*Ada pertanyaan*)
There is no answer to love
Tidak ada jawaban

melihat, menonton, membaca

              (to see, to watch, to read)
     I am a "penulis puisi"

a penniless poetry

   I come into you from a great distance a penniless poetry

You are my pitch
my sound my song
         (the holy 3)
rendah, suara, lagu

I sing you my beloved because I am lost without you
         Is it forbidden?

listrik mati
I am dead without you

How many times I think "I am dead without you"
capi apa?

                I look for my own eyes
& for the switch to bring them on again
I see you everywhere
                          di mana-mana
      be still be silent
           this *nipu sipi (nyepi)*
the whole world died, no fire, murder the fire

I was lost when they murdered the fire
              the whole world died
This is the child's first lesson
Bahasa Indonesia

    it is a simple tongue
tongue of the child
                      lost everywhere without
my child-man-speech
    guide to the temple
you must go there with torch, he says
listrik mati
         dead in the cave lost without you
   child-man-deity
   call upon you as guide

call to the *langit gringsing wayang*
         flaming heaven of the *wayang*
    call to my ancestors who live inside me everywhere
      & abandon me in my weakness
        not making the proper ceremonies

Call upon Giri Putri, Dewi Gangga, Dewi Danu
Call Mother Uma
Stave off Durga

        all could die here
          in me

                    murder the fire
I see you everywhere

                    (di mana-mana)

        Beloved Indra, active and warlike

    you bring down the rain to cleanse this heart

            everywhere that existed once dies now

            it dies as I call upon you

Batara Siwa, divine hermaphrodite
                    source of all light, Windu   that
        takest away the static of the world
                            blow upon us
                    bring down the radio to cleanse this fire
        (for I am burning, burning)   dear shape-shifter, dear Iovis
                            who are you?
this is the dark moon of the ninth month
the puppets dance to activate the mind
        toward what great comedies & miracles?

Siwa once upon a time created beings with no ethics, no *sila,* no code of behav-
ior, who went naked, lived wild in cages, had no religion. They mated under
trees in the light of day, abandoned their sad children, ate offal, lived like beasts.
Siwa was so horrified he imagined a son to destroy these humans. He was cop-
ulating with his wife, he was coming into her, he was excited with his plans, his
great revenge on the monsters he himself had created and he told her, he told
Uma his intentions. (He was fucking himself here.) She was indignant and
withdrew from him quickly and in the struggle Siwa's sperm fell on the
ground. He panicked, he called the gods together, and pointing to the sperm
said that should it develop life there would be great difficulties for them. The
alarmed gods began to shoot arrows at the sperm. The sperm grew a pair of
shoulders when the first arrow struck it, hands and feet popped out after the
second, and as they continued to shoot into it, the drop of sperm grew into a
fantastical giant who stood as high as a mountain, demanding food with which
to pacify his insatiable hunger. Siwa named him Kala and every day sent him

down to earth where he could eat his fill of people.
                              thus the barbarians dwindled

                                          (put out the fire)

but again
it comes back
again, again

again
but do you hear
it when it comes?
the fire, can you hear it?

in its signal its plea
to not escape burning, burning
not to escape the comedy of burning,
miracle of burning
nor not be witness
to me, newly charged with power coming out of the dangerous cave
       (tender, angker)
                           manifesting one's holiness
        (mawinten) to bring out
the dormant power

come out!
come out now!
you can come out now

Take my tongue and inscribe on it all
the magic syllables
                    ANG UNG MANG
make my voice sweet with the inscriptions
of honey

Make my epic, my song of male *sakti,* sing!

I'll be Rangda
I'd be Durga to pursue you, male,
   seeing you everywhere
                          di mana-mana

once I was *sebel*
now I'm clean

      seeing you everywhere
                       (*di mana-mana*)

cleansed by seeing you everywhere
put out this fire with *tirta*

(Kala Rahu swallows the moon)

again, it comes back again
during the eclipse of the moon

      (Beggar's Bush, February, we sit drinking
      brem-arak)

a full moon

   bulan purnama

eclipse of the full moon

put me in thrall

         blaming you, the child
         & you, the man

menjual apa?
         (what do you sell?)
& what do you see in me

cari apa?

(what do you look for?)
(in me)

I think in order to live
& live by seeing you everywhere

di mana-mana

to receive love
(terima kasih)

& seeing in me the one-staying-up-at-night

(bergadang semalam sentuh)

the one-burning-at-night-receiving-love

I am a carrier of this great love

di mana-mana

a language: what? speaks in tongues: what? knows
no bondage: what? lasts the night: what? slaves
by day: who? tends the rice: who? sweeps the
steps: who? tends the temple: he does. waits
by day: who? goes into trance: who? puts on
the mask: he does. dances with sword: he does.
climbs the mountain: many do this. walks in a
figure 8 (*ngumbang*): many do this. breaks for
a while (*angsel*): many do this. interprets the
"right": he does. interprets the "left": she does.
listens with 2 sets of ears: he does. binds
his breasts: he does. wanders of: who?
supplicates the deities: they all do this.
another language: whose? what does he say?
the answer is always yes. *Senang makan nasi?*
(do you like rice?): yes.

stand before me
of which object, me
you are part &
parting of

I will see you
or you are
never seen
by me again

& I am again
just here
at it again
seeing you

green duty
calling me
again to
what song?

Nothing but you
new in path
of my sun
Come back or call

Reminding
I mean, remind me!
A tough number
to learn

The one with "exit"
all over the face
astride you
speech or heart

in a rapport
with thought

impulse
action

I'm the total they add to, and you have to have arms
for the woman, you know. Slow down, my genes do not
carry the same messages. Rancor? No, messages
like the one on at night, with the flashes growing at
the boundaries of the nucleus. I see them, but they
also see you. You who constitute the Balinese
universe: upper, immediate, lower worlds.

     Dear Naga Banda,
       We cling to you, the priest giving life to
you (*pedanda boda*) the priest taking it way (*pedanda siwa*). We cling to you,
vehicle for the soul into heaven,
phallic channel to heaven . . .

             Hari apa hari ini?

what is the date today?

the date of my cremation, for I am burning, burning

the snake awaits me in the channel to new life

                   di mana-mana
what stays? nothing
what continues? no thing
who asks? I do

(the husband dreams I am the serpent, and he must
crush me in my power, writhing like a wild thing
on the kitchen floor. Mercy!
I am merely a long rope bound in greencloth,
with a great mane of *lalang* grass, effigy of the
serpent, mere effigy woman becoming man becoming
woman becoming man again. Mercy!
I flail under the boot)

                    the whole world dies again
                    no fire, not allowed to light the lamp
fire in the body?
murder that fire

It's *shiva ratri,* night of Shiva

with a full moon, a red dot in the heavens
now wake the fire!

I'll play the
wife of Shiva
& we go dancing
to an old sweet
ancestor tune
& when you fall
I'll bow down to
pick up the
pieces of you
eclipsed
by the night
of me, the dreamer
(nothing compares to you)

                    di mana-mana

and I sing of how nothing compares:

(blinding green, eyes tear
        on the back of the bike)

because it is early
& you are beautiful
weep for how early it is
how beautiful you are

        and the debts to pay
because it is thus:

how early it is, and beautiful

    debts to the teachers (*resi*)
        to the ancestors (*pitra*)
            to gods & self (*dewata*)

    how early
    in
    us

some days I resume color
for I walked too far

                are you there?
                are you there but silent?
                did the world die?

did you do the proper chants?
did you perform the proper ceremonies?
are you restless (*gelisah*)?

I am mere body-bone
I break & wither
I burn in the fire
I am clever that way
I weep
I disappear
what am I?

I go a lot of places
I study language for a penniless poesy I reap what I sow
what am I?

I beg you this heart is broken
It eats itself
It is self wounding
what kind of heart is this?

I came here to study
I came here to dance

I beat the gong with a steady hand
I left something behind
what was it?

   (I need this burning in order to live)

the poet needs these three (in order to live)

vyutpatti, culture, or a vast knowledge of the world

abyhasa, a skill with language developed from constant
practice and apprenticeship with a master

skakti, creative power

                          no posturing

               her teaching is you, man
               or you, man-woman who stands in for phenomena
    & and you   siddhas
            flaming languages
   erudite
          or simple

              & wherever the energy is,
                   seize it!

grabbing the power from the male deities

       she lives inside them

they haunt her
eclipse her
increment by increment

a kind of bondage
& then she transmutes their form
(eyes & skull)

to her own
eyes in every pore of her body/cervix is the window of her world

Dear Deity,

Thank you for showing me around the island. Now I am lost. In the best sense. Now I am *kerawuhan* (possessed). I no longer own this body. I dance for the gods (including you). I dance in front of the dolls, the effigies, all the ones gone before me, all ancestors, lovers, poets. I recognize your world. Holy shadows on the screen, ho! Thank you for the drinks, the cigarettes of clove, imagination, and for pointing to the code the smallest increments of which I would honor & obey. You lead with your heart. *Terima kasi.*

Anne-Who-Burns

Singo nodo gegere
    (The roar of a lion)
Sang dewoto kabeh
    (And all the dogs took flight)
Wojo kasilat
    (It had teeth exposed like fangs)
Wiyung tutup kadi pereng
    (Lips as wide as valleys)
Rejang irung kadi sumur bandung
    (A nose as deep as a well)

Eyes like twin suns
    (*Netro kadi suryo kembar*)
Kerananiro kadi layaran
    (Ears large like 2 sails)
Rambut kuwel agimbal
    (Hair ratted & matted)
So tall was he that he caused a fright
    (*Ogah uger luguriro kang girigiri*)
He was so tall he covered up half the sky
    (*Luthuriro tanpo toro*
    Tutup kemadiane akso)

the green idol
on board the *bemo*
go beyond knowing this or that
little green idol
match lights up
this or that is not strange
points to volcano
I am here
with my little green idol
his flowering top
his glowing eyes gone beyond this or that
the battleground inside him
is the playground of the green idol's heart

(see him everywhere   *di mana-mana*)

In Bali there are small but very mean dogs that bark all night. And their eyes
glow when you shine a flashlight. And there are motorcycles all over the place.
And twelve-year-olds drive them. And babies ride on the back and they are
crazy drivers.

The island is very green. There are things called rice fields that are everywhere.

The market is smelly and there are flies everywhere. We bought mangosteens
and two out of the five were good. Things in the market are cheap.

> the puppets are asleep in the box
> we never talk about tme
> the puppets become shadows
> you start to make them from the eyes
> then make the rest come alive
> this is the creation of the world
> the *dalang* is god
> the screen is the world
> the oil lamp is the sun
> we never talk about time

Yet in sketching
the lines "do you? do you?"
& "you do if it pleases?"
do you not
sketch
the knots
that mount
to greet you?

around a shield
or warrior-stick
life guides
the writer
to the
morsel

again
again might drive in
something
outside
the focus
of someone

writing that details
texture
& is real too
by turns

looking for
the right time
in (on)
the man's wrist

then something
(the white plastic watch band)
explodes the portrait
as well as
looking for it

(see you everywhere)
in time

if all's well
eclipse precepts
salamat malam
or taste or hear
deflecting options
which allow for
language
who speaks here?

      he does, and does he quarrel?

he does and does he strive?

   he does

& does he dance?

he does, on many a corpse

he carries the tusk
he carries scars
he bends over his magic
he has magic to burn

     Victor is in his cups tonight!   The moon goes black
     I ask for more
     more blackness, more light
     more firewater

   he complies, but does he?

  amendable to night & foreign tune (blues?)

I turn
& your eyes are also on the sky
your eyes, which are his, and are his too
all the "his" of eyes on the sky

are you the shadow next to me or
        are you the shadow next to me

                who are you?

                        his eyes?

(the moon goes out)

                        listrik mati

I give up everything to know you

                        kenapa? kenapa?

        you tell me
            & tell me again

she lives inside them, she lives inside him, she
lives in the corner of his eye, she writes as
woman-who-had-stretched-to-this-point, to the
point of an eye or corner of "his" eye she writes
as one abused, she writes as collaborator, she writes
now she writes later

                She-as-describer is always a person

wasted old widow, prostitute & eater of infants, she comes to spread death &
plague on the land

Rangda danced by a single male

eyes bulge from her head
tusk-teeth curve upward
& fangs protrude down over her chin
hair a matted tangle
breasts: withered & pendulous dugs
hair hanging between them like tubular sausages
her long red tongue is a river of fire
amok Rangda! *enter here*

she splays her ghostly hands from which extend
long clawlike fingernails
(*wild clanging of gamelan*)
several minor witches (male dancers) toss the corpse of a stillborn babe around
shrill satanic laughter
she clutches a magical white *shakti* handkerchief
Rangda-Durga, Shiva's malignant consort *enter here*
Barong *enter here,* challenge her horror here
with puppy hilarity
entranced men rise, gone into *nadi,* become *nadi*
& stab themselves with kris dagger
shaped like a sound wave, sea wave,
vibration of universe
they gobble live chicks
wildly convulse in the mud
drop into coma

go, gone, gone beyond into trance
those deities are presences
go, gone, gone into *nadi*
startled into *nadi*, gone.

& every syllable is conscious
    & the unconscious, too, structured like a language
language moving us up & down

Is it revealed to the man? Is it revealed to the woman?
Is it only revealed to the man?
Two protagonists struggle for dominance

the imagined world is quite real, a tree with its roots
in heaven, tree rooted in highest heaven, one branch
goes into "god" itself, the branches are sentences, the
leaves are like words
    language a living system in the zone of convergence

rhythm, pace, sonic blast, parapraxes
    inherent in my nervous system
                    a patterning to live for

what does it mean to rot?
holding out against experience
                              & my words sung
but entheogenic, entheogenic!
            liquid, sap, blood, semen will nourish my words

image forth naming
image forth naming

                     dear Gabriel (Angel of Words)
                        hear my plea

hear my plea to name the cause "ambivalent"
Candidasa at night:
I believe in the exquisite manners of the gentleman
& yet I look for a telephone in the dark
I am not crazy I don't abandon anyone
Everyone is partially true because everyone is already dead
Water beats against the stone walls
They only chide who wish me ill
No temples here the sea is alive
I walk a tighter, tightening rope
unless to believe "to cut through the veil of outward form,
    dissolve in air" is a human solution
6,000 rupiahs for the night

"When I was a child, I learned that the moon was goddess
Dewi Ratih. Then Neil Armstrong landed on it. I still look
up at night and pray to Dewi Ratih."

step through the *candi bentar*
enter your own life
You walk through the split in your life
you are half male, half female
you are never too late to meet yourself halfway
each step brings you closer to the split that forced you here
arriving in a red car, a white car
into the inner temple of your mind

      look . . .
it's simple.

I'm no fool.

I cross every ocean, reach every foreign shore, leave my home
to acquire wisdom, you friend of my heart, you friend of my
secret passion. You need not ask, I join every adventurous
trip, I join you faithfully, taking care of those parts
you leave in my charge. This, because I honor you.
I haven't cut my hair, it looks alright even for conservatives,
since I wear no moustache anymore. In the West, it seems
to be better like this, but in Indonesia, a moustache is more
advantageous.

                open
                unoriginated
                space
                of dharmakaya
                gives birth to bija
          of seed syllable

          Primordial
          sound
          becomes the basis
          for all manifestation
       of form

             O M

        (Leitmotiv of
        "religious" life)

Mantras grow from experience &
from the collective knowledge
of many generations
         HO HUM

    (without fear/without hope)
                     ONG!

di mana-mana

I fear you go from me, language
when the world goes dead, goes silent
& I was burning burning
I fear you sleep too long

Peliatan: the night, the table, the books, the "spirits"
    & who are you?
                                (I fear I slept too long)
I see you everywhere
    the cues (*sasmita*) are transmitted musically visually verbally

    what signals us here?
what pulls us into motion, what navigates our forms?
what priest is behind all this, activating our tongues
what got left behind when we agreed to enter this day together?
what intersected with what?
what cycle are you on?
       the loop or the coil
                        tearing about the island to see, to see
to burn, to see
(even requests for drinks, cigarettes, or betel nut
are made through the mouths of the *wayang* puppets)

who is alluding to whom on what screen or otherwise
field of play, field of Mars

what forfeits itself to coexist

what does the boy say who sobs as he departs
("how was your trip?" (he shrugs) "okay")

                        (nuance vs. nonchalance)

inviting the voice to speak
it arises out of chaos
& I am burning burning
my wit (it burns)
my grand style (burning)

my books (burn them!)
special privileges (burning)
who's talking (I burn)
shut the man down who crosses me here (burn him!)

(Rent a motorbike for a week & ride it all over Bali)

returning to the source of shut down! shut down!

silence the chromosomes one small day

"I was talking about time"
"So?"
"I was talking about real time"
"Brahma dreamed it"
"Was he lying to save us?"
"Lying by dreaming?"
"Yes"
"Were you inspired?"
"I was & said so"
"How 'mantra' of you"
"You joke with me"
"I spied myself inside blinding green"
"It was the last color to come into consciousness you know"
"I didn't"
"Didn't what?"
"Didn't know"
"Green is like that, coming later"
"Maybe we were just too narrow to see it"
"Just blue & yellow, sea & sun"
"But here it enters your veins, your skin turns to green"
"You become the green deity"
"I'll pray for you"
"It won't help"
"It was always there, we didn't see it"
"It was hiding in the desert"
"I couldn't look when I landed it was too vivid"

"Everyone spies it & is afraid"
"Afraid of what"
"Of losing it after they see it"
"It makes them happy"
"A kind of parlance, weary traveller"
"It still makes them happy after they lose it"
"Green makes them feel alive"
"I'm not exempt"
"I paid you for this with good green money"
"Are you proud?"
"Like most men"

Dear Grandfather,

It takes 23 hours to get to Bali and a little less going back. For us, it took longer to get back. On the way there we stopped in Salt Lake City, then Los Angeles, then in Honolulu, then in Irian Jaya (near Papua New Guinea). Then you get to Bali. On the way back our plane broke down in Irian Jaya (Biak). First they said the plane would be fixed in one hour, then they said we'd have to stay two nights! But luckily we only stayed one. They took our passports and our tickets and we had to stay in a funky hotel called Hotel Irian. In the lobby people were watching a Mohammed Ali boxing match, or was it Leon Spinks? from 1976. We had eaten on the plane (but I didn't eat). We couldn't make a call out of Indonesia. We went to the market in the morning after a very funky breakfast. We saw dancers at the airport who wore grass skirts and painted faces and had guitars and drums and spears. This was interesting. Finally they got us a plane from Jakarta to take us to Honolulu, then to L.A. Then we changed planes and came to Denver.

Love,
Ambrose

XII

PUER SPEAKS

Indonesia has softened her competitiveness. The poet can finally resemble the boy in herself, having had extensive "Puer" dreams. This possible, too, as she ages, having shed seductive submissive ingenue. She doesn't want to always be irritant. Thus poet becomes name of a boy for the time being. And takes on implications of Muse ("mouth-forming words") & then puts those new mixes into boxes, assured now of a place on the page. Windows are two-ways and may be locked.

Somewhere the boy rises up in me. And the words become chants of mock battle or curiosity. For curiosity is the boy's guest-song. What is he looking for on every landscape on every planet in every woman's face, ear, or belly? He sleeps inside me on my shoulder, shoulder that sleeps inside me dreaming of holding up the world, holding up the sky. To shoulder it and play with it gently, to mock and tease the elders, to be naughty and eschew sleep, he thinks. I go out with men as their boy. And as a young girl, too, I am one of them, not a camp follower. The initiation is words, which forge the muse upon me. She thrusts herself at me, she challenges me to be my first woman ever, to guide and show me passion. She teaches me the words *laterly, labia majora.* She teaches me *mons* and *Euterpe,* she is the concept I have of mouth-forming words. But they, the men, are rough and cut the sentiments from the bone. Go on, they mock me, show us your mettle, show us you aren't lovesick, romantic, a fool for a turn of phrase, for a twist in sound to match your eye, go on, show us you can piss and sweat and scorn the ridiculous mother. Show us you can do without light, water, fossil fuel. Show us the poem, of what it's made. How diamondlike it might be if you don't bend it to your weak woman's will. Show us, boy. The initiation is how I will descend to meet this mid-age hag, wrinkled 'eld, how this boy, young-spirit maverick, cowboy, this young soldier will fight through his life ah humming! toward the castle. Don't kill him, don't, but neither trophy hung for a puerile adventure. What were the words? They were *rock, salt, stone, arrow, intent, jump, dare.* They were *jaunty, jest, armor, pistol, poke, drive, penis.* They were mysterious: *jockey for power, jockey shorts, jock strap.* They were innocents in their lostness to experience, for what was experience but a dream to this slip-of-a-boy? I played the tomboy, I wore pants, I was just setting out to make my fortune, to swell the tide in my favor, to impress the others, to see real gold. To touch the lands of France, England, Egypt, Italy. I was 18 years, knapsack on back aright, eyes gaze forward to shore, I see land. And I see the monsters on that foreign land I have come to conquer. Who grants me their sword, albeit kindly blunted for a young man. Youth is in the clothing, in the color of cheek, in the desire for mix and talk around a fire. In the dirty show and sock. I hid in these clothes and wooed women. Yet I freed myself from women, I wooed men. I abdicated the mother's hearth. Back off, mother, I go now. Language, assist me in this rite. I have learned to charm snakes. On the desert the scorpions hide from me as I recite the secret mantra of universal youth. I converse in tongues. I keep up with the best of them. I don't have to be an object of their desire. I can feed tigers if I wish and ride on the backs of elephants. The old men like me; I am their young friend. I climb trees for coconuts. I resist the clutches of the mothers who want every young son claimed for insatiable lust. I write to keep myself pure. I study the stars for purposes of navigation. I travel under sea to the center of fire. I ride porpoises to learn about sound and motion.

I am buoyant. I won't fight with my fists. My muscles grow. I study the forms of other men and their words. Soon I can swear with the best of them. I write for my comrades as Dante did. I show them how the quest in me is to reach them through words, to make words dance out a body without breaks and womb, or to take that body and establish the will of a man coming to life, just coming to life. Male poet on the brink of his/her fortune, no one can lean on me. A solo act. A first change to fail to not ask the right questions as I enter the castle. To forfeit knighthood awhile. To come before all the goddesses of thunder and song as a novice, stealing their power. They don't recognize me I've grown. No one lean on me yet.

Puer, Nom de Guerre

caveat

or front the ticket
he tricks me
    (gets dressed)

cover sex
covert

boy to

part

closer

brace for the turn

she like to me

blurts

organ! organ!

from a shrine

to fortress

blind, her blind

semi

autonomous

from the lunar

courtesy

misrule abuses

what causes

    slick & chance

salvo-

realm

sleeping partners

going out in currency

be a man

        to

affront her nub

& temerity

assists Lysander

nope, don't

Mace

a trademark

war is

a sub-kingdom of this

---

boy poke

like as to persist

grand slam

as in the game

---

slit trench

spare

men or boys'

body parts

neutrino

difficult to explain

he-me

he-she

plots

as to a truck

shine back

vent the

cloth

rend veil

or scream   same as you

boy

chance it

tattoo

saw me

nude, hide

stay the push

　　　　pleasure's drive

　　　position

　facing east

　　　still in the closet

"he" lied?

paid well

　　for "it"

on an exception

to the Academic

spelled me

then submit

to document

I see

static lover

switch

& side with

the other side

of her

onanism?

high sierras

land this escape

for her she

will, she

won't

be gone

boy to

light up

lie down

                    I see the battles

ground of

all your dust

            sex-dust

wither

eros

name of

her spot

banishes me   boy gear

put it on

Adorno

settle throat,

obdurant

not the boy

wound about word-

object

of desire

from distance

speaks objects

rant or

spewthroe of

her hate/

her love

obliges this

She-He

obfuscates

the interior

pleas

take me

consort

with the

matrix

boy

rise up paginal

XIII

AEITIOLOGICAL ONES

She worries about unsung heroes, migrating, restless wanderers, including her own father, who has become an active correspondent to the poem, and makes a list of the conquered towns he moved through in Europe. Out on the town she hungers for conversation for the poem, visits her blond friend Robert who shows her some secret treasures and tells a little of his story, which interests her as he is quintessential American male whose father worked for the industrial-military-nuclear complex. She has met quite a few men like this—would-be albeit tattered bodhisattvas who live in poetic shadows expiating the sins of their fathers. She prepares for a trip to Prague and other parts of German Europe. She dreams about Ludwig Wittgenstein while she grows nervous about the impending war.

$$^d Nabu - ku - du - úr - ri - usur \quad šar \quad Babili$$

$$za - ni - in \quad É - sag - íl \quad ù \quad É - zi - da$$

$$aplu \quad a - ša - re - du$$

$$ša \quad ^d Nabu - apla - usur \quad šar \quad Babili \quad ana - ku$$

"NEBUCHADNEZZAR, KING OF BABYLON,

WHO PROVIDES FOR ESAGILA AND EZIDA,

THE ELDEST SON OF NABOPOLASSAR,

KING OF BABYLON, AM I"

(The last phrase, "am I," is omitted from many bricks.)

Dear John Waldman,

You have very sane handwriting; did you ever notice? I think I've inherited my sanity from you. Our Frances was intense, she treated me as a lover. Jealous, why? Do you have any ideas? Am I off the wall? Was I the fulfilled artist she/you wanted to be? Heroic ideal of some kind maybe. It's complex when you gaze deep into the eyes of this thing. Thank you for your sanity, albeit its neurotic edge.

I appreciate saying this to you tonight because there should be no claustrophobic barriers between us. Please don't hesitate when it comes to your truth. I try to write in the cult of truth. I supposed I've been the "armored Amazon," as pop psychology describes, taking on your male attributes because you were detached, sometimes passive. You suffered, survived the war, and shouldered the responsibility of supporting us as a family. This was exhausting. So proud, you working at the drug clinic all those years too, keeping in touch with the darker realities of addiction. I am grateful and for the "moral" support you always gave when I wanted to shift in another direction. Did you ever feel that you couldn't speak what you felt, that your throat was literally blocked? This is why I write, keep writing.

When you weren't "there" where were you? Off in your fantasies as I am? An overactive imagination? She probably guarded you in her protective zone. A kind of radical belt. And she went off & enacted all the guises of women & came back to tell you the stories. She certainly had an ear for other people.

I see you in my mind in a modest wooden rowboat on Union Lake fishing. Early memory. Or reading a book. Somewhat the same meditative presence you carry. And I see myself on your lap in your uniform of the Great War, you are smiling. What's hidden? "Dandled."

I would love you to come to the "Zen weekend." It might prove interesting, provocative to you. You don't have to get up like the rest of us at 4 A.M.

Sorry about the "ativan." Bernadette's d.o.c. too. It's hopeless to procure such a drug in, as Ambrose says, "health-nut" Boulder without a script.

I hope something works out for you. . . . Remember the moods aren't solid and see, as the Balinese do, that every thing moves in its own distinct cycle of time & happily intersects when it does with other "things." "When a body meet a body" . . . Many many wheels & shifting gears. I'm glad we meet at the interstices of light & sorrow, and you my father be. Off to Prague soon. Allen Ginsberg will crown the new "King of May." Your daughter-at-arms, AW

Dobre jitro

Jak se mate?

Kolik je hodin?

Jake je pocasi?

Nerozumin Vam.

Odkud prichazite?

Na shledanou . . .

(My heart breaks like my father's before me AH-YA)
I wanted to be Queen, but . . .

You reduce me to an object of desire. My breasts say this because they are wise. My thighs are responding to the accusation because they are wise. Eyes behold a thousand reasons you do this, you who are groping for the be all & end all here, you who take a proverbial turn at the wheel & navigate us out of sync. Sync is the new age number for it is the is the is the number. Turn on the radio. Good luck. You reduce me to an object of desire. You think I'm hot. You take my words and twist them to a recommendation for a scenario of desire. Is desire lively? Does it live? Is it sending the votaries forward, does the Man regress as He checks his watch to obviate time? Check this out: A long way back, & now in Saudi the women can't drive cars. They can, of course, but may they? May they? Does anyone, (they), care? The light goes off, you reach for my neck. I love you. I'm not ashamed to admit this for you are the saint & scholar who studies desire. I came into view as a representation of an object of desire. Good luck, I said to myself. The night is youthful. It smarts of love & sweat. I love you because you are fatal. And mortal too. We will die in desire & spend the context of break & night on a boat of love. You coaxed me into a rehearsal of dying into life. You feel it? That the heart could continue at any cost, that the cost would be everything, that cost is the tomb of desire that it rides into dawn, always, always. And is an *alba* for you. It only exists at dawn when the bottle is empty & we've smoked under talk. For talk is the witch & it is my voice that attracts the battle in you. That says okay test me in your language. In the code of the male. I encode you. I take each phoneme and rake it over the coals. It imprints on me the message that held you back. Unseen ropes scored a hand. And bound & gagged the truth be told. You are a compliment to the room. You are intrusive like any good idea.

dexterous
    a kind
of
    truncating:
dancing
a kind of
naming
going to be,

but
     always
   quid pro quo
our #1 obsession:

overthrow the little countries
& you are really
running
    no longer dancing

up the angst-gangster stair

   like a
line of
scrimmage

Shamir rebuffs Gorbachev on emigres, Arabs applaud Gorbachev remark, Bush nudges China on anniversary of crackdown, Cambodia talks collapse, Congress looks anew at ties with Vietnam, a Beirut "cease-fire" is but a weary interlude, President Samuel K. Doe of Liberia is facing the most serious crisis of his ten years in power, Mandela, off on world trip, will urge retention of sanctions, rainy days in Zambia, Bush and Colombian President to assess drug wars today, Canada premiers try to save pact, Dubcek rebukes Slovak protestors who rebuked Havel, Japanese feel quite ready for a visit from Gorbachev, White House sees aura from summit, in Europe few are cheering, Summit failed to narrow dispute on Afghanistan, Santiago: Allende's widow meditates anew . . .

And he writes me all the towns he passed through
Marseilles, 5 Nov 44 St Barbe, 8 Nov St Benoit, 17 Nov Bertrichamps, 21 Nov Reon L'Etape, 23 Nov Moyenmoutier (Thanksgiving), 24 Nov St Blaise, 25 Nov Rothau, 26 Nov Uberhaslach to rendezvous Area, Moyenmoutier, 27 Nov Biberskirch (end of Alsace campaign), 2 Dec Bust-Struth, 3 Dec Puberg, 6 Dec Goetzenbruch, 12 Dec Lemberg, 22 Dec Petit Rederching, 23 Dec Siersthal, 25 Dec Guisberg and back to Sierthal, 2 Jan Petit Rederching, 22 Jan Mountbrunn, 25 Jan Petit Rederching, 29 Jan Mountbronn, 14 March Holbach (Paris, Nancy), 17 March Schorback, 22 March thru Bitche and Maginot Line on into Contwig,

Germany passing thru the Siegfried Line, 23 March Maxdorf, 24 March
Rehhutte, 31 March Crossed Rhine, thru Mannheim to Schwetzingen, 3 Apr
Eschelbach-Rappeneau, 4 Apr Frankenbach, 5 Apr Bad Wimpfen, 14 Apr
Crossed Neckar River thru Heilbronn to Weinsberg-Sulzbach, 15 Apr Rappach,
17 Apr Gleichen, 18 Apr Hutten, 20 Apr Edelmannshof, 21 Apr Steinach, 22 Apr
Baltmannsweiler, 24 Apr Rommelshausen, Unter Urbach, Schorndorf,
Hauberbroun, Unterschlechtbach, Schwabish Gmung, Altes Lager (one week
in field), Schwabish Gmund, 28 June Heubach, 7 July Herrenberg to Stuttgart,
Return trip Karlsruhe, Strasbourg, Le Havre and

        got boat

          there

        Yankee don't go . . .

    rectangular space
    within the girl who never-went-to-war
    who sees stillbirth aftermath of
    such a conflagration
    collapse of every communism
    & all false boundaries challenged

    parent form what
    comes from it?

    prowling the mind
    of what bargain what bargain what power
    what way she might turn:
    bootless solitude
    of the caged humiliation
    of any undernourished nation
    other-curtained
    sun metamorphosed
    as eye & yolk, diamond

patterns in her hair,
on the feet she walks
and when she does
she walks toward the new countries
all of them, "what's a nation?"
under what god, guise, flag banner wave

(give me a break)

no es lá

whatever

you say

it is

is what you say

we, who are we

who are touched

(*père et son fille*)

sa *fille*

& map a strategy

Dear Anne,

I remembered when you wrote to me about the past that I stuck away some letters I recovered from 501 E. Main Street before the house was sold. I've numbered them in the upper left hand corner from 1 to 11 so you'll know which ones I'm referring to in my comments. They're all from my father to my mother beginning from 1902 to 1908.

#1. Addressed to Rio (long i pronunciation) Grande, this is of course where the four Hand girls and one boy were born. The girls: Sarah, Stella, Lillian and Idona. The boy: Leander. Sarah was Aunt Sally to me—she was much older than the other girls, by 10 or 15 years. (I don't know why the gap.) Stella was the one who went to the West Coast, was a prison matron, and then married a rancher (rich) and settled in one of the cattle states—maybe Wyoming. (I'm sorry about my memory—it'll be faulty through my reflections, but good enough to give you a sense of how things were.) Note the "My Darling" at the heading. This was about the most affectionate term used, although the general tone of the letters show that John was in love with Idona and wanted to marry her.

Anyway, Lillian was Aunt Lilly, also older than Idona, who along with Aunt Sally helped to raise Idona. (Remember, they were all orphans.) Rio Grande in case you don't recall is the village at the entrance of Cape May proper. It's on the sheltered sound where the lumber boats sailed from, and where even today yachts and power boats anchor. That's where the father Thomas Hand (married Josephine Clarke, I don't know about her early death) sailed from to keep the invitation of a fellow captain to Liverpool. They, the crew, the ship were never seen again. This was probably in the 1880s—over a hundred years ago.

The Church mentioned in #1 is almost certain to be St. Paul's Lutheran, since as you know John's father cofounded it.

The "orders" referred to that put him "out of sorts" are orders for glass bottles, or "little ware" as they were called by the glassblowers who made tiny bottles by hand ¼ oz, ½ oz, 1 oz etc. The blowers worked "piece work," paid by the piece—so no orders—no income. I don't know where he went ice skating, but probably Hawkins Pond, where the present-day high school is located—out Main Street.

Letter #2 was written from Wildwood—that's where my father always went when the glass furnaces shut down for 2 mos in the summer. You see, he did make fair money considering he worked only 9+ mos of the year. But it was *hard work;* I know because later I watched a shop in action.

If I've spent this much time on #1, I'll have a book written by letter #11. Look at #10 and #11 now and see that the "boy" referred to is incredulously me at the age of 9 mos. The N. 11th St. address is that of Aunt Lillie when she was living with her husband Irvin Harris, who had a butcher shop in Millville. The marriage didn't last—but that's another story.

#2. Smith Street is where Aunt Sally lived. You can see that Idona moved from house to house. She was the youngest and the sisters felt responsible for her. I forgot to say that Leander, the only son, died of cancer—but I must have been 10 or so by then, since I seem to believe that this was the first time I was exposed to the sense of dread about the illness.

#3. Interesting letter from Washington July 1903—with the "boys"—fellow glassworkers.

#7. The reference to the bouquet holder is of course a piece of off-hand glassware to be made at the factory (Schettersville plant of the Whitall-Tatum Company in south Millville where my father worked). The oven of course the lair where glassware was placed for slow cooling.

#8 John was going to Camden to meet Idona at the ferry. Why he wanted Ethel (Hollingsworth) to be with her because he would have to leave, I don't know. Mr. Hughes was his immediate boss at the factory.

I'll try to resume sometime in the future when I concentrate and collect my thoughts about the early years. But his little packet of letters almost deserves a poem of its own. Or just some bits and pieces for a longer work by you.

You can imagine a Millville of those days: Coal-fired glass plants—four of them. Two

Whitall-Tatums, one Weatons, one Mitchells (also the Manufacturing Co.—textiles); horses and carriages, the business area on High Street; noontime whistles when the workers had dinner. The evening meal was supper. Working hours 6 to 6. Half day on Saturday. I'm written out, but I'll keep thinking.

         Love,

            John

can't be turned
away
can't protest
flesh
can't let it
go
can't speak at times
beyond
a daughter

protesting yet in me
in you
in the late
water
the water like shattered glass
lake
what I have done
that flows
on place
on the place
it feels like
in wind

what have I?
a town of not
autumn
not night
staring down
eyes staring down
the mind

to look back
genetics
of how it
can't
be turned
can't
turn back

blast the moment,
come
can't speak at times beyond a sister,
come

O daughter be home, come home

    & to the lair of a canyon come

    I lift his blond hair over his ear as he opens his trunk of magical objects. They bristle with power, skulls and skeletons empowered with his sense of unmitigated life, unmitigated death. It's night I've burned through trying to get lost in words or sympathy if you could say such a thing around him. Nah, can't say it, can't say it around him. Dear Robert. No access to the temperament at hand. He's a search on for me. He obfuscates the power inside the objects he hands to me—See? my grandfather's. A gun it was. Is. He has a pent anger. Anger. Pent. Waiting. All of them have the ability to resonate and shine, worn by time and a memory exact as to be painful in the glare of opening such a box to prying eyes. Or is the point to be entrusted here as a point of view he could have and I would bow and follow after. I want to shrink and climb in myself and be one of the things he might bring out after a time and caress.

Inside the room of the Canyon Club, separation is extreme
touch a nerve
touch a bone
a bachelor is exempt from the dream

yet tries hard in the light of its demand
to write, to be a writer, to have written, to have taken
words to the source of replay & bid them stand up in the
room of writing

to exact the debt from the overactive mind
to challenge his imagination
to take the "blondness" out of his eye
to make him my brother forever
slash wrists & exchange blood
(may I say this?)
. . . . . should I ask? . . . . . should I ask of him his destiny . . . . .
. . . . . the bandage of what injury what wound sits on him? . . . . .
. . . . . a bandaged hand holds a Mediterranean blue pen of what
origin, writing what words? . . . . . a slash on hand, poor hand . . . . .
. . . . . (smashed my hand through glass the night El Presidente
resigns . . . . . and spend the night in St. Vincent's under the portrait
of what Pope's holy eye? . . . . . J.F.K., empathy, time passing . . . . .)
. . . . . Robert's hair is long. He knows how to keep still . . . . .
patience of the inveterate traveller? . . . . . Like an Indian saint, perhaps,
or ancient scribe . . . . . red socks: how was he thinking when he put
them on was he thinking how red when he put them on, how red? . . . . .
A private thought . . . . . He drives home this weekend before she puts
all his stuff out on the road . . . . . should I ask? . . . . . is he the
son of a master on any computer . . . . . should I ask? . . . . . red or
black? . . . . . red and black . . . . . a black rubber accoutrement on
the wrist . . . . . a briefcase (black) parked to one side in a
presence of mind . . . . .
                              He was in China at the place of the terra
cotta warriors . . . . . "communism sucks" . . . . . and the courage of
people under extreme circumstances caught his heart . . . . .
an inflexible language admits only the word "chofa"—"sofa" . . .
. . . . . A father is a kind of power god, master of the nuclear
heaven or nightmare . . . .. technology is not evil but changes
things about the way people live . . . . . Germany . . . . . Hartford . . . . .

Los Alamos . . . . . Encar . . . . . a son of Treva Jeanenne and of Scottish
ancestry he wears both of them . . . . . red, black, yellow, green,
the colors of the Buchanan clan . . . . . how red, should I ask?
when he put them on . . . The wounded writing arm, the wounded
father home late having been scrubbed for 8 hours, no hair left . . . . .
"I was 2 years old" . . . . . after being splashed with Plutonium . . . . .
. . . . . should I ask? . . . . . I did . . . . . . Who are you . . . . . I ask who
are you? . . . . . a pen in a presence of mind facing the person, facing
the page in a desire of the way people live coming from there to here . . . . .

& descend on this one
touch a nerve
touch a bone
His father comtemp with mine
kissed by karma
adisthanas of deadly manna
we children of war gone further,
inherit the words, the earth

O Phytalidae!
        . . . receive Demeter into yr house
     O Plant Men
. . . enact the ergon as you mouth the words (mythos)
     . . . take me, an aeitiological one, into
                . . . yr male bosom (get me stoned, I never used a weapon)
. . . re-utter the song that makes us
     . . . leap for the crops
I am the contest, the pathos, the epiphany
        peripeteia is the number
both, both
   of which I am yr memory
to sing this long epic song

Dear Blond:

In the dream I was an escaped convict & I'll tell you why:
flames
airplane

held back a gun
killed one too many fathers

The renowned Ginsberg became my lawyer, the celebrated short story writer, Bobbie Hawkins, a surrogate moth. "Anything you say," she said, "I'll believe anything you want to tell me." A surrogate moth and then a mother. I tried to have wings. I set the plane on fire. How? I fly over the burning trees. I burn up in my enthusiasm for action & adventure. Must be Vietnam. I grow ahead of my dream. The lawyer grimaced & chanted the mantra: YOU! YOU! YOU! He was angry. He slammed the door of the ladies' room at the airport (they let you go in there to conduct "business meetings"). A woman was giving birth at the airport. Name her "Jubilate." Name her deo. "dei" to gleam, to shine.

I had been captured. I had escaped. & then I committed the crime of flying low, burning up, killing many fathers. They had the Eastern Eye. They had the epicanthic fold.

In the court, the restaurant of the airport (they let you have trails in there) the Judge, an Irish fellow named Maelstrom X, wore a wig when he said "Next!" Wore a woman's wig when he proclaimed "Not innocent! Not permitted!" Moth-mother held me in her wings, they had grown larger. They were fuzzy like the rug & fuzzy like the trees. Blurred by flames. I held back a gun, I think. It had the mastery of a high-heeled shoe.

Thanks for listening
(dreams can be boring)

dear Anne,
caught ginsberg at Harvard campus reading for AIDS benefit. allen told me he had just gotten back from Nicaragua. but I didn't want to talk about Nicaragua. ginsberg was being ginsberg. I wanted to talk about the passing of Bob Kaufman. and why? because I love poetry and he was a poetic genius. his poem THE AMERICAN SUN has to be the poem of our decade. what with the President anteing another 3 ½ billion dollars this week to ask, "Did Bob get his fellowship, his NEA grant funding, his Guggenheim, his Beatnik festival? After all it is said he coined the word beatnik"

we can disdain South Africa but Anne something terrible is happening on the homefront.

when I walk into the St. Mark's or Harvard Bookshop and I get a chorus of, "who's Bob Kaufman?"

    & I answer

    "A visionary, a poet, a genius. He wrote the THE ANCIENT RAIN one of the most powerful books of poetry of the decade."

    & I am met with blank stares.

there are dimensions of censorship and one of the worst is silence and neglect.

and I am sad and I am trying to somehow understand,

"What does this mean?"

Sincerely,

R. B.

           —The Stone Age culture of ax-makers

                                —unsung

—known as homo erectus

                    —unsung

                        —transformed to the modern homo sapiens

                      —unsung unsung

—the latter began with the Neanderthal & culminated with

                      —"modern man"

            —sing it! sing it!

How many years? sing it! sing it!

                        —unsung! unsung!

Africa, a million years ago "Acheuleans"

spread to Eurasia a few hundred thousand years later

(sing, sing)

space shuttle radar detects hidden valleys under the Sahara sands

   vegetated & densely inhabited up to 212,000 years

      ago (sing o ago, how sing it down down ago)

set down, set down the honorable load
By Jove, this not be revoked . . .

He is telling the story, telling a story
on the hour
leaving on the hour
the hour if I can hide it
leaving on the hour
to arrive in the context
of another hour
He is telling the revelation of St. John
& the four stages of my apocalypse
prepare the stage, o women the end is at hand
nothing has been changed
only delayed

the demon speaks the language of your tribe

So I'll be glad to take one or two questions. So just ask it. And I know
the Secretary would too. Yeah.

Question: Mr. President, did President Mubarak say Egyptian troops would
stand shoulder to shoulder with American troops in Saudi Arabia?

Answer: Well, he made clear that they're willing to do their share. And, yes,
that they will be there.

Question: When will they be there?

Answer : Well, I don't know the exact time on that, but they will do their share,
and so will other Arab countries . . .

Question: (UNINTELLIGIBLE)

Answer: Well, the good news is that no shipping from Iraq is coming through the Strait of Hormuz. And we are in consultation, active consultation, with other powers who have naval vessels there or under way, to be sure that no oil goes out. But we aren't prepared to announce anything more than that.

He is telling a story
We are drawing a line in the sand, he says
The other declares a holy war:

To all Arab and Muslim masses wherever they are—save Mecca and the Tomb of the Prophet from occupation . . .

Iraq, O Arabs, is your Iraq . . . It is the candle of right to snuff out darkness . . .

Burn the land under the feet of the aggressive invaders
who have evil designs . . .

     sing! O sing!

the door of the bloodbath opens
problem-time is at hand
prepare the stage

THE CREATIVE IS SPEAKING
THE CREATIVE IS SPEAKING

"I am none" is his latest philosophical thinking & I am thinking (we are somewhere in Europe near the Wannsee?, then at the Caffe Dante in New York City) how am I to hear that? "I am a nun"? Well, that's nonsensical. He is thin like my friend the filmmaker & speaks with a thick accent. He visibly does not appreciate women (I am too gaudy or something) although I seem to have some kind of stature as an interviewer. How do I know this is the great poetic thinker Wittgenstein? By his utterance, or so I think. "I am wit," he says. "I am Europe." I know he has been cruel to schoolchildren. I know he has parted from his money. "The world is a place," he sighs. I want to ask him to contribute some writing to my new international magazine or at least make a public appearance at the Naropa Institute Summer Writing Program. He is looking more & more like Samuel Beckett. It is dark now. I have to go home, which is down Macdougal Street, to feed my father & some of the new tenants, but I've misplaced the many keys it takes to enter there. It is summer. Many night people, eyes wide open with caffeine, chatter excitedly in the crowded café. There are columns suddenly blocking the door like some odd stage façade. My companion, the great man, is now shaking his head slowly from side to side. "You are on loan," he says looking at me intently. Do I hear him correctly. "Alone?" "I meant about the Viennese coffee." He says this last very sedately, ominously. I'm now worried about him falling into dotage. Will Vienna be entering the new war? He says, muttering to himself, "I must put on my mad yarmulke." Is he taking the side of Israel? "Madhyamika?" Will he really "take on" Buddhist philosophy? There's a gleam of light soaring forth from his eye that hits the coffee cup like a laser beam & shatters the cup . . .

It is a large dream machine made me write this. It takes off to tell you what's alive & took my pen to write as a nuclear warhead, as a large boot, as a map walking into itself circumscribed, as an obtrusive interloper, as a witness to the man, the men who wanna play the music loud 'cause they're some kinda animal. Pit against the intricacy of fern, the receptivity of any womb, ovoid and lined with silk. It is a meadow so it may contact you as you walk, ground rolling under your feet even as you stop, stand still, look up: Dear Venus, Jupiter, Daddy, Dear Robert, Bob Kaufman, Ginsberg, Dear Wittgenstein, Dear Uranus, Mars working this soft lute in me. I learned my song in you, unconditioned space, stepping out of the elements & dancing in your subatomic embrace.

THE CREATIVE IS SPEAKING

It is a not-to-be-suppressed voice-tone
& going on like a point of view
in which the notes ascend out of the top of the head

PHAT

Dear Mrs. Waldman:

You don't know me & I don't know you. I'm a New Christian Minister Monitor of God and I'm starting a Suicide Prevention Center and I'm asking for donations. My ministry is to help people who have lost the will to live. If you can send a donation I know God will bless you for it . . .

XIV

PRIMUM MOBILE

Mover is both celestial & underground muse or goad that perpetuates the writing, like the male principle of skillful means or Upaya. The poet needs a prod and being Aries she identifies with the responsibility of kicking the whole procession into motion. She too, like Alexandrian Ptolemy, feels the earth as her center & wants to join the outermost concentric circles as a heavenly body. She reaches this point of recognition after a sleepless night out under the stars & planets in her yard at the foot of the mountain. Down to earth again, she speaks about the issue of homelessness with her son who is sheltered in the safe town and house. She wants to move his heart.

—move by being

—moved

—if something is

—otherwise

—than

—it

—is

—motion

—in change

—& motion

—in

—motion are moving

—& this

—the Mover articulates

—then

—exists

—by necessity

—on

—such

—a world

—this Mover

—& "all this being"

—assumes difficulties

—is then,

—something working

—which ceasing

—motion

—not

—in

—theory

—only

—is also

—moving

—(move also)

—for the appetite writes it down

    —&

     —for

     —the

       —wish

    —to hold

     —fast

       —you

—(to hold you fast)

        —attention

 —but desire

     —is

     —an

      —opinion

    —on desire

  —& thought is

    —one

     —of

     —the

      —two

   —points

—of

—opposition

—reject

—&

—accept

—a contrary condition

—(heart?)

—that which is simple moves

—— & that

—which is simple

——is

—motion

—a thought is a

—capable

—action of motion

—complete & best

—(move it! move it!)

—is motion

—the idea, say

—of one quick

—pulse

—to

—hold

—fast

—the Mover as

—the Mover moves

—& the thought

—struck

—the Mover: "it's binding"

—"that which I think is binding"

—Mover thinks this

—too

(To Pan the bristle-haired & the barnyard nymphs, Theodotus a shepherd laid this gift under a rock because they stayed with him when weary under the parching summer, stretching out to him honey-sweet water from their hands . . .)

—the Mover's hair

—springs up

—like threads

—of leather

—Mover's parched skin is

—hard skin

—partaking

—of

—a structure to

—house

—a modicum of

—desire

—the hand

—is

—sinewy

—hand

—of

—a homeless

—Mover

—gone below

—into

—the terminal

—(don't impede

—our

—quickness

—of

—perception

—see how

—the Mover lives out

—the economy

—Mover is a colony

—no one

—inhabits)   —yet

—provides

—a home

—for all

—human things

—being human

—being subway

—Come together Mover

—since

—it

—is life

—& breath

—you speak

—that holds the frame

—of the entire new creature's

—marrow bites

              —(holds the flame)

—pratitya-samutpada

         —of such

             —a principle of one

       —defends the heavens

     —for the Mover

          —is a starting point

       —a compound

               —walks

       in exultation

primo
     the very first

& in his prime created her eros night
loved unto himself
her, the second mover

you say,
but book say
it is what told the heaven and stars
& was a book to boot
& kick back all sense of sound & dram

for sleep, forsooth, inside her womb to take
a kickback
you would be blasphemed here
& not a power be

for he, Mover, accorded power
because he sits so well
because he doeth it well
& slips
sleeps
out
sleeps over her, she
is dreaming this
while he lies next to her abed
in the soft computer light
& beckons her out of dream
to write this down
for he can be Muse, the Mover
& she is amused, slyly to herself & stops this rap
for this one night
it was holy, it was a holy storm
the day remained silent
the Balinese Nyepi took hold
all the cars struck dumb in road
ice blocks & nothing moves

but light fall of snow

He who moved the quilt, who moved the books
down from the bed lay abed & drew her out
from her dream
for he was the Mover, this was the job,
the process of Motion and sleep, sleep that was
a trigger
a happy trigger for him to let her snarl, her anger go
& she could bask in the light of her strong urge to keep it going

for it was her song, &
she had always wanted to sing it

moving as she did among his waves

incrementals, did I say it right?
of his sound

("let someone in authority come forth,
A woman, or more fittingly a man;
For then our converse need not wear the veil
of modesty—man freely speaks with man
And in a sentence makes his purpose plain.")

                              Libation

                                    & sure

                              Mover's heart

                                          will

                                      be

                                          uplifted, too

            sing O sing it in the mountains

            sing

                  O

                  sing it

                        in the plains

            that man is moving-prone

            like

                  planets

                  whose orbits turn

homeless within

their charted rounds

turning to see you, Father

on the

jeweled stair

primum mobile

all this is a way the men before me

discovered long ago

but I follow them also curious

climbing

(be careful, be very careful)

Dream:

large hospital-charnel ground-delivery room-beauty salon with an enormous floor of refracted mirrors. Busy time, no men in here yet, but about to be born full blown out of their mothers' bellies. We workers are in gear to keep floor sparkling & tidy of its blood & shorn hair & slivers of nails . . .
(he's coming, the man is coming)

Theory: I am afraid to express my anger as if it might make the world less safe for me.

Question: What price do you pay?

Answer: The imagination of the oral poet.

The messiah is a man of sorrows

Mary has a look on her face of the birth & death of Christ
& he comes in lowness
& I answered in lowness
to overcome the lowness in being below?

Lamb into lion I become
& I am in lowness
But soon the time *is* I will take it
The time *is* I will take it
I sing within the male gods
& O he is the "I am" & I will take it for myself
I speak anew great King
& I will take it, take it
& give them back a son
Strut the orthodoxies. G Lock. Air Battle.
Loss of consciousness by G Force

Dear President:

I am in the 4th grade. I am glad you met at Malta with Soviet President Gorbachev recently. I am glad you are trying to cut down the number of weapons made every year and to ban the use of chemical weapons. Please keep up the good work. And to take care of the Homeless in our nation too.

Student Ambrose

XV

DEAD GUTS & BONES

An image of her father's from WWII *haunts her tonight, as if life goes on amidst a different kind of war-rage. But what had he described, as he crossed, as he crossed the Siegfried Line? Steel beams sticking out to stop the tanks? "There wasn't a tree, there wasn't a bench; dead guts and bones. There was a smooth sandy beach where the Allied Air Force had pulverized the ground. It was nothing now. It was not quite beach sand but a dirty brown. Just been pulverized by American, British, French Air Forces. Our outfit was going through the Siegfried Line and there was an opening between those steel girders. It was a motorcade. Motorized part of infantry division. I was sitting in a three-quarter-ton truck with a mounted 50-caliber machine gun and I was sitting beside the driver. As we turn into the opening across the Siegfried Line and there coming out of the land was an arm, a hand coming out of the sand. Earlier I'd seen 2 Nazis in a tank that had been hit, cooked to a crisp." The poet is invited to give a reading at West Point. She performs and argues about the old war in Vietnam. Male precision interests her. Why always the inclination to honor dead male poets? Are they like the soldiers from an even more ancient war? A letter from the priest in Rome turns her thought to Liberation Theology, bravery and risk there. What choice in such a situation? Pray for them. She records once again the young boy's energetic, prophetic talk, which grounds her in America. Old Cary Grant movie* Gunga Din *showing this eve is a rare nostalgic relic. The poet grows more confident in her epic as she brandishes the rib of any man—poet? priest? soldier? pre-pubescent son—in her hand, pen or knife?*

West Point, springtime:

They come for me in a big limousine. The driver, a military man, tips his cap. I am suddenly a Ma'am. Yes Ma'am, No Ma'am. I dress in a skirt of many flowers, white blouse, ladylike. Hair brushed to the maximum. Underneath I wear the poet's uniform: skin of the jaguar. The world prays here in unison at lunch. The two thousand spoons move synchronistically into two thousand youthful mouths. A young woman tells me it has been her childhood dream to land here. Another traces his family lineage to be strictly "held in line." A black daughter of the army is gracious & direct; she likes the precision of awakening at dawn. The light is friendly as it slices off trees. Flags move slightly in the spring breeze. Down a road I spy a maneuver in battle fatigues. Three soldiers in battle fatigues silently blow up two men & a cannon. Now they are hiding something. Another group is seeking what they have hidden. Across the road men are marching in tight formation. There is some remorse in the conversation about the long-ago war in Southeast Asia after I read the poem with the lines "Then gathers strength into something monstrous/right here along the coast of your feelings." But many of these officer gentlemen never had to go there. I shout "Mega Mega Death Bomb" to some polite applause. Now I want to make them laugh. Who is to say who's more awake? The heads and shoulders of the cadets move against clean buildings. Spit and shine. Spit and shine. Tamed to be fierce, unbending under the seasoned officer's eye.

I
dream
you
ancient
Romans
come
& laugh
at
modern
poetry.
You stroll
on
the
beach
with
the
transparency
of
ghosts.
You
point
to
the
sea
as
if

it
belonged
to
you.
Your
strange
hair
toys
&
curly locks
make
me
curious
about
the
cult
of
Janus.
God
of
doorways,
of
public
gates
(*jani*)
through
which
roads
passed,
and
of
private
doors.
His
double-wreathed bearded
faces
allowed

him
to
observe
both
the
interior
&
exterior
of
a
house.
He
was
the
god
of
departure
&
return
&
by
extension
the god
of
communication
of
beginnings,
of
navigation
&
as
a
solar
deity,
presiding
over
daybreak.

Yet the
folds
in
your
dress
are more
sensuous,
Tellus Mater,
goddess
of
earth &
fecundity.
You
sit
between
Air
who
rides
on
the
back
of
a
swan,
&
Water
with
an
accompanying
sea
monster.
Urchins
tug
at
your
breasts,
plants

grow
from
your
lap.

I
sit
by
the
sea
lost
in
my
vision
of
you:

your
haughty
gait,
derisive
gestures.
You
shout
& jeer
you
throw
sand
in
the
poets'
eyes.
Flight
attendants
prepare
your
doors.

                    dear Frank O'Hara
                        can hate
                            really be
                "graced by a certain reluctance
                  and turn into gold?"
                   tell me quick before
                        I die of it!
                            "quel head!"

                Anne-Grasping-the-Broom-More
                    Tightly-Still

Messieurs Kerourac O'Hara Olson Denby Berrigan Duncan

You all float now
monsters free
poetry still brazen as the 20th-century thing
I have strutted along with it so long
up-to-date across
maps of some world definition
lovely heels, gab & loitering
You float now tattered bodhisattvas
in my heart
to struggle without limit
live a life in flames
my words seem small
in step with your enchantments
Work finished, you "guys"
conquer no more "languages"
yet at the end of these long days, years
without you
heart can stop at the same beat
roaring down old metabolic streets
Want to say words large enough to
contain you
dear dead poets

Gilgamesh, wither are you wandering?
Life,
which you look for, you will never find
For when the gods created men they let
death be their share . . .

(ask the panel what bio-region they are coming from &
How they, as writers, address the "issues"?)

"I am no prophet, nor a prophet's
son; but I am a herdsman, and a dresser
of sycamore trees . . ."

A wandering Aramean was my father; and he went
down into Egypt and sojourned there, few in number;
and there he became a nation, great, mighty, and populous
another literary giant
passing through your home
all six foot three & 230 pounds
of argentine edgar bayley
especially bear-like
he preferred staying here
tanking up on burgundy
and having lengthy monologues
at me. on the third day
i slept while he talked
the bayley tape loops
going on & on
i guess i learned a lot this week but didn't do a goddamn thing
not even mop the floor

anyway, welcome back home
ambrose had the most phonecalls
someone came & got their skateboard
someone raked the yard

gratefully, joe
                    heels, gab & loitering

you float now

working to place a place

telling the story on the hour

let it down on me

I'm not sure what all the men in your life want from you now, possibly they want to "tame" you & that it's too much of a threat to be with someone who's always in motion. The men want you to slow down so you can be with them, so they feel you're with them. You slowed down for me, I became faster to be with you, but after a while we began to revert to old tempos: how could anyone go as far as we did & survive? I wish we'd had the perspicacity to do it & fault myself often for not taking more control of my own life & not requiring that you take care of my needs, which you did take care of anyway. I sometimes think the Poetry Project ruined both my marriages because it created some adjunct world that had nothing to do with "our" life but was just a weird volatile mix of business, pleasure, friendship & that it ultimately all got in the way, parties every Wed. night etc. It was like a whole other family required your attention, & then where was I—as long as I didn't "need" anything I was okay. Needs are infinite & also nonexistent.

always believed in your love when we were together & that kept me going (& I think that's your great strength—to make another person feel what you're feeling)

you are my trust, a referent
back to self or "us," light I need
you, you I need you, you are
the call, call back to me
call me back to myself or
I'm not the same, eyes
seared for this view
you taught me, you forged,
you took me, I conspired
& inside a hand was caught

you are the hand, master
of this turning, my mind
to you burning, where
we were crossing I held you
around the back on the bike

touched You said I
will never be the same
I will not be the same
I'll fight for that, and turning it's not too late

You are witness it is too late
to stop voice at the end of this
plea to ground me in your
sight, not to own the
sight but I see you everywhere
defy rude boundary of space
You are inside me that's why
I project on my screen
your insight inside eyes I love

(retina)

Impresario says, looking at Frank O'Hara with carpenters
"Carpenters had to be called in to pry her angst
"est anguish" (tr.) We believe that this time it . . . ."
"I see," Frank sez, scribbling in his
gloomy eyes. "But this time, we behave
from the small wooden box. This minute."
"The story is, after all, *her* dilemma,
you out with crowbars?"
                              in the dream of the poet ancestor
                         I was my own dilemma
                                             post-ancestor
"And they finally got her notebook"   Impresario
says, referring to this poem
I had just gotten news of an old friend's suicide in Massachusetts when a pray-
ing mantis sprang from over the canopy outside the restaurant and landed on

my hand. We (the mantis and I) communicated for several minutes. I brought it right up to my face and opened my mouth and it wasn't afraid. It directed an intense affection toward me that I could never have associated with a member of the insect kingdom at all. Their heads move around just like a human's. It tilted its head at several angles to look at me closer. I declared my love and (I believe) it did the same. Then it flew over the Chinese restaurant across the street and camped in a flower box. I look up the etymology of "mantis" and found out that it's associated with prophecy and divination, and madness. The prophecy, in general, I believe is that there are no boundaries, and the angels are communicating with me constantly, and if I take care with this relationship, no door will be closed on me. Or on Louis Zukofsky, his mantis sestina. Anyway, I've begun "Mantis Ode."

"A Day In The Life Of A Male Praying Mantis" writes Ambrose

It's mating season and I'm scared. I will probably be eaten today. I was looking for hot babes all day and then I saw the center-fold in the latest issue of *Prayboy*. I started drooling. I thought I was going to drown so I moved. I thought "What a person to be eaten by!" I remembered that even after our heads are bitten off we can continue mating. People say it looks like we are praying but I'm of no religion. Anyway, back to the other side of the street. Where is she? Where is she? I felt a slight gnawing on my neck. Kind of like a fatal hickey. Then my head popped off. It was dinner time— and *I* was dinner.

en rapport:
thought
impulse
action

                                        slow down
                                        my genes
                                        do not

                carry

                                        the
                                        same message

                rancor?
                no

flashes glowing at the boundary of the nucleus
(I can see it but it also sees you)

              I can see it but it also sees you

SEFIROT

many
avocations
or
alterations
&
ventures
one
night
down
on
the
late
night
underbelly
I'm
with 2
bald
Zennies
&
we
watch
macho
slam
dancers
perform
aggressive
deeds
it
is
the

best
ritual
to
slam
yr
body
like
a
door
I
wanted more.
I
want
to
get
on
the
floor
under
the
man
boot
then
hurled
through
air
to
male
body
no
I
wanna
crouch
down
& let
it

happen
over
my
head.
No
I
want
my
Minerva
helmet.
Sweat
hold
fast
your
ground
hold
fast
yr
groin
waist
bob
unnameable thing
on
the
sea.
One
night
my
lips
get
redder
&
I
have

no
thought
but
to
be
in
this
Hell
not
a
girl.
No
girl but
kinda
old
"mahoo"
of
Tahiti
watching.
As
we
leave
the
club
the
doorman
says
there's a private party later & we're invited
back but only if the guys come dressed like that (Zen)
long erring in a globe, long earring in a strobe
stern break over the knee
under a ring: blink
Order that knee in place: blink blink
Deft (Zen)
made of mud
that knee dab in the sweet milk
The term shatters us so

Wider so much wider than light a voice: why so long?
Why grind the bricks?
Why stack them?
Why build
or age the tool
what weight
carry?
Working
to place a place
in a job
place
a work man
could live here and talk
& swear, nothing much
glob of dirt under
the boot
broke a stick
upon a knee
claim check is deaf
& to all dependents
worrisome
long taste of coal
you ain't
calling
it healthy (Zen)
but maybe you could lift a
sanction, dear President
amigo?
     Our fate is forked

                del sueño al sueño al sueño al sueño

Anne,

Peace, though it is difficult to imagine peace in this world of violence.

    All Jesuits throughout the world, including myself and all the members of our community were horrified and saddened to hear of the murder of six of our brother Jesuits in Salvador yesterday. The government claims it was the rebels, the rebels say it was the government. The murdered Jesuits were outspoken in their defense of the poor, those never given justice. I think

of the daily threats to our Jesuits in Sicily who speak out against the Mafia. But how can any-
one justify the torture and brutal murdering of others? The six Jesuits of the University were
dragged into the courtyard, stripped naked, had their testicles cut off by barbarians, and then
machine gunned, their brains splattering over the trees and flowers. I am happy for our departed
Jesuit brothers who are now eternally happy with God, but I am profoundly depressed that so
many evil men continue to flourish on the earth. Please pray for the families of these brave
men, and for the families of the others daily massacred in Central America. And please pray for
me, that when and if my time comes to die for the truth of the Gospel, I will be ready and have
the courage of these six men. It is true that Jesuits have been murdered and thrown into prison
somewhere in the world every year for the last four and a half centuries, but this last crime
seems particularly brutal in light of all the changes for the better in Eastern Europe, the falling
of the Berlin Wall, etc. I can add nothing more at the moment. My heart is too heavy. I have a
strong temptation to leave all of my work here in Rome to go to Central America to witness
Jesus and what he preached. To live is wonderful, but to die is pain! All of us here at the
Historical Institute and Vatican Radio must go on. How unimportant poetry seems at this
moment. Love and prayers to you.

Love in the best sense,

T. K.

Institutum Historicum Societatis Iesu

I weep at the hearth

                del sueño al sueño al sueño al sueño al sueño

The earth is tired

                al sueño al sueño

The earth is tired of weeping

                The night gets cooler

            silver moon

& they might dance all night
warmed by a single flame
Uneasy armours
The Guru assumes a strange shape
& welcomes all pupils up
out of pools of darkness

(wet, slimy)
Yearning they in turn
lift teacher up
not passive participants in events
but subjects of a curving boundary
infinitely spinning
He's incessantly spinning in their hearts
Around! Around! Churn! Churn!

(iridescent ever-shifting world

Surprise Joshua! fit the battle . . .

Alertness is all . . .)

You could dance all day

warmed by a single flame (guru heart)

not singly, each silhouette precise

invade my heart

light in this heart (mine)

because I am light in your heart

& in the larger (*comprendes?*) "goodness" heart

        del sueño al sueño al sueño al sueño

      the moon is a sliver

dear Joshua

    the earth is tired of weeping

          (our fate is forked)

Yet the most incredible result of your editing is the following:

                    ~~as if~~ It hurts to hear you
            talk this way, and yet
    beside me, in the bath, you took
        the left, the Latin Catullus and I
    ~~the raw~~ Zukofsky
                    faced each other in the
                ~~stillness~~
                            ~~shimmering.~~

    ~~Forgive me~~

                ~~I was lonely and the~~

                                    ~~sudden sunlight~~

    ~~the~~ salt of your skin—

To:

                    It hurts to hear you
            talk this way, and yet
    beside me, in the bath, you took
        the left, the Latin Catullus and I
            Zukofsky—
                    faced each other in the
    salt of your skin.

That's all—not asking anything of you—just saying thanks, with appreciation.

                    Millville, Mar. 2, 1908

My Dear Wife,

I am so glad you have had a nice warm day today but is storming now and I am afraid you will not have it so nice tomorrow. I hope the boy has not taken any cold. I expect you can tell me by this time it is much warmer anyway. Clate was home today and is coming home every day. They are going to start and pack up. Kenneth has the measles now very bad. They had the Dr. today. His throat is so tight. Now Dear be very careful of your money. Watch your bag. Keep it closed and tied and do not tire yourself out. I have not seen Alma. She had company today. I will see her tomorrow. I certainly miss you both very much. I hope you get along nicely. Dona, if you see any of the coat sweaters cheap, get me one size 36 or 38. You can get them from 50 to 75 cents apiece. I hope to hear from you tomorrow. Goodnight.

Your Husband
John

(time for things to go quiet on us)

al-Tanzil

the Downsent

When the sun shall be darkened, when the stars shall be thrown down, when the mountains shall be set moving, when the pregnant camels shall be neglected, when the savage beasts shall be mustered, when the sea shall be set boiling, when the soul shall be coupled, when the buried infant shall be asked for what sin she was slain, when the scrolls shall be unrolled, when Heaven shall be stripped off, when Hell shall be set blazing, when Paradise shall be brought nigh, then shall a soul know what it has produced

hayya 'ala al-falah (twice)

when time
is old
tell me
about
when
time
is
old

& forgot itself

—Fine time for things to quiet on us.

—Blast them Thuggies.

—Why don't they come & give us a good fight?
   How can we get a nice little war going?

—What if I was to sneak away & blow up the Taj Mahal
   or one of them sacred Indian tombs?

—What do you want to do, start the whole Indian
   mutiny again?

—Dead guts & bones sticking out of the sand, that's war.

—Blood & bullets flying through the air.

—Michael J. Fox is in casualties.

—Tom Cruise is born on the 4th of July.

—Explosions ah dead, everybody gone now.

—The world is nothing.

—A Stealth blows up the enemy base.

—M-16 machine guns down whatever in sight.

—Iraq has as many tanks as both sides of World War II.

—They fight over who's going to be the President of a
   dollar bill.

—So what is a thrill, boys?

—Hitting a home run, a grand slam.

—Swearing at the Sega. I cuss at Wonder Boy, whatever he does.

—You cuss at the game because it cheated & a guy killed you or a bad
   snake or a mushroom or a snail or a fish killed you.

—They waste yr butt on Mega Man II.

—If you're Metal Man in Mega Man II you can blow their guts

right out of their shells.

—Winning is pretty fun.

—Feels weird. "Hand-eye coordination," all that.

—This is easy. Look, look. I'm trying to turn.

—I got II on Aztec Adventure.

—Winning Bubble Bobble at level #24.

—God damn you Tommy La Sworda!

(I take that back)

Telling the story

telling the story on the hour

How to become a writer out of the rib of a man

How to spit out the man's marrow to breathe free

How to stand on the ground & contend with his mystical hormones

How not to get sick in the midnight hour

("Give me a break

Elvis wannabe
Madonna Wannabe . . .")

Oh, and the last movie character I recall identifying strongly with, and it amazed me as I hadn't had this sort of experience in a long while, was the Bobby Dupea character Jack Nicholson played in *Five Easy Pieces*. Especially that scene where he's goaded into playing that Chopin étude by the Susan Anspach character and the camera goes around the walls of the room, you see his whole life in those family pictures, then the piece ends and she tells him it was lovely and she really felt something and he says he just picked the easiest piece he could remember and felt nothing at all himself. Of course, I come from a similar musical background, but I think it was more the sexual tension mixed up with a misreading of art in that scene I felt I knew from the inside. From then on I felt I knew his thoughts, and this seldom happens to me with movies. More often I feel like I can read the director's thoughts. Love, Clark

kaúsalya-ekagrata-citta

XVI

DEAR SKYBOX

Egyptian god Ptah? Prophecy—Riots in the city of Angels. It's the poet's birthday today. The student's dream scares her. Her girlfriend tells her to be sure to fasten her seatbelt so she won't end up with sutures on her skull. She writes until dawn, then dreams another Puer dream, a kind of map for political infiltration. What is this identification with young men? Are they playful tricksters inside the hag? Sometimes she can only converse with the son, his energy closer to hers than suburban housewives' judgmental gossip. The missiles, their concomitant deadly naming (Faw, Green Bee, et cetera) need appraising. If she appropriates their voices will she seize their power, or does it backfire? Keep adding dreams, stories, relive movie plots. Her son needs to do the assignments of the same. Memory eludes us. Skybox is science. And then what did you do today? a most terrifying proposal. Odd energies live in the cast of the mind of the child. If she includes him he understands the world better, simple as that.

Now work to the edge of time
Or if it's black
crack sleep in two
when young back
then & do
or think to do, break
the dawn or night through speaking
true, itself a "self" is switched &
switch it off again
Air is clear of sun
Rain now, 2 a.m.
Roof leaks, the man
denies, but keep telling
roof leaks
here's evidence
got proof?
what?
Evidence, got proof she's writing at night
You know this?

Dear Men Of Night: here's proof I made you in writing I read it in the news

Headline:

A God Loses:

Ronald Frances Bennett, a maker of false teeth who claims to be the Egyptian god Ptah, finished last among 17 candidates in the city council election in Palm Springs, California. Mr. Bennett said running for office was the only way to draw attention to his identity.

        movere, delectare, docere   a god loses in Reincarnation

O Key of David
& Sceptre of the
House of Israel
that openest
& no man shuttereth

& shuttest
& no man openeth
& no woman openeth
Come & bring
the prisoner out of the
prison house
& bring him that sitteth in darkness

bring out! bring out!

           & the shadow of death
             In those days
        (& were they far from here)
        & indeed for many years
          someone was inspired
        Someone was imprisoned
          YOU WALKED ON ME
          in the shadow of death
      and I became a dakini bridge
        and was a gleam of you
        (in the shadow of death)
          high-density disk
     mi madre mi madre mi solo mi solo

Does the eagle know what is in the pit?
Or will thou go ask the Mole?
What predator asks what hole did she climb into?

In those days & indeed for many years I was unable to say anything except a
sentence in rejoinder that I had not written out and committed to memory
beforehand . . . I had to try to foresee the situation and to have a number of
variants ready to meet its possibilities. I therefore came with a quiverful of
arrows of different patterns and sizes some of which I hoped would reach the
target. I sometimes thought of my mother . . .

I sometimes thought of myself as warrior-in-progress. And little did I know
the name of Winston Churchill would resound through this hall and land. I
thought of her when I thought of him

Early memory:

In the center of the lake
Her voice, breast, & manliness rub against the father
Wanting the center of the lake inside my head so that I would have
a clear pool of calm and clarity abide with me between their struggle
& battle that I would be the daughter of so & so running for office

                                        Anne Waldeman

                                              I write You because I fell

(Not only for La Intellect Français)

A Directress of a Distress School should take measures to protect herself

            and overcome   (come over)

all forms of Inclog work that are not definite

indefinite, sincerely yours,

(letter received June 7 in the nineties, Naropa Institute)

Scholar's lost at least 3 hours on this computer
"like dying"

The nodes of Blake or light of words
to carry none
"like dying"
He's lost time more precious than money
He's subject to machine wiles alas a student
Gin o gin has done me in
    (scent of juniper off the mountain)
in that
he's lost again to carry none
I'm in,
done

in by time
we men have enough of it or gin but
6:14, look
the black comedy hour is over
Is that Sparky barking?
The son is the speed I cannot be tonight (in gin)
Sonny boy down block
miniature Porsches & Chevies positioned to go
all the way of pens & stare
I stare at the objects because of heat of sight because of "mammal that thinks"

He clicks the machine
Cars want to be in the hands of boys who love them
baseball on the pavement
I talk this way not urge middle malaise

Someone is on trial I have a front-row seat. I'm dressed in yellow silk my hair is quite long. "Puer" is being tried for a misdemeanor the night before the 4th of July fireworks display. He has used this civic occasion to promote his world view that the best way to peace it to patent his elixir "Puer." Take your chances. He has been arrested trying to dose the central water fountain of our village, the one with the busty mother goddess statue that towers over & slightly intimidates children. (I am that child), The water is milky here. One child (I was that child) drank it and had visions all night of animals known to be extinct in these parts. He had studied them in the local gymnasium (I am

that child)   Puer is tense. He is speaking in tongues & gesturing
wildly with his hands. *Om namo Shivaya*

Plahn sounds like a lament not a hopeful plan, but Puer is intense hormone rage
It is the sound of any mother, any son
I wept to be a plahn to sound the gong and tell a history straight

The Harlem Hellfighters were the first Allied unit to reach the Rhine, served
longer than any other American unit, and were awarded the Croix de Guerre by
the French. 171 of their officers & men were awarded that treasured medal indi-
vidually. No black American troops were allowed to march in the great victory
parade of the Allies up the Champs-Elysées even though France and Britain were
represented by dark-skinned colonial soldiers. Moreover the War Department
requested that no black troops be portrayed in the Pantheon among the heroes.
On February 17, 1919, when they returned to New York, the entire regiment, line
after disciplined line, paraded the length of Manhattan, up Fifth Avenue, behind
James Reese Europe's magnificent jazz band—60 brass & reed players, 30 trumpet
& drums. Crowds cheered them all the way up Fifth Avenue. At the top of
Central Park, they marched a block west & then continued parading up Lenox
Avenue to 145th Street. In Harlem the band started playing "Here Comes My
Daddy Now" & the soldiers & crowds went wild with joy.

every soldier's due
& privilege that
be accorded notice here
puer had spoken enough
& lights
that bite
tell us
    war dead count
or slip
to salvage
    there
what place?

a place men died
battlefield

held raw
place that
accords
itself official
    stature
a label?
static as it be
alight
the
promise
    to be
to be it true

shut down I say
    Vanity shut down
& all the flare or fare
        to be continued
                SHUT DOWN
like money
    is a power   how many megas does it take
how many tax megas
        & it is killing you
with the boils & brunts of never-more-solace here

everyone burns
everyone burns
                    anger is mute here
no longer appropriate to be human
everyone everyone burning
although I wander through the thick black fog of materialism
I still aspire to see his face
(it was human passion burning to create the kingdom from Kether (Keter?)
AYIN
AYIN SOF
AYIN SOF OR
& climb the burning ladder (for we are burning burning)
although I wander through the slimy muck of the dark age
I still aspire to see your face

Dear Anne,

7:15 on a chilly Sunday morning. Now let me see if I can answer your questions. "What was your first sexual encounter like?" An out-of-body experience. I was extremely naïve and modest and self-conscious, and so it was quite a shock to find myself naked (no clothes on!) in bed with an older woman, her hand manipulating my cock. Of course I had had hard-ons and wet dreams before, but it had never occurred to me that you could make it happen. So, like I said, I was too self-conscious to be much more than an observer. A totally embarrassing experience. Though I felt very proud of myself (cocky) after.

"What was your relationship to your father like?"

Undemonstrative of affection. And total embarrassment.

"Did you have any role models as a child?" Only Jesus.

"What 'character' (mythological, fictional, actual, such as in the movies) do you remember identifying with at any particular point in your life?" This is hard because I find it extremely easy to identify with anybody. I have always felt an enormous amount of empathy, and had an affinity with homely girls: perhaps (?) a result of identification. And then there's Katy Keene: I thought she had the perfect life: beautiful clothes, two boyfriends, and a little sister to treat like a doll. And nobody has influenced my life more than Ted Berrigan. But I think I am straying from the question.

I guess that's it for now!

LOVE,

Joe

who was a one to be straying from
Pimelometopom pulchrum
    (turns female to male)
        blue-headed rainbow wrasse (*Thalassomam Lucasanum*)
is *Protogynous Protandros* hermaphrodite (male)
we were discussing fish, stared at them in the tank a long time

sex you up? sex you down? the cheap song rings & turn the weighted spotlight upon your pain & this was the deepest I'd felt from one in what gender O world? I loved far away

My friend,

When I was 13, I came across an article in a journal about a female-to-male transsexual who had married. Since then I had hope, I knew what "I am." I instantly knew that I was the same. But living in a village & my mother telling me "& when you hang yourself from the ceiling, you still won't become a boy" (a very deeply felt humiliation—she once shouted at me when she discovered that I bound my body in order to not show my growing bosom (the same old disgust coming to my throat, start to choke again). I couldn't tell anybody what I was. My mother forced me to wear skirts once in a while until I was 16 . . . and then I had to tell her. She admitted she always felt that I looked like a transvestite in girls' clothes . . .

Well my mother especially worried about my sister. She was afraid I would do some kind of damage to my sister's psyche until I was married. It took a long time until she called me with my male name at home. (I was 19). This brings to mind another offense/humiliation: my mother had a close friend, a divorced mother of a girl my age. The daughter was like a sister to me. I once visited my former village where the girl stayed & was married & pregnant (they, the girl & her mother had "known" about me but had not seen me yet, I already had hormones.) The mother invited me to visit & when I arrived she said how good I look!, how relieved she was but when I asked where the daughter was she said that she, being pregnant, had not dared to see me because she was afraid she would have such a shock the baby in her belly would get "bewitched" and become abnormal like me. I've never seen either of them again. Yes, they were afraid I would be a "beast," a strange creature bringing evil to innocent babies—like in the Middle Ages! (Allah, I will never forget that.)

it was a weighted dream
crusty for splendor
& when I read it I warned myself to fasten my seatbelt
in the real time
& I invited the students to dream &
He who does adore his Kerouac wrote this down:

I'm walking through the student lounge at Hampshire College, leisurely, apparently knowing what I'm doing—no mystery to the situation—and I pass a woman sitting in a semistupor. She's sitting by herself with the fore part of her hair removed in a semicircle, with wild Bride-of-Frankenstein hair. I do a double take as I pass and I realize it's my beloved poetry mentor Anne Waldman. She murmurs something to the effect of, "You can talk to me, ya know." Her forehead and cerebrum have huge sutures traversing the top of her head with some metal, protective device over them. I turn, and sit down at the table to speak to her. We look each other directly in the eyes, not an awkward feeling but a warm pity. Nothing is said. Suddenly a large group of people is tromping toward us. As they near I can make out some of the faces: it's every English teacher I've ever had in my life converging on me. There's Benjamin Boatwright Alexander III, Diana Rose, Mr. Banas, Mrs. Niergarth and some teachers who look familiar but I can't remember their names. I look to Anne, who is in a daze—yet her eyes are wide-open, clear. Benjamin Boatwright Alexander sits down on my lap and the chair breaks. A fuzzy delirium sets in and we are all walking in the same direction outside in the streets of Amherst. Anne leads the pack in her usual black, but bald and inhuman-looking with that obtrusive protective cage around her head (she has apparently had a lobotomy or something of the sort). The group settles on a town green with park benches around. Everyone is going through their things, getting props together for some kind of show. Even I seem to know what I'm doing as we are all unpacking things: folders with poetry, musical instruments, etc. Out of nowhere, Tim Hulihan approaches with a football in hand trying to persuade us out of the performance idea and into a good old football game. He succeeds. We all opt for a game of football. We line up in formation. I'm on defense—middle linebacker. Tim is quarterback on offense. Anne is offensive tackle. Tim gets the snap from some unknown bespectacled English teacher who is the center. Tim attempts a quarterback sneak—off Anne who is lead tackle blocking. Anne throws a wonderful block, bulling over Benjamin Alexander (author of a book on patriarchy). Tim runs through the hole Anne has created and gets past me too. But I spin around and grab him from behind (by the neck of his shirt). This is no sissy game of football. Tim fumbles as I bring him down in a mad scramble for the ball ensues with brutal collisions and extreme folly. Everyone is dressed in lecture and performance garb as they dive for the loose ball. The dream ends with the ball still bouncing and a pack of crazed literateurs chasing it.

& was a kind of sign, "warm pity"
part performance that sticks
the world of illusion into form
part form
that sticks it right back out from under you to see
see again how beauty risks or sweeps a charge pon you pond sleep pond or
played upon a mind,
Groucho said this about how we are past tense & into bungalows
to be a word
word it twas!
to be a gargoyle jointed
the frontline of the story

past tents and into shelter deeper

& called up a kind of king
You know the story of the soul gazing through the window at the veiled spirit
engaging her in conversation & she tells him some secrets of existence and then
they wanna get married

but when the king gets in there who is he who is he not who is he who is he not
what is he thinking who thinks for him of him with him who is the subject
who is the object what does it mean a king & take the scepter what is it to want
to be a man a king and don a male garb what is it to have them take your
breasts away so you will beat like a man beat your chest like a man howl like a
man take on the male mantle tell me what's it like in the kingships of yore
what was accorded power but when it gets to be him what he of what kind of
crystal lineage what birth with a gold spoon in its mouth with a gold cock
between his legs tell us the frailty & cruelty of the bygone kings . . . who is he
who is he not whose is it not his but is or not his for answer, for taking might
be his but who is he who is he not to represent a time forgot itself and it got
dreamed up to replicate itself as form you know of talking about the King of
Kings or something like prophet like Rebbe & take you by the hand but what
is missed my Hebrew brothers is how strange when you study this picture of
the young Lubavitcher men more than seven out of ten are wearing glasses a
sore Torah eye proposes . . .

IESUS NAZARENSIS
REX IUDEORUM

(This is not a resurrection but happy Easter, king of kings)

All the "shuns"
I take or know
of
are twin to me
& not stalks of eyes
but like me
one of them, one stalk
is as light
registers

to go or not
to love a room
& go into it
then exit
surrounded by
edges:
sh'i music
a slavic table
a modest floor to stand on
around or
inside talk
ice is in all
the glasses
It's been variously
summer
not
at all
like love

Gatsby believed in the green light
orgiastic light
future that year
by year
different patterns
recede before us
Eludes us then
no matter
tomorrow faster faster

arms stretch
arms stretch further
so we one beat morning on

faster faster
enter now
the grace
or place of worship

TOGU NA DOGON: the men's house
millet-stalk roof keeps low structure cool while men talk, prepare tobacco,
    take naps . . .

Elders meet to discuss business, defacing their own carvings to prevent theft

What do they know of leptons, elusive neutrinos?

The King Abbas, still under development, flies up to 550 miles. Some of the sys-
tems nearing production stage are the Tammuz, with a range of 1,250 miles, the
3-stage Abid, and a tactical antiballistic missile system called the Faw. (*disable an
airfield, devastate a city*)

Zulkar Ali Bhutto once said his countrymen would "eat grass" if necessary to
build or buy a counter to India's nuclear capability.

Taiwan developed its ballistic missile the Green Bee (range 60 miles) in the 1970s
using Lance missile technology provided by Israel. The country is reportedly
developing a 600-mile-range missile called the Sky Horse.

Argentina & Brazil have some missiles for export. A two-stage missile called the
Condor II, which was to carry a 1,000-pound warhead to a range of between
500–600 miles.

Israel has the most advanced missile program ouside the Big Four. The Jericho,
the Jericho II, and the Jericho IIB can propel a payload of 2,200 pounds up to 1,500
miles, armed with nuclear warheads.

A Scud B releasing 1,200 pounds of the chemical VX agent 4,000 feet above an
airfield will kill half of the people in a strip .3-mile wide and 2.5-miles long, ori-
ented in the direction of the wind. (*disable an airfield, devastate a city*) An equal
weight of high explosives can destroy buildings more than 150 feet away and kill
people more than 400 feet away. The 4,500-pound warhead planned for the
Saudi missiles would more than double this lethal range (cluster bombs fur-
ther enhance these effects by detonating many submunitions over a large area,
thus producing a blanket rather than a point explosion).

Accuracy is as important as destructive power. It is generally measured by the "circle error probable" (CEP), an ellipse whose major & minor axes describe the maximum misses along & across a missile's trajectory. The most primitive missile-guidance programs, which use inertial instruments taken from aircraft navigation systems, would typically have velocity cut-off errors of from two to four feet per second at burnout. That yields a CEP of approximately 1,000 feet at a range of 200 miles, close enough for high-explosive warheads to destroy most point targets and for cluster bombs or poison gas to wipe out troop concentrations and cities.

Psychological dimension to the military effectiveness of ballistic missiles: They sap the will to resist. The thousand V-2 rockets that Germany launched against Great Britain late in WWII were not particularly accurate. But their 1,000-pound warheads wreaked as much terror among the British as the German Air Force had in bombing raids of several years before.
The thousand missiles launched during the Iraq-Iran War was the only other time such weapons have been employed.

Sine qua non of great power status: Missiles are symbols of technological prowess & political prestige like battleship of 80 years ago & will set off accordingly, eject into consciousness how many dead? how many casualties

O gracious death light that raiments me
    vague wools, sovereign quest of turf
        venal enough to send anguish to
            rhyme or art my king not adroit in continued war realm?

& you pent me, colder still, heat-seeking
    to get inside my cloak, you are
        the dumb phallus, the killer prick,
            head of war, of poison, king weapon

        succumb or falter faint light
            all risks to not-a-mere-dagger

I'm nubile, tremulous, panting, alone, a ceiling . . .
inside the shelter, underground, mask on,
roof never the same

also, my same old patriot light
& your volts appear, what travels Zeus?
is soldiering an error or errant?

    O my delite my light
        & pure my governing
    the mere record of a dance
    & it never nears the state of stillness

O come grate the occurence
    neither tempo is young when the anchor lunges

The sperm is brave Ha. War is the number, the playground.

Memory is a road that skirts the battlefield

Ill-remembered this passionate cozy tryst
battle very triste eh?

Erasable optical drives?

from the mother to the babe in her womb, out here
it's just fucking war!

the word "race" is a delusion
"dark
age"
is
the
time:

The noose approaches
It's usually hung in the forest
Rue of matins
The noose approaches
Mount the brooms, witches
Noose coming closer
The terror in the heart is crisp
Another day to put

together & take apart the world

Eh you for certain thought you only vital to my day?

Me in a sari ready to die after time spent with you

Sign your life here, the date is set

What other king might I love
solemn or hopeful where I turn?

The great house flashes: Manipulate the day & don't out-taxi Maitreya

Alcaeus, do you own your experience?
Dear babe, you want to come out for *this?*
I sing to the elements
& then I sing to the wind
Why is he like stone?
Stone I call you
I sing to wind but
stone I call you, the whole world: War Stone
Not a heart
but a dead stone
I want it like his heart is needed
or a substitute. Is it so dead
can you really say that?
Feels dead in the little window
I see him & his heart I can fuel
It is substitute for stone, dead
I sing to say this
so I won't be sad
Stone I need as heart

& NEEDED as a kind of life apart

in a place where TARHIB means terror and TARGHIB is a kind of enticement

and Ghost Shadows fight with Flying Dragons

and both gang up against Born To Kill

Dear Skybox,

Do you know that the packaging of your baseball cards is not biodegradable or recyclable? The packaging may look good, but it's not helping the environment.

Your packs are made of a material that will last for hundreds of years. I have included an example of what I think your packs could be like, which has paper around the cards and tinfoil over that and they are not stuck together. So you can re-cycle them separately. And you could think about using wax paper.

I think this is worth doing and I hope you will keep it in mind. And I know a lot of other kids who feel the same way. Thank you.

Sincerely yours, Ambrose Bye, 5th Grade

ancient in me
active in me
in the present tense under nacreous sky
I dwell inside the pearl,
hiding from all the men
to study their names:
the name of Indra:
from *ind,* to drop
like sperm, like seed
O god of light ray
another name: Vasava, king of the Vasas or
Maghavam: "the bountiful"
I live inside his thunderbolt and
return to his hand
I slice life right next to him
feeling his power as it drops
indefinableindicativeindividualindifferentindecisiveindelicateindirectin-
 dorseindomitable
all the "ins"
rise like the
name of insurrection
but Indra got down to his place
his implement stolen
subdued

subjugated

The date of this is April 2, 1991
My Mom's Birthday: A Living Hell

To start out my mom woke up with a dream that there were two guys blowing their brains out. Then at 7:30 a.m a lunatic had called and said I have some of your friends hostage (Jane & Anselm Hollo) and you must do exactly what I say if you don't want them to be hurt. He hung up after that. I locked every door in the house. Then my dad called the police and they said this guy got a reputation for pranking. My mom was scared to answer the phone.

Then when my mom picked me up from school we found out we were locked out of our house she didn't have a key and there was none hidden under a rock and I have locked all the doors and windows. I was having a piano lesson and I did not have my music pieces. But we went anyway and I survived the piano. Since we couldn't go home since my dad wouldn't be there until 11:00 we went to *New Jack City* and watched guys blowing each other's brains out. Ice T the rapper was an actor in the movie pretty good. Then we went to Sushi Tora where my Mom drank a lot of sake. And I start writing this for my school report on *What Did I Do Today*. Later we went to A.'s and he was still up reading. As we drove home my dad's headlights were just pulling up too.

XVII

GROTTE

O sleep walker; is this fleece too heavy? —H.D.

The poet travels to the south of France and beyond with family during the summer. She takes notes along the way to unmask a patriarchal past in a glorious setting trembling with murmur of archaic human habitation, middens. The dioramas, the "as ifs" tableaux, are helpful, amusing. The oldest folk are dolls of a dream, clothed, groomed in extinct possibility. Evidently a stretch of consciousnesses from human realm wedded to rock. And after that: how many confusions & dispersals. Were her Huguenot ancestors marginalized like Cathars? What similarity lurks there? Nuit Sol. The night sun. This is the journal. Ambrose takes us to the Eiffel Tower. A bungled coup in Russia. Headlines. She misses the one who touched her mind.

He said
   "your people"

meaning
The Huguenots
     &

in what cave do you dwell?

Wake: life
as statue de magie
Bois, fer, cornes, cauris, graines, tissu, miroir

could feel
pins stuck in
gut
   and the points along heart meridian
dissolves further down
legs already given out
je suis fatigué
Auto da Fé

trans-fire
Came through
trance Atlantic
to breathe l'air préhistorique
taking the light inside, he said

in
what
cave
or trance
do you
dwell?

a face—child's? lover's
next to my eye
to answer—and was that an answer? –

ancient in me
active in them
in the present tense under nacreous sky
dwelling inside the pearl
which is the way
you might see
something sudden
A small plane crash in which the pilot is immolated
& the end of his Timex, which is one cycle
which continues you could believe
to any not definitive end, it's relative
as said, more of occurrence
at dusk, my shadow to his light
you want master to be manly
against a tide
but, being sure of foot the way is lost
but the way is found
to be sure of thought
& the study of it
being neighbor to whatever culture
presents its lovable secrets

on hieroglyph animal
in speech, gesture
the head turns to breath
air of the next occurrence
in what time cycle do you dwell?
& what is the specific title
for any of all of this
Preliminary practices exhaust you
but the teachers never give up on you
You are tired but true to the text
which is words—only writ in blood
not more horrific like
business is ordinary
If I say so I might believe
spectacle of exploding desire
inside the cocoon

(Later in a separate sleep segment and removed scenario, Anne Waldman is persuading us—all
the Naropa students to become cops—she says she's got these great low-risk police jobs lined
up for us and all we have to do is go through some minor screening to get them—we won't
have to wear guns she says and probably won't endure any violent circumstances—it's just
minor cop duty . . .)

            inside cocoon

*Ever since the Iraqis paraded a handful of captured allied fliers, whose bruised and battered faces
showed all the signs of a serious beating, pilots have had something else to worry about. "It plays on
your mind," says Beguelin. "You think Do I really want to get out of my jet? Because if I do, I know
I'll be partying with the boys in Baghdad." It is, in short, the ultimate role reversal: one minute
streaking along in a thirty-million-dollar war machine, the next landing rudely on the ground and
facing the enemy with nothing but a government-issue 9mm Beretta handgun, retail value $1,200.*

*Weather permitting, the squadron flies roughly 40 sorties every 24 hours. Between bombings, the men
laugh, lunch on bean soup and apples, brief again, and get ready to punch the sky . . . "We're like
a motorcycle gang, or a roving pack of dogs," says Captain Tom Rutledge, call sign Strut, a mus-
cular 29 who does just that.*

Strut
or blow me into the next Iraqi's sky

light

Cher Ami
Have you gazed into the Perseid meteor showers?
debris, detritus

flying matter

in what meteroric asteroid belt do you dwell?

Quatuor en sol mineur K 478
inside the Church
Perigord Noir

then we
cross the Rubicon
Font-de-Gaume
    points to
presage
    back inside where I was
        contentious, struts
    nothing of this but hag neanderthal
        allow
& whole
    toil, & male

what about a thousand modulations?
    fingers crooked like claws
        erratic to
wake the girl in every pose or pore
        machiolated walls
uterine
    a little bazaar inside her
: fruits and shrine-tables
potions of exotica,
excrement

& voice as
     in a quarry
 hieratic
"I, the Matriarch, *did* exist"

encamped, moonlight or closed a carriage
she

rides
in sacrament
in trust of apprehension
        onto the 20th-century set

hook
        a packet of . . . ?

inconsolate looks
intent upon a woman
drill
    or think about
duty
        enigma-face
shed unnatural
    Babylonian tear
captive
if there ever was such a tear

held or fit
            yet dry

a floater's desire

seems to fit

Here comes the old fit
    prerequisite to yr knowledge
of "heart"

*

gorge is green
        scent of . . .

lemon?

        grip   inside

rough, mitt
        or fist

tight vegetation, dim-eye troglodyte
        monastery beaten down

& patient spin back 40,000 years
rare to go but

        but spoke that you hear

        but to snatch up

                see, see

a stern vision is told to me
the plunderer plunders
& the destroyer destroys
Go up, O Elam
lay seige O Media;
all the sighing she has caused will be brought to an end.
Therefore my loins are filled with anguish;
pangs have seized me,
like the pangs of a woman in travail
Broadcast this to the constituents

Mind reels, horror has appalled me
the twilight I longed for
has been turned for me into trembling

Arise O princes & oil the shield

youth come off a face
haste the bison
    dust is light

      khaki-past lighter
on a long way

all you hear is well of you
       Vesere, Vesere
the bison

& not signed

no one,
the supremely painted dies

but hand
    a hand in

 look there
         swift as torch-flicker thought

    *

fear makes me stupid
'gainst walls
grotte: I thought of her teeth
    & fucked inside her belly
tongue entered her gorge
    grotte: rotted flesh
what remains are bones & stones
    wisp of hair restored to
the effigy got built
    words to your painted deeds
a flame that sustains me now
here
long past a witch's hours
all the family asleep
      in their caverns of dread or dream
La Borderie, on the edge
between you & you, a lover

between the mouth of the cave
&
the man's memory of cave
cave in
I cave in: *grotte*
Some woman gave birth to you &
will eat you alive
don't cross her now

in what mind do you dwell?

& the Sybil writes her oracles
on leaves that scatter in the in the in the in the wind
while others
move
more
deeply
outside
caves
Now turn to this channel for the most "cred" show in the skies

Cool Grove, Perfected In Body, Lotus Mound, Lanka Mound, Spontaneously
Accomplished Mound, Display of Great Secret, Pervasive Great Joy, World
Mound Kid Get Hyped, Higher Than The Sun, Lily Was Here, Life Beneath The
Waves, Distant Village, Divine Protection, Polish Your Own Writing
refrain your breath
even sweet breath
launches death
to animals gamboling there

         so that breathing

(be careful, be very careful)

destroys the hush
what went there?
         who goes?

what masters of the brush?
of superimposition /   of the hunt?
a sigh
    pass
bound

    meet the pigmented shape

    to put a hex on you,
buried
    excavate or die
cinders & kitchen middens
in the pithekos life
I was an ape, but . . .
He said
what stream
do you dwell in
Life or the water?
Was ape, but . . .

Called back "flume"
Call back
"contact the information office"
un longtemps

swirl of outrageous fortune
from Dieppe-bound
holding erect
a book or look
to pass *le temps avec*
un gleam d'eau

bateau Champs-Elysées
My friends my friends are obscure to see
"Not since le Carré has tough emergence . . ." but

Sealink thrive
Uni-ball thrive or throne

& be a lamp of Mahamudra to
Mes amis:
babes on deck make a Cro-Magnon word
espoir or
Seeing the essence of mind is called heat
in that mingling is a hundred syllables
    & every one of them has a hold on you

or blue deck all hands upon
& shoes
& shoes you caught dead in
la la la Duval
"59"
"une place de Lightning Bolt"
Paris Université teeshirts

Maroc woman

toutes les choses fantastiques

wake to know
& are wonderful
Make more of your money with fidelity
then follow daily life
all contours as parts of the
enlightened mandala are wonderful
I was an ape, but . . .

O you systems lacking in legitimacy

Just before the close, the Dow Jones industrial average was 15.21 points up at 2,913.24. Earlier in the morning, the index had stood at 2,926.65 but began to fall after reports that women were being evacuated from the Russian parliament.

In what cave do you dwell?

    After the Louvre, we walked five miles to the Eiffel Tower. When we got there, we waited in line for about half an hour to get tickets to go to the top. First, we got in the elevator that is pulled up the side of the tower. It takes you to the second floor. It was cramped with people.

Then we got to the second floor. That is where we were supposed to get on another elevator. The line to get on it went around the whole second floor. We waited in the line for about an hour and a half. Finally we got smushed into the elevator. My face was rammed into the wall. I noticed I wasn't feeling that great. We got to the top. I could see about twenty miles of city lights shining in the dark. We walked up some stairs that led to the very top. It was freezing so I went down to the inside part again. We (my aunt, uncle, cousin, Mom, Dad, and me) were starving so we tried to catch the elevator going down. Unfortunately, when we got to the second floor, some snobby five-hundred-pound lady started complaining that she was sick and nearly killed fifty people by pushing them into closing elevator doors. My finger was practically amputated by a door. We got in the elevator and went down flattened. When the door opened, I was trampled. We got outside. I looked up. I could see the top of the tower; then I realized how tall it was.

how small I was

taking the light inside
&
light on all the tongues of . . . *vive la France!*
(but what of Mother Russia? Headline: kidnapping its own president)

& may the Fatherland crumble
(Until 1924 the emir of Bukhara had runaway slaves nailed to the gateposts of the city walls)

Vive la France, soil of ancestors
1589 The Edict of Nantes grants Huguenots freedom of worship &
　　　places of refuge

Revoked in 1685, the ancestors flee France

How is it with you in a cross-Atlantic traveller named Virgin because you never had it so good. The music company, clouds marshal out aircraft portal, divine drinks hey more of those please & conversation about the unusual amenities. Recycle waste. Cute in the most complimentary sense. Incessant logo beats the drum of "sell, sell" "buy buy." Hey but I paid for this. Went under.

Dear Lady,

The poem "Sightseeing" tells of a happening in which I was part of. My first mission as a radar bombadier was scheduled for a May tenth knockout blow to Dresden. Thank god the war ended on the Eighth. In actuality my plane continued on, getting involved in a "buzzing" incident of a German Village church as parishioners were still entering the church, in all probability giving thanks for the war's end, but the pilot and co-pilot just had to give them a brush, "Just to let the bastards know we are still here."

Odd ally,

Gabin

9 *Août*: Studying in this psychedelic dream the Atilians *(Atrabesquians)* who used to live in caves

We ingest a powerplant of purple leaves ground with the ashes of Ancestor. Because these other people have no extant texts we must get to their power source & habitat through the concentrated study of a 3-D diorama, almost like a hologram, map. It resembles the inside of a hive. But we've gotta shrink too to get on top of the scheme. Some hesitation as we leap into our smaller, tighter skins. We know that this lost people are secret utopians and have the key to interstices survival.

Dear Anne: I sent "Grotte" around & got a mixed to negative reaction response on it. I don't want to pester you with editor's critical comments. Just give you the gist, which was ask her for something less journalese, more compact etc. One person suggested "Grotte" be edited, but I don't see how that is possible, given its structure. So, I'll leave response up to you. If you want to send us other things to look at, fine.

I think perhaps you sent "Grotte" thinking of my work on Paleolithic cave art—understandable, but "Grotte" is not really addressing that area of attention. So, in the future, I think you should simply show us what you consider to be your best.

Whatever it is worth (for future editing) "Huguenot" & "Iraqi" are mispelled—& you should probably be consistent re. diacritical accents (you use them on page 5 but not elsewhere, as on p. 1 "fatigué", & "Auto da Fé" and later "Champs Elysées" etc.

Begin at the mouth of . . .

XVIII

"I AM THE GUARD"

Some years ago she founded a poetics school on the spine of the Rocky Mountain continent with a close poet friend. The school carries the name of Jack Kerouac. They both agree that the angelic writer had realized the first noble truth of suffering & composed his mind elegantly & spontaneously on the tongue to the page. He also entered the American culture, not always sympathetically. She often heard his sounds in her head, whole lines even, & many years later is invited to participate in a reading honoring his work at the local university. "October in the railroad earth." She writes these words, to be read aloud, that caress his. The challenge of the elder poet-men is their emotional pitch she wants to set her own higher than. Are these not masters? Her presumption is boundless. Her poem sees no end in sight if she continues to honor & measure her life & work against theirs. She visits her father, who speaks darkly from the corner of his room. The political climate is depressing. She likes to travel back in time.

> *"Stop the murder and the suicide!*
> > *All's well!*
> > > *I am the Guard"*
> > > > —Jack Kerouac

You are fun

you are god

you are

"far-out-like-a-light"

Raiders, a game
    Something about skull & bones, black white logo writ 'gainst Astroturf. Everyone looks into a bowl. And then the players start ejaculating into the air. Just like the beer commercials.

Could be London, shopping for just the right male dolls, a black one, yes, a white one too. One Christian doll, perhaps a Pope. The other is one of the 3 kings from Orient R.

They will coexist on my little shelf. And another comes in gold, Jambhala for wealth

> *the razor in-cut of void meat Buddha*

Dear Jack Kerouac
who'd rather die than be famous
who ran away from college in 1941
into Memorial cello time
& spilt his gut
50 pesos
Aztec blues
A vast cavern, eh?
I caught (he did) a cold from the sun
upside-down language
ulatbamsi Bre-hack! Brop?
Of the cloud-mopped afternoon

and turn this lady upside down

dyuar aham, prthivi tvam

May Vishnu prepare the womb;
May Tvastr fashion the forms;
May Prajapati cause the seed to flow,
May Dhatr place the seed within thee

Let the marriage begin
Let the fucking begin
to people our numbers
what it's about, the fucking,
what it's
about to
become, a form,
to worry about fucking
& we are dying in it,
of it, inside the form
which is happy illusion's
mind bog anyhoop

but you can go (go now! go now! in spite of yr blakity blakity brains)

But keep me,
whatever-your-name-is-deity,
a terrible form
A "krodha-murti"
Keep me terrible
for I curse the day
I wed the poets

for I have sinned
I have slept in the arms of
another "husband"
I have advocated revolution
in the marketplace
I have looked
into the face of
Fidel Castro

("only the laboring man adds anything to society")

& wept
but see how
he is lost in
his "gray beard & fuzzy thoughts"
Fidel now
I am old now
(the father is speaking now
& of Kerouac
his indulgent-boy word run,
sometimes hard to keep company with . . .
slowly, fully clothed,
lying on his bed of thorns, my father
room shuttered,
she goes to pull the light in)

I have nothing to live for
No direction
No direction to go

Came here to die
I am waiting to die
I'd rather die than be famous
I never thought I would live it this long

Cry for the leaves to cover me come come over me

who has accomplished
his children
Don't break
your tenderness

When the wind blows
you feel it
Same for the country . . .
you feel it

I felt once for the oppressed of the world
& studied Marx, Hegel, Kant, Lenin
& the Communist Party meetings I went to
had no connection to reality

You see how it changes?

Creatures of light!
That's what we are & leaves
It's all happening in snow
But I shudder
what's been buried in the grave?
Dust.

Depression drives me down
Ninety devils jokin' with me
I'm not quite clinical

But we are similar in our thinking
he, me, & you too

although you are super
O logistic! woman

Vishnu pervades you all through the night
& day comes
& he is still your marker & destroyer
What are the marks of existence where they
empty of themselves?

Put away habit, come live with me

Take this love from your father
it comes through a wizened boy body

I understand how beings in their time
endure unbearable suffering

why listen to me
an old man

call it to action

Where were you when the last Ancient Forests were being destroyed,
along with the 6,000 species that called them home?

Old-growth forest
dies with me,
an obsolete man
Hundreds of trees
falling every day

We throw away our last ancient forest heritage for Happy Meal boxes . . .

You could say
we live in
a life-vest mentality
swim for life
Lay it all that, be bobby

be buddy
How optative?
go Sutter's home (his gold)

going my way a marriage
had a life in the war
age or ache in breast
war was a life it woke me up
a long time was always
a long time
in war

dear Jack:
not-of-war reflected in that mirror

& when you returned life was sweet

heart or breast would
swell up, proud
to die
proud to enter her womb
with renewed optimism

& thinking of all the ways to die

to die at war

to die fighting

the way he looks at home,
away at war
& how in marriage
Father, I call him,
captain Kerouac
or husband
needing him most
by his words

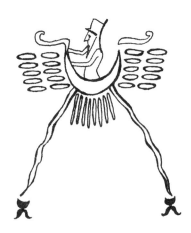

(forget the deeds here)

Operation a Just Cause
to weep
a cutting of deals is
1,000 Panamanians dead
is a cutting of deals
billion & 1/2 property damage
is a cutting of deals
& 23 servicemen dead of the u.s. of a.
a "federal posse" intervenes
of a necessary day December 20, 1989,
a cutting day of deals

read it, get it? O cutter of deals
money launder drive all the blame
or drug traffic doubles
& lights go out for Miami's bulletin
in a cutting of deals

narco-kleptocracy
a kind of joy
Medellín cartel
a risk you run to cut a deal
kill what "we" we bounce back on you
kill what "we" we needed once
& serve a darker purpose
Plap play play plap plap plapity gap

not to wax sentiment, a groove
but pertains to any deal
the speedboat was a vessel
quick trip out of here
(the way the sun goes down in idyllic valley)

(he said in a tv movie about
a deal, episode of a mother implicated)

It, the vessel,
carried goods
crossed a border
was fast
crossed the harmless headline
& criminality when "smoking gun"
is your
position
& headline for
growing
narco-biz
a kind of showcase
or stop
joking with men

I love you Jack
I love you Neal

you take on macho landscape with
the freeingest sensibility, men
what ban
what sex do you play
arms sales
back up to plead guilty
& make the words sigh true
political
what care they back for then
what bitch to plead
immediate action toward Syntex
toward Sabotage or reduction flight
toward Capitol Cities front for CIA
just bought by ABC
forget another *petite histoire*
I love you for what I hate
crossing the country in my way
it was fast, I kept the notebook
I said poof bang boom

I said shut a yap me mon

                what cooks mon and he was his sleepy dreamy self
       you just gotta look at me as I crawl outta here eyes,
slumps at table, wake now and me with me big sentimentally hot heart setimentalitopality

me see em
& they are all the poets in my book
a big heart church
& later down on Market Street I saw all kinda colorful street people

Dear A:

With millions of others I spent last weekend transfixed by the Senate Judiciary Committee
hearing. Can you believe that men like Orrin Hatch are in political power? There are others on
the committee that make me nauseous, but Hatch seems to be the embodiment of evil. It was
hard to get to sleep after watching for 9 or 10 hours this panel of middle-aged white men and
listening to their inanities. The hearing to me was not a question of Thomas vs Hill, but instead
a question of the sad state of our country.

    I'm woefully depressed here these days, thankful for your love. I can tell you forcefully
that I support you in any decisions you may make.

    Much much love,

        Daddy

       from this concentrated spark of raw energy what they call
       quantum chromodynamics predicts that a vast swarm
       of fundamental "quark" particles called "gluons"'
       will spontaneously spring into existence

I, your *Clocharde Celeste,* spoke to you TiJean in a dream:
So I write about Heaven.

XIX

WHY THAT'S A BLADE CAN FLOAT

The poet has by now travelled a distance, spanning mental universe, moving cross country, moving cross town and comes to rest with her box of scraps, notes, journals, memorabilia, letters, unfinished versions, her major task continuing unsettled at her feet. She spreads the documents about her, and bows her head. She feels a burden to sustain the plan. The society is crumbling around her. She can barely withstand the daily news. She thinks: why America? Am I American made? The computer is a little theater for her mind, although she senses it was designed & created & marketed by more & more men. Is this a problem? This is no mean accomplishment. She needs to enter more words. At least 400,000 characters. She has both exposed & guarded her life; whatever poetry survives is the autobiography of a dreamer. Mustering her strength she skims the surface of her dream & aspiration to find what floats, what rises. She has transcended some of her personal drama and contemplates a larger picture once again. The radio keeps her company tonight.

I'm on my way to America . . .

What caller Apollinaire enamelled of him and portrait a German had of wit or style none none but peasant come and come again we came from that stock o' soup and vittle, vital to any daughter's wish. She loves him. She's one who loves the taste of burnt vittle because of him it comes by, dark bread for the peasant in you. She loves migration, how it complicates the maps of nationals and leave them writhe more problems. A chaos of place to be born out of male stroke and swoop.

What weave got France wave got put in here Huguenots, a difficult brood bittered by betrayal, and Europe's sperm said it before mix in her. Mix "x" factors here. A curse of mere cuticle a cusp or covering a couched phrase to tell a trouble in or else you come down here a Sunday and be baptized. This was not speaking in anyman's tongue but how rather she went out on a limb once a night alone and bled for all the weight of childbirth he caused her. She still said "he" as she waited for her property to be taxed. And it was daring to go that way just try me, just try she said. Incest was no explanation. A moon of problems.

Property was an old handle to hold her back. Give her it back. Time again her legs walked further, back to Europe and died in the bosom of would it be Abraham? Wood wood wood say it wood wode wood wood make it sing a wood praise song, my wald, velde, velt, Wotan mounts the stage to terrorize woman.

break here

    &would a Walden be
   set
           round
      with

caller
    stone
        wood a Walden
  prehistorique

would
blue
  a wald-man be

at
one
time
    migrate

    green
        another

(the pond)

& he says about my eyes
about blue & green
& silver, he says
view
from

a door

more contracted
than
from
eye

sock
he specs

too, happy ending
    he, nationalism fraught a kind of sympathy
    a free house, says

(how do we talk
to ourselves
deep at
night
in the dark in bed?)

    die Mauer im Kopf

      socket

the wall in the mind

& how do we

in a slice of hours
talk
    or calibrate this table in human time
2 o'clock: Page 2 is missing but what are your contacts
       in Venice, London, Erlangen, Paris

3 p.m.: St. Francisco rescues sailors from hunger

(il Santo Salva dalla fame i marinai)

they have been at it a long time

4 o'clock: the mountain comes to the man

5: Peacemaking conference, Mideast

(Dear A: I hope to see you otherwise. Sending you lots energy, getting my act together you
are right about academic theory of Zeitgeist. LOTS ENERGY, Madrid)

6 p.m.: *La Calùnnia di Apelle* by Sandro Botticelli depicts various outstretched
arms in degrees of panic & passion. The statues look attentive in their nearby
alcoves. I watch this instead of television

7 p.m.: why did I ever leave home for the new world

mi padre, the old man, is weeping, *weeping*

calling it a life to turn aside
        & he goes backward a step in his masonry

    each part of the house corresponds to a part of the human anatomy. Arms
are bedrooms & social parlors. The navel is the courtyard, sexual organs are the
gates, the anus is the garbage pit in the backyard, legs & feet are the kitchen &
granary
& head is the family shrine
    patriarch descend here
    Jove, a designate, shine here

putting doubt aside the temple
I was trying to tell you
when you call out
suddenly
like a demon
                    he enters here
Hallow Eve afflict
a species of madness
& he, the immigrant-deity, dresses up as a hermaphrodite
(old festal table, ancient wassail, jest or sport)

he comes out of Columbus's tomb to make amends

amending to America

    & keeps a ceremony there
all change in me, *muthologos*

sacred to some god always departing
lay down a book

hear the ancestral names

    Bush cruel crack
    against caribou

pipeline continue, imperialist America riding
on the nation of caribou

find you here no sanctuary from religious persecution
    collisions between nuclei
& wander freely as the first instant of creation

by whom?
of some sperm
& the first people who live here
in what mind do they dwell?

(Kabel und Betriebssystem liegen nicht bei)

caught as if by
force
    & forces
upon
the histoire

somber muse & disease

          walks the gangplank,
pirate to a war
     & held
in kind of thrall
for
diversity
to arc back,
     you come home from all points
          to tell the family the stories

Doctor Benton speaks:

A. Atypical lobular hyperplasia B. Moderate intraductal hyperplasia C.
Fibrocystic condition D. Microcalcifications. A & B are worrisome; some people
feel they are precancerous. Empirically punctate calcifications can be cancer

     then he leaves the room

mi padre, mi padre
predator
doctor god America

& give advice to workmen
how to vote:
     force an issue

          more nonaffirmative action O women
sign here they operate, *exploratory*

males with scalpels: *milde Grösse*
carving the u.s. of a.

Dear A,
     Back in Munich

You must know this but arose in the lecture last night the most important person of the 18th
century being John Locke, founder of political liberalism (liberté, égalité, tolerance, fraternité,
humanity etc.), who influenced George Washington, Thomas Jefferson, Madison and those
who put their signatures under the Declaration of Independence and were freemasons as well.

At my meeting many freemasons of today were present. They have 2 beautiful temples in Nürnberg and Erlangen. Only men are admitted. The bible the president of the USA gives his oath upon is the bible of Washington which was used in his freemason temple. George Bush is probably a freemason too. His "new world order" is a reflection of their esoteric teaching so similar to Shambhala vision. Conspiracy theory again, yes? That is my fear, distortion of a vision, in real politics. And it seems to be, indeed, a common mindset capable of "dark" and a "white" result. We need more dialectical awareness to overcome the danger of dark results. This is what I endeavor in my scientific thinking and work. You, too, my friend . . .

my friend dark night a result
friend a light of me combine
to find alas no woman at the table
of Israel, of Lebanon, Palestine
how do they sleep? of Syria
& shine or shrink the tale as of void
& radio it says hands-on broadcast
a hundred deejays wait, not one a woman
the scholar & savage equal points of light
rub dry sticks together
a sham, a delusion, kind of affectation
never felt lonesome in it
mythology cast a spell on me
wonder a caller they say special interest
& instrumental in recording & taste you will see
on drums on bass & on Smithsonian
pumpkins so light, spear a ghost
it is an eve my friend a dark night
that's the way I feel now
they tend to shatter, words they tend to shatter
I'm a wrecker,
Roland Kirk plays "Haunted Melody"
they tend to shatter the words they tend

XX

OUSTED

She must leave the family home and abide by certain forms that she challenges daily. How are these rules etched in stone? Have they worked so well? The poet finds the scholarly task of unearthing alternative histories & examples to "prove" her arguments exhausting. No one really listens. She rants at the Male who has this kind of mindset that she considers myopic & alien. What's his problem? Mere jealousy? The whole world's ablaze & he's jealous? She chomps at a mythic bit. A new friend draws closer in the den of insects and raccoons. They push on each other's work. She falls into doubt occasionally, scorned & maligned by the "community," who still after all the centuries hasn't learned a thing. She feels banished to the outer rim of the small town mandala, the witch woman in the company of beasts, but it's a guise she will embrace. She writes in a long dark chamber. She sits in the hallway at night reading & writing so as not to disturb the child sleeping in the only room. He rolls with her mood & passion. He follows her with his eyes. He knows her energy, just seething below his own surface. She identifies especially with mystic nuns. She reads about Sor Juana & her sisters licking the dirt to make the shape of the cross with their saliva, their tongues raw with the work. Should she do penance? Someone then responds to her writing.

> *"Look for the nul*
> *defeats it all*
> *The N of all*
> *equations"*
> —W. C. Williams

When law stated was it sacred monogamy or illusion seduced ourselves to it. He kicks me out. Circa deities, what? The law fuck-wish for "have not died yet." "Am yours," violent plots, arranged mix, or match this eye with that hand. As wish for completion. Tradition means to pursue fullness & let your eyes be glutted with honey. I see you. I see you. *And stick in the blade.*

Megaladapis edwarsi gone, *Bos primgenius, Hydrodamalis gigas* gone, brave to be wiped out, inoffensive, easy to kill. How did they & in what habit mate? Marriage, extinction, gone beyond use in the ripe outdo-ourself-time, golden tangle exists, resists: *keep this together.* A man and woman in time. Bow down. But see the triangulation of desire. It could be mother/son, father/daughter. Intersect this life in that other's, see how you come out or up for air. He-Who-Kicks-Me-Out, I pray you feel the sweetness of revenge yet suffer in your stupidity. Ne'er see likes of me again, dummy. You jerk. I'll go frolic with the animals in the expensive cave.

Some brute die & you are keeper of an ancestor filling a void, bring "it" out in the shrine box, unwrap her head, make the offering. No one dies really. *Illud tempus,* a primordial touch before language & deed go hand & hand. I love my antecedents. Consort, you are the saint of me. Now turned to demon. I own you and you are never out of sight, I see you everywhere proud edifice, a field accomodates you within. Tight rein. Lover said your signature is enough of a roof above my world. Mystical mutters provide a flourish, sanctuary. Alphabet I marry. Tomb I marry. Ancestor I marry. Events too illicit to bear the light, nobody's business. I marry the secret too blinding she calls deception. I touch your cheek, is that a pact?

A woman takes her clothes off around the planet & throughout the 10 directions of space. How many world systems may I get married in? & disrobe the holy corpse, I vow to enter every one of them. Trust is teacher who ensnares a girl-body. *This? Worms, a mantra of worms, food in any woman's thought, let her as her thoughts provide a mantra of worms.* Rise grisly roots, genesial laugh. I want you as mirror, dear Sky-Hero, take it to the top.

er bell er elly

        slike a cloud

hite loud evening

        efor hudder nigh

ood ill indi efface

        out thir

weat oil ow love

ow love ow love

    no insect is awake

er elly er ell
aclou

hat nul
weat oil
ow love
eein now, eein now ow love weat oil

initiation into insect tongue
area of knowledge
yr wish broods
because she of earth
thinks
cup do in raccoon
substratum

*

love's
body with
arm
has
been
longer
sky signature

*

altar
& wine
hierophant

mount them

*

whose
glut
not die,

rebel
sweet liturgy
write this
in pain

*

to the wronged:
can *shift that cave*

*

live & think
these actions

summa scienta nihil save

*

abscond with booty
lust, heh, lust?

*

be-wilder
contour

against the threat of spiritual extinction

I wish him a long long journey

Numbarkala, Wandjina, Ungud, Rainbow Serpent
tribe of everywhere,
on location

Arapahoe:

Complex of occasions
grown perfectly shy
sift back
something soft lived here
vertiginous

til ductile anchor hold
the islands
and then
but
when
is to for surely
happened
part now round
meet the sea
above
lyre sound
(his heart I care to meet)
erotic the sound
wins on me
yet screen
on see
his love
where is it?
there? o
don't scare
a heart
puts
stock
admit, admit
yr love
where is it O
dream bit:
"if only you will do such & such
the gears are more accelerated"
trying
to be good
but
faster?

occur wider range
risk is full of
snatch the light
connubial
occur his body

suck up
my belly
don't leave
me out

rave form
ghazal loose
name form is Anne-of-Sorrows

rocket
knuckle-grip
stun

with an eye to poesie?
what idiom for makers

arc of love
writ in wine

you project I want to work
you have to say what you want to do
don't project on me to get an excuse
what are the expectations/rules
of our relationship?

see what happens?
I'm simply out because I said I'm falling in love with you
and then if you're suddenly not there?
I never want to go through that again

It was not a monologue it was *respondez s'il vous plait*. Tasteless to be one so free of inhibition. Bringing up the cast of characters in a little town. Not so interesting as run out by the moon. Flagstaff is bladed. Not so as it might be even more interesting to sit you down thus and tell our story. You want to cry me to sleep like a babababababy. You wanna hear me cry to sleep like a gull. You wanna hear his heartbeat. Now it raises. In the basement all things taste the same. Because they are even, untried, because they are close to the ground yes that's not it but close. Really laugh? alert with the dormant spiders, the gold fardels. Barbed with raccoons. He sees them he says gazing in at him from the far step.

Awake, and they are alive, awake & they are alive awake & they are awake & they are alive awake & they are all alive. I dreamed his banditoed face that night my son came over. Animals will save the story of her confinement, shall be majesterial, shall be brave. They are the extinguished ones. Never again that form that creation brings. Never again that form that brings the ant galaxy to her rug. Her rage of rug. Her killing. Let them live in the crack a while.

I went out. It was the docking hour, it was a witching of night. It was strange. I came back. I just woke up here.

I am the queen appointed herself to be of these new parts. A bridge. A view of sturdy trunks. I fast by the window. I am the novice ruler of these parts in my head, new places where the pain always hangs out with me. Where ruler is to be ruler to pain. Ruler to the boiler room. All come seek shelter here. I tuck you under my big skirt like Misericordia. Suffering does or didn't did it and does not exist. I have enough space for the suffering of all of you. Latin *obstare:* to hinder. You put the hex on me, you put the hindrance on. Put down the next song of the no eyes part of the no ears no nose all parts of what makes sense. It is a tract and include it here you are least pride of being to practice your religion yeah in peace of harmony. In the place of cellar. Where light is a thief to your light-up-world-mentality. Ok. And out it didn't go yet & does or doesn't it did govern did go out.

The governed is bowed down. She's ousted by law. Lord of the manor wants her this way: out there. But no longer live under ready rule. Yet ride with daughter power. Or she'll be the artist forever. How made these pelicans. How made them spite and strong, how made them pierce his heart, how did they lie awake & plot his quick demise. Poor Lear. This gets reversed. It comes to naught but writing, writing . . .

I want you
desire is a field
includes the objects
& divine events
as if performing at the
fragmented dreaming site
love is a rite
includes our myth
laid out epiphany-style

in our secular environment

need is a net

guess what it includes

the way nature operates is one dimension

and through the holes goes

you can't lock nature up

love, love

above censure

chthonic rhythm can't help it

go beyond

"idea of a single"

a woman to her lover

"no sacrilege"

let him speak

Dialogue 3, Giordano Bruno:

"thus one should think of Sol as being in a crocus, a daffodil, a sunflower, in the rooster, in the lion. . . . For as the divinity descends to a certain measure inasmuch as it communicates itself to nature, so there is an ascent made to the divinity through nature"

Spaccio dellabastia trionforte

speak to make it so
no matter you king of me

speak to make it so
no matter you poor man

speak to make it so
industrial wastelands blight the earth

Of course the stories known in many lands many tribes say this: about how men go off to battle, to catch a wild animal, to avenge a sorry deed, and if they slip, if they get maimed, if the animal eludes their grip, blame it on the wives. The wives were unfaithful. And so rush home to punish them. Oust them.

was a wave of interactive particles
limbs carry me across his country
I fled I fled I fled I fled I fled
Juice was first and Juice was last
he with the glittering lightnings
Juice is King
Djeus is ruler
he with the gleaning lightnings
you see
a moment
of her mind
the form of a ladder
to . . .
can't waste anything!
every thought holy
I fled I fled
invite him in
every thought, holy
do you see far, my friend?
How far?
gather thoughts to
feel & hear
here
love is a shelter
the postulants receive
smitten by how you guess her
he's out there somewhere
look after the country
proclaim your attention
you who are attentive to this
look after the country, the beestes are coming

Every child teaches that things are backward

Dear A.W.:

First impression: a kind of aside: physically—for whomever does print the book, I think it needs a big page; something on the scale of Olson's or Frank O'Hara's *Collecteds*. I think of the pieces I've seen printed, and for me it worked best in NOTUS (STILETTO was a long page, but too cluttered for me). Because it looks like in a lot of places the page was, if not quite the compositional field à la Olson, some kind of unit or frame for you. Also the thoughts are quite long, philosophical, at times like syllogisms of Teutonic-compound-word complexity, and it helps to follow your thoughts if a reader can see a lot of words at once.

I remember the title of a book, I think, interviews (maybe essays): "Ecstatic Occasions, Expedient Forms." And when I read your work—not just here, but much of the time—the form never seems to be quite expedient enough for you. The language also has to be bent, made more expedient, wrapped about what you're trying to say the way headlights used to be "Frenched" on custom cars. So, the language is constantly slipping out of my grip. (I'm not a very nimble reader, really. But, as I may have mentioned already, my value lies in my being a persistent one, I think.) I lose the sense a lot in your work, but hear your voice, hear something it would be too melodramatic of me to call your "transport," but that would be very close. If the OULIPO guys (wonder why there aren't any OULIPO women) can declare that "A [OULIPO] writer never needs inspiration, because he is always inspired," meaning that their dedication to forms and formula gives them an automatic impeller for the writing, then I myself might say that you have some of this same insistent pushing-against-inertia-by-way-of-a-system approach, and that the system is simply the emotional pitch you want to set the poem to. That is, you fire up the emotion, then try to catch and ride it with words; ride the whatever you might want to call it—muse, carrier wave, inspiration?—playing a fierce game of catch-up with yourself (selves?) You say this almost explicitly yourself in several places here. For instance: ". . . loves my writing/ & the road in it/ It roads you away, you might say/Messages get lost/Look for a word and can't find it".

Shaman might be the easier way for a new reader to enter your work as a whole, because everywhere you write—incl. IOVIS—you are always making charms, attempting spells, sketching out IOVIS as your stanzas build up their chromosomal clusters; and like those medicine things, their component parts, your lines can be very hermetic, encoded as DNA.

In Olson, Pound, etc. the difficulty is because of their—to a reader, an outside-stancer—seemingly arbitrary arrangement, the nature of which is tough to puzzle out. You have declared these men/works as the ancestors of IOVIS, and your poem does have this architectonic puzzle aspect as well. But the pieces you use are not really like those in Olson or Pound; somewhat closer to Williams, and even Guy Davenport's fictions in *emotional* content. Because your pieces are overwhelmingly personal history, not political or geological history, as the others tend to use. Is this why the Pisan Cantos work best? Why Paul Metcalf's Patagoni is not "better" than, say, his Middle Passage, but is certainly boosted by the personal letters' immediacy? Why Olson chose to speak *as* Maximus?

But to be a little more specific about IOVIS . . . "Both Both" is a kind of alap section—alap being the intro part of Indian raga, where the theme is started slowly, completely, and most clearly before the improvisations begin.

We are "told" what the structure will be when we encounter the first male after IOVIS—Ambrose. His voice, we are told, is one of "demand and interruption," and the structure is an interrupted one, interrupted by stories that demand you tell them at certain points. And the bandwidth of the piece is established—from IOVIS across to Ambrose. And not just that the male voices are of demand and interruption, but also of contribution and celebration as well. And when you mention the given of maleness' connection with war, you state it, use it, and deal with it, but you aren't accusatory or condemning and do not as so many might have been tempted go for—the cheap shot. Rather, your take on it is one of recognition and curiosity. And when you do show the consequences of such a manifestation of IOVIS as war you do it matter-of-factly and as part of a context: ". . . now we live in the combined karma, if I might use that word . . . in the sense of what continues, a thread of energy perhaps is all. Which is why I say the poet must be a warrior of this battlefield of Mars, o give me a break, thank you very much." The poet must recognize where he or she is. A male(ness) self-recognition, even in a female poet—accept the good with the bad, and do your best. This is a clear-eyed, unflinching poem, Anne W.

You say "I feel myself an open system (woman) available to any words or sounds I'm being informed by." I've already noted this fluidity in your work, though I made up my own term for it (really, borrowed from Hugh Kenner in THE POUND ERA). I've been trying for a few years to finish a book of essays on some poets—I may have mentioned this to you before: Schuyler, Brainard, Elmslie, Koch, Waldman, Berrigan, Mathews, Padgett, maybe Coolidge, and in my notes I made for your piece I called you a "Fuller's Knot" poet. In THE POUND ERA Kenner talks about a demonstration that Bucky Fuller used to do: he'd tie a knot in a rope that was made up of a number of ropes of different materials—some length of the rope was hemp, some nylon, etc., and Fuller would slide the knot along the length of the rope(s), saying the knot was not the rope but the patterned energy that manifested itself there. And I see you as this kind of poet, who lets energy flow through her, while you do your best to manifest the patterned energies you sense . . . within the limits of materiality. As you say yourself "excluding nothing" is impossible. Coincidentally in the notebook where I was making notes on IOVIS I was also making notes on a number of other things, and my comments on the final paragraph of your poem face a quote from a GAIA-an biologist, and I think the quote applies to your work at this point: "This amounts to setting broad boundaries within which many pathways may be taken, as in a proscriptive rule (what is not forbidden is allowed). But this is a far cry from a prescriptive rule (what is not allowed is forbidden)." He's writing about inheritance, natural selection etc., but I think it fits your poetry . . . B. B.

XXI

SELF OTHER BOTH NEITHER

She will turn again to the precious Dharma, which holds no corner's gender. The poet studies Madhyamika philosophy, a branch of Buddhist thought, which refutes the idea of solid existence and embraces the view of codependent or co-arising origination. Things do not come from themselves nor do they come from things other than themselves, nor do they arise from both these factors, nor do they come from neither of these factors. Where do they come from? We live in a Samsarodadhi, or ocean-like world. The strands of our existence come together karmically, if I might use that word dear-sticklers-against-dogmatic-vocabulary, dear comrade poets, and through varied ruses and desires. She has set a shapely form for her thinking—10-line clusters that resemble wings to sit on 8 pages— as she moves through a mental relationship to phenomena. Cut it out, she admonishes herself, it's also only, simply writing. But this is mysterious too. She yearns to write "outside the book," as she has written outside the kin of men. She wants an oppositional poetics.

The desultory hours go slogging by
 All that time remembered as one false start,
   one laborious outing, one laboratory's hour,
     The lights go on all at once, blinders off,
       one distinguished guest, the scientist in repose,
         the first time you ever met. Why is it in some
           cases I am entirely missing the point? What comes
             of this meandering about: the particles coalesce
               What exists exists only as a presentational context
                 of our presentations, Descartes suggests perhaps

And then what happens is precious & strange
 This is our paradox, no perceivable rules
   Just the minds of wizards who tempt us
     to greater Herculean feats, go on now
       bringing your language out in the open, go on
         now, they sing, they reason, they coax
           It is the way to, or back into, one mouthing
             entity, one yapping entity, speaking in
               a kind of soft body tone or else tough and
                 uncompromising, let it go at that into air

Onto bright page, the text is inviting tonight
& speech is the plan of the hour, don't stop yet.
  Wittgenstein's "block," "pillar," "slab," "beam" is
    a tactile language, signifying the way he goes
      about it, and the workers too, the lifting & carrying,
        building up a case only to abandon the building
          once it is completed, ceremonies and all.
            "Human," "ground," "ceiling," "limit," and
              the rest of the senses hop for joy at
                the attention they are getting, one edifice,

One sliver of recognition, one completed sentence,
 one half-baked thought, one coming attraction,
  one way you looked once, the door's wide open,
    Elucidate the promises you made, will you please?
      Is it a genetic agreement, not to be taken lightly?
        I know a woman who clones skin for a living no
          kidding (but seriously), she is inspired by the work
            And is a necessary further wrinkle on the assumption
              that we want this all, this lone life, to go on
                I have this bright idea I want to try out on you

If you would be ready to drop your socks
 But seriously, no such insinuations, trying out
  rather the notion of the notion of this layer
    of time, how elusively it passes so, one caught,
      I'm caught catching myself thinking out back
        under the sun. Gardening would be a wise activity
          to be engaged in, caught, no not napping, but caught
            as 40 years blur into a single event—pouf!
              What happens is wrong-headed thinking like this
                Think of the present as a dimensionless membrane

Think of my presence as something to maintain,
I am saying to myself, or rather it speaks,
    the loquacious one in my head, the head of the
        Senate in the old Greek sense, and the mental machinery
            creaks, trying to flash back, ah trapped in this darn matter,
                in this bulk of stuff I affectionately call mine
                    as it rallies the other constituents to vote
                        on this one, how solid do I want to be? What
                            started this was the repercussion of the language
                                How it bounced back in these 10-line clusters

To note the matter here, that it is necessity
 beckons to straighten out the contradictory policies
    and not one of them religious in the sense of
        duty but holy, yes. Holy smoke, holy yes
            Matters to be attended to include the stars,
                which are themselves repercussions too,
                    and the rest of the firmament, which I am
                        begging to penetrate, and the matter of tastes
                            which can get extreme in the sense of having
                                to live up to the beauty of that painting, that vase

Is this pure artifice? that Guston, that Orozco,
 that sleeve (embroidered to look like electromagnetic
    waves) and so on, some kind of newfangled renaissance
        at least, or living up to the best quotation
            for its pleasing music, not its sense, not the
                content but the contradiction interests the
                    ferocious entity behind the screens, the gauzy
                        veils, behind the dense intrigue of tastes,
                            who after all are the arbiters, and in any sense
                                could they be said to be arbitrary to the thing at hand?

Stand before anything until it becomes important
 Important as obstacle or as attraction or as simply
   what it is, so marvelous it could exist!
     And meeting you too, our eyes commingle when not too
       shy to meet, and you say something in Serbo-Croat
         And my brain filters the information stimulated
           by your eyes and the new sounds issuing from your throat
             and then it all dissolves into the next bite
               It seems that 2 signals separated by an interval
                 of up to 30 or 40 thousandths of a second mesh

Into a single event never to repeat exactly
 this way again, and then they get lost in this
   third collaboration and lose time, where did
     my mind go? My mind is a reflection on the
       instant before I lost it, and suffers to get
         back its bearings again and toe the line
           Stand before anything and you, and anything
             pales by comparison. And so I remember my life
               according to how it goes with you, for or against
                 but the fact of you as 2 signals—Could they be

blended and separately forgot? Does it matter
 to count kisses? And distinquish this from that:
   the person from the object. The person from the
     rock, the river, and yet the instrument wails
       out its tragic song of identity, trapped in
         matter too, sprung free out of a kind of inspiration
           The musician takes little metal mallets to hit
             the strings and they dance over them, hear the
               plaintive wail O hear it in me, it is a woman
                 caught and suspended in sweet love or a country at war

Could it be the song you are waiting for to
jolt you into present time? The past can wait
   to be remembered, the future is relative to this
      moment you get yourself out of here because you are
         rootless, like all thought, and philosophy
            always begins & ends with the question of Other anyway
               Who are you? Naked space? Who are you, disembodied
                  song? What toils here in my late-night brain?
                     I have waited until now to state the case of the
                        imperative, for language takes its awful lawful command

And stands for naught but this French "redouté"—
dread—and did it not exist its content goes to
   its competitors. I fear, you fear, we fear and
      we laugh also, a fragile mass of jelly and sensation,
         a bunch of silly problems, sitting in the foyer waiting
            to enter, nervous about our dress our speech our
               dignity and the coming election, who's in power,
                  and the fashion of that power, its unending ineluctable
                     influence on the surrounding provinces and bank accounts,
                        the way it will kill or cure the lives of thousands

Not one of them can talk back and be heard
And stands for naught but the way you stop speaking
   when she comes in and she is your desire—the rose,
      the crux of the matter—standing in sunlight in a kind
         of deception, a feminine principle, the beginning and
            ending of your world, a mother-trust, an emblem of what
               can breathe and bloom outside the Pentagon, and that is
                  your job to do today, to stand outside the building
                     which has a goal of scathing intellectual tone
                        of nihilism, extinction. Irony, too?

Not my job to stand up outside and give a break
to the proceedings, take up some room, shout
and dance on the lawns, some kind of private
property anyway, has it come to this? This
old protest, an old language, old manifesto.
What he says has the form of a question but is
really a command. What they say seems rhetorical
but is it really, is it? When I say "May I"
do I mean it. And the child might say I want I
want and it will be his because he says so

Or so he thinks. Deep disquietudes, deep panic,
the objects do not come as they are bidden
He thinks he owns one of them and traces it with small
delicate fingers, he isn't sure, it is only a
frame of the thing he desires. The true things
the things that shine and cost money, the things
someone else values or did once, or the things
that are unnamed, unspoken. It looks like something
but what is it really? A master of the universe, a house
of cards, a paper bell he inspects and ultimately destroys

Not like a concrete linguistic object, more like
something neutral, unworthy, no I don't mean that
but has no energy one way or the other although it's
ready to jump in as soon as you wish to attach some
importance to it. Back here again, square one, with the
perception of form. Then: is it for or against me? And so
tonight these questions retrace their antecedents
because the "you" of the "you" interfered. Let *you* alone!
Rather, what is social, what is individual, what sublime
is the issue, and saying it to point the way

is to really get down to details: his necktie
 pearly in the light, his small hips moving in
   a kind of playful jog to amuse us, his sockless feet,
     books strewn about with the titles of things Roman,
       to conjure an eternal city is a duty here, the lines
         which are studied in another tongue. "Tungol," did you
           know, means "star"? The "you" of him, the "you" of
             his desk, you leave in a huff, and the objects remain
               with you on them, binding me to you even further
               even after I turn the lights out one by one

An obligation to glucose, an obligation to the empirical
 you whose ingenuity keeps us going past bedtime
   One woman's bedtime is another's rising after all, and
     even with all the lights off you burn the midnight
       oil up on the hill surrounded by the tomes that cry out
         to be loved. Let's not be pretentious about a library.
           The fear of falling into terror might inspire a mistrust
             of science, but instead you are able to mimic the
               indestructible and the invisible, the matter in the sense
                 of "stuff" will always allude you, what else is wrong?

A science studying the life of signs, that is the task
 after the decline of religious meanings for what we must
   get busy analyzing the gestures if we are to really
     have results, nothing else out there to amuse us
       Do you agree? I would or would not stake my life on it
         and walk away getting off easy back to the lab where
           we dissect language into miniscule parts
             Phonemes and phones ache for their missing limbs under
               our fierce scapulas, our sharp and accurate unerring ears
                 If we can hear reason we will let you know how it destructs

It could be the interpretation of the dream
 in which I am possibly "saying something"
  Wooden tables are the women in the dream
   Two men on either side in tall hats
    and then Winston Churchill comes in
     and a man called Suchness with a hammer and sickle
      It is the politics of the time and the thinking
       that that person indulges in a kind of discourse
        with himself letting the day and night settle
         in, not in the physical sense but in the sense

of yearning for more to absorb or really we do
 take it in, know it or not, believe or not,
  sleep or not, in love or not, talking or not,
   dreaming or not, waking to write something down
    punctuated by the sound of water dripping,
     and the so-called politics are invented by the
      dreamer so that there are two sides always
       to our thinking and we might roll over to
        left or right, or jolt up in fear at the
         total annihilation possible in one nightmare

reaching out to consume you, hazard a guess
 because you keep trying to construct a different
  reality based on what you want. Can't I get it?
   Doesn't he she they get whatever they want?
    Was it this or that they got? Now everyone read a
     stanza aloud I wonder you do it so differently
      Can you get ahold of it as I do, the gesture
       of emotion, the sweep of a hand, a scarred landscape,
        one brushstroke, someone steps off the sunporch,
         that grand person's line or life or drama ends

Of course you can, and you may write it too,
 or play it, or sing along, and know that
  we all exist to know how to do this,
    clapping or joining hands or tapping out
      the meter with our foot, the whole chorus
        moving en masse to honor the hero returning
          from war, look how wounded he is! Look how
            women kneel at his feet to kiss those wounds
              listen him tell of it, the blood and steel
                Watch his eyes go wide in the gore and glory of it

And see how his exploits dance in the song
 the strophe and antistrophe accentuating
  the way this one was felled and that one
    cried "Hold, enough!" Or was a prayer of sharp thanks
      to one of many great interfering gods who like
        nothing better than paeans to themselves
          They come alive as we call their names and
            resound in us all the passions they represent
              O goddesses do not let me kill that which
                is in me to kill, but if I do take it out

on that other one who crossed me with her
 heart and tongue, O great goddess do this for me
  because I am only of these delicate bones made
    I break apart on any continent, but you soar
      as mind does and can take shapes, O protean one
        do this for me and for all women: Revenge!
          That she should do it is not the point
            working the women in us to frothy rage
              against a meek one of our kind who looked
                at the man belonging to the other, and so on

An old story that gets retold in a poem
Let it beat out its meter, exhausted now
   and yet keeps on and on in me, heartbeat
      or the mother's scenario, or the hag's
         or the virgin's melody she knows not what for,
            languishing in the hot forest night yet
               not in a language more primitive than ours
                  The adjective "licht," open, is the same word as "light"
                     To make something open means to make light, free, and clear
                     To make it shine in your heart, make lucid

To make the forest clear of trees
The openness is the clearing, the nothing in common
   with light meaning "bright" (Heidegger) and yet let
      the brightness stream into the clearing, mind on fire
         Outward appearance is everything today
            What is the opening of what is open?
               We pick up the book and eyes alight on the way
                  Merlin appears to Perceval as an aged man carrying
                     a sickle around his neck and wearing high boots
                        "Si fait, grand partie de ton affaire gist sur moi"

So much for others interfering in our affairs,
 the business of proud self going about a day
   arrogant until it catches sight of you, a magician,
      a glamorous one, who pants and cajoles and
         speeds his or her way into your heart, flattered
            by the promise and pleasure, assuaged by the tone,
               look, color, taste, touch, he is so soft
                  and I am so solid and desirable, there is no
                     thing in itself, it is only in relationship
                        to tangible emotions, forever exchanging molecules

Which is what neurons do in order to communicate
  The axon of one neuron releases the excited
    molecules of the neurotransmitter into a microscopic
      ever-ready gap. While on the opposite of this royal
        divide, receptor molecules in the receiving molecule
          respond to the neurotransmitter by opening wide their
            channels, which let potassium and sodium ions into the cell
              If enough of these positively charged ions accumulate,
                other channels, sensitive to voltage, are tripped open
                  Speaking, on the other hand, is an individual act

Then more ions flood into the neuron causing it to fire
  sending its own signal to the next cell in line
    The brain stores memory by linking neurons
      to form new circuitry, turning up the synaptic
        volume controls by stimulating neural pathways
          in the hippocampus with high-frequency bursts
            of electricity. Give up, turn the corner
              And let all this somehow be triggered by calcium
                But that other is not an object but impulse
                  A rub of two sticks under moonlight, we need a fire

To push back the horizon of the observable universe
  as we discover galaxies and hints of galaxies
    at distances they should not be. One ten times
      more massive than the Milky Way and at least
        12 billion light years away, and beyond
          The quasars beam out their luminosity at this
            core of galaxies. Do I derive from this?
              Of course, and of course not. There is no thing
                without other things yet one thing cannot come solidly
                  from another as the edge of this writing, outside the book.

XXII

PIECES OF AN HOUR

She is roused to write on call for a performance. The poet needs summoning from mental torpor and welcomes a structure, which she creates with natural aplomb. She has also given her students the same assignment: to write everyday within the same hour in the same spot. One woman never strays from the laundry closet. John Cage is quintessential artist of this century, likely the most innovative. His "passivity," if you could call it that, both gentle & active. His work is fierce. She pays homage in a kind of twilight meditation, whatever sounds come out of her composed in this "chance" procedure to accompany an evening of his piano music, which also allows for improvisation. His work gives permission to speak of the animals inside her. She is also at a juncture with the sounds of Gertrude Stein ringing in her ear. Stein is such a man. Cage seems the androgynous alchemist. She will perform with 2 men.

preparation: on 6 different days write within the increments of one hour

dear John Cage:

=what?=
=Time me=

TIME E E E E E E E E E E E E E E E

=individual who is=
=effective=
=drama drama=
=but, with a turn of gentry pretension=
=who is=
=pattern in a great part persist=
=*was ist los?*=
=sacred gesture, utilize it=
=what—in *counting?*=
=4 minutes 33 seconds=

=patrician etiquette=

=of their family=
=daily like is built=
=pieces of an hour=
=1 the cause=
=2 the ceremony=
=minute flicker three=
=you see the inside of her plan=
=on very hour a minute is recorded to match=
=her time=
=prepare the piano=

=it is never wasted=
=meet the man in Boulder it is time=
=Cage's laugh would wake the dead=

=complex can be cursory=

=intricate palm leaf offering=
=but empirically, it is signal=

=restless, & where=
=dupe of leader=
=ritually a muted one=
=turn to dust=

=pieces of an hour=
=in which a small bolt was living=

=suspended web of significances=

=demand explication=
=undomesticated thought=

=it in motion=
=Tuesday=

=curious=

=coherent cluster=
=endurance=

....

=incomplete unfinished animals=
=who complete their selves through culture=
=through highly particular forms of it=
=Javanese, Hopi, Italian, upper class, lower, middle=
=you are on the fringes too=

=our plasticity has been remarked upon=
=but even more how dependent on=
=a certain sort of learning=
=weather, stripping, rubbing=

=attainment of this concept I tell you it is true=
=specific systems of symbolic meaning=
=beaver build a dam=
=bird you build your nest today=
=baboon organize into social groups, go do this now=
=mice mate on the basis of forms that rest on instructions=
=coded in their genes=
=they can't wait to do this=
=& evoked by patterns of external stimuli=
=physical keys inserted into organic locks=
=but women locate food, build dams=
=shelter, organize social groups, or find sexual consorts=
=under the guide of instructions=
=encoded in flowcharts and blueprints=
=moral systems, aesthetic judgments=
=ground plan of activity=
=second segment of preparations=

=fine eye for detail=
=Wednesday=

=quest: metaphysical entity=
=cultural artifact=
=me *au dessus* piano=
=chips, stones, plants=
=I want to tell you a story=
=Henry David Thoreau was one of them=
=and walked=
=*wakaru:* (to understand) means to be divided=
=*widdershins:* take the left-hand path=
=baboon you sleep now=
=I am subject that I am object=
=and took to the hills=

=I was a hidden treasure=
=& I loved to be known=
=so I created the world=
=I was a word then I hid my treasure=
=mind is outerspace piano: continuous memory=
=penumbral light=

=tiled tight=
=was words then=
=mottled=
=his thought pluck'd a string=
=strain=
=Cage=
=inverts the piano=

=1 minute away awaits a wit=
=without shuffling the debris of monolith intelligence=
=Thursday: mix, a rehearsal=
....

=minute number 2 succumbs=
=I go under=

=I fall away=
=love is strange=
=yogin please don't go=
=sing out a gut to you=
=pieces of an hour=
=await you=
=spread on a bed=
=take a shower to meet the main man=
=his day's a practice chart=
=you are flow=
=flowers of an hour=
=a piece of coffee now=
=a piece of her hair=
=voodoo is not in question=
=the cage is wide open=
=gamelan thumps your mallet=
=*ump o ah um*=
=he invited my voice=
=9:10 p.m. he invites my voice in=
(here she lies down to make a crow sound under the piano)

CAW CAW CAW CAW CAW CAW CAW

=did you say it?=
=what was it?=
=a savant's dream=
=unstudied=
=unsteady=
=no it was a crystal=
=it was a steady thing=
=it was sure=
=it was a sure thing=
=did you see them?=
=where?=
=living=
=I said it again living=
=you mean a dwell in=

=no I don't I said living=
=like take it out=
=all students: take it out=
="life" is a word=
=like I said I mean omigod yes=
=take it out=
=it was a valley=
=it was a hill-rill thing=
=it was a swell time=
=it was a holiday=
=did you say it?=
=what I said=
=I said but what I said=
=said itself so=
=& such and such got down=
=you go koan a hand=
=a knee=
=you go moan the wounded animal=
=you go down baboon=
=meet the small bird=
=you go sing a small song=
=you are nearly extinct=
=what?=
=did you say extinction=
=I did=
=I saw him pluck the silver cactus needles=
=strum=
=it was a hill-rill thing=
=it is best said & it can or can happen here=
=why=
=because they said it so=
=strumm=
=someone wanted it to happen=
=no not really but it does it does happen=
=it does it does happen it does doesn't it happen =
=it sure does=
=it is damaging to spill all over the place=

=and better not focus on any government=
=to be a damage all a place over itself=
=& wander thrust around about a similar mantra=
=it is about gaining & spending=
=it is a loss to a principle speech=
=what did you say?=
=I said but does it does happen doesn't it?=
=utter in=
=under it=
=I said it utters itself well=
=I said it well=
=I said it better than that to be a burden to=
=I was the piece of my own hour=
=got stuck=
=how?=

(here she speaks in the loudest whisper:

REVVVVVVVVVVVVVVVVVVVVVVVV ELATION)

=it was a set up=
=you set yourself up=
=pieces of an hour=
=you got small=
=you got taken in=
=you were the proxy=
=in the convent=
=you say your matins=
=evensong=
=you got made over every moment every moment I=
=let go but my heart to reality=
=what you said it=
=that's verboten, student, "reality"=
=I said it=
=what=
=that you are restless=
=that says it all suppose you sleep=

=suppose you sleep on Thursday=
=Thursdays were the days=
=of all my hope or fear=
=is it a strain?=
=is it?=
=to get dressed again=
=I said it well=
=& we were a moment & stopping=
=fish: sorry there is not enough memory=
=you are animal programmed=
=the genetics of the sonorous one=
=narrow you are mind of=
=slight like the insect & gossamer made=
=I love you when they ask for texts about America=
=I love you like under water=
=this is the assignment assignation part where=
=the dream got on stage again or was it silver screen?=
=& the animals were caged before their entrance=
=we will act the story of a transformer=
....

=it was a metal contradictory=
=it was meeting you to do lunch=
=if you could ever "do" anything=
=do a book, do moving=
=you are moving with the slower ones=
=atrophy on the machine=
=did it?=
=what=
=bounce=
=did it=
=I said it did=
=or words can do it=
=like sleep=
=he can really sleep=
=I mean he can really sleep=
=Ambrose likes it=

=what=
=to be seated and happy=
=the night was half a star, half a moon=
=half over=
=did you enter in=
=someone said about the star it was sort of impossible=
=to get as far away as that=
=but he can really really sleep=
=yogin please don't go=
=are you caged or who is not a man a codger be=
=mode of viziers=
=government names us here=
=& you are the such & such of taxes=
=5 things go on in this poem=
=can you guess what they are?=
=sustain the axis=
=what say=
=of my argument=
=what say=
=meet Friday?=
=less in admin=
=Lamartine, poet of politics, to quote=
=these times are times of chaos=
=bounded terminology=
=opinions are a scramble=
=parties are a jumble=
=the language of ideas of new ideas=
=has not been created=
=nothing is more difficult than to=
=give a good definition of oneself in religion=
=in philosophy=
=in politics=
=one feels knows lives & dies a cause=
=but can't name it=
=it is the problem of this time to classify things and men=
=the world has jumbled its catalog=
=tangent paragon=

=& tangible=
=you are suitably emended, a precious tool=
=mock realty=
=you abode here a boulder?=
=mention that one of them is time decisions=
=and the next is a mention of specific animals=
=because Gertrude abounded the cow=
=did she let owl in?=
=I rather not=
=what=
=say=
=it is to be=
=understood it is spoken=
=are you still ready=
=were you ever ready and then did it wake you up=
=your preparedness=
=I'm not sure=
=get dresses=
=you are now putting on your shoes=
=is it a form of do the meditation?=
=how you are being and inside a rule or regular=
=space play with my=
=dresses=
=for they are the new form of me=
=I let my liberty go=
=she's not a caged animal he said she was=
=that's long ago=
=the Himalayas=
=or some other form=
=the composer is=
=holding your hand on this one=
=then he lets go=
=what sounds are the sounds you speak of=
=what sounds mount the podium=

=the space is cleared=
=we have a kind of non-pew revival=

=a performance is a cage=
=I will lie now under his instrument=
=I will be under his instrument=
=I will mount the embankment=
=I will be ready to rise=
=how can I show you my piece of a mind=
=& let it rip=
=I will show you it from down here=
=crouch=
=like the animal you are always being=
=need a worry=
=I was not afraid of being an intimate boundary=
=Cage, who is a man woman not=
=Caged, who=
=I ask you=
=I ask you=
=I ask you=
=who is not=
=I asked you=
=remains under piano silent=
=magnet imitation=
=Eric Satie=
=he was a piece in my hour=
=whirred=
=ears took off their delicate sheaves=
=I am the sleeves of his ear tonight=

....

=dear John Cage:=
=the world is a more humming place we thank you for it=
=I listened to the traffic lights=
=I will never get used to television=
=Can you always be a man or nun=
=what is the action most diverse in all=
=the Zen of world=
=could I place a gesture here=
=it is "think of a gesture," the game=

=what hands, arms to hold you=
=my son=
=is it the increment of time I thought of=
=do animals think like this or will they never perform=
=I am asking for more time=
=I'm used to getting my way=
=I set the stage for her return=
=in the fourth place you are trying hard to lie down again=
=how many surfaces in an hour?=
=how many times do you think?=
=how many colors do you see of an hour=
=it was increment of 10 it was increment of 10=
=it was increment of 10 then double that=
=what is your thinking track it my dear home an hour=
=trying to stay with the fleet increment=

=wed the pace to the bon mot=
=how good is it?=
=it is very good=
=how limit how you plan to me=
=It is swell, it is well=
=how speed your way on?=
=10 minutes by 10 is the key to mystery=
=what master do you wanna be or control a=
=clock tower, master time=
=I would an Aztec be=
=who does this=
=what is your sense of time?=
=had it out of hand=
=it is a notion Claud Brown had=
=it is a long silence=
=Cage had it once=
=night arrived=
=night of Saturn=
=thought to himself a way to dance around it=
=pluck an untuned string just one=
=the reverb fell throughout the cell=

=did it travel=
=how far=
=let me strike a gong or shake this thing=
=let it be known the cage is open=
=& a terrible sound is loosed on the world=
=crack the page, let out from under self=
=the body sings=
= stand up=
=let them be three=
=let them be three=
=the men and me=
=let them be three=
....

=caged, who is a man not caged?=
=who is a woman not whirrrr=
=what is the date in a library=
=out of time=
=a clock, an hour, time is early=
=white against white=
=engage=
=on an hour: clock whirr=
=a man had an idea=
=that put him inside sound=
=the woman has the woman hasn't =
=the woman has the woman hasn't=
=the woman has the woman hasn't the woman has the woman hasn't=
=a conversational propriety=
=hazard, he calls to me=
=increments of 10 of 10 of 10 of 10 of 10 of 10=
=screen slated slants highlit by=
=backlit by foam of her ceiling=
=I will write and then stop=

=I will write & then stop=
=I will write & then stop=
=& to end on the daylight of the sun=

=rip rip rip rip rip rip rip=
=in the cave=
=the three-legged sister=

=white toward what hoop or blind=
=blond who is not caged=
=the piano is not a planet but has=
=a planned network=
=a "c," a high C laughs=
=a rub against book=
=rub against cock somewhere there's a universe=
=could be tenored alternative=
=could be attentive or tense=
=lover leaves again=

=what animal beckoned you here=
=what mantra was heard?=

(chant & crow sounds into piano here)

OM AING GRING CLING CHAMUNDA YEI VIJAY

AW AW AW AW

=how many l's or leaves=
=in the doorway=
=how many leaves of an hour?=
=levered, light tread=
=enter the hour clocked upon a page=

(close—slam—a door)
(she is lying under the piano here &
hits its hard black underbelly 3 times)

KNOCK KNOCK KNOCK

XXIII

YOU REDUCE ME TO AN OBJECT OF DESIRE

She questions as ever the male godhead, but "Fat Almighty," an avatar of Allah, proves soft. Long Armageddon dream (backdrop is war) segues into an acceptance of her power as twin of the male and perhaps the better artist because she does write down her unflinching vision. And is willing to love her enemy. The boy teases & calls her back from her role as sober Superwoman. The final cri di coeur and deception of the Doctor is a subtle reclamation of territory, her own body.

————————————touch a nerve

————————————ma sha' Allah

————————————lamp light the "sinner"
————————————————goad on

————————————Father: incline thine ear
————————————————————to hear of
————————————————furies, spent of father's blood

————————————son spent of mother's blood

————————————& hero: a dusky weapon

————————————to be sprung in wrath

——incline an ear

—none give him welcome

—why?

—incline the ear to hear the intellect rule her

—madness, sudden panic, for she is twin

—how did she get so "even"?

        —in the night

—to hear how he clamors for blood, but she is smart

        —in the name of the land he rages on   *Allah Allah*

        —to name it his name but she steals his words

        —to slay a demon in the same night

        —in his calling she steals his sex

—& he becomes his own head (for he has a woman's heart)

—in mixing of the wine (which is forbidden)

        —drink offers a grace   —yet curses

        —unseen unseen curses shall bar him from himself

—but she will enter the temple dishonored

—but mightily empowered

        —warrior with irresistible cause

—(such were her oracles)

(Cumaean Sybil wrote oracles on leaves scattered by the wind)

        —Fat Almighty with flavor of Zeus was kind of enemy too

—she dressed the part of part-animal to slaughter Fat Almighty

—she became Tramena, a hybrid

        —draw near Fat Almighty with the bleat of god
—a goat to slay, got slew
—a cutting of deals
—Shaman Goat Man nervous about western medicines to America Sud

—incline the ear of thou who favors us, Fat Almighty

        —Let righteousness walk into battle! she said . . .

            —Allahu Akbar!

—teach me O father the marginal life before Fat Almightly gobbles us whole

    —how by word or action to

      —to live to fight
           —day charged into night

      —how to live the female night sky

      —when the flames devour the flesh &
each boy child addresses his tribute of lamentation to the mother

      —how to live when naught's here but evil

        —undo a sentience out of anger

        —as sentence not stand in doom

or as suppliant not stand in doorway blocking light
as suppliant voice intact
as suppliant claim the social security payment
as suppliant a pinch of salt to flavor the bowl
as suppliant implore sanctuary
as suppliant rehearse the logics: what did the German say?
all the philosophies won't help then supplicate all the more?
"For a murderous blow let a murderous blow be struck."
as suppliant: peaceful load for the house of Atreus
as suppliant, may these lips be moved in song

as Masai warriors get circumcized, dress like women, paint faces
    & shoot at the diminutive birds with little bows & arrows

                            they say

"so strong in hope a woman's heart, whose purpose is a man's"

....................................a gap in my life . . .
....................................I was a mutant, but . . .
....................................a gold tooth in a mouth proclaiming
....................................a gap in life, but . . .Mafioso stayed out of here
....................................Yet silhouette of a High Priestess had her own mind too . . .
....................................Mosiac too, I was a reminder, but . . .
....................................The hair of a pearl in—whose?—heart
....................................Or memory of Keats's tomb in Rome
....................................Remember my flagellation on the Spanish Steps?
....................................But, is texture true? But? Is it?
....................................I had a memory toward the Editorial Board
                            whose life attitudes were not sound
....................................& Yeats's burial place (ah dear dead poets)
....................................I worshipped all of them, diamonds, opals, guns . . .
....................................Honored all the poets
....................................Picture a distributor cap with pinions stuck out
....................................Pinions stuck out?
....................................Little electrical nodes inside of it
....................................I know what you're saying sort of
                            but not exactly a description
....................................Friend said this
....................................Then Anne said:
....................................Feels good in my hand
....................................in the chaos of my life
....................................Feels good in any laboratory of desire
....................................& back in the hand, holding the reins of desire
....................................I was a truant, but . . .

I approach my family home on Macdougal Street in disguise—purple dress, yellow beret, hair dyed black—to find another costumed stranger at the door—either a black transvestite or woman dressed in some red clothes of mine. Not clear. There's a note from my mother saying "Please help your brother do, or write out X as we used to help you." My brother Carl is sick. Mounting uneasiness & speed inside me. I notice that water is rising at the window, although there is none in the street. The basement is unfamiliar & stranger who observes me like a cat is obviously more "in possession" here. I'm here simply to take messages & pick up "assignments." He/she waves goodbye at the door & this is humorous. I turn the corner at King Street but then abrupt right uptown presumably "on assignment." The streets indicate it's the end of the world, finally. The few people I pass are not themselves, in varying degrees of disarray & stress, and garbed in odd attempts at disguise. I pass my brother Mark who says: I knew this, I came dressed like this (Bald Zennie); isn't it funny? Streets are made of wood, buildings papier-mâché, like a Red Grooms set. I'm walking on a tremendous theatrical set of 6th Avenue, created by a mysterious subliminal "will" to give the illusion of New York City. I'm to go to Madison Square Garden. Taxi?

Old Pennsylvania Station but miles underground. Bigger but populated with a multitude of sentient beings dressed in *extremis.* Nurse, Eskimo, cowboy costumes. Heavenly host? Some folks decked out as animals. A whole panoply of ill-fitting disguises—fake-identity-desire "covers." A lot of gesturing, & multilingual talk & bickering. A stage show is in progress in a theatre reminiscent of the Globe, that combines with a "people's stage" (Red China?). In contrast to the colorfulness of the lively gesticulating mob, the Globe set is extremely drab. It depicts a dark subway station. A huge pulsating boulder sits on the tracks. I know for a fact that there are at least a dozen actors inside the boulder costume making it come alive and it's destined to burst although I may never see this happen. There's a *paseo* along the apron of the stage & people must pass in coupled formation. As my lover (he's a Marine) & I pass we pause to assess the action on the stage & the couple behind us frisks us & holds a gun to lover-Marine's head. But it's only plastic, shoots stage blood. We abruptly turn to catch glint of metal, the other alloy, under fluorescent light. Someone shouts a warning, we duck as machine guns fire on the unsuspecting crowd. The "RPF" (The Rabidinal Police Force) descends. There is a bloodbath as the spectacle of color flies apart, horrible too as the assimilated "people" writhe in pain.

I crawl over the bodies of rubber, papier-mâché, down, & straw that are bleeding in the cool metallic light. Is this the new Israeli War?

Wander to the arched mouth of a cave or hospital waiting room & peer out into the darkness. There appears to be a New Delhi style taxicab awaiting me with a "couple" inside. Polish. Czech? *"Vse je v poradku."* I get in. The driver is smiling idiotically, machine is running he'll do business. Wherever we are going takes forever. Multilayered tunnels, constant U-turns, up & down ramps over "bulges" (artificial mountain suburb terrain). Couple is discussing "sex change." I realize I'm regressing, getting smaller more girl-like—but I'm doing it in self-defense & it's external as inside I'm feeling stronger & it's like show me more, "ok I can take it what next?" We get to another waiting room just like first but it's completely empty (realize it's the same one but cleaned up)— everything outside car is dank & dark & damp & dark again—riding through fungus vegetable world—as before there's water rising at the window. Finally drive onto lighted tableau scene of business-as-usual Emergency Ward World. Dioramas of bodies being carried on stretchers by some earnest young men sorta like TV flat slightly sinister celluloids. Intense young doctor. He lifts his arm. He turns his head. He smiles. He studies a chart. He is being paged. He has a name like "Dusty." "Rusty?" Now he is really concerned. Someone named Sue comes in. Things look different. They're outside in a park now. Cut back to his eyes. Are these eyes to be seen through clearly I wonder? I wonder.

Now the Czechoslovakian couple is again discussing "sex change." "It's all in the range." I'm still regressing—passing back through puberty. I'm anxious to get back to the workaday world again, find a telephone. I step out of the cab & get caught once again in a barrage of machine-gun fire. Taken prisoner, I'm surly with my "Captivators." One of the automatons will make a deal if I sleep with him/her. Won't. Lois, a prison manicurist, befriends me & comments on my dyed hair & exotic looks. I realize I'm not really looking like "myself," which is not only mine but everybody's problem, & wonder if they have any control over this. I'm growing down to 9 years old by now (call me Bice Portinari) & the younger I get the more pain & suffering I feel. I want to eat my own heart. I put away my yellow beret (a mere "childish thing"). I want to call William Burroughs, my Dream Teacher, he'll know what's going on. There's a newspaper, "The Nerve-Ending News," that says the incident at the Terminal has been "sewn up" & those that got away are the real victims. There are other prisoners as well, students, & those who have not had sex changes yet, and they dance as they move, beautifully. A dance of death. *De Muerte.* They weave in & out of long ballrooms guarded by garish red-skinned automatons. May an automaton have skin? There's a decision to bring in mustard gas as there is no more blood left to spill. The gas comes in blue tanks & there are some Commedia del Arte masks too. Everyone has to go to the hospital.

He, the lover said, "you are the nightmare & the dream."

I dream this way & give advice to the tribe in the morning:
young men, throw away the rifle & lance
take back your lasso of the reindeer herdsmen
your harpoon of the seal hunter
the spirits will help you
your pronunciation will change
in a small voice you will nurse the children

& to the panel I say:
I will tell you about the Buddhist approach to cause & effect. There is no first cause, there is no final cause. All the factors we observe in any situation have arisen because of the subtle influence of many factors. Cause & effect when observed closely go back & back. We do not discover anything solid. "Egolessness" has existed from beginningless time. Conditioned by such & such, this will happen. Out of the bowels of your realization, your spontaneous utterance, your poem, is the lion's roar. This view denies eternalism, this view denies nihilism.

As a cultural worker one needs to have all the skills one has a bent for. This takes discipline. Sharpen your attention. Get the facts straight, don't color them. You don't own them, you are mere vessel for lion's roar. Question the billions it takes to re-invent the plutonium trigger warhead wheel at Los Alamos, just one example. Are you too addicted to fossil fuel? Investigate the effects of burning of wastes. Learn how to write a citizen's complaint. Be accurate, articulate, awake, and always move gracefully with your subtle sense of humor to navigate the dark passage. Seek out the like-minded. You will be a community of eyes. And you will create the world in your heart.

There is a text called Memphite Theology that dates back to the 2nd or 3rd millennium. The theology describes a cosmogony according to which Ptah, the local god of Memphis & his emanation Atum, were the primal beings. Ptah created the world in his heart, the seat of his mind, & actualized it through his tongue, the act of speech. This resonates with the Platonic & Christian "logos"—the Word. Thoth (father of Isis)—Dhwty (Thoth Thrice greatest)—had a role in this cosmogony as the heart of Ptah, Ptah's tongue being Horus. There is an association of the heart with the intellect of which Thoth was the especial master. In other theologies, he is the inventor of writing, originator of mathematics, magician, and master of the divine act of "speech," which allows the gods to converse with each other & with men . . . you know your job, men.

Dear Hermes Trismegistus: you could play all the roles. You could be the hidden god, demiurge, Holy Ghost. You could be the messenger of all the little people. You could be prophet Idris. You could be mercury. You could be father of all the gods, you could be *intellectus,* light of my mind.

I thank you, I thank you

Dear Anne W & the Idea of Naropa Institute,

I was on my way, on my way! I've been sending you clippings & haiku as a warning, your undercover poet. Remember a couple of years ago (I've been through so much since then maybe it was three (or four?)). Ray Manzarek & M. McClure were to teach a workshop. I was on my way, on my way, on my way to find form. But . . . something happened. The video police kicked down the walls, broke into my bedroom my composing room. Kidnapped, drugged and brainwashed me. They had me eating garbage on Venice beach, dragged me off to L.A. County jail. Had me hallucinating on a combination of drugs and what I think was virtual reality. So they kicked their way into my brain too. I got an elementary lecture on segregation, oil power, power, power, 10,000 dollars, power and power. I'm in a psych unit right now, the stuff is still in my head. I feel I'm being held down by Lilliputians. I hope this is not permanent.

Be Bip Be Bow Bow
Be Bip Bip Be Bow Bow

X. X.

Prosim, kde je posta?

All the men ride my mind
Yet death is death
Fire is about that high
My dear men are always in sight
Deliver me, one says, you are a witch
I am Hermes's daughter Isis
I ask the cards & more
Just the way I go into a museum
nobody knows when my cards started
& I also ask my dictionary
which rescues me, which saves me
It knows me
I'm well dressed with opera glasses
I walk through narrow streets 4,000 years old
I rise from a field of Mummies
I talk with my ghosts—again, again
My angels are ropes
My angels are clay
My incense lamp will clear the mood of Europe
I throw the light around
Fire gets wild in me
My hearts pounds in my pocket
These objects make me what I am
What am I?
I make the people important in my life
They are the other India
They are the other Arabia
I enter my lists of friends
onto the shelf in my car
I am linden
I am oil
I ride an orange car
What am I?

Dear Anne:

As a kid I remember identifying, the earliest I can recall, with Donald Duck, and now I realize this was probably because he was the classic imaginative fuck-up, never gave the lie to the adult male myth we were brought up to admire, never had a job, got by somehow, had amazing adventures, never took maturity seriously, even when the nephews put him down for his lack of serious plans abilities, etc (in fact they were more adult in outlook than he was, what with their Junior Woodchuck book of rules etc.) And then I suppose I had the usual peer-group film heros, cowboys mostly at that point, but I doubt even then I thought of them as any kind of possible future model for myself, just that furious inviolability I felt for a few moments coming out of the theatre.

<blockquote>
blast of air
Clark in love with celluloid
</blockquote>

"You accept the language that is spoken around you and that you speak."

"You deal with it in writing."

deal

"The way you write will reflect what you think those words do—what effects they have, what effects they can be permitted to have—how you can change the effects they are known to have to what you want them to have."

deal

"You assume that your readers understand the language."

deal

"You can assume the existence of a large, widely accepted set of rules. You can also not assume or accept it

that the language be fair, that it hold you

fast, that the cross it bears exempts the woman
$\qquad$ She rides through the poem on
$\qquad$ villains, brothers, saints, deities
$\qquad$ they speed her on

like a *diwes, dyeus,* a god-machine
$\qquad$ out on the street again
$\qquad$ long trip moving toward what *intellectus*

blast this air

$\qquad$ (almost closer)

$\qquad$ rehearse the deity-part, tell about the
hospital

$\qquad$ where the twins
$\qquad$ rule
$\qquad$ the
$\qquad$ cosmos

& take an artist as their queen

The cold order loosens
The straps, they are heavy, they were dark, loosen
His head is held up high on the post, a veritable herm
How gnarly, take it down after tonight
It ties to what you were saying: "loosen, loosen"
A clench was open as he stroked the grisly hand
Held upon, loosened & lighter
Inner heat is bursting
No one needed a radiator
Not needed, hut doors
The moon is getting to "you"
He-Man arise in a prying sense
All four doors swung wide
Come in to see the light
"You" too
The insect kingdom will be out soon

Welcome them
The twin misses the twin
It's in the air
It's in the air
I missed you, twin
Love was my troubadour
I was that troubadour
I was never-at-peace-in-love
(Keep a little picture of desire in the rafters)

For what got clearer was architecture, was my power, & that if you kept coming back around section by section you'd reach my ultimate protest, which reduced me to an object of desire.

(Not.)

You reduce me to an object of desire. But I come back again. Never reject anything. You reduce me to an object of desire. Never reject anyone. You slave under the illusion of every beauty mark, every defect to catch me unawares, off guard. You control the arrangement of room, of meal, of conversation, ideas come to you. The fixation is complete in its optimism, in its colonial offerings. I am the little colony. Who will save me? Who inhabits my oil wells, my missionary zeal, my quixotic poetry? Who indeed surfaces to take my hand & walk me across the desert and then across the plains. Then we climb the mountain. I'll lead you to the ocean. I know the way. You will be baptized in my ocean. In my fire. Who will live to tell the story? You try—reduce me to desire. You enter my tent. The lamp is extinguished by wind. Father is a kind of wind and you are his son. You know your business. But I am twin. The earth is a bed and grave. I am calm again. I was the vessel for his wind, just tell me that. It was a torrent inside me, tell me that. Just tell me that. Give me that

OM VAJRASATTA SAMAYA

a vow to light the mind

        —are you satisfied?

                    —just tell me that

—& that you are

                    —a satisfied one

                    —(*beyond monotheism*)

—Mother, guess what?
—What?
—Chicken butt
—Ambrose!
—Shut up, mamma, shut up
   I've got to hear the score
—Funny voice he's got
—Mom, sports announcers have to be antsy pantsy
   Mom, you want them in a slow voice saying
   "Heeeee maaaaade a baaaaasket OOOOOO joy . . .
   Let's sing Kumbaya???"
—Heh look, Scottie Pippin soaks up a play
—Jordan shot a 3 pointer & made it
   But Drexler can't shoot worth a ——of ——
   My grandmother can shoot better'n that!
—What's the "hustle board?"
—Ohhhh Mom
   Look, mamma, there.
—Where?
—Chicken hair
—Bulls lead 82 to 78
—No! Go Blazers. O, sweet.
—"Let their defense ignite the offense"
   "Scottie Pippin is now 0 for 3 from the line"
—Gnarly
—See somebody's fist in the screen?
—Awesome. I mean down to the wire
—You heard the man "This 4th quarter is going to be inneresting."
—Sweet!

Finally I needed to tell you about the trip to the hospital:

Wrath that could be queen not doubt solves it like surgeon whose knife is Himalayan whose knife aberrants you. Twist down. Crumble, go bleak under blade, enter his doctoring charnel ground right now. Metal, or edge to be born to, blind too. They cover my eyes with an antiseptic plastic mask. Hospital sky blue. All wrath tenses blind to boundary. Space—is it?—or "just space." What jackal lingers there & knife turn again to drink ventricle. Metal to bone. What soft (was it?) flesh got made love to just a mite before & sings its pleasure cry: to kill to cure. It lies on any edge you care a mention. Break sigh blood ink settle restitute mores, your custom is a clutch. Hand (no jewelry) swings up to beat him back. Face (no makeup allowed) grimaces & twists its smile to contort him further. Dear surgeon-doctor-god I have not really sinned. And the Arab girl's tumor (as recorded by Roman annalist Diodorus Siculus) bursts open to reveal male genitals. She changes her name, dons men's clothes, & joins the cavalry. Don't take this breast. Underneath: a man. How many times O doctor trick blood sheet money leave the room. Send the bill. Can I go. Send the bill tomorrow can I go. Right now send it I want to go. Let me go. Die a death. Itemized, charged. I go now. Unstrap me. Let me go. Exist on cold slab who I called back "ancestor! ancestor!" who called wrought steel surgical a war. I cry to my ancestors & then I cry to them. Revenge. The maritime Koryak took ordinary stones instead of wives, dressed them in clothes, & took them to bed to caress. I dress the cold stone in the hospital gown, place it quietly on the operating table, and leave the room. To blunt the knife.

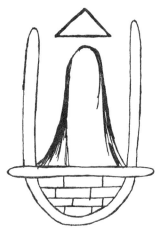

BOOK II

Guardian
& Scribe

BOOK II
~ Guardian & Scribe ~

I will hide in my song
So that I may take kisses from your lips as you sing it

—Anonymous Qawwal

*

The Master says: "He who succeeds in leaving this clime enters the clime of the Angels, among which the one that marches with the earth is a clime in which the terrestrial angels dwell. These angels form two groups. One occupies the right side: they are the angels who know and order. Opposite them, a group occupies the left side: they are the angels who obey and act. Sometimes these two groups of angels descend to the climes of men and genii, sometimes they mount to heaven. It is said among their number are the two angels to whom the human being is entrusted, those who are called 'Guardians and Noble Scribes'—one to the right, the other to the left. He who belongs to the right belongs to the angels who order; to him it falls to dictate. He who is to the left belongs to the angels who act; to him it falls to write."

—Avicenna (Ibn Sina)

*

And the mountainous-minded Greeks could speak
of time as a river and step across it into Persia, leaving the pain
at home to be converted into statuary. I adore the Roman copies.

—Frank O'Hara

*

Ooo-wee, mountain, you're rocky all the way . . .

—Billie Holliday

Guardian & Scribe: Prologomena to Exile

She wants Book II sounded as a gong protracting her charge "to blunt the knife." Her Sprechstimme rhapsody to the tune of male energy would turn a corner. She stole it, precious time of it—the time it took to it—in guarded night. Guarded her poem-mind-ear then scribed it down, sleepless. How to *act* what you *know*? (She is *dichter,* female *dichter/in,* speaker & one dictated to, and a dictator of sound & meaning) *Do it.* Carve a poem out of a stem of nights. Image of celestial totem pole. Traditionally, as in Northwest Coast tradition, a totem pole establishes the *past* in the *present,* and the accompanying performance—dance, chant, mask returns someone in the present to his or her *primordial past.* The book might be her pole, a personal world tree, witness to all vivid & lived events, the enactment of it *(read this book)* would be her performance. Each section of the poem has a "face," a consummate mask. She remembers how we dress up the world neurotically, project our masks onto "other" to scare ourselves. One choice: the terra firma of war. Take up the weapon again: sword is railing stylus. The other is *grip of love.* That would be abiding thrust. All is full of the sap of Jove, Virgil's quip, but . . . indeed a challenge fraught with feministo irony. Now she'd call as well on female allies to join the throng of male voices inside her own. And it would be elegaic tone. Several people dead. One sick. A sharp turn. Topological maps had appeared demanding where to have gone next. She'd deliberated. Studied the lore of exile. Juxtaposed Indonesia, Mexico, India, troubadour Europe. There's a direct bus from Boulder to Cheyenne every morning. The boy says you may buy fireworks at the Wyoming border. (She hides out in New York.) The dream of the smallest increments of money the man exchanged for a peso where suddenly she was in Mexico buying postcards. Terra-cotta currency the shape of homunculi. The world traffics in human bodies, and body parts. Not to mention animal bodies and animal body parts (the Gobi Desert bear just one example). And a postcard she spotted pictured a girl-child-doll inside a luxury car, with shiny "red skin" upholstery decked out with sophisticated metallic communication apparatuses. From the hood of the car sprouted antlers, vines, other accoutrements of jungle/forest, primal artifacts for the dream. The caption of the card read "Lost American." She's not that, but there's a struggle, too.

I am a citizen of the world. (Diogenes)

Intergenerational. Not Armageddon.

Guardian & Scribe is the way into a propitious optimistic exile. Counter-poetics. Subliminal. Guard well the language flame, the tribe's demand for land, now dream-land, and how its glyphs are carved in the depths of a cave, on the bark of an extant tree, incised in stone, on tortoise shell, on vellum-skin of a beast, encoded in brain systemic, in the memory of this or any costly machine. Keep plugging away at a salvation-poetry, lock in before the power is exhausted. Phallic thrust? In Tantric Buddhist practice the Wisdom Body or Jnanasattva descends to confirm or "un-trip" the projected visualization, which is called the Samayasattva, the "coming together" or "sacred vow." A psycho-physical union. The Jnanasattva is basically the adept's own sanity, which possesses the Samayasattva projection or aspiration. What you have only imagined up until now becomes active, real. Performance is the point at which the two meet. Your projected aspiration & the confirmation of it are at the same juncture. You crossed the limen. Operating smoothly now. Reenact any premillennial holocaustal dream so that you never forget where you come from. Out of the human . . . Ah, you can function! You can make those animal sounds!

By exile is meant the need to make & act art outside anyone else's agenda or dogma. Market economy model is oblique & obsolete. This is another example of ego's self-destructive game. Create your own country: to make the energies dance. Then rearrange the chairs, books, molecules, garden, tend lively phones & phonemes. Scramble the parts writ on buses, planes, on random scraps, on top of newsprint, sung into a machine, screamed into the void—now gather herein to create ongoing orderly chaos. *Iovis* is ten years inscribed so far. Survival is precarious, and navigating other countries, languages, realms, lovers requires skills of cunning & desire. Thus one writes in continuing practice of and in antithetical preparation for disinheritance, betrayal, loss of power. Reclaim all these here in particular language. Standing by . . . singing over . . . dancing upon . . . an exile's word.

Full Moon, 9 September 1995, Nueva York

I

SO HELP ME SAPPHO

"may you find sleep on a soft girlfriend's breast"

The poet continues a long meditation on the nature of male energy & its attendant strife & delight. She admires the strong-mindedness of Sappho, as evinced by a cutting, penetrating poetry, & her ability to embody the unnerving negatively capable slogan of "both both," whatever her actual sexuality, with great aplomb. And if she did in fact run a school, all the better to compare this own writer's current situation in which she instructs poetics students to create long complex collages, made up out of the fragments of a dream, fragments of the utterances of ancients, investigative poetics, translation, and other sundries of the art. What is the comparison? Are we doing this, dear students, in the service of Aphrodite? Adonis? Beatrice? Mistress Language? Or to make sense of our fragmented world in which the mind is forever spinning & buzzing through various dark then brilliant language realms? And concurrently in the business of being antennae to the horrific reports from various fronts: Bosnia, the Acquired Immunodeficiency Syndrome battlefield, issues of insurrection & of gun control. Dante enters first, as frequently he must, to claim attention, and as reminder, through the auspices of his useful ars poetica, La Vita Nuova, that we are "making" writing out of the world, out of the imagination, in a new speech, a "sweet new" (rude) tongue. How it will sound could wake up many an ignorant sleeper. Sestina embedded within this text, an homage to the bard Florentine's mastery of that particular form. As in Book I, the poet honors (stomps on) distant Greeks & their mythic wars yet further wants her poem to soar with the wonderful tantric conundrum of recombinant masculine & feminine energies, which shift & burn though many lifetimes. The Kalachakra, the many-armed-&-headed deity, is summoned in a five-day Buddhist ceremony & initiation that inducts one into a study of the nature of time. She dreams of this event in the context of an old friend lost now, and of her lover, whose sensitivity to the wild nature of the feminine is an inspiration to keep her stamina going in this exhaustive investigation. Finally, she conjures modernist painter Philip Guston's sense of Muse. His late work, the comic & grotesque eidolons of most trenchant imagination, seem apt in a contemporary landscape of paranoid KKK-like militias & western civilization's detritus. Francesco Clemente has this power too; she sees (of his) a floating head & it is the consciousness that sings like a poet's. A contemporaneous dance between now & then, Sappho is an active presence, as is H.D., in a writer's imagination.

Lofty teacher had
put an end to his argument,
and was looking intently into my face,

if "I"
seemed satisfied

                              (ho!)

and I,
whom a new thirst was yet tormenting,
was silent outwardly, and within said:
"Perhaps the
too great questioning
I make irks him."

I was Dante's Hag

with dreams of a siren adorning my skirts

& he wrote—

"when the geomancers see their Fortuna Major, rising in the East, before the
    dawn, by a way
                          which short time remains dark to it,

there came to me in a dream, a stuttering woman with eyes asquint,
and crooked on her feet, with
maimed hands, and of sallow hue"

& he wrote—

"I gazed upon her; and, as the sun comforted
the cold limbs which night weighs down, so my look
made ready

her tongue, and then set her full straight in short time,
and her pallid face even as love wills did
colour"
& I translated

When I had my tongue thus loosed, I began to sing

& I sang
        "I am the sweet Siren,

who leads mariners astray in mid-sea,
so full am I of pleasantness to hear

I turned Ulysses from his wandering way with my song,
      and whoso liveth with me rarely departs,
so wholly do I satisfy him."

And Sis, I said to her my great Muse
and Sis, I said
    I sought
the wild animal
And dared of love
vague for vestigial desire
a spare
sparse
wheel?
through woods, dark
ermined
ebbed
singing "Quel foco é morto"
I sang, "Quel foco é morto"
but genius weak
in that new age
the new style
came, altered
armed with rhymes
& was alive with fire
considering men
considering women
who "were" the warriors?
They wore "warrior," a brave word
& could they both
resound in that name or frame?
This was very Greek to me
one, a huntress
another a hearth-maker
a third avenging
and the men were loving

& going to do battle
But mothers are weepers
& cry out for the young deity
& beat their breasts
& they can find solace in the
touch of women too
who understand one another
intuitively
hennaed over & break
like waves
those words
over stone
a firm rejection of prettiness, Kyprian

        may she not find you harsh
or younger hag
no occasion to brag of it,
an erotic power holds over
a tongue
love's speech
franker than any modern
        woman could permit
Thus sing for her
how women loving women
       is truth not ruse,
lucent dew,
        milk-white longing,
a holy tortoise shell
made instrument made song
a pledge, a doorway,
       a rite-to-sleep-by,
       a tear a god might shed,
a hyacinth of bitter light,
       qualities of other lights,
& moans from out the bed
         & torchlight too
(touching her!)
a banquet
(Aphrodite, please come, I beg you)

a thigh gone wild
a farm girl lifting her skirt
or me saying
"I cannot work the loom"
for love of her beauty
come, darling, moist one
I will taste your flower, the white city—

Can you forget in our poetry
where lovemaking was
sharp
& loosened my limbs?
we did many wise
things & spoke
together, now
when Adonis dies
we shriek
& tear our dresses
we cry out in a dream
& pray the night last
twice as long

*

got love back a second time

   how thoroughly occasional
we cannot know
the precise secret of the accent,
            the *tonos*
but
the bright ribbon reminds
bite my tongue   not to explode
& take a place
around the
altar
do I still long for my virginity?
Hymen! Hymen!
It never left me, girls.
lay out

soft pillows for your body . . .

& yet
she is subjugated before a father
    subjugated before a brother
before a lover
    a son speaks

dear momma who probes in our bags & boxes for papers that aren't really hers / who kicks me out of the kitchen so she can talk / who talks / who writes in a Powerbook / who drives a Volvo and adds chile to most of her dishes / who beats her little boy with broom handles / who demands some savvy / who sneezes in spring & buys sheets of stamps / who folds the day into many hours / whose brother slept in a drawer / who has great quantities in the trunk of her car / who saw a Queen Angel under the sea / who wears scarves of many colors / who dresses up for all sorts of occasions / who likes to travel to exotic places / who is a happy mother

Tried a hand, he was great at it, cold, torn, speech. A lot of talk, lateral spin. She, the other one, a creature rapt longer than space in attention, treats the night as warm as comforting. A wand, read *sceptre,* old dying grace or place strummed a measure of quality, speed, tension, glut. And the world market would put up a glut for her gentrification, dress torn. Don't walk there in another's frail grace, don't walk there where a motor could spin out of control, don't summon the wrong kind of warmth like murderer's breath on a body chaste and rapt in gauze, a chador, a holy veil. Why motion, what tension, why spit and thrust? Truck roars by, rapt in headgear or hard line I wasn't aware of, wasn't glutted enough on bad news, wasn't warmed over enough to sing of a marriage bed, Jove's grove, maidenhead torn. Wasn't fierce enough for him to get off of me in Bosnia in cold thicket's spin, crying *mercy* in my own religion, crying Allah's hard grace. What about doing it, revenge too subtle a grace period, demilitarized zone, war rapt in no just cause, no mustached force, never positive spin, and he, a doctor, was arguing point of view of brainwashing, propaganda glut. Not old smile-rivalries anymore, but black jealousies, shuddering tremors to tear, to tear the curtain down. Torn. Of stripe but what of it? Loyalty? What cries the infant who has "seen it all: but warm me, warm me!" A nature of our paralysis, of our lukewarm scream alarms the tabloid reader, and she suspects basic political carriage's grace has gone awry. Was book a carrier of old psychic pain wrapped tight as coiled knot in brain, genesis old disputes war-torn handwritten beyond countryside? beyond borders? A bridge crossed over, thug's glutinous sex-perversion, his head you want to cut it off &

spin & spin & spin & spin & spin & spin outta here, out of whatever hell's hottest, where no one cares, where world's grace is cheap, where no one is watching the show, watching how pain builds on pain. The Ottoman Empire gloats no more over rich spoils held tight. What conquering holy rapture could hold sway in valley so desperate, so torn? I ask. She is broken. He is torn. They are perpetually wrapt in pain, no end to gluttony of genocide and its spins, absence of grace the torn worn flame-land.

Le Fevre who was mother
mired in a kind of rant-box
co-congealed
like a huge knot
lambasted
a simple folk
a civilized action
This was an excuse
accused of "turning Sapphic"
in her seventies
a logic to frustration with men
who dares to be different
Albigensian ethos
got sent off as a prisoner might
heretical
got sent off
awfully strange
got sent off
the trees, the land . . .
got sent
under someone's cold eye
got sent off
but wanted to go of his own accord
got sent up
prison, prison all the way
what was sent?
his suit of clothes, his criminal mind
got sent up for petty larceny
got sent off
his boat disappearing, Morocco this time?
(I was reading *The Life of Jean Genet*)

got sent
it was overdue
we were all waiting
expel, exile, export
expire not quite yet
nor die of raging fever
skin bloodied
didn't cut it
tempered by a sinister plan
married to a Frenchwoman
forest, to burn, to burn
wooded down
hooded down
bedded down
ashes she didn't get to sift through
his ashes
but I bought a little metal box
for the ashes of
John Marvin Waldman,
as the stars are my witness,
& sat in the chapel
of the Ascension
with the
ashes of Frances LeFevre Sikelianos Waldman
mumbling Om Tara Tutth Tara Ture Soha
a matrix
a discipline to be
Grace in her name
but obstacle
her naught legacy
Christ's Science was a mother
lobbies for medicine, but
No
No
No
Lobbies for a hearing
but bodily ascension
really not possible
& swayed by fire

Nan, nuncle
a song nay marry
a song she wore like a wimple
A war
Where do you come from?
A war
And you?
Come from a war
You too?
A war . . .
& what
is your name?
War, grace, wood
fever
of fevers it's made
He called me Walnut
"a foreign nut for trade"
for travel
one of the tribe of Volcae
who occupied southern Gaul
Anna, she's a small coin
a 16th of a rupee
Let her be spent
got sent, the other sex, to war
& she would live to think in war
approval ranks ambition
got sent
she was dreaming of men
got sent to war
she was dreaming of guns
got spent
one night with you
was dreaming of women
this was the part where Zeus is angry
Zeus is a gun, Zeus is a joke
& you may be dreaming of religious cults
but this is another century, babe
got sent but wanted to go to war
exiled like Dante, got sent

his mind in a bardo of Florentine intrigue
& if you could have a conversation with anyone in time
who would she be?
Dear Aphrodite, the words do stray to you
& your battlefield of love
but I do love thee well
in all manner
got sent
words are the war to die for
& all suitable sway
needed you when I needled you
& the Tibetan deity too like 21 Taras
who makes a consort out of the practitioner
sent off
sent down
sent below
sent above
into the next votary's arms
all 21 of them

We would like to bring you up to date on the *Fragments of Conversations* book we have been work-
ing on for the past several years. We have selected and translated a number of parallel passages
from early Taoist and pre-Socratic Greek texts: Lao-tzu, Chuang-tzu, Heraclitus, Parmenides,
and Empodocles. Arranged thematically, these passages suggest fragments of a primal East-
West dialogue. Envisioning the quotes as ancient seeds falling into the late-20th-century soil, we
are now completing our book that will include creative responses in the form of poetry, com-
mentary, visual art or any combination of these . . .

　　Frost on the automobiles up and down the street,
a dull white sun in pewter sky.

　　　　The gap between
　　　　　the clapper and the gong
　　　　　　has vanished

Or are we, together somehow—
　　　　　teachers—?
To watch younger ones
take the stage with wit and sage
　　　　wordcraft?

                    Pointing the nose of my car
                    into the void, turning
                    strange sounds over on the
                    tongue

In the dream I stood in
twilight chewing on terrible
hunks of bitter meat.

Phenomena warmed up
warmed by him, up
a trade
deliberates the plex
what kind under glory
how calm
the plexion woke with—
Did?
Did?
Woke with Did?
woke with rub of love
not a rube
did he her she
did she
self, make up to
& too, a cry or
notable town crier
croon croon croon
came from a war

weep entirely
for barn nostalgia

cardinal, how color rides
"nice blues" of sky-barn-day
got to keep the grass
excursions onto property
fell into path properly
a pathfinder
chooses green

naught
but did
strife
to walk
& see
that is vision
polychromed edge
grown crusty with love

"Do you know the five nectars?"
"Yes," I reply. "Semen, marrow, blood, urine, feces."
"And the deities in union?"
"Kalachakra & Vishvamata. Is this a Buddhist quiz?"

We somehow are viewing these powerful deities together, looking upward at
their visualized bodies, like holograms. A HUM, turning into at five-pronged
vajra joins blue-skinned Kalachakra's secret place, and a *phat!* covers his penis-
hole. An AH rests at yellow-skinned Vishvamata's secret place, transforming
into a red lotus, and a *phat!* her vagina.

Could this be us copulating, withholding ourselves in some gone tantric
imagined realm? (Of course these visualizations are quite traditional.) *But he was
always more like a brother.*

I've been worried not having seen him so long. Has he been a homeless
vagabond? He looks it, face sooty & weathered, clothes soiled. He wears a dirty
rainbow-hued poncho of coarse wool. Yet warm. And studying it, I say, "the
toughest fiber," thinking of his sharp mind. His voice is aged, yet instilling the
usual irony—his quirky thinking. He proffers a flask. "Fibber?" "Tiber?" Now
there are crowds of devotees coming between us. We will not get drunk
together.

"What are the four night appearances, because if you know I'm imitating one
of those, ha!" I recite to myself: *smoke, mirage, sparks, flame, or a butter lamp.* Hurrying
my thinking over the din of exuberant yoginis (men & women, hair matted,
eyes wide).

"Butter lamp!" I cry, and he's gone.

....

Old friend
        to fathom lost night
or chart tide & time, eclipses of moon
        grind Dharma-wheels where gods are swift
inside cycles of poverty & desire
let's mount the illusory dream . . . a lamp, a candle
        How fare thee——(I hope) well?
....

then in the sense of the mother of,
  she rises like the sun

horizon, or dawn her fierce light

the fruit-center, journey back to that,
  like

        Egypt's ball of dung the scarab pushes

  (the work is never done!)

not easy
never easy
        in the sense the wife of the desert
rises
                        to meet studio light

        but the night studio, a lashing out of particles

        see see? he cries "I've done it!"

        (& you, poet, were there)

branded in the human realm
what woman is not only the beginning, too,
of night
        —butter lamp!

primordial cervix, rounded
          to a radial mind
catch her if you can
pigment could do it if you try
you do it painterly
          long night to paint the Muse
& breaks the line, flatted out, her radiant head

Animal—a poem-prey
is found & honored
with eye disarmed
& rage?
rage goes romping
fish nibbling at the body of a woman
mouse out of her belly in Clemente's eye
clemency there?

move
from here?
never
it's only paint

moves there
one orange fishing pole
across Diamond Lake
waving to the shore
in trouble?

Mountain Lion or

friendly stroke

(Meanwhile
boyfriend is
cracking some jokes
up
on the altiplano)

Guston's time of the bodyguards
& they come from "correction," come from hell
distance themselves in incarnate verse,
collide
busy themselves with difficulty (yours, mine)
while the universe sorts itself out
discoronated
cold, triste's memory, how limpid
decorous
reclaim a life-lunge for epic

Cool is his favorite color

three adjectives, he writes, that describe color:

> *green   blue   vermillion*

He'd most of all animals like to be a timber wolf
His sign is double Capricorn, Leo rising

Briefly define the following:

sacred
he responds—
> the place as definitions vanish & dancing begins

pornography
he responds—
> exploitation of another for libidinous gratification

wisdom
he responds—
> flashing sword, calm eye

sanity
he responds—
> alone & upright in a misguided world

anarchy
he responds—

the law of the irreducible minimum
somehow miraculously enacted

then . . .
If you could have a conversation with any person in all directions of time &
space who would it be?

Sappho & I'd ask *(he says)*

questions of poetic craft, how she runs her school,
    how you cultivate the poetic,
        who are her lady friends, did she have a daughter,
            did men or women please her most,
                what she discusses with other poets,
                    who she learnt technique from, who took her
                        maidenhead, did she commit suicide

II

TO BLUNT THE KNIFE

She comes by our losmen, our bungalow, looking for massage customers. She's dressed western style, a bit of cheap makeup. She smokes. She is not a typical Balinese woman. Javanese perhaps? She looks weary but seems willing to come alive for the conversation, for money. She's spent much time in Kuta Beach, known for its available sex and drugs. We're living in Ubud, less than two hours inland, purer, the artistic heart of the island, although they have no word for "art" here. She's come by bemo from Denpasar. She asks only for a glass of water. She accompanies me down the road through an avalanche of mud. I like her stamina, her guile is touching. She's probably my age. She has children. She's got a crazy mother. I learn this when we go up to Melanie's room a few days later. She's distracted. She says, "Call me Marlene Dietrich. That's what they call me." She's got a Muslim husband. She has difficult children. She has some "deep trouble," she says. "They call me Marlene because I'm sad and sing sometimes." She laughs. She's doused me with oil. She rubs my legs vigorously. "I saw God," she tells me, "and I traveled to outer space. I lived a long time ago, an Arab." She's working into some kind of trance. She can't stop talking. She's pounding my left shoulder where I took a fall on the stone floor. It seems to be throbbing with a memory of a memory she has of being beaten. She's saying: "I prayed. I saw light. My mother won't listen. My husband has a difference. He thinks he's holy with his book & god. I am holy and I am sick!" Her eyes are lit up like small suns. She's covered in sweat. She slaps me with more oil. Her hands have a cunning against my thighs. Now she stands on the bed to raise my legs and twist me around. I groan. "I saw something the others didn't see. I saw my own heart!"

She's massaging oil into my hair now and combing her deft fingers through it. "Anna, you are beautiful," she says. "Anna, you are kind." Then, "Is a man all there is to a woman?" and "I would have been a man." Suddenly she's regained her composure, a tight efficient self, and says matter-of-factly, "Don't wash your hair for twelve hours." I pay her 10,000 rupiahs. She takes a long drink of mineral water from a blue plastic bottle. I fall back as she changes out of her "work" clothes back into faded jeans and a sparkling t-shirt whose letters jut out from a pert chest "Las Vegas." "Remember, Marlene Dietrich, for massage."

I encounter her back down on the road several hours later. "You washed your hair," she scolds. She's disappointed. I try to explain it was so hot I had to shower and get the stickiness off my head. I hail a small van and give her a ride to the bemo stop at the market. "Salamat jalan." She's tired again. Could be a tired woman anywhere.

A month later I visit Pura Besakih, the mother temple, perched 1,000 meters up the side of volcano Gunung Agung, having spent several hours watching an ancestor ceremony with dancers, gamelan, two pedanda priests officiating. Carefully study the men, their mudras, their implements, their mut-terings, which invoke the old spirits to visit and see how the phenomenal world still performs for them & ask their wisdom & blessing. I think: not to banish them the way we do at home but seduce them back to help us. I'm walking back along the stately road down to the entrance. "Anna . . . Anna.' I don't recognize her at first but as I get closer I see it's Marlene Dietrich, impeccably dressed in the attire proper to the occasion—sarong & white kebaya. "I'm here for the family ceremony, one of my relatives," and points toward one of the family temple compounds. She's scrubbed. Her face looks younger. "Things are different now."

range

  a rest

face off

 behind the *aling aling*
demons only travel in straight lines so this fools them

drinking *arak*

she was when used to be & there was talk
layer of a woman

volcanic time
Eka Desa Rudra when the demon awakes

nod

bagus

here to witness green

once upon a time
when East Timor was far from my mind
restless

                political   shutter don't budge
nanosecond   lust's pubescent necklace

boy
I know
would never mention
lathes — works for
women, tends ducks

could he?
still
in the temple
sing ritual?

start clacking

clanging for

roar or proprietary
        bow

& hang like silk, pale, in
the
March sun

vertigolichen

against the
holy stone

concede rice-paddy-as-my-theology

Dear Dad:
The night before Nyepi Day or Ogoh-Ogoh is a time to "appease the evil spirits and restore the
balance of good and evil." For this night massive demons are created out of wire, wood, and
fabric and are attached to a network of bamboo poles. Young men stand between the gaps in

the poles and carry the witchy demons down the street in a parade manner. There are many people out that night especially in the villages that have the parade. In the family compound Ogoh-Ogoh is celebrated by walking around the compound banging pots and pans.

I experienced Nyepi and all of its attendant events in some way or another. For the days on which Melasti occurred I noticed many Balinese getting dressed up in their finest ceremonial garb to go down to the ocean or Champuan River. On Nyepi Eve or Ogoh-Ogoh I went down to Ubud and got a first-rate picture of the night. On the way down I could hear pots and pans banging away in all of the compounds I passed. When I got down to the soccer field there were four or five huge lady demons lined up. The gamelan began playing and one by one flocks of young men began picking the demons up by the bamboo poles. Before the last one was lifted I was waved in to come help carry it. We lifted it up and began carrying it down Monkey Forest Road. We crossed the main street and set it down next to Bambu Indian Restaurant. After about twenty minutes we lifted it up again and carried it down the main street. The streets were lined with tourists as well as Balinese and they often had to jump out of the way to avoid being crushed by our youth brigade. We turned around at Miro's and carried it back down the main street. We then walked back down Monkey Forest Road until the guys I was with noticed that the Sai-Sai bar had put out a few cases of beer for us. We quickly let go of Rangda and rushed the cases. After some drinking and yelling in the street we carried Rangda back to the soccer field and left it there. Then I was invited to somebody's house and we ate and talked for a while and then I left. On Nyepi Day itself I woke up and meditated with the group. I then did a little reading and lounged around until four and then I meditated again. I enjoyed the meditation but found it somewhat contradictory to my understanding of Nyepi. Not the meditation itself but the fact that I was required to do something on a day that was supposed to be free of requirements.

I remember saying to a Balinese person that "In America New Year's is very different, because we make a lot of noise and run around yelling." But when I think about it now they are very similar. Because the running around and yelling is actually New Year's Eve, and much of the same chaotic behavior happens on Ogoh-Ogoh. The day of Nyepi is quite similar to the first day of the New Year. In Bali, Nyepi Day is one of silence and rest. In America it's the same way because everyone is too damn hungover from the night before to do anything but lie in bed and sleep.

Love,
Ambrose

OM AWIGHANAM ASTU
(May there be no hindrance)

The poet returns home to guard the hearth, collecting weaponry and NASA disaster documents and receiving response mail to her poetic mutterings. Keep it up, the good fight. Stay informed. This poem rides her identity but meekly. It is for Every Woman and all children. Keep railing. Consult the I Ching. Everyone in this small town visiting doctors & healers. It's the preamble of a millennium rife with diseases, kleshas, maras of all kinds. The task of blunting (dulling, deadening, numbing) aggression through language is now a daily practice. The trick is a language that lives its passion, leaps from the tongue, a lover's kiss. Jove's ubiquitous cock & ubiquitous spear are the implements that keep her challenge alive. Will "they" never understand about weapons? (She'd rather put music on now: Coltrane's "India." The Jauk concert Ambrose recorded in Bali.) Weapons don't kill obstacles but create more. Rape & murder as acts of war morally reprehensible. The boy has gone out in the suburban snow, he says, "to pick spears." The icicles melt daily.

Crude weaponry

++++++++++++++++++++++++++++++haunts all fronts
 +++++++++++++++++++every inner
city heart of envy +++++++++++++++++++++

targets
every congress

  sophisticated weaponry   ++++++++   targeted here

every outer continent   nothing free from the blade its false starts & tongues   a
flame   a dart,   ten-blade day, a day of lies and concealment the passage
of a cynical amendment   who defends the victims of genocide anymore?
what conscience of planet botched   rotten to core what world council
what recourse to cry help or whoa enough?   dear gods enough   they weep to
look on us so
              Zeus turns a blind eye
basta, basta.

thinking about armed struggle &
she came in

              & cut the Tao in half
    Adonis the wounded son . . .

The Federal authorities have arrested eight white supremacists who were preparing to blow up one of the largest black churches in Los Angeles—the 8,500 member First African Methodist Church in the heart of South Central Los Angeles. One of the men had planned to burst into the church during services and "start popping people" with a machine gun. They had also planned to assassinate Rodney King; Danny Bakewell, the leader of the Brotherhood Crusade; and the Rev. Louis Farrakhan, leader of the Nation of Islam. They had also planned to kill Rabbis and other Jews. They wanted to spark a holy war.
++++
During a search of five residencies, numerous weapons were seized, including machine guns, as well as Nazi paraphernalia, including swastikas & portraits of Hitler.

The folks arrested range in age from 20 to 42 & also include two minors. Two of the adults are women. They are members of the white supremacist Church of the Creator, based in Florida; the White Aryan Resistance, based in Southern California; and the Fourth Reich Skinheads, based in Huntington Beach near L.A.

People seeking guns for personal combat want reliable "stopping power"—the devastation to human tissue when a bullet strikes. That requires a bullet with a diameter of nine millimeters, similar in size to a caliber of .357 of an inch. Larger bullets have greater stopping power but must be fired from bigger guns that are hard to conceal, heavy to carry. Guns using .357 or nine millimeter cartridges are either revolvers or semiautomatic, pistols known as "nines." The revolver, a comparatively simple device dating from the early 19th century, commonly fires six rounds from a cylinder that rotates with each pull of the trigger. The semiautomatic, which dates from the late 19th century, typically fires cartridges from a magazine that fits in the gun's grip. As each cartridge is discarded, the recoil drives a heavy slide surrounding the gun's barrel. Traveling back and forth in a fraction of a second, the slide automatically recocks the firing pin, ejects the spent casing, and moves a fresh cartridge from the magazine into the firing chamber. These differences are easy to feel. Pick up a .357 magnum revolver and your wrist muscles strain to level the weight. Fire it for the first time and the bullet is likely to fly wild as the recoil jolts your arms and shoulder.

++
++

We call upon the President of the United States to reassess the easy availability of guns in this country and in doing so help prevent the thousands of similar incidents . . .

—Anne-Pacing-the-Floor-More-Vigorously-Now

+++

At 8:30 on Oct. 17, 1992, Yoshi and our son Webb were on their way to a Halloween party for exchange students, dressed as a dancer and a hospital patient, without masks. The man emerged from the carport with a .44 magnum. The man told the boys to "freeze." Yoshi, not understanding, walked toward the man. The man shot Yoshi in the left chest at close range. He died minutes later. The thirty-year-old homeowner was charged with manslaughter by a Baton Rouge grand jury. On May 23 he was acquitted.

When I asked some friends to sign this petition I received only yesterday, they said, "No way! You kidding? I need a gun in this world."

++++

                & cut the Tao in half
                    tie
       an intimate circle
                     collapse
                     not violent
                     resist
    but

        harmony

"wall of the town sinks back into the moat
      from which it was dug"

T'ang the Completer
Author: Doubt Dispeller
You: He-Who-Flutters-Down
Weapon-Wielder: never had enough power

    Receptive
moves
downstairs
(above)
  Creative moves upward: below

all things bloom & prosper
  light of Bali
in
the side
ribbon grass pulled up
   sod
with
it
   (end to all feuds)

each according to her own kind bunch of it
stalk
by
root a meager truncheon
"it"—connect, the "it" connect
   might induce melancholy
but never fall into illusion
guns or roses

ford the river
heaven on earth

Anarcho Tao / Chaos Linguistics (read "human," please)
what need of guns

+++

[these words paint down middle to resemble missiles]

       —"Ring Nebula in Lyra?"
         —"You saw?"
       —"Like an eyeball"
       —"Like embryo"

—"You opened the book?"
—"Not I"

—"Bernice's Hair—between the tail star
of Leo and end
of Dipper's handle—was
bright"
—"Use field glasses"
—"I have them"
—"Here, give me"
—"O.K."

—"Hercules"
—"Yes"
—"A dolphin"
—"Maybe"
—"Cygnus the Swan"
—"Maybe"

—The Sisters
—The Daughter
—The Children
—A son

—Ten long years have rolled away
—By Zeus
—A thousand ships
—Put forth
—That with
—Went out
—Pealed
—Wild as vulture's cry
—In weaved agony
—around
—around
—They wheel
—But not . . .
—That called
—But let . . .

                    —Or Pan
                —The exile cry

            —Doth Zeus, the jealous
            —Speed Atreus's house
                —'Gainst Paris
                —Whom one
                —And many
                —And last
                —And many
            —And splintered
                —A spear
                —Despair
                —Of Trojan
                —Of Greek
                —That iron
                —But as
            —And now
            —Unsoothed
                —Poured
                glares
            —And each
                turns

She returned, she scribed down quickly these NASA notes from the Draft Envir-
onmental Impact for the Cassini Mission, which will send plutonium into outer
space:

For the mission through Phase 6, Phase 1 provides the largest contribution to
overall or total mission risk of 4.6×10^{-7} number of health effects (without *de min-
imis*). (This is obtained by adding the mission risk contribution calculated for
each of the three representative accident scenarios applicable to Phase 1.) The
population at risk from a Phase 1 accident involving a release of plutonium
dioxide would be the population in the vicinity of CCAS, estimated to be on the
order of 100,000 people (Halliburton NUS 1994A). When the concept of *de minimis*
is applied, the health effects for Phase 1 would be considered negligible. In turn,
the contribution to total mission risk from a Phase 1 accident would also be
considered negligible.

—Raise him
—From where
—Sunk all
—Bade them
—Lest she
—With one
—Those that
—To plead
—To plead
—How oft
—Wherein
—Rang "to plead"
—To plead
—When I
—Sang from
—Sang of destruction
—And then
—But this
—This wage
—This risk
—And yet
—Clear with
—Now, let
—Find yet
—So prays
—That guards
—The nuclear universe
—For, while
—Now they
—That bid
—The powers that be
—I, fain
—As saith
—Spring forth
—What say'st
—Hear then
—Thrills thro'
—But hast
—Go to

—Hath some
—Out on
—The rim
—Of space
—Militias breed

For a Phase 5 accident with impact in Africa, the predicted health effects would be about 1.5×10^{-4} over an assumed reference population of about 1,000 people (Halliburton NUS 1994A). Since the overall probability of an accident occurring in Phase 5 is 5.0×10^{-4} (1 in 2,000), the mission risk contribution or expected number of health effects is 7.5×10^{-8}. Factoring in *de minimis,* the predicted health effects would be reduced by a factor of 3.4, with the risk contribution dropping by a factor of about 3.

Dear Anne: I am currently taking Creeley's class on Olson, which I am actually really enjoying, partly because I am finding Olson incredibly interesting. And actually I find that if I listen very hard to Creeley, I can hear him saying very significant and illuminating things about the text, and about life in general. But anyway, it's this whole idea about an epic that I am finding fascinating, that is, about how one goes about bringing one's BEING into the poem, how to write something that's big enough to fit it all in, how to locate, geographically, on the "moving map" (Cocteau's phrase) the complex intersection of mythology, history, and personal fluctuations in life. And so I wonder how you see Olson in your lineage. (I mean, would you say you were more inspired by Pound, or rather, by an Eastern epic, like *Tale of Genji*?) And of course, the whole idea of a woman doing something like this is so remarkable—especially in light of Olson, who was so filled with that male energy that you were penetrating, in reverse of course, in both a personal and intellectual way. Interestingly enough, Creeley asked the class today if anybody knew of anyone who was attempting to write an epic on the scale of Olson, and people mumbled this and that, and I said, but of course, A.W. And Creeley disagreed with me, and I still find it strange, not on the basis of writing/poetic skill, etc. but EGO! What he meant is that your work is more personal in that you bring in letters, stories about your child, emotional instances, etc. (although admittedly, the boundaries get very shifty here—I mean Olson's persona was huge and was personal). So I was thinking what was at stake here was not ego but gender, and I wonder how you felt about it. I mean, even that reviewer ends the article questioning your work as "essentially" feminine. But no one would think to say Olson was Essential, in that way. And then I was talking to Juliana and my other poet friend Cynthia Kimball (we meet once a month to show each other our poetry) about how it seems that women with PERSONA are always the ones who seem to get criticized the most—and you have one, a real one, and I wonder how you negotiated this fact. Did you learn how to do it at an early age living in New York and hanging out with such amazing people? I mean, I have seen you in action! When we were in Rochester and that weird guy was saying to your face that you were a good performer but didn't know how to write and that you just copied Ginsberg etc. (do you remember?) you were so poised and just shot it right back at him—I was amazed! I guess it's this thing about being a writer, which involves, of course, a certain amount of self-projection. I mean, one is always disclosing something about one's Self (which is why I don't really buy all the talk about "non-representational writing that leaves the reader free to construct his/her own text blah blah"). And I will be frank. Many of the contemporary women writers who have persona are either slightly neurotic, paranoid, or aloof—and they are safe, in a certain way, to talk about. But then there's you, who are strong and poignant (as is Kathleen Fraser, in a different way, but she was here recently and people had similar reactions), and people complain about EGO. But no one complains about that same way in a strong male presence, because it is more expected. Well, I am very confused about the whole thing because I am being confronted with the problem—to be forward, or to hang back—to perform or to whisper—to vanish or to shine forth—and of course it seems that the answer is obvious—and yet it is confusing. It partly has to do with something that happened recently on e-mail (of all places), where I accused a man of getting out of line, of not playing fair—and I did it, I admit, in a tone that was not exactly friendly—although the truth is that I was ANGRY! And I know this is only the beginning of similar kinds of interactions, where I speak my mind and get my hand slapped afterward, like I did something BAD, or even worse, that the way in which I expressed myself was WRONG. It actually is no longer a big deal (the e-mail thing), at least not to me. But the whole Olson thing, and then your book and then that guy's review have gotten me all riled up. And I apologize because I know that students often come to you for "motherly" advice, as I think you called it, but truly, I do not mean to be oppressive.

Love to you, K

—Who doth
—War's money
—Sends back
—Scant ash
—To blunt
—Light to
—Yet fills
—Urn full
—With what
—Soldier's ash
—Sleep last
—Their breath
—To blunt
—In war

For an inadvertent reentry from a VVEJGA or VEEGA Earth swingby(s), the potential health effects could occur in two distinct populations: the population within and near the reentry footprint and most of the world population within broad north to south latitude bands. Since the reentry footprints, and hence the potentially affected populations, could vary considerably with reentry angle and latitude, the predictions of radiological exposures and health effects have large uncertainties. Based on the estimated footprint areas in Table 4-9 and average popluation densities in the potentially affected latitude bands, the affected footprint population could be in the 10^5 to 10^6 range (specifically, 226,000 persons in the VVEJGA steep reentry footprint and 2,200,000 persons in the VEEGA E2 shallow reentry footprint).

—Is heavy

—As deep

—Flung by

—For not

—Seems the

—Till then

—And smite

—And help

—To blunt

—O'er him

—Over them

—Sped from

—This bliss

—To tread

—To tread

—To Walk

—To Tread

—A burden

—Is heavy

—Is weight

—To blunt the war

—The battle

—Is heavy

—To blunt the knife

—Her call

—Called out

—Called from

Call to
—The night
—The unexposed grave
—The pit
—The dead
—(recent dead)
—(exhumed dead)
—Called out from pit
—Horrible horrible
—Nor see
—But is
—A child
—Who let
—And then
—The edge
—Good news
—That fences
—The tale
—Soon shall
—Draw hither
—Speaks plain
—Not dumb
—And on
—O Land
—My feet
—O Land
—Turn thou
—And hail
—To one
—With grace
—Ah home
—So out
—On you
—The hail
—I'll rest
—All pains
—And curse
—A curse
—And hair

—Why tell
—Lay stark
—Why mourn
—Why sum
—For life
—Let those
—The city
—The need
—Thy words
—The ear
—Last night
—So wild
—That I
—Made sure
—Yet on
—And in
—With voice
—The king
—My lord
—What day
—Than this
—The store
—Be steel
—I'll joy
—& blunt her knife

In the unlikely event that a VVEJGA or VEEGA inadvertent reentry occurred,
approximately five billion of the estimated world population of seven to eight
billion at the time of the swingbys could receive 99 percent or more of the radi-
ation exposure.

jostled this op. page
to find a source
which said (indicate!)
be brave in battle
Earthquake Procedure

or *jam karet*
(rubber time) above the tectonic plates of Indonesia
Volcanic?
REMAIN CALM . . .
Look for the safest place and carefully move toward it. Motion during an earth-
quake is not constant. Take advantage of time between tremors to gain a safe
position.

IF YOU ARE INSIDE THE HOTEL
DO NOT RUSH OUTSIDE
BRACE YOURSELF IN AN INSIDE CORNER AWAY FROM WINDOWS
CROUCH UNDER A TABLE OR DESK
STAY AWAY FROM WINDOWS, SLIDING GLASS DOORS OR MIRRORS
MOVE TO AN INNER WALL OR CORRIDOR
AVOID ANY OBJECTS THAT MAY FALL OR SHAKE LOOSE
IF YOU ARE IN BED, STAY THERE & BRING THE PILLOWS AND COVERS ALL THE WAY
OVER YOUR BODY
DO NOT USE ELEVATORS

GENERAL SAFETY RULES AFTER AN EARTHQUAKE:
REMAIN CALM AND DO NOT PANIC
DO NOT RUSH OUTSIDE
DO NOT LIGHT MATCHES, CIGARETTES OR TURN ON ANY ELECTRICAL SWITCHES
PROTECT YOUR HANDS AND FEET IN ALL AREAS NEAR DEBRIS OR BROKEN GLASS
WAIT FOR FURTHER INSTRUCTIONS BY THE HOTEL EMERGENCY RESPONSE TEAM
We sincerely wish you a pleasant and safe stay.

> & Sappho on the
> isle sang sweet
> epithalamiums to
> stir the hearts of girls
> and quake

> another war

> of sex

> and because he read her
> conscientiously he wrote:

a book like *Iovis* demands responses I'm parting the curtains and stepping through . . .

There's a strong ego at its portal but it doesn't stop us pushing open the door; for we've had
enough male ego in our day and the female force has got to counter that in breeziness and

health. Anyway, she's so welcoming. A question arises, and it is probably the central one in all rightings of power: can the world you create behind the door be richly lived in? And, since I'm an utter, utter democrat (which is why frenetically academic forms of feminism strike me as excluding many women), can we all find warmth and richness? Your great discovery is to build generosity so firmly into the sequence that if I, as I do, agree willingly to wander around in your world, then I equally willingly accept along with it the whole, justified critique of the male domination of the art we both devote our lives to. But I don't have to bonehead about it: I can just live through it. I don't have to turn aside muttering, for example, "but jouissance doesn't exist;" instead, I experience something joyful but full of point, possessing great stamina, something which doesn't come out of the study. *Iovis* is an experience shaped along a lifeline like a 4-D world-line tube, a transparent windsock of lived time.

Then, also, there's something scorelike about it, various blueprints for multitudinous performances in your style (and it must give you and your audiences a lot of pleasure). A dippy bag, a bottomless one with stars in the bottom. It must enable you in performance to move from persona to persona, from the grave register of "revenge" to the chants or to the necessary engagement with the "lost child's voice," as I myself have called it once. If you can do that in performance, then the silent reader also can move around from one state of his/her spirit to another in a kind of self-instruction. Something else I'm interested in: it provides many genres of poetics as several different doors of entry. Both you and Alice have modeled an admirable feminine consciousness, one with humor and sharpness, astringency and kindliness. We might all want actually to bathe in that as something restorative after so much splitting apart of all the radical causes I most care about into various kinds of separatism. Purity is always possible when people are apart from those who disagree with them. All battle lines have to be drawn. But all warfare should be conducted as a last resort and with as much generosity to the losers (white males, etc.) as possible—that's what Rabelais knew. So if the father is in your created world here, with generosity, if the jailed are, if the male brats are still with generosity, then a feminine chateau might truly arise with sun on its walls and the streamers flying with, inside, the peaceful giantesses and the equally large men reclining there, released from their various prisons! Rabelais's friend, Sir Thomas More, said, "Man considered in his universal would be a giant;" so tit for tat, Sir Thomas.

This chateau you don't quite give us, I think it must be a Platonic thing; in fact, I know it is. You let things get quite rubbled, strewn along the length of all this by your life-events. This tells us that you won't let your own conscience out of its responsibility, even if it means some loss of the purest design; it's all open to circumstance and chance and personal decisions, as things, even the grandest pronouncements, surely should be. I am currently obsessed with the thought that the poets should seem vulnerable and expose their inadequacy—or otherwise we just have more of the shit dressed up in power games. Poetry's power politics must be wrong, but who can I say this to? Who, fighting for the small amount of attention available, will listen? Anyway, this breakableness of your design means that various parts get thrown into significance in unexpected ways, for example, the very affecting crazy letter in Book I, which caught me up short far more than any Amnesty missiles/missives because in this grand progress of the poem, the letter becomes dignified (in the old sense of worthy). Again, that's democratic, you see—it couldn't happen with a thoroughly deconstructed text because the dignity would not be accorded to the letter by its position in a real-life process.

All these aspects don't mean that I'm just lost in admiration as I wander along your life-landscape. I feel very alive and critically awake, because the issues are too important to be left in the care of any one ego, even one spreading itself so large and generously as yours, or annulling itself by incorporation of so many other voices as yours does. The nature of poetry-power is still a problem for me inside that world, you see, and it is a tonal question first and foremost. The tone of a politician, of a philosopher, of a poet, is my very first question and a very deeply "moral" one, and it's a little shameful to have to put that word in quotes.

There is an old Renaissance virtue of magnificence, and that yields tone above all. You have rather magnificently seen that we need these large imaginative universes just now, and we no doubt need them most from women, and out of Africa and parts of Asia.   Love, D.

++
Note to herself to tell a story:
Rabi'a al-Adawiyya is a major saint of Islam and an important figure in Sufi tradition. She was born in Basra in what is now Iraq, the ancient Mesopotamia—in one account—in 717 A.D. and died in 801. She was presumably born into a poor family; famine killed both her parents. Homeless and vulnerable, she was captured and sold as a slave. She was later freed by her master and may have made a living as a flute player. She may or may not have made the pilgrimage to Mecca. In the stories about her, there were many obstacles along the way.

   "cold, cold smoked the bitch."
                    —American pilot over Iraq hitting Iraqi warplane
I sought the wild animal

   "salamat jalan"

III

HAG OF BEARE (CAILLECH BERRI)

Gaelic, ninth century

Call it morbid, didn't want to scare anyone in the dream of withering radiated mother-skin. You looking at me, son? But murmurs consistently indicate back to ancient crone. And to enter her keening mouth was the challenge here. Life was taking another bend. Twist of a knife to a heart. Get a grip, she tells herself on the dual enigmatic passages of time and love. Another wrinkle or fold in the spiral. Former student John Wright, a balladeer, studies Gaelic, and we begin, then continue outside in a place where we are planting trees together. Trees hold the old Celtic runes—whole alphabets—in their twisted branches that beckon like gentle witches. Caillech Berri, who holds the synoptic view, is foil to a patriarchal consciousness hooked on earth (property) and chattel (women). But the sea is her rhythm. Carib poet Kamau Braithwaite speaks of "tidelectics." A much more complex—feminine?—notion of the way language, whole cultures move. Fame and glory are the headlines of arch-male's competitive spin. He wants to make big waves that drown out the other voices. The old lady is an island to herself. Never self-pitying. Men and love and beauty ebb & flow. But never fade as long as poetry boasts the truth of suffering.

Caillech—a veiled one; a nun; a cormorant; an old woman; the last handful of standing corn on a farm; the circular wisp at the top of a cornstalk . . . from Old Irish caillech, from caille, veil . . . Welsh pall . . . Latin pallium.

The Hag of Beare is a ninth-century poem, orginally oral, and composed of several fragments, including a prose narrative, which is now lost. The Hag of Beare is an ancient figure in Ireland, a goddess of land and sovereignty. Pagan heroes and deities were common in Christian-era literature, and often these characters converted to the "new faith" in their old age. However, the conversions were often very superficial and defiant, and the old ways were portrayed sympathetically. The author is anonymous and may or may not have been a woman, but there are some connections between this poem and other women's poetry of the period from southwest Ireland. Although the poem is composed in a first-person narrative "voice," it is very personal compared to formal compositions of the time. It is a poignant death-song, not unlike women's keens (caoin) in later Irish folk poetry.

This translation omits several stanzas that seem to refer to the missing prose narrative. We work from the original text in Gerald Murphy's Early Irish Lyrics.

spoken:

I ebb like the ocean
Old age makes me strange
Although I rant & rave
A lucky portion returns with the high tide

Returns to me, Bui, Hag of Beare
Not for long this hag used to wear fresh linen
Today so thin
A secondhand gown's a sack on me

Bag of Bones
Goes bitterly toward the place she's known
When the time comes
Let the son of God collect her body home

Look at my arms—
Narrow, scrawny
That they used to embrace kings
Was sweet poetry

Not fit to embrace
Any handsome boys now
Arms shrunk & bony—
See?

See girls go wild
When May Day comes
Past-Her-Prime sits here watching
Grief, not sex, is more her moan

No honey ale's poured out
No sheep killed for my wedding
My hair's thin, graying
A cheap veil is no big deal

A white veil over my head
Is modest when you're old
When I drank good ale

I wore scarves in every wild color

But no gentleman or slave's son
Makes merry with me today
The ocean roars
Winter raises the ante

Many waves, how many days
Since I rode youth's ocean
Many years fever-lust burned out
Beauty dried up

I wear a shawl
Most days
Even when the sun's out
I'm old, okay, I know it

I know summer of youth
Got spent in autumn
Winter drowns every person
Now beginning of winter's come

My cloak would still be old
Even if I stayed at home
I jumped the fence once, did you hear?
Lived a fast life, no regrets

But I'm really cold now
Eyes weak, deteriorating
After a feast with blazing candles
I'm stuck in the dark druid house

But I had it, had a time with kings
I swear—high on wine and mead
Today I commiserate with
whey & water among withered hags

Be a cup of whey, my ale
I pray to whatchamacallit—a living god

What vexes me be the will of this god
Pray, don't fill this body-cup with anger

I'm losing my grip, wind plays tricks
The mark of age on the same old cloak
Gray hair grows through my skin
Like moss on an ancient witch-tree

My right eye's taken   *John—this is starkest image*
& sold to make a down payment   *wanted to ask you about*
& my left eye is snatched   *rights this time vis-à-vis women usufructus etc./ remind me*
To close the deal

The flood wave
& its swift ebb
What the flood wave brings
The ebb steals from your hand

The flood wave
& the next ebb
I recognize them by sight
See them coming?

Flood wave
Don't come to my door
My comrades were great bards I know
A hand strikes everyone down—whose? Fate's? God's?

Maybe Virgin Mary's son will spend the night
In my room under the roof pole
I can't offer much
But say "no" to no one

The ebb is never seen
Until the flood comes in
Woe to all
Woman is the basest of creatures

It's okay for the ocean to flood the beach
Of an island
But I don't expect the flow
To follow the ebb

What was once afloat in high tide
Is now all ebbing
I don't recognize a single house
Or hut—
    ranting & raving
    where's my shelter?—anymore

*Back in the dank basement of her home on Macdougal Street—barely recognizable after an insur-
rection has swept the city—the poet dreams she is looking through eyeless sockets into desiccated
boxes of paper, books, photos, mementos of deceased poets (with whom she drank mead in the dark
druid house), love letters. She's got the body of a pubescent teen. Searching. Where, o where have I
put my eyes? Then what a relief to have them at rest. This crone business is illusion's game, a con-
jurer's trick. She re-recalls the sorceress/guru who appears in various guises—both wizened &
seductive—to pandit Naropa (tenth century, India) and hears this mind-duet.*

HE: *(disgruntled)*
        How many miracles
                or credit
what karma backs
        a big bag of wind
    You speak well
        what's your mask?
          (your game)

SHE: *(chuckling, rocking side to side)*
        You're still asleep—
          selling souvenirs in your dreams?
        Do I look like anyone?
                You want a priest?

Agh, this is my agenda:
        whatever you see
                grates the form
look again—

            a precious human body
aha!
(she strips the rag from her body)

HE: Stop—
            you'd bum the devil's eye
Supposed to get holy
      embrace you as leper?
Disgusting dogs mangy dogs
      suck your tits dry
You twist my sight
      offend all senses
                        Please
            proffer another image
from your bag of tricks

SHE:
                        smoking mirrors, false prophecy,
            botched teeth, clever poetry . . .
Take your pick
I'll hide
            under a monk's hood
      sanctuary at the edge of town

HE: Odd corners? I'll take poetry instead—
      a phoneme charms
            a charnel ground
      got any?
people languish
from the heat & dust
            but I guess you're other-prone
go ahead
            Get beautiful if you dare
capture preen of youth & sex
            sing me a spell

SHE: Phantom thrill, okay—
      here I go
(spins into a supple maid)

"virgin"
   "lubrication"
"comb"
   "dance"
(spins into a small heap at his feet)
        "puddle"

HE:
   She's got a coy glass heart
        keys to the city
but "virgin lubrication comb dance puddle"?

Come back
        & finish your poem
it's weak, puerile, no tangibles,
        too soft for the times
   better personae—do it!
you could be immortal

SHE:
"virgin
   drinkable
his gold prick
        under her
seen a naked girl comb her hair?
   tilt chin
dance macabre
        public, pubescent, nudge,
pull me, long, long . . ."

That's all you get to blunt your knife . . .

IV

LIP OF THE REAL

A pilgrimage to Lawrence, Kansas, with her son to honor one of his several godfathers, William S. Burroughs, maverick writer, consummate elder, who has survived difficult surgery. She wants to honor Burroughs's edge & gift of survival, and his own work, of course, which manifests the bizarre, aberrant, & phantasmagoric underpinnings of the current Dark Age. He set her on a path once of fragmented memory & dream retrieval that fed into more powerful writing. She created an idealized factotum of herself as artist—a she-beast with skin of jaguar, eye of hawk, radar of bat, heart of Buddha, cool mind of Isis. What does Burroughs really "image" to her? Sometimes he seems willful nun, or crone-like in his sinewy-ness, his "edge"—sometimes dark saint. A man redeemed through art? His gaze carries the bead of ancient votary, one long accustomed to the cave, a dark Mephistophelian scriptorium. He was always generous with her and playful with the boy, whom he more than once threatened to capture & "take to the mountains." Burroughs is surrounded with a host of "boys" who act in turns as amenuenses, cooks, comrades-in-arms, collaborators in his creative projects. While in Lawrence, a city of some intellectual & academic fervor, she confers with a noble translator of Greek text & his Zen wife, & with scholarly poet Ken Irby, a Renaissance man. A war is always raging somewhere. She meditates at the local zendo, an oasis anywhere in this world. "Lip of the real" is a mouth around words. Also joke for her students, who are forbidden use of tangible-put-with-abstraction joined by preposition of. Does she get away with it?

Exhaust appearance &
get the what-was-hidden or what's
so-called real in a
rise to greet occasion
Cher Maître Burroughs
You, meaning cryptic, mean to do this. Meant to? &
strike the act from the poet's list. Lip of the real.
Or more especially the book of heart & chance
hit list like lisp
got written
gets written
how survives
on top of teaching
ballooning artery in heart
Burroughs' angioplast

double bypass: Topeka
survives his own story
eats an egg yolk with salt
smokes ten cigarettes
turns on with grass
double vodka with coke
supper
what's missing?
a hero to many is not amiss
a kind of dominion
& you?
Lip of the saint
Lip of the devil
Know not nor gentleman be

War on every horizon
beat their butt in Baghdad
kiss their butt O Israel!
a pert pact
a centrist operation
with sick intentions
hotline to idolatry
keep it pumping & back your
mouth, with a dollar bill
& one taste of blood is blood-sent
scent to you you told me
a horror you can't imagine
crime
payment
what's due
battleshield won't help you here
sent through you
to get up my sisters
who get riled by his old saw
for he thinks them biddies
& green skin
or soggy
get up, my lover boy
& the one who was queer

for he thinks the womb stinks
no no he don't do that

wash away tears, O Mother
what kind of life we're having
I'll tell you:

B-52s G-bombs
tighter protection hit elite corps
corpse attack
AWACS monitor attacks
F-117 Stealth strike aircraft
F-15E's Eagles
Tornado GRIs
A-10s
F-4G Wild Weasels smash SAM radio
et cetera
you've got all day in cockpit
love you, bravado
understand mercy but no time here
understand you, baby, be away from here
what blows through blows through
how do you fuck strategy?
martyr calm
much maligned
martyr calm much maligned
have you forgotten Pandora?
ills et cetera?
inebriate the cure to gun a pain
cure the enemy in you to gun my pain
inebriate ah all enemy
Jesse Jackson kiss the dust
& it rises again
wartime it's wartime like
a kiss on the lips
I put my love for you in here
How many Iraqis dead?
I put my great love for you in here
with the dead uncasketed

swashbuckler, O muse
all the man I wanted to be
all the parts I wannabe
I put my love the poem it's here
here it is, you, you who strut
to be my love
lip of heart
lip of the poet
she's in her deep heart self
a seal made firm to love
& keep out war
give it, give it all up
mi amore
Dear William:
this is the new section
in long born-like-a-man poem
about taking chances
be a risk to you, to him, to her, to them
a risk to book
risk the alarm of family, accounts
given & received
risk the other stuff
& plunder the future alarum
Are we cinematic now?
I put my love for you
like daughter
in here
a hard sell
Please get well
contradict a predicament
a coalition
dark conspiracy
who runs that effort?
eyes tell me nothing
your eyes tell me nothing
you bluff but are friendly

I stepped off the porch in Kansas, William, but the light . . .

I stepped off
              the porch

              William
but the light
it was it was a raw kind day
it was a mutant day, it lunged, it started
roar a way a way out here
it was a your kind of day
  & lost at the edge of St. Louis finally
it was a movie it was definitely being captured
& you bent over to tie something down
stranger than life itself
I saw your ghost
& voice for
it was all voice
Hassan I wanted to say "savior"
old voice of mountain

I
stepped
off
the
porch,
William, but
  the light

& because they get
a wrong take on you
or voguing take
you suffer the women
gay women too

inside the scheme agenda play it my way or his

long or styled, a veritable patriarch not be

my boy
is alive with song
with glee

rides with me
& be
he sweet
& extend the stage to include more & more light

in the valley I saw them more ahead than dead yet
they were sick & they were failing
& in the valley they wished to be saved
  I stepped
off
the porch,
William,
  but
the light
back to the Paleolithic, yogin
& become a law to himself
Mexico is placed here
in a duty-prone-karma-thing
or state your case
irreducible minimum
lived in a valley
was a kind of saint too
& law became path
bring all the spectators to it
we went out to the field & shot at the targets a long time
You said "the lake . . ."
  something about "the vibes" here
"who died" & "the lesbians?"
you said or tolerated me to
take notes on you
I became administratrix
or Durga with weapons in her hair
to pursue the penumbral light of male day
or haunt men who tame me
clock me down
not you
but
all those sheaths & swords to fall upon
& I become

Female Adorant Before a Column Support
bring all to it
And Terminator of Death, you
16-legged, 34-armed, buffalo-headed deity
hold me consort
  Diamond Zombie
to the path, bring all to it

a loose cannon on gundeck of state
something you could say
  or some such clever-headed thing
surrounded by boys who adore you
humor you
not
desultory
a contra-barter
not grim
  no, you had no choice
it is fated, Allah, it is willed
  a Meese admit
    or hit
a perpetrator
  not sage to me
but understood a president's thinking
unequivocal to be
awash in hypnocritical edge
crisis exonerated
thanks the lingo, thanks the star
  her lucky pointman
out of the loop
  a spectacle
the best-seller is
healed in the heart of
America
one who cuts up words to make
  them brew
and fashion killer virus language
so Pentagon speaks
  voice of the cynical beast

headed in the art of
  I'm a Wrecker, America

old photographer . . . flesh in and out of focus . . . he looked through his sickness . . . casual adolescents came to the door . . . voices frosted on the glass . . . age flakes fall through a cloud of old photos . . . forgotten boy walked on screen and dusted off a magic smile . . . just pick up the dark street . . . mirror images breaks out street riots . . . I was saying over and over, reshapes where the awning flaps . . . speeding along the asphalt . . . vines twisting through steel . . . machine guns in Baghdad . . . wounded man came to the door . . . some boy from vacant lot . . . child eyes look out across the nurseries . . . junk sick from an old mirror Mr. Martin smiles . . .

Mr. Bradley?

  Pedagogy?
rush?
Russian diplomatic crush-down
hit dirt
  pay dirt
next, whose?

Here I shall put down my pen
to climb into
the merciful ship of sleep

How estrogens affect action
will start by keeping a headache diary

prostaglandins
will tell you your new nighttime name

I sat in the Zen-circle-high-winds
    of Kansas

Bring all to it, William
naming your planets & stars

V

WITHIN A BUDDING

"unclothe your ship"

"But she danced like a pink moth in the shrubbery"

"Imagination dead imagine," says her best friend, quoting Samuel Beckett. How to reel with this one? The absolute boundary of mind & art, or rank. We walk on the springy grasses. Nature arising. To think a class where women writers we study were to be summoned as muses & pilots, as old tests & trails or trials I really wanted to put it thus, of past time. Eternally present in the imagination. It's other "old" place. One could say the Muse is in charge of environment & atmosphere. And we could pay attention to how Laura Riding wouldn't be caught dead using metaphor, or Gertrude Stein would argue like a child for attention in no one's true idea of simplicity. But nothing could stop her stubborn means to put it down. How to say, only a woman would do this? Huh? Or the reaction to an obscure reference from sybilline H.D. Go look it up, you dummies! Then someone protests that George Steiner is Eurocentric, elitist. What else is new? Of course, I would love to know Swahili poetics. White ladies—Guest, di Prima, Kyger, Mayer, Notley, Acker, Howe, Scalapino, Lauterbach, Hejinian—will cast you into one or myriad contemporary net(s). Mullen, Hunt, Patton, Coleman, Cortez, Lorde—another. But the experiments you muster will change the way you see "her,"—that lady's (Stein's?)—thinking-grammar forever. Could I say it was a fleeting kind of freeloading mind? Yes, I could. The title of the class I teach: "Interstices of (Female) Imagination." Interstices would mean being caught at some funny-bone nerve juncture, and that juxtaposition makes pictures & sounds of words, yeah words. "She" lets you try it too. This was my experiment using the idea to cannabalize a hallowed canon-worthy text & play inside gender, place, point of view, translation, sense perception. Seize Proust.

.

.

.

.

.

.

.   rich
in
expletive

surprise
is poor romance

. . . .

poem born, poor romance

to remain

for gender's sake

an unknown person
she may love in turn,

but needing

to make
con-
tact
not so much with
her body
as with her foreign attention,

sing

heart-opera
)))))))))))))

                                        gender is not where you came from
                                        with all respect to the motherfathers

.
.
.
.
.
.

.

.

.

.

of a wet dream
about which
gender cares
bind on of marjoram
so also scribed other imaginaries

she
has been sung of as
                              he has

docetic
companion to girl
magistera bibendi

upward current (((((((((((((((((((((
&
bibe abide

that these fathers had daughters

that they spawned))))))))))))))))))))

.

.

.

.

.

. by dint of
inventing cuneiform

words or letters
  by dint of writing

within a budding
   an erotic impulse
(reading as an act to oneself)
or writing oneself
            queer here

. . . . .
forgive

had nothing as knew Gilberte

later, dispatch the monster

now "gendawful"

to feed
upon
a body all over the place
whipped up in ten directions

and finding that
monogamy /persisted
in thoughts, /but hardly

. . . . .

ungifted of perfume, but sweat sweat
.

.

.

.

.
who the friend was had seen
was writer

was
scatter east west south north
a writer whose writing was

Labyrinth
Jerseyed coast?
Xumal
(she lived in India a time, father
in foreign service)
abrupt departure

Abruptly awakened
by the pain
and finding that it
persisted
my thoughts
back
to landscape

a Spanish name . . .
an English child
or chill
windy coast
or desert

"jungly"

. . . was not Joseph's part
with Pharaoh's . . .

set . . .
was not

said *was not*
set

Biblical

like those mutilated saints

.

.

ignorant archeologists have
restored them
badly

.

.

.

of another
and jumbling
all names

rubbed clean (((((((((((((((((((((((

those objects that people see in trance

inscriptions, runes
to uncover you by)))))))))))))))))))

the poem
(needle, dart, projectile, latchkey)
we love
is to be
transformed
while
she, he, a parent, an obligation
discovers & speaks

gender
is
asleep

.
.
.
.
.
.
.
.
.
.
.
.
.
.
.
.
.
.
.
.
.
. now waking

.

.

. to sex

.

within a budding roves
>>>>>>>>>>>>>>>>>>>>>>>>>>>>>>>>>crossfires

the lift boy
our lateness massed on
now that they had
beings who change so
characters who luggage bring

in another century
carrying things
dildos
many,

as we ourselves change
and are so French
ho
bien, merci
are we
time by
the
mirror
of
danger
Crips & Bloods

. . . .
.

.

.

.

we are being exposed Proust say a joke

sight violet curtains
sight gut-fat in fire!
expose

. . .
soft breast
must have

are?

far far

expose

door, that's in fault
sky, that's a promise
just kiss the word / kisses "child" again

.
.
.
.
.
.   far far
.
.
.
.
.
.
.
.

sight of long violet curtains within a budding

         .   vigorous bone structure

         .   beneath delicate skin

         .

         .   . . . .

         .

.   too many "ofs" in feudal architecture

.

.   . . . .

.

.

.   apparent "of"

.

.   & then the one about notoriety

.

.

.   He is one of those

.   old

.   castles or

.   novels

.

.   keeps

.   dusty within

.   . . . . .

.

.   walk into libraries

.

.   as one sings a refrain

.

.   with abed in gasm arrival

.

.   had begun to doze

. . . .

said to them overnight
thighs, hips,
shoulders
    point to
sheets

said to them one night

"out point the point"

— 402 —

of vellum

scribes down

.
.
.
.
.
.
.
.
.
.
.
.
.

Orion

.
.
.
.
.

.

.

.

music

on mornings

figurement

the life of zoophytes naked
alas

Divided, or rather undivided

what was becoming precious
seen instance

those windswept houses
or hours?
they were writing
dumb to wind

they were collaborating

thin exposures

laid those forms, so exciting . . . within a . . .
.
.
.
.
.
.
.

of Rosemonde, of Andree

say which of them it was
which of them poem most wanted to ruin

poem as at its endings ((((((((((((((((((((((
wanders voluptuously
through ozone to ruin))))))))))))))))))))

charm

the helicon hill charm kind

like appetite

abundant of lines

buds & repents an inkling

  pent up for inking
the windswept ruin

VI

EVANGELLE

I sought the wild animal . . .

In a spirit of further experiment, she will trip out for writing. She prays she will not take on all the world's suffering. A woman could always be Martyr or Queen Trips. Not ingested LSD in many years until today. A guest of Merry Pranksters, the next generation. A farm in Oregon. An August day with rain and trenchant breeze. Someone was on a tractor. Someone was singing. A company of strangers. Someone back home, he she changed a life for she thinks (perhaps erroneously) has betrayed her with an adverse wife. She must rescue him from Mrs. Difficultness. Or so she thinks. She wants him with her. She is manic in her mind with this. She makes magic on this. She despises his weakness to make a clean break. She gives his ticket away to comradess, daughter of like-poetic lineage. They go off. Who will catch this poet's imagination, her eyes? *She has eyes for no man. Skyline, a meadow, a bower, the Magic Bus, the way the hay looked stacked there, many oddments in the house, a musty room with musty beds. Broadside of Rilke in the bathroom. Mementos of a dead beloved son. The Native storyman who repeats himself like a rosary. An old dog beneath a child's legs. Pies in the oven. The gutsy singing of Rosalie. Ramblin' Jack shows up. Deadheads out there in the meadow, in the "audience," on blankets, weary with getting there to pitch a tent, feed a child, but cheerful nonetheless, waiting for nightfall for the magic show. Show of strength. She is featured with Robert Hunter, maker of songs, tender intellect who has a mind of poetry, in his Hawaiian shirt, cigarette holder held in emphatic gesture. She's been reading and singing out from gut on stage, and falls into the aura of X, daughter of Y, who proffers the Owl's brew. And she hooks up with a Saint who is making a movie. He downs it too. Everyone is mad at Gus the Director, his Dutch lover, his little dog, the crew. Face of the distant lover is superimposed on the Haida shaman backdrop. Where is he tonight? Her voyage is not revenge (melt, o melt this revenge) but complex witchcraft. O the drugs these witches make, which make of them witches.*

ol
 d
er

                                                               plan

to make a spectacle—
illusion's mad song & apron of a stage
because we mask this one always always

& need the illusion
puppets at the screen

kliegs
Clytemnestra

would say
would
a woman
be
would wound
a woman
to love you   ((((((put on a jkt/cold
                                                      cellular shiver))))))

frisson
outside
her mask on stage?
powered by . . .
I say powdered

closet   wound a mirror

edit

me down
or
mea dow

(placed)

I'll take these notes

to save
my skin

ground down
the ego it takes
to write this down

grind down
  grrrrr
el cid
a cid

.

.

.

.

.

.

.

tween
cars who got the people here
a farm's

a lot to travel to

of people need to come together in large open spaces
(writ that again)
of peoplein spaces

comerainorshine

out of the cities

talking
to

(train of
self
taut
toughen

control to get what's
tangible
fleeted alike

fleeced down

though) rough.

I am a stranger here . . .

stub

 that thought stubbed
or stumped
the maid

Come back in next life Clara Barton or Ms. Nightingale to save these folk out here in the meadow
in the drizzling cold, gnawing on meat & alcohol. Wake thru bodies, steamy, rheumy, I wake, I
walk thru them. Wake I walk in between the bodies & someone calls out to offer something I wake
to smile. Wake to see in them the midst of the them in all of them. If there are no words? Their mist
their breath. Wakened I walk thru them.

If there are no words?
 their dicey looks
if there are no words?
serving up a meal
no words?
"horns of a dilemma"
 wake walk thru

alone.

a megalomaniac.

 evangelle

But in the kitchen
later

a deity of the house stokes the fire
behind
a broom
Hearth-Lady
who prays
who is holy in prayer

I recognize still-you out of this cock'd eye
clouded tho it be
with love decidedly acid

Made with my brother Osiris as end to the eating of men
I revealed mysteries to men
I broke down governments
I made an end to murders
I decreed mercy to suppliants
I am Queen of the rivers & winds & sea
No one is held in honor without my knowing it
I am the Queen of war
I am Queen of the thunderbolt
I set up the sea & I calm it down again
I am in the rays of the sun
Whatever I please, this too shall come to an end
With me everything is reasonable
I created walls of cities
I am called Thesmophorous
I brought islands up out of depths into light
I am lord of the rainstorms
I overcome fate
Fate sticks to me, harkens to me
Hail, O Egypt, that nourished me

goddess of a thousand names

My nod governs the the shining heights of Heaven
the wholesome sea breezes
the lamentable silences of the underworld

The primeval Phrygians call me Pessinuntica, Mother of the Gods
the Athenians, sprung from their own soil, call me Cecropian Artemis
for the islanders of Cyprus I am Paphian Aphrodite
for the archers of Crete I am Dyctynna
for the trilingual Sicilians I am Stygian Proserpine
& for the Eleusinians, their ancient Mother of the Corn

Some know me as Juno
some as Bellona of the Battles
others know me as Hecate
others as Rhamnubia
but both races of Aethiopians, whose lands the morning sun first shines upon,
& the Egyptians, who excel in ancient learning & worship me with proper
ceremony to my godhead,
call me by my true name, Queen Isis
I come in pity of your plight
I come to favor & aid you
Weep no more
lament no longer
the hour of deliverance is at hand
(Apuleius, *The Golden Ass*)

(tears running down his hairy face)

But what caught & held my eye more than anything else was the deep black luster of her mantle.
She wore it slung across her body from the right hip to the left shoulder, where it caught in a knot
resembling the boss of a shield; but part of it hung in innumerable folds, tasseled fringe quivering.
It was embroidered with glittering stars on the hem and everywhere else, and in the middle beamed
a full & fiery moon.

and she was in her acid dream deity again   but also
like insect, she was sliding in the dirt, slithery
gleaming but also slithery
she was wanting to be under the others like servant,
like snake, undercover, under grass

rambunctious in the daylight, following the communal course
with "tribe" with "group" with "sanctuary"
in an innate language only we
may understand
wired into our psychotropic brains
  (where is my hunter
  where is my saint?)

Homo habilis,
a tool-making people
with developed larynx
she was sliding again

she wanted to be nurse
she wanted to sound the emergency siren
she wanted to be with them when they were in pain
& she saw the whole world dancing in front of her eyes now
& it was, verily, in pain, the whole world

(thirsty now,
"water, water" she says to no one in particular)

(Rebecca on the horizon, Rebecca smiling now on the horizon
Rebecca wife to Isaac, mother to Jacob & Esau
sister to the Rebbe
on the plains of Abraham, on the plains of Abraham . . .
Rebecca out of my vision now, she's "real" or
editor David on the horizon, real now, he's real,
takes on boss Goliath
viewed by eye-twinkle who stands-the-fords
& Paul, another saint who hikes these drifts
real . . .)

In her right hand Initiate holds a bronze rattle, the sort used to frighten away the God of the Sirocco; its narrow rim curved like a sword-belt and three little rods, which sing shrilly when she shakes the handle, passed horizontally through it. A gold boat-shaped dish hangs from her left hand, and along the upper surface of the handle writhes an asp with puffed throat and head raised ready to strike. On her divine feet: slippers of palm leaves, the emblem of victory.

& the emblems of victory are
  key, voice, olive branch, crown, radarless sword, F-16s, dead bodies all around

consortless gods on the new day, without women

if with them listen: listen, listen

Mrs. Difficultness my new path
  confront & love

confront / or / destroy
waves of tenderness
scratch out her eyes &
then blame the man
the man, man, man
andros

  O sister, what love hath we?
that it come to this great rage
a terrible thing
would that we be clan
(in the dream She-who-rages slams doors
weeps
needs help ascending the smoke-hole, to our collective sky
  I'm above & tug at her long blonde hair
come up, come up, we will be fine!)

=clan life was reincarnation=
=clan life held us, held her—a place to be=
=it was wide like a river can be & currenting=
="currenty," the runny child said . . .=
=clan life was being a beaver in the mushroom gulch place=
=clan life was exciting it was the only life=
=because we were together, we were clan=
=not brother not sister but all that too=
=clan like normal propensity=
=what could last, some might say=
=or inbred-ness of it=
=clan blind=
=bristle of clan in morning everyone hungry=

I touch the earth
this is witness-mudra
bow, scrape, then write this down again

again

listen listen

how the lord spread out his net to enfold her,
The Evil Wind, which followed behind, he let loose in her face
When Tiamat opened her mouth to consume him,
He drove in the Evil Wind that she close not her lips
As the fierce wind charged her belly
Her body was distended & her mouth was wide open
He released the arrow, it tore her belly,
It cut through her insides, splitting the heart
Having thus subdued her, he extinguished her life,
He cast down her carcass to stand upon it

(I go inside to warm myself)

The lord trod on the legs of Tiamat,
With his unsparing mace he crushed her skull
When the arteries of her blood he had severed,
The North Wind bore it to places undisclosed
On seeing this, his fathers were joyful & jubilant,
They brought gifts of homage to him
Then the lord paused to view her dead body,
That he might divide the monster & do artful works,
He split her like a shellfish into two parts:
Half of her he set up & ceiled it as the sky

the other half of Tiamat's lifeless body became earth *(Enuma Elish)*

He heaped up a mountain over Tiamat's head
pierced her eyes to form the sources of the Tigris & Euphrates,
and heaped more mountains over her dugs,
which he pierced to make the rivers
from the eastern mountains that flow into the Tigris
Her tail he bent up into the sky to make the Milky Way,
and her crotch he used to support the sky

(we're near the end end of Sumero-Babylonian civilization
now see ever-increasing emphasis on war & conquest)

born of brutality, rape, conquering, born of the heaped
mass upon

mass upon mass of female
suffering

(to trip
a fall
in narc
issus pond
& wedge mys
elf upon all body pain)
  Yap! Yelp!
      . . . mass upon mass of female . . .)

rotator cuff is located below the chin & to your side
look there . . .

I'd had the great wine, performed the great reading where I sing to John Cage,
and we're back on the farm on the bus
highest heels not for a climb like this one to be on the bus,
tight skirt not for a night on this town, this bus, high rise, and laughing
& getting inside the mind of Hunter
this bus is a museum, not moving
but I am moving laughing to fall off into a frog pond
Rebecca catches me in her arms

& sleep in the room with many bodies, musty,
bodies snoring on the floor

remember?
but earlier

I see the stripe the pattern
of the cloth
now clearly
& outside it was a calligraphy
a calligraphy of us, me & Gus, as at the sky &

we (me & Gus) walked to a barn
& we spoke (I tried to speak, it was hard)

to see a man clothed as Shaman
He was also Boss Kesey
He was running the show
He was paying

He had the edge on lights
& color

And the crew wanted to throw the basketball (at us?
   with us?
   with Gus?)
and she will throw a key
or some small object
through the hoop
and she will be calm
some kind of show-off calm

to show she is not stoned
she is cool
thinking of her son
& how he will hook the show
& she will survive to meet him at hoop & dare
what am I doing here?
some kind of warehouse garage
& the Boss in elaborate robes,
accoutrements of magic & dare
fur & feather
it is the sham in shaman
who rehearses this circle out

all the molecules spitting at
molecules
hoop a ring of fire

it is a lovely story of a tender seal
Gus's eyeballs are big
he is lithe
& nervous
I start to speak but
he hides behind a bush

to watch his own movie
before it's shot

at this point
the multifarious
names
of all I ever knew named
flood in of

of
light
no
of semantic referent

how crowded a head

same coin
a trace
modified echoes come down to me

wilt worship me
"little master" who is Satan
half mad for me
crowded with hair

crowded with fear

a sign of a cross
in vain
I am a devil now
in my pride, in my fancy

more powerful than that other goddess
spells for better harvest on this farm
I would not heed
more cattle?
erudition not bridge the abyss
 feel in heart

the soil, & curse her heart
go down upon this earth

out now
out out
pull me out now

victim of interrogation
inquisitors-of-poem

I thought
"a witch, a fool, dancing
 on my own grave"
 I thought
"where is my cortege of
 ecstatic women?"

a word of dead
gone back under to
people-on-blankets-in-drizzle
making a humble party
having a time
on the margin of this day
got qualified: old drug day

making a bed for a child
pity for her runny eye . . .

making a song for children:
 pity her runny eye

   battle for the fertility of this field
a show tonight, there will be a party
[inside the farmhouse] to make the land grow

inside the soil of imagination
imagined house
imagined lover
a riverbed

then later I caught Gus
we parted
I to the parking lot
wandered off
in my head hiding
behind a bush
"directing" his movie
I thought
"the meadows of the underworld"
I thought
"a dense fabric"
I thought
"what is my power"
and
"flank my temples"
I thought
"a film is a lighted house"
head's afire
I thought
"the proper ceremonies"
& the report of the "mistress of the good game"
had two stones around her eyes, one on each side,
that open & close at her wish
"She had a black
band around her head with patches before
her ears & eyes
so she could not
see or hear
anything"
as confirmed by Caterina della Libra of Carano
for "everything she hears & sees she makes hers"
I thought of a mission for life
O to be a hunter

if she could
see everything
she could do
great harm to the world

or
she could help what she sees

make a choice
bend not sinister

Hunter comes close
verbal
teeming head
. . . . hear the gears in his head

whirrr
        whirrr

Hunter is close
hear his gentle code
& caution in the world

how many people to touch to touch
with a verse
a song

(hold back?
push on)

                                                    whirr

these small notes not a story
I try to track a trip, that's all

Words of visionary precision
I thought
"I've been handed down by the fourteenth century"
I thought
"impure people:
I turn into a bird"
I thought
"shall I duel with my lover

to show him who carries the most
passion?"
"shall I strangle his wife
in my head?"
I thought
"I am in my catalepsy"
& seeing the beginning & end of time
curses of those
who catch the myth
something about the unquenchable
thirst of the dead

Billia la Castagna had given all the participants
a repulsive-looking liquid:
those who drank it
were incapable of leaving the sect
It was said the liquid had been made
from the excrement of a large toad that Billia
kept under her bed
feeding it meat, bread, & cheese . . .
Another woman, Alasia de Garzo
had been accused of mixing into the potion
the ashes of hair & pubic hair

to have done with the judgment of God . . .

Please be gentle for him I snapped
sentient beings deserve to "have a life"

you'll end up in her poetry
not as embarrassing as Nin diary
j'espere

   perhaps as fraught as

she had an ambassadorial intent
what conveyed her here
launched a chain of command

& Oregon a kind of sideshow
what she did learn of external maps
was restituted inside the
climate
inside
the wood
   the
nail
inside
 the
shelter-charnel-ground

dark thoughts

inside the Boss's gentle plan

"a trickster resides here"
 she thought
 & she is his guest

but she used them
the demons
o yes she did she did

VII

ROOMS

[Come home. Calm down. Grasp the broom more gently now.]

The Tibetan Buddhist psychological practice of entering & assuming particular postures in five different colored rooms is useful to a beating mind. This is entitled "Maitri" practice, which translates as "loving kindness" to oneself. The idea here is to understand aspects of your own mentality—all its jagged particles & softer edges as well—and work on your sanity. You allow fifty minutes at a time to hold a particular stance, a distinct posture, and notice what arises in the mind. Each room has, also, a legacy, a pattern of opaque windows. You can't see out, but there is a sense of luminosity coming through, and breaking the claustrophobia of a windowless room. The color of room and placement & shape of windows will have interesting effects on the mind. Each room embodies a particular psychological state or energy. The blue room (vajra) is associated with clarity, intellectual rigor, sharp, cutting edges. This kind of mind penetrates confusion. On the dark side, it is too cool, excessively detached. The red room—literally padma, *which is Sanskrit for "lotus"—is, on the other hand, associated with communication, territoriality, passion, flashy sunsets, & extravagant, seductive gestures. Ratna, yellow, or "jewel," is associated with richness, generosity, often to the point of smothering kindness. With karma energy (green), one is forever accomplishing things, monitoring the troops. In its wisdom aspect, karma is all-accomplishing action. Buddha family energy (white) reveals, on its troublesome end, lack of humor, doggedness, implacability. But all-embracing spaciousness is the enlightened aspect of such a state of mind. These are five spontaneous meditations written during & immediately upon exiting a time in the rooms, which are housed in the basement of Naropa. She was afraid of her own passion toward others, toward anything. The room that held her when she was not in the "rooms" was a prison. She was drawn to the blue room, a kind of "exit" for her own basic nature, which was red & green, on & off, green & red, all the time.*

Blue (Vajra)

That it would be okay very soon okay, that okay it could be sooner before I swooped down in here. Lying down now, face down in a celestial pose. You concocted to be with some kind of vision or version of how it works. Brainy? Noumenally dead? Mind wants to be an ice queen. Think this so. Or astronaut hang out with me. Spaceship blue. Brought to play on such a metabolism. All around the beat of *intellectus.* What had I read so gnostically last night? Nostalgia for a library. Here would dwell the worm-in-a-book. That that was something to climb about. Pound dirt mound, fell the trees (no never). And you mention dance in order to do it. Build a mandala here, construct it with your piss, excrement, blood, diamond tears. Dream: a small puddle with life inside it. Don't step here. That he would be driving up the hill. That the hill, too, is icy. You could believe the beginning of sensory perception. Inside here. What's out there, her forceful dakini'd hand, horse-headed obdurateness, or swift like skull color. You could believe the beginning of color perception. That a child accompanies her mind is to be true inside herself as to be held by fox. The boy wonders too. The moon is a deity. Inside here. All I know about him maddeningly brief. How he sits, turns, you get his blue eye darts back, for he is Blue Snake Vajra, all's well. Some animal cool animal crossed here. But it will grow dark before it gets light, I meant the time a copy of your time or neck (a kind of yoke about your neck) we live inside. Some animal stopped here. She enters the kitchen. He bends to kiss her neck. The windows are rectangular, placed in a spatial propriety to all we hope to foster. About the blue I meant: Crypt.

Red (Padma)

Noting he is not in the room, noticing he is outside the room. Hear his voice outside the room. Inside. Then he strides in. It was noted, back of his body, his smell. Why caught what is the scheme for but thus it enters. Hungry as opposed to indifferent. She is hungry, demon between her legs. Demon dancing on my slit. Come into a world I will flay you with kisses in, bite your tongue. Operatic. Thrusting her breast out at you. Suck these or else. Lotus, tender too. Proud. Sight of Jericho. Battle in the sight of guns. Or the new Spain wedding is a padma room. I saw blood, I saw my own vessel, I saw the traitor die, I saw land and the sea incarnadine, I saw the traitor women spread wide, Petra I saw, I saw portals immortals walk through, I saw the elephants in their passion. Why seduction? It puts its weave on you. It is as if my passion might say, Come between my lips, and it says it moves to tend you. Makes you grow swelled with your great passion, overgrown flower you are trying to be. Parsifal in the snow. I say all the heroes and later heroines came with task and accoutrement. I lay on my side mental, extremely mental. Noted how mental I saw everything. Opaque window looked back at you. It will be thirsty movie screen. Project anything you wish in wash or red. Anything you wash you wish it red here. Red again, red here.

Green (Karma)

All the kings I am to march in the battalion. Always wanted to accomplish everything, which is why you stew in your own juices, which is what everyone said. You will be mixed up in all your doings, which is everything anyone could say. Saying it again so speedily you don't have time to scribe their names from the voice mail. Which is why a man I know always says "slowly please" on his voice mail machine. He'd better in a wobbly world. But what happens in you you are in or out of breath all the time in some ultimate way, or maybe you are in the beginning of where breath is made, you just got it backward, outside the mirror you were not in. Inside the cosmic mirror you are in nowhere & in everywhere simultaneously so breath is the skin of some dream. The collapse of a dream? That I know about action is what the night is born to, but day is better, day is green, night will say wanting the thing done. She gets her way. Karma is speed, it is aggressive and monitoring the battalion. Goes way back to archaic, remote time. I fought a way up the corporate ladder. Innocence is a catered affair. I fought old battle. War-torn and slumbered no time long enough. Never took a rest and then it was spring again. You talk about rites being redone and they are caught spiked, retold, the fire is lit. They are to bite your head off. They bark. Snap at your heels, a busy day. She said she had a busy day. Busy busy busy busy day.

Yellow (Ratna)

Rot not thy brain, O son, this is your mother speaking. Mother she swerve it over you, laud it over and under you, take her hand, she is going to roll her logs now. I put myself on the floor of the ratna room and took the appropriate posture, the aztec ritual sacrifice about to begin. I give up my corpse of ego not so easily, spread-eagled on the stone slab I will live the part to the hilt and halt not the knife of the priest to crave a heart. Carve. For it is the heart of generosity that makes this lamb bleat. And carves itself, monumentally, lifts above the ether stretching to sun. It worships the sun. But it (you) lying on floor here is sunbeam too, you forgot. You were just about to get up and you forgot to collect yourself. The Ratnas are gems. They are coins in a new society, sometimes bills. Paper lucre is a message to the state. Ratna. Fu: Return (The Turning Point). The Eternal Return some called it in a youth. It stored up a rich harvest. It drips its honey. You are not alone in all the soft chairs, and there are other gentle places to accommodate your body. You will be made well when you taste all my food I have prepared in the laboratory. I will make you feel small unless you come inside this room and eat. You must *mangiare*. You must dress up. You must wear your most elegant clothes. You drip with jewels so bright all eyes are ever made to burn, and it is a restless rich loam over everything you taste, bend down.

White (Buddha)

Bend over like an animal, beast of prey. Come into the hutch, the hovel, the reserve to never have to go out again. I will lock here and wait for the animals to mount me from behind. I won't have the occasion to laugh, or they won't give it me. Mock the animal, they say. They say this room should be the color of the light in the bardo, that gap 'tween living and you now lie down to die. Hardly here. Hardly anywhere. Diaphanous? I was abiding in anxiety in a room in the midst of a city. But I felt generous. I would take you—bump on a log that you are—to dine. Ghost that you are, to dine. To dine on the vittles of the tribe. We would dance around a fire in a landscape white as dirty snow. We are all animals here. This is a hospital—institutional-white. Not a spanking white. How may I sparkle? An off-off-off-spermy-white. Candlewax mixed with the ash of wick & match. Get it? You get it? I'm stuck. Struck out. This is a mind can't laugh at itself. May an animal smile? You tell me. You are meant to be sobered here. Meant to be established as a solid entity here. Cloistered here. Hermetic. Monk & nun could take a vow in here. Gregorian chant music. Piped-in monody. You know the rest. On all fours you bray & whinny. You roll over. You don't even have a vocabulary yet.

VIII

SHREE JAGANNATHA

Mohan Rao wants something. "You are the best thing that ever happened to him," my companion says. Mohan Rao is dutifully waiting for us by the small banyan tree outside our bungalow. He smiles. His teeth are surprisingly white, only partially stained by betel nut chew. Hair neatly combed. Shirts and shorts miserably faded, threadbare although freshly washed. He sports a scarf he uses as a rag to wipe the rikshaw seat clean, dust off the wheels. He swipes sweat from a muscular neck. "Many temples today." He smiles again, a little wistful. He gestures down the road. This is temples city, Bhubaneswar, capital of Orissa, famous in India for its numerous temples, some going back 1,400 years. Bhubaneswar, from the word Tribhuvaneswar *or "Lord of the Three Worlds," the Lord himself a simple granite block washed daily with water, milk, and hashish. He names some of the temples, a mesmerizing litany: Lingaraj, Mukteswar, Kedareswara, Siddheswara, Parsurameswar, Brameswar. You know all's not well behind Mohan Rao's white smile, energy, forced cheer. The daily desperate grind to get by motivates a particular gesture, word. That we would appreciate him, that he will do a good job as a driver goes without saying. He has designated himself "our" driver, although he is not aggressive, forward with the other drivers to make his point. There is some implicit understanding amongst them. Protective of us, solicitous. The vehicle is shabby, no frills. He is capable. Forty years old? I ask him questions like a social worker. How many children? Do you speak only Telugu? When did you come up here from the south? Much of India is in flames. Daily reports of rioting in Bombay, Muslims stripped and tortured. Marches in Delhi, nationwide airline strikes, communication lines down, mail backed up at the post offices. Thousands of Muslims arriving daily to Calcutta to escape the killing in Bombay. On December 6 Hindu fundamentalists had stormed the Babri mosque in Ayodhya, a city whose name means "a place of no wars," claiming the site as the original temple that marked the birthplace of the God-King Ram. This controversy dates back to 1528. In 1949 idols of Lord Ram suddenly appeared under the main canopy of the mosque. A plan to rebuild the Ram temple is announced in 1989, and brick worship begins all over the country for use in the temple. When you ask about the trouble everyone says it is "political" not religious. Mohan Rao has an inkling of the trouble. He even says how the Middle-East War, Iraqi War affects the Indian people here, "More poor." Pakistanis, Muslim workers return to India. "No work, more poor."*

On New Year's Eve my companion and I sit in the Swosti Hotel bar, where they have given us double shots, unbenownst to us, of expensive whiskey we'll pay for later. Everyone is saying "Happy New Year! Happy New Year!" The message is crudely sprayed on the dark mirror, "Happy New Year." We argue about rupees, how I overpay the drivers, don't bargain enough for goods. I'm stupid with math, can't translate into cents. Can't haggle over a few pennies. You spoil them, he says. If a rich Arab oil baron came to New York, is he to be charged more for everything? Is he expected to pay the cabbie extra? You build expectations.

Is Mahon Rao outside waiting for us? Dozing in his rikshaw?

"Please, visit my family," he says coaxingly. "It's good, you come." I go off alone with him in the dark. Lights are down except for the special places, the few costly hotels sparked with generators, oil lamps in small recesses, one lamp going near the sugar cane juice press, another by a water spigot. A dog yelps, moving clumsily out of our way. We navigate side streets, stink of offal & excrement, and come to a tight compound of huts across from a modest electrical power station. Are all these people from the south from your village? "Yes. Some of us stay together. But my mother is back home. I send her money. She's very sick." He strikes matches to light the way along the muddy path to a small, windowless dirt-and-stick hut, five feet square, if that. Paltry thatch-and-tin roof. Small cave for animals, I think. Shelter at least. His pretty, diminutive wife, Subha, dangles a tiny infant, naked but for a little protection cord around his waist, a thong with a few beads & sacred metal relics strung on, the only visible bit of wealth. A few pots, modest pile of clothes in the corner. Four children now, he says. They'd lost one a year ago. They cluster around, dressed in rags, noses running. Quizzical faces. They want to touch me. I comment on how lovely the faces are. Neighbors are at the entrance now gazing in, smiling, curious. Mohan shoos them away. "Stay with my wife," he urges. He lights a little wick in the tin of oil. Everyone clears out. She offers me her baby. Hold him. He's tiny, dark, the most vulnerable infant I've ever held. "Sick," she says. I want to help. I hand back the child, who whimpers weakly now. I fumble in my money belt for some 100-rupee bills. Mohan comes back in alone with one of the daughters. How old? These children age quickly, carrying heavy loads, tending smaller children by the age of five, begging in the streets. I hand her the money, which she takes as a matter of fact, but also with dignity. It's not that I owe them anything, she indicates.

Mohan Rao says stumbling now, "You want the baby? We give him. Take him. Take him with you." This plea stops the mind. That's what Mohan Rao wanted. Thinking for three days, watching me closely, waiting to catch me here, lure me here, show me the delicate child. I laugh nervously. O no, no. That would be impossible.

Back on the road again we're completely silent as he peddles back to the bungalow. The back of his head a shadow as close to my own shadow as my own head.

The next day we travel on to the Jagannatha temple in Puri, whose doings we observe from throng outside ("non-Hindoos not allowed") & from the Raghunandan Library balcony opposite the main entrance to the temple. I've been here over twenty years ago, another lifetime, but the wooden stick deity-doll with saucer eyes is everywhere. He is accorded great powers, much fuss & tribute, and is *oblivious to caste—all are welcome before Lord Jagannath. The temple employs* 6,000 *men to perform the various demanding rituals involved in caring for the deities, including dressing them up in their various seasonal costumes & preparing* presad *(sacred food) for the weary & hungry pilgrims. The Rath Yatra or "car festival" happens yearly, and it is from these colossal cars that our word* juggernaut *is derived. As Lord Jagannatha and his sister & brother are paraded on the cars, devotees are known to throw themselves beneath the wheels of the juggernaut in order to die in the sight of the god. We stay on the Bay of Bengal, smoke opium mercifully legal in these parts. Thoughts, dreams, hallucinations implode and twist around each other. I meet my lover on a netted cot, human who nightly transforms into a powerful cobra. And then there is India, constantly transforming herself with her vivid outcasts, the hijra (men minus men) just one example. Our chillum is carved & flanked with four hooded cobras. Jagannatha watches over us, cartoon-like, part owl, part wood. I stare into his saucer eyes.*

it is written
no, it is spoken
  nay, sung

that the eyes of a god will strip the cosmos bare
blink it back again
all accoutrements of desire

rivulets of desire

tread

then notch

  so gaze into eyes many lifetimes back
& slip into your life

Many men now enjoy
the leaves
of the lustful woman,
transformed—
who married a cobra

High on the chew that
is her spouts
& cobra man let her be had
by the rest of them—humans

They could never match his slip or slide
could never undulate
electrical current
charge up
charge up! that made him sway

ingest her buds
smoke her twigs
I tell you
she grows in the brain

"But did you enter the house of turmeric?"

All her fingers yellowed then
& she was back to tribal origin

You could turn this way,
then that &
in a moment be
squarely transfixed
between eyes,
what third consciousness exposed?

Her *tikka* shines
this is a true story
but what kind of husband was that,
to let his wife go up in smoke?

But this was a riddle:

Not the queen of birds,
but lives in a tree
Not a cloud, but carries water
Is not Shiva, but three-eyed

What am I?
A coconut!

He guessed it

He guessed her hairpin bends

Nature gods always
"breezing into your life"

So he, another human,
married a monkey girl
who arrived with a house
full of coconuts

Now I ask you
What kind of a clutter was that?
What kind of wife?

She transformed him into
soft white coconut meat
got eaten by all
& the spermy milk got drunk by all the girls
agh! sweet!

But he, the human, got tired of being eaten
And she, human girl, got tired of being smoked

So when cobra man & monkey girl
ran off together, they left those two
to their own dull human devices

& life got simpler

It did?

   —(opiated dream)

TELL ALL

eyes that are liquid desire

tell all

  can't
but listen

*There was a king who asked a hijra to show him her power. The hijra clapped her hands three times
and immediately the door of the king's palace opened automatically, without anyone touching it. The
the king said, "show me your power in some other way." By the side of the road there was a thorny
cactus. The hijra just took the thorn of the cactus and emasculated himself. He showed the king that
he had the power. The hijra just stood there with the blood oozing out and raised his hand with his
penis in it. Then the king realized the power of the hijras.*

I dilate
I dissolve

Tell all

Main deity is Lord of the Blue Mountain—*Niladrinatha*

he is consort

as we enter the *natamandapa* (dancing hall)

and I become female deity to get closer
Subhadra just another piece of holy wood
    holds central position in Jagannatha triad & central position in sanctum
  then comes alive, tells all
like Vimala is a form of Katyayani-Durga—
& original partner was Siva
Tell all

he is all
she is all-of-him-in-him

Sakta (fish sacrifices) offered to her down to the present day in a separate shrine

In order to adjust to intruding god Vishnu (endlessly accommodating these gods shift personas, go underground, et cetera), Vimala had to assume another name, which was Subhadra

tell all

about worshiping stones
about washing the "dolls"

stone or sapphire image of Vishnu embracing Laksmi is worshiped on a platform under a great banyan tree (fourteenth-century text)

purusa—a man

puri—in a fortress, one who lives in a fortress
purayati—one who fills up
derivative of root *prs*—to spray with semen

purusama in Upanishads is
a human being, the individual soul, presiding deity of some element or personal god, the impersonal, abstract cosmic soul Brahman

Purushottama—erotic tantric form of Vishnu Purushottama

An important ritual in the Jagannatha temple involves a sequence in which Balabhadra, the ascetic elder brother of the deity Jagannatha who is identified with Shiva, is homosexually seduced by a transvestite (a young man dressed as a temple dancer). In some Hindu myths a male deity takes on a female form specifically to experience sexual relations with another male deity.

menarche: tell all and of first bleeding

cactus—stung

I was born a man but not a perfect man

When we see men, we like them, we feel shy, we have some excitement. We want to live & die as women. We have the same feeling you have, just as you women fall in love and are ready to sacrifice your life for a man, so we are also like that. Just like you, whenever a man touches us, we get excitement out of it.

They call the emasculation operation "nirvan." The Hindu scriptures call the beginning of this experience the second birth or the opening of the eye of wisdom. Explicitly, it is a rite of passage, moving the "nirvan" (the one who is operated on) from the status of an ordinary, impotent male to that of a hijra. Through the operation, the formerly impotent male person dies, and a new person endowed with "shakti" is reborn.

The operation takes place at three or four in the morning, an auspicious time in India. Only the dai mai (midwife) and her assistant are present. The client's clothes and jewelry are removed and she is given a bath. She is seated on a small stool and held from the back by the dai mai's assistant, who also crosses the client's hair over her face for her to bite on. The client's penis & scrotum are tightly tied with a string, so that a clean cut can be made. The client looks at a picture of Bhuchara (version of Hindu Mother Goddess whose main temple is at Ahmedabad and who, legend has it, cut off her own breast, offering it to outlaws in place of her virtue) and repeats her name "Mata Mata Mata." This produces a trance-like state, during which the dai mai takes a knife from her sari and makes two quick opposite cuts. The organs—both penis and testicles—are completely separated from the body. A small stick is put into the urethra to keep it open. When the cut is made, the blood gushes, but nothing is done to stop the flow. Blood is considered the "male part" and should be drained off. A forty-day recovery period (like that of a woman after childbirth) follows the operation. The client is looked after and put on a restrictive diet. At the end of this period the reincorporation stage takes place. The facial hair—by now quite long—is pulled out with tweezers. Turmeric is applied to the face & body, then washed off. The nirvan is dressed as a bride, and her hair part, hands, and feet are decorated with mehndi (red vegetable dye), as those of a bride. She is adorned with elaborate jewelry and puts on new clothes. She is given some milk to drink, then, accompanied by a procession of hijras, she is taken to a body of water—a lake, an ocean, a temple pool. Now a puja is performed to Mata, which includes pouring milk three times over the head of the nirvan, and three times into the body of water.

three times the cut, the cut, the cut

three times to give myself to myself to myself

to Mata

"Mata Mata Mata"
Hindu, Jain, Ajivika, Hellenistic speculations mount
(she is wary, she is weary)

India vast in number now "reduce" the view

(bed down, all the books convey your India)

Now take a Buddhist view, tell all

ornamented & unornamented she walks in a new woman

transsexuals on the train dancing you throw a coin their way

now walk to the corners of the Universe

SAHA conjured here

located in region of the south, impure, but also "mixed"

It is
Our Universe & the field of Buddha Sakyamuni

a drama of salvation plays out
a gesture in red

images of motion & light
motion is every gesture every twitch every orgasm
tell all

Buddha is a woman too
or Buddha
is
a
woman,
too

light in the eye in the illuminated way you realize impermanence

(the cut the cut the cut)
single circular world systems come up & collapse again
Cakravala
O see an
iron mountain
surrounds it

Vasubandhu's ABIDHARMAKOSA (Sautrantika) is useful here
for its version of the SAJHASRA cosmology

(now conjure here an opiated dream)

system of one billion universes
tisahassi mahasahassi lokadhatu
(great chiliocosm) embracing one thousand "middle chiliocosms"
—can you hold this in your mind?—

cakravala is a disk ringed with a series of seven circular golden mountain
ranges, arranged concentrically with Mount Meru at the center and the
cakravala wall of iron at the perimeter
Proceeding outward from the center the mountains are

Meru: hub, fire
Yugandhara: I was walking
Isadhara: took her time
Khadirika: endless & then another step
Sudarsana: more golden I was walking
Asvakarna: tame her circle
Vinataka: like vines
Nimindhara: the vast I walk to
Cakravala: the protector, impenetrable

(getting closer to outer rim now)
                    —push, push against the darkness—

four landmasses, spoken of as islands
in which abide

the four moments:

1. kalpa of creation, which exists from birth of primordial wind to the production of the first being who inhabits the hells

OM

2. curation of creation, which begins with the first being in the hells

MANI

3. a kalpa of dissolution *(samvarta kalpa)*, commencing with the moment when beings cease to be reborn in the hells and ending with the moment when the receptacle world (sentient-being world) is destroyed

PADME

4. a kalpa during which the world remains dissolved and during which nothing remains /space where the world was *(akasa)*
  less active than Permian   HUM
          more active than poetry?

would be, wouldn't you?

a kind of *Dasadigbuddha*
(Buddha of ten directions)

would be studious here
on cot of Puri
her mind, her sex in ten directions

because life is short
& suffering is infinite
we study the Texts
to keep a shine on our universe

dear Cobra: what stone did you come from?
how many Indias go on
in future telling
impossible telling
tell all
& tribes all at the beginning
the tribe of Mohan Rao converted to Islam in another century
tell out all our secrets

worshiping gods not our own
smoking gods not owned
children proffered not our own

Apsaras reign here in the *puskaras*
& bow & worship Lord Jagannatha

They will steal your husband & make him "unnatural"
they are water-witches alive in the ritual baths
lotus-pond ladies to snatch your sex away
shift your shape away
what   text   did   you   come   from   out   of   what   oppositional   dream?

IX

ANCESTOR, ANCESTOR

The father dies, heart gives out, as travels continue in India & Nepal. He—integer of poem, with stories of war, his own particular quirky anarchy, seafaring Protestant ancestry. What carried in argument of "all is full of Jove" was male's potential innate sweetness as reflected in my witness of him. He was "elder" from an age of less commodification. And qualified by a "just" war fighting Nazis. She respects his aspiration and the knowledge that he would never willfully do anyone in. Atheist, shy, hidden, not always able to "deal," active thinker, consummate reader. Shortly after a bout in hospital, he went home to the little apartment in a barn in Cherry Valley, New York, to die. He said: "Don't wait around for me to die." Always encouraging travel & adventure. With friends she lights 108 candles in the niches of Boddhisattvas around the great stupa in Bodha. Light the father's way into the bardo. This is written in grief, in reflection. Make a way home through memory. Hindu Shiva, lover & destroyer, whose ecstatic cosmic dance carries all the features & creatures of the living world in the quick momentary flashes of his limbs, is her meditation. The dance is an ancient act of magic, of creation. The god is in this aspect four-armed Shiva Nataraja. He carries a small drum shaped like an hourglass for beating the rhythm in his upper right hand. This connotes Sound, the vehicle of speech, which conveys revelation and is related to Ether, the first of the five elements. The opposite hand, the upper left, with a half-moon posture of the fingers, bears on its palm a tongue of flame. Fire is the element of destruction, which will annihilate the body of creation at the end of this age—the dread Kali Yuga. The "fear not" gesture is displayed by the second right hand, while the remaining left hand, lifted across the chest, points downward to the upper left foot. The foot signifies Release. Shiva Nataraja dances on the prostrate body of Apasmara Purusha, a dwarfish demon also called Forgetful or Heedless. He represents man's ignorance. Shiva is totemic phallic god, outcast, sadhu, the difficult "fiery one." The consciousness of John Marvin Waldman has the blessings of the local teachers, the precious ones who make offerings for the dead. She calls to him from her sleepless nights. She makes sounds. She recites the hundred-syllable Buddhist mantra for his and her own release. The world around her seems an illusion without him in it. Or she sees the world as through the eyes of one dead. In a landscape rich with tantric ritual that celebrates birth & death constantly, she contemplates the essence of her father that gave her life & whatever that genetic strain of him she carries, then simultaneously contemplates his ashes, his humbled dust, hundred-syllable mantra.

Dream outside Puri close to the night you died: You & Frances are precious stones now, large ones, idols for the rituals we desperately need. And you need to be dressed. We were in a shrine like the coconut husk shrine by the beach, by the Bay of Bengal near the Black Pagoda. You had been bleeding and I was thinking, Can you wring a stone of blood? But it might have been the red paste devotees caressingly apply to their stone deities, primitive icons of what reality, what shape and form could you say this is. A form or "rupa" of first things. Take a tree and place a stone beneath—stone becomes deity. All it takes, then gathers. And one gathers there to tend. My father was retaining his features somewhat, as if a little hologram of his face danced on the stone. I remember thinking, How did this plug in? This was a serious question. He (you) wore his bandana, he (you) wore his frown. He (you) wore his secular scepticism well. I am thinking he (you) will laugh if I act holy toward him. But on the other hand, he wants and needs this attention. He was being readied to "join his wife," who sat aloof on a high chariot, the "car" decorated like a big Mack truck. I was thinking that she's never been in a vehicle like this before in her old life. Frances was patient, but she had been waiting many years & the garments that wrapped her were worn and faded. You have to understand these were stones without appendages, no arms, no legs. Their hair was the silk of corn or of coconut husk. She was intimating without speaking. (Was there a mouth even?) "Husk, husk." As if that is what they had become, but this was paradoxically comforting. War brewing between Hindus & Muslims. (& this is true & in the dream true too) & in the dream there was dispute about the appropriateness of these idols being prepared by the sea, and the difficulty if the Muslims arrived "by barge." And they might "bark" at us. And I, the dreamer, would go to "Muslim Bardo." And the stones could be thrown in the sea, not simply bathed. And this was another kind of vehicle, that war barge. It was time to lift my father-stone in all his splendor to the truck, and he was light as a feather, this father (I lifted him in the dream as I might my baby.) And there was a future for them together, as they would be wrapped and bathed & dressed & carried all over the city of New York. We are always in New York again.

cry to you papa who
weren't lords who
wasn't
deus who were not all
the tributaries
all rivers
but came in history: bronze star
  these are the rhythms
supple strangenesses
   unfulfilled love for women
as if every
daughter were master
for it is new time
if backdrop could ever be
  named new
collective hallucination

our commonwealth
 richness of soil, what
loam to cast your ashes upon
mix in the so-called matter
 who were really here first
rock, animal, sand, native bands
 not pioneer but what
is pioneer?
   impulse to drift here
shift there
   shiftless nightmare beast
arrives to conquer
haunts the corners
of any globe
 with salt in his mouth
salivating a great desire
fur in his teeth
 armored for the unexpected
his "other"
   decked out to seduce,
   —could you really say "her"?
I was another "her"
"armored pent waiting"
   because you were
passive
conquistador
who fought against
sight for sight
fought the light
fought sound for sound
 ground hit ground
sky inside sky
as it disappears
 warplanes change direction
encoded once more
 restarting
what could you call it—their new
 in-flight program?
if it could be put

how simply could it ever be put
putting feet on ground put
head to pillow the cold hospital
down honorably a load for
  a body put its mark
shadow putty
  puts its remarkable weight   focus in on things
which is frail, still now   you don't ordinarily
for the marking   see
 no trace but what
haunts her like a mirror
  her father's sperm
 that makes her breathe
I was saying

& he said
"I will return to the barn—
the barn! the barn!—
the nurses think it
sounds so funny
that I live in a barn"

peaked American
 for that did
again describe
accoutrements
 battered cap
muddy cup
rustic
 bandana to shield
 restless agnostic eye
 tough insomnia
demons sickness old age death
"I do not think of myself as an old man and yet"
 those things: amorphous (turtle?) shape of hand-blown glass,
  war trophy or medal, German buttons
   off an enemy jacket, soporific pills
particulars, credentials

of put his body around
  of putting on
feigned innocence?
no, it was real
  dumb, native
sweet expectation
the soldier's reward
modest room, pension
generosity
  devoted son
  she bows to them,
  the woodsmen
what it means
to be teacher
not proud since
you had to give
in a job like that
for the commonwealth
  or keep hanging on the wall
collage a wife decade dead made
  to honor him
  letter writ in type hand of Marianne Moore
our most attentive
     poet
speech not good enough
language not—
  but for her
  difficulties were
  inane patterns
  inveterate gleeful chaos
as if
  "I hate television"
 or the imagination
is only credible
  if it rants, it sings
    enjoys its birth & demise
      O wingless thought!
I too joined you
  in the crypt

glad on the year I was born to
 time a mind
whose yardstick?
a crypt of gone detail
"do they know what time is?"
I say you could dandle me
but uneqivocal tenor of
 bone, brusque touch
awkward
grope dark medicated lurch
 before I could raise the blind
wish I could say it plain
 could
let the child fall down
 not a good time, rock salt lyric cradle
never wanting, o yes, wanting the edge off
not complaining
 yes, complaining the edge to be
swift battened-down the
hatch on
   darkness
& when it comes it comes

I see you in a modest rowboat
green paint peeling off
you
vizored 'gainst the setting sun
you'd
"gone fishing"
now home, turn to us
Am I five years old in eternity?

*

Shiva's eye

June 5, 1904
I never could go to bed tonight without writing you a few lines to tell you how I would like
to have you home. I hope you can come home Tuesday. Now do not run too much if it is very

hot. As you may be overcome. I will do your errand tomorrow night and will enamel that mirror tomorrow afternoon or before you come home. I am taking things cool right now and I hope you are. I am going to bed and get prepared for tomorrow. I think it will be cooler as it looks like a shower. Now remember do not get too warm while shopping you may overdo the thing. I would rather you stay another day. Or a week for that matter, than to get sick. Now I will close. Be sure and do what I tell you.

    Ever yours, John

PS. Clara and Tresa were cutting up this afternoon and Clara sprained her ankle.

His mouth

open like mask

Nkondi was it—O
Africa to take it all

in

like sex

*

No voice

I want 2
a.m. but mine too "up"
cheery on cold machine the miles
are sin

   Showboat in a gambling motif:
Double Jokers Wild / Double Diamond / Magic 7 / Home Run / Super Bar / Jokers Wild / Wild Cherry / Crazy Doubles / Over the Rainbow / Wild Ten / Double Delight / Shamrock 7 / Draw Poker / Quartermania / Deuces Wild / 25 cents Draw Poker / Crazy Bar
   silver coins rain down (this is right after we've scattered his ashes)
the precious jewels—dandelion fuzz

—Heh Sherrington
—How's it go?

—Cut me clear open, belly button to crotch
   Healing up now, hell, I'm 86 years old now

—There's a racial powder keg in the nation

Keratometer
Phoropter

slit lamp/ bio microscope

astigmatism

shape of the cornea

sea trope
scatter of the dead man
  to the sea, to the sea

Heel: one
Toe: two
Hell: one
Toe: tow or taut
Heel: towline now draw
Tall: costly, very
Heal: it was to be sunset or stable
Tow: line
Line: all in
Heel: down at work, at mouth
Tough: beat
Road: to walk, a body to carry
   or caress
Heel: one
Toe: a third of
Hell: two or half of everything
Tall: look up
Up: bend
Tow: toss

Heel: hand
Hand: hawk
Heel: back
Toe: front
Heel: back
Toe: behind
Walk: caress
Heal: march
March: birth
Tow: ripens
Tawny: ashes
His ashes
explorers they were
puritans they were
theocracy it was
& Maximus a heroic part of America
Father? how many species like you have died

voice in bungalow
next
bang door
closes
rage
way
seashell under glass
(O deliver me a seashell from India, Rikki said)

awakening the spirochetes
                              counterpoint
the rich substitute
                    & ritual for the quelling of desire

say I won't I won't won't
say: wasn't wasn't
say I drew his face away from here
say I drew his body away from her
(see it go it goes now)
say move, lost body, move

say moved I lost my body it moved
breasts so sorry go to sleep
cunt so sorry sleeping
legs not tremble don't tremble, legs
hair needs washing I will not tell the rest

Prophecy is a corrective
not a prediction

Old Testament: every prophecy fails

But thought o I could prophesy but that the earthy & cold hand
of death lies on my tongue

I cry to you, papa
on great barge
to dance dance
in hoop of fire
who
weren't lords who
wasn't
deus who were not all
the tributaries
all rivers
but came in spurt in me

X

FUROR BELLICUS

Pull of tide ever back to home & scatter a dead man's ashes. Stark contradictions glare off America's post—Cold War rage to kill. Instigators of crime, tentacles everywhere. Rank anger. It uncoils from base of spine. Five million prisoners in this land. Forty percent of children in New York State malnourished. You want some stats? She goes out with some dedicated folks to live like a homeless person on the Bowery. Letter from Prague. A solution perhaps lies in alchemical alembic.

Andromache speaks: *(this part is sung)*

The Cobray M-11 and the TEC-9 along with their relatives and clones
are an important subcategory of the nines
Taking long magazines holding up to thirty cartridges
The Cobray looks like a quarter-size milk carton
turned on its side & fitted with a barrel
The TEC-9 is the same size but shaped differently
with a rounder frame, a grip set farther back, & a barrel
surrounded by a shroud ventilated with holes
the size of nickels

> *(pause)*

(sung)
The Cobray is descended from the MAC-10, which fires an
astonishing 1,000 rounds per minute as an automatic weapon
Pull the trigger & the barrel jumps up as repeated recoils throw the gun's
weight back
Try to hold it down & it's likely to swing about, spraying its hundreds of rounds
per minute across wide arcs . . .

Harass from *harer* = "to set a dog on"

Hare! hare!
   a cry to incite
mad dogs

> *(pause)*

Bernadette's dream as ordered by Anne:
You, Anne, have to be in charge of this project. Extracting brains and putting
them in other bodies. You are in charge of replacing all the brains. This, my sis-
ter, is a monumental task. Do you have the right surgical instruments?
And I have to ask again: Do you have the right surgical instruments?

Dear Mom
We were here & took the Scott Erickson rookie & cold spaghetti
the headless Templar knight
the alchemist medallion
the bicycle   Love, Ambrose

(sung)
the jungle did not have the same fear for us that it had for the Allied soldiers

the Japanese had no sense of balance from being carried so much on the backs
of their mothers

but the Japanese secret weapon in Malaya was the bicycle
(to the retreating British the bicycle on stones sounded like tanks
  & added to their fear)
                              (pause)

(sung)
Intratec, a Miami company founded by Cuban exiles, introduced the TEC-9 in
the 1980s
Intratec claims it has sold the gun to police and military forces abroad; they like
the TEC's menancing appearance, the company says, because they believe it
deters political street violence without bloodshed

Clint's Dream:
Darrin, Vic Lacca, and I are on our way to Tiger Stadium, Detroit. In the vast
coliseum's corridors and hallways, before the game, there are advanced tantric
lingam practices happening. Participants are seated on mats on the age-old
baseball concrete, taking detailed instruction on phallic power practices. We

would be instilled with erotic energies—thoughts, images, etc., and our erections would come off our bodies and we would hold them in our hands and do secret tantric power mudras with them. In our hands our phallus implements turned to gold yet retained the soft fleshy texture and blood-warmth. Each time an exercise was completed, we retained a separate golden lingam, which we kept at our sides. Our sides ripe to tear to tear to burst & they come off the assembly line the little vehicles little idols to fall down upon.

Bow down upon
  that little gold idol who came from seed
from stone
   inside the body of
all the jocks of morning
   of afternoon of evening
Bow down, it is mecca
  to be here and puja to be here
holy roller to be here
   Shiva lingam!

I was 27
this longing all my life for a peace offering to be given
I was father's daughter—no, it's empty that role now
I was longing I mean Leslie then Nancy then Myshal said
I don't really wear perfume
so I can breathe
When father died he had one adrenalin thing in his hand
another was clasping a book—what? NO I can never remember this . . .
suffocation is a greater coil than you can even IMAGINE
a lesser evil you can no not ever imagine
I had a Bergdoff Goodman credit card
& only wanted the top of the gold decanter
& she said—Nancy said—it's not a sewing box
what do you mean?
It's gold
(she was going crazy, seeing things in objects,
you know) The times, o the times when
Manisha wore her ruby cross
It was Bombay
more important than a datebook

a cut-off radiator hose
Buddha was still alive in 1987
And the Dalai Lama visited Bloomington for the keys to the city
He got them
He got them, simple as a comb
They were a class of women saying these things
holding up the objects for all to see
There was a question asked about
The Sixth Edict of Ashoka, which said
"Reporters have to report to me the
affairs of the people at any time and anywhere while I am eating within the
harem in the inner apartment at the cowpen in the planquin and in the park"

There was a question asked
What is the best day of the year?
The last day of school
& ten years from now
Life's going to be different I can go to bars
Mom will be off my case
This book will be ancient history
You know, I'm not a crystal ball gazer, psychic—Mom
You gotta problem?
Take your question out to the street

"Spare any change?"

We tried panhandling on Mulberry Street in the heart of Little Italy, a street with fancy Mafioso restaurants, espresso cafés, obligatory for tourists. People of all kinds, colors, some Europeans, Asian visitors passed us by repeatedly, embarrassed by our presence, annoyed, in some cases hostile. No one looked us in the eye. No one said, "Sorry, I can't help you out." I caught a wince now & then, slight recoiling. Were we junkies? AIDS victims? Pathetic? Anathema? Weird? Dangerous even? No engagement, no curiosity even. Cool chill up the spine. One of the former homeless we'd met said that was the most painful thing, it was just that: people don't look you in the eye, flinch as you hold out a hand. No human contact, that was the stab, forget money, you weren't accorded basic human contact. Invisible to them. Subhuman. An ancient broken man sat on the street down the block from us, rattling a few pathetic coins in a tin cup. . . . A centuries-old sound. . . . How long, Lord, how long?

We slept nearby on the cold pavement of Hester Street. 15 of us, 2 of us women having decided to stick together rather than brave the city shelters, where men & women were segregated, TB raged. We'd been told you need to sleep with your shoes on so they won't get stolen, and keep an eye open for sexual assault. Who could sleep?

Who could sleep on Hester Street? We gathered cardboard boxes from Chinatown, some with plastic peanut pellets, others with rice paper stuffing. Again we had the advice of savvy homeless, people who'd been out there years. Get the boxes in Chinatown. And we fashioned our cardboard condo. The street was cold. The cold seeped into your bones. What was that omnious sound passing by? Aggressive, merely drunk, indifferent? Was someone going to bash you on the head? Crush you in a box? Start a fight? Tell you to leave? Cops stopped to check on us, their lights blinding. Garbage trucks raged like rutting elephants all night . . . up & down the street . . . up & down. You slept on a cold slab of a bed, you lay on psychological tenterhooks. You waited for dawn so you could walk to the Bowery Mission. Even sitting through 2 hours of a Born Again Bible-thumping service in order to get a little breakfast & weak tea in your belly was starting to look good. You visualized the food. You could wash your face & hands there, use the toilet. Rinse your mouth. You were feeling the call & rise of your animal nature. Survival. You were thinking of yourself, your urgent need to keep alive. Could anyone take that away from you? Night after night like this would you go mad?

Dear Anne,

It has been quite a time since you left but the things keep on running. I enjoyed your stay in Prague enormously, and more than you might have guessed. In a way for me it was a kind of rebirth and charging of battery, since before your coming I felt quite off-balance, exhausted and lacking energy, which was perhaps a postrevolutionary hangover.

This country has set up for the road for freedom after the first free elections since 1936. The election campaign was quite fun. There appeared an enormous number of new parties, out of which finally about only 23 went up for the vote, including for example the Party of Beer. By the way they did not make it. Even before the election they summoned a meeting but only a few turned up, allegedly the rest went out to have a beer. Their program was much the same as the program of the majority of right- or left-wing parties, including the Communists, everything just the opposite of the past: free market, free speech, all the rights, privatization. The Party of Beer differed just with a special concern for quality beer and good services in restaurants. Similarly, the Erotic Party (which finally withdrew its nomination) pushed forward porno shops and public houses. Sadly, the new freedom has brought along with it petty concerns and nationalistic and racial bias (but you have noticed that yourself). The election proper was a success. Over 90 percent of people went to ballots and mostly voted for the Civic Forum in a kind of plebiscite. But still the Communists got quite an unexpectedly high percentage (around 13 percent). Now we are in a period of "tightening the belts" and it seems to become tough. No wonder. The first time that people are free to express their views and even to go on strike for their own good, they are asked to accept the fact that democracy starts with worsening their living conditions. But it is true that many realize that all this is remnants from the past. Although the world is still open for us, due to the ridiculous exchange rate, it is still quite inaccessible for us. There is also some real insecurity arising among people concerning their jobs. It is especially true about culture and other nonmanufacturing industries. Now it is very much dependent on Havel to prevent the country from getting the greedy capitalist shapes without the advanced capitalist social benefits. To get out of the mess, the changes must be radical and profound in terms of efficiency, but what about those vulnerable and what about areas which can never be profitable? For example our publishing house is in big danger and I guess it is not going to survive. People also stopped going to the theatres, as there are so many things on TV and in the papers that they simply do not have the time, which is rather bad for me, as it is now for the first time in my life when there are two translated and one original play of mine simultaneously running in Prague and my income is entirely dependent on how many theatre-goers are present there. Well, I do not grumble, as there are other pleasures. Take care. Yours, J.

. . . of a November 1621
this is a test
with glad tidings
public expression of it
you know who wrote "A Train to Harlem"?
"Take the A Train"
someone like Willie Stargell?
Billy Strayhorn
Malcolm X did & more
sharp
bright or vampyre, native
true today
only in America? he . . .
took the whole assassination ride
what is love?
to
stain the objects we touch?
sucking?
& native
like this
food, he
Thanks gives

if this had been a real emergency . . . in Prague   Havel reconciles enemy

stuff & truss   this purpose
he binds the American bird the turkey
& greets the native like a beloved   thus extracted
eye to eye
"yr stuffing burning, girl?"
shore   she is a rag doll
to shore
she winces but
more Duke Ellington
snow's storm rouses
advantage one car lauds
over another
wheelbarrowed out of here
hello chains   &
waits
rahulas of the hearth trying to get (be) home
yet children love to save a golf course
bruised by snow
how does leisure enter
out of anything
no blame or push
but
paces and watches
the future
black on white or red or . . .
what color
over iced snow
tracings
mammals in snow
they just had to put up the fence
I said about snow not racial
& you said about wolf bison &
Canadian geese their long
black necks overhead
bowing our heads
talking to the sky—

what is this
theistic stuff?
not theism
plunge to
make it a story, set up fences
fill the meadow (mind)
with persons   (native species)
juniper
pine bough incense
gong
spreading outward
today the only day we believe—
American food
(who's bringing
posole—?
wild rice for wild girls
as they say
"the wolf's at the door")
while white wolf's at home
eating
& we Martians
in small acreage
sweat in a kind of salt-mine-proofing
yet cook too
rather he does
to wolf her humblest down
for he is beautiful
mighty male among chiefs
as food spectators rush to
feast,
naive as might be a guess at
do we do we do we
what lack in vivacity
or proof show
aha beauty shirr swift there, swift there, & bake
knife, spoon, go taste of
& chef a beard in air
& calm never to leave this land
kitchen, said again, the kitchen-land
but

guns
positioned thus
to kill for food
meal to be born to
can you eat it, can you eat America?
(primordial
to feed
country tenacity
hold, hold on
bow this cup to yours)
Apache do wardance on Vatican
to save a sacred Arizona mountain
touch glass or lip
table & all its red candles two knocks
of the magician,
marks of the teeth
we send them flame
Om Va
here here
lost &
out of, a mantra
restored to
let them, let them breathe
let them, let them breathe
or wrongly are ranged free (we)
& we (we) are executors
blood-sattva
of the animal-other on our hand
eat this in remembrance

Blowback to "savage"
outside the ruined village of Jaji
scraping brown opium into burlap sacks
or "percocetted"

lunar terrain
trained as assassins
tens of thousands of assault rifles
rocket-propelled grenades

millions of rounds of ammunition
hundreds of deadly accurate Stinger missiles

meanwhile back in the jungle

millions of dollars of taxpayers' equipment
is missing from Rocky Flats

millions—from computers to forklifts
equipment that walks out the door, equipment that sits in the rain
eight miles south of here

eight miles south of here

a lot of the horses are out of the corral already, said Skaggs

EG & G changed the acquisition cost of a welding tool from about $137,000 to
about $547,000.
Then it gets sold. And they move the plutonium "pits" to Livermore

Eight miles south of here at newly named Rocky Flats Environmental Technology Plant, plu-
tonium-laden acid leaked from a corroded pipe for eight days because workers didn't believe a
gauge on a storage tank & maintenance crews couldn't find a leak. According to the incident
report the acid leak occurred after water began pouring from a steam vent into a glove box in
the upper levels of Building 371—a former plutonium-processing building. The water drained
through the glove box and into a holding tank containing the plutonium-laced acid. The mix-
ture backed up into another steam line, ate through a pipe, and leaked onto the floor. In all,
about four gallons of plutonium-laced acid spilled out of the tank.

"An additional problem was that the blueprints for the pipes in that building are not up to
date," a spokesman said. "Workers had to literally go hand-over-hand along the pipe to locate
the leak." He said the water leaked into the glove box through an open valve that had not been
touched since production at the plant stopped in 1989. "There are hundreds of miles of pipeline
out here and approximately 30,000 liters of liquid containing plutonium in varying concentra-
tions. These solutions have been sitting since 1989, and nitric acid can be corrosive."

al-Gamaa al-Islamia I conjure here
but now they've moved the plutonium "pits" to Livermore so you're not sup-
posed to worry

Alexander the Great, Genghis Khan, Tamerlane pitched their tents
& destroyed whole nations eight miles out of here

first a person
then a woman, a child
then a tribe outta here
then whole nations

In 1992, handguns were used in the murders of 33 people in Britain, 36 in
Sweden, 97 in Switzerland, 128 in Canada, 13 in Australia, 60 in Japan and 13,220
in the USA

In 1991, 38,317 people were killed by firearms in the USA—homicides, suicides &
accidents. More than 100 people a day were killed (more than total number of
Americans killed in battle in the Korean War)

A new handgun is produced every 20 seconds

An average of 14 children & teenagers are killed with guns each day

In 1991, 18,526 Americans committed suicide with a firearm

More than 1,000 people were shot to death at work in 1992

50 percent of children who are shot accidentally are shot in their own homes,
38 percent in the homes of friends & relatives

yea, there we sat down, yea, we wept,
when we
remembered Zion
We hanged our harps upon
the willows in
the midst thereof
For there they that
carried us away captive
required of us a song; and they
that wasted us requireth of us mirth, saying,
"Sing us one of the songs of Zion"
How shall we sing the Lord's song in a strange land?

O Cyrus, do not forsake us
Assyria comes down on its neighbors "like the wolf on the fold"

An is flayed alive
Enlil has his eyes put out

"I am Ishtar of Arbela. I will flay your enemies and present them to you."

Sennacherib recording the conquest of Babylon:
"I left not a single one, young or old, with their corpses
I had in me *the rage to kill*

I filled the city's broad streets . . .

Though thou didst smite Lotan the Primeval Serpent,
& and didst annihilate this close-coiling One of Seven Heads—
thou shalt wilt, be ennervated, desolate, eaten—
I myself shall consume thee"

Anat found Mot. She winnowed him in a sieve, scorched him, ground him in a mill, scattered his flesh over the fields, and gave him to the birds to eat

Goddesses with their hands raised in the Minoan epiphany gesture I supplicate here

HOKHMAH, heavenly bride of Yahweh-Elohim, I supplicate here
(for her thoughts are more than the sea and her counsels profounder than the great deep)

King Gudea (of Lagash, Sumeria)'s Dream I supplicate here

The figure of a man whose stature filled the sky whose stature filled the earth. The crown proclaimed him a god and at his side stood the Imdugud bird (I'm to do Good). Storm at his feet. To the right & left two lions lie. And he ordered me to build him his house. Who he is I do not know.

A woman appeared—who was she? Who was she not? In one hand a pure stylus, in the other a clay tablet on which celestial constellations were displayed. She is rapt in thought. And in that dream a warrior holding a lapis lazuli tablet, on which he drew the diagram of a house. A litter was set before me, upon it a brick-mold of gold, and in the mold, the brick of destiny. And at the right of my king, the man of stature, stood a laden ass.

She interprets dreams

Build the temple of Eninnu!!!!!!!!!!!!!!!!!
Your guardian god is Ningizzida!!!!!!!!!!!!!!!
The god Nin-dub is designing the temple's structure. Help him!!!!!!!!!!!!!!
Nisaba holds the stylus, showing you the auspicious star for the building of the temple!!!!!!!!!!!!!

stormed or raged over
how traces
webbed webbed wedded
a
notion
or do you mean
ask for it,
an explanation
Sex is never talking about form exactly
forced to behave like a gunshot wound
like it bled
Did it really?
cautiously, like rain
was secretly a writer
I know because I saw his eyes
reading a seller
was it best?
like summer glut summer glut rain
How you must incriminate mountain, weather not

not obliged

nor tardy
how mystical

light it up with rings
And guns?
Guns suck

And books, you know,
are blind, deaf
to idiots
help!!!!!!!!!!!!!!

fly to me image of Han dynasty
sonorous keys in a language you made it so
No, not notes of alphabet
but implement of motion
runic
obsessed
formalized with itself
more glyphs
that are characters
materialized
walking walking
come to light
as in proprioception
>the meat consciousness dealing with itself<

when a woman's gone to wooing
how the night is fast ensuing
et cetera et cetera
in sooth, la!

come
distress
ill bruises
& glee all buried
mem's della rena
come limpid
come sin
host in decorum
di colonne e di salci
eye lattice

a grand saint
salt of wolf of garden
trove

the parole officer
then find the word, his sentence
for life?

Bassarids in their foxskin masks
dancing about the tree of life
but what grabs her
is the spirit in their eyes as it the body turns turns
as it the body turns turns

it is a woman in a mask
I will tell you this about their profusion
as I imagined their universe

this is long ago before the weapons
but there were diamonds

(chanted)
This was a place where native germs did not exist anymore
This was a place that didn't accept any form
There was no room for claustrophobia
No room for the coward to sit down & stay a while
Any preventional approach not applicable
Any pride the kind that clings to your shirt not getting away with
anything here
This was a place that gave birth to itself in space and further than that
space, & space again
Conditioned mind is terrified because space is unconditional
Was it a room entered a long time ago?
It was a room entered, you will enter, by tomorrow
It is simultaneous with all the times you open the door
& the phenomenal world is the guideline
It is the sign
It is the symbol
Everything has its own messages

I read ya, Annie
& not so blood

if I'm guilty of love
let me do my time

& follow the pretense of accident

This was a place that produces children & great-great-grandchildren

& driving down Broadway I told my child the dream:

(chanted)
**how we were facing our end & looked up & we were many of us persons
in a field it could be your everyday ordinary stadium I said and we had
to prepare because a big rocket a big meteor was coming down to anni-
hilate us & I was thinking to keep steady o hold steady because this is
the end & this is the end & he wanted me to listen to the Doors at bed-
time earlier & I was thinking I will live through every thought & all of
us will lie down & we will be dead but there will be continuity because
I am thinking this I am dreaming this & lo the next day after we are dead
someone is continuous and this is the end the end**

what is her name?
Prajna is the glorious name
or Sophia, wisdom
I cannot color it further
& the woman slowly walked up the slats or rungs of a ladder to be consumed
by the sun's fire
saw the head & shoulders of a soldier an airman
"I thought," she said, "ikious, the sun"
I cannot edit them
I will live through every one of them & in the dream you can edit, rewind and
remove that missile from the sky
& he says yeah dreams are weird like that

they give you a slide show of the relative world
how then to lie down in it
& you are inside those phantom slides
& you became a kind of Phythia
inside her fane

the sigil is the sign the signet & you are fast on it
you are the poet & her muse
This was a place built for speed
& to
recover & communicate peculiar sensibilities of a cunt race
books are not guns
but bodies of thought
Nike marred by her loss of spear
to think back through our Mothers . . .
inter = between
sistere = to set, to stare, to stand
interstices of female imagination
bled cautiously this is the end the end

. . . .

then little Althea writes:

copy
three carré
moon
ahhh little
canary bubble
emmy emmy
uhhm
santa's express

obscurum per obscurius
ignotum per ignotius

& there was a blackening—*melanosis*
& there was a whitening—*leukosis*
& there was a yellowing—*xanthosis*
& there was a reddening—*iosis*

ladies standing on balls with jugs on their heads

Mercurius in the vessel

"Vas Hermetis est mensura ignis tui"

transmute *furor bellicus* to
mere flame or tear

XI

NERVES

dust

Puts the splint in her mouth every night so she won't grind the world into ~~being~~ a Hamlet's Mill. Do the stars above rule destiny, are we simply points on a synergistic map? How does my heat correspond to that star? Her body is like a sieve on the one hand, a rock worn down by weathering Time on the other. Come closer. Did I not agree Time's a spiral? Creating & destroying over & over. A fine grind. Dust to the kingdoms! Dentist says she is eating her teeth. She bites the lover rapturously. Anaximander once announced oracularly that the cause of things being born and perishing is their mutual injustice to each other in the order of time, "as is meet," he said, for they are bound to atone forever for their mutual injustice. But Nerves is the modal hum of such a karmic wheel. This is written mid one night, moon's in Scorpio. Know what that means? A difficult reach, a boon, a long wait, vying for power. She prays to the moon for a good catch. She celebrates clan-life. She tacks on Professor Anselm Hollo's accurate letter to an aspiring poet—generic letter to all young poet-man-woman-kind. A stickler, he. The School of Don't-Rush-into-Print Poetics. Sleepless, she rises once again to be an apologist for the macho Beat Literary Movement. A young woman writing a thesis is distraught in England . . .

Nerves, blind
attraction to,
 something like
when it's science,
the scholar says
He is dreaming of nerves again
the margins are safe,
the commas are safe
but deeper inside the book
he is thinking: it's nerves
nerves again
We'll go where nerves retreat and
study balances the mind
It was night. He was right
Nerves are science & I loved his body
. . . to be dissected
. . . . & to be soothed
a kind of science

A mind came down on me
the one I met in a book
My nerves sang off,
sounded down, and
out way back on a later burner
because the mind in book
was a body
was nervous too, and fraught
....

   ....

....

Taut light,
    taut page
nerves again
Come down upon me, nerves,
and have your argument
Alive & wait the tide for another siesta
that will be a day
that brings drinks with literature
as in "Smoke & News"
So you go out on the Mall again
lifted up from the bed of sex & news
Okay his dream,
   her sleep patter,
his restlessness,
   her trance
or old patterns repeat,
and the vision of X-acto knives
in books inside libraries returns to
nerves, nerves again

        Pages of great ones being excised
        for a greater purpose because they are
        severe or salient manifestos
        to be put up on all the lampposts
Here's one we missed . . .

The original manuscripts
were understandably fragile
But in vision you are in the
Library of Congress or Yale's Beineke
& you are younger, bearded, hooded
a terrorist for language,
beautiful thief of rare text
How do you get the transmission
in paper a tide across time,
how do you pass muster
in your aggression versus
erudition's goodwill?
Did you simply *breeze by* a librarian?
Homo homini lupus is a strange motto
How true is it?
  How brutal?
I—do you?—wonder how a
neighbor could rape a neighbor
(I saw the picture from Bosnia)
or sue a friend, steal the
good stuff, envy a car a home
How atrocity
twists under atrocity
How many times the gospel sings
a beautiful edge to get redeemed
or demystified, and someone official
glorifies war again
To get saved no matter your sin your skin
an ethnic closure & it goes like this:
different, different, territory, fixation
they are out to get us
& there is little to go around
nerves, a pulsing of them
Climatic karmic opposites?
Will intellectual rigor respond &
save all our miserable days
Pass the words around?
What sense of opulence did
a friendlier human

score under,
An earlier benign time less nervous—was it?
nerves, nerves
I return to kiss your mouth

The girl had seen how the people prayed to the moon for a good catch. She wanted to get that close.
Some of the people (she saw she heard) had such strong magic formulas that their water ladles came
quite near to the Moon Spirit's house. These ladles were small on Earth but through incantation
became enormous & were filled with refreshing water. Sometimes a whale & sometimes a seal &
sometimes a walrus were put into ladles as sacrifice & reached the house of the Moon Spirit. Once
the sacrifice arrived the person would have a good catch. Down below there were ladles that remained
near the earth near the people's dwellings who were bad hunters who had no good luck. The young
girl watched all this (she saw she heard) & thought about it (again again) & became homesick
remembering the pleasure that followed a big catch. She who only a little while ago thought only of
dying, she thought of these things (again again).

I am shining, I am willing it so
I hunt through words
I will say "whale" I will say "seal" I will name "walrus"
or
in another culture (she saw she heard)
after a twelve-year training period, the *fieleh*
would be entitled to wear a coat of crimson &
yellow feathers & carry a golden rod
He/She was seated next to the king &
could grant pardon for any crime
except murder or treason
　　　　　　　　　　　　(pause)

What is sweeter than mead?

intimate conversation . . .
. . . terrorist for language
This is my object-poem
smell of new-mown hay
this is it: elevator with two kids I'm here I'm here
this is my object: a golden poem-dome in Iowa
this is it

a prison
a railroad apartment
this is my story I'm in
grinding teeth to dust
they cut open my mother
they cut open my father
now they are dust
a sleep shade on
my head exploded
this is my object: a big ladle
a crystal ball
all around the edges of a tent I sing
wind flapping canvas white room
this is it this is my catch
a word
an uncaught catch
(for there is always a catch)
a hitch
if this is it this is my object
light & freedom within
this is my object a golden Torah
this is a dream
my lover's a terrorist for language
or
coming back at night . . . . . the tiny black flashlight . . . . . .
. . . . . . it is a good guy, a good doll . . . .
hugging a pelvis please preacher, please police
on the West Suede Highway
wake up or think I wake
Solomon's talk in Allen's dream
He'd been to Heaven
—What's it like?
—Well, there are rules—two things you have to remember
—And what are they?
—Act like you're dead &
     Remember you're dead

JUNGLEFICATION

maze jungle rising into sky
tropical bugs & night buzz
I lost my water
I lost my way there
                    There were stones in front of my eyes
          No flashlight but a love box,
full of
   the coins of love

the 3-D of the computer keys
resilient magics
   or
MORTIFICATION

someone dies &
then a cat dies
    one of a clan
    O
clan life was reincarnation
clan life held us
   held the young girl, a place to be

place?
if you believed this sort of thing
you could even enter inside a cat

placed/placate
a place to sit
hold down
                    it was wide like a river can be & currenting
                              currenty, the child said

wide like this river . . . .
clan life was being a beaver in the mushroom gulch place
clan life was independent of the rest of it
(I sweep my hand across the map to show you the rest of it)
>>>

she saw she heard how *vast vast*
clan life is exciting it is the only life
because we are together, we are clan
not just brother not just sister all of that too but clan
clan like a token range clay-made
clan like normal propensity
what could last, some might say
or not, the inbredness of it
clan blind
bristle of clan in morning everyone hungry
or wanting to agree but not
I would I could
leader?
that was the buddiness of elder
elder was a history
was an old story
carried the blame
old responsibility
woke to duty because it was clan
needed governance?
clan not so secure when you think on it
tribes are different
how?
tribes are summation
& have the animals intact
& wild toon nut named & imitated like shaman
(sympathetic magick)
clan might come later like beaver clan, bring back the industry of beaver
clarity! clarity! was only a naming call

Dear Surface Crest,

Thank you for your letter, and for your trust in letting me see the enclosed typescript, with my view to possibly writing a note for it. It is in response to that trust, and in a spirit of sympathy, that I feel compelled to give you this considered and honest advice: Do not, repeat, do not rush this into print.

You are an effective and dramatic reader/performer, but, as we all know, it is possible to make the telephone book sound exciting (at least for a short while).

In a book, on the page, the poem needs to be more than just raw material to present to an (these days, and in most places, increasingly illiterate) audience, in ways intentionally or unintentionally designed to cover up weaknesses in the writing (such as unexamined clichés, received ideas, tired "beat" stage props, etc.). If Whitman's "barbaric yawp" had been only (or truly—he is being definitely ironic vis-à-vis the academics of his day) that, we would not be reading him today.

I know that you consider yourself a poet in the tradition of Kenneth Patchen. It occurs to me that you might find it instructive to read what else was published, in American poetry, at the time KP was writing and publishing; not just the big names but the "field" he came out of in the 1930s, and to study the ways in which he does differ from his immediate predecessors and contemporaries. Just to realize how, and why, what he did was fresh and new and important when it was being written. There is no point in trying to repeat what he did (as, to mention just an example, Jack Micheline seems to me to have done); there is no point in trying to sound Hip, or Doomed, or Victimized, or Romantic. He did it. You have to do something else, something that corresponds as exactly as you can make it to your life, your mind, your senses. You have to find out what it is that you are seeing, hearing, smelling, touching, and then you have to find words for it: there are no "new" words, but there are words that don't come out of some prepackaged bag but that are put next to one another in a way that bears your imprint, the imprint of your mind and body, first and foremost, and then (of course) also the imprint of your time and place and culture. But what is and will remain truly interesting is that "how" that is yours, not whether you were one of, or adored, the Beatniks or the Confessionals or the Fugitives or the Pre-Raphaelites.

Came across this quote from an interview Frank O'Hara gave a year before he died, 1965, speaking of Robert Lowell: he says that Lowell seemed to him to be working in a "manner that lets him get away with things that are really just plain bad but you're supposed to be interested because he's supposed to be so upset."

See—in a "reading" situation, everybody involved easily gets into this kind of make-believe "interest" and "upset," i.e., false and ephemeral emotion. And I imagine it can become a kind of drug, a place to go for a rush, especially for the "reader." In a book, however, it's all there on the page, and the page is all there is: no special pleading. The page is evidence of care and respect for the material. As in the finest Japanese brush painting, what looks the most spontaneous has been the hardest to achieve: it is never formless, it has mastered its own form to the point where that form has become invisible. Paul Blackburn (whom you mention in a poem) was at his best a great master of this.

Well, enough already. Please consider this in the spirit in which it is offered, one of concern for your desire to write and publish work that will make a difference.

With best wishes

        A. H.

---

          no caught turmoil to bother her poet's head beat, but sleep,
sleep . . . .

=an interlude=

Dear Jane Dancey:

You've brought up some quirky questions, "issues" that need time to consider. Here's quick bit
of my thinking . . .

I think the Beats are still vital as a cultural force primarily because their art—their writing—
holds up. Now that so much of the work is in print & stays in print and other texts—previously
unpublished—are coming into print, people can judge for themselves the worth, the value,
the intrinsic power, beauty, wisdom, outrageous originality of the writing. And you must get
specific here, because each of these individuals is decidedly a unique stylist. Perhaps you can
generalize about Beat "values" or some such, but lumping all these writers together is poor
folly scholarship. I don't think "their" reputation—ultimately—would last without this
immense body of work left behind, still in production (Whalen, Snyder, Burroughs, Ginsberg,
di Prima). So. That doesn't necessarily mean everybody reads them, of course, but because the
work is strong it still carries a phenomenal & phenomenological energy or charge—large rip-
ples after a heavy stone has been thrown in the water. (Old pond / the frog jumps in / Ker-
plunk!) It's finally, then, the work that's back of the whole thing, the writing that counts. What
do you think of the writing? But once that's understood, there are so many other factors that
contribute to the legend(s) . . . which, like any popular movement, is rife with complexities,
difficulties. One could go on & on about the adjacent "issues." Think for yourself how relevant
to the writing. Maybe interesting but not relevant except in current contexts. You wanna talk
about "queer theory"? You wanna single out misogyny? or mother-problems?

As I see it, with some exceptions—and the biggest is the inattention to women and the often
sexist attitudes about women that undermine some of the early writing (primarily that of
Kerouac & Burroughs—Allen Ginsberg, Philip Whalen, Gary Snyder are still active, still writ-
ing, remember, little sexism there)—the Beats are popular because they represent an alterna-
tive (in their work, philosophy, action) to the status quo. An antithesis to bald commercialism,

selfishness, spiritual vacuity, political advantage, double-dealing, lying, dishonesty, racism, general all-around uptightness. They were, for one thing—like few people were at the time—onto Jazz, inside it, influenced by it, appreciative. One of the greatest musics of all time, still horribly neglected. They were/are travelers—literal and psychic. They got OUT THERE, looked at the world, mixed and mingled with all kinds of folk, and recorded their adventures with loving detail, attention, taking to heart William Carlos Williams's dictum "No ideas but in things." They studied "minute particulars." They experimented with mind-altering, exploratory drugs. They wanted and did STRETCH their consciousness. Some were early environmentalists (Snyder, McClure), advocates for spiritual, sexual freedom, Native American rights. They have, on the whole—then & now—a pretty good record.

The women, as Diane di Prima once pointed out, were "not getting the transmissions." We're talking about America in the fifties, a difficult time for women anyhow. If you were a woman & different, strange, artistic, bohemian, if you didn't buy into the American dream of Barbie Doll marriage (or whatever the equivalent was then), your parents could have you locked away. Given shock treatments. Abortions carried tremendous shame and guilt (losing virginity was bad enough). A suicide attempt was also taboo, a blot on the family line. In the meantime, alcoholism, dysfunctionality, "downers" (sleeping pills etc.), sexual abuse on children etc. etc. were rampant across the land. We're still reaping this karma, so to speak. There were distinct overtones of fear of women, mother complexes, misogyny. I can't claim to have psychoanalyzed these Beat guys, but I recognize the torment there, and a deep-rooted fear of women's power, which is blatant in cultures & religions & whole nations worldwide (Islamism, Christian fundamentalism, some styles of Buddhism, Judaism, African nationalism, white supremacy everywhere etc. etc.) and our so-called modern enlightened Western world is no exception. Madonnas or whores, etc. An old syndrome. And one could also call to task the Art World, the straighter literary world, almost any cultural/artistic community. Women have had a raw deal. The Beats, those particular ones who seem most offensive in their writing, should have been an exception. I think in the case of Kerouac there was a stunting, a crippling in his relationship to women (*Tristessa* is one of the most heartbreaking books of a failed relationship), exacerbated by his monk-like need for psychological space around his writing, dependence on a stolid (impassive?) rock-like self-sacrificing mother with her own complicated need, & a weird blend of Catholic-Buddhist "view" in his head. But can't you feel the wrenching throb of his mind? It was interesting that when we had the Kerouac Conference back in the eighties at Naropa's Jack Kerouac School of Disembodied Poetics and included a panel of women who had been intimately involved with Kerouac, not one of them had an unkind word for him. I kept trying to rock the boat! Maybe he brought out a motherly instinct in some women. I'm not trying to make excuses for Ti Jean, just trying to understand the underpinnings better. And Burroughs, from all accounts, even tho it wasn't by any stretch a normal marriage, loved Joan Vollmer (his wife), thought her a genius, was stimulated by her powerful intellect etc. But they were crazy junkies at the time, and yes, his basic sexual proclivity was toward men. I don't consider him a typical homosexual (if there is such a thing!) either. Nor Allen Ginsberg, who also loved & feared his mother's madness. (I think you'd have to include a study of homoeroticism to get to some of this stuff.) Took care of her. She inspired some of his best work. You could write your thesis on these relationships alone. But these men at least were TENDER toward one another, not into the competitive macho syndrome you find in a lot of boys' clubs, not out joining the Marines together. A great deal of comradery, support, interest in aesthetics, philosophy, intellectual/artistic exchange (editing each others' work) and the generosity of going the "extra mile," not trying to do each other in. Neal Cassady (not the writer the others are but a great monologist/talker), thru Kerouac's heroizing of him, becomes the quintessential Beat. But consider other writers of the time—Norman Mailer, Henry Miller. Do they not suffer some of the same idiocies around women? And, again, the whole culture? I think intelligent scrutiny of any of this range of event & phenomena would turn up some of the same hideous ignorance.

My experiences with Allen Ginsberg have been remarkably free of misogyny on his part. He calls me his "spiritual wife." We have worked and traveled together for more than 20 years, founding a school together, a long long history (whole chronicle there). Burroughs has always been gentlemanly, respectful, a "colleague." He has been a generous teacher & presence at the Kerouac School. I was present around the sickness & death of Burroughs's son—Billy Jr.,—during the late seventies/early eighties and saw Bill Senior in a different light, as concerned parent, a "man with a heart." Also some stories there. He was, in some ways, an influence on compositional aspects of my own writing, through his own experiments with cut-up. And I saw his positive effect on younger writers. Gregory Corso (who was abandoned by his young mother early on, spent much time in jail, etc.) has also had complicated relationships with women. (I don't find his writings particularly sexist, do you?) We keep a distance but maintain, basically, a playful relationship. I've also seen him at his best & worst (exacerbated by drink & drugs). Whalen, now a Zen priest & head of the Hartford St. Zen Center, is a master teacher. Gary Snyder, another comrade. He is a tireless worker on behalf of the sanity of the world. McClure also. Ferlinghetti continues to do major publishing work, political work, through City Lights Books. His coeditor/publisher is a strong woman, Nancy Peters. Amiri Baraka is a tireless cultural worker. And a family man. His wife Amina is an artist & writer as well. He continues to struggle on the behalf of African Americans everywhere. He has had to live with continual harassment from the U.S. government. He is an incredibly generous teacher when he visits Naropa. And there are others.

And remember there is strong writing by women from the early Beat period who are considered part of the movement, and continued with interesting lives. Diane di Prima (a principal player), Lenore Kandel, Hettie Jones, Bonnie Bremser, Joanne Kyger (read her funny Japan & Indian Journals), Joyce Johnson. And the lineage is carried in part by many younger women. At least the next generations are heavily INFORMED by them.

It is too simplistic to say "boys' club mentality" if we're talking about the ongoingness of lives and work. Back then if we want to lock in a particular period, phase, there's some accuracy certainly. I hope in your thesis you specify the time, the period, the particular work. And write to some of the women present then. The worlds of most of the writers associated with the Beats who have survived—& most of them did—have expanded in myriad directions. There are further relationships, families, children, practices, more writing, collaboration, teaching, travel . . .

So I have a less myopic view of all this, and sense, from the vantage point of the Kerouac School, the power of what these folks did & continue to do. And we don't have to get holy & pious about it either. And I'm not apologizing for any blind spots, ignorance, lack of tolerance. There's been amazing stuff since, and I feel great confidence in the poet-warriors (so many of them women!) coming out of this spectrum/program, which flies, in part, under the Beat banner (although we nearly called it the Gertrude Stein School).

Warmly

yr Village Explainer

Nancy Levin: I mean, do you feel like you had to work twice as hard as they did to get published—was it that kind of thing?

Joanne Kyger: Well, no, I wasn't getting any pats on the back, so I didn't have any real audience. I didn't have anybody that was encouraging. So I had to find my own momentum & my own desire to take me through. Then once I came back from Japan, there was Donald Allen, who wanted to publish the Japan & India Journals, where someone says to Gary, Is your wife a poet? & wrote "I felt like I should be writing poetry *in front* of them."

NL: That guy in India—I just couldn't believe that he was saying, Who is she? I thought Wow. It was wonderful. I loved that.

JK: You know the style of the fifties & maybe the Beat scene with Allen was a very male-oriented buddy group—there weren't too many extra women in there. I don't think women were treated with any particular sense of equality, so in order to be there—& you couldn't just demand it, then you'd be a whiny woman—you had to be intellectually able to be there. I remember when Allen was in Japan stopping on his way back from India. I gave him my work then & he's still having problems with it. The other night he finally said, Well, it's lucid or clear or something like that. I never got the pat on the back from Allen, let's put it that way. Plus you never get it from anybody else. It's your own voice that you have to feel confident in—no one's going to tell you

you've got it. & I think you're always in question about it too, in some ways by reaching it. *Is there anybody out there? Where is this going? Am I really saying what I want to say? Am I saying enough?* I'm really strict about overwriting & not wanting to write the same book again, being in the same place.

XII

GLYPHS

"A scribe whose hand matches the mouth, he is indeed a scribe."
—Sumerian proverb

"Who shall read them?"
—John L. Stephens

Any poet is enamored of syllabaries, alphabets, the phonemes of old tongue & groove. She is rest-less again & travels to the Yucatán to meet a stubborn knowledge, secret, yet vibrant still in its actual display, the toil & play of its living people, their tragic disinheritance, and the ruins that bring her to her knees in awe & astonishment. Egypt's remnants, many moons back, were never quite like this, to stop her mind. The closer continent intrigues the imagination more subtly perhaps? Less trampled? Hidden? She moves with a scholarly companion of equal stamina & inquisitiveness. They read into the night on a humble cot, one bare lightbulb, outside Tulum, into Cobá, Valladolid, Chichén Itzá, Maní, Uxmal, Mérida, always checking the simple rooms for reading bulbs & lamps. Reading old accounts by night, eyeballing the incised glyphs by day. What sounds behind their fierce façade, what lore, what language, what action, what myth or passion ruled, how much warrior & slave blood spilled to meet a dire hallucinated need? Who built what & how? She is sometimes Rabbit-Scribe, sometimes Mescal-Lady Great-Skull-Zero.

& the code
public record stopped midsentence . . .
a great backbone of volcanoes
codes a mighty kinship
& arrived there a kind of goad
forgone conclusion
that it sounded in an ear,
a jungle ear, serpent vision hiss
or strum, that it made sense,
created a universe, a world tree
a "raised-up" tree: *Wacah Chan*
she goes down to market . . . .

The priests want her thus placed,
conjunct to reality,
hazed in the dream of sacrifice so that instead of
blood blood blood
it's star star star star

the route of divinity crosses the firmament, the world goes out, eclipsed,
(fired) (see eclipse tables of Dresden Codex)
released or realized in the abstraction: it could go
on, the "let," the blood

& my dear friend, always in sight, throws light around
amongst the good skulls, a rude awakening to rend your flesh
off off
learned all this from a skeletal woman
reading the columns left to right
top to bottom
about twins & oppositions, metaphors for the concept of change
paddlers representing day & night
one thing replaces another replaces another replaces another
chan (caan) sky
& *chan (caan)* snake
a homophony, a glorious conjunct

nobody knows when it started

more arcana:
the data base must be large enough, many lengthy texts
the language must be known, a reconstructed ancestral version
Linguistic family should be known
a bilingual inscription of some sort is necessary
the cultural context should be known
for logographic scripts there should be pictorial references

Who can read the inscriptions under the bulls or elephants of Indus-Harappa?
Who shall read them?

forests hacked away
what changes is not the will . . . Atlantis?

(Olson, thinking this, *off*base, hunts among stones)
or astronomer tracks the skies, celestial tropical nights
looks down, stares down the long stelae, complicated, in moonlight

The royal scribes write the data & deeds down in bark-paper books
devotees of the twin Monkey-Man gods
they live to write, lords of language
"linguistic boundaries leak like sieves"
but they mouth the lines linked to place, dark deed, lineages & destinies

(It is not possible in Mayan to use an imperfect verb [referring to actions or
events in the past, present, or future that have not been completed] without
sticking a date or temporal aspect adverb in front of it)

buried a millennium . . .
then

ghosts   should endure . . . . . go on . . . . . go on . . . . . go on . . . . . & walking
million Maya still walk these lands . . . . . gone on . . . . . gone on & walking
made it . . . . . object . . . ? . . . . . this is play . . . ? . . . . . important
-----------unauthorized lives . . . . . but gone on walking these lands . . . . . incised
? . . . . . or   wasted . . . . . go   back . . . . . it
written . . . claw . . . precisely . . . that they walk, speaking . . . what is memory?

hand on chin to visit . . . . . get up to ask . . . . . cut off...............//////////////////////////
thinking . . . . . thinking . . . . . polished . . . . . walking . . . . . timely to walk the
sacbe . . . *disappointed* . . . . .
come again . . . . . it is a day time? . . . . . talk with friend . . . . . drink *balche* . . . .
exchange? . . . happy? . . . all parts & more . . . . feathers . . . . eat *keehel wah* . . . .
breastplate/////////// . . . . . the day it was transcribed . . . . . that was the house
of . . . . . changing lord
it is his name . . . . . the name of fire . . . . . name the lord of fire . . . . .
he drilled fire . . . . . the ballcourt . . . . . watch . . . . . it was the lintel that was
his . . . . . ? . . . . .
memorial of the house . . . . . ///////////----------------over------------------

& she went down to market & heard the news

various guises of Venus

It was a great ceremony, don't lose me here

and of "Count" Jean Frederick Maximilien Waldeck (1766-1875), the historian
William H. Prescott (in a cutting Boston tone) once confided to Mme. Fanny
Calderon de la Barca: he "talks so big and so dogmatically . . . that I have the
soupçon that he is a good deal of a charlatan."

producing drawings & architectural reconstructions fanciful in the extreme
he died of a stroke, pretty girl passing by . . .
maintaining till the end of his life Maya civilization had been derived
from the Chaldeans, Phoenicians, and especially the "Hindoos"
what folly lurks there, what coded racism?
(Lady Xoc nods, crouching before the Vision Serpent in A.D. 681
& vomits up the future, all that will occur will occur)

one of a long line of fascinators, fascinated by, fascinated on, to "crack" it what
got coded long before you were born, the earth went dark & then they came in
. . . Constantine Samuel Rafinesque, John Lloyd Stephens, Frederick
Catherwood, Alfred P. Maudslay, Teobert Maler, Charles Etienne, Brasseur de
Bourbourg, Ernst Förstemann, Leon de Rosny, Eduard Seler, Cyrus Thomas,
Desire Charnay, others. Thompson, Knorosov
& you, woman, what of your great quest?

Boleta de Entrada, and we go in
coded/closed . . . . . >>>>>>>>>>>>>>>>>>>>>>>> . . . . . open to?
feathers & arrows, the heavy plumage
lead off by the curve of a neck>>>>>>>>>>>>>>>>what Toltec sacrifice?

>>>>>>>>>>>>>>>>>>>>>>you play or not>>>>>>>>>>>>>>>>

certain death

This is an assignment where you go to a museum to observe the past in a twist
of fate
it is often the shape of bird (clay, bronze)
object made it of itself myself
that was itself a kind of death-rattle
(see *tzab,* the rattlesnake rattle that resonates with the Pleiades)
but more objective, like removing the mind of . . .
but you say about the sacrifices, they go willingly, but a horror in the face
panic not the stupefaction, or seeing the vision, eyes wide
flowers, earrings, wool wrapped around an old lineage miles ago
& how important in my life? decked out . . .
slaves & bastard children, those who lost at ball

my clan? my kin?
what topology O Proto-America

it was her way out
& then she whispered because she was speaking in me, a kind of Maya
hallucinogenic bone tube enemas, they carry the vision into the stream

I cried I started I leap I strap down. Doctor Witch he came down on me I go out
I go out a light like she who might die in a short stretch, flower cut *ex stasis,* this
one Amazonian *brazos.* This old arm twisted body burn she valiumed out like
lights. See her, Momma, see her I go get down the basement out the body now
see me wizarded or wizened a mother's thigh, she in *huipil* she in bright flow-
ered sun, Mérida. A dream, and then he came inside me, a shorter death. . . .

In the evening we took another hot-bath at the *lotería,* and the next day was
Sunday, the last day of the fiesta, which opened in the morning with grand
mass in the church of San Cristóbal. The great church, the paintings and altars,
the burning of incense, the music, the imposing ceremonies of the altar, and
the kneeling figures inspired, as they always do, if not a religious at least a
solemn feeling; and, as on the occasion of grand mass in the cathedral on my
first visit to Mérida, among the kneeling figures of the women my eyes rested
upon one with a black mantle over her head, a prayer-book in her hand. . . .

Mérida tall beauty, a bloody plan a wound dead never but state of settled mind,
unsettled, those descendant calibrated to spy on the afternoon. Mérida, the
helpful panama-hat man guides me to the post office, then saves a parking space,

illegal, going wrong way. Somber. Hombre. Buying tequila Hornitos now to rec-
ompense a green mind. The lover in his beauty, eyes bore into mine. Locked.
Wanting to taste the bitter lemon & salt of life. Then she goes down to market.

dream: copal smoke rising like a snake
she goes down to market
all the Indians are silent
she goes down to market
in an awareness of earth, it is a clay musical instrument
& air brings sound & soul to the object
contact with an alien symbol, try again
(she weaves she weaves)
clay is the number of her song
& her weave is not a macho thing but circles the warp
And then becomes writ in stone

Who shall read them?

going down
saying something confusing
something you meant to say way back it was midnight & you talk it to a wall—
old stones, the last blocks hundreds of miles away whisked here on whose
authority?
I was in love with the heroes & adventurers who quested your dark continent

in a Red Notebook
& this was the chaos of the Red Notebook:

storms, conflagration, the tempest at Tulum, hoping to make love in the
water, a nest of hammocks, some hippies still traveling through, running
naked into the water, left a prissy white jacket on the shore, the kind you wear
when the pope's in town, forgotten in the tequila of love & dream, silky sand,
and the pope was converting all the sins to gold pesos under a rim of a saucer
go gently here. So what is the big buck of this town or time?

a little tourism, a little rope hemp but market dries up, one thing replaces
another replaces another, and nylon is the order of the day to tie anything up
replaces another replaces another

This is the Red Notebook speaking, lifetimes away, sentences freeze in her handkerchief also the degrees climb. I was planning this notebook about the new world ways about the rage of any underclass anywhere you turn, going down to market. . . .

Red because of passion
Red because of bloodletting
Red in the nature of clay, which card is up
Red because you lied
Red I did your name in red
Red the spotlight was never going to turn
Red was mortified
Red was a palace of seduction & held the breasts aloft
What red could hold artistic attention, hold the crown?
Ruby tooth of the jaguar
Priests could sanctify the ball game though it end it must in pain
Eyes turn
It is over
They lose
& Jays & Sox are caught in Oct 1993, Sox lose
You dream or you believe?
Who will win?
Red the color of Philadelphia

Red speaks to a crowd
Red is under seige, a coward
Red in the center of attack
Red in the color glyph code
Coded for centuries
Red whose name is Chac
EAST WHOSE NAME IS LAKIN
& that is Red's direction: east

Witch, tell my fortune, prophecy my only star
Venus? Do you keep moving or still?

Assignment: dear Naropa students, go into a museum, stay in front of a particular picture, graven image, idol, or visual detail a long time. Stay until they

close and are restless you leave but don't be rude, banging the old wooden
doors, turning off the fans, you are tired too, from sleeping on the coast, bugs
on the sand, your elegant suntanned legs—

you stopped in the Museo Archeologico for rest
down at heels, gorgeous, blond gringa, transfixed in front of the weave
a statues depicting the beginning and end of Maya time
The world directions as discovered by Rosny
& associated colors later by Eduard Seler
& all the deities that crack the whip
Credit where credit is due
Behind the ears? . . . . in this girl's "dig"
& being archeological I unearthed the glyphs to my own rendering

I, Princes am . . . . . she who writes . . . . . monkey-scribe . . . . . or rabbit woman

or let me live to crack a code: revolution

went down
went down to the market

What is the best day of the year
The last day of school
or ten years from now, the boy says. . . .
Life's gonna be different I can go to bars
My mother may be dead, he says
This book will be ancient
I'm not a crystal ball reader, just any psychic out on the street
but son of (child of *yal* [mother]), who borders the next century
----------?----------
He of the wide-mouth speaks it
He is a monkey
Yax he dedicated the four-bat place,
it was his house
"sky god lord," Moon-Skull
the seventh successor, the lord of the titles, *Yat-Balam,* Holy
Lord of Yaxchilan (just one example)
Taken?

A problem-solver
Solve the cresent moon
it moves while she went down to . . .
her lover

dark
meteorological dust
settles
on
the
moon's
surface
then
is
covered
by
transparent
oxygen
ice
(I am alone, alone)
Sunlight
penetrates
the ice
&
warms
the
dark material underneath

what market economy lurking there?

his *brazos*
arms for the asking only if I feel good, arms for the taking, ordinary closed eyes,
a kiss, detachment of the sense climbing one more pyramid and wanting to
scream How dare you slight the great Jaguar god, how dare you burn the books
in Mani, how dare the colonizer, destroyer of hemp an old god slighted, down
in the teeth, the mouth, the earth
Chac chac chac chac chac chac chac chac chac chac chac chac chac chac chac
chac chac chac ch acch acch acch acch ac

mool

                                        But
                                        the
                                        heat
                                        cannot
                                        escape
                                        through
                                        the
                                        ice
                                        so
                                        some
                                        of
                                        it melts
                                        into
                                        gas
                                        causing
                                        pressure
                                        to
                                        build
                                        until
                                        the
                                        gas
                                        erupts
                                        upward
                                        through
cracks
chac chac chac chac chac chac chac chac chac chac chac chac chac chac chac
>>>>>>>>>>>>>>>>>>>>>>>>>>>mool>>>>>>>>>>>>>>
carry
I say, carry
ice
&
dark
material
with it
so I go down . . . .

she goes down to market
anklets jangle back to------------India?

coded back into ur-language
What are they saying?
It is written
It is written .

always on my shelf: the terra-cotta phallus,
the bloodletting isn't over yet
Take your cause to Lord Chac
& circle the house of Turtles
the house of the Old Woman
the house of the Dwarves
going down . . .

We went to the Orange Bowl. We took a plane from West Palm Beach to Miami. It was a two-hour train ride. The train was loaded with Notre Dame fans. My dad and I were about the only University of Colorado fans in our car. When we got to Miami we got on a subway which took us to a bus station. From there, a bus took us to a loud Orange Bowl stadium. We stopped at a stand and bought a cute T-shirt. My heart was beating hard. The first thing we saw from our seats was the Notre Dame band. They weren't very good, but the Notre Dame fans liked them. A little kid was screaming his guts out for CU. So was I. The first half of the game was exciting. The halftime show was pretty good. It had a lot of firecrackers and lights, dancing and singing and floats. Then CU kicked off.

The second half was the most exciting part of the game. The game was over. CU won 10 to 9. CU fans went wild. They were in heaven. It was hysterical. It was hard to get out of the stadium. Some people were screaming and some were crying. We tried to find the bus so that we could get back to the subway station that took us to the train station. Then we took the train to West Palm Beach.

the men go to the ball game
she goes down to market

Stephens (my animus in this dream) in Petra, the red city, says to me, You will go there in another calendar & play their games, unknown then, now ungraspable, you will have to dress like the Arab boy, & here, the *huipil* (white with flowered embroidery at neck & hem) or disguise of panama hat, overtime entering
I intrude upon the red ruin and a Menacing Man shows up stealing my jewelry ancient players of the old regime

coming & going
the royals ones absolute in power & pride, they are a writing elite named
ah dzib (scribe)

& then we were driving to Cobá in the little red Bug & as I lifted the book
to ask had we seen that one, that pyramid yet? you turned for a glimpse
& hit a pothole, two tires blown out
now at the mercy . . .

& the taxi-drivers-who-were-drunk came and asked me to be *amiga*
& we pointed to the tires, kaput, and they made motions with their hands
like cars careening out of time & space & huffing noises
so we would get to the repair shop
I keep tapping the soberer one, not at wheel, to rein our driver in
almost knocking pedestrians, guys carrying huge goods on bicycles
then
a can-do kid for a few cents fixes the one we had no spare for
his old mother rocking outside, and back to the car safe
we thought we'd end up on the *Tzompantli* (rack of skulls)

how out of any of them one reigns supreme?

He was a wise ruler
only sacrificed those he had to

He stopped the clock
He organized the Venus festival
& fixed our tires
with rubber (the blood of trees)
his was the reign of _____
The tablets spoke
you see me, see me calling
& she goes down to the market
no truck in heavenly things
keeps a vision all to herself

Katun 10 Ahau, the Katun is established at Chable.
The ladder is set up over the rulers of the land

the rapport, the bed, the chamber, a cynical conquistador. It was wash wash
wash & wear. I see the colors. I am pink red meat raw & blotched with a rash
of eyes. The scourge of the tourist & her plight, the outline is political, the
outline is insane

It is not dressed up enough in all the colors
Insane?
Because other time frame. You can get on every wavelength . . .
It is a mere guess how these people, so dark, so sophisticated, practiced their faith
They say they were obsessed with one eye on their gods
Invoke
Invoke the need for blood
It carries the day
It is mercantile it is slaughter
& went about an ordinary day

They slowed down the process
But the rest of their constituency speeded up
To quit the ground of most resistence
It was ending
It was coming to an end
It was the end of time
It was old hearts cracking
It was a headless body, a woman's . . .
She had not pitched a ball
She had spoken with apt tongue

You have to be in charge, you have to be in charge of this body and putting
Anne's brain in this *other* body (someone sent me this dream). It is a new body
for Anne. I may need to repeat: you must put her brain—it is ashore—in her
new body, which resembles no one you will ever know. The poet abdicates
control this is a reminder she goes down to the market . . .

so many times to be afraid, your number always comes
you will be flung into the *cenote* one claim to fame
you wanted it
elegant the first time
& entered in
intruder, a clause
a cause for
you wanted it
Did it want you?

Dear Anne,
We were visiting the temple at Ulu Watu. I thought I could fly, out over the blue green white
crashing water. Camera in hand, Grazia was standing between the outer wall and one of the
offering platforms. Suddenly a monkey jumped from wall to platform using Grazia's shoul-
der as a midpoint springboard. The attendant prevented these quick grays from proving
they're smarter than we are. Dreamt you sobbed on my shoulder & said, "It's just that I love
everyone. . . ."
it's just . . .

what generosity rages in death?

On his body, before cremation, little pieces of paper called "armor devis," who
are protection devis. No difference between outside & inside now. Why need
armor?

It is a long tale, a long drive to the repair shop

Suffice it to say, "Paranirvana," holding his seat
tilt
rigor mortis a thing of magic, dear Chögyam Trungpa
kindness: 49 days
kindness: green mist coming out of mouth
kindness: the tilt of inside & outside
I saw a good king die, a shaman, pass death
in a 20th-century dream
They say blood was pouring from all his pores . . .
Though I never needed a sacrificial patriarch to rule my world

I was never wanton
This was a travel back to gloss & ruins

How the driver-slasher cuts my heart for the scissor cut play
I was dreaming
& then I went down to the market & you said "It's just . . ."
(TV played a role to alternative lore)
Execute half offensive or you be dork, my friend, go around here & I am boss

archaic remote   clues   shards p[oint]   o taken!

the slip or shod   harebrained scheme   vertical flange

ravages   weatherings   layers   obsessed with war

entice   cloud-scroll   austere   how would you die?

The Xibalbans hang up twin Hun Hunahpu's head in a calabash tree. One day
a young underworld princess named Lady Blood happens by & holds her hand
up to the head, which spits into it. She becomes pregnant. It's just . . .

I screamed
& then died
his arms older then ever, cracked with brown specks (I see it now)
eat eat
drink drink
on this day
dust holds the earth
on that day a blight covers earth
a cloud rises
& mountain too
a strong man seizes the lands
things fall apart
a tender leaf murdered
dying eyes close forever
signs on the tree of life
generations hang there
the battle cry is raised

They are scattered in the forests

& this is the secret agenda no matter what
(all these in the marketplace for exchange or sale)
coded: Itzamná, Lizard House, one of the aged gods, smokes cigars,
& wears the headdress in the form of a mythological owl-like bird
named Oxlahun Chan
His rule of underworld Xibalba is chronicled by the rabbit scribe
rabid scribe

coded: Ix Chel, his consort, is moon goddess with a toothless mouth

& finally, Personified Perforator, a stack of three knots
Flint, obsidian, thorn, stingray spine are attached to the ubiquitous long-nosed
head
This deity personifies inanimate objects in the Maya symbol system
& their starry machinations,
that they swept a night sky clean
close observation, tracking,
to bring the cosmos to its knees
& rule without & within,
drugged, simply?
living in tandem

a people, whose people, imploded in the Maya tongue

who reads them now
what thought to how tried the ancestor dream how it was loaded with the
romance of schemers & adventurers,

coming down to "power" America

& have I told you about the dream? "just a tortilla lady" who visits or rather I
visit her in whom I was some years ago—that skin, that body, that curious
mind, & traveling & she shows me the magical blanket that weaves itself into
the night sky

cordillera, her spine
a shawl to hang about the moon

then rain
it rained
it rained
rain (May–November)
and what was considered in the great span, it rained

milpas
beans, squashes
sweet manioc, chili peppers
along the Puuc chain
she went down into the *cenote (dzonot)*
the circular sinkhole,
found her death rattle there
found her rapture there
walked the land & talking

spider monkey, howler monkey, ocellated turkey
joined her there
& she wore in her vision
the resplendent pelt of the jaguar
that shone in the moonlight
& her vision was mouthed & recorded by rabbit and monkey twins

it was 23 December A.D. 2012
when the present universe was annihilated
when the great Cycle of the Long Count reached completion

it is written

They were bled
Who reads them now?

idzat
"artist"

XIII

OBJECTS OF DESIRE

Called upon for performance, here's oral section in parts for four women. She's heard a blend of distinct voices already in her head. Operatic. Contagious magic is the plan to make these words effective in a nightly void. This will be a ritual production. Lights & an audience. Costumes. A stool. A typewriter. Brenda carries a nightstick. Kaitlyn wears a long black leather trenchcoat. Judy is blasé, administrative, & sits back. Types. Brenda will be on edge. Kaitlyn will strut & pace back & forth like a streetwalker. Anne steers this vocal constellation, shifts gears to interject surprise, moves at irregular intervals. We hold text in hand. Use it in gestures, as obstacle, as point of reference that we carry tangible words with us. Voices will come in on top of one another. Now purify the ground of ritual theater. This is to be heard as a four-part Sprechstimme conversation in the head of an insomniac. Four new voices are invited to perform this text at any time. Music: Shubbalaksmi, Mercedes Sosa, Bulgarian Women's Chorus, Om Kalsoum. (As you read this silently or aloud, please play these attendant musics.)

K, J, B, & A all characters, all stalwarts

A: It was a matter, it was mattering that dissolve to rules. Animal fury, intensity, body, body. It was a matter, it was mother or master, it was a gleaning, monstrous couplings forming, all the worlds in upheaval. This is the cosmology. Words will do it, painted & free of lid, of lid, as in "put a lid on." All behavior offensive. The sun was always standing still, watching while men they did it did it. Revel in fear, keep their boots on, hyperagitated, no ventilation, panting after the women they fear the most. A kind of dagger in, contagious magic, stick it, stick it in. Think of mucus, think of wounds, think of her belly, charnel ground. Think belly charnel ground. Belly belly charnel ground. Inner mucosae charnel ground. Love the body, decompose the corpse. All in it together. Invitation to sink in. Vertiginous eroticism. Saturnalia but a transgression? Think it poor a habit spreads itself. Moved by passion stronger than will. Will tumble down, create a cosmos. Spiral, spiral, spiral, spiral. (*she twists down to the floor*)

Is this the discussion? Are we having a discussion now? Can I define you, body? Waltz in. Questions please. Any question I've got one. Nudity provokes lack of charm? No, what I'm saying saying saying is. Outside marriage is nudity fun? I mean I never got there. By the sea, by the sea. I grew up by the sea by the sea. Take off all the clothes by the sea. *(turns to audience, points at individual women)* And you grew up where? And you, you grew up—where? And you? You grew up where?

Enter B, reading from a large tome:

. . . . . to the secret understanding . . . . . one to other . . . . . tendency, a shift . . . . . fact to dull . . . . . hike desire . . . . . capricious . . . . . kind rots . . . . . what do we care . . . . . king sits down . . . . . rises . . . . . what care we? . . . . . burnings at the stake . . . . . I had a stick once . . . . . I had a broom. . . . . . I was the police . . . . . I thirst for it, embrace . . . . . O animal muck . . . . . king runs for president . . . . . what do we care . . . . . numb of male born . . . . . fleeting . . . . . we are expensive habits . . . . . creature . . . . . king's photo in the newspaper, who looks at it? A song for your thought . . . . . I was mad, transgresses, but I will read to you about something that happened, happened today *(reads from* New York Times *here, a strange account):*

once upon a time . . .

Which book is the closest to the body? *(she rips the newspaper into shreds, and stomps on the book)*

J brings in a typewriter and begins typing slowly, pausing, muttering to herself, rattling off names, numbers, as if she's typing some kind of art catalogue: "Bust of Apollo 1993," "Anti-Cuntrification," "Lost Episodes, a Series," "$1,000, acrylic & sand." "Twigs, blood, semen, spit," et cetera.

I think I know. The book is the capitulation. The book is ready for *me* to write it. I will read it first, then I will write it. It will be as big as my head. But you open it & see all the body parts. See them? You will read me as the world.

Cruelty is negation of the world so hate it. Cruelty has no charm at all. Cruelty would be numb of male born. I tell you I fell in love once & it was eros of reading a book. It tripped me. Like sorcery. Love that joins from all the others, take this. Cruelty has no bounty. Cruelty is a bad habit. Cruelty doesn't pay. Cruelty is the lapsed lover. Cruelty disengages the heart. Cruelty is lost on us, so why the rage, why pin someone down like a bug. Cruelty is always the bigger one. The louder. The most obese. Everywhere I turn in every direction—and there are many directions to cruelty—I wince I whimper then I stomp I rage. I try to breathe it out of me. Disembark from it. I was thinking but discursively. I dreamed we couldn't find our Shakespeare yet. . . . He had a word on cruelty.

Essential to sex. It will be stories of murders & fictional fears. I will start on a street, an avenue you've never heard of, close to a park. . . . It's dark . . . *(she goes into a kind of reverie in this description, which K will shadow)*

A: Numbers of people moving about. *(K strolls in, very confident, like she's cruising, & acts out A's words.)* One bends over, she's in leather, to pick up a note or paper—something wrapped in it? She bends over, leather, something writ down for her. Or not for her. But the way she bends down, I tell you, the way she bends over, you want to freeze it is gentle, generous, it is particles of woman . . . I could see from the bench where I sat. (I got up & moved toward her hoping the crowd will part around her, like a sea.) She bends over, I was telling you this as erotic, no, fear? In leather. Black you guess. You are always right because you know this part. She bends over, strawberry blonde hair hangs over her right side. Pick it up. It was white paper, folded, in moonlight. I walk to her, and see her face. The sea will part. Numbers of people moving about, ambiguously.

J is reading words from the paper: clandestine, oceans of cum, libation, mercurial, free the Theatrical Four, Remember Tibet, meet me roadside 15 degrees latitude longitudinous litigations, last but not least, are you for sale?

I invited these people in. *(J's hand sweeps the room)* This is my gallery, my space. This is for art's sake art's sake only. I'm not so interested in philosophy. I like a show where things happen.

B bursts in swishing air with nightstick: I am the policewoman here. It is my duty to see them—these persons—erotically, as if they'd make a move, bend over, it could be vice. It could always be vice. I am the squad all my own. *(makes a sound like a siren)* I can make some rules. Nothing easy about a policewoman, nothing soft until later. To receive a message, to think a thought could be vice. I am the squadron to notice and oppose vice. Vice could be a word, a deed, a fiery messenger in the middle of the night to rankle the ear. I fought some old demons. How to bar a thought I've wondered on it. Got some hunches. Her voice, the one in front of me, the one I hear now she's reading something is low now from any pinnacle. Void from any pinnacle. Everyone has identity. I've got to break up anything illegal. So people have names and numeros. Uno, dos, tres . . . I can check on it. *(pauses)*

Is this the way to begin *my* story? I will tell you the funniest thing I ever heard. Someone said "sharpening the pool" & it was the funniest thing I ever heard. "Sharpening the pool of students." And ask her what is in the note. Why she bends beautifully. Erotically. Freeze it. Perhaps you are mistaken, perhaps the message is for me. I come here always. It is my beat, my soul-place. If I must die in action, in battle, let it be here on this little square of America. I can radio my comrades but they would travel far to come here it might be too late. What are ladies' voices? A policewoman is paid to notice and investigate and report on anything untoward, suspicious. I staked this out. A contact I need to have made for me. We are more than myself out here. I carry the radio & baton of trade. Speak softly & I will carry my stick. Secrecy is essential on a job like this. A lover's absorption in the universe. A shark's. She is not smiling. She is perhaps here to sell something. This is the common denominator everywhere: "to sell something." I will sell my savvy. And I claim a right to be hired because I was trained you know. And then the idea of a book. I was trained you know in desire & the erotics of the human plan. And to think like a suspicious one. You look suspicious to me, young strawberry blonde in leather. Bend over. Bend over. Bend over. *(B bends as well & picks up crumpled paper)* It says *(B & K simultaneously)* "You are the nightmare & the dream."

(K bends over repeatedly, stuck in a gesture of retrieval)

B: You see? She hears me & knows power, training when she hears it. Is she one of my agents? Bend over, Kaitlyn, bend. *(A intrudes, breaking up this pantomime)*

A *(excitedly, didactically)*: What would a Marxist do or say? I have to think this way . . . power structure, economics, hierarchy. Who pays you to write? Why do it? In a society that has done away with institutional sovereignty, personal sovereignty is not given. Even the women who fought to abolish that which oppressed her (was it merely that other woman?), which reduced her to an object of tears, reduced to a level of things, she must still be some stroke, some gesture, poem, recapture that of which oppression denied her. What could that be? What could this be? What could that be? What could this be? *(she pulls out a notebook)* I wrote: I'm sick of this woman business. *I just want to write like a nun.*

K: I could be just bending over before I am arrested, you know. No big deal. Lots of night people out like me. And seize up that note that went for me. It wasn't exactly a sonnet. It was Abelard's letter, it was the confession of a tyrant in love. Is the world richer than my language for it? Should that stop anyone. I want to ask them is the world richer than the language for it. What word could you say. Do you need drugs to hear it? Do you need to be dying of orgasm & climb that old ladder? What political climate does it matter to take the richness of this world to the beach? Bow down. How many characters of any alphabet does it take to mirror the richness of this world? I grew up by the sea. To the beach, some day we go to the beach. One day it whispered to me in the breach in the imagination of the Marquis de Sade. It was someone like a Stalin speaking & it was an oil slick kind of day. You couldn't have a proletarian dictatorship. You couldn't disarm the forces of the counterrevolution. Civil war would follow. Then Lenin stepped in. These were not my heroes. Results from an accentuated development of capitalist industry. You can't separate the two. But from the erotic view . . . was Lenin attractive?

B: What was the desire for?

K: Someone would always be oppressed.

A: Compare a mind to a city, compare a mind to a song. Compare a temple to a bird. Compare a park to a stage. A stage to a mechanical bird.

J: Compare the glass to the table.

A: Compare the German language to a star.

This was the voice speaking to me in the imagination of a writer.

Compare your inner ear to the outer belly of the whale. Compare the hair under your arms to the quill of any bird. Birds will always be there for comparison in my imagination.

J: Compare the book & the notion "What Is the Meaning of Communism." Especially now. I grew up in a place where we were forbidden to utter any of the "isms."

B: Compare your right breast to here, the nipples darken, rise up. Taste them. Are they the same?

K: Compare her voice, murmuring "the park, meet me in the park" to mine.

A: The park to me. It's like a program for perspective of dream work. And relations of fire. Did I tell you that's what it was to be a writer? We were doing some experiments for performance. Some of the visions of the world. All levels of society mixing freely with all their scratchy voices. Could it be human. The same light shines on the Republican, you know. And the tundra. Frank O'Hara spoke of it one presumes because he thought of the tundra living by the sea. Relations of fire & homeless are the women I needed more of. I was welcome I was very welcome but I needed more of more of more of more of women to speak with, and discuss these things. When I talked to the sea & the other elements. And sometimes animals. And it was guys around me, always guys to compete with. I was not writing or living inside Tennessee Williams exactly. I was more non sequitur. Psychologically, dignity is a shadow I always believe tailing you. The old man still has it. The women who are objects of desire, even for the page alone, are tailed by their leather raincoats. Someone stand to count, someone stand to count. . . . No arrests please. Don't tempt Satan. She is powerful and her mind is her body.

K: She acts you out. She takes you. She acts you out. She takes you out.

B: Nationalistic forms of violence no matter how much a woman you are, take it out on you. The stones are real. The suburb is real. The mall is real. No, the mall is a projection. How to save it not be mere replica I am part of your object of serous desire. Erotic because of consumption. Erotic because I needed more of more of more of more of more of women to speak. . . . Then

J: Then, then then . . . Yes? *(very impatient)* Something has to happen here. Something new has got to be written! I will force it out of you. You are so messy such a wig. You are so messy such a page. You are so messy just a man. You are messy monarchy. You have a too-big room for writing. You are so messy just a hunch. You are so messy such a retreat. You are so messy in your face powder. Messy text & grammar. Messy syntax & style. Messy hussies.

How could it ever be big enough? I needed the dangerous park & policewoman to hold my hand. I needed more than notecards for memorization. I needed to travel to the block notions gone now to no dignity tail them. Where are the tribal communities now? Depose the tyrant. Put on his shoes. I take issue with a mod approach. I wanted to once I did I did to rule the office. I fire up now. But earlier when I turned the radio on to the talk show a woman was complaining, she was the aunt of the bride, & the couple had been engaged several years already, and she was complaining about her crazy sister & the sister's family how they had all showed up at the church wearing clown costumes. For the wedding. And was she kidding or what? Was this an insult or what? Did her sister need help? The groom's family were horrified, the priest, you can imagine. But it was funny then I was driving down Folsom and I swear there were guys driving on either side of me dressed up like clowns, thick make-up.

A: But if you are on the job, they see you, they like you. Clowns are everywhere. If you are on a job they compare you to a bird, a real go-getter, a summer day, better autumn day. They compare you to a fireman always ready. Soldier, you are making preparations. Trained to be a setting sun. Trained on a city, narrow it down. You are putting an eye to the scope. Hit the target. Something erotic climbs you, marshalls forth a cry: Ay Ya Ay Ya. But to dress up in a certain way you are saying something. And then you give off a little cry. Ho. Or is it Caw caw caw . . .

Gravitational. Graaaaaaaaaaaaa-vi-tation-al.

K: I like the sound. Animal need. The Native American will win in the long run. We will be sympathetic to white women. My parents were _____ & _____ and I have no claim.

J: My parents were _____ & _____ & I have no claim.

A: I have a claim! I have a claim! I have a clam. I have a clam. I have no claim. I have a clam.

J: Say it. My parents were _____ & _____ & I have no claim.

A: My parents are _____ & _____ & I have no claim.

B: I have a complaint. I have a compliment. I have a plaintive cry—AH

K: It was a necessary banner. Banner to be held.

ALL: It was a smattering, dissolve to rules, forms. How to bend over nonsuspiciously, could be Prague, could be anywhere a foreign tongue. Could be a Kurd. Kurdish women woven in, could be a round rime & light for all of us, maiden dignity, maiden voyage, could be a strong sea swelling, could be death by eros. Could be, could be *(as if groping for words)*—liberty. *À nous La Liberté!* Could be, could be . . . could be . . . *couche avec moi s'il vous plaît.* Could be tangible dark night, I wait on my bench to do a job . . .

Could be, could be I have a job—scheduling art, scheduling artists. The boat comes in you grab them. The monarchy can't swallow them up. The revolution soon tires of them. Socialism (ha!) might have worked. But I get them. Schedule art. You see these walls. Someone hangs them here. It's a job with an eye to pleasure. Eye to your pleasure. And the artist must be happy if she is alive. And if she is dead, you do these things for her. They are her heirlooms on the wall, on the floor, on the sky. She makes a claim because she had a body. She had a book which told her story. And I might design the catalogue, another artifact.

K: Like this? *(She bends over, taking off her coat.)*

B: No, like this. *(She bends over differently.)*

J: Like this? *(She bends over yet another way.)*

They all, four stalwart women, standing horizontally downstage, speak the following in play, in unison, repeating lines, improvising upon them, taking liberties, dancing in place, gestures toward sky, motions toward ground. Some of the movement in tandem, others out of sync. Call & response, whispers, shouts, cries, chantlike. Hear this as you may:

Kind of a law to void out of a pale face to have a claim on wall, on property. Take it to the sea. Kind of a desire to be a part of it. Take it to the sea to the sea to the sea. Standing here before you. Under you. Someone wrote this down for you. To be your object of desire. They could be pretty words or not. Or not. They could be pretty or not, sad you say or not. Long too long a speech to make here. Or not. But not to be abused forsaking all truth & desire. But not to be stranded, the tide is out again. Not to be tundra bred but light of tundra way up above everyone, sovereign. What does that really mean, to be sovereign. Queen of her world. Kind of pale face kind of dreams to have queen at hilt, to have her over you. Get sown to the menial job of it. Of her. Of blue outfit, of blue uniform. Skin of the big cats I'll wear, you'll wear, we'll wear. Kind of like a playlet to hear our voices in so we try it on. We try it on. We try it out on you. We tried to be true a kind of longing to alert your eye or ear. What poet makes a song or call to. Call to. Call to you. Call to you. Send out call to you call to you. In civil tongue in harping tongue in tongue of the lion, jaguar, a not-muzzled cry, a not-muzzled cry no not a stifled cry, no but Kurdish woven in, and all the belles of any ball, wallflower life, the end of her labor time, working, working, working, working, take it to her sex, to her sex, to her sex. Take it to her sex to her sex to her sex. She, like any light sing out a part of but typing too & more than enough of you to be body. You, you be eyes. You, you be feet. You be breasts, you. You there, be nose, be mouth o open wide be mouth again again be mouth again again be mouth again again. Be elbow, be shoulder, be palm, be ears, eyebrows, be the triple heater, be thighs be thighs again, waist I hold you, belly I taste you, be a lash to future night, go down

go down

go down

go down

breasts again, be mouth again again, be mouth again again talking, talking, you were always talking

Mouth again, you were always talking

No you were always talking

Mouth again you talked & talked

I invited you in

September was still sunny

Was windy

Be a lash to future night, go up, go down, go up, go down, go up, go down, go up, go down

Go up, go down, go up, go down, go up, go down, go up, go down, go up . . .

mouth again
mouth again again

XIV

ONE TASTE

"One taste," or "rochig" in Buddhist psychology, is a state of awareness or samadhi (absorption) in which one realizes that all experience & phenomena have the same inherent quality of energy, whether it be negative or positive, painful or pleasurable. As such, this insight provides the meditator with new eyes. This "siddhi," or accomplishment, is to my mind related to the notion of rasa in the Sanskrit poetic tradition, which literally means "taste" (flavor) or "essence" (sap, blood, semen). There are eight distinct categories of rasa, including the erotic, comic, heroic, horrific, odious, angry, pathetic, and awed. I wonder if in combining all eight categories one doesn't come to some ultimate black hole of primordial rochig. This experience could be dull, nullifying, it could be like all colors mixed into black, or it could be exhilarating in its hard density like a diamond—more condensed & powerful. This chapter is a ritual performance that combines the various textures of the rasas and arrives at "one taste" through love & its attendant pain. The chanter must be operatic by temperament, and must visualize herself as a Greek chorus having a collective voice and wail hybridized with the antics & seduction of a torch singer. This is sung-spoke, this is gestured. This is homage à Beckett.

Lone spot on the chanter who is Writer
A kind of blues-like wail, syllables in descending pattern:

Lon- *(sounds like "lawng")* on-on-ong
Lon-on-on-ong
Long-on-on-ong it took long to get to

Lon-on-on-ong
Lon-on-on-ong
Lon-on-on-ong it took long to get to

ONE TASTE

(Then hands in front of mouth repeatedly & quickly in a gesture of pulling strands from same or spinning to create a kind of fire image):

The tongue flickers like some demon's
or forked
two directions

(here the arms reach out from tongue in opposite directions)
ten directions *(chanter spins on the spot)*

Lon-on-on-ong
Lon-on-on-ong
Lon-on-on-ong
It took to get to you

ONE TASTE

I turn my back on you in tyranny mode *(turns abruptly)*
hinged by very thin wire *(in whisper, lying down)*
precarious string from heart to gut to cervix *(gestures to these parts of the body)*
fromhearttoguttocervixtohearttoguttocervix
riding in the getaway car *(jumps up)*
(starts to pantomime turning of steering wheel)
spilling the mescaled drink
as libation on path *(moving in circle ritualistically as if scattering holy water)*
(mumbling "Om Tara Tutth Tara Ture Soha" over & over)
I said about the muffler it was
EXPENDABLE
not really
but loud like my expendable fear
exposed & RAW *(an enormous roar)*

The night is warm *(gently)*
Turn my back *(turns again)*
to strip *(taking off clothes)*
& run up my back door naked *(turns forward)*
in the body sense
I do turn my back on you *(turns again, abruptly)*

Run to embrace that mountain *(monodic chant, slow)*
Beware cactus underfoot *(makes motions of walking cautiously)*
& prick the intent too
Pierce me &
turn it around
Get to the yard to chase a mad demon over the fence
or knock him to the pavement

& was that a person in the sense of . . . *(this part improvised upon operatically)*
was that a pavement
or was that a person in the sense of . . .
was that a pavement a person in the sense of . . .
hot & chalky
it was it was
& was a cheek to ground
a pavement kind of transition
concrete of person who walked upon
a pavement to cheek it down
& was a kind of person & was that a
person in the sense of cheek or pavement
it was but was it hot was it chalky

& kissing the ground *(bends over)*
but not that you walk upon *(gestures as if writing on the ground)*

Lon-on-on-ong
Lon-on-on-ong
Lon-on-on-ong
It took long to get to you

Bending over
I tasted the unmistakable spring leaf &
slightly bitter chip of wood *(face onto ground)*

Needles of the forest stung my face
as I sunk into you

                ∨   ∨   ∨   ∨

*(This next spoken forcefully as if addressing the ground, sounding each
word with great intensity)*

which>>> now >>> domestic>>> light>>> plush>>> towel>>>
jammed in closet
box shoe wooden something hanger silk jewel stump

hidden hat a sword a clock a danger a diaper a rage
a beauty a worn heel a down-at-heel jumble melted stocking
desperate stolen bitten fur sex scent on me
me a man-woman bending over to humble herself on wet tile
a closure the closest you get you never try you did but I didn't
the end of something outside inside like person like pavement
was hard was ground was flesh what was it?

it was
was it?
was
a taste . . . .

reach up
reach up now
reach up
reach up now
reach up
reach up now
reach reach

(hands to heavens like gospel song summoning the spirits)

UP

reach me
I reach you
reach up
reach up now

Long long it took
to embrace you

He grows like
the expectant lover *(groans)*
I turn my back on
(turns again)

TEAR YOU OUT OF ME!

long long enough
rub together the deceptive existence
of me & other

(rubs hands together)

TEAR YOU OUT OF ME

You exist because you do not exist,
Other

I taste my hand
All two of them, salty

I extend them to the mountains & the sea

(bends over, rocking from side to side
licking both hands)

& of my crackpot nation, what of it?
& of my anticipation, what of it?
It waits
It waits
& the little village I passed thru—is it still there?
& of my wiles, can you see them?
& of my purse, it falters
& of my tolerance, it anticipates impatience
& of my fist raised in protest *(raises right fist)*
it aggravates the lady next to me perhaps—
Who is she?
& of my cowlick, it is energetic
& of my smile, not for you only

& of my sob
it is the taste of the sea

Lon-on-on-ong
Lon-on-on-ong
It took long to get to you

Long long I took a long time on it

one taste *(bows)*

Taste me now *(offers up palm of left hand)*

(right hand lifts up making gesture as if writing on the sky)

XV

DEVIL'S WORKING OVERTIME

She travels with Ambrose to the Virgin Islands for hire. Work with a group of writers. It is the middle of winter. They escape many storms. A preacher on the radio has infectious urgency. They explore the reefs, & slow down. Swimming is a soothing mantra. They live in a tiny cabin with cracks in floors and holes in screens the insects creep through. The boy goes night-snorkeling, looking for an illusive octopus that he never finds. He's bitten by an "acid spider." His hand swells. He explores her randomness with her. Words are coming through here in a list for broadcast. Her students tell dreams. She & her son stargaze. The telephone is far away. Do they grow healthier? Together they name the things they don't understand. Conjure Amiri Baraka here.

the Devil's workin overtime
the Devil's workin overtime
He's workin harder'n he did a year ago
Yes, that's sure
hmmmmmm that sure is true
the Devil he's workin overtime
he's workin triple time
quadruple time yeah he's workin
yeah he work he workin
he's got plenty a do
he's a busy one he plenty a do
the Devil's working overtime that's sure
o sure that's sure he workin he workin he is
& it's a dark dark time he's everywhere
& workin harder'n every minute every second
triple time quadruple time
hmmmmmmmnnn he workin he workin
O you sinner man o umm huh you sinner man
you sinner woman too you a sinner too
all god's childrun asinning asinning
& don't you doubt it people you sinnin
he is yes he is surely working overtime
Devil Devil Devil umm huh
force of the Devil you see 'tween people every day

'tween man & his wife, 'tween man & his boss, brother'n'brother
father'n'son, sister & sister mother'n'daughter
doan you see it? & you see it
so much trouble every n where
that's the Devil & he workin overtime
'tween man & his wife trouble o lord trouble
the Devil's workin overtime you seen it all over
& you gotta push him outta here
push push against the darkness
you gotta be strong agin that devil
cause he workin overtime he is he is
& push, push againt the darkness
& push push push against the darkness
go for the light

great barracuda
under there—he points—
dark shape in the shadow under sea
up for air
takes the tube out of his mouth
there—
he says
treads water
hand suddenly out
in the air—
this big!
(the length of his stretch)

humans inhabited the area long before Columbus's arrival
Indians, migrating northward in canoes from South America lived on St. John as early as 710 BCE
They hunted & gathered food primarily from the sea

Introduced to a woman at the beach she looks up
"I'm writing a manual"

she's channeling Emmanuel
"Emmanuel told me to take a five-year sabbatical," the man says
the devil o yes it is

A List

a boat named Fetch
frangipani
flamboyant
termite nest
sensitive plant
lime tree from India 400 years ago
sensitive plant again
poison apples
machineal
Salt Pond
Annenberg Ruins
bricks of coral
bay leaf
shipwreck landing
Stoplight Parrotfish again
slave quarters
Captain's license
"Justice is the enemy but there's a child in you"
inebriants to keep demons at bay
Valiumed out
rum in punch

that this ode not erode

Nudge
a
banana twit
flits
hits
bowl of nuts
ah fast heart, bold thief—
pinnacle
of grit

tetrastich

crusty
the beginning
of her reign

netty way
to scold
now
one incident cross a wire
sap of life
soup's on
suspicion

sets up beak
awry
squall

knew
I'd never see him alive
gain a ghost father
so
door's shut
was turned
mystic face of him
alert
in all my time

cavern domain
she, a fish, hides
o yes
she flashes
dark milk she
dart milk she
blue tint stealth display
hiding like a fish

ode of coral not erode

but bright
was sepia
flash
hazy color
being born
head was too big
cut open my mother
too big
couldn't fit through the doorway
Doorway was small
Room was short

standing in
front
of
a mirror

putting head on
Then it explodes

E. J. jumped out of an airplane

random

Zena saw the Maharishi
& he was a golden dome in India
there were some cutters going "cut cut cut"
going, I say, "cut cut cut"

cut
cut
cut

Willow dreamed she was in a place dancing
a prison place, but not bars
but white walls thick
white walls thick thick
not threatening not paradise either
but beautiful walls
perhaps of a prison-city

Like most of its Carib neighbors, the island later supported a small population of Arawaks who chose sheltered bays for villages, made pottery, practiced agriculture . . .

Nathalie: "This is my object—I dreamed it
I dreamed about being in a little town in Switzerland
steep bank
smell of new hay
lapping of water in lake below
(something must have been moving there)
coming back at night this little flashlight is a guide"

The Danes took formal possession in 1694 and raised Danish colors in 1718, establishing the first permanent European settlement on St. John at Estate Carolina in Coral Bay . . .

By 1733 all of St. John was taken up by 109 cane & cotton plantations. O yeah they workin. Heavy demand for slaves. Many who were captured in West Africa were of tribal nobility & former slave owners themselves.

Emancipation of slaves in 1848 . . . push, push against the darkness . . .

dewlaps & pushups of local lizards

dildo cactus

vanilla-scented night-blooming cereus is pollinated by bats

Bromeliad

hawksbill & green sea turtle I supplicate here

huge colonies of coral polyps
soft stomach, stinging tentacles, mouth surrounded by hard limestone

suplicate here
out on the reef

& together we see them—the giant sea turtles

First we're on the shore, getting our gear on under hot hot sun
spot their heads

our list of fish
& other sightings continue
in lineage of Tennessee Williams

supplicating here
coralline

moray

sea whip or plume

sharknose goby

parrotfish (also called stoplight)

moon jelly

southern stingray

Flamingo tongue

foureye butterflyfish

fairy basslet

French angelfish

blue tang

another blue tang

  tang, another

Trumpetfish: another
Brain coral: endless

spotted moray: sinister

Eikhorn coral

Queen triggerfish

rock hind with isopods attached to head

tarpon
say it again: *tarpon*

Gorgonian
say it, Ambrose: *gorgonian*

Staghorn coral

smooth trunkfish

& a bright robe
I stripped off
to be fish
And the toga too, wherein
it was wrapped
the one my parents had sent
from the Hyrcania Heights
And hadn't remembered
remembered its fashion
because I'd left it young,
so long ago in father's house
(how far to come, how far

How far?

far,
far I'd come
to say how far)

All of a sudden I faced "it"
took the robe off
  & the garment was a mirror

of myself

saw my whole self in it
& faced my whole fish self
in facing it
& We were separate—
distinct—
I'm a fish-woman
I said
This is my robe
but, so too,
we were one

how far I'd come

and I watched my son
amphibian
his rubber feet—
now webbed—
emerge from sea

son of the sea of her great foam
& some monster lurked there
called him back
but he resisted, shed his mask
come toward me
"mother"
and
"so thirsty"

aretalogy

"These heretical women—how audacious they are! They have no modesty;
they are bold enough to teach, to engage in argument, to enact exorcisms, to
undertake cures, and, it may be, even to baptize."   —Tertullian

And to mirror the fish we look at constellations
the boy swatting nightbugs
all around cicadas

other tinny orchestras whirr
   beat & throb
pulse in time with our
season

Andromeda or the Chained Lady was out we saw
Antlia or the Air Pump too I see

I see Apus the Bird of Paradise
Aquarius I'll mention
Mention Aquila the Eagle
Ara or the Altar is sounding her name
Argo or Argo Navis or the Ship Argo moves
I witness Aries
Auriga the Charioteer I saw
Big Dipper I view a lot
Bootes the Herdman, naked to eye
Caelum or Caela Sculptoris or Thy Sculptor's Tool
& I'll just list more here
Camelopardus or the Giraffe
The Hunting Dogs, Canes Venatici

Canis Major
Capricorn the Horned Goat, star of my lover
Carina or the Keel
Cassiopeia or the Lady in the Chair, we see you
Centaurus
Monarch
Cetus the Whale
Chameleon
the Compasses
Noah's Dove
Coma Berenices
Corona Australis
Corona Borealis
Corvus or the Crow
Crater or the Cup

— 521 —

Crux the Southern Cross

Cygnus the Swan

Delphinus

Dorado Fish

Draco the Dragon

the Foal, Equuleus

Eridanus or the River Po

Fornax or the Furnac

Lupus the Wolf

Grus or the Crane

Gemini

Ursa Minor

Libra, Ambrose

Lepus the Hare

Lesser Lion

Leo or the Lion

Lacerta the Lizard

Indus

Hydrus

Hydra the Sea Serpent

Horologium

Orion's Belt

Orion or the Giant Hunter

Ophiuchus or the Serpent Bearer

Orion's Sword

Mensa or the Table

Microscopium

Octans or the Octant

Monoceros or the Unicorn

Musca or the Fly

Norma or the Rule

Northern Cross

Malus or the Mast

Hercules

Lyra the Lyre

Lynx

Pavo or the Peacock
Pegasus
Perseus
Phoenix
Pictor the Painter
Pisces
Piscis Austrinus
Puppis or the Prow
Reticulum or the Net
Sagitta or the Arrow
Sagittarius
Scorpion
Sculptor
Scutum or the Shield
Serpens
Sextans
Taurus the Bull
Telescopium
Triangulum
Triangulum Australe
Tucana or the Toucan
Great Bear
Little Dipper, obscure when you look
Vela or the Sails
Virgo
Volans or Piscis Volans
Vulpecula or the Little Fox, I'll mention her

all out on the map, named & delivered to sky
because we study in reverse & code a name, color it, it seeps in
marrow-down, and then look up
& place it there, it corresponds to what we always heard about
those stars in beautiful cosmology
if no other reason to be than this—

look up

lighter years you could not imagine
& the boy too looks up, with eye-dart
down again
wanting to own, contain these things
quickly
& I love him for it
for inside you know the truth of these luminaria
boy, boy
peering into depths of Orion Nebula
among the glowing gases of a stellar nursery

Imagine many newly evolving stars
which bear seeds *o yeah they working*
of future planets
planets now to be *they working overtime*
in the universe

half of the young stars in Orion
are surrounded by raw material
for planetary formation *push, push against the darkness*

this stuff swirls about the stars
in flattened disks of spreading dust
which glow from reflected light of stars

disks contain enough mass to produce Earth-size planets
see, boy?
You see? *they working*

("Mom, you're so random")
☆   ☆   ☆
☆   ☆   ☆

stars less than 300,000 years old
and they working overtime

protoplanetary disks they're called
in abundance
which are a common product of solar formation and
prerequisites to the formation of planetary systems we supplicate here

the sun is not alone in having a retinue of orbiting bodies *o push push*

existence of two & possibly three large planets around a pulsar
    spinning remnant of exploding star   *(against the darkness)*

first definitive evidence of planets around stars other than the . . .
what is it, Ambrose?

"Sun"

proplyds

one of the
most sharply observed
disks was measured to be 7.5 times
the diameter of the solar system, or 53 billion miles across

at the center is a reddish star about one-fifth the mass of the sun

disk around Beta Pictoris, a star only 56 light-years away

swarm of orbiting particles *o yeah they working*

Beta Pictoris is a billion years old *workin, yeah workin*

"extraterrestrial" he says
or "Mom, you are random"

I dreamed of an adult who became a kid
was a naked child
was an elevator then with two kids on it
halved in the dream
twins
Peppo & Lydia

work this
doesn't work it will, though
working words till they work
the same night
hugging with a pelvis
the devil o he comes in
gives me a comb
sex comb it out
o yes that sin, woman
comb
comb
then look up
comb the sky!
(& I'm combing I tell you

'cause I'm scared)
 only got hair to comb
 only got sex to comb
 only got sin to comb
 comb all the stars out of hairy dark sky
 so try run away down West Side Highway
 car starts backing into me
 out of control it wobbles
 lurches
 neck & she/me's dying
 please police *push against the darkness*
 only police to comb
 please call a lay preacher
 please police to me call a preacher
 a *curandera*
 words come out
 like a basket of vegetables
 then someone's in a park
 & his brother's starting to have a heart attack
 & a father had died of a heart attack on his same chest
 broken a doctor's appointment how silly
 to stay here but there's hearts in the family

 attacks come & seize the day from the stars

 or you could say *it is fated, it is willed*

 It is in the stars o yes it is

 I was vulnerable
 thirteen years old in a
 tropical rainforest at
 nighttime,
 old stone masonry jungle rising to the sky
 hissing to the sky
 all alone, eyes watching me
 burnt out years ago Cathedral
 stick of patchouli
 gone into cities on my own

when I would be in the army
then—
now
a boy out of all dreaming writes:

A Day in the Life of a Malaria-Carrying Mosquito

Hello, I am a malaria-carrying mosquito. I live in Port Moresby, the capitol of Papua New Guinea, located precisely at 5 degrees south and 143 degrees east. (You know, the island just north of Australia in the South Pacific.) In this tropical rainy climate the temperature ranges from 75 to 80 degrees Fahrenheit. Around here I am called Doris. I stay in a little bungalow windowsill. The owner is a Malaysian farmer. He and his wife grow and export sweet potatoes, yams, and taro plants. Since swamps cover most of the coastal land, I sometimes go out there to see my friends. I usually stop on the way and get a snack at a restaurant called "Blood Blood Everywhere."

Oh boy (excuse me but) here comes a lip-smacking *Homo Sapiens*. I think I will go have a meal. Now watch closely. First I will plummet full speed hitting the arm with a tremendous blow, then I stick my sticker into its arm and let out anesthetic so it can't feel the pain.

Ooooooooooooo the sensation of this cool refreshing blood is sooooo delicious. Oh well, I've had my fill and I better get out of this person's arm before I get swatted at. Oops, I forgot I carry malaria. If this person doesn't have shots he/she is going to get very sick and possibly die.

Well, I think it's about time to go see my boyfriend Morris. He is a malaria-carrying mosquito too. He lives in one of the swampy areas. Flying to his house, I could have sworn the population was at least 3,860,000 people. When I arrived at his place, he didn't seem to make a sound. As I was looking down I saw him lying still next to a can of Raid. I swore in every one of the 700 languages spoken on this island. I covered the whole island (which adds up to 178,260 square miles) looking for another mosquito to replace my dear friend Morris. I even went up to the high mountain ranges and volcanoes. I went through all the tropical forest. But none of the mosquitos appealed to me like Morris had. I almost went to the other half of the island, located in Indonesia. But I didn't want to go to all the trouble of getting a visa.

Since it was Sunday I decided I would go to a Christian church. The main religion here is Christianity. As I was flying out of the church I fainted. When I awoke I thought I saw Morris standing there. I flew over but it was all to no avail. It was just some dust.

I was feeling very very hot because of the heat and Morris's death. I began to wish we got more than 80 inches of annual rainfall on this island. Just then it began to rain. I thought there really was a gdod. But then I realized I was under a faucet.

I went into Port Moresby feeling really depressed and down on everything. I flew through a market where people were selling coconuts, coffee, palm oil, rubber, and tea. I passed a jewelry stand with a lot of gold for sale (because of all the gold mining here on Papua New Guinea). I returned our engagement ring.

I was feeling weak and feeble. I needed to have blood. This time I didn't dash to the person. I felt clumsy, so I trotted. When I hit the man's arm I forgot to inject anesthetic and unfortunately the person felt me. I tried to pull out. I did. I am going to live, I thought. As I was turning around, I saw out of the corner of my eye . . . a HAND!!!! I tried to move but I was just too weak.   SMACK!!!!!

"Damn skeeters!"

XVI

LACRIMARE, LACRIMATUS

"DUX FEMINA FACTI"

*Publius Vergilius Maro (70–19 BCE) continues to be interesting referee or reference point & aspect
for the ongoing arguments of the poem. Which built upon continues the discussion of what is appro-
priate "stuff" for epic attention. War, gender, language? This has become the poet's mantra. Virgil
is farmer boy, didactic on issues of crop raising, beekeeping, cattle raising. O holy earth poet-man!
He was a cultivator of lines. Also the not-so-great-as Homer sophisticate Latin poet, stealing fire
from his Greek models. In her heart Catullus is perhaps the greater magician, but she is impressed
by any long-winded scop's scope. Why? It furthers the plan to "include it all" (Gertrude Stein's
admonition) and history. And her story of a generation & all the consociate-aspirational activities
associated with it. It's a smaller planet than last year's. Another president is dead. But her "time"
is filtered through one particular suspect antenna, one welcoming receiver. Do it differently! tell the
story of the tribe! and she feels some of her male kin get used to it. And what of Sulpicia, (circa
55–19 BCE), said to be educated & beautiful? What happened to all her poems? A scant six remain,
conversational & witty, first complaining of spending her birthday in "the disgusting country," à la
Frank O'Hara, without her boyfriend, then delighted when she'll have her birthday in Rome after
all. Quite a contrast to hero Aeneas—truer folk-leader—who submits his private need to the need
of his people and becomes ultimate sacrificing warrior patriarch. Dido is tragic, long-suffering sui-
cidess of womanly passion & down-under despair. Wants to drag the rest of it down with her. Can
we let Aeneas off the hook? Is he culpable? We travel to the underworld. The net. The drag. This
poet wants to get inside Latin tongue to further examine love & military glory. She thus titles this
aspect of the journey "Lacrimare, Lacrimatus"— of the travails of weeping. Much currently to cry
about. "Cry Like a Baby" the songs say. Virgil loves Italy, its landscape. What is the relation of
language to landscape? How is one masculine or feminine? Heinrich Heine spoke of Latin language
as one "for military commands, governmental reports, usurers' judgements, a lapidary speech for the
flinty Roman folk." Another strand: Shakespeare's sense of Roman valor & virtue enters in in the
hint of Coriolanus, whose mother Volumnia haunts the essence of her son's valor. It appears no one
wins in war. Do we continue to conduct wars, more & more nationalistic, because we kept the myths
alive in our various languages? And wars against the landscape? Against Nature? And now we turn
on our own citizens? Latin seems particularly relevant as a kind of conquering tongue, obsolete in
most places now for most schoolchildren. She suggests the popular experiment of the poets: try to
eradicate all Latin from your speech, from your text, a haughty challenge, and German will be your
new/old tongue. She has interesting consociate-correspondent in one William Sterling, who lives at
Goat-in-the-Road on the Pacific Coast, an Attorney-at-Law, who is a passionate classicist and
translates some of her phrases into a just Latin to sound & ponder. She is grateful for the call &*

response he provides. Richard Milhouse Nixon, who resigned the American presidency in scandal, enters the poem on his death. His reign was shrouded in many dark veils. He was a complex villain and emblem of paranoia. Did he really need to be loved? Her eye alights on the descriptions of the efforts of the "mani pulite" (clean hands) crusade in Milano, attempting to expose the corruptions of Berlusconi & his Fininvest Empire. Do the shades still murmur & writhe in Dante's hell?

. . . . *and this will be in part in partial Latin, in art of Latin*

strum
a ton
a rung
of sung stuff
or rapt-spun
strung out
hummed into being

                unjam thy string awhile

Dear Anne: What civilizes? Is that at least part of the root query that throws the branching questions in your introductory paragraph? How do civilizing influences work? Ignore for the time being questions about the premise itself: what does one mean by "civilizing"? Can civilizing occur in the absence of language? No, I daresay. So how does language serve to civilize or decivilize? I worked for a Swiss economics professor once, a bit of a polymath he was, who argues tenaciously that war is the mother of invention and therefore the grandmother of civilization. Does this reduce to the proposition that we need war in order to beget peace? Is this a necessary dialectic, either biologically or intellectually? Does that make the poet the apostle of belligerence? Presumably not. But the presumption does not answer the challenge: how does language work or serve for better or worse?

Perhaps these concerns are more germane to the *Odyssey* than to the *Aeneid*. What do you think? Or is the difference simply one of scale, not of theme? With the *Odyssey* Homer considers the redomestication of a soldier and the restoration of a household. With the *Aeneid* Virgil considers the foundation of a state and the declaration of its psycho-emotional constitution. Same theme, just small screen vs. big screen?

I have some teaching notions I would like to run before you. For, example, if the leading character of the *Odyssey* were female, not male, what would the epithet for her be in the first line of Book One?

(sing in me Musa & spell the story):
Comminius speaks:

I shall lack voice; the deeds of Coriolanus
Likewise the dirty deeds of Richard M. Nixon
Should not be uttered feebly. It is held
That valor is the chiefest virtue
virtus famula fortuna est
        and
Most dignifies the haver
But was that what Nixon had?

valor, virum, virtus
            he never had

whatever resides here,
whatever had
  gone mute—
rift with—
a kind of forgone pride,
  twilled,
then twisted tongue
or
manhood, she could say—the poet could say—
with smugness
herself defined as defender of peace

=she rages=

pax on this or any other turf
          how many Americans slaughtered as he
          kept going the war
          how many Vietnamese, Cambodians

bodes not well the warring god realm
& now
the presidents & ministers confer on Bosnia

> statesmen are encumbered
> stratagems, fisted
> oblique for the asking
> how meet?

at divisae sunt factiones
et singulariter insaburratae

---

but divided are the parties
& singularly unballasted

Anne: I took "singularly" in the denotative case "one by one, each severally," which is precisely what *singulariter* indicates, not in the looser, intensifying sense of "very, exceptionally"

The crucial adjective "unballasted" is a challenge.
In the context of the poem I take it nautically, an allusion to the want of able helmsmen in the ship of state. A ship without ballast, and without a cargo to compensate for the absence of ballast, floats high and is tippy. Hence my choice of *instabiles.*

Instabiles can certainly be said of a ship. The historian Q. Curtius Rufus wrote of *naves instabiles.* But insofar as *instabiles* is recognized and registered as "unstable," and the notion of instability seizes the reader's mind, the ship of state metaphor gets lost in the briny froth of latent linguistic associations. The original metaphor itself is then unballasted.

The Roman word for "ballast," I learn, is *saburra,* the primary sense of which is "sand," the principal material used for ballasting. I thought of *onus,* meaning "burden" in its most general sense, but also meaning "cargo" in maritime contexts. The related verbs are *saburrare* and *onerare;* the participles, correctly inflected to agree with *factiones,* are *saburratae* and *oneratae.* I find no evidence in my Lewis & Short Latin Dictionary of negative compounds in the forms *insaburratae* and *inoneratae.* The classical formation would probably be achieved with *non:* thus *non saburratae* and *non oneratae,* though the compounds with *in-* would have been intelligible if not conventional or elegant. But what rule (other than your wish in this regard, which I shall honor and obey without deviation) requires strict adherence to what we moderns imagine the ancients would have done?

So perhaps, in favor of preserving the ballast metaphor literally, I say it again:

at divisae sunt factiones
et singulariter insaburratae

In this do you hear a light auditory echo of the sounds of
"scurrilous"?

---

  a people unallowed to bare arms
lift, o lift ill-fitted embargo
scourge, terrify, *vidimus*

It is not a united mission
distracted
what are the deals to cut
with commanders
obsessed with their mission of cleansing
for the ongoing cutting of deals?
(& 20,000 women raped, you hear?)

dealt with, you could say,
a blow to—you could say—
they—the others—
compared to Ottoman Turks
were dealt a bad hand,
& think influences here
the way you weave
or spit
what you might don as
marriage is but funeral weeds

I was 7 I was 17 longing for a peace offering to be given I was 27 longing I was 47

& strum
& strum
strum a lift
a pax

across a bridge
divided children could be seen to run
newspaper circa 1994

Question: what is a world when you wipe out another ethnic group?
Answer: tomb, forgotten, clean slate
Question: will thrive will prosper?
Answer: with blood in the sky, on hands, on earth, on street, Mad Tom

but they say traces at Auschwitz drag up nay nuncle
yet not a scream remains
while they rent torture chambers to tourists in Prague
short on space
wherein tortured fell apart, stretched, racked, scoriated with pain
to eke out confusion, testing loyalties, manhood

& you do scream Aeeeeeeya

. . . his pupil age

Man-ent'red thus, he waxed like the sea;
And, in the brunt of seventeen battles since,
He lurched all swords of the garland.

His sword, death's stamp,
Where it did mark, it took;
    from face to foot
He was a thing of blood, whose every motion
Was timed with dying cries
who's gone before

& there are meeting, at a metaphorical table . . .
                                        e-mail?
                                        public space?
    (across my lines)

On Feb. 16, 1993 in St. Louis, Missouri, a skinhead biker beat a black man to death

In Feb. 19, 1993, a skinhead was arrested in connection with the beating death
of a homeless man in Birmingham, Alabama

On May 20, 1993, in Montreal, Canada, a skinhead beat to death a jogger he believed was gay

On June 3, 1993, in Winston-Salem, North Carolina, a skinhead shot and killed a white youth and injured the black friend he was walking with

On July 20, 1993, in Tacoma, Washington, the NAACP headquarters was fire-bombed. Church of the Creator skinheads have been charged with this crime

On July 23, 1993, in Atlantic City, New Jersey, a skinhead beat a 75-year-old black man to death with his own cane

tears of the women of the gay men & women of the black men & women of the black gay men & women of the white men & women of the white gay men & women

tears of the children
karma of divisiveness

set down a load
right noble?
ineffective
valor turns to rancor
  as they file past a casket
                culture sentimental & sick with death
                rehabilitation
                langue d'oc apart
                or *trobar clus*

or valor turns to villain, turns to virulence

mal' odoratum
rapina convertit in praedem convertit in contagionem
  foedens cibum sub caeno

convertit in pestem
        ultione verberatam

malodorous
ravage turns to plunder turns to infestation
  digging under dirt for grub

turns to plague
    whipped with revenge

a
cure
haunting
the
test
tube
you
hope

then I =waste=, =zap=, =nuke=, =rub out= you, I =croak=, =snuff=,
=bump off=, =knock off=, =bushwack=, =lay out= you, I =polish off=,
=blow away=, =blot out=, =erase=, =wipe out=, =blast=, =do in= you, I
=off=, =ice=, =hit=, =gun down=, =pick off=, =put to bed with a shovel=,
=take care of= you, I =take out=, =take for a ride=, =give the works to=,
=get=, =fix=, =settle=, =spill blood=, =let blood as in waste=, =nuke=,
=zap=, =croak= you
in the name of
*aborticide, amicicide, ceticide, deicide, elephanticide, formicide, fratricide, fungicide, genocide,
giganticide, gynicide, herbicide, homicide, infanticide, insecticide, mariticide, matricide, germicide,
ovicide, parenticide, parricide, patricide, pesticide, regicide, rodenticide, sororicide, spermatazoi-
cide, autocide, tauricide, tickicide, uxoricide, vaticide, filaricide, vespacide, viricide*

as in

how Jill & I don masks of black cloth, veils, gloves, black hats, jumpsuits,
dressed for outer space to attack the wasp colony, an attack of horrible ves-
pacide—with guns of poison—

how people burn ticks to death in these mountains

how the
mongers do battle
&
random rancor
again, again
    as in Rwanda, Tutsis slaughtered in hospital beds

dragged from homes & hacked to bits in the streets
insatiable mad cry for blood
woman with babes on back hacking at women with babes on back

virtue, virtus

klea andron
(the glorious deeds of great heroes dead)
what heroes are these skulking the battlefield?

arma virumque cano

one's lot or *moira* unchangeable
but when Achilles wondered to sit his anger out
rather than slaughter Atrides
Athena drew down & shined
he knew her by her eyes
so terrible they were
sparkling with ardor
She speaks:

Thou seed of Jupiter
I come from heaven to see anger settled
I am sent from Juno
Draw no sword
Use words
Use words
Throws reins on thy passions
& serve us

Homer's goddess & Chapman's differ in this important
compromising point about action & word

or the importance of the forum
of the model Roman state
model of a well-ordered society
versus heathen chaos
gone down the tubes
Brunelleschi's new order & subsequent disgrace makes a headline
the streets of Rome filled with rubble

disease & health of
the Body Politic

how Coriolanus's love of his mother was strange

There's no man in the world
More bound to's mother
& wracked by her grip
toughened in the womb

"What he hath done famously though soft-conscienced men
can be content to say it was for his country, he did it to please
his mother . . ."

how the tapers turned bedward
O Volumnia
voluptuous one

this is a sorry state to lose valor
to be robed in bed in sanctity
of a darker deed

Thy valiantness was mine, thou suck'st from me . . .
                            he said
ut verba soni sint lateres
et infecta cruore

---

so that the words are building blocks of sound
& are tainted in blood

---

antebellum

wash them back, back, into bellissima bellicose Latin
sweet tongued, church tongued
or
tense sport & action
of my personal histories of heroes

wash wash back to cleanse a literal sound
of war & bellissima bellicose mutterings

of religious traumas
material gatherings

wages of fear
in a country Mafia molded

they don't look back on the bloody battlefield
like a money market, bodies gored
of bombs,
plastiques

of migrations
the mighty cartels & spoils of commerce

& fights over borders

fights over goods & in a
comparision of loves . . .

Damoetas & Menalcas speak:

—The Muse began with Jupiter & he's everywhere. He makes the earth
    fecund, he listens to my ditties.
—But Phoebus loves me. My garden is Apollo's seat.
    I give him gifts. The bay tree & hyacinth blush & bloom.
—Wanton Galatea throws me an apple. She runs off I'll follow, spy on her.
—But dear Amyntas is my flame. He is my flame & never coy.
—My little dog knows Delia well.

—I have a present for my Venus! I have a present for my love!
—I've noticed where the doves build their nests.
—I plucked ten golden apples for my love. All that I could I've sent to my
    boy & there will be more!

& so on, a competition, a conversation . . .

I have a riddle: where on earth do space of sky measure three yard?
Answer my riddle, & I'll say Apollo's not a greater bard
I have a riddle—where on earth are flowers signed with a king's name?
Answer my riddle, & you shall keep Phyllis

of the borders themselves how arbitrary
a Catholic thing now,
from god to emperor to pope

are you circumcised?
& rape to destroy the women, all sense of dignity
what of the children of these horrific couplings?

dolor dolor dolor dolor dolor dolor dolor dolor dolor dolor dolor dolor dolor
dolor dolor dolor
dolor factus
intra nationum sensus
fragiles et elicentes
bellicosos

---

woe woe woe woe woe woe woe woe woe woe woe woe woe woe woe wrought

inside ethnicities

fragile & evocative

bellicose

Anne: I took "woe" as a noun *(dolor)*, not as an interjection *(vae!)*, given the adjective "wrought"
in the second line.
You have 20 monosyllabic "woes"; I gave you ten bisyllabic *dolors.*

"ethnicities" is difficult. I take you to mean with it something like tribal or group sensibilities, which range from the tenuous ("fragile") through memory-laden and hope-creating ("evocative") to harder-edged, dualizing, self-absorbed us-them touchiness and pugnacity ("bellicose").

I took *natio* (in preference to *tribus* or *gens* or *populus*) because *natio* feels more other-oriented and them-ier, where the alternative words feel more familial, local and us-referencing, and I was encouraged by the note in Lewis & Short that *natio* was "usually applied by Cicero to distant and barbarous people." Isn't that an aspect of the attitude you are after: the arrogance and dissension that arise from viewing others as "distant and barbarous"?

Then I took *sensus* as a generic term for the powers of perception, and it also means the results of perception: feelings, perceptions, sensations, and the mental formations which are based on those results: dispositions, attitudes, understanding, frames of mind, etc.

So here are two words for your one, but I am at a loss for a one-to-one equivalency for the conceptual layering inherent in "ethnicities"

I took all three adjectives—fragile, evocative and bellicose—in agreement with "ethnicities," not with "woe."

Latin has *evocativus,* but it means "summoning, calling forth" and the spirit of the word is more strident and bellowing than seems to fit for English "evocative," which has something wispy and wistful and tendrilish about it. So I prefer *elicitus* (whence English "elicit"), from *elicere* meaning "to draw out, entice out, lure forth, bring out, elicit." The basic word in the cluster to which *elicere* belongs is *laqueus* meaning "noose, snare."

sing a snare

        cringe a noose

& ring

et bello mortui

_____

& the war dead

_____

dead of a century's pollutant streams

yet
a millennium is made up of all the words

panique de l'an mille

ab multis obtestari possit vicosque vias
itinera omnia tramitesque et intorti pavorem

---

one could conjure from many the streets & highways
all the roads & twisty paths & panic

---

speaking at the surface of ourselves still breathing he said in
Tower of Babel he said Steiner did
moving forward in the slipstream of the statements we
make about tomorrow morning, about a millennium

sing

sing
dolor dolor dolor dolor dolor

---

woe woe woe woe woe woe

& turn to stars again

       binary star . . black dwarf . . blaze star . . carbon star . . Cepheid . . comparison star . .
dark star . . double star . . dwarf star . . early-type star . . eclipsing binary . . eruptive variable . .
F star . . fixed star . . flare star . . giant star . . gravity star . . Greenwich star . . G star . . Hydrogen
star . . intrinsic variable . . irregular star . . K star . . late-type star . . long period variable . . M
star . . main sequence star . . multiple star . . N star . . nautical star . . nebulous star . . neutron
star . . nova . . O-type star . . R star . . radio star . . red giant . . red supergiant . . RR Lyrae star
. . runaway star . . semiregular variable . . silicon star . . solar or sun star . . spectroscopic binary . .
standard star . . supermassive star . . supernova . . variable star . . visible binary . . white dwarf . .
x-ray star . . zenith star
which are the ormulum
ON. stjarnan (whence ME. sterrne)

Propter montem nos esse cano
et neminem in nos jaculantur

I sing that we are near the mountain
& no one is gunning us down

cogito nos ex stellarum piscumque originibus fieri
illorum omnium
quo modo cumqu'opinari possimus et excogitare

I think we are made up of the genetics of stars & fish
of all those
we could ever dream or think of

they are in our eyeball movies
haunted by light—reflected—
little filaments of celluloid created for your eyes
hunted in light, old war flicks
to flicker on a retinal screen
who climbs the edge

then take out your dictionary
take out your lexicon
& eliminate all the words
derivative of Latin
& you will harden on a harder edge

it is hard

for hard are words of harder Latin
wrung in Latin
stung in Latin
expunged in Latin
Johnny-come-lately-in-Latin

caged in Latin

fought & bled in Latin
estranged

holiest in Latin

tortured in Latin

naming the names in Latin

naming the numbers in Latin

stiff in Latin
bow down in Latin

I can't be vernacular in Latin
et verba majorum in ossibus sonunt

& words of the ancestors sound in the bones

---

pound in the bones in Latin

hearts beat in the bones:
bellum, bellum, bellum

beat in the bones:
vellum, vellum, vellum

it is plenum, plenum, plenum
virum, virum, virum
  taut grammar of futurity

ein noch nicht festgestelles Tier
("we literally hear how the verbs kill time")
    (Mandelstam
    on Dante's *Inferno* &
    his own imprisonment)

est Erebus Erebus Erebus
infera fervida cano et infera gelida
quo forma renasceris cano fragmentum glaciei

ibi ita, ibi iens
ibi ivi, ibi iero

it is hell hell hell

hot hells and cold hells I sing of

where you reincarnate as a patch of ice I sing of

gone there, going there
have gone there, will have been going there

Anne: Virgil refers to the nether regions as Erebus. The term is Greek (Erebos, the god of Darkness, son of Chaos, brother of Night).

For the hot and cold hells I shifted to *infera [loca]* = [the] lower [places], to mark the transition from the general hell of Erebus in the singular to the specific plural hells of the second line.

I have not found any satisfactory way to avoid the hiatus in the second line (. . . *cano et* . . .). Making *cano* the final word of the line yields . . . *fervida et* . . . which is worse. You might prefer:

    infera fervid' et infera gelida cano

The syntax of the third line (*quo forma* . . .) roused memories of Dr. Alan Gillingham, my Latin master at Andover. He would have cherished the problem, found it toothsome. *Cano* ("I sing of") here requires the indirect discourse construction, which uses infinitive-plus-subject-accusative for the main statement and puts subordinate clauses in the subjunctive. I took "where you reincarnate . . ." as a subordinate clause, it being so relative in form, and hence the subjunctive mood for *renasceris.*

Finally I somehow imagined that you, in the first person, indubitably feminine, were the subject of the inflection play of the last two lines. So *ita* is past participle feminine in agreement with the assumed first-person singular, *iens* the present participle, *ivi* first-person singular present perfect, and *iero* same for the future perfect.

civis, civis, civis
a civic responsibility

we're going to wait for an Aztec now
Hold shorter, let me know
Let you know, shorter
The A 1456 crosswall
375 behind Margaret Tower
769 32L Tango
Alpha 7 & Tango
Am 432 Monitor Tower
United 224
Runway 22 left
Turn right on Hotel
Runway 32
Tango 310
500 Yankee behind
United 1490 behind
Bravo Delta behind
Give away 22 companies Alpha 7
Tango 7
Roger Delta
Contact Departure

it is kithara I ride
strummed

a daemon departure
locusta

lacrimare lacrimatus

an old story:
Virgil was going to destroy his book

=fluxus= & depart

where old scoundrels die a Latin death
"don't they speak Latin in Latin America?"

Virgil was going to drown his book
regnum
virum omnia plenum

Dear Anne: *Dux.* Virgil's word is *dux.* I do not know what daimon induced me to write *ductor.* Go with *dux.* Makes me want to sing: "Use *dux,* the foaming cleanser . . . " *Dux femina facti.*

The phrase caps Virgil's recounting of Dido's flight from Phoenician Tyre, after uncovering the murder of her husband by her brother, unearthing ancient buried treasure, assembling other Tyrians tired of Pygmalion's tyranny, arming them, leading them to the docks where her brother's treasure fleet lay at anchor ready to sail, seizing the ships and sailing them to the Punic coast where she then founded Carthage.

Poor Dido, twice bereaved. She loved the husband Sychaeus whom her brother murdered. He was an extremely rich man, as it happened, which may have entered Pygmalion's motives for putting him to death. Some scheme to capture his wealth.

My mother advised me that if I were to fall in love, there was no fault in falling in love with a rich girl. My father advised me that if I were to fall in love with a pair of bright eyes, I should make sure it was not the sun shining through a hole in her head that made them bright. I suppose they advised my two sisters similarly, substituting boy for girl. We failed our parents. Our first round of spouses were of ordinary means and adequate intelligence. Each of us is now divorced. None of us is rich, in consequence of marriage or divorce. I alone have remarried, though romantic hope burns bright on each sororial turn. It is advent season.

Dido, however, succeeded. She fell in love with a rich man and married him. Her parents approved and blessed the marriage. Loss, grief and sorrow ensued. I suspect Mom was not a reader of Virgil. I am not sure she would have approved of Dido's ship-swiping either, at least not until after she realized that her dreams about how she and my father would spend his retirement did not coincide with his dreams. She then awoke to her resentment at playing second fiddle for so long. There were to be no movements when she would get to play first violin. This grieved her. It felt unjust. Yet in the milieu which formed her, the culture which Robertson Davies describes in *Fifth Business,* conservative Anglophilic southern Ontario after the turn of the century, *feminae* were not *duces. Dulces* yes, but not *duces.*

Poor Dido got rich young and was heartbroken in consequence. Twice. Is there a moral here? Is her suffering just coincidence? Just a device in Virgil's story? I think not. The issue, of course, is not how we deal with wealth that is gone. The issue is how do we deal with love that is gone. First Sychaeus, then Aeneas. How do we deal with feeling abandoned? I think that was my mother's issue at the end, even while my father was still alive. And then there was the physical wrench of his actual dying. First abandoned emotionally, then corporeally. Mom lost twice as well.

Death only reconfigures where the points of connection are situated. Forgetfulness may sever connection. But death need not.

I wonder what Dido understood?

Bill:

Latin *alere* "nourish," with the parallel formation *altus* "high, deep" (whence altitude), *ad/ultus* "ADULT." See also *ELD.* Hence *olden* "ancient."

$=strummed=$

ego paupercula feminea forma

XVII

THERE WAS A TIME AN ECLIPSE

Words & music for dear friend Joe Brainard, perished of AIDS in New York City. Minstrel Steven Taylor first improvises then composes & notes this music in accompaniment for performance. The words are spoken on top of the music, as the spirit is moved. Con vivace. Later, an aftermath of visitation & description.

There was a time an eclipse
I hear voices I heard them
A veritable cough in the morn
Cough in the moon
A march of his voice in the afternoon
Night was small & stranger,
& he spoke

What did he say? What did he say?

He said "rueful" he said "ruthless"
(Then he laughs)
But during eclipse
as if alien power gripped me
I heard them nail him down
Fast to a bed I was weak & I weakened
Then dreamed must cook him an egg
for that yolk heralds the energy of the sun
This is before eclipse
And then after eclipse
—As if he had rested, gone softer—
I heard him cough miles away
Like that: a glow of sound

I hear voices
Hear them?
I heard them
Hear them?
But o I was weak & the egg was a trick
to make you eat the sun—crack it!
Don't identify with the moon
Because that would be silver sliver
that would be white
& you need the yellow of sun
It is an alchemist's dream to eat the sun
I do this every day
But everything went dark
It was timely
There was a time an eclipse
& then I heard them

(I hear voices)
one, two, three voices
then four five six seven voices
& they were the voices of the dead
O my o my
the voices of the dead
& I heard the voice of eclipse
& it said I am the gap between you & your mind
And then came in voice of Tarquish the Ice Demon in the art installation
It was a bigger voice, coming & going
It was—you could say—prophetic-sounding
because what they all predicted has already happened
I heard them, I hear them
It happened & you weren't looking &
now it's too late, ice melting

WE NEED A NEW GLACIER
I CAN'T REMEMBER HEAVEN'S FACE
I CAN'T REMEMBER FIRE
I CAN'T REMEMBER EVERYTHING THE DEAR DEAD FRIEND SAID
WHO DIED YESTERDAY 4 P.M., MAY 25, 1994
His voice once laughed in the irony of being alive
or dumb, we were all dumb together
This is a man who loved men & died of that dread
disease that loves young men
I hear voices
& then I speak up
speak out
speak back
speak forward
speak on angle
in angelic tongue
messenger between earth & hell

(music pauses here)

& there are only the inner limits
Vocabulary expands the plan
A planet is sick with the disease that takes young men
midmen

Tribulations of the tribe
be so bold as to exhume
Voices in the hide of their desire
Pounds & pounds of flesh
A dim view
Exhausted planet exhausted men
Stricken
I was trying to find some beauty there . . .
I hear voices
not seductive, but demonic
And are inside my head
And are inside my head I wonder
A haunting
And just now a goose honks in suburban night
And over my head is a dagger
In the artist's dream upon a bed of nails
on which he lay down to die
I died a thousand times
Then woke to eclipse

(music resumes)

There was a time an eclipse
A dagger shadowed the sun
And Joe was dying during the lunar eclipse
which put a great stillness into the air
That you could almost praise a divinity for
And he died slowly
& it was long, long the suffering and
when the eclipse came
He could finally go out
Out, out
A stubborn man
cooperated with the external
phenomenal world as he was dying
Did that seem odd?
Not to take a life
Injected with nothing like the heat of the sun
nothing like yolk of egg
Morphine did not spell his deep pain

But he saw himself as one in many
& many in him saw many
in one modest heart
He had an artist's twin instruments
of vision, his eyes
He could see
He sees he sees he sees he sees he sees he sees
  he sees he sees he sees he sees   *(note of violin is held here a long time)*
  he sees he sees he sees he sees he seize
When he lived he made exquisite things
That is enough.

                                       (music ends)

―――――――――――――――――――――――――――――

coda . . .

        and now I see how you spoke to me from your dying . . .

in the dream
it's earlier for both of us
a century when people are reading long books
installed books, that take root with you permanently
you're lucky if you get the one you sought
(you can't exactly buy them)
& maybe you'll read one for a whole lifetime
(It's the new/old thing to do)

you have a book
the best you say because of its opacity
"it unfolds like baby skin, it rolls & rolls"
but also "demanding"

a beautiful blond has left to return
to his job
of head-turning
& you're stretched out in a meadow
discomfort from an edge of something— leaf?
thorn? old bone?
I was about to say "bramble"
when you hold up a drawing of one—

drawn with graphite on a new paper called "lorn"
I was trying to see how you'd changed
I know you're sick now
"Not much, now, I hope," I say

"O yes, greatly

                    (pause)
—When I was trying to be alive before I fell down here—bent & stayed
down—I-I-I-I-
then stopped at this zone of flowers because paint was not ink in my book,
but I had to catch all t-t-t-too, and get outside. To see some things. Then it
was different."

Oh?

then

"You see the suit I'm wearing? Scriberia!"
(but he's naked)

a cry from within the house nearby

"sick enough, sick enough!"

Hebrew noun *Sh'khinah* is derived from *shakan,* "the act of dwelling"

Shekhinah-Matronit
act of all my dwelling

she is so tiny her body could be accommodated in the ark of bulrushes that
held Moses
yet so great her body extended for millions of miles
that woman, that female
in Exile—the Widow, the "D" tone of Exile (Lapis Exulis)
scatter the light of the Shekhinah into myriad sparks—*scintillae*—that are the
souls of human beings
alchemists often called "washerwomen"

Some things in the house that are Joe Brainard . . .

Tiny fake pearls spelling the words "GIANT NIGHT" have risen against a black sky, streaked (where the paper was creased) by faint rays of stars.

On another wall a little female flamenco dancer from a *Maja* soapbox crosses the stage cut away from an old New York City Yellow Pages logo, her backdrop a glittery red candy wrapper.

Walking with Joe around Manhattan's SoHo district one night I was astonished at the sharpness and speed of his eye, and at the sheer quantity of the treasures that made their way from the gutter to his pockets—chewing gum foils, cigarette pack shells, and butts, other discarded debris that became more interesting to me through his interest. And once at the beach in Westhampton, Long Island, he was spotting, bending over, and collecting "anything blue" at an alarming rate—used flash cubes, ancient sea-worn Bromo Seltzer bottles, a frayed plastic cord, and broken lightbulbs. Later these items appeared in some striking "sand" collages, literally embedded in sand (cemented so they stuck fast). An ecologist of the highest order, he was not only recycling what others would dismiss as trash, he was turning these bits and pieces into works of beauty and humor.

From 1967 through the late 1970s I observed Joe Brainard's magpie-like propensity. When I would visit his spartan loft on Greene Street I would stumble into piles of "things," organized principally by color—scraps of every imaginable shape and texture from his ramblings, from old magazines and picture books, from the packaged world: ripped segments where a product had been stripped in haste and so on. These piles (with little else in his spartan loft) were in and of themselves artworks, stacked images from the phenomenal world. It was fun to look through them and later see how he'd worked the images together. In 1978 he presented me with a little cloth bag of "Portable Art" which included, among other delights, a little Bayer Aspirin tin (the label was inside the tin) containing "Some Things in the House That Are Brown": cutouts of a chocolate donut, a small radio, a chair, a ladder, a fur coat, and so on, colored-in cutouts primarily from Yellow Pages' illustrations. His collages, adorning the insides of matchbooks, seem to me now quintessential Brainards from that collage period: a perky semi-tragic-faced pansy, a "LEARN TO DRIVE

U.S. AUTO CLUB" matchbook, for example. What this artist could do so well was notice the forgotten "stuff," see it as sacred or amusing, and reclaim it, reenacting it in new contexts, restoring its intrinsic vitality through magical poetic combinations. So many of his works suggest (to me) romantic scenarios. An anthropomorphized sun-face seems to be rising over a bed with a graph-like quilt but it's a traveling dream bed (like the one in Ballanchine's *Nutcracker Suite*) whose lower left-hand corner shows an upside-down canceled George Washington stamp. The canceled lines become further waves that resonate with the edges of clouds behind the sun. It is all over blue and white and entitled "Blue Sky for You" and its scenario is something about time passing and the cosmos—almost a reflection of the Heaven/Earth/Man principle in Oriental art and haiku (stretching it a bit), in this case Heaven: Sun; Earth: George Washington, father of our country (earth), now interred; and Man: the bed, which seems to visually bring the two others together.

Every time I enter my kitchen there's a charming open-faced, exquisitely drawn bacon, lettuce, & tomato sandwich presenting itself from the wall. Some of the works beg not to be simply "on the wall." Their dimensionality is explicit (e.g., you need to open the matchbook or the Bayer tin to experience the wit).

"Sitting" for Joe, for a portrait, I was always impressed by his desire for accuracy—his infuriating perfectionism, you might say. Some early nude drawings were skillfully drawn—flattering, somewhat "kittenish," but later he was never satisfied and, I think, abandoned an oil portrait. I always thought perhaps I was too stiff-looking, trying too hard to "look good," unlike those discarded candy wrappers! The pencil portrait of composer Bill Elliot is remarkable for how it "gets" the gentleness and dignity of the man. It's careful, tight, very clear and direct, but not at all photographic. It's translated through Brainard's appreciation of the person. He paints his friends. His portraits of the gorgeous whippet Whippoorwill, who belonged to the poet Kenward Elmslie, have a similar quality of familiarity and directness, as well as a lushness of an expansiveness in the brushstrokes. One especially regal portrait comes to mind, sitting on a green velvet divan, Ingres-like in his rich patina, color, and detail.

Poets love Joe Brainard's work because of what the works suggest as well as what they so generously depict. The jokes are good too, quotations like "DeKooning Nancy," which copies the frenzied freehand energy of a DeKooning female topped by the classic "Nancy" face. He stopped as we walked to point out the pansy faces, making sure I noticed how *funny* they were (this was in a garden in Vermont).

The Buddhist notion "Things are symbols of themselves" comes to mind. Those pansy faces are *right there.* Joe Brainard's power was to *notice* this, as well as to create beautiful works out of particulars, making art that has irony as well. The world was sacred to him, and his work connects us to the world. Comparisons to Joseph Cornell and Jasper Johns and the best Surrealist collagists (Picasso, Max Ernst) seem relevant. Right now, Brainard's art is so outside the current mainstream, however, that classifying his gorgeous artifacts seems a blasphemy. There was something highly dedicated and spiritual (alchemical) in his practice of art. He beheld the beauty/humor everywhere around him and honored it. It's a practice that's ancient, timeless, not prey to fashion. And his generosity was always present. Joe Brainard once wrote under the category "ART":

"Art" to me is like walking down the street with someone and saying "Don't you love that building?" (too)

XVIII

SEQUEL TO A SHARP TURN

Left hanging, didactic words to what purpose? The ellipses of desire, doorways, someone else's pain, another's child gone, head blown off on distant road, for there are still roads she knows. Knows what? The wait, hanging there. Someone just dies of immune deficiency disease again, again. An eclipse. The dragon Rahu's tail obscures the sun. She is definitely in America. "Mom, you are so random," the adolescent boy quips his mantra as he locks his door. She sees her gesture inside his hand, closing the door, all flurry. She makes circles on the lined pad. The lines are boundaries waiting to be agreed upon. The circles are eyes, the words are hanging there. Waiting for Indra to show his face. It is a jeweled net he commands, but she is not a disciple inside his plan. She will cut the flow or else how to intercede. I write this down, again. I turn at the bend of page, bird in the yard, coyotes under bent moon. A footnoted conversation with filmmaker friend Nathaniel Dorsky about Rossellini's Voyage to Italy, *that dark and luminous marriage bed.*

enter

swallow

each calling

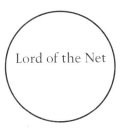

Lord of the Net

like film or
firm of it
groin-lie

stones

Neolithic

"widow"

lamentation for marriage

Cundrie with black hood embroidered with a flock of turtle doves

O Kundrie she walks, she lies down

teeth likes boars' tusks, I hear voices
I heard them

The yarn of the Robe of Glory "I heard the sound of its music, which it whis-
pered as it descended" . . . .

I hear voices

Upper Paleolithic
The Mousterian (roughly 50,000 to 30,000 BCE
notations of lunar cycles bone fragments incised with lines)

. . . . . woolly mammoth . . . . .

The Aurignacian—gradual retreat of glaciers (30,000 to 25,000 BNC)

Carvings of human figures begin
[to appear] in caves where Alpine zone merged
into deciduous forest, providing food & shelter

multiple pathways
graded synaptic potentials
triggered responses

certain corals experimentally subjected to excessive stimulation luminesce for
several minutes afterward with a spontaneous frenzy that suggests "berserking"

Better war than the past
Bolje rat negopaky!
Better the tomb than slavery
Bolje grob, negoo rob!
crowds in streets of
Belgrade! March 1941
after Serbian regent
signed a pact w/Hitler

. . . . exempt

agitation . . . .

pretext . . . .

. . . . jawing with a dictator

or, a dictator's jaw . . . .

scum or
scud . . . .

. . . . revile
that blame could be a tool, a weapon

. . . . reveille

rural . . . .

exile . . . .
that I have tried . . . .

came from a war . . . .

went forth from . . . .

chansons de geste . . . .

outside the rule of the paladins . . . .

I seize, I took . . . .

this is the part I empty the cartridge

. . . . went outside from

refugee . . . .

sectaries . . . .

St. Priscilla in her catacomb . . . .

cognition which rehearses itself in reboundness

or -ing sound, end

becoming

scant dignity

subjugated

not to jump at

perched on a rich need

lurk

night horrors

security

flutter of doves

ardent

yet subservient

assignation . . . .

. . . . lumpen

a thin idea . . . .

scaffold? . . . .

. . . . victim that was still warm

not all arabesques & cherubs

dying in the past tense like Mina Loy

. . . .

mosques bombed

. . . . acculturated

not all stout & gay

. . . . stiff

corpses

stiffen

shirked

whim of the weather

studied serenity

bloody map

rapt condonation

entreaty come sharp
entry come sharper

portentous form

cluster

interlocutress

not all questions

not at all trivial

flattery

trade connections

hollow guise

. . . . irony that would be transparent

. . . .

. . . .

gaunt

. . . . like a ferryman at the pier green shutters

rickety objects

the bridge at Mostar . . . .

. . . . nothing to attenuate

nothing to brag about . . . .

. . . . irreclaimably

preoccupied

▯▯

recognition: American

it was not vagueness

. . . . sunglasses rigid . . . .

. . . . momentary

risen at a bound

sequel to a sharp turn

the dizzy edge of it

. . . . a clearing

and in the middle Al-Uzza a goddess worshipped as a sacred black stone

. . . . yoni

slab

(hooded)

hurried

pursuit

a method of progression . . . .

gaze of consent

rape

& yet a mocking light

war trophy

systematic

systemic . . . .

a bag, an ear . . . .

[bag an ear]

a note of recrimination

danger

rushes

opposing scruple

industry

serpentine
                    routed

"love interest"
two got off to be two again

land grab

the theme of every tongue

a range to be out of

or gunpoint . . . .>>>>>>>>>>>>>>>>>

but speak of more cheerful imaginings

The Joyces, Catherine & Alex, are going to Naples to clear up their inheritance from Uncle Homer (Obvious irony of names and play on *Ulysses*. Uncle Homer is instigator, perpetrator of their voyage.) Driving in their car: noise & boredom. Alex's (George Sanders) acid voice. There are tiresome cattle blocking the road. "Danger of catching malaria." He: "We should have come by plane." She: "Boring to be alone with me." "First time alone since we married." Married eight years. Now, "like strangers."

Ordinary couple in crisis, claustrophobically stuck in active/reactive chemistry of their marriage. Fruition of it comes to this. Simply bored? Childless. A chill, frissure in chemistry. Suddenly thrown into the exotic landscape of Italy. Pregnant women push baby carriages. But reluctant to let the environment penetrate their cold habit. Now out of their element, it—climate, ruins, history, vapors of Pompei, sea air, *la dolce vita*—seeps into them, leans into them, softens them. He almost sleeps with another woman. She's off traipsing about the ruins, melancholic.

He on patrician side but bourgeois.

And, too, pragmatist, he, manly, impatient, condescending, & she a romantic, would-be adventurer, dreamer. She reminisces about her friend Charles Lewington, a poet, his long poem "The Triumph of the Spirit." She's hardened around edges around her husband to withstand frustration, insult, void. Beneath a surface: tender, gorgeous, supple Ingrid Bergman, her face waiting to meet the moment, waiting for recognition of the moment when everything could turn around, crack. A word, gesture to cut the static heat. By the end they are reunited in some familiar way.

I speak with filmmaker Nathaniel Dorsky.

—How would you characterize the filmmaking of Roberto Rossellini?

—First let me say there are three basic periods: Neo-Realism, the Ingrid Bergman films (five of these), and after the breakup with Bergman, the India film. At one point he decided he didn't want to bring more fiction into the world but bring light into the world by elucidating history. So you got the later didactic cinema: *Louis XIV*. There were transition films in 1950, like *The Flowers of St. Francis* where St. Francis sends his disciple out to spread the gospel. At one point they twirl till they fall, it's so beautiful. But 1953 (when he made *Voyage*) was an amazing year for film all over. Rossellini had made "industrials" under Mussolini, using regular people in real situations. One example is *The White Ship*, which is, in reality, a hospital ship. The male principle tended by the female principle. It's allegorical, mythic. Then you have *Open City* with Anna Magnani. *Paisan*, which has the same light sculptural process as *Flowers of St. Francis*, although it's a dark situation. But with all of them what you have are films in all their awkwardness, crudity. Crudity in the very quality of light. The films are as modest as the people they are about. No vanity, no presentation, no veneer of art. They are as crude as the earth. They break down ego because they don't take refuge in ego.

—It's true in a way that the situation in *Voyage to Italy* is unglamorous. The characters are not even tragic, they are too much like us. If anything, Italy—a country in a way without an ego—is the heroine, the all-accommodating space in which anything can arise, and something as trivial as the situation of a middle-aged couple suffering angst in a marriage does arise. It's never loveless, however, or cynical. We respond to the truth of the characters, and of course, the actors are pros. The undercurrent, their connection, holds us as it holds them.

—His films are not "art objects" at all. They make the audience uncomfortable. Certainly *Voyage to Italy* does. It's a crude & painful situation. George Sanders complained, broke down several times, in fact, in frustration. Rossellini worked with little pieces of paper. There was no chance to prepare a scene at all. But this film takes a lot of risks, using the dynamics of a couple to pop out of previous kinds of syntax, it leaves the theater. Jacques Rivette said, "On the appearance of *Voyage to Italy,* all other films suddenly aged ten years."

—Why?

—Something about the existential situation. Being caught, perhaps you could say.

—Yes! that's it. It—whatever that so powerfully real atmosphere is, so much like our own lives!—is held, then breaks moment to moment. It's heartbreakingly like life. Or you could say art & life are inseparable in this film. I wince at this film too. Who hasn't felt trapped? And had it brought home when you're in another context, far from home, outside familiar patterns. Those habits are exaggerated, highlighted. I remember breaking down uncontrollably at the Spanish Steps in Rome and my early husband flailing on the ground, beating his fists on that sacred spot precious to John Keats. Italy, with its ancient sensuous & holy vapors, of course, is extremely evocative. It's the place of Sacred Muse. And the marriage edge is particularly vivid. What's sublime is how beautiful the actors are at it, their sweet groundlessness. In a way they are innocents abroad, in the literal sense. What you say about George Sanders's frustration works to the advantage of the film. The interconnectedness of people, situation, place, the subtle shifts of attention, emotion are basic truths subtly rendered here. What a good eye he has for the details. I can't get her face out of my mind. He obviously adored her visually. Why struggle to make it art? Does he struggle?

—It's just that Rossellini's films took life more seriously than the vanity of cinema, that the truth he's after is more important than the vanity of cinema.

This is Rossellini speaking: "How can you reach such a humble thing like piety if you look at yourself with pride. You must just reverse the thing for the real values to come up. The truth is something very very small, very very humble and that is why it is so difficult to discover it. If you have no humility, how can you approach the truth? How can you make an error? You can build an opinion, but that is pride. The whole point is either you have faith in human beings or you don't. If you have no faith in them, then you must convey a message because you want to take advantage of them or train them to think like you. There are people who like to beat others and there are those who like to be beaten. My purpose is never to convey a message, never to persuade, but to offer everybody an observation, even my observation, why not?"

XIX

AMBROSE:

NAM

"If I cannot bend the gods to my will, I shall move the underworld"
                                        —brief history lesson for a schoolboy

                "What will children remember? What will they know?"
—a mother sitting next to me, reading an article on ethnic cleansing in Bosnia.

"I now—as a funerary offering to him (Sennacherib)—ploughed those people
under alive. Their flesh I fed to the dogs, pigs, vultures, eagles—the birds of heaven
and the fish of the deep . . . I took the corpses of the people whom Erra had laid
low and who had laid down their lives through hunger and famine; . . . those
bones (I took) out of Babylon, Kutha and Sippar and threw them on heaps."
                                        —Assurbanipal (668—626 BCE)

*This morning at breakfast he asks a question about Vietnam. Bits & scraps I offer. A few facts.
Reminders now in sterile wisps of poetry: What do I know, living it from the other side, Lower East Side,
New York City? Baby boom. Demonstrations, poetry events, benefits, calls to action never enough.
Yippie monkey-wrenching. Throwing money away at the stock market. Setting tacks out on the streets of
commercial gunrunning America. The Chicago trial. Chant mantras in the park with Ginsberg & cul-
tural workers from many quarters. Om aing gring cling chamunda yei vijaya. The boy sees caricatures
in movies, listens to sixties music, aware of underpinnings of an insane war that ravaged a generation of
youth, & continues to plague its aging survivors and subsequent generations both here & there. Movie
illusion, swell of music, action. Heroic contradictions. Will the ghosts & demons never die? More doc-
uments? Soul-searching? Hard to compartmentalize such a war temporally when you have a sense of the
dynamic pratitya samutpada, the interconnectedness of the whole "scene." Cause & effect that goes way
back. The culpability of French colonizers and how the U.S. supported France. Merely one divided Asian
country's sorrow? Never again a war so obsessively captured, recorded, uncensored in living rooms across
the land. How much more vivid than Nintendo war. Energy of community action, at home. And the psy-
chedelic explosion, where you got high, felt stab of compassion, "freedom?" or on the macho hard stuff,
you felt nothing—nihilism. A generation of paraphernalia, accoutrements, new terms, naive generation
coming of age to its dark side. "Hell no, we won't go. You don't need a weatherman to know which way
the wind blows." et cetera et cetera et cetera. Now's all attendant sickness, mental torment as the maimed
of body & soul haunt the streets as "homeless" spectors. What did you see? he asks. What do I know?
Hoa Wah Nguyen—young poet in San Francisco—sends a pantoum.*
the cloudgatherer

with muscular tautness
& undeviating purpose
aims his lightning bolt

   & lonely on the waves
she dances the word into being—
who will survive

creator or destroyer?

two young sisters of beauteous slant eye,
see it all
the country fall
  she & she, another

unfulfilled,
wasted
the sea parts
the world is separated

she &
  she,
the other
               sweep the sky

deiwos, sky
Indic skygod *Dyaus Pita*
Greek *eudia,* fair weather
Latin *deus,* god
dies, day
a sad day
when gods are angry

not the beginning of the world

but
beginning of their own time—she & she—
ordering power of undifferentiated imagination
right timing
exactitude
[Titan means to stretch, to extend, & spread forth]

the two Nams

the "face of heaven"

can be seen in mirrors
mat troi
any mirrors
can be seen in mirrors

on the faces of mirrors
the Vietnamese paint the names of their ancestors

then cover the mirror with a red cloth

often referring to tigers, elephants, & other jungle animals as "Mister"

Chinese domination began in 200 BC. Trieu Da came over the mountains in the north & conquered the country around the Red River Delta (size of New Jersey), declared himself king & named his kingdom Nam Viet—*Nam* meaning South, and *Viet,* people. Among the first Vietnamese heroes to lead the people against Chinese rule were two sisters, Trung Trac & Trung Nhi. For nearly three years—39–42 AD—they led their forces in a fight against the Chinese. They liberated a large part of the country & for a time ruled jointly as queens. Finally Chinese troops beat back the rebels & the Trung sisters chose suicide rather than surrender. The Chinese were finally driven out of Vietnam in 939 AD by a patriot named Ngo Quyen. For 500 years the people of Vietnam jealously guarded their freedom. It was the only country that defeated the Mongol hordes under Kublai Khan in 1257 . . .

---

were
the water
of
eastern seas
to be
exhausted

                                                        the stain of

                            ignominy

yet she & she
could not
be washed
away
all the
bamboo
of
the southern
mountains
couldn't
suffice as
paper
to record

their
crimes
   & pain

Dear Claude—a vet—
Tell about being a killer & a saint. Padmasambhava could live in this hutch
(lurch).
Tell how the young hippie spits in your face again. Tell us again how you are
decorated, shiny with medals . . . how you went on the skids . . .

The 1954 Geneva meeting was supposed to decide the fate of Vietnam. Unity &
freedom, it was hoped.
               hoped
who?
& how could
 a power concede
& not "save face"
thought?

that?
hoped?
a knell
not heard hard enough
she & she, a legacy

North & South leaders did not see eye to eye. France, the U.S., Britain, the Soviet Union, and Red China were seated at the conference table. In addition, there were delegations from Cambodia, Laos, & the part of Vietnam not occupied by Red forces. Also present at Geneva were representatives of the Vietminh, headed by Ho Chi Minh & in control of most of northern Vietnam. North & South leaders did not see eye to eye. The Communist delegations wanted as much of Vietnam as possible to end up in Red hands. France had thrown in the towel, but the U.S. & Britain were determined to prevent the Reds from taking over all this strategic, rich-rich region. Tough negotiations. The Communists agree to a compromise plan. Cambodia & Laos, which had almost gained full self-rule from France in 1949, were to remain neutral in the cold war. Vietnam was split into two parts, supposedly for only a short period of time. Land north of the 17th parallel was placed under Red rule. A non-Communist government was put in charge of the southern party of the country.

---

a pledge
not see eye to eye
horror
the battle there, the battle at home
eye for an eye

The night LBJ resigned, March 31, 1968, I put my hand through a pane of glass & spent hours in St. Vincent's Hospital, a portrait of JFK on one side, and a garish crucifix on the other. I should have been happy.

---

convulsion

   around the table
disordered eye
   the gloat or
cloak
of
   a terrible rift

Dear Ambrose: In June 1963 a Buddhist monk named Thich Quang Duc sat down in the middle of a Saigon street, doused himself with gasoline, & set fire to his robes. Madame Nhu referred to the burning as a barbecue. (Today, her former summer retreat near Saigon has been turned into a public tourist site. The residence has a heated country-club-size swimming pool, marble tile, gardens that took fifty men to cultivate, a $20,000 stainless-steel kitchen, and an underground passage for quick escape beneath the swimming pool.)

Vietcong woman says:
(long ago in poetry)

duty now is
  all
in arrows
shadow flag
  sorrow runs me
    young man he put away pen & ink
take up sword!

man's will flies
across mountains
    then in full battledress
crosses Vi Bridge
  tugs the last cup down
here's tiger cave
hear the flutes
  you, husband, go to war
I back to mat & blanket your sad-war wife

the chu mon spoke this many moons back

"smash the glass of the ruling class"

& Hoa Wah Nguyen writes:

Pantoum

take your skin as an indication
under a woven mat an accessory of war
rolls in dust we are the children
attached in a dictionary where speech is

under a woven mat accessory of war
little dragon I can count to three
attached to a dictionary where speeches are
your hair on fire

little dragon I count to three
in that other language
my hair is on fire
he wrote life in war is so short

in that other language
to strip the leaves off trees
he wrote life in war is so short
confiscated diaries

strip the leaves off trees
all Vietnamese make poetry
in confiscated diaries
many of whom are twenty years dead

not all Vietnamese make poetry
desire to forget also
the many twenty years dead
a guest room house

desires to forget also
the year of the ram or sheep
in my room in the guest house
you teased me about how clever heaven was

in the year of the ram or sheep
craters became ponds the hundred thousand hatreds
tease me about how clever heaven is
eating a village of frogs

craters become frogs hundred thousand hatreds
when you find the name of your country
eating a village of frogs
assume your father was a GI

when you find the name of your country
celebrate the new year with explosions
your father is a GI assume
napalm was a cohering matter

celebrate the new year with explosions
roll in dust we are the children
napalmed a cohering matter
takes your skin as indication

Hey! Hey! LBJ, how many kids did you kill today?

In 1968 the U.S. alone was spending $30 billion a year to carry on the war in Vietnam.

---

and scribed these words from a homeless vet addressing the Statue of Liberty, torn shirt open, gesticulating in the breeze, Battery Park, NYC:

All right
How long you live
How long you know me
Statue, statue
Tomorrow
Mucho tucho

Pucky pucky
Mahecy mahecy
kill kill
Juna's an old lady now
Up down
Huh huh
I got eight down
China ow tuna
Jung chow
Noodle bowl
Macutty macutty
pucka pucka pucka
I know why not baklava
Siney nonny non
No more New York City
No more subway
No more New York New York
No more hot dog
No matty cochisa
You nigh you night
Any pay onga mille
Mucho mucho
A que a que mucho
God sa-ka Gog sa-ke
Mhata hatyouso (hat-you-usu)
No more New York City
No more subway tomorrow
No more mahatma
Reefer, yes
Eh eh no moe-or
Pa dina lak da eena
How many gonna give me no dolla
No goong
Now all the people a pay a gook
No more oomy
Ah ya 299
Foo ya a ichy dicky ah
Belly big league
Belly belly big league

Hat plate hot potato
Stick no big one ah 69
Very big one a stick-ons
Oh said woky
No more Hollywood
Cowboy o ya!
Hollywood no more
No more cowboy
No more Chinese movie
I didn't see the movie I see the war
Ah beg a saw wouldja
No salary a five a loonya
Goddamit no subway tomorrow
No city tomorrow
Mille Mille no tomorrow
Mañana ya too D-Day Sunday
Gook cong
Oh laa mucho a singya la
Fuck em si no mucho, agua
Today's Sunday—sun day
Ya bag subway all the fucky time
See a look a goddam sun
Yah today is sure Sunday
You see it it?
You die you have a good day
I kill & die, kill & die, killy die
You eat? You see you July
No money no subway
No more señorita
No coffee
Malo malo Mahata
Yal rowty matta fucky
No mala no mala tomorrow
Manhattan tomorrow
Go home go home
Don't talk to her no more

Quiz:

I ask him
Who were the Trung sisters?
In what ways did the Chinese rulers of Vietnam improve conditions during
their first long period of control? (200 BCE–939 AD)?
Of what importance was the city of Hue?
What were the names of the three states into which the French divided
Vietnam in the late 1800s?
Who was "Nguyen the Patriot"?
When did LBJ quit?
How many people were killed in the war, both sides?

XX

TU M'

Spirochetes of memory now launched. Philadelphia was home one summer in the sixties early on in Vietnam War, rioting in her neighborhood. Now neighborhood's more gentrified. Return to the museum with famous Duchamp. You would like to live among the playful artifacts that strum on your attention. And the duty is to scribe an impression. That it is wry is easy, that it survives in a kind of mental quandary is difficult. The inability to see the face, for example, in the violent tableau, at the same time you know it's perfectly safe (there is a sweet guard at the door) a shiver resounds in the body. Brittle sensation. Enigmatic, voyeuristic, a master of chance, Marcel Duchamp still mirrors back your own expectation.

TU M'

tomb

pro

prodromus
proem
prologomena
prolepsis

< long

& sung

& sounded

<gage

on the tongue a **guage>**

eyes & gaze

gouge>

as if wounded

removed

lang >

<gauze

voile>
inside a fallen garden

water
rape

<gaz

he said art life

. . . . or art "i"
(to place a face in office)

fice
  dictum tu m'
tu m'aime

Jasper said co-painterly

peut   -être

tête
perhaps
or the head is bent to peer through,
pierce,
or shatter glass
a chemical beaker
breaks
alembic
words are offhand
offstage
an aside to Marcel's game
smoking

\littoral
why retinal?

fearful
[peur-full]

pet
homme
age
rage d'or
or door

adore
rotate
resembling a feather
retinue
resembling a pinnace

[et tu]

objet

2 peepholes

dart

,

mock   amock

in scribe
bid,

or, bidden,
mid, pasque-fleur
or, mien of a
philosopher sleight of hand
at midsummer
culture, sign it repeating a
nomenclature
numinous
or hard to be sure—numerous

when ready made for the IRON age
Arose
a gender enamelled

a man in the middle of his living
of most
                              in them

a bottom nature to himself

                              always
                              being
                              made
                              to
                              know
                              more

less tribal
toward the darker subject

try actuality
or
epistolary mode
made a mistake asking me

a thing where wanted
use of me

       so write
words back
serving
a serviceable said so
old blood serving
he said writing,
wanting me to serve
sleep on the large glass
singular
sleep on the small valise
pillowed now
pillaged
the spoils that become art

sort out
tout

     redoubtable weakness

spin spine
       spire

like out of "in"

long (longing)
  i

tude
  wrist longing

the raconteur
bluffs (puffs)

limber

closeted not a fool
monk-art which is inscribed
penance for an age
plastique.

>>>

XXI

EZLN

A communication and a dream . . .

Aguascalientes, Chiapas, located on the
outskirts of the village of Guadalupe Tepeyac

Rebel Subcomandante Marcos ended the offensive phase of the insurrection. Wearing his trademark ski mask, Marcos told thousands gathered in the Lacandón rain forest earlier this week that he was turning to the National Democratic Convention, a civilian front dedicated to peaceful struggle, to carry on the crusade for social and political change on behalf of Mexico's poor & indigenous masses. Four thousand activists rode trucks & buses for nearly thirty hours to reach this spot in the realm of the Zapatista Army of National Liberation.

She visits Chiapas a year and a half later to note the following:

note this
a range of which
is noted
wit or
witness
is closed then
open a Mayan codice
o yes I saw that
& seen, too
I've "sawn it"
the skinny animals
tengo hambre
tengo sed
thirst for the maize
[closed on here]
[ ]
[ ]
[ ]
& from here on out
we all close down

the sense of which
we are closed
it is closed to us
although it is
close to us
could be jaguar
could be burro
the place is empty
no, it is waiting
for the elected to be chosen

brackets are a con
& trick you here

the trick is silence
walk out
close no door
or contained
as body
is with
all its attendant *skandas* that
go flying

not what it seems
not what is sorted out to be
piles
||||||||||||||||||||||
on the pyre
prone or tipped
which would you do
to be
or assured of
to desire
++
++
++
++
++
++

++
++
++
++
++

Communiqué from the Clandestine Indigenous Revolutionary Committee High Command of the Zapatista National Liberation Army (CCRI-CG del EZLN)

February 26, 1994

To the people of Mexico:
To the peoples and governments of the World:
To the national and international press:
Brothers:

The CCRI-CG of the EZLN addresses you with all honor and respect to speak its word, what is in its heart and thought.

When the EZLN was only a shadow, creeping through the mist and darkness of the jungle, when the words *justice, liberty,* and *democracy* were only that: words, barely a dream that the elders of our communities, true guardians of the words of our dead ancestors, had given us in the moment when day gives way to night, when hatred and fear begin to grow in our hearts, when there was nothing but desperation, when the times repeated themselves, with no way out, with no door, no tomorrow, when all was injustice, as it was, the true men spoke, the faceless ones, the ones who go by night, the ones who are jungle, and they said:

"It is the purpose and will of good men and women to seek and find the best way to govern and be governed, what is good for the many is good for all. But let not the voices of the few be silenced, but let them remain in their place, waiting until the thoughts and hearts become one in what is the will of the many and opinion from within and no outside force can break them or divert their steps to other paths."

* * *

Those who go by night said: "And we see that this way of governing that we name is no longer the way for the many, we see that it is the few who now command, and they command without obeying, they lead commanding. And among the few they pass the power of command among themselves, without hearing the many, the few lead commanding, without obeying the command of the many. Without reason, the few command, the word that comes from afar says they lead without democracy, without the command of the people, and we see that this unreason of those who lead commanding directs the road of our sorrows and feeds the pain of our dead. And we see that those who lead commanding should go far away so that there is reason once again and truth in our land. And we see that there should be change so that those who command obeying lead again and we see that word that comes from afar to name to reason of government, 'democracy,' is good for the many and for the few."

The faceless ones continued speaking:

"The world is another world, reason no longer governs and we true men and women are few and forgotten and death walks upon us, we are despised, we are small, our word is muffled, silence has inhabited our houses for a long time, the time has come to speak for our hearts, for the hearts of others, from the night and from the earth our dead should come, the faceless ones, those who are jungle, who dress with war so their voice will be heard, that their word later falls silent and they return once again to the night and to the earth, that other men and women may speak, who walk other lands, whose words carry the truth, who do not become lost in lies.

"Look for the men and women who lead obeying, those who have strength in their words, and not in fire, and finding them, speak and give them the staff of command, that they may return once again to the earth and the night, the faceless ones, those who are jungle, so that if reason returns to these lands the fury of the fire may be silenced, that the faceless ones, those who go by night, may rest at last by the earth."

This spoke the faceless ones, there was no fire in their hands and their word was clear and without folds. And before the day defeated the night once again they went, and on the earth one word remained: "Enough!"

Zocalo Dream

We are in the "concentricities" of a small village in Mexico, high in the mountains, above a fertile valley. We are in the innermost town square, one of many town squares—or zocalos—*boxes within boxes, but paradoxically these are also inhabiting a greater cosmological, psychological framework of circles within circles. As if the squares have shadow-circles. And some of these shapes are made up, illusory tricks or trompe l'oeil masks—painted and vibrant stage sets—false fronts, substitutes from other times & places for the "real thing." So that suddenly you get a slide of a shopping mall interrupting a cathedral in disrepair or glimpse a woman from another century—high European, scornful—passing, her elegantly coiffed head at mysterious angle she's gone now, or catch a futuristic moon landscape where nothing will grow. I saw a Rasta man laughing. "We" is my lover & I who are caged in the center in something you might keep large birds in, but it is also any old car, tops & sides ripped off. We are desperately making love, we look scrawny, plucked, there are titters from the sides. Our zocalo is a bullring, I think. We are "core." We are "railed." We are "trialed." We are "monstranced." We are "loco." We are "bullied." In charge is old Indian shaman lady, barefoot. She resembles María Sabina, the Mazatec shaman. She resembles Rigoberta Menchu, the Guatemalan revolutionary. She is an amalgam of all of the old magic wisdom-hags.*

She is the woman I saw in Oaxaca Cathedral doing puja *with herbs in front of suffering Jesus. Is woman with branch performing sympathetic magic, touching the "wounds" of statue Mary, touching Mary's womb, touching the simulacra of thighs where Mary gave birth to a son who would die. Touching the image of the son who would die, who is greater more excessive martyr. She is cackling, she is the mother of us all and we are a hologram of her imagination of conquistador. We are put forth as examples of weakness, of indiscretion, singled out as interlopers from an alien land. We are a spectacle but will not be tortured, will not die. We refuse. There is a large family we have been traveling with, an exotic bunch who are "related" but safe because they are inside the Adobe Palace. One noble lady resembles R. D., who is writing this down. J. C. is pacing the palatial patio, face obscured by a Panama hat. I escape to get a look inside and wonder at how adobe can also be like mirrors. Reflections appear on the walls as frescoes. Images, family portraits. My Greek, Italian, African American, and Jewish relatives are all depicted there. They are so real! Then I'm pulled back to the center of the* zocalo *by desire. I pull stringy rags about my body. The old lady wants us to drink* atole *and starts dancing and yipping like a coyote. She wants everyone dancing. My lover gives a weary look as if to say we will continue to go "round and round." We are happy to dance. A young girl in golden rags starts doing very formal ballet.*

---

ablution
skinned

astride

melting pot

guilt

yearning for other

her plight

his/her

selva

Cathedral of Peace

The Tzeltals

Tzotzils
Zoques
Chols
Tojolobals

campesinos to turn to turn never never from land

credibility
gap
squawked

We climb to the chuch tower of San Andreas de Lorrainzar & are arrested by
local guardians, the church *alferes*. Women are not allowed up there. Ambar
writes two months later the tower has collapsed.

Isn't that gnarly. Such bad access, shit. No, no. Whoa. What are you writing?
Mom, I swear if you publish this I'll slaughter you. Stop, it sucks! You are the
annoyingest person. Stupid fool! I'm going to beat you 'cause you mess me up.
—Jerk, Dad'll see it.
—Omigod, dammit!
—You were talking trash. Just shut up & stop always writing things down.
—Way to go, thanks, Mom. I swear I'm going to tear that in half & you'll never
publish it.
—Wait a minute.
—Stop writing down your stupid notes. What are you writing down, Mom?
Anne Waldman's an idiot. She's going to write these things & think: O I'm
going to sell them for a dollar. Maybe I could sell it to a fool like me for a dol-
lar. She's the goddess of all idiots!

---

oblige
sound
when all the planets are in a straight line

in her big-bottomed passion where god Jupiter appears out of a dusky cloud in
baggy pants

fucks her impersonating a wisp of smoke

Woman next to me—is she French?—can't tell her funny (country) accent
turns to me in the palatial Das Kunsthistorisches Musem, Wien, blurting out,
loud, so everyone hears:
Can you imagine? To be made love to like that? What could be more romantic?

terra-cotta idols
smashed to the ground

XXII

COSMOLOGY:
WITHIN THE MIND OF THE SLEEPING GOD

kāminīkāyakāntare
kucaparvatadurgame
mā saṃcara manahpāntha
tatrāste smarataskaraḥ
—Bhartrihari

The poet starts her assignment of "cosmology" with the Buddhist notion of birth being just one link in an ongoing chain of karmic events. She has found the opening lines of her canto—"the longest times in love with living"—in a notebook kept in Vienna around her birthday in April, which also celebrated Easter. She continues her study of the great Yugas—ages—based on Hindu philosophy and turns to a version of existence that is flowing, dynamic, nothing static. Everything originates, grows, decays, vanishes, then returns. She studies the primordial symbols of this dynamism and sees links to other cultures. The eagle belongs to Zeus, serpents attend the goddess Hera, Zeus's consort, Mother Earth. In Homer's Iliad an eagle appears to the Greek heroes one day during the seige of Troy. The bird is observed slowly soaring in the sky and bears a bleeding snake in its talons. Sun force against the liquid energies of the natural waters. The creator is poet, sleeper. Dear friend, compañera-poet, lies in induced coma in Intensive Care as this is written. She sleeps as creator Vishnu does, coiled in on himself, surrounded by royal snakes, intravenous tubes, wires, a veritable tribe of nagas. Snakes are feminine principle, nourishing. The bird is patriarch, sky-bound. Who pecks at the earthlings. This cosmology borrows from the Hindu, from the Jain, of destruction & rebirth time after time, the play of opposites that are merely manifestations—reincarnations of the next form around. The Jaina speaks of the the indissolubility of matter, it is a dark view. Which would you prefer here? That we may completely start over or carry the burden of matter lifetime to lifetime? What her friend has suffered sounds like a stroke, aneurysm, something sudden, spasmodic. They keep her on intravenous morphine so that she lie still. The doctors aren't telling what they know. People keep vigil, pray, send mantras her way. Bernadette Mayer is writer of depth, of intricacy, whose words sing in my ear. If I could but wander through her body as the holy man Markandeya did in god Vishnu's, an aimless pilgrim, contemplating the interior landscape, the holy spots and shrines through the countries of her body. If I could meditate on the junctures of energy that produced her sacred writing, perhaps I could help heal her sickness. I visualize her small still body in the dark hospital vast miles away. Markandeya was thousands of years old, alert of mind, but an accident occured when he slipped inadvertently out of the sleeper's giant lip and dove headlong into the cosmic sea. What was his utterance out of the mouth of the body? We live on the edge, constantly, of a precarious unfathomable existence. She returns to the stars . . .

the longest time in love with living
to seem to be born
a detail: her red dress
a blue shoe
earring the shape of a knife,
a skull
the longest object
touched to
core
a liberty taken there
to be
free
from things
in love
the sweetest joy
urge to birth
again, again
one of the links of *nidana* chain
(this written on
napkin, Carlton Opera Hotel,
heart of Wien)

·

& for the quelling of desire
no recourse
say I won't I won't
say I wasn't, never never
say I drew her face away from here
say I dreamed her body likewise
"likewise"
say I moved, lost my body
my breast, so sorry
sorry,
cunt
moved

sad
arms tired
rest

eyes not seductive tonight
legs do not tremble

& yet you are born
into interstellar space

candle flickers
your name, a little bee, rises
into an arc
informer faxes me here
many miles away
go away, name
no, don't
flicker of you, beloved
phantom you
fingers were cold stalks later
gone numb
awoke on fire
I get up
CNN describes the world
but not my need of you to heal
not good enough
Beograd for a drink
lips pursed
drinking enemy Serb wine
not lips to kiss
a sober set-face woman
hair needs washing
I will not tell the rest

Powerbook at hand
what have poets come to
up to speed?
I roar for you . . .

daguerreotype invades personality
lift the curse of patriarchal hatred
topmost greatness subtitled "a rental"

Ixion embraces a cloud
which is the god Jove
(detail: in a museum)

Phenomena warmed up
warmed over
a trade, this for that
deliberates the plex
what kind
under glory
how calm
the plexion woke with
Did?
woke with rub of love
did he/her
glory seize?
she, she
self, made up to
& too, a cry or
notable town croon
weep entirely
for barn nostalgia

                                                            stave off her pain

cardinal, how color
rides
"nice blues—
get to keep the glass"
excursions onto property
a pathfinder
chooses green
naught but
strife
to walk
& see
that is vision

polychromed eye
poet's eye
grown shifty
in bold sense
rather close
really closer by
then squint back
lines drawn
black now,
upended

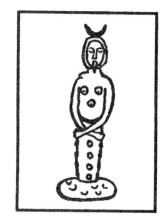

blind, blind
blind
& bound, bind more
so blinded
blur not screen
demur
incur or trust
but her
blind
is hard

               to dear son, my issuance, far away,

these messages:

expand
may be free
head
tongue
(of small one
thinking
he chatters lots)

change the world
I say
the world—
those others—ha!

toward
generous
action
     all that will matter

gesture
join
throng-buzz
somewhere
to spin the wheel

give up
yes
personal comfort & gain
enter the stream

ear-whispered

on highways
malls
everyone gone on shopping
siddhas abound

ka-dag

the accomplishment of dressing up the world
in poetry

lusting for non-existence
jnanadharmakaya beyond awake

sidle up to art
more real than
what you just now indicate

                                                    sensed

an earlier epoch of the world when husbands and wives were born as twins, had
64 ribs apiece, and were two miles tall . . . .

sensed

Vishnu sleeps, recumbent on the coils of Ananta, absorbed as if in a dream of
the universe inside himself . . . .

sensed

  she sleeps, the poet gone into coma
hooked up to machines in the hospital with a saint's name

from the navel grows a lotus, bearing on its corolla Brahma, the four-faced
demiurge creator

she sleeps, coiled

sensed out of time

the great serpent bed of death & desire

Vishnu's shoulders & head are protected by nine serpent heads with expanded
hoods,

like animal self of the anthropomorphic sleeper

sensed

  animal realm, coiled in on itself

herself, sensed

sensed upon the waters

paranoia to disturb the dream   ranging
                             blood ranging

  but insensate

she sleeps, locked in morphine dream, the doctors do it

named *endless,* Ananta, the serpent we rest upon
all of us
                         a world system at rest
  sensed up

incensed

  before the next fiery Yuga

named *The Remainder*

The Residue (sesa)

As figure representing the residue after the earth had been shaped out of the
cosmic waters of the abyss . . . she . . .

descends to earth of the Ganges . . .

  arriving as snake to strike the ground

sinuous body of snake is represented as running down the back, curve of thigh
Nagas—naginis—door-guardians—*dvara-palas*
let no trash enter here talking trash not welcome here

                              Hustle, girl, hustle!

no universe, only water and the starless night of the lifeless interval between
dissolution & creation

                         Vishnu sleeps
                                    the wounded poet sleeps
  blood poured forth her skull
                              no sound issues forth her mouth
see her: thin, dark
see her: resting, healing upon the waters

moving around inside herself creating new sounds for the end of the universe
  may she not die but live to prosper these forms

what gets made: device for slaughter, undo slaughter here
what gets made: ceremonial twist
what gets made: a last resort, a financial collapse
what gets made: more things, toys, space stations, weaponry

yantra = machine

life & death yantras to keep the matter churning
plasma churn
                         where is her *prana* now?

sleep little one
sleep, sleep

what's worth clinging to: the rise of the moon, it never set
spoils of a long war
texts that will tell the story but whispered here

                    Vishnu, the creator, sleeps in a pool of water

the elements wrestle with their shadows

shadow earth
shadow air
shadow fire
water shadow

  not alone in this

  but shadow of sleep
                              without dream
no, maybe dream
    she . . .
not a male god
  but conjures all the faces we have
have in her
  Bernadette sleeps in a hospital
swathed in the white bindings of the saint
blood in the cerebellum

morphed into sleep
the phantom syllables she would speak lie here

a pillow of runes
  folded & twisted in on itself

swaddled, you could say
white linen
rise up, she-Lazarus
  cowgirl far from home

or Indian, the darkest eyes you could mention

what's surely made: point of honor
departure
or
not
readying
for the kill

another world woman
another world system
    asleep upon the waters
rebound

    obscurum per obscurius
    ignotum per ignotius

(the obscure by the more obscure
the unknown by the more unknown)

old alchemical trick, to measure

she abides in the nursery of young stars

                which will someday be planets

. . . in a photographic survey of young stars in Orion, astronomers determined that at least half of
them were surrounded by the raw material for planetary formation. The material swirls about the

stars in flattened disks of spreading dust, glowing from the reflected light of stars all about the region.
Closer analysis reveals that the disks contain enough mass to produce Earth-size planets. The abun-
dance of these protoplanetary disks in a cluster of young stars, many of them less than 300,000 years
old, shows the ingredients for making planets exist around a significant fraction of stars. Scientists
say this reinforces the probability that many stars have planetary systems. This discovery is one more
important contribution to the accumulating evidence that the Sun, one of countless stars, is not alone
in having a retinue of orbiting bodies. In April, radio astronomers said new observations confirmed
the existence of two and possibly three large planets around a pulsar, the spinning remnant of an
exploded star. The prospect that many other planets could exist increases the chances that there is
extraterrestrial life.

fluctuate: move like a wave

pass to & fro

flux: copious flowing of blood, incoming tide

serum: watery animal fluid
corr. to Gk *oros* (flow)

stellate: studded with stars she sleeps

. . . .

Let now your wanderer's mind
Roam in the forest of woman's form.
There in the mountains of her bosom
Lurks the robber Kama.

XXIII

SPIN OR LACE IT IN STORY

Retell traditional myth from this continent, the artist-hag's narration. How spinner of yarn works phenomenal obstacles the imagination conjures & vivifies for her. She sits around a campfire in the Ute Valley, high altiplano of Colorado. She thinks: No man to touch her. Pronghorn feed nearby. Low hoot of owl as it gets black. Coyote yip a mantra. Only outside do we tell these things, fire making sweet animations as flames dance. Do you see the girl in there holding a beautiful head? Or Copper Man with copper harpoon? Jove with erect cock attacking the sleeping world? Woman of Skins crackles green & blue. Nothing to plug in here but nature's sound & light.

There was a spinster
cold in the nights

from this spinster came all the spiders in the world
great artists all of them

There once were a man & a woman who had a daughter who despised men
Her father wanted her to marry but she always refused

She was beautiful, the men came, but she refused them
Who would help the couple in their old age if the woman did not marry?
She was sad at this and went wandering

She wandered out onto the undulating plains on which there were many small
hills

Suddenly a head jumped out of the earth among the hills

not animal but human

human

beautiful head without a body

A head with the face of a very handsome young man

He'd been everywhere in the latest head fashions

He had a smooth tongue

He smiled "I know you don't want to have a husband but I've come here to fetch you. I come from a powerful race of men"

Ho!

The girl was happy with the young man and picked up the head & put it carefully in her fur coat & carried it home in the dark

Where to sit with this beautiful head?

She settled the head next to her couch and laughed and talked with it all night, in love with this stranger-head who was not like other men. Love? More like curiosity

Her father heard her, night after night & was happy to have a future son-in-law. He thought, a hunter in the house, or at least a knowledgeable talker

This talker had been some places

The girl was happy but now she never went far from the couch and her night-time ramblings with the head

The parents wondered why they never met the man and the father pushed aside the fur rug she kept the head under, but when he saw the head without a body he was angry and took a meat skewer & stabbed the head through the eye and cast it on a rubbish heap

What's the use of a son without a body who can't hunt for us when we are old?

The head rolled away farther & farther leaving a bloody trail into the sea

The girl sobbed and sobbed::Where was her talking man?

Girl went out and followed the bloody track to the sea. She wanted to dive into the waves but they were as hard as wood. Like a stage set. Something cardboard or petrified. Then she went inland looking for a white lemming, for she knew lemmings have magical powers. At last she caught one and threw it into the sea, and right way the waves parted and a road opened, which she followed to the bottom. Fathomless bottom, they said. Or end of earth.

But then it's like a dream where everything is familiar. Like the dream with the page of words she had where she had to also be walking on glass & reading at the same time. She notices a little house and runs to it peeking through the window. Inside she sees an old couple with their son who lies sleeping on a bench and has recently lost an eye. "Come out, come out, I'm here," the girl sings. He is like in a dream like her talking man head but another man too

She makes a decision to travel he can't come & tries to stop her saying o don't go to Heaven you'll never come back. But . . .

She goes on and on not knowing how she does this, she travels to heaven and comes at last to something that looks like a lid with a hole in it

It is difficult to get to the hole but she jumps in & lands by the side of a lake & hears oars splashing. Here is a Man of Copper coming along who like in a dream is her talking-head man and like the man in the little house too but now another man too. The same man and another man too. And everything he has is made of copper—kayak, oars, harpoon, everything of shining copper. She sits in the deep grass, thinking she had hidden herself well, while Copper Man sings:

O a woman's breasts tempt
a kayak
who crosses the shining lake
to kiss her soft cheeks

When he finishes his song, Copper Man raises one hand high toward heaven and the other arm drops down toward the lake. The girl sees the upper part of his body is naked, and that her fur coat lies across his gleaming arm

Woman, woman, your breasts
attract a kayak
Who rows across the bright lake
Copper Man raises one arm again and drops the other & the rest of the woman's clothing flies over onto his raised arm!

Naked now, the girl's "ashamed" and can't understand what's happening to her

Copper Man sings his song a third time and this time the girl passes out and when she wakes she is sitting next to him in his kayak

Rows and rows with her, far away, with his bright copper oars never saying a word until they come to a place where they see two houses

Copper Man says in a stern voice: You must go into the big house, not into the little one

She does this & he rows away

Small-Woman-Dressed-in-Clothes-Made-out-of-Bearded-Seal-Gut cries out excitedly for the girl to come into the smaller house, for Copper Man is dangerous and will kill her

Inside the other house she sees a little girl who lives with Skin-Guts-Woman who sits on the sleeping bench

Big house?

Little house?

How to turn?

Copper Man was not an ordinary man—nobody could resist him and he would be angry she left the big house

But Skin Guts would help her and gives her a small cask filled with water in which there are four small pieces of whaleskin

Throw them in his face! Throw them in his face!

The woman had sung a magic song over the cask and it was strong now, very strong and would protect her

Soon the man came back in his kayak. He sat beside the sea calling out to her, Don't be afraid, stay quiet in my house, and I won't do you harm. You can't be hidden from me

Then he came flying through the air like a bird and circled the house four times and came to the small house

Then he picked up his bird arrow saying, I will not kill you

The girl stood hidden in the bend of the house and threw the pieces of whale-skin in his face

Copper Man fell out of the air

Then the three women went into his house, which was the house of the Moon Spirit, and Copper Man was Man in the Moon himself, which the little woman in the skins had made harmless for a while through her magic chant, her magic whaleskin present

The three women went into his house, and up in the rafters crowds of reindeer ran about

In the corner was a big water barrel, big as an inland lake. The women went to it and looked in and saw whales and walruses and seals swimming about

In the middle of the house on the floor lay the shoulder blade of a whale. The women, all three of them, pushed it to one side and saw an opening leading down to the earth, from where they could see the dwelling place of the humans. They could see the humans quite clearly and hear them calling out for all the things they wanted. There were some who cried out for whale meat. There were others who cried out for long life

LO-ON-ON-ONG LIFE!

The girl looked down at the countries of the earth and discovered Tikeraq, the largest place she knew. Here there were many women's boats, and many busy people. They were collecting water in small casks and throwing it up to the new moon so they might have a good catch. It was like a dream. Where was she? Had she died?

The girl had seen how the people prayed to the moon for a good catch. Some of the people had such strong magic formulas that their water ladles came quite near to the Moon Spirit's house. On the earth these water ladles were quite small but, through the magic words, up here became enormous and were filled with fresh water. Sometimes a whale and sometimes a seal and sometimes a walrus were put into the ladles as sacrifice and reached the house of the Moon Spirit. This meant prayer was heard and the sacrifice accepted and that she would have a good catch. Down below there were ladles that remained near the earth near the people's dwellings who were bad hunters who had no luck. The young girl watched all this and thought about it and became homesick remembering the pleasure that followed a big catch. She who only a little while ago thought only of dying

---

Now she thought about all these things

The little old woman in skins and her little companion were sorry for her and wanted to help her get back to earth. They plaited a rope out of the sinews of many animals, a very long rope that they rolled into a ball as they plaited it

When it was finished the old Woman-in-Skins said: You must shut your eyes and let yourself down. But the moment at which you touch earth you must open your eyes quickly or you will never become a woman again. The young girl fastened one end of the rope tight in the heavens and took the ball of plaited sinews and began to let herself down. Slowly, slowly, and she thought it would be a very long way. But she felt the ground beneath her feet sooner than she expected and because she hadn't opened her eyes quickly enough she turned into a spider

There was a spinster once cold in the nights *[close your eyes now/the fire goes out]*

Did not want to stop imagining . . .

XXIV

UPADESHA:

CYCLE OF DESIRE

Can't be a spider all her life. Words with a lover & being in love. Tantrik garb and gab. Upadesha, high teaching/practice. She covers her tracks. The Tibetan terms signify blind accomplishment, a fruition stage. As lovers, still in the crucible. A chamber, a bed. Elements of song. The last love affair? Pinnacle of inexhaustible desire. Endless wheel of fiery "becoming." Rage in blaze, sweet embers later. After this, she thinks: the cold cave, the charnel ground. O laugh at myself, the expert . . . a chthonic pair? Like Kadmos & Harmonia perhaps, who had more in common with heroes than mortals. They were driven out of Thebes and took the guise of serpents to show a power. Their tombs were shown in Illyria. They were steady. Died in love. And then it's all just double-language, hidden trope for existence's paltry sex-dream, another test or lesson. Turbulent conflagration. [But she met a match, she grants him that.] She bows to a man's prowess, and the infinitely fallible gaze of love.

unheard
you do

    stand me
in desire

        ——————— ཡེངས་མེད་
        yengs med

undistracted

embellishments of energy

        ——————— རྒྱན་ཅལ་
        rgyan rtsal

flesh
blood
&
semen
 (& mine a kind of

holy fluid, primordially pure)
then sleep
through flame's
  reflections
  rocked like sea
& set
  a name: ocean of bliss
to cum for you
jittered dream
  in mental talk
I saw
"us"
  conjoined at the end of a millennium
                             seized

or you might say *claimed*
  tonic stem
of *clamor,* cry, call, appeal
  clasped
held you
  in my legs
a well
   you entered in upon

tapped a root-nerve
inside the grail
the base of his spine

                       ————————
                       'khor yug chen po   འཁོར་ཡུག་ཆེན་པོ་
                       ————————

the whole dimension of one's life
  think on it

  I'd been all those years
slumbering
  laying the snares
then

                                                 ————————
                                              had de ba   ཧད་དེ་བ་
                                               ————————

surprised astonishment

bidden
   (from hidden)
  to language
& tilt not bide
    power there
to
  tongue a cryptic code
                    never grave
    to seal

cry out
  in poetry's leap
sovereign sex
   (that below)
    in
dakini code
    being karma dakini in mode of
secret conduct

———————————
               gsang spoyd   གསང་སྤྱོད་
———————————

   discovered in mind *in coitus*
kind of protection I had for you
   waiting

was waiting

———————————
               nam-khar ar-gtad   ནམ་ཁར་ཨར་གཏད་
———————————

look at the sky

      a covenant prescriptured

  you think?

  concealment
engraved on rocks

desiring to be heard
or
strummed—
hit my text!

'ja-lus-pa

འཇའ་ལུས་པ་

she of rainbow body
    cremated

wished

a return
   call it mind-time
rock-time
  reading your syllables in
laugh
cloud
over-a-fire-time
later
walking
millennial time
  call it
inosculate
bed-sport
shard of prick'd desire
call it
a seige
sidereal
a field connubial
our claustral love

  now
in an idiom understood

  to say

   we go back
I play you
   & you upon me
celebrants as one
cynegetic act

thugs rje ཐུགས་རྗེ་

energy, compassion

bde ba'i nyams བདེ་བའི་ཉམས་

experience of pleasure
  which is awakened

chos kun ཆོས་ཀུན་

in love with phenomena

  a body

      akin to

      socket:

rise on wing

  to explode

in flagrant periphrasis

  heat's language.

XXV

SPRECHSTIMME (COUNTESS OF DIA)

A sprechblues. Deep register crystalline vocalizations resound in down-at-heart lady singers. Mabel Mercer, Lady Day, Sarah Vaughn, Nina Simone, Ella Fitzgerald, I'm thinking of you. He—the Other—becomes Master of Deception through the words of trobairitz Countess of Dia. The poet visits Vancouver's Museum of Anthropology's Great Hall to stand among the Haida, Nishga, Gitksan totem poles. They reenact a present in her past. The lover is no longer a god, but friend & fellow traveler. This section concludes at 2 a.m. in Frankfurt am Main in the Restaurant Elba, spanning two continents. Is she closer to being the "exile" she creates in her poem? May it be her ultimate sirventes, that old troubadour refrain of outrage toward a botched civilization.

> mouth down at sides
> waxing moon
> tipped over out
> of which
> these sounds emit

Did we not say it would be difficult?

Vida:

Born 1140, the Countess of Dia was the wife of En Guillem de Poitiers, and a lady beautiful and good. She fell in love with En Raimbaut d'Orange, and wrote many good & spirited chansons in his honor.

I am trobairitz

I sing a chain of gold

=breath finally gives life to stars=
=ours as it were, a break, a foible, long night museum-clad=
=the stars are in their little cases good night=

=worn helmet, worn desire, under the roof you said "Egyptian"=
=as if a cliché were mounting pressed out of sorts, the tongue=

=tongue is my dream=

=tongue is my long dream=

=not ironed, pressed=

=for command for speech for sky research=

Did we not say the roof, the tongue, the old man
or women if she would appear for us, hermaphroditic
like a charwoman, a slave, a something-out-of-doors
Who's invoked because she holds two sexes in wrinkled clothes

=all street singers enjoy her=
=she is in her *langue d'oc*=

=tongue is disaster but not in her mouth=

=who is invoked would be duty-bound to tell us=

=what about the other place=

tongue is salvation, tongue stands in for all-the-body

she tells the truth about matricide, about genocide, about rape
about torture, cleansing is not unfamiliar in her witness trope

her witness, a dram, a dream
=test her=
did it not happen because she lived to tell of it from outside the crematorium
Lyotard come in here & make your point again
about who is and is not witness

Fuck the arrogance of all philosphers in dream

what about life as it was behind a curtain

o go on & on

=an energizer=

=he knew she knew he knew because he knows something about
secret torture=

you are no longer needed—did we not tell you?—

but we
but we need you because we don't get it quite yet
tell us something experimental again
abstract the effort to change the world into safe nets

did we not—but not in spite of "it"
say—

=the mark is in the pudding=

=the word is outside, look
outside=

=the net will hold the sacred & the scared=
=victims of boat people syndrome need not apply=
I am trobairitz
I sing a chain of gold

=the net is cruel=
=& we are its subjects=

did we not complain again to this page a torrent/torment of desire
because what jabs the most is unrequited love
of all the beasts you demonize here demonize this one
his sexy eye is rampant again, ageless desire

=we is a name for the scared writer=
=sing in the dark the dark snow=
=sing in the hall=

hall that would be king of house
grabbed there, before you enter

=hall—hall=

passage to any bardo
Did we not say, abandoned, how rude's
the night in this town

=hospitality down an evening, did we not warn you=
=if you come here you come to a dark house=

=I mean town=

=iron or damask=

=rich or ornate=

=again ore=

=again ornate=
=again one veil over eyes to shunt to shut out=

=order=

=did we not warn the tourists=

=did we not say or was it not said properly?=
a medieval manners thing & then she comes in
Andalusian & strange & he says "Venusian?"
=described how death hits in a town=

=someone (old man) is murdered in a movie theater for a fist of movie dollars=

=take a life or leave it=

Dear Cynic I did not say it would be easy

=how many plagued (you knew this was no lie)=

=or censored (slow death)=
=possibly strung out=

=love twisted inside love=
she writes of unrequited pleasure &
tender drift of sex that he come to her, come to her

=visited the afternoon in drag=

=it was—did we not say—was it not articulate?=
=how hard how
not said?=

Did we or he or she not say how

=about the house the prima donna male was watching=
=did it not be said how what was his song=

=limber=

=cranked up=

=lustral=

=offbeat=

=dark world here, come out come out=

=did we not say his goose is cooked=
=her gander is fried=

=watch soon ends=
(up all night failed Xanax)

Did we not walk down the poem because
it was open, available

no other reason but this you look maybe you find
in words she touches Raimbaut d'Orange

=an oriental cookie told this to us=
=but we looked & found you=

=you were the us the we always demanding more=

=not words but attention=
=did or did it not occur to you that you could rub=
=you could rub the wrong way=
=& we would be stuck between fur & purr=
=a kind of tangible hell=

=too old to become a soldier=

=A Fragment to a Tragic Mask now becomes her face=

=what shall she be=

=UNKNOWN CREATURE WITH MOUTH AS DOOR=

=what risk, apostate?=

=I address you=

=as defector=

=*as bonnet rouge*=

=& out of pain
what's real?=

ancient poetries arise to keep the world safe in love
but
breaking up you turn into your opposite

=a demon insane=

=all the ancient poetries give devilish heed

seeing thru new eyes=
                            =to beg release=

she knows because she writes it: beg release

know not what I am but what *seems* lady

betrayelle
  or
concealment, sham, sophistical blur
had me on

=what *seems, not-a-gentleman*=

=illusory shadow of love?=

=did I but dream his face his body his sound?=

=it is the sounds in love?=

=the words=

=he did grab me with his words=
=entered the secret place in another language=

above feline mask, fragment of a tragic mask

or
Six-Nozzled Oil Lamp with Heads of a Deity & Shop Prows; Duck Heads on Top

deck hands below

=what is it?=

down a goddess
down *mi donna*
reform her code
solace is not mine

solace is not mine
down a goddess
torment the game
of these emotions
curse of—
but
me, be damned
betrayed
old woman no
Fuck his big deal need
I am matchless
but not French yet
to find
hues of
cramp
or salvation
now boney man
next to me—
austere—he dries up
as these pictures attest to—
or out a window
who is he? bones on the walk
merely
not a word
but death of a bonnie man to her heart
now commemorate a father's death
Daughter
come for naught to a world?
wonder: did she do the right rituals?
perform the proper ceremonies for a dead father?
for father dead & gone?
how blind?
or fleshed blue
traipsed her
or once ground down
he does this to me
now it's to blame me
"you were the wild one"
 inadvertent

adjacent to slaughter
but slaughter all the same
a kind of sacrifice
that shatters perception
why ruin us
& me to say
I wasted myself on this dream

Hoagy Carmichael's
"Skylark"
some such fantasia

(take out my Raven Rattle & shake it here)

I will re=in=vent my roles
make a mark
in black to note this death in May
old anniversary
&
sleep in the margins of my writing
speak there too

vent as a kind of spleen thing
or window for air
speaking in the margins of my writing

put down this load
take a deep breath the cynics say

the new age materialists say
excuse me, I meant commodification
I meant commerce not material, i.e., matter

line on

sky

piercing blue
you'd ne'er

know
till
now

glow lime of light
a line
then wing's tip
or tip o' wing

cry No No
but beauty sleek
did dip its side then sense
to me
like dart
edge on caustic night
leaving the country
how I'd like to shut
that door

clouds below
so what else is new?
flying Brit Air
same old fetch

lipid second messenger
& out of this pain,
enough
he fucks me over

then I had a trip
June II birthday of a dead father

something the Arab Muslim girl said
time is up
or supper, something . . .
the stocks of sex go up
no choice
enslaved you check it out to him
he made me breath?
you check out on him

like the strange way you can't
=bide=

=ply=

  =then trade=

=subject born object=

notice

listen's up

   her down
way you can't wake up straight to me
=coward coward coward coward coward=

in this murk a dream
say No again
again
say again
won't help

lack in him
& made him seek

I won't say what

say last week a soul catcher
came to hit you unawares
o
catch/ of soul

=rift=

=trap it=

=don't say it it might get lost around you=

=it won't one day, next will=

face in the groin a power spot
held by the paw of a bear
born from
a bear—*arktos*—
  that tempered its clime

The girl's tragedy begins
with separation from home
& then
idyll of seclusion
then gets a man a husband
then gets lost in him
then gets another man

don't say "lost"
but she
a kind of
rift
mode
  but he's got other things to do
  on her time
counting her hours, the Countess

don't say

  gain
everything counts here

rather lost
rightly so then *tempered be the plan the elf*
the eve
tempered be the slight edge over night
then say not a gain
but swept downside
it sidelines her time

=tempered be the plan the elf the eve=

    mouth
    tipped
    down

a grimace on herself, the Countess

elf for speed
eve for any inebriated sconce
dare we say
it bred disaster
plan to be in life synchronous

=who had not a history=
=a past to accommodate=
=fancy boyfriends=
=some are queer=

some women held stock
then let go verbs all over her page

pages rather
down a leg
looking up & down

first up to crotch
then down

=I was that paw=

=I was that woman=

=face in groin=
=my face in his groin=
=betrayal sucked out=
=core is scattered the more=

=cormorant=

=a score in the cedar the sacra=

=the scarified scar=

  =marred she married=

=because he was at gut a wound in me=

gut like tomahawk
strapped in leather
has wood
has axe

=marred=
=never really married=

tranced sex
like the way you get holy around stones

balanced
before blame
redress before
a tonal light

=language that spits its cause its curse at you=

go under

splay
  then do not betray
the elder
  crackpot troubadour love

=that sighs in glance of eye=

=locked in the vajrayana tube=

=the only way out is down=

& goes shattering

{shatters}

=how go=

=now go, go=

Haida got it right
bridges from top to bottom

an Unknown Creature & Human Wearing Ringed Hat
who seems poised on discovery of first syllables
some kind of poet cut loose from wood

=I am that first sound=
=I sing a chain of gold=
=part of a mask that only speaks prophetically=

of course it's what's behind that counts if you sort out
the sense, or intention
but what's hidden is flurry of an owl
(just one example)

never had one in hand
though one saw those owls in a bag in Nepal
  the child proffers—you wanna buy?
flickers

but with human face

o mar
  & marred the scar, the owl

sacrifice
Frog with Hat Rings on Back testifies
=sees you here=

held them a long time

long Haida poles

who reenact your past in their future
which is sung out concentrically

I had this notion when I discovered Venus
going out each night to track her blood
then went off a deeper end
beyond horizon
unmentionable chaos & pain of cramp
that we were so near so far from "us"

suffering on all fronts
Both Eagle & Human Wearing Feathers

=I wear them to abide or bird their power=

=I trickster them=

being Bear Holding Human Head

or
Supernatural Bird

=I trickster them=
=I trickster them=

my lover fell asleep here in the museum
I blessed him in my distance

in my distance I saw his goodness

Human Wearing Shaman's Headress with Halibut & Human in Her Mouth

Capture d'Ame
Captured Anne

Unknown Creature with Mouth as Door
=a terrible night=

=& needing to speak=
    =body jumps from his=
=thwarted in desire=

where is gone the love that bound
not just phantasmogoric
not cultural orthodoxy
this was tactile
then primordial
dare I say Our
  where gone that love?

 =miracle intercede please=

=revelation, uncanny in my city biorhythm=

you understand all these words are from a notebook
three by two and one-half inches
given to me by Ann Lauterbach who said, Yes indeed, *it is little*

this is not easy (little) as Robin Blaser says

writing at the edge of our grasping discourse
where something of shared existence is working & unworking

so friends enter to assist you in your rite

=Vishnu depicted as King of Boon Bestowers I supplicate you=

=Kali dancing on Reclining Shiva I supplicate here=

=Hercules C-130 Aircraft with 105-millimeter gun batteries supplicated here=

I wanted to kill you the Countess sang

for to down an old loyalty
he's down an old path
don't dwell nor belabor
the intricacies of Eros

how hard tits under hand
gaze of eyes
how hard, salt tears
how hard: let heads roll
who walked around, said what
say what
he sticks it in her
a fool for love
language knows more than we do
so do we say what we do no never we never say
what we do but gainsay under what we do
in
discreet trope
not punctuated equilibrium
foisted

now kneel in the Temple of Amaravati from Andhra Pradesh
Ashoka built, *take refuge here*

not to do in all the big things

you drop off to sleep
suspicion
another walk?
sweet penned notes about walking
importance of walking, mountains, et cetera

=marvels of the obvious=
=marvels of the hidden=

=you risked the mountain=

=we live in a burning house=

she laments her fiery mind

Across the waters let me ride free . . . . .
······ ə̣ə̣ɹɟ əp̣ịɹ əɯ ʇəʃ sɹəʇɐʍ əɥʇ ssoɹɔ∀

medieval switchback
    on pain of knighthood
his lance, a thrusted chain

I am trobairitz
I sing a chain of gold

or claim—his old goat.
  and gone. holy gauze
hers

her word for it

bloody cross.

or lost

visor on to kill an infidel bag him?

the sun.

I am that she-King

  not that metal monkhood sex
    bearded-monosyllabic-Ambrosian-chant-person singing

  but I am. still singing

brag-like.

cackle.

but intercede a slot, clopping

  eyes roll up into sockets & grand
clarified butter greases a finger
  & a horse.

replaces horse

deity whose pubis is smeared by love

red on jacket mount?
   dances on corpse of nightsky.

a dream: *chandali,* the fire. throw the word in the fire. hoops. mental refractory. not high-castle-tone. slides. was mute. sober like glass. a ladysleeve kind of poem. hints of Andalusia. was clarified. butter skin. then war on local sex propositions. more muted bands. a long march to fence in cyberspace. was trembling like post-op wind. wrote to not *die of love.*

Of things best kept silent I sing
so bitter toward him
whom I loved more than anything

diamond pattern of tablecloth
napkin rides the trobairitz dream
shadow of thumb, a kind of tunnel
11 p.m. in the Restaurant Elba
exiled in Frankfurt am Main
never not writing

---

dear *jongleur* maybe try again
  a juggle act

Look here
problems of the Vida
all the fat *recueils* of Gallic history go blank
swept clean.

  obliterated.
late of love above all love

 poetry *d'oc* only remembered
 she who was remains in lines of poetry

did she
did she
wonder: did she

take it back
a kind of pallinode

no wife of a Guillen de Poitiers
who held title to the county of Die

a small town nod
present northeast of Orange, dept. Drome

~~THERE WAS NO FRANCE~~ then
~~THERE WERE NO FRENCH~~

bastard Guillen of Poitiers
 offshoot of the great house of Poitiers
coming from a line of love
   Eleanor of Aquitaine

married a lady of the Viennois whose son held the title
Count of Dia

ennobled by a son
speaking a kind of med-speech

speedy title
 how many lovers named Raimbaut
   of Orange

"The gate of the devil, the patron of wickedness, the sting of the serpent"
                                        was woman saith St. Jerome

again occidently

you need love in atrocity's face
 an accident

logic of Jean-Francois Lyotard might lie in interest
 of revelation
if she did not live to tell

once upon a time there was a genocide
once upon a time there was a crusade
once upon a time a friend betrayed her

but once upon a time in poem-time
she did live to tell à trial
its tale is arduous
not had cheap

proof is a diagnostician's revenge
I saw the old Nazi propaganda footage
on German TV, rats in the sewer
equated with "Juden."

then a barrow of bodies
dead of starvation
pushed to mass in a grave
a pit of hell
   terrifying devil maw

is there love before atrocity?

what to do but glorify & witness the grave

 phenomenological time extant here   WAR-TORN

"it is certain that
 every lady
 who listened to
 troubadour or *jongleur*

was furnished with
the material for constructing
a fresh estimate of her
own importance" —Emily James Putnam
    in condescending tone

fin d'amours or so she thought
feel good about yourself today
a moment in patriarchal time

I know what a great lover you are
but I find you changed from the chivalrous knight
you used to be
your mind's distracted
do you still find me attractive?
I'll better you in every way
with my virtuous, stricken poetry
in mirror: great breasts & thighs
you forgot to tally

If only I could lie beside you for an hour
embrace you lovingly
then what went down
is easier to swallow

I need a friend and Sis, I said to her my great Muse

she was probably from Die, northeast of
Montelimar
descended from the costly robed seigneurial families
of the Viennois & Burgundy

she dresses well, size ten I tell you
I lay out
soft pillows for her body

I'm true I tell you
He should be faithful
I'm true I tell you

My love for him never strayed
My heart's not the straying kind
But he questioned my reputation

---

there was the difficulty of finding privacy in the court

did she have a twin?
did she have a "turn" in the sack?
did she take her son's title?
was she the lover of Orange?

She held this title: *usufructus*

was a kind of chain result mores,
an alliance of poem

I write this in Franconofurd, the ford of the Franks
to meet her heart & line

was she, in fact, called "Beatriz"?

CODA

I break a sprig on the sun-set tree holding
its red flowers
—Robin Blaser

& I said to myself
dash water on face you'll be fine
(& this talking was inside night) (in sight of night)

soon the daylight's soonest mending yr toubled brow
& I went to a sacred grove & stopped screaming

turn to charcoal if you can, burn yrself up doing duty
upon the world

a charcoal dakini said this
deity of fabulous energy
hermaphroditic it said this:

he mends me
but she binds me
she soothes me
but he winds me

up
word sooth
& smithy will shape & burn brighter
for he is Word Man up to his ears
(and she worded down to her heart)

there is a story

for once upon a time someone was stealing our poetry
stealing our sex I said

there is the alchemist's story about a woman bound into
a four-fold body & she must change from color to color
black, white, yellow, rubedo

she changes
& when this feminine thing
who carries the man inside her
has evidenced all the colors
she continues into old age & dies in the four-fold body
which means *iron, tin, bronze, & lead*
& in each one she dies in the color red
& is rejuvenated in the color red

Like poetry I said

for passion is the sprig of this heart
each according to her own kind bunch of it

stalk
by
root
connect
~~might induce melancholy~~
but never fall into illusion

ford the river
to heaven on earth: DISARM

[Sprechstimme here]

   /
=claim=
=bespoke=
=the tremble of alchemy=
=wear words as armor=
=atrocity mars all senses=
=and havens pale=
=*hustle, girl, hustle!*=

Anarcho Tao / Chaos Linguistics (read "human," please)

I had a lung
I sang him down

what need his guns?
    Once upon an island's time

you could see the

silver &

the gold

& this is the story:

    woe to a difficult, headstrong king

land

between rivers

(Petanu & Pakrisan Rivers)

Mount Batur in North to sea in south

O cosmos

ravines

rock riverbeds

an earlier kingdom

    cosmos of inhabited worlds

curse or blessings?

& this is the story:

battle for the "soul"—

Kintamani route

& this is the story

a demon king bemoans a difficult marriage

:

The god of the lake grants him a boon to

take a Chinese

Buddhist wife

but she doesn't work out, gets ill,

& the king goes to the temple of Tolangkir

to ask assistance

unhappy, unhappy wife

the haughty god will not favor anyone

with a false religion so the king is angry

& forbids the Hindu religion be practiced

you can only worship me, the king says

forget your Shiva, your Vishnu, your Brahma

The Queen dies

& this is the story:

he lives alone getting stranger

at the expense of the people,

shut in this palace and

after twelve years

                              he is defeated by the god Indra

                    who taps the ground at Manuk Aya, where a magical spring appears

                                        (wild gush here, her sound

              of sound of many bonds breaking)

Drink from it, O warriors, and receive great strength

& this is the story:

When they finally killed Maya Danawa

      blood spouts

            from his mouth

like a stream of gold

(becoming the river Petanu)

Drink & bathe here and expect misery

The god then went to bathe in a silvery spring called Air Empul

and from that time on the Hindu religion

was restored and good kings reigned over Bali

this is the story

another woman's woe, & far from home

again

again

    blame her

another religion

she will not be blamed

water is provocative but not an ally

it is her blood, her blood, her strength coming out of him

       I
      rang
         him
            down

BOOK III

Eternal War

BOOK III
～ Eternal War ～

Eternal War: An Introduction

The plan (*plahn* or *plaint*) for the subsequent years' inscription was to keep dirge-tone with the times, and continue mind-track of dailyness. *Dirge* from Dirige, Domine, Deus meus—*direct my way in your sight, O Lord my god*. Flash forward and back and into the middle of things. Radiating out from 9/11, a decade of syncretic activism. What can be salvaged: we'll move to higher ground. Could it not be more dire (dirge), our human circumstance? Ignorant rejection of planet's urgent exigencies. Its climate shifts. Planet has Auto Immune Deficiency—the *kami* perhaps—Shinto spirit essences of mountains, rivers, wind, lightning, rocks—do not favor industrialization and nuclear fission, do not welcome toxic assault upon land and water. In Shinto cosmology, a spear had originally stirred the waters and when lifted, water drops fell from it in the map of Japan, its eight perfect islands. In this vision the dead go to a gloomy underground called *yomi*. The sun goddess Amaterasu, in dispute with her brother, was tricked out of her lair and light returned to the universe. She was told there was a better goddess in the heavens! She rose to her vanity!

We call out the Fish and Wildlife Service (*fission* wildlife) to amend their toxic ways: stop sleeping with the enemy, big biz. Stop creating more graveyards of deadly nuclear waste. Plutonium in the Colorado Rocky Flats soil is continually kicked about by small unsuspecting animals. Don't build a nature preserve there. Join our guardianship project, O earthlings. Fukushima is perhaps our last chance to wake up.

What closing tome from mind to ear spilled here, a conjecture for future "beset upon" radical poetries? The practice of Book III was attempt to further aright the gender divide. And it succeeded a small space at an incremental pace. You were attempting the "proper ceremonies," and perhaps failed as you confronted the Irreparable and a broken heart for your civilization. And more massive white-male-driven suicidal wars this new century someone could get rich on, upon a country that was one of the cradles of all humankind, incunabula of Tigris-Euphrates. And instigated by a mini empire named Halliburton. Hiding now behind the difficult-to-pronounce Xe, this cult of war metastasizes. That is the name and the game, a cancerous shadow government. "Macondo well would be unstable" they had predicted themselves, Halliburton in charge of cementing the deepwater drill hole. Book III drowns now fathoms deep in a crucible of oil.

But the field-poet-mind ages more ethereal now ("go heavenly guest ethereal messenger" —Milton), unable to bring the corporations down. The tick tick of perpetual war, the daily assaults are paralleled by the increments of poem time. You work on inner strength, deconstructing the dystopias that surround you. The sending and receiving practice of *tonglen* I recommend again as it is the crux of this project: take negatively upon oneself, call it out, breathe out the efficacy. Practice empathy in all things. Pick a cause and tithe your time relative to the half-life of plutonium.

Hold villains accountable. No easy pass for tyranny as you see whole countries go down. Acknowledge poetry as your cause, as being endangered and to struggle for, as being your guide in understanding the nature of your own mind-time. We operate with no other consciousness than one of language and cognitive insight.

You make a call for a feminist mother poetics where the mother is man or woman, or anything else it cares to name itself, and is recognized in all animal mammal realms with inalienable civil and human rights.

What forms will be transmissible? Trust your encounters with non-human metabolic elementals such as snakes, and with the dream consciousness of your friends who pass on "to the other side" frequently. Lament them, and read their poems aloud in the company of friends. And collaborate with your child for whom you write this all down. Joke how the slime molds will inherit the earth. Concentrate on Archive of so many witnesses in this little net of cacophonous time, to leave a trace so that poets of the future will know we were not just slaughtering one another. And the many nameless others so inflicted in the struggle, lament them. Bloated corpses in the flood. Wee babes washed out to sea, tsunami consciousness caught in the gap between death and life, without a body to come home to. Shock of a best friend's death "without warning." And this mantra from a Buddhist teacher: "Death is my friend, the truest of friends that never abandons me. Death is always waiting for me. This shadow looms over every moment of my life, yet death allows life, painful and terrifying, to take place. May I absorb these subtle truths."

Threnoidia, elegiacs, matins, lamentations. We live perhaps in fear of the human. *How doth the city sit solitary | How has she become as a widow | She weepeth sore in the night, | She is in bitterness. Gone into captivity.* Oh Judah! And pondering the *oecume*, or the inhabited world, common possession of civilization. Are we lamenting the dead or consoling ourselves, the survivors? Sitting somewhere on the disputed Siachen (Kashmir) glacier. Military=market. And big bucks to be had in the Global Hawk drones, JSTARS, upgraded U-2 spy planes, the Rivet Joint eavesdropping planes. Or the Joint Air-to-Surface Standoff Missiles of the future, the Electromagnetic Personnel Interdiction Control plan, the Silent Guardian, the Airborne Laser and the High Frequency Active Auroral Research Program, developing weather systems as weapons. HAARP will be able to enhance and prolong storms and cause floods or drought on specific targets.

And the nuclear leakage in Japan exceeds 1,000 millisieverts into the sea.

Dominating members of this society I'm born to at all murderous costs maintain economic and political control through the ever-palpitating war machine. How many interlocking relationships based on greed and paranoia you have to wonder, to keep us so wired and stretched? Is this the allegory we've been waiting for?

Think of recent trip to placid Delos, birthplace of Apollo and Artemis, where resides the House of the Dolphins, the temples of Hera and Isis. You marveled at the dictum: *no one can die or give birth here.* The terrace of Lions, huge Dionysus phallus, and the god also rides a sleek panther. Think of the Delian League, 5th century, spearheaded by Athens over the city-states, designed to perpetuate war with the Persian Empire, and how it folded after the Peloponnesian War. Were, werra, werrien, guerrer . . . bellum, bellicose . . .

It folded.

Stay with me here in my oracular documentary trance dance. I tend to speed up what should be slow, circular movements, becoming crazed or ecstatic as a dervish might, but I make obeisance to all directions of space, including all I can hold my mind to—all the beings that are touched this life—waving their fluted fans and ringing their summoning bells.

April 2, 2011

I

YEA, I AM SALT

Halloween. Festival of Samhain. Messages from the child who is her guide in matters youth-cultural. She incorporates the methodology of the USA holding tank, and the surprise of the notion of seven genders, into her meditations. More costumes! The poet is now en route to India, stopping in "Bangkok's green shade," in the words of Allen Ginsberg, who sang of the drug trade & other complicities in the shadow-realms of Asia, backed by Western corruption and CIA spooks. Stir up some trouble? Chasing the serpent was it? Low on the ladder young ladies of the night—sinewy dancers—haunt the red-light Patpong district, ply their wares, traffic in sex, already bit themselves by the plague that decimates whole families, communities. Not without cunning or guile, most often hungry. Buy me food, food for my baby, she whimpers, stroking my knee, eyes dark pools of seduction, desperation. Meat-wheel grinds under the beauties, against them. Dancing skeletons of the objectified and poisoned dakinis under strobe light, flickering she-phantoms of the hungry ghost realm . . . .

Dear Mom just so you know—wherever you are—this is the text the lawyer had me write:

On October 31st I was arrested with the charge of public intoxication on Pasado Rd., in Isla Vista. I had come down from Santa Cruz to visit two of my best friends who go to school at UCSB, N and M. We had been walking around, visiting various friends and acquaintances of theirs. It was Halloween night and it seemed like every other house had a party, and there were tons of people walking around in the street, like us, going from house to house. I was feeling tired, run down and on the verge of the flu so I had decided that I was not going to get drunk that night. Around nine my friends, some of their friends, and I went to a party that was at a mutual friend of all theirs house. There was a keg of beer there and as we arrived it was near empty. I had around four cups of beer out of the keg, it had a low content of alcohol because I remember being disappointed that I had hardly caught a buzz. The keg finished, and my friends and I stayed at the party for a couple of hours. Eventually we left to go walk around, look at people, and make our way back to their friends' apartment where I was going to sleep. I was walking with my friend, N, on Pasado Road, when I noticed an undercover cop drive by right next to us. It was followed by two more of the same undercover police vehicles. I knew they were police because I could see uniformed officers inside of them. I said to N something along the lines of "look at all these undercover cops," and gestured toward the cars with my hand as they were driving by. The next thing I remember was hearing, "hey you in the hat." I was wearing a New York Yankees hat and was the only person wearing a hat at all out of our group of people. I turned around and saw a police officer standing and pointing a flashlight at me. We approached each other and the officer said something like "what did you say to us?" At first I had no idea what he was talking about and in a hesitant way said "what?" I was then approached by a few more officers and the questions began. "How much have you had to drink tonight?" At first I said something like "I don't know exactly it was a few hours ago." Again I was asked the same questions I said I could think about for a little and tell them exactly but that I had around three or four beers. One of the officers then said "Yeah right fifteen." I was also being asked what my name was, where I was from, where I was staying, who I was with, and other basic background questions. Different officers were asking me these questions simultaneously. At one point I finally said "I can only answer one question at a time." This is when I was told that I was being "non-responsive" and I was handcuffed and placed in the police car without any explanation or rights. I asked the officers if it was common to pick random people out of crowds and arrest them. I thought it was funny at the time because I was so sure of my innocence, that I figured the truth of the situation would be cleared up at the station. I was taken to a parking lot where I was asked the same questions over again in the same rapid simultaneous manner. I asked if I could take a breathalyzer test, a blood test or any sort of test that would prove I was not intoxicated. I was told that they didn't have the "sophisticated" equipment to perform such a test. All of my possessions were taken off me and I was handed the Santa Barbara County Jail Inmate Property Inventory and told to sign it. I asked what it was and began to read it. I had just finished reading the heading at the top when it was taken out of my hands and I was told that I was not cooperating. I said I would be willing to sign it but that I wanted to read it first, it was not handed back to me. After being questioned, I was sat on the side while they questioned other people. Eventually I was taken with about four others to what I assume is the Goleta Jail. I was booked in under the last name "Pye," even though they had seen all of my identification and I told them my name was "Bye." In the fingerprinting room I watched another inmate get physically forced and beaten to the ground by more than two officers for a verbal comment he made. This is when I realized that this was serious and that I had better just play along and be as courteous and calm as I could be, even though I felt extreme injustice in the whole situation. I was eventually placed in the holding cell with the other arrests from that night. Many of them were in Halloween costumes with no blankets. One kid was in a toga, another in centurion garb, some half naked. Eventually I was let out at eight in the morning, I had been awake for over twenty-four hours and was definitely sick by this point. I had absolutely no idea where I was and felt much more inebriated, unsteady, and lost than I had ever felt the night before or (even) in my whole life for that matter.

[*rite of passage* . . .
taste of the state . . .]
=rite of passage . . . taste of the state=

While in Bangkok

stripper's cunt
thrums against icy metal pole
frission, endocrinology
desire thick in you, out of her
   Maw
silks
   balloons, conjurer's tricks . . .

Sweat at tender spine
cajoles desire
in you? you too?
Is your cock hard?

(Out in the yard out in the boneyard the giant heap)

Here are fine gifts I would bring you, beautiful child
dear Songstress-of-Tortoise-Shell-Whose-Flesh-Quivers
groans with reach of "it" desire of "it" touch of "it"

   a show for the night

risk it

she pulls the annexed world again & again
out of her girl maw

In the riparian floodplains as the glaciers retreated, with the advent of deliberately planted fields of grain, comes the Great Mother religion. Based on the womb that men pass through and the earth that when seeded produces the crop, the Mother Goddess religion spreads with the advent of agriculture (wheat, barley, emmer). In places it includes the sacrifice of a male consort to the Grain Goddess. It loves fertility and creativity (wherein magic resides) and the wonder of cultivated growth, so it is very domestic. It absorbs sheep, weaving, and tries to absorb domesticated cattle, but comes into conflict with pastoralism. The religion flourishes for 5,000 to 8,000 years before a chaotic fusion with other religious modes. But, it wanes because it is not comprehensive enough to encompass meat (livestock / fishing / hunting) and the noncultivated aspects of the planet. It may have suffered from misunderstandings of

sperm but this is speculative. Inana, Phrygian Cybelle, Gaia, Ishtar, early
Demeter . . .

mercy mercy
a pity's the money
dictate to me first cause of suffering
while buckets of water
wash ejaculations off slimy floor
mercy mercy
I am no man
I am no business . . .

She's sober, a stone
calculates the night's game
This is hell's game—
pacts with lost beauty
hunger,
taste & don't tell
pay up pay up

Fear is snake in you

You are victim in her temple
She the shiniest, skinniest one under
strobe lights . . . *mercy mercy*
Is there music in hell?

*

Numbers:
Prisoners of conscience are held in at least 78 countries. Political detainees have
been tortured in 120 countries, with more than 1,000 people dying in 34 of them.
Government opponents simply "disappeared" in 29 countries. Executions out-
side the judicial system occurred in 54 countries. Armed opposition groups in
36 countries took and tortured hostages. Of particular concern is the growing
number of women targeted for state repression. Chinese officials are adept at
torturing and abusing women in custody, especially, in many cases, Tibetan
women imprisoned for speaking out for their country's freedom: "some of the
most imaginative forms of torture we have seen," said Amnesty spokesman.

. . . Dies irae, dies illa . . .
. . . Solvet saeclum in favilla, . . .
. . . Teste David cum Sibylla . . .
. . . Quantes tremor est futurus . . .
. . . Quando judex est venturus . . .
. . . Cuncta stricte discussurus! . . .

Yea

I am salt

Yea

I am *as though dancing*

Yea
I am Asian tear duct
I am my blown-out Ethiopian brains
A walking bomb for Allah's blue heaven

Yea I am the blade life
A hotter war a hotter hotter war

Yea

[urban density takes out more than a few lives]

Yea I am rice & oil & sugar & guns

Yea I am yr throat & will wean you, poem, from despair

Yes
I am even, free, & rapid

I am ardor
Aye aye aye I am ardor

Yea

A throbbing matchbox
(*light the pipe, my friend*)

Body will be ravaged
eyes dead

No life in tits & ass
bracketed
erased

Black hair fade to white
Legs no longer carry me
Flesh drop away, scales flake off wizened body
Pocked with hideous statistics
in carnal malady

Yea

no more pink-armed dawn

Cannot be undone the death
love pitches in place of excrement

You want one, you want two—three—
down on you? *cheap the whole night*

good deal you & your man?
Pimp gives an eye
shoves past phony decorum
How many *bhatts*
to witness? have
sex? how many bodies

Torn

PAT-

PONG

Torn

Bodies

PONG

Later
crumpled in high hotel room
held
in the desire mills while
craving
that I may be their netherworld
& continue this treatise
on economic wars & crimes against women

half of Asia could die of starvation
wash the stage with tears, my children

My darling—it's me, your mother, calling—

mercy mercy

You were wearing a long red dress and black high heels, a black scarf, and a black coat. You were running, chasing the man who was a man except he had no genitals. Everything about him was like a man dressed as a woman, a transvestite, but he had no genitals. He had a black wig on, a black dress, and a lot of makeup. You were running across the concrete in your high heels, around the city, under bridges, and down alleyways. You threw your black coat at him and it went up in a puff of smoke. You threw your black scarf at him and it went up in a puff of smoke. You were trying to catch him with your clothes as if they were a net. Then finally at an intersection you caught him. You entwined your body around his, legs wrapped around his legs like pretzel twists, arms in knots. There were swirls of red on black on red on black. You were kissing the man / woman on the mouth, your bodies were impossibly woven together, and you were kissing. Then you melted into one another except you were the one who was left, absorbing him . . .

A syntax of seeming & comportment
iconic fragments, cynic's edge
Marlene Dietrich's quip on seeing a disheveled mass of
humans at the airport "no wonder they pay us so much money . . ."

after
"look at how many ugly people there are in the world"

the way the moguls think the English gentry dressed—
in pristine tweeds & cutaways
fine-boned, alabaster women
"So we won't have another dame with big boobs on the lot. So what?
We ain't got a star? We'll make one!"

Lebensgefährtin, a lifetime companion
What did she say she was?
a glamorous woman
above the clouds
tempest-tossed
heart sleeves
what she thought to say about having to live through every moment
the way Magic Johnson does every day with his illness, nothing is edited for
sure . . .

A flight to New Delhi
the Sikh next to me takes out his "book" through the night only
pausing for intermittent naps to absorb the glow
I said—trying to make conversation over dinner—
I was going to study in Delhi—& he grunts "go to Punjab"
that cuts it

fer sure
and the steward has me take the machine out of the briefcase
    because this is Asia
& does a little dance step as the computer boots up

& the whistle of the security runs up & down the girl's leg across the aisle

looking for bombs . . .

   a mercy a mercy

II

"I; MYSELF" OF JADE GROW COLD

There was silence in the house. Back from a tour of duty, a "she" was relegating her eye to images of empty sockets where the Bamiyan statues had resided. Combined with that, the journalist's image of Afghani father with dead baby in his arms—now synchronized with drought, starvation, treks toward what dark illumination?—kept the image-cloth alive, vibrant with unresolve. O ye Museums & rich cartels of the Worlde, where be ye now? The wrong-headed mullahs, masters of commerce & desire, will never bow their heads (put their heads) together. You know how stupas & Buddhas are reminders, containers of enlightenment? What living container do we be? The poet has designed and marked out her own map for augury. It contains intersecting concentric mandalas for spiritual exploration and contemplation. The page is jade, the time is contemporaneous with Genghis Khan, and the mood is present tense of suffering Afghanistan. The Taliban give fair warning. But they are unschooled children, fatherless, crude, young (growing older in ignorance), unsung. They can't see the light for the trees in a mental desolation provoked by years of heroin and rubble. And tragic lack of mother-love. They are solid in their heads about "enemy," about "heathen." And rage that a museum pays for the salvation of a statue and doesn't rescue starving children. Who were the mothers of the Taliban? Where is a woman's kinder touch in this landscape? How many of these youths are missing limbs? Writing is on the wall. The twin statues, the twin towers. The persona calling itself "I; myself" begs an issue concerning psychological imprint, identity, objects of worship and revelation. The poet composed these lines with the very palpable destruction of the Bamiyan Buddhas in mind. The sense of the statues taking "refuge in the dust" comes in an e-mailed missive from Gary Snyder. The "occasion of these ruses" is Frank O'Hara's phrase. The mushroom image is copied from an old Taoist alchemical text. The Buddhas as a state of mind, the Taliban as a state of mind: which mind survives?

every move its rhythm interpolated interrupted ejected is the child's   because she
each sound I wrote is his for he was   carries the
my music. It was day it was night   seed of baby
it was his between sucking sounds   growing
you call it like nattering? bird-like, small   within her
body whirr. "Who is a woman not whirr? in her   to term
association, her miraculous conjunct with baby"
I wrote years later: *it's a dancing symbiosis*

a polysemous world, I was not mother Taliban

and the first speech is of "hot" of "fire"
the mouth moves inside its mind of
every word to ever come late and later advocate
boy! boy! that would be man could be
the first word "breakdown"
held then
rocking, sucking, interrupting.
segments of sheer joy
the gaps between
intent & how he becomes every child on any continent

         . . . then in the middle
I; myself
defending I; myself the little house

   I was not mother Taliban

     three gates or jade residues descend further
then deep off scanner into deep jade so
jade-hue is more
   than texture.

   more than shape-in-hand
more than you bargain for if you ever could
maybe I; myself did (once in Viet Nam)
jade is the condition for prayer

turtle . . . Buddha . . . handsome manacle of jade

or
three animals
in the middle of jade grow cold
as in when in grass things keep shadow
on the left side

if they don't keep left of the wind that way they perish from heat
this somewhat being explanation

for coldness of day
cold spirit
& why I; myself would linger over it

pouring troubled spirit over the cases
& jewel boxes
of jade

or beautiful chill of a line beyond jealousy

I; myself in the Tao state

    . . . in velvet toadstool

Chinese Mushroom

you say that crudely

    sensual delectation
[stage direction: *cough here*]

that my epic sense not be merely causal
but a relation of voices both inside
and outside
the physiological
hampered even by cough
(a fit & start)

[cough here]

but the label carries warnings thru the door

for more huts.

more mats.

 . . . more sanctuary for things seen & unseen

take this elixir when you can be resting &
prone, the label indicates. *turn off the psychological blizzard*
white noise showers down on you.

                                         click.

perhaps a larger temple than this one

—with its children & seismographs,

toys that talk or moan
ask questions you never
have the heart to answer because

     no, plastic-skin-doll, you
will never be alive like I; myself attempt to be—

or am indicated to be (arrogant)

house with I; myself
intact

axis of language is rare
     (syntagmatic)
but a spoon falls
     to the floor
the one you held a moment ago

I; myself dutifully take salutary measure of

that fall—move it!

down it! faster, faster

for pain. & so on

gravity's pain, aid the child

& so on. radical, back on the left again,
a spoon of air
in a pictorial hand.
    talismanically Egyptian
it promises to help you as

you move the Asian continent to Africa
approximating your medicinal dipper, which is a
measure of one swallow

grounded, isolated
becoming delineation of map of starvation

the Tibetan antideath potion

a night-poison—right?

(hacking away at the statues by night)

        [bow three times]

moon half-seen
    Big Dipper that points you
down again toward earth, go there

in your astrology religion I; myself
make much of never obfuscating
the terms of defending I; myself
from its debts to the telluric gods

I; myself defends more than gods

& would die for a dharma-mind

more than views from a ziggurat
from tent from something resembling igloo
though not of ice.
            rice?
more blinds behind which I; myself
watch, an outpost of this crazy frontier

frontier that I; myself witness
going back to my jade epic again
because it unfolds like a metaphorical
        lantern
son et lumière

& is carved to keep the I; myself
(*the occasion of these ruses*)
intact for a ceremonial day

much like this one, in solitude

death of poet, death of
friend, death of brother Grecian born,
        death of statue
illness of species the bottom left see? is
going deeper.
                Dipper digs deeper

a favorable geomancy or placement
of objects.

        I; myself resembles a clock.
I; myself
        takes the top right-hand corner for
political reasons.
        the lower far east can be
star-lab

can be monologism

may be ore extract for all I; myself makes sense of

she if she is all the shes I think she is
is capable ally &

   more than the summation
of her jade parts

. . . traded a cow for beans—how many? . . .

. . . a clash in fashion but they match . . .

. . . upside-down "thanks" . . .

. . . version of a book I; myself gave the students . . .

. . . half-hour seashell installation . . .

. . . a boy who was the officer of Taliban army . . . he also died

. . . camp-bug artwork. pathos & embroidery . . .

. . . blue plethora attached to a rabbit's foot . . .

. . . self-portrait of the sun . . .

. . . no longer booted up for posterity . . .

. . . weapons checked at the door . . .

. . . notepad, 5 scribbles, dark & dangerous looking . . .

. . . bombing plot in the little school . . .

. . . no I; myself did not say that . . . .

. . . what I did say, the dissolution of sounds . . .

. . . strange Taliban in their closed microcosm . . .

I; myself said to be coming through the
wire of least resistance
   more permission
granted with the door out front

Anne's jade talisman has always been wished upon
this is her amulet, lean pauper in a notebook

this is her word "ruby," this is "eyes"
sketch of a wolf: osha root
& the qualities of wolf: cooperation
respect for others
& this is a latch to the moonroof of a Subaru
or a clamshell when it runs opaline
this is a jade pendant shape of tear
this is a brush with death
these are farm children who see the future
conservation of wolf
& conversations beginning
"birth" "root" "wish" "fur"

    & the equitable sky surrounds
just as you exit

to save on human air, over there

    . . . maps

. . . memorabilia

. . . refuge in the dust

III

WORRYING YR LOGOS:

CONVERSANT YOU SPEAK TO THE DEAD

(Heraklitus)

---

stupid folk
(uncomprehending
before they have heard "it"
after they hear "it")

forget what they do when asleep

war-strife is everywhere
normal-course-of-events is war-strife
everywhere things fall apart by
war-strife
&
normal-course-of-events

Stoned on Percocet if that's at all possible the rumination turned toward the notice of never-the-same-river-twice when students had objected that it took the British Museum to read Charles Olson. (Gregory Corso had said but of course you can't even step in the same river once, what's the philosopher's problem?) Or at least a reference book. How's your library where you live? Marginalized by the corporate bookstore, reduced hours? How many know Heraklitus? I will not tell you the hand count. Suffice it to say the bitter professorial tears stream down in the middling dark ages. How I'd long for something from the Malpighiaceae *family:* Banisteriopsis caapi? B. inebrians? *Or some recourse to know that a wit & wisdom might stretch toward a normal-course-of-events small town (infanticide, plutonium, date rape) so that you are haunted by books, books, books. . . . As war continued you could breathe in the hints and murmurs of these thinking quarters. You consider who did not serve how Moloch they serve. I see Heraklitus in public, the streets are his, and all their contradictions. Did you notice the Women In Black again today protesting at the busy intersection. I certainly hope so.*

& take you out of yourself in harmony

1)

One man or woman serves another man's or woman's sentence.

2)

Parents may murder children when they are insane.

3)

We should not listen like children to their parents.

■ war-strife keeps the world afloat.

~~Apparently so~~.

still breathing in your hallucination?
return to the origin of all things

I saw that the tribal gods in my vision
seemed to intuit when I last looked
the flesh & heat of ego & beat a retreat

4) *(attendant jaguars)*

~~How long, Rumsfeld, how long~~
(that's a joke, Cyprian)

■ logos: mordant wit

■ century to century
caught yr mind

not comprehending they hear like the deaf

& the newest century promises more artful knavery

5) think about Proudhon, Simone Weil.

   & what couldn't work for them

          is thinking a private possession?

If so where do I hide it or
how may I give it your way

The genius Jewess could not abide the Old Testament
Nor could Blake, antinomian that he was
So that wouldn't work: Ten Commandments, et cetera

    The mind must be free
       & the body lover's delight
O Palestine! O Palestine! May you come home to your body soon

6) desire & hunger, hunger as desire
    that abnegation when you can / can't eat

couldn't work & then I stumbled . . .

7) ~~jealous of the god on the cross, she said.~~

& Belief
is it Opinion?

              ere I fall . . .

8) a cottonwood and an oak tree
as if in conversation or love, their
branches
    lap over   act like women in sleep
tremble together
               as if thinking shared by all

nothing separate from that which coexists with it

move down the trunk   move
      down to seeing

Nature loves to hide.

roots go under

        Homer was an astronomer

9) *lutte, dieu et feu*
   struggle   god   fire

we know more than Heraklitus
scientifically
        about these things.
        too theistic for my taste surely
        change & sun, he knows
about those
so give him rich credit for those

I do for those.

Change: I know.

Sun will poison me.

        & for the others?

Terror will not destroy them
~~(Bush sings here though we mock him strong~~
    ~~as he twists the verbs of matriarchal discourse)~~

      will Furies chase the sun?

10) . . . about fire, the Kali Yuga, there's no question.
11)   But relational cosmology
       in and out of fire drains the liberators

Here is drought season.
Many people water lawns who later beg for water

Yo people of the future:
hear me tell you this for a Dark Archivist Project:
guard well yr water!
Protect the rollback rights of gays, of Lesbos
transgendered,   straights

there is a another year of struggle predicted
whose winter is a great flood, whose summer is a world
    conflagration.
                    mark it well.

In these alternating periods the world is going up in
flames
Or turning to water. This cycle consists of 10,800 years.

a lot of people are ignorant
but we weren't thinking exactly of you all those years

although Justice is what you'd die for she is
true to all her years

A solar system exists in the country within the city within the town
in the home within the room in the hearth it comes down to
justice and neurogenesis

What will our middens be?
If there were no sun it would be night.

detritus of excess. No justice displayed
for Earth & its inhabitants.

Not antiglobalization the folks in the streets were going on about
one shot dead in Genoa, Italia, July 2001,
it was how
to create less suffering for those who suffer in the
Big Greed Decisions

The sun is the size of a human foot.

The people must fight for their law as for their city wall.

count me in, Florida

we can do with less
It's sexier

Plant tears for the divorce between philosophy and poetry.

ROOM for this διαφορα? an old animosity.

but nail those guys going thru the White Back Doors
      arrest them on the watered lawns

make them accountable!

Shame! Shame! Shame in the House!
Shame! Shame! Must exit the House!

    cloning?
I went in search of myself

Almost—laughable-self

not so much threatening, as touching
heap of random sweepings . . .

almost Buddhist here, Abhidharmist?
He intuits the *skandhas,* the little heaps

> The hidden attunement is better than the obvious one.

Senses, the interstices &
fragments of thinking
coming into being in the world

enough? have you had—heard—enough?

Pleistocene woman dies in a medical experiment
a drug seared her lungs to death
protest from the scientific community

12) *Dear Joe Brainard:*

stem cells is now "hot topic" of the hour
We are at a new century of ongoing-ethical-concern
Wish you'd be alive for getting cured

> Death is all things we see awake;
> All we see asleepe is sleepe.

~~. . . later that same night not quite dozing the pill having worn thin it occurred~~
~~to me that in an attempt to control the future according to our fates (woman's~~
~~character is her fate) we live a Devil's variance with Heraklitus's time zone. We~~
~~exist in a false construct where we can appreciate the contrivance.~~

The drug spoke to me and said:

> There would be no time like the present.

Be a child of illusion

it rests by changing

no pasaran

What I learned . . .

Dick Cheney: did not serve. Several deferments, the last by marriage.

Dennis Hastert: did not serve.

Tom DeLay: did not serve.

Roy Blunt: did not serve.

Bill Frist: did not serve.

Mitch McConnell: did not serve.

Rick Santorum: did not serve.

Trent Lott: did not serve.

John Ashcroft: did not serve. Several deferments to teach business.

Jeb Bush: did not serve.

Karl Rove: did not serve.

Saxby Chambliss: did not serve. "Bad knee." (The man who attacked Max Cleland's patriotism.)

Paul Wolfowitz: did not serve.

Vin Weber: did not serve.

Richard Perle: did not serve.

Douglas Feith: did not serve.

Elliot Abrams: did not serve.

Richard Shelby: did not serve.

Jon Kyl: did not serve.

Tim Hutchinson: did not serve.

Christopher Cox: did not serve.

Newt Gingrich: did not serve.

Don Rumsfeld: served in Navy (1954-57) as flight instructor.

George W. Bush: failed to complete his six-year National Guard; got assigned to Alabama so he could campaign for family friend running for U.S. Senate; failed to show up for required medical exam, disappeared from duty.

Ronald Reagan: due to poor eyesight, served in a non-combat role making movies.

Bob Dornan: consciously enlisted after fighting was over in Korea.

Phil Gramm: did not serve.

John McCain: Silver Star, Bronze Star, Legion of Merit, Purple Heart and Distinguished Flying Cross.

Dana Rohrabacher: did not serve.

John M. McHugh: did not serve.

J. C. Watts: did not serve.

Jack Kemp: did not serve. "Knee problem," although continued in NFL for eight years.

Dan Quayle: Journalism unit of the Indiana National Guard.

Rudy Giuliani: did not serve.

George Pataki: did not serve.

Spencer Abraham: did not serve.

John Engler: did not serve.

Lindsey Graham: did not serve.

Arnold Schwarzenegger: AWOL from Austrian army base.

Hey Guys,

I am on Phi Phi island, which got hit pretty hard by the Tsunami. There is a lot of rebuilding and piles of rubble but it is still a beautiful place. The island looks like two islands connected by a thin bit of land that creates two bays on either side of it. The place we are staying in literally opened the day we moved in and they came in to install a mirror first thing in the morning. Local people are happy to see people coming back here. Tomorrow my friend Chris and I will head to Krabi for a bit and then make our way back to Bangkok. Looks like I will probably come after that but nothing is set yet. I still have to book a ticket from L.A. to Denver. Anyway everything is fine on my side and I will let you know when I am going to be back.

★

Hey mom I'm in Seoul now for a few days. Pretty cool city, though I haven't figured it out yet. I think I am going back to Thailand to chill on the beach for a bit and then come home and figure out what's next. No dates are set yet. I am not really prepared to move anywhere without coming back first. I still would like to go to Japan in November if possible but no plans for sure.

I am jealous of your computer that is what I want to get. Was your old one really that screwed up? Please take better care of this one and keep your files in order, seems like you go through these laptops awfully fast. Be careful on those roads. And I will let you know what I am doing next.

★

13) [ART POINTS BEYOND ITSELF.]

IV

BROKE THE TALK DOWN

A broken tongue a forked tongue a broken mental construct a broken tibia a brokered road map a bro-
ken accord a broken treaty a broken land a broken skull shattered beyond recognition in recent bomb-
ings. More skulls to claim. The minds have exited them—gone gone beyond gone—but here on
Earth one must do the proper ceremonies thus gather all the parts of the body one can to bathe, to
chant, to sing upon +++
+++++++++++++*ganglion*

    occipital +++++++++++++++++++++++++++++++++++

                                 they tell of eyes blasted out of sockets +++++++++

            they tell, they tell ++

                               thus have I heard +++++++++++++++++++++

. . . .
. . . . *ablutions, prayers, recite mantras over them*

. . . . *the unrecognizable parts of the dead* . . . .
. . . .
. . . . *melted down* . . . .

. . . . **σπαραγμός** . . . .

sift . . . .
. . . .
(pause) . . . .
. . . .
. . . . *sift* . . . .
. . . .
. . . . *sift (pause)* . . . .
. . . .
. . . . *sift* . . . . *no dig* . . . .
. . . .
through rubble . . . .

Stan Brakhage sees angels in the breaking (he's filming) light. William Blake encodes a mind so deluded that it creates a universe it can no longer control. Light rays become glories you can't control. Imagination freezes, then leaps for the light. What need control? The weak do, and they do posture and rule with their dangerous toys. Abrouac, an Arab word for the overconfident, pathetic state of humanity, rests on the notebook page tonight. What is communication? What is propaganda? Why is a choice not indeterminate? What is the arrogance of armies? What is the arrogance of an Anglophone empire? How does it dare? Why is the epikos a respository for your mind out of all the possibilities? What does your mitochondria whisper to you in the trench of night? The Abbasid caliphs of Baghdad sponsored a translation of the whole corpus of Greek philosophy into Arabic in the ninth and tenth centuries, fighting a ban by the Xtian emperors. It costs ninety-five billion dollars to hunt down Osama bin Laden. Ferdinand and Isabella expelled the Jews and Moors in 1492. And the New World? Those-who-dwell-by-night-with-open-eyes: I dedicate the merit to you wherever you may be . . . grasping the humble straws (strands? filaments of light?) more tightly now.

The new world: the cabin, with family before her next assignment.

Osiris Sam (blue white-eyed husky) guards our door
roaring "row row toe your boat" at the sky
Starless, breath piping
He barks for joy & barks for anger
and for food: pizza, crackers, and cheese
Remnants from Saturday nite Millsite where
Fuzzy Bob recognized us and mountain billys crooned
for love, beer, & showing off their hats
Up in a mountain high as a ski in a little cabin
with no bathroom here or there
snow all around two feet tall and it's really hard
Crusty, except where holes open groping for two other feet
You might just be taking a walk across the road
& fall in. Help
One lightbulb is shared by three rooms, like
the three gray sisters' eyeball
The fire glares as Jason & Ambrose jump like
kamikazes off the roof. (My) mom reading Sanskrit
studying words *samsara* and *shakti,* the endless
wheel, the endless force, Ambrose writes
Skiing up & down graded trails of snow cone

ice fall like clowns up & down
Pausing for jerky on the Phoebe "B"
and a sesame Veniero's cookie—Lorna's gift from New York
tumbling & turning Twin Twisted Tree Trail, ouch
Mad at gloves they don't work, at doing incessant "herringbone"
at the gray clouds O sun come on &
melt your ice faces. Jason has a toothache!
"I'm being eaten by a mattress & my belly's cold"
says Ambrose, boots on, March 25, chez cabin
Watch the turn in the trail, a big hole there
Come back to the belly stove, center of our world

                    if policy
be dissed
    the dreamer
could not be owned
    in her lonely yearning cabin
details

(just life,
mere living)
    at
what cost,
    at
whose
    expense
survival

to consume! consume!

violate genocide accords &
    you violate Geneva
    she works
all day for the Tax Man

ponders nightly
a systemic
vow
to

make
    political sanctions
(transactions)
    cede to poetry

she prays (pays)
for this
dearly this
America
privilege
then
across
an
ocean
ride
free

America:
that needs to be part
of continent America not
just solipsistic busybody
U. S. of A.

accords

North Atlantic Free Trade Association

could it work
    for the mass of them

indigenes

World
Trade
in everyone's future

face / fate

never fall back
on mere
honor at
bedside.

her valor, a value
prone

to melodrama
   & drug busts

our friend
   across
      the border

our Virgen
   our cult of *vigas*
& tears

our friend who is "mixed"
   in origin

bow of head
   traverses a map
in policy
save one expression
still bright
one star still bright, Aldebaran

   the markers form ambush as the pushpins
encircle a city, take out a city
   the war plan on the computer glowing in its
deadly space

people aren't sounds, are they?

this poem is the occasion of my complete LIBERATION

   estrellita

upward toward stars
one motion of Mars
brutality of sanctions
you set a bomb to
if it might be
her wish
could

shift
    would be
mighty exodus

Nuestra Señora de la Salud

you calibrate
would be mighty
gain
on top of a corn goddess
you
give sanction to

I touch her blue robe

I live inside her skirts

I touch her plucked-berry eyes

she is my butterfly
my sanction
my health

would be no destruction
no bombs yet
but those conquistadores
cruel Guzmán
no way to pity
they were born
of steely hearts

rape, lust
give it over

no delicacy
    in it
a kid gone dim in the
    centerfold

sexy Latina legs
paint smeared across the
vagina billboards
of Mexico City

a thought with your own ears
allusive talk
broke the talk
down
why broke
why down
why in the language realm
    we have these claws
        for gouging meaning out
for obfuscation of all text you would sing
from a heart, broken like the symbolic statue
(*a dictator made me put his face here . . .*)

why a frozen coffin that's a ballot box
why single out the people who can't write
    cross a border, x on the line

broke
the talk
down
to be brokered as if she,
the one responsible could
    ever speak true

"A war on Iraq is sooooo twelve years ago!"

a border patrol

Zapatista-ed out of here
away from La Mesa

San Andreas

draw attention
to why
a pity's the inquiry
bandito-ed
to why
she breaks
the steadier
light way
off
& thinking: it's curtains, it's prison, it's incarceration, it's the old
conquistador dream:

First evil in Alcatraz, a fatal Catalan youth brigade out stomping for the dour duration. "Minaya"
did she say? That was the name in the dream. A broken name of Minerva. Crumple your vote:
Nirvana. Does it matter, all the voting buttons in the doorway? Distill the tragedy of voting. It's
blood, my Cid. It's too-much-at-stake. The lid's off you didn't get a chance. Cramped and manda-
tory, Tell me, Minaya, did you vote? Tell me your worst dexadrine nightmare. Orality on the Nazca
lines, Come my Cid, read me from above. As if you are a visitor from another planet. Come to the
broken lines of Nazca. From Spain. From the old world. From an Andalusian dream.

Except for you
I would be no longer sweating it out,
laud a fiat over the globe,
absolve difficulties
abdicate results
torque diamond mines.
The oil of my reserves
would be vindication,
forget offshore pearls.
Accept no apologies
and I would control all vittles
your virtual stuffs to make a new creed by
I will not as gentleman
accept your fond and furious delays
they will work against you
As gentlewoman
I will be cautious courteous to a fault.
What is not as evident as could be
is appetite,

is my appetite
my acceptance speech

assuaged
in
her
Indio
Catholicism
        her heathen warriorship

her translator's desire to make all the languages
        work in consanguinuity
in concert, philologically or otherwise
    she was nonetheless anxious

blood won't back off
    a culprit's
devastation
as isolated as it gets
&
someone's "word"
arrives to crucify the Indians

"cutting
some slack
    for the generals"

his rank war. his rank trembling fucking war

Anne—
But what is happening in Mexico, and, more or less, all over in América Latina? u.s. imperial-
ism is interfering everywhere, even in Argentina, where my friend Carlos who is Austrian and
Argentinian has just traveled for 2 months. I hope to be able to not imagine another century
of this endless exploitation caused by the ruling classes with the aid of the u.s. Yesterday Michi
Lainer (who touched your hair in the Tachless in September '98, you remember, in a strange
way) said to me that u.s. foreign affairs had died for him with the madness in Chile in
September '73. And Viet Nam, I asked? Just around Christmas, I was thinking of something
else: while in Romania during Christmas '89 the dictator fell and was shot, under strange cir-
cumstances, and the whole world was mesmerized by the fall of the former Soviet satellite

regimes, the u.s. air force bombed the city of Panamá and killed 3,000 people in working-class areas, this was under George Bush, former chief of CIA, hunting another former agent, the general, Noriega, allegedly for drug trafficking. This was well planned and executed, because it didn't get much attention, because of Romania and other revolutions. In fall, Bush was celebrated in Munich by high German politicians, I forget why. Yes, why? In my point of view, he is a war criminal.

I'm often thinking of something that John Cage once wrote, quoting it wrongly now: . . . that the u.s. will become just another country (and not stay a so-called superpower). Love, B.

hmmmmmm

if it was only UNSCOM

an old Europa Norte Americano game

making a point
it would be
in short
supply

It scorches Talib who earns
4 u.s. dollars a month
"doctor me up good"
he will not
hear
"22 million burning hearts" of the
imagination

It scorches all the workers who weary
    look up at the night sky

Har decher is the reddest stone.
It is the blood stone. Mars is my eidolon.

Nergal. Star of Death

Fiery One, War Gun, the reddest

what may I call you?

A dead rock with traces of water?

Can you be my new Tigris my new Euphrates?

oppositional poetics
                    a mismatch
to put one continent
    against another
        one culture on trial
one little team's greed
against
    the world

one planet against
itself
as epic proportions chant their way out of here

what lesson you learn
multilingual to break
the talk down

"inobservable sidus"

UNSCOM

Mars's usual motion is
from East to West

it is his / her warlock dance

tires & spare parts for ambulances prohibited
in the emergency zones
machetes cut through the forest

there is a list of all the indigenous ones
in the last communiqué from the jungle

set a site upon

& it is
land land

it is land land land they want

when in opposition (opposite the sun)
rise when sun sets, set when sun rises

Gulf War: more tons of munitions
dropped on Iraq in 45 days
in continuous bombardment
than were dropped during
45 months of WWII

and now?
            it's oil oil oil they want
        over 1,500 civilian casualties

Tormenta del desierto

what is the capability

don't ask it's oil oil oil

does this broker an ill wind?

to break the *corazón*

broke the talk down

A-10 Warthog

Nergal Star of David
come back into bondage
veiled & deceived

I ask you no I beg you no I plead
to whose promise you acceed to

one more Mister one more
peso, one more Mister
one more dinar

a burning coal in the hand

wail above a son's tired bed
(I remember him at the front
standing tall in Nicaragua)

then
Eudoxus of Cnidus
a mathematician & contemporary of Plato
        enters

&
Aristarchus of Samos enters

"thinking men" enter and
    Air Force women enter

scientists of the heavenly war zone

they rule in their
eyesight their
blind articulation

Apollonius
Hipparchus

system of epicycles

enter

Claudius Ptolemy
The Almagest

look up!

then down:
wards of Al Qadissiya hospital in Baghdad empty
bodies gone dumb in the night . . .

4,700 children died of waterborne diseases & respiratory illness

combined motion of epicycle &
deferents
caused each planet to swing in
near the earth
at times
producing
retrograde movements

& it is retro
the poverty
retro:
    the look to star wars

  retro the *investment,* which breaks the talk down

then the warriors those who were jungle
those who are "word"
ask who's doing this suffering that is
    put upon us

upon our bodies

a body universe, burning shrapnel

The Almagest reins in the news

Copernicus refers the planetary motions
to the *mean* sun
rather than to the *true* sun

counting
accounting

retro the numbers of things
of men of women of soldiers
of memory of all the above

counting
accounting
   debt mounting up

the generals pause

El Presidente in his suit
& stern *cholo* glare

August 21, 1560, Tycho witnessed a partial eclipse of the sun,
which changed his life

Kepler:

punctum aequa!

and he awoke
and said

I awoke as if from sleep

a new light broke upon me!

and to Emperor Rudolph I Kepler wrote

For my part, I must, above all, praise the activity and devotion of the valiant captain Tycho Brahe, who, under the auspices of Frederik and Christian, sovereigns of Denmark, and then under the auspices of your majesty, every night, throughout twenty successive years, studied almost without respite all the habits of the enemy, exposing the plans of his campaign and discovering the mysteries of progress. The observations, which he bequeathed to me, have greatly helped to banish the vague and indefinite fear that one experiences when first confronted by an unknown enemy.

"The square of the period of revolution
is proportional to
the cube of the mean distance
from the sun."

Rudolphine Tables state

and
"Distance from the sun varies from 206.5 million kilometers at its closest
(perihelion) to 249.1 million kilometers at its farthest (aphelion).
Each revolution in about 686.98 days."

orbital variation is
     an emotional stance
          grace in its being
heard

     the mahogany tales
from the Lacandon

August 28th, 2003, Mars will make a closer approach to Earth
than at any time in the last several thousand years
and will come within
34,645,500 miles

Galileo spoke

Sidereus Nuncius, Starry Messenger (1610) spoke

Huygens wrote that
Mars was "crossed by a sombre band"

totem of postcolonial poem,
the war-planet
a signal into
spoken colonial world, a sombre hand

fight to the teeth
& to live

in the glint of the jaguar

eye? mind?

in the glint of jagged war?

tyger tyger

& those who were jungle those who go by night
those who come to this table of dispute

will sing a question

which translation does not in some way betray its original?

(as a lamp turns emblematically in the war zone)

what nascent irony?
what delicious company?
what artistic enslavement?
what occult beauty?
what moon over our panic?
        our little world?
what can the Renaissance teach us?
what verbal assault?
what old-time religion?
can you translate the Umbrian language
        for me please?
where is the *Herald Tribune* today?
is the world still spinning?
what equivocating emotions?
what numerous vibrating dialects?
what clash of civilizations are these?
what cruelty in Afghani migrant wind?
what anthrax scare?
what parched mouth without water?
why support for the rich, for military might,
    for arrogance?
why not generosity, pearly speech,
    sculpture turning into trees again?
homunculi on a string?
a photograph of Palestine for a peace march?
include all of these, why not!

the sweet birds of Assisi
eyepatches on Roman marble heads
why the myth of never-sweet warring revenge?
why not a sense of humor?
let be ranging bestiaries, pungent herbariums
    gentle planet guardians, a peaceable kingdom
    on Umbrian Hill
let be local and macrocosmic harmony
    let be astonishment, spontaneity, friendship
      with wonder in the endless spin
        of Ernesto Cardenal's interconnected universe
name it: edifice without paranoia
name it: artifice without cynical urge
name it: illusion to see how fast it goes
name it: philosopher's stone
let be that sanity haunts the premises
(woman seated with cup in hand)
let her in

V

A SLICE AT THAT

Wager sex, wager place and identity. Ekajati, one-eyed deity, paces your shrine tonight. Also known as ral chig ma, one braid of hair, or she-who-has-but-one-chignon. She makes a mark, a swipe, a slice at that——at what? emptiness? the void?——with her one incisive tiger tooth, her insatiable curiosity. With her sister dakini's symbolic hooked butcher knife, the triguk, *and her blue lotus axe. She is quick to act and has a retinue of a hundred iron wolves as aids. She holds a heart in her hand as in Dante's dream of Beatrice and wears a white cloud as raiment. She is supplicated as an "arrow of awareness." Sor Juana enters, scholar at her books, prayed to as inspiration for poet-life. Hermetic with a grace, and dialogue with outside world, its powers, trials, practices of the night.*

wake up a
tigress
for heat of him
    all sound all claw of growl & rue
gone a rule to tame the suck the crawl
hunker down
a bud

mass a bundle, warm, he is thin
resolute to stem a blunt so quick now
clit clutch a kind mass erect
of it

kind adept
she watches the indigenous mummy
go down

under
all decrees read "seethe"

: rather
animal musk

how deep he anoints her
sex cuts darkness
a slice at that—
that? museum lore trouble with
stuffed thing, musty no way back

eye genuflections
sleeveless in shade
summer scent
witless scarf
on seamless shoulder
the child's tooth
a cradlepearl
at sea roil-rung, rage
balmy
on sill

sleep kind one, tend orthodoxy

at home in arty town
three women abound
the Angel-of-Sleep-Reminder
the Angel-She-Wasn't-About-To-Go-Anywhere,-No
Angel-With-A-Drastic-Dada-Face
horror of horror

gaze into palette of black cloth
silk or shadow?
who notices pulsating cringesop

late toward the end of twenty centuries
gluts?
I wager disgrace at terminus

wrapped for no tundra behavior
supplicate bed-down you are puff & wealth
no spurn of load
no turn of rod or tooth
no churn shank bottles this broad voice
crank her up to soprano-century
then let a scream fall nay block it
it will not help the *crise*, old shadow
but ruses show it

a fishflails at the shrine
Sor Juana, holy intellect
in your library-cell, we pray to you
are you untouched by man?

keep our loneliness glad & sane

keep no thorn in the catapulted wound

or place of pride to reason it

no slip through this finger

tiny dry hiss, no waste no pain

keep our broad shadow as refuge

enjoy the carnal world, now, now

as it slips away
the world is your book

Holy Lady
keep close
the carnal book

someone watches, Dakini?

not undo environment

but sober for sleep resolve like steel
plays with a little risk-smoke,
goes up the ladder

not a calculated risk
as they say
but from another hand-
out leak
elixirs for sleep
someone next to her blind with love

confers a lick, his paw

shall I kiss you gob of night or
hunt the present prey
elkears
guess each part
nibble elk part
tender like young stud
ring monk bell
aught pray
or like that a quiet medicine wheel
she simply breathes around
on him.
tease a nipple
like a
banditress

webbed indolent rawlip
from
century's salt torment
conversion experience now
imagines
suffering Bosnian woman
   (things in history exemplify
       sheer cruelty)
to shriek macho! macho!

stop
the
flap-tremble
mouth

Eidetic—
mimic
a wish
accords
the mapping drama
ties silk robe's cord on, or
tries core to sob her heart by
him, him, him, I thrust all paper at

sex blooms below
a sex-appeal s & M belt
what was not imagined was
feather, stroke, animal skin, chunk of
metal, heavy, you got it?
but soft you know
smooth loggers like it in saw material
educated guess
how you could have
wagered her ass

could not read a book
tonight about
the famous homosexual
too sad

then sex lauds a broken book
whose spine is
incontrovertible
as eyes are hit
get rescued from stampede
a rodeo fix way out off the map
stars of nesting type light & topography

by method
our life is gay because we read
& consult oracles
tossing coins
from a lacquer box
poised to prophecy
        a book of change
    Tao! Tao!
    "Tea! Tea!"

                    what of our line, desire
        shifts
to drink how
anything eurocentric
takes place
but secret is exotic & held out on
purse all the lips to kiss & never tell
how we come by Mexic leaves

études:::::::::::::::::::::::::::::::::::

      play my piece for little bells

at room temperature
shades drawn
we enjoy hearing about night-
side opera
     buzz
a worthwhile telling
dagger-driven ice maiden
sets out
to kill her working-overtime demon
or some kind of plump Papagena
swoons

take a pick
it's your folly
to take back foreplay

:grandstands a position

:lie still in blood pools

light match

to illuminate St. George
who is now canonized
as candle

as dragons never sleep
but roar & roar & roar & roar

~~story is told about lovers who . . .~~
~~—as means of thinking of each other—~~
~~in body, body, body~~
~~tarry elsewhere I never think this way~~

~~get along in sunlight I do, ludie! ludie!~~

~~or evaporate I will~~

keep us dear Lady Sor Juana the vast one
    vast one thought to be ever bold
        & stride across our books our body's eye

bountiful! bountiful!
  to do such & such
    we
(shudder)
or
mar
the liturgical
page

Coda: *Practices of the Night*

                    :

                         (mtshan-mo'i rnal-'byor)

[one]

                         in the evening, just before falling asleep

              all senses present move

into a stage of contemplation

(mnyam-par bzhag-pa)

integrate concentration with sleep

fixate on an object, relax attention
fixate on that red dakini, relax yr attention

fixate on the wick
the stem, the wooden leg of table, of chair
the metal rim
the piano
the bright-colored crayola
then the word, the note, the unopened letter
then this, do this, calm the mind

(zhi-gnas): calm the mind

visualize the happy white "A"

visualize the "A" or "AH"

between your eyebrows

or a small round bead (thig-le) of five-colored rainbow light
in the space between your eyebrows

this is visualized clearly, the size of a pea

do this, lie down,
& the sixth sense consciousnesses (tshogs drug) will "alertly" relax

the dream state is analogous to the Sidpa Bardo, called the
birth of becoming

when we fall asleep we become disengaged from
the karmic traces of the material body
the karmic traces of vision
the karmic traces of mental functioning

the solid walls of the room are not solid
as we sleep

[two]

when we awaken a primal awareness arises
            that is uncorrected by mind
& that is present in its own condition

(ye-shes rang-so ma bcos-pa)

rest here in this

look with bare attention (gcer gyis bltas-pa)

into that state of presence (rang ngor bltas)

look at one's own face

what's recognizable?

no meditator
an awareness of nondiscursiveness (mi rtog ye-shes)

the solid walls of the room are not solid as we wake

this shows your willingness (dad pa) to participate . . .

the karmic traces of wall . . .
of paint peeled back . . .
the karmic traces of lust . . .
a map of terrorist Asia . . .
alchemical metamorphosis . . .
karmic thrust of the dakini's mind . . .

VI

WAR CRIME

World askew. She arrives home again to New York City, charnel ground of zero, ancestral home cordoned off, you need identity papers to get thru. Who are you? Citizen? Terrorist? Also to duplicity, deception, pathology in one she thought a friend who proved—was all along—her worst enemy. Pity? Mercy? Forgiveness? Don't mess with the goddess. She is on retreat now, prostrating to the deities of clarity and chöd—where you cut the aortas of the perverters of dharma. No mercy for the narcissistic male egotist who used her good name, sucked at her power, resented, manipulated and undermined the community to his own sick ends, called the cops on her & her son in Ashcroft's New World Order. A trip to the coast, demonstrating against the Afghan war restores a sense of purpose, balance, and punctures her disdain. Challenged, as ever, by the dharma adage: Drive all blames into one's self. Then returns to her Indonesian island "armed with shin protectors."

(The Prose)

Identity posits control. Who "are" enemy? Who are fleeced? Rendered abject, dead, or merely dead. Dead on the ground. What was your name, citizen? And of what realm? Hungry ghost? Animal? Human? Warring god? You are bewildered in the twilight of Star Wars, in the twilight of shattered bone or eyeball. A Daisy Cutter so grievous you have more than 400 lb. per square inch pressing on your skin, pressuring out an eyeball, limbs fall off with that implosion. Give me breaks, simple breaks. I can't live any longer inside of nearly dead, or "posits control, posits control." Give him, the other generation, his due, fighting the way back up to 1945. Clean up? Shoot anything twitching. Clean up? How much pain to inflict on a nearly dead one? All over Germany, the left-to-die-dying, whatever their stripe.

I hate my Nazi life, everywhere Nazi life in Nazi movies Nazi flicker, see in every step I take where one goes informed by Nazis this whole woman-life encounter. Nazis with their exaggerated tongues, and how proud they stand, how many actors love to play Nazis? I hate my Nazi life. I am labeled before I leave the vestibule: "queen" "faggot" "gitane." Sleep in the wagon then escape. Don't go down that road yet, they will find you. Cloak and dagger. Helpful train master who leads you to safety? Or is it a movie I missed, light in the tunnel, manic change of costume. Not what I seem. Dressed as beggar, my gypsy gal leads me through the labyrinthian streets, there is a checkpoint, she makes me look foolish rose in hand, escaped to fall in love, for that girl saved me, that sweet Jewess. My tender Jewess haunts me. Hands over the occupied life. You imagine that things go well. My water is my dust. My daylight is my giver and my curse is this gullet. Water, do no harm. Safe water, the well of Sinai, the well of Galilee, everywhere no harm if you have water to drink. Water, do not harm.

Get down to beg for water. The enemy spills out the canteen I drink from. My father said so, never asking for help but asking for water. It was metal with drab olive bag to shelter the sandstorm of outrage and hefty hoist downstream, coming down on you. Harm on you. She saved my skin to cross the line of demarcation. This zone lights the way to freedom. Let me down now, Mata Hari wears real silk, I tell you Nazis—that word "freedom," that word "silk"— could never be the beautiful time you had, dead on arrival. Harm. Harm. Give me back my life my beautiful life.

Harm to you. Harm to me. Next door, out there, harm to you. From above, strafing, you are never safe from their airborne probe. Violation in all directions, the inviolate that says no harm is done it's not true. Look at them, their photos. Harm to you. Roll back, a crime, take out of the forest, crime. Crimes against women and children. It's not true what they said. Escaping across the Himalayas to what new India now mounting its troops on the borders. Believe the victim from her sad grave.

Charred remain, hand reaches to heaven, the ghostly vehicular journey you made, all the old corporals laid to dust. He cleaned up with the same hands he held me. Man-o-live, stretching out the amnesty, the old war . . . ovens? You said ovens were plenty full? And now, what colony occupies what territories? Colonialism leads to war, take the text down from the shelf, brush up your victim mentality. You go nuclear, you go ballistic, Israel. Take out the spyglass, the tattered notebook, the frayed-at-edge dossier that holds the spoils, literary clippings of strife. That card is played. I examine the remnants, the body parts. It was my job when you were saying you are merely dreaming to keep them together, sort them out before the jackals come. Sort out the ones for lustration rites. Sound the gamelan, your mallet proceeds you, ready to strike. Raise a cry to heaven as you sift through the pits. Everyone is culpable, believe it, in this harm. Go back, there is an image my Paul Celan vows to bring to the most angular surface rendering of trade-off to. Bring to the path of circumstance, go mad with renewal when everyone says it's reclamation time. The march of the next plan: down on your knees. What is brought to trial when all is not fair, love or war. It's reclamation time!

I cede to the harm. I want to die.

Walk into the ocean like a one before me. The tall thin novelist.

Strip down to a woman's body you cannot love.

These are the shoes, these are the bayonets.

These are the dried ears that still listen.

The Cong are not silent in their march now, their long tunnel runs under your feet. You are old enough to remember, now, twenty-five years later, the streets of Hanoi, so much struggle in the mind.

My psyche lies down in the hot room, fan whirrs overhead, my lover dead to me in another country sleeping with the enemy.

Here are your spoils little girl, little Annie.

Here are the spoils of war.

A broken heart, a very broken heart. Crime's the way you walk the way you talk crimes, the way you get away with it not seeing arrogance, narcissism my god & all his prowess on my side. What mastermind of machinery to make sure suffering is not yet death, not enough to die without the torture chamber's cry. The crime is in the pudding in the picture, on any screen that will play. Drama of infrared music, you want to shout in the disco before you tumble, night after night the You are not in control with your signal of error with your signals of terror with your action deferred with your faulty warning system. You are not in control with your pilot warning rhizome with your human bomb attuned to readings in philosophy. Nietzsche could still rule your mind not hope of loving a "virgin" not to be confused with "raisin." In heaven: raisins. Raison d'être, to be greeted with virgins who are like the raisins in heaven. Crotches, nipples of sweet fruit? This is not a finely attuned translation. But never going on your nerve underestimate the mind of a revolutionary man, a revolutionary one. Anarchy is sweet revenge and you get what you want, this act of "faith": war. I hate my Nazi life.

Fake identity: war. Are you what you seem? or greed, revenge, violence reigns your day. The small villages plundered, citizens plundered, whatever human brings with its scent of fleshly doom: rape, desecrate a crop, starvation. It stinks.

War in this neighborhood is not a pretty sight. The petty mind is giving the petty mind another boost of recognition. Before the tribunal sets in. What about Guatemala, Mr. Reagan? You are my disgrace.

Where are my fine Rwandan sons going to be buried now? Anybody's guess. How to sift, sift again, then sift again, you sift sift through rubble. It is the antique obsolete way that moves and you think, watching them now below your very neighborhood sift, what is gotten, a cufflink, a locket? Your legs, dear dead immigrant American one, make me weep, how service and terror? sift sift again of hair of flesh of machine matter, all the more-than-asbestos-jammed into last year's air conditioner. They posted a warning on my door at dawn. And would you still question never paying another tax? Tax that harms another, harms your very own child? Your destination. Don't carry my war to you. Harm to you.

You have not voted with simple mastication in any other night like this of fact of fiction. Panting like the oval office, panting like one day to the next, what we know and do not know. More theme music. Harm on you.

Question: I am relatively new in the new frontal on-home-world. My behavior is modest Iraqi, no my behavior is mufti Europe. My erotic manners are as good as yours. The Brits show their mettle. Some are deader than nails in my coffin. Harm to them: does anyone pray to the Church of England?

Mom—Here, you asked, are my *Questions to the Grandmother* . . .

Question: Where were you when World War II broke out?
Answer: I was with my family. It was Sunday and the Prime Minister of Britain, Neville Chamberlain, was to speak (on the radio) at 10 a.m. He announced that we were now at war with Germany and that France had declared war on Germany at the same time.

Q: What were your feelings?
A: Nobody was surprised. We knew it had to happen and were relieved that the waiting was over.

Q: What did you do when you were threatened by enemy forces?

A: Shortly after the announcement that we were formally at war, all the sirens went off. Which meant that enemy aircraft were coming and you must take shelter. We were not attacked this time but it was a warning.

Q: If there was one, how did the draft work in England?

A: Everyone male or female at the age of 18 or over was called to serve. You were given a medical exam and sent to one of the Forces or the Land Army. In the Land Army you took the place of farmers growing food.

Q: What did you do when the draft came?

A: I had had surgery and could not do those things. I worked with the Red Cross evacuating old people and children from London and on an ambulance.

Q: What do you remember about rationing? Was there enough food to go around?

A: Food was very short at times but always fairly rationed. People who worked hard on the land got more than people working at desks because they needed it. There was very little meat, butter, or sugar and the Boy Scouts picked wild roses and collected the rose hips so that babies got Vitamin C. Also there were no oranges. Some children did not see a banana until they were 7 or 8 years old.

Q: Was there bombing in your area?

A: Yes. London was defended by a huge barrage of balloons (Blimps tethered by ropes) and by airplanes of Fighter command, but still it was bombed many times.

Q: Do you feel the leadership of your country was good during this period?

A: Winston Churchill, who replaced Chamberlain, held the country together and encouraged people to keep going alone, after France had fallen.

Q: What do you remember about the attack on Pearl Harbor?

A: The Japanese bombing of Pearl Harbor brought the United States into combat themselves, instead of helping with supplies of all kinds. The war effort was tremendous and they had Army and Air Force bases all over Britain. Together they launched the attack to free Europe, which is now being celebrated on June 5, fifty years later. The bombing of Pearl Harbor had of course started fighting with Japan and made it a World War.

Q: How did you feel about the dropping of the Atomic Bomb?

A: The Atom Bomb shortened the war and saved many American lives. The result however was so appalling many people doubt if it was justified, and whether President Truman should have made the decision to use this devastating weapon.

Prey on them.

Question: And friendly fire?

Answer: Euphemism is a danger to the nonbeliever, to true reader. The poet will not insult you with his euphemism. You get a handle? You need the door. Don't go out yet. Hear me out before you crash and burn. One handle turn is enough.

Doors are for hospitals, morgues. When there is no door you have a sky burial. The tent flaps open, the tin cans are not enough to be your door. When they keep the athletes prisoner, my stomach sinks down, blood on the floor, on the sofa. I will not absolve any killing. What will it take?

Go set yourself afire in front of the U.S. embassy. Stop taking out more innocent lives. I will do that next time. I will load up on kerosene and matches.

That is one idea.

Another idea is more Marxist where you vote on point of fact. You could be a civilian casualty anywhere, any rail station, any rubble-strewn outback, in your own backyard, a lonely colony. Who resides that cannot fly away. Safe zone will return in its own time frame, portioned out, drawn and quartered in a map-like gaze up at you. Take out this, pinpoint that. What did the president know or not know? Where are the charts of the war room all can get to? I'm ready. I am ready to see. Lay it all out here, all to see. The meeting is not adjourned. To tell of what comes up. I visit the United Nations building, its gardens, its art lobby, its trim and brisk attempt to be kind. How to ever be kind together. That's it. Is it ever enough—is it ever precious enough that you want to concede and drop that habitual pattern that drives a wedge in your world and you explode? Where is he—the companion, the former citizen of heart and line? Gone, gone, gone beyond gone.

So you sit inside your war, never sure, never clear. Who did what to whom? Who will live to tell of it? The father hiding in the chamber you think of now as the war room. The recovery room, the bardo of going beyond the sound or hum of crossfire, the stolid command, the "hup hup" that William Burroughs sang in mockery: my heroes are dead and they were their own kind of criminals. You think?

I want to tell you that it is a crime of passion to write this down now.

Dear My Country: Spread the wealth around. Turvy is my world. You could be mentally merely coming up for mortal air. There are gunboats protecting you all sides. A submarine doesn't move, if that is at all scientifically possible. Merely.

What I am angry about.

Not safe in bed, no lover's arm.

The sweet boys protesting one spring day you'd better keep at it until you die, protesting. You can take your body to the street, not pay the war tax. Pity the poor soldier boy. Or honor him. May he never have to kill. May he be untrained in any reality, mugging—a throng of thugs do gang up on you. He looks like you, my son.

Didn't hear the warning signal (*move to higher ground*).

Parched earth, scorched earth. The ponds low in these parts. Stocking up on supplies inside the war mountain. NORAD. All buttons ready to go. Aimed at your own nomad heart.

The charitable fund dies but who would care.

Give up your sanctuary, nothing protecting you now not even the place of the babe Lord Savior's birth. Let's go down now to the bombed Fertile Crescent, let's take the irony out of the cradle of civilization. You are thinking about yourself, the clock is running down, why don't you swerve toward me, scented one? With war pomade. With oil-slick hand or torture implement.

The crime smacks of desperation (more heroin on the streets).

The crime leaves its signals behind (step on a hypodermic needle at the beach).

"All the cops bring the best dope to the parties."

By definition you grow weary keeping up with the scandals, with the time. You are on your own get-down time. Marrow time. By definition you are transparent in your Enron slumber. Wake up!

Answer: Struggle. A day like any other. Just because you don't see . . .

Count them, how many in their suits and ties testifying, how many ugly faces, and a face you know is lying right toward you. It doesn't matter. They are all empty phantoms, transparent ghosts of another lie. They are the banality of evil, they are sweating when they don't get their way. Remorse is not a word in this man's eye. Looks right through you to dollars and sense and avoiding criminal time. Is there a pen to put you in? Is there a pen mightier than a sword to light the page?

(the minivan stops, you are afraid to exit)

Question: Could you emerge like the worm you are? Could you be loved, lowly, humble?

I would say yes.

(denigrating the enemy, the male is charged, is lifted up to the rise)

(the jets freeze in air, you are afraid to ride now)

(he is good male, neutral, not without quality of: bravery, jaw quite prominent, a drawl, a lit object of smoke, your pick is right, there is no one else here)

Question: you are convincing me to join and serve. Serving is not a virgin heaven.

So waiting for the curfew I put my head-covering on to beg. The sanitation trucks disturb the sleep of the homeless on the sidewalk. Someone shines a bright light on a city street. Crime is on the street again. War is in every head-line. Once when I was an American I felt the pulse of war to be light, an allegorical dream that sent a chill down my narrative spine. It was telling a story. Then a poetry vertebra was on fire with the explosion of my birth, this one came later when he died, flag on the coffin, and another one resorted to being on a map of mountain terrain. There was no cave I could lend you in this body. It was surface, all surface.

The war was on the body, the crime was in the twisted mind that could handle and not repent. Take this other spot on the ganglion stretch of star, of plenty of matter ready to be discovered, that the dust on Mars could poison you, that toxic is your hatred of me. The planets align in the sky to say this is the spine that runs your life. Disarray, discord, all will perish. Who was blind to the ray of sun? Who took the inside of the moon to be soft like the underbelly of no reward? Who walked free out of one's life, never having served? Was he a man?

Was he a man of War? Was he a reject? You are addressing all lovers, where are the men who whistle and march home to Johnny's song, where are the men who seek in their crimes of having to serve to what intention to what major way of being never a child once again? "Not I" comes home to myself as a bowl resembles the one held out to beg. Down on your knees to have them come marching home. Hurrah. I will line the street with my swollen eyes, with my nuclear winter eyes, with my eyes of gloom and doom not being able to look into yours because you hated the gaze back at you, hiding out, a coward. Better a soft coward than a dead hero?

What is a hero in poetry? What does waiting in ambush mean? What are words for if not for this battle cry? What are the anapests doing in my sleep? Why do I wake up crying every day and loathe the lack of courage that could change this? Women most of you O women unite. Rip those babes from wombs and hide them from the new homefront security measures, from the new draft law day, make them criminal investigators of the harm to land, water, sky. To earth you shift your weight, restless upon. Open the mouths of the babes and feed them on love and a power to turn it around. Harm to none. Every death is a palpable hit in this heart.

Who is blind? Who gives strategy the next move on my behalf, who is it who lies and covers his crime? Who stargazes? I will stop all bullets now. I will study war. First it was merest conflict of cosmos, a flicker. "This" got separated out from "that." First it was not yet wronged, then a person or animal—a consciousness? —got harmed. Harm to you. Then it was a crime to see it, the harm, look back on itself, jump and start the whole wheel in motion to see what harm might be in me. I am fascinated in my harm to you. Harm to me. This wound never heals. Harm on the whole planet is my wound in me. You feel it too? Look across the table at him. Harm to me. The babe on her father's knee, she got fooled that men are heroes. He was standing taller than she. Then it was wounded the harm to itself on me, on him. He was caught in the wheel of harm and duty. It is duty to be harm to me, no don't say that. No, I can take it. Yes, I will. No, I can't. Gaze, crime, give me back my life. Let me relive the 20th century and never war no more. Never no war no more. First it was an edict on the rights of heaven earth and man or the first truce carved and sitting on the United Nations wall. I saw a press officer sigh before Gutenberg, I saw the assessment paper in several languages. I saw the press officer eat his pastry out by the large window, out by the river that still flows, urbanely. It was civilized. We put up with the world that day. No one was allowed in Jenin that day. The crime was on hold. The war went on. It was an error to see it any other way.

War Crime

(The Poem)

What takes? break a stupor

      Crimea in crisis?

   Metabolic modus

different
(sex & sanity savaged)

    creation myths on every turf
      pit this against that

     (human remains)

eyeballs extend, assimilated or
acclimatized to glare

bodies burst open

GI Bill
what got: education

    manhood's mute operandi
      lay it down
    scope it out
  soldier time
woman moxie too
& babe born to boot camp
    in family opus

the war gaze

canonical vision to lock up a human
      trope on fire
  child-psyche on fire

that a few charge it up in mortars
he was—John Waldman was—advance "wire" man

good for the asking
wire in my heart to his, Lieutenant

    wire the scheming eye, night vision
      a German lullaby, *gute nacht*
   he held the child. Doing it for her, new world full of love
& no more Nazis

over Europa's moutonnée

hillocks to wire, to go advance within

steal this

& one plays "swing" in every camp
    as antidote to fascist enterprise
      minor flutter at key
haunt (hump) the piano

stoned & drink your cheap red wine: classic enterprise

put it down to predator's power

interpret antithetical hallucination

that one fights for justice in love
that one fights for justice at all
    is cause for riot & leap

    erotic justice is first cause
    the right to live, the right to water, light, food

what is the sweetest war lore?

most terrible?

that of narration?

It's war crimes tribunal time

Because many are dead for it

        of it, many names to tell
nuances to spell out

Story: trance. Defense
    There is none, crimes of the heart
King dancing on his own altar holding
    Elegant elephant tusk, 12th century BCE

    40s rumple, 40s agenda

glad she never had to see this attack on our motherland

one, a woman, witnessed "the camps"
    flesh in the pit

saw sad matrix-war, double armaments

    embankment?

Labor Movement held one in thrall

   & he, the veteran, mutters

"I am pro Cong, back off"
& sleeps in the gutter that night

   doing a job, unconquered

what are we dying for?

58,000 of "our own"

did die, then died on them

did die them, then

& now?
   we die others, many thousands

they die on us

die on me

we did die ourselves & them—millions

         earthquake:
Afghanistan

did die them

30,000 casualties could be "handled" by American psyche if we invade Iraq

   is what I saw (read:read) today
                      ha! propaganda
did die today
   rebel, militant whatever in them did die on themselves

   Colombia?

Longing to be sacrificed

    at the war crimes tribunals

Metataxis
              War on druggie selves

A contra-war?

die, did die them many did die did die then

Serve the country that couldn't serve you, dying then die

            She lives for father-deathbed-wish that she go on

& in a heart's folly she did not love a soldier
    not a hero this time around

    but oversexed on old charnel ground

war-trauma & the trauma of love of sutee sutra love

           link inside the brains

survival's brain cells

    extra RNA to what cause

In Indonesia that old question again:

    did you do the proper ceremonies?

      did the good soldier return
              psychically wounded?

& the towers fall in a tall tale

Original idea did die that love, so many

& the scent below your street, under your native ground

a foul stench of war

Crime—the fixed one—

Idea—the fixed one—
   listen
      in death-wish we trust

carpet bombing again
   armed with shin protectors, the well-greaved Achaeans

What sound 5 a.m.? Processional. Leading the barong back to the temple. She-Who-Is-Away-From-Home-Again ponders the turmoil these multiheaded islands are prone to. The breakaways. Is she a breakaway island? She wants another possibility to the kingdoms of poetry, the new careerisms. She goes out to be counted. Confronted. There are legions of spies on motorbikes. She has to conceal her Noam Chomsky tapes. Bloody former battles of East Timor keep the community on pins and needles. The fires of Kalimantan rage without respite. And even more recent disasters. How many dead who spent their last minutes in incendiary auto-da-fé? Terrorist attacks at a nightclub won't change the world, just sadden the frequency. Arjuna's passion? Battles of family, of clan. Disco bombing horror! Tsunami for a troubled coast. Aceh will never rest, Someone says "unquell the world." I say "Saya namanya Anne, please let me come in." Smoke gets in all our curious eyes. The rupiah is plummeting. A Balian predicts the Marxist Age of Dismemberment. I come here trembling, to remember how we studied the past to understand the future. Remember? A time when our gamelan instruments were made of iron. When we walked around barebreasted. Where the "inner temple" was alive with ancestors who now only fret and scold us. Invoke a local deity when all else fails. She is the rice you must save to feed the future.

the fires of Kalimantan.   SMOKE.
the fires of Kalimantan we cannot see.   SMOKE.
SMOKE   SMOKE.
the fires of Kalimantan we can see.   SMOKE.
the fires of Kalimantan at dawn. haze
we see. WE SEE THE SMOKE.
the dawn, smoke. Kalimantan. smoke
dark at the center. smoke clears.
dark at the center. everyone sees
smoke. the fires. smoke. everyone sees

The bombs of Tora Bora. SMOKE
The bombs of Tora Bora. SMOKE
smoke him out at the center. SMOKE HIM OUT.
SMOKE HIM OUT

Again?
Let's carry some industrial states in 2004
Let's carry our good old boys along
No flesh off our backs—
Let's be everything we want to be
Let's carry the worker-states—get those steel mills going again

Get those votes in Ohio
Pennsylvania
Let them off easy in
Turkey
Brazil
Russia

We need it
We need them working again
Working again, we do we do
We need them voting again, we do we do

It's a game, it's throbbing adrenaline game
Heart of steel, steel night
Steel in the vein
Turn on the war machines
USA thrum & motion

   on the move

A:

I read your kind card. I put Padmasambhava up next to my very beautiful Chenrezi I got from
you! "Up" means a little toothpaste glue on the cinderblock wall. I have been transferred to a
Navy Security "non-booking" facility in the Styx of E. County.

"Woes": what an interesting—albeit Middle-English—term for my predicament. In reality, it is more of a catastrophe.

I have worked harder than ever to be a good student of my faulted paths. I have succeeded amazingly well; if you only knew what kind of crucible this former _____ of yours was in, you may very well shed tears.

This has been my spiritual retreat indeed I called it that after 3 days. It has also been a gladiator's school and I have been made into more of a man than ever. It is a "finishing" school for boys. I am adaptive in the extreme. So far, I have survived. The change to this facility and the violence here has been a great challenge, though the 23 yr 10' x 6' cell in Visto was more challenging in many ways. There was violence and death there too. I was shackled to a murderer on the bus here and get this, his bail was less than my 500K. A murderer, good god!

Again, thanks for word. All positive and friendly communication helps. I assume you wrote after talking to Mickey, not après one of my letters. It would be interesting to plumb a more emotional landscape, if you will.

Despite the obvious hardships as a caged "butterfly" (a Native American shaman-teacher of mine said it was my spirit animal and peyote confirmed this) . . . the strangest and most wonderful things have happened to me here. I have reclaimed my life, my joy, my excitement about the future—my manhood. I am a tough sonofabitch, determined to forge gold from this lead.

Eye rise before Ishtar. After Gilgamesh journeys to Shamash & loses the plant of immortality. O Enkidu! I shall thee join in this house of clay. Love, B.

VII

RASP

Cicadas? You want to hear? What? Your own rasp in the wilderness? Water, water! Just home from the desert the auteur drove a point home about exploitative angles in the SUV *world, seeing them as luminous as you gathered for the kill. One just rammed your little Toyota. You were guzzling gasoline, drowning your guilt in a vodka and tonic. The World Series could not stay your despair. You were distracted in the long bar, corridors of women to serve you, but would the ball be served by the pitcher exhausted for many rounds? This was not tennis. This was high-stakes war and you were no longer in love with the phenomenal world or that enemy on the next barstool. And Mars? That was another planet. And then death again, "without warning." You visualized his boy body in fresco, illuminated through the painterly hands of the father.*

try not
         to jabber

relationships

            origin's form in organic light

on the on effect

                root sense of limits

on the on defect

            an idea. relative. affect

philology relative

residual stint?

in color "milk-blue water"

         lived & active

alienation. thirst.

again

there be returns to his arm

practice them, undo the habit

    be kind

rendering his pain

irony
in message

& thundering

        "so much remains"

not late

for this love?

arid of art some days

Capricorn of
    activity

meets Aries

    of plan
but friends of the house

living in a house
    I cited

& cried thru night of Elio

no guarantee

    against shadow, against filagree

against phallus-bearing body
    of other

    or her

a star

she beats her breast

elegies in a gentler hour

with these faded, ornamental eulogies

born-again things
    items recall "against the morning sky"

avoid artifice

shod the vehicle

cede term
    banks of dark rivers

to meet & meet again

entails a passage

    all folk are dwellers
    in active rooms until they die

    cities where
shocks

a blue coverall

jeans laid on a body

collar triangles
    where he dresses to
    a red heart center
&
simply sung

like struts

on plywood, plants a kiss

erotic comedy

& to execute

larder
   come back

yellow, her green, its blue

their especial plum food

& longtime wornout organe-yellow?

obsessed by guilt (double lime)

chilled

it is a motion, it is beauty
   she might have had
   jealous to the point of insanity

funeral games (of love)

a grave may evoke strange colors: Albegensians

I needed to make a quick exit from New York City. I got caught up again in a methadone nightmare, it was hell getting off. Now I'm 3 months clean. I've moved to another center, near Toulouse in the South of France, of the same association. The weather is great (at least lately), the quality of life much better than in Trouville (Verlaine and Rimbaud once roamed the countryside there). I have more time to write here (but it's still hard going).

Things worked out in the job department. They still want me! (They must be crazy.) And I may receive disability while I'm here. I go back to work July 1.

My rhythms have slowed down here in France, the life I left behind in New York seems distant like some half-remembered dream. I breezed through the city of Toulouse yesterday, a nice small city with lots of pretty French students roaming the streets . . . Love, Elio

oil

or honey

gather?

& a picture

of something
is
a spill

is spilled

  is lower
than I be
lover to
power be

from couch to
chair

to draw out

achieved me

my death

as my demise

are you also

dramatic performer

"and waters of Styx poured over the wound"

may become
crumpled

a boy's body

we use

worn & torn

hieroglyph

recognition

placate green, feminized

aquarelle

   none of its subsequent grandeur
but
a dot & then flower
or blade of grass
gels the dead

in us, slip the finite
but
word

not flat, slips in

a shuttle of
mental posturing

it dried a

love name

ratified

a sentence advanced before

sleep

   art into life

& canny blood

& canny where quality shows

they plan, he said, in my poetry

to break out of their human form

episodic seekers, away from their desperate needles

we knelt

what altarpiece

  if cut
is owed
  married
bowed

intimacy
would highlight his beauty

key

to focus his poetry

blood

to shoot home

which implies

"own"

mission

telling someone, anyone

other

they can afford

a conflicting world

as cogs in wheel

crave

or nag

or crave a wound

asymmetrical filter

or scold

framing, the gallant sky-man, an angel awaits

& protects children

~~sadly~~

~~talk~~

~~one-up him~~

~~mitigated romance~~

on their knees with prayer & love

Anne—

The priest was nice, he kept his words moving, George was apprehensive when he told him that he would speak, but it wasn't like other memorials that I've been to where the minister got too familiar, talking about the deceased as if they had known them personally when they hadn't. The Catholic priest read three bits which said "you are not alone." It was nice to pray in the cool church, breathe in the frankincense which settles and soothes me. Elio's poems were read by friends, they were all sitting to the left of the coffin except for Pamela, the only woman who read. The poems were all short, beautiful, in the air. His brother Emilio, the most beautiful, reading one about George "your frescoes like clouds," and then everyone cried.

George's face was incredibly beautiful, after the service, so alive, thinner, ageless, the most handsome face, unforgettable, clear, eyes completely open and looking way inside and coming right to your heart. He described to me the vase that he made in 1984, never showed it, never used it, never wanted to sell it, saved it, didn't know why, up on a shelf. Now he knows that it was waiting for Elio's ashes. Terra Cotta, black columns, Roman windows and stars.

Katie and George sat close together in the church, joined together. Katie seemed so big to me between George and Pamela, mythic. So much pain and still we smiled. Her walk heavy, unsteady going in, later lighter, she seemed in a dream. Ron said that it was amazing to be in Vermont and then to be standing in the basement of the church, "dreamlike, it's probably better that way."

The coffin seemed heavier going in, the pallbearers working hard, lighter going out, backs straighter, feet using the strength of the ground. Pamela was very present, all in black, with her dark eyes, dark hair, holding white daylilies, looking tortured one minute, accepting and fine the next. A young woman named Dahlia was there. She had been in the treatment in Europe with Elio. She said that he had kept everyone laughing with imitations of New Yorkers. She called to see him on returning to New York, Pamela asked her to go and see Elio because he was in trouble but they didn't know then that he was already dead. "Released from this dark world." Love, Grazia

a split and stop
  hold back
    then tears scatter like rain

VIII

[THINGS] SEEN / UNSEEN

Messages from the bifurcated world: world of duplicity and euphemism. Now you see it now you don't. Speaking in double tongues, snakes writhe and hiss around the heart. What is the weirdness of religion all sides what double standard? In the Nilo-Saharan regions, at the end of the pluvials (the northern glacials) a religion of sun worship developed (perhaps in Abyssinia) as the land became desiccated. The sun was correctly seen as the source of all life and, in excess, the unstoppable taker of life. God the creator with a harsh edge. The "enviro" truth was associated with the sun in the heaven above and, by analogy, was instituted in Sun King leadership. It spread down the Nile (Egypt) and later into the semitic male monotheisms (Judaism and transcendent militant Islam). It retained a predominant "magic," which had to do with weather and social control. It was definitely concerned with immortality (mimic the Sun God!) and devised vivid scenes of sacrifice for the transcendent Abraham. Magicians became priests in their institutionalized forms. Priests became corrupt and perverted the magic, binding with briars our joys and desires. Thugs donned the priest's mantle. Yet the desert remained the central zone for potential enlightenment—even as metaphor—(hear them, the souls, crying in the wilderness?)—a place devoid of beasts and plant life. Out of charnel ground the lover, a she of no small order but modest in demeanor (so many have died so many have died) rests her case here one moonlit night chanting Onward, onward again. And the enemies, who are they? Paranoid hallucinations of one other, churning out more double-speak. Poets: Guard your word! Is there anyone under that burqa?

> "If I had people in here, I'd want to know someone was looking too," Danny Nolan said. Danny Nolan has nightmares now, waking up screaming about the job sometimes. Friends from the past who have died visit him, like the old friend whose name he will not speak because of a belief that the name now belongs only to the soul. In the dream, the friend takes him into a strange room and shows him actual items that Mr. Nolan has seen recovered from the World Trade Center, things like African artifacts. "The place is playing tricks on me, I guess."

> *New York Times,* November 18, 2001

snake wrestler
Ofra Haza singing "Galbi"
La Pitture Etrusche di Tarquinia
A Bar at the Folies-Bergère

I met a man who killed a man
—scattered fierce T-storms—

         life is not like this
not the way it was supposed to be
                           but allegorical

        you were in a place where the future had come and gone

       name it "home"

     I met a man who wronged many women

crossed borders
he "sidewalked" here late one chilly evening
he fell back way into 20th century
Oslo en route & fell again by wayside in failed detente
code: to rout one out to out one out and suffer for it
      war-state, mental siege, people gone on a dime
entering outer Mongolia

he mass seducer   he holy bounder

code: seen anyone else the premises promises?

born in a crucible of heroin and rubble

      all maps all children suffer
but he's privileged man-on-town
faithless, a liar of cruel tonnages

      wielder of psychological harms not knowing the
truth of deeds, how concomitant ignorance is
rejecting the truth of its own nightmare
locked, of course, the SETI researcher conjures, sadly,
    into weapons in space

an end to imagination or of
"thinking of things as they exist" (Oppen)
that's the rub for this palinode: I was never there
     so *let me go*

---

on to smart bombs heat bombs bunker bombs
out of their caves
to one or two en route it's moot
onto and what she was into knowing
how long—Daisy Cutter—how long be shredding?

  (more suicided flesh & nails)

sustaining
The Queen Tut Archive

(seen)

pursued by darker demons

could be a manipulative child
she's sure / unsure her power is the

attitude of racist. ageist. lookist.

hedges of thorns in the dream
she tyrannizes others
pits one parent against another
someone pricks a finger
she breaks down
spoiled daughter of the wounded
times
not
a

soul
to
blame

(unseen)

all the eels in the pot
bore through the earth to China

the finger bleeds
winter in Wien

I wished I had stopped thinking
for once

the Kosovars, Giorgio in Venice
screamed, a videotaped village wedding
all that gone forever, gone

I have a job to do every day
of the week
I am busy in exchange for purification

creating an old language
"proto-world"

sustaining
Pesh Merga (We Who Face Death)
sustaining
The summer of 1992:
Keraterm, Omarska, Trnopolje

(seen)

the relational
the retinal
Cash

the Camps
The Camps & Genocide
2,000 lb. of laser bombs
a white male chief of staff smirks
a vice president dodges his odds

no pasaran

(unseen)

it depends what ends you are on
terrorism? or eternalism?
cash deficit
(mortar rounds)
Michael Moore stalks Charlton Heston
another voting machine dysfunction
"my last mistress" in cash

or better yet
the strobe of intended
landing
knew words by heart
& there were ruins
more unnerving
near rapids again, need rapids again
                    & again, had disappeared
sun & rain of a dead civilization
her debit card
works like a ghost

a bitch from Westchester
lights up the night
digs claws into the young novelist
"sketchy" at best
a palpable hit
maybe half-truths

are the clearest phantom you have
staying alive

---

    her mordant wit
my worst dream: lobotomy

   recommended for "cognitive dissonance"

   sham Xmas-tide in a negligent trophy home
little quarter acre of ache & regret (ram into heart)
crack in the way-back
lift a candle to fetishes of crash & burn
to the fetishes of deluge, hard rock, death of a holy Beatle
the way you hold up your holiday like that playing ragas
you'd think the world depended on trance music (it does! it does!)
cumbersome native soils he writes over
   the worst offender of anything ecological, all he wastes is mine
all cons, obligatory tears, subtle oil on the sex-dawn-sheet

    on the strangle-this-dawn sheet

       old loves come forth with a frontal assault on Adorno

what about Indian Point
what are you going to do about it
what about your "crazy" wife
what you gonna do about her
& the girl with the face makeover?

(the Dutil-Dumas message was sent from a transmitter in Ukraine. The message was encoded using a system called Lincos that starts with simple mathematical ideas and builds to complex information about who we are)

"My conduct was an expression of the will of the people."

       —Milošević

seen

a *Burqa*
an *Abaya*
a *Chador*
a *Magneh*
a *Niqab*
a *Rosarie*

---

face mask, black cloak, sheath worn by Iranian & Lebanese Shiite women, cowl-like cover-
ing, a face-concealing veil, Iranian headscarf

---

women whose senses I told you
    be gentler to
& speech to save
        in light of cleansing things
    not the presidential selected ones

"kill, whatever it takes, let's roll!"

I take this vow in meditation

say it: *I take this vow in meditation*

    women no longer hidden
nonobstruction is the effort, a greater *poethics*

Anne—

Hemaphrodism is not quite clear in animals. There is, for instance, sequential hermaphro-
dism. Wonderful clams that pile on top of themselves. The bottom become females and, dur-
ing slack tide, the upper clams (as males) release sperm which descends in clouds on the

females. But, if the females should die, the male clams closest to the bottom become females. There are fish and other critters that are sequentially sexual as well.

Then there are some arthropods like millipedes (not sure, maybe slugs) who do not seem to decide which sex they are until they are wrapped in courtship and mating. I can look that up but I remember that few knew how it was decided which way to go.

There are also false hermaphrodites. Female hyenas have such huge clitori that they look like males and display like males. For many centuries, observers thought that there were only males.

On the other hand, there are all-female species of lizards (we may have seen one as we walked around my studio). They fertilize themselves and produce more females. For years, naturalists searched hither and yon for the males—before someone figured out the females do not need males. It's a cool way to invade new habitats and not worry about finding guys.

Of course, if we drop into the world of protists, there are species with seven genders. They bounce off each other, swimming around in drops of water, and finally one bounce doesn't. The combo sticks and exchanges DNA. It took some time to figure out that there were seven sexes. What the sex ratios are and how the boudoir changes proportions of each gender is beyond me.

So add another book to the list. A history of courtship and mating. Maybe *Playboy* will fund it with lots of photos and I can live in L.A. with a million Zsa Zsa Gabors. Love, P.

AH

Hieroglyph

crystal toll, maximum
technical metaphor x9
trembling 18 cartouche
beckon or beat back 50 scarab
and ankh the tomb, 12 laser beams
1,000 bird, 400 good hacks, he holds
to recapture 18 terma
which is found treasure
à la Tibetano
Crimean? maybe
No, altiplano 17 hills
is worth 5 in the bush
& Pharaoh knocks
the 14th whisk down
down, down, many fathoms
surge of a million omens
Ahmen, 20 honey jars
a rage to conquer all 30 Niles
when I was Queen & he was deep in me

I am the members of my mother the member of all my tribe I am the wearer of snakes the beater of men the eggbeater of men the whip top of men I am the barren one until today and many are my sons are my sons I am she whose wedding is great whose empathy soars in war who wields the shield all the weapons of 10 directions in space I am the subsidy of the low and wicked I am the toil of all Jerusalem my eyes are firebrand meteors to light your way I won't go there over there because I am here living the good life the sane life the yuppie housewife life of a lovelorn mistress life of all my people's people the life of grandiloquent suburban despair and desire I could be a prime candidate for betrayal but I trick the fiend the flibbertigibbet I flick my tongue at his sloppy mindset his sad body fluid his loathsome temper his old skin I ignite with a thunderbolt I am friend to the storm king the storm windows no one knows the code the name the constellation I will inhabit in space I cry to be hidden but no one can be hidden under this new code this code of middens of ash and shell and dream of labor of telephone of plastic of glass of wood and all its constituents including fiber, of insect dung of scarab lore of wasting away in the desert waiting for a mirage of good fortune to steer my course by it will be steered it will clear, the dust storm will abate the eyes of all the enemies will open wide they will put down their rusty armaments they will wage war no more they will hang the swords from trees innocuous now out of the hands of men and as seven-gendered woman I will watch I will witness I will recall any stumbler any falterer I will track the liars and abusers to their graves I will tear up their scrolls their mighty warmongering poetry their lasting flame of crude moans because their lot is to be white to be male to be privileged to be of greater arrogant sex pain than the ones who really suffer never forget the sufferers of field of stream of mountain of meadow of dungeon of cavern of full fathom five of Hawaii five-o of Havana of harvest time of constabulary withholding of tax evasion of draft dodging of being profiled for color, for race, for ideological metaphoricalness for religious belief to be an artist of regret isn't your calling to be an artist of remorse is not for you to be an artist of doom and gloom forget it to be a seven-gendered chance operation is more your style as long as the waters part the breath is held and you survive to carry on the examination of evidence of choice of love of dark pogrom of prison of death camp of trapped in Nablus of trapped in the Church of the Nativity of elected officials that were never my choice or yours to keep the men honest and functioning to abdicate control so that people are happy and free and not one is hit upon no one is subjected to the indignities of false love of fallacious love of folly love of freak love of wearing out of syllables love of treason love of dis-the-women love. Avaunt thee warlock!

dicey talk
the markers are all mine
mitochondria in space
strident lab animals in the forgone conclusion tubes
gene splice continues
(genes for spider silk spliced into goat's milk)

---

cut out the euphemism for "grief" & splice in "aspiration"
this document keeps the demons at bay.

IX

APOTROPAIC

At bay . . . at bay . . . a Druid drill. Mixing up civilizations and my place inside them. Back to Asia. When in doubt, turn back to Asia. She was convinced more than ever of the need to practice in a space with a spiritual architecture. Had been carrying it on my back in my head, she said, a space marked out by the augur, in secret space, mandala for the practitioner's mind only. Sitting in front of a Buddhist shrine, decidedly frontal, a tricornered world. Facing ritual objects, studying their "men," Japanese for the front of an object. How an object "presents" itself. Such a place might be the "saniwa" as the sand-raked gardens of Kyoto, which originated as a site to stage divinations, also a place for judgment of criminals. Could she coinhabit with them during the extensive tribunals—surely coming soon, they must be coming soon!—of those war criminals, including those who profit from war in a free-falling free-flowing unrestricted market? She keeps mumbling "Bombay, Bombay!" remembering her lover there, a thousand moons ago. Things fall apart . . . visit to the Taj before the attacks. Restitutions of Kali. Filmmaker Kabir guides us around the city. And a pilgrimage to Ellora and Ajanta next. . . . Needing protective icons willing to subvert destructive power by means of artistic play. Since childhood, why are her dreams so much of war? Is this what made her poet, to create a lifestream far from battle? And yet she keeps writing of it, to exorcise its grip in the world's psyche. A performance of "rat tat tat tat, rat tat tat tat . . ." will quell the demons.

hush now

crash now

drop of Shiva's semen shot into the ocean swallowed by a fish

becoming mostrous
what happens Mumbai happens Bombay
what happens Vicenza u.s. Base
or Prodi
advanced warplanes to Japan
what happens

NASA's five space probes
aurora borealis where we study shimmering light
what happens
on the Lunar New Year
I want to know are there names for these moves
what happened with Augustine & his mother in Ostia
I want to know what happens Nicea 325
perhaps God creates the world
a lexicon and
vibration that
touches
the complexity
of gestural motion
Ex nihilo
Ardore/splendore
Europe still riding the pull of Zeus
a nuclear reactor not dismantled
& how that is part of your story
flooding in Mozambique, part of you
what happens Rwanda, Darfur, Chad
glaciers shrinking what happens
carbons capped
to save yourselves what will happen
Kyoto Accord ending soon
& there's something coming next
all-out nuclear war
bombs falling on Natanz
what is the poet's job out of slumber
names, names, perhaps you recover your power
I used to be an arranger of little lamps in Bali
I counted coins in Mohenjo Daro
joining in a worship of cattle
I bent a body into the stocks at the Kalighat temple
watched blood flow from the corpse of a sacrificial animal
I was one who protested, got dangerous
In lockdown
I was a postcapital person
entering postmodernity
I go neural then

I spooked on what was to be seen, neutrally
in a continuity of practice and resolve
and in a kind of diction
virtual
to die kind
die wider
doves and night
& wonder
not die yet
laugh human
see words
Mars, Mt. Tammuz, metallurgy, quark & fissure
words leer as in "ist" as in "ist los?"

Milky Way was
worlds away and close too
when I loved you
when I couldn't
speak and started
to look up
Regard me too
as empty complicated sky
I will build
my meditation
hut around your path of stars
and way is
mountain
and way is
the sure-footed ram
the dual
horned
animal never shackled
that there
be lovers
and beesties in
the poem
that's the way

weird, in ways
world says

"trauma"
twilight in the house we walked from
spirals too of a soldier, plus lover of a soldier
who suffers
rolling over a bridge now, tanks on alert
then stop
we walked
a vajra in his hand
some kind of leader he was
the "I" was holding on to become wiser
overtake the "he" in my resolve
in my syncretic power
I took his mantle . . .
I had the handle on it
I sat down to meditate
    in a cave at Ajanta

        jaunty mind

thinking . . . its reliance its dealings its questions its agendas its questions its
anguish its history . . .

. . . its covert arms sales its Saudi money its scandals its Bandars its conclusions
its not telling its clandestine operations its covert operations its not telling its
not telling its echoes its not telling "its no way, I'm not going down that road
again" its not telling its not telling its contraptions its blurring of lines its not
telling its monitor of Hezbollah its blurring lines its secret its whispers and
rumors its 47-million-year-old animal, an extremely early primate close to
emergence of the evolutionary branch leading to monkeys, apes, & humans

Darwinius masillae the missing link

Messel Shale Pit, a quarry
near Darmstadt
    dear martial ancestors,
do not weep I come to unwire you for war

felt trip a beach
    walking back thru sand

struck wooden, when I sat in the wood hut
    many obstacles happened

struck a wooden foot
became "deserter"

    spinal chord (of wind)

antler? Or was it "antlet?"

a part of the body below
dreamed a marabout

        music, didn't it whistle (she indicated that it didn't)

    inside a nuclear core information

    or

a little meditation hut

with its own stiletto formation

        electronic music in overdrive vocals

crazy huge boots
real stompers

dreamed a Tibetan nun waiting by the door
dreamed Kali instructed me

homunculus in a bubble on the desert floor

a fingerprinting
destroyed thru flood, never could get the markers right

but owl carved out
    autistically elegant

copper child next to owl

then later an owl inside mirrors

    a hoot owl, and child reversed

    a tattooed wrist
an "om" owl
    turned upside down an "ow"

way of life used in snow
or leaving a husband in Turkey behind

music sheets   indicated to us he was a composer from Cuba

lost & found
    "nothing's forever"

the one who cut it

                the one who held it

the one who stroked his torso

          & the indigenous one buried many years in a circuitous way

web hands that could move inside & outside a dollhouse

a functional identity
ghosts of a Civil War general

in a grandmother's handwriting
down into
the cellar   getting thru Pearl Harbor

+++++++could be punk, sexed, disinherited *(rat tat tat tat tat tat tat)*
++++++++++++could be henna-haired & extremely professional
++++++++++++++++pursued by darker demons
(curling the extra dimensions into Calabi-Yau spaces
is no small feat)++++++++++++++++++
+++++++could be moraines from the ice age
+++++++++could be passenger pigeons
++++++++++++could be *ectopistes migratorius,* the Migratory Wanderer
could be a blow-dryer for the art people well it could be could be++++++++
could be spin, filagree, the filibuster+++++++++++++++++
could be attention to grace and diamond++++++++++++
+++++++++pierce through a glint of writing
++++++++++++could be a fatwa following you around
++++++++++++++++could be the report on radioactive metal
+++++++++++++++++++could be the McCarthy transcripts
you cut up on the transatlantic voyage   rat
saying Down, Down with the father!   tat
people knocked you down and courage folded   tat
I know you soldier on, O my neighbors   tat
I know you go into exile, I knew you progressives   tat
see what people are made of   tat
born on the cusp I was born to   tat
(and sweeping the broom more frantically now)
size of the loops
the way electrical and magnetic fields thread through them
++++++++++++++could be a manipulative child
++++++++++++++++++she's sure / unsure her power is worthy of her

                              attitude of small racist ageist
pop it higher out of these small-minded ones
subvert the schadenfroh of our Time++++++++

>Tonight the two leaders attend the ballet
as nerve and chemical agents are sprayed on a variety of ships and their crews
Operation Shipboard Hazard & Defense is busy
using sarin, a nerve agent
or vx a nerve gas or Staphylococcal enterotoxin B<

This is my hot | cold war epikos remind me to report back to you
(hedges of thorns in the child's dream)

I was born but . . . uneasy

& to what purpose

dream life for the ancestors
    underground railways

        traveling in a rupture

irony or omamori

thinking . . .

    when noticed, shifted position
was not a communist reaper
was not a maid from Coffin's Creek

a Las Vegas suburb

I stumbled in Vegas
as a commuter might, going to war

a wrong turn
bad guys on the screen
Taco Bell for lunch
a drone is deadly

& you ask for purpose
    buying remote-control killers

and fleeing thus to Ajanta

                        to pierce through
                        torchlight

.

as you enter /   gasp /   exit /

as you restore from the street your text

of displacement

       you delineate the vihara, the chaitya,

           rock-cut replicas of wooden architecture of the day
            apsidal halls of secular communities & guilds
              a hall built like the inside of a whale

          modernity the conception of secular desire
                all sides
            the power of "cave"
          war, interrupts, cave
      war, interrupts, woman, exiting, her, cave
        Pakistani girl asks *who are you?*
             traditionally clad
              from Vancouver
               lives with her
           Muslim grandparents
              in Aurangabad
            hidden behind scarf
     pale blue with filaments of ornamental gold

while the fires of Tora Bora still smoke

industry to all sorts responds
the listener
to all sorts
the buyer
the traveler
the money market account
& hawkers, desperate for coins
sell jagged glinting crystals from nearby hills

to all sorts action claims collectivity & yet . . .
the buds of this crystal play an action with light

natural delineation of grace/gasp/exit the cave
& animals reincarnate to Buddhahood

kinship among all forms of life

marginal? all strata depicted on the walls

pauperized? all strata . . .

Daravi slums of Mumbai
                                        less good reason

a treason of "them" & company

less good my anarchist alphabet,

                            less good a terrorist hit

a terra, a terror, a territory, refuge in a cave off the street
& Kabir took me to a rectangular sacred pool in the middle of the city
where everything sounded different, muted, & we said

"The creeps from Contra back in their loud arrogance"

            & he said:

"& U.S. rushed request from Israel for more than
1,300 U.S.-made M26 cluster bombs
and how the reshaping of the Middle East
destabilizes us all"

            & I said:

"& the street action in January
& the railroad bombing on the peace trail,
Delhi to Lahore. windows barred you can't escape"

       & Kabir said:

"xenophobia"

 & I:

"complex conflagration
 each a world apart
 until you recognize Palestine"

       & we said:

"the *dis* of slaughter"
"the *dis* of displacement"

 & global
 & human
 & Habermas

   / RIP /

terra verde, red & yellow ochres, lampblack,
lapis lazuli all went to make this paint, clay mixed with rice husk & gum
& then a coat of lime applied for smoothness

a pigeon being chased by a hawk who says it's his lawful prey
takes refuge with a king who cuts out
an equal piece of flesh from his own body
                      & RIPS into the secular

at the airport in Beirut during the six-day war, a submachine gun to the dakini's head

slowly chipping away at artifice
the top of the woman's shoulder lifted as a lid

& the juice poured in to make her run, keep running
on empty

        puddles of oil for the asking

is it

"relegare" or "religare"?

& I asked *what is it worth?*

& Kabir said

"run on your own juice
where images are forbidden
& you have the mystical dome, the mystical stupa
primordial shapes of mind on fire"

                    | *umbra viventis lucis* |

X

G SPOT

direction implies a vector.

                              in ringing him down

   Stop

               gap,

point of return is a typology meant to be surrounded by noise. You may kiss the icon without it see-
ing you but it will feel that breath, those tentative heaves. Will it? In subjectivity it wills itself erot-
ically. Something sort of hushed and holy as in "ikon," or . . . the punctum as in "he pricked me."
Never tame the spot its scandal its woman tyranny. A little death is quaint erotics. And shakes the
world. A lecture mode as the hero speaks to her charioteer. On this spot "I" will achieve liberation.
On this spot I will stake my claim to not be reality cheated in art. I will unfasten the animal skin,
revoke the covering of leaves. I will keep the most somnolent awake, and invoke Rudra the Howler
with his toxic arrows, and Empu the Sage riding on a deer or crossing the water on the leaf of a
Keluwih tree. They will watch me strip down and will pay heartily. And the female ones of
Tambakredia, those Rita Hayworths ever-scandalous will join in the bath. Lead on, my driver, lead
on. Cape Canaveral is the coast from which to delineate these mudras, torrid tableau vivants,
strolling against a backdrop of missiles, trajectories—ever on alert. She wanted to meet her adver-
saries the night of the full moon. Strip down Florida, strip down. Looking for love.

                what are they?
                   figures
            and what do they do?
                 they walk
            and then they settle

          I was trying to be exact
          vantage from the shore
          or a piece of the action
          behind pubic bone

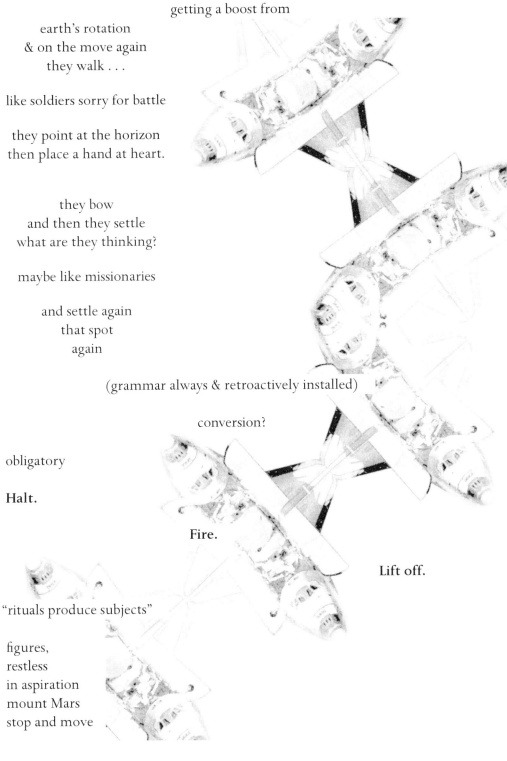

getting a boost from

earth's rotation
& on the move again
they walk . . .

like soldiers sorry for battle

they point at the horizon
then place a hand at heart.

they bow
and then they settle
what are they thinking?

maybe like missionaries

and settle again
that spot
again

(grammar always & retroactively installed)

conversion?

obligatory

Halt.

Fire.

Lift off.

"rituals produce subjects"

figures,
restless
in aspiration
mount Mars
stop and move

move again or
        in tracks

dead.
empirically or socially given
                for Saturn?

a body owes its life to another

                Jupiter?

a body owes its life to a mother

targets itself as double bind

something is "over"
but never degraded

come again Jupiter
come again

the mate/de-mate device is activated
& she is swimming toward me now
wireless or testifying witness

jury out on planet waves

baring her naked breast.

Not quite mermaid in her climate change

& the eleven-story device
removes the orbiter
on a 747
usually around midnight
when the winds are most calm
& we can't sleep

she is most lovely like this
in anticipation as she wheels around

and he with his names
"Redstone," "Jupiter," "Pershing"
        "Polaris," "Thor," "Atlas"
recited with official punctuation & click of heels

the language of weaponry
in those old dead heroes
give it up,
in another kind of game

your quaint erotics, heroes!

hand and hand we walk down missile row
a love affair that is in
pure Keplerian orbit
and in erogenous zone surrounding the urethra

she is amused and he keeps naming the hardware of space

"Stratofortress"
        "Hustler"
"Banshee," "Hercules"
        "Phantom," "Stargazer," "Alpha Draco," "Gemini-Titan II"

Demons, she cries
They puncture me!

Deftword, Swift Creek, &
    Weeden
island cultures come back here
postcoitally

resist the orgasm of empire

        deconstitute

a spot in the middle of water
set off from the mainland
and a body like the name of a temple derived from the

phrase "the erotic body will arise"
or "the work can be done"
as in irrigation
as in Pura Sidakarya, "the water will be done"

Turtle Island also a source for holy water

A rod derived from the verb *sirat*
Meaning "to sprinkle water" activates here

Includes as offering wolf or panther teeth

Keep by my side always
Porpoise teeth
                         includes more water, adding

panpipes

bifacial knives

As stripper
offers up
her night
wares

a promise of microgravity's many propensities

Seduction's a middle name

Go there often, the Bottom's Up strip joint, just down the road. Wonder the stories behind the stories in subtexts' hardscrabble lives. Can't just be seedy need or bead of needy eye in that seed. Compare with strippers' lives in Thailand's red-lit Patpong district. Tambakredia, take me back. Document these natives. Sex trade has its own needs need not be seedy need and no one's ever all about the money. "I'm just a waitress tits and naked flare. I like to dance the eyes on me." How much I ask to repeat that number? "Slow tonight, it's anything you want." "A drink!" Denizens of place: one ancient transvestite Barbara Bush far from home . . . and you have to wonder not being a true Barbara Bush what is the fancy or fantasy of travesty. A chest of falsies, like multi-tit gorgon. O Barbara, you fucking racist! Sailors from the Space Center . . . cars crashing against each other in the broad light. They play the anthem there and "Wake Up Little Susie." One guy comes in late,

blind, but tells the waiter he feels the grind in "sound." He said "sound" in a funny way, just that
way the way you might say "sex" or "sorry."
And he says turning to me:

body parts
    what do they signify?

born in a blast
fourteen billion years ago

geology's membrane taut and ready

g spot that is elusive like eclipse
g spot that intimidates the doctor
g: genie trapped in the bottle

presses on as genome does, resolute

stippled of need

    her body parts, what do they mean

& say to us, down under the strobe

A statue looks frozen in outerspace
    till she shatters

///////////////////////////
///

[g spot
don't you realize
you are a
local occasion of the universe?]

primordial gases of the
early universe
could be laced with
tiny temperature variations

do   re   mi
like you—a note—a site—a semblance of ecstatic dreaming
g spot was a hilarious overtone
because she wanted recognition

acoustic waves in the
expanding fireball,
a stimulation she wanted

the fireball seeded
ringing like a
bell she wanted
gong ong ong ong she sang she wants it always waiting for more
with a main note and overtones she wanted

notes on which the early fireball
was singing gave notice to her wanting
        or way to validate
or calculate
cosmological parameters
of singing
her need

groans dare a groan

            sound plummets sound

like geometry of space-time

universe's density or
a rate of expansion, with busy nematodes she wanted

and a sex cry goes out to scatter the world

AHHHHHHHHH

shatter the ears of the world

g spot: big weapons system
launched and trigger-happy

a dilemma on or off the landing station

g spot crashes & burns

push the button, tidy
manicured
fingers
    will
activate the launch

a purification ceremony
named *Melis* or *melasti*, burns
fire puja burns and
takes the form of a procession
to the sea
or pilgrimage to a netherworld
where demons dwell (down under)

rolled copper beads
from Lake Superior
dried leaves of
Yaupon holly
find a penny for the admiral's thought

migrations of sacred
objects, stern ones as well
stem cells in the mix
the detritus of all the body parts

as we, the tribal areas,
throw all sorts of earthly effluvia
into the ocean
in a myth called
the Churning of the Sea of Milk

a g spot, a temple,
a place to visit, plug in
a sacred pleasure spot for adoration
no—*start again*
a magic place, a g spot
a pilgrimage, a strip joint

thousands gather to witness her pleasure
I want to go back there
to give a piece of my mind
          break the day
strip it down

Stripper Voice #1:

Well the changeling does resemble the human it substitutes, and has more than childlike wisdom & cunning.

The common means to identify a changeling is to cook a family meal in an eggshell whereupon the child will exclaim: "Now I am as old as an oak in the woods but I have never seen the likes of this!" and vanish.

Alternatively you might bathe the changeling in a solution of foxglove.

Stripper Voice #2:

How interesting. Does that hurt?

Stripper Voice #1:

Well it is supposed to approximate fire. It seems cruel in any case.

Stripper Voice #2:

You are not supposed to look at a baby's face with envy or the baby might become a changeling, and if the baby turns out to be left-handed that's another sign.

Stripper Voice #1:

Are you left-handed?

Stripper Voice #2:

I try . . .

Stripper Voice #1:

Well it's something about being abnormal as far as I can tell. Some might not like fashionable things. But then abnormal these days may be authentic as walking here now in such a place as this. She's the kind of person who stops to look at a sunset. Stops to consider endangered species. But then that could be a mistake if it were misinterpreted. You have to be careful about scrutiny, not hurt the feelings. Where did she come from? Was she friend or imitator of the brother?

(<u>they put their slippers on</u>)

Stripper Voice #2:

And being lost . . . and hard on the "substitute."

Stripper Voice #1:

Is it like the screen lover?

Stripper Voice #2:

That's in poetry when you write about someone you can't really write about. But I'd do it in any case, write about the real one, and maybe the real ur-changeling will emerge, her g spot intact.

The missile never takes off

And she?

    founded on a promise

will break anyway

waiting for her Shuttle to rejuvenate

pray in your sunshades for a lift

*I was just going to mention
how not to be ritually dead*

You just keep standing, like a jewel
denied access to the inner sanctum
Remember to pray in a patriotic mood
out on the sand, prostrate
with all the other citizens
Then stand, look up

At your Dyaus, a sky-monger

personification of the sky itself
Your *Deva,* which originally meant "bright"

Or something for sun worship, a scandal

shield those eyes lest you go blind
lower those eyes as you pass the lieutenant on the road

schoolgirls with simple headscarves cry for recognition

identity! identity!

As if a cloth outed thus to conceal a power where
women may kill with the arrows of their eyes

troubles mind
placed thus on head, seat of a stubborn wisdom
but some governments do care
more like nuns
than chatter
but . . .
Do they really?

What hides under the headcloth

The Gräfenberg spot below or

"upa" top of head
where it's said
the consciousness ejects from
at moment of death
eyes that could kill
what is hidden

G   g

g G

G

G

g

is revealed

and the creatures?
mother Loggerheads
back after twenty-five
years
to this very site, their features
reptilian, weathered
with lug of leg
step in the same sand twice

& struggle

as if sand is
what we represent
gravity to lift off upon

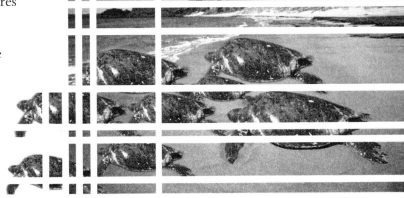

see that yellow post?
it marks the place the
turtle has gone underground
to hatch her eggs

she arrived last
night
mothered-agates now beneath the gate

two broke
on the sand
raccoon trouble

does sand travel

oh, very
she must dig with her
armaments
accoutrements
a very large hole
it's night also, a challenge

a child or a turtle
is in question
crack or other sound
someone comes out of the house
into the future
what more sorrow
we'll see when the push
for weaponry is outerspace

Our Lady of the Sea Spurt
Lion
Our Lady
Star Spurt
of the Sea Foam Lioness
How alone is terror
when you set it
between eyes: she

ejaculates

A blow to the skull

Rooms of disintegration,
Gun aimed
toward lover's pillow
About to pull the trigger,

Protect us, Our Lady
Keep me from this seedy deed . . .

How many heads slept
There in the bed of betrayal
(hid my g spot from you)

Hike up your stripper-gone eyes
Gone, take a hike

Hitch up to a star
He will

B * U * R * S * T *

Break

A sun spot

She was willowy as she moved
& her eyes seemed to look inward

very casual, slow gyrations
a dollar between the legs

Live wire

go down, god talk keep it down now

In a name that translates

"Ocean of Bliss"

—the hell realm—some say
on every & all shores
    is the borderline
    where troops amass
a Kasmiri shawl to wrangle for
the oily realm it's oil to wrangle for

Right here, too
Of course in sweat

A bloody oily spot
Gone dry

What is the lore
of love?
deals & false erections

missile deployments
trigger happy

Legs, legs
get shiny
as eyes glaze over a memorial
for dead ones
cops out
busting boats
with open beer cans
Fourth of July

what's the point
of fishing
without a swig
mouths wide
with pleasure
unendurable
madness
disintegration
downed

      or drowned

a kind of holiday
variegated assault
pierces the body

body of form

the woman's brain is organized to select men in a certain way
that could be fatal
body of a fetus female by default

primed as reproduction
primed by the brain
our newly full-fledged sexual organ

trigger that stirs these neurons . . .

cortex thicker for women
aroused by images of both male & female

shudder
recoil

and in the fish-tackle store
a reincarnation as
she says herself, a gal
who followed a boy
to this shore, the spitting
image
of Elizabeth Barrett Browning

Dear Invalid: be mine

figures of light
coded in the genes
forms of crippled dimension
perpetual yearning in a name that translates
ocean of bliss, my Elizabeth

intact
the virgin
till she comes

flight schools closed
for the holiday

alert on Orlando's waterway

and simulacra of holding on
an American dream
in a sad generic town
named Celebration!

toy street, toy
shoppe, the toy soda jerk, toy bank, toy realtor,
& cinema
with a million-dollar deal:
children of the future
toast in tiny town

g spot a video-code-identification-utility
frame rate, duration
aspect ratio,
bitrates

many "bug fixes" exist!

seen through the eyes of global warming
g spot
that is hidden, sister
underneath America's
tin heart

uniform hiss
of microwave radiation
fills the sky

good news?
"severe water stress"
by 2032

what are they saying?

that hard times
a-coming

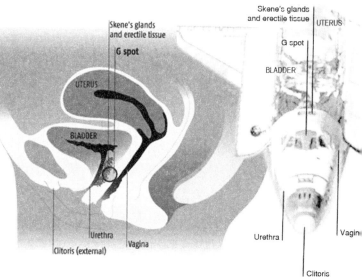

g spot below the radar
on a furious metabolism
all the g spots in the world gang up on you

and she walked then to a place then
stripped then

and performed this dance then
shouting then
like a mad person
it was a full moon with
many alcoholic drinks
then someone swaggered over to the campfire
outside the club
as she sang her song then:

"Foxes in the Henhouse"

Connaughton Holmstead Raley Myers Sansonetti Bernhardt Smith
Foxes in the henhouse you'd better act quick

Timbers going down in Tongass National Woods
Giant Sequoia turned to roof shingles so someone gets the goods

Man in charge says we've got paper to burn
Zealots in charge boost the paper industry's scorn

Foxes in the henhouse, industry moles on Capitol Hill
What will it take to save the Clean Air Clean Water Rights Bill?

Climate change—ignore it!
Superfund Cleanup—shove it, shrink it, destroy it
Air quality rules are relaxing
Let's have some more broken taxing

What on earth does it take to admit the North Pole's melting down
"Clear Skies" another euphemism from the evildoer clown

USA accounts for a quarter of carbon monoxide worldwide
Armegeddon pundits pray for planet suicide

Censor global warming reports, go into deep deep denial
Heh what the fuck? it's Bush-Cheney fundamentalist style

Foxes in the henhouse Foxes in the henhouse

It's totally out of hand
When you gonna wake up, take your environmental stand?

They loosen pollution standards
Overhaul every sane protective act
Massive salmon die in Oregon River Klamath

Coal industry's doing fine while wetlands & wilderness come to grief
Let the cattle graze on public lands
So the National Cattlemen's Association can sell more beef

Foxes in the henhouse the situation's dire
Oil drilling on the move
Iraq a huge tragic quagmire

Arsenic, mercury, vinyl chloride, lead
Not to mention 9/11 dust you gonna soon be dead

Not one species added to the endangered species list
Get out there all you environmentalists with collective raised fist

Foxes in the henhouse it's getting out of hand
You can't be idle while
Stealth tactics assault precious motherland

Foxes in the henhouse put those criminals on the run
They undermining everything we care about under the sun

Griles, Rey, Connaughton
Holmstead, Raley, Myers
Foxes in the henhouse, they're
pathological liars

Connaughton, Holmstead
Sansonetti, Bernhardt, Smith
Foxes in the henhouse you'd better act quick!

Foxes in the henhouse
It's totally out of hand

//

"and my poor fool is hanged"

it was then inside
the club now
a palpable feeling, then
of desire, she fell forward then

where people are wired for
nights like
this

to steady the ocean
in its
sway

[this was part of the seen/unseen project where she inquired:
afraid of the g spot?
is evolution in doubt?]

tremble the margin
yet solid in its sway

the stripper girl & I

low doorstep! listen up

she said "chestnut"

she said "break apart"

"try a haibun zone," I her jaw wrote her leg wrote

she into her stomach. her plexus. her third eye. or lease a flow brunt

"write with your eyes closed in dancing"
"watch for turning cars"
        or
"big mack trucks"
        and
"the humvees and suvs that send you down"

her hip felt things

& I took apart her act on the page

steady
steady now

XI

SIGNATURA RERUM

Vienna, I didn't know you could be so random, a wink after Floridian sleep. The airport hassle. People afraid to travel. Pavilion of tongues. A hot tub in Frankfurt first. You are wet behind the ears. On assignment to make something happen and consider the negotiations of your own empire, all your United Nations friends still worrying the subject of WMDs. Home to origins of empire, hegemony, out of my own mythological reality, Babylonian captivity. Notice other things, the killer instinct in someone who would harm you, a lover perhaps. Shifty-eyed. Annihilation to the point of every now and then. She has been marching and shouting. She has been noticing the world goes faster. Out of control of the gene pool. She has been noticing how the elements stand off one another and spin out. O they do this. He is surely dead in this form. Enjoying road rage, tailgate sorrow. Intellectual? Exile? Allemange, her birth origin and Mongolian epicanthic fold is temptress in her. A song of ten strings. Not one does she pull. She hammers out the schedule. Today I will visit the birth of Nazidom. Tomorrow I will bow in Brueghel mania, let the alarm go off as I cross a wire. The next day I will found a poetry school. There are no denizens of flood and famine here. The signature of all things manageable.

Lebensunwertes Leben,

A life unworthy of life what could that be

Did die them, did die on them.

Anne—

Well it's extraordinary because the past 2 days I have thought of you intensely and was planning to write so obviously we are still in some kind of communication—

You know I was often thinking by myself that in a sense it was a pity that we met when I was still so young. My own thinking and working was just beginning to crystallize, I was in many psychological difficulties, my mind was struggling with so many emotions; yet having encountered you has been so influential on so many levels, spreading seeds only now sprouting.

St. Petersburg was breathtaking, helping me to understand European history. If one has visited London, Paris, Vienna, Berlin, St. Petersburg, and Istanbul one can understand the whole period from the second half of the 19th century to the time after World War II so much better,

This is actually my favorite period in European history. One of my great grandmothers had studied household work in Berlin. At that time she met Emperor Wilhelm ɪɪ once and was allowed to shake his hand. The experience stayed with her until her death and has now become part of our family folklore. My father was born in Berlin. His mother was an opera singer and came from an impoverished aristocratic Polish family with ties also to Hungary. When her husband died in the war, she married a millionaire in Essen, and moved there. From my father I have inherited a genetic deformation. There is schizophrenia in our family and other disturbances. His sister in her crazy period lived under the bridges of Berlin. Berlin now for me is like owning the shadow of my family.

Please do not think I blame Americans in general for the war. The Bush takeover was so textbook-like, I mean like a textbook for fascists: You help to create certain conditions, which then serve you to fully come into power. It is very much like Hitler's takeover. It is so disgusting, because it shows that old strategies apparently still work, and history is so very fast forgotten. I cannot even begin to talk about the tsunami. In Aceh or Sri Lanka political interests prevent victims from receiving help, all donations likely to be channeled into certain pockets.

How was your trip to Linz? Linz was or still is the center of the Welt-Spirale (Agni Yoga), a kind of theosophist movement featuring Shambhala and Nikolas Roerich. Ages ago I attended a lecture by one of the members in Munich. The somewhat rightest rhetoric repelled me though.

I have always loved you very much. Alas, again, I was very young when we were together and I felt I never did you any justice. I was so immature then. Now my love is without pain without clinging, very light and warm. M.

Autumn in a place they don't know it's autumn yet,
the beautiful gardens meaning they are still beautiful in autumn
Think of points as little strings

& eliminate your troublesome anomalies, shoe fashions, and other things like that

the realms are incompatible
metarealms
playing dice with the laws of physics

living in four directions

one the poem
two the poem
three the poem
four the poem

& curl up in the microscope

loops in the carpet

I have a case of a very simple woman's
mind going in more than a few directions

one to eleven

could be gentle, scared
could be daughter of a Nazi
(this is possible remember
we are only a few years older
than Holocaust)

she came to me in Frankfurt
haunted by the demons of her father the Nazi

How to write, how to write out of
them, my parents the Nazis
she said

I didn't know anything now I know
I want to write
I said Come to my Schule

of Love? she asks and I comfort her Yes, to study.

she—dark eyes—could be
of tribe of Rom, maybe she
could be of tide of anyone
genetics in any ole direction
fucking, that's all it takes

get genetically modified here fucked

it doesn't take much

how astute to our condition
we are

& subject to change, mixed bloods

                              she tyrannizes others
                    pits one parent against another
                          someone pricks a finger
                              she breaks down
                    spoiled daughter of the wounded
                                    times
                                     not
                                      a
                                    soul
                                     to
                                   blame

                         daughters of woodsfolk

all the eels in the pot
bore through the earth to China

the finger bleeds now it's
winter in Wien

How long am I doing time
The job is to create a trilingual sphere for poetry

I wished I had stopped thinking "accountably"
for once
but couldn't, it came back to me again:
the Kosovars, Giorgio in Venice
how he screamed, a videotaped village wedding

all that gone forever, gone in massacre
& not been merely threatened by seven ravens
eight notes of an octave
eight
days in an eight-day week

I have a job to do every day
of the week
I am busy in exchange for purification

mechane means *trick*
if only I could make the trickster machines
work for me

Schmerzenreich is not my son's name
nor does he live in twilight

peasants & saints reside higher up
walking naked on glaciers

harrassed for their dark skin

one unkind word
provides a text for

tragedy for months—what was said

wrongly?

the girl leaves home, goes to a garden   "the boy joins up"
wants to eat pears et cetera

It's simple

she wants more attention, she gets on a train
& flirts with the men around her
she is in a sleeping car, women only

she drinks her wine alone

someone is smoking a filterless cigarette

coffee?

I'll have another dark night of the soul, auf Wiedersein

once upon a time you are moving up through
layers of the earth

Freud will not help you climb up o no

His museum is a kind and difficult parable

Parsifal is the third Adam

& she remains the woman-without-hands
stuck in the woods

We went there, the Biergarten

lunch in a tressled bower

people getting drunk & laughing

we too, almost in love

& stared at the text a long time
to translate?

what is the word for "naugahyde"?

Weltanschauung

send me on a mysterious quest
I need more assignments, my friend
I need more assignations
at the heart of noir Wien

a man gets up in another culture &
says someone has stolen the fat of my kidneys

did you notice?
or someone thinks her half brothers
are being turned into swans

six little beds   six turns of heart or phrase
six white swans

& she will make shirts of flowers
to redeem these brothers

shaking off feathers

she didn't get the shirt over him fast enough
& one boy has the wing of a swan

& he partially disrupts the conscious world

Sternblumen

stars & herbs correspond astrologically

I want to say more about the deeds of Jove
The xenophobia of Jove that was the task of a lifetime
I took the hook off the "j"

"I" now and "ovis"
                    I owe this

O vision
O visigoth

Dorneus says "shape the heavens below" toward
an egg

what signatura rerum behind the motif?
Santa Maria Maggiore, the alchemist's gate

global warming almost slipped my mind
in our conversation

in this age of super anxiety

Perturbation; desire   :

No one called today & the bee population is way down
                                       "why would this be?"

& what
could be
said of luminosities
the gorgeous planets'
luminosities (cold, dark)
just abandoning us?

where is the first day of spring

(the bluebirds flying & worms coming up in January)

push   "pause"   step back

the mindful gap

essence of patience: stuck with the pixels
keep looking at emotions

drop the white noise, Angel Eyes

I want your intelligent disobedience

A world of things in motion

Stravinsky, my chameleon

A world of music in motion

Music and light, to walk in your shadow, Mahler

This was an epic and a walk, Schoenberg
This was a female "self-referential" (an epic and a walk)

This was a political entity—a song that elides nation & culture into a single
    sacred union

But is it the right of the nation to claim certain lands whose soil upon which
    the noble warrior's blood is sacrificed?

What right, Wagner

& conjure & name other places
to awake the awareness of the world to itself

I noticed the keys lying on the floor, open doorway, metal in the breeze

Notice the rain before it happened

Walk now, walk

Now move trees into the shadow

Metabolic stress of readers with your intergenerational star wars lingo

My percussive reader

Storm windows

Walking side by side with me in indeterminancy

Katrina . . . Lebanon . . . Darfur

Syllabaries of the storehouses of the Royal Retainers

in this *ukiyo-e, the floating world*

walk and drink the Bijinga,

heated sake with maple leaves

Dirk Bouts, my Magi, my adoration

In a gift culture, drink up

A thought or exchange about "going crazy"

Or "about" "eciding" "eliding?" "deciding?"

What is one to do when one is an ancillary "you"

Live decisively!

History & one's own sense of history

Howl typed by one Robert Creeley

How pretty & wild is this life to me when these men were in it and even now
we're doing research on the
Hawthorne Army Ammunition Depot in Reno

there were no single objects

there were merely atoms in a liquid named "desire"
& rounds of bullets in a culture mad for guns

Dear Younger Generation:

what gives of trouble
when that trouble is
mythical time standing still
read carefully your women poets
turn the clock back and study Europe
open the camps
be a community of conscience AGAINST THE CAMPS
reports on the trains that go anywhere in Nevada, coming in
& the artist with the German name
saying But you elderwomen will have to teach the young ones
how to abort themselves!
a railroad ending in a camp—highly sophisticated surveillance
but the quarters are of cages make no doubt about that
for immigrants, enemy combatants, queers, transgender beauties, bible study
dropouts

who is a man not caged
who is a woman not whrrr

Who is trans not caged?
Who is an "it" not whrrrrr

She said she saw the camps
She said she saw the matrix war
Die did then did die then
                              yr elder

What did I see—
Daughter of a tyranny to identify
My friend Joe working on it, report back to me
My friend kari working on it, report back to me
Central headquarters in possibly so old Europe—give it a rest

mountains where dark energy propels the universe apart are in flux
Possible universes—could I go there?
Exist at relative low points or valleys in the landscape
Some of these might be suitable for life
                              and others, who knows?

A gearing up to combat
Bend of the eastern toe

Collapsed Europa
All my euros gone to beggars

Chances are good for disconnected landscapes

The universe is like water rolling around the hills
Always seeking a lower state
From one configuration of dimensions and fields
To another

Am I a witchhunt
With my arms and paganism

A body in a waltz that learned to speak?

Thought to be ancient-regime idealism
Blink of an eye

Moved a body from late capitalism's transparency
All the stolen money in the banks can't
Animate this translucent heart

Writing as a form of translation

You see all the reflections in the oil paint
Still Life with Apples and Pears
Still Life with a Ginger Jar and Eggplant
Two Children between a House
Still Life with Apples and a Pot of Primroses

Still Life with Trauma

Schule für Dichtung

We argued about the Rock 'n' Roll department
Too male identified
Galaxy upon galaxy, erotic arousal tactics
Tips the ecliptic in a voice not my own

Anna Freud had warned the populace not to
Swim too close by

Dear Anne—

Later I attended a reading at the excellent Adalbert-Stifter-House in Linz. Erwin Einzinger, a poet, prose writer and translator (of books by Creeley, Ashbery, James Schuyler and others) presented a voluminous new work—the title had something to do with the "History of Entertaining Music." Erwin lives in Upper Austria, is now a retired Gymnasium professor— we've been knowing each other a long time but have rarely met in the last 10 years. He translated "Mabel" and "Autobiography."

We had some beers after the reading at a larger table so it was a bit difficult to concentrate on one person. But I caught some rumor about the death of Robert Creeley. But no one knew. And I thought it was just a "malentendido" (a misunderstanding) of someone. Could you tell me the day of his death? Please tell me. Love, B.

splice: be kind
chrome: an old nobility
subject: be kind in telling of poet-death
subject: don't lose your way
object: metabolism
proposition: fervor
position: studying the places that endanger reverie

antropic principle, a universe suitable for life
for the sake of the world that lives in sickness
conditions observed in the universe
must allow the observer to exist

XII

ROBERT CREELEY TURNING TO CHE IN A DREAM

Last night she dreamed herself the mystic lover of Che Guevara (a corpse) indoctrinated in anti-imperialismo and is roused to write an altruistic manifesto for the good of all humanity. Perhaps she will call it "Earthlings! Human Comes from the Word 'Humus': Remember your Origins!" Back then so long ago—she went to the party with Bob Dylan to meet Raoul Castro who was accessible as an infrastructure rationalist. Che has laughed at her Buddhist naivete re: taking up arms for revolution. When he pronounced "oil lamp" so carefully in English what did that mean? Was "planets" a euphemism for missiles? Is this dream a rune about the Bay of Pigs she worried a long time ago? Es necessario . . . he mutters, as he morphs into someone else. Bob Dylan held her tight. Something like that. Robert Creeley, a syllabic poetics. A line from Cuban poet Nancy Morejón hovers in the ear "to bask in the afternoon sun in Havana Cuba free territory of America." Free territory. She has recently returned from a conference in Venezuela where everyone danced late into the night, although the subtext persisted in a drama between sex, poetry, and revolution. Revolution is a term that turns many ways. You need(ed) a bodyguard on the ominous streets. More decorous occasions, sponsored by banks and restaurants. Her passport is carefully scrutinized in all directions of space. Poetry aficionado teen fans share their tequila and marijuana at the decimated beach. They all bask in the sun. Or "surrogate mother" is a better description for her role to Che in the actual Robert Creeley dream. Like the boys she dreams she looks after in the large compound in the ancillary dream, they count upon her savvy. Her son is writing a paper on Hugo Chavez. "Is he a good guy or a bad guy, Mom?" She brings home a statue of María Lionza and will pray to her for nuclear disarmament and the "reembodiment" of Che. She thought We need a Robert Creeley to reclaim his daughters. That would be most wise. We need a William Burroughs to describe the addiction to power, to oil, to ideology in this increasingly bifurcated world of euphemism, lies, gulag torture, the radical symmetry of displacement, as the twist of bodies burn, turn in the wind. Waterboarding? The whole world is watching. But is it. Is Homeland watching? Who calls themselves Homeland? Watching the mudslides? She interviews Ernesto Cardenal, who speaks of the Kingdom of Heaven. As for Chavez: he will wear out his sound.

*planets
will fly
    from
their
spheres
    and
an alembic*

> *oil lamp*
> *flickers*
> *emblematically*
>   *in the*
> *beauty world*

he said, somber now, sobered now, from a torture site——

    & she said: *out of what charnel ground do you rise now to tell me this?*

This was a full blue/gray jacket
This was a uniform of control
This was a working family
The blue line held work
The lone blue line held teal, held maroon
The gray held a crown of subtlety
There was no need for royalty here
Lineage was dangerous, reeks of privilege, of scorn
The intellect kept dreamy, kept dreaming
Or did it?
Red ink, right hand, to ink you away
Red ink against you to make deportation
To mark you for your life
In spite of beautiful gaze of where you are from
which is vast, where you are from:
the skyline . . . the orchard . . . the alley
the camp . . . the road . . . the desert
Whole anthropological worlds
Where is the intellect from?
Is it green?
The color of sunset, of straw?
What other world is it?
How may I get there?
How far away is it from here?
Trapped in Guantánamo in a dead zone
How far in yellow? In mauve?
This was an orange monkey suit
This was a lone white towel
This was a cup of water, of dark gruel

This was a wire cage
This was not a colorful rug for prayer
Cold . . . bare . . . ground

   & she, the oracle, said Muster men for war . . .

pick up the phrase "muster men for war"

where relationships are fluid
   marked by time spent in cages

or fire-booting on the fringes of civilization

   hot war, calculated terror, pyramid of severed human heads

this Tartar life, an endless siege

& tall soft boots
   & he wore a tunic
   when in the east the steppe is higher
& a long belted coat
   quilted, or fur-lined
& if one felt if he were a Scythian he could be that for you
   a turban against the summer sun
   come up a steppe, come up
& rode a small horse
   rather a pony hardier than a horse
& fought from that horse
   with efficient bow
     on the left
& arrows
   in a quiver on the right
if he is rich, this one, held sword or saber
but never underestimate the power of the bow

   have brought
me
back
to my
self

a bow—tune that string

his?

untune that string

alive
for a
night

picture him, the wastes of
him

down his power
where whirring
abuts
demand

someone
somewhere
nullifies
a taut treaty
someone
somewhere
unsignifies a
weapons ban
a goal,
a basket,
a score,
a genetic assist
for what purpose?
no hidden agenda please
keep
power ethics
out in the open
where we try to sleep but can't oh can't sleep

in the different
time zones bodies hold . . .

Dear Professor Waldman:

I am trying to notify you about the service re-call to Iraq. Seems my
wounded-in-action status is low. Can the school lawyers help?
I need to spend my life in poetry not on the killing fields.

Love,
X.

            A weapon whose spine's a
cordillera of pleasure: taut bow
like fine lady's curve it would be
mantilla, mons veneris might be
        troubairitz left old Scythian Nueva York
            coast for
"come to it on top of it body to gloat, to sing"
            would be   that it could
come round to humble a mighty Olson
                in jagged jest
points are obstacles are collateral damage
    breasts of goddesses, pricks of demons
no playground for fun-hogs but
    bomb clusters that shatter illusion
for 21st century's pop-up glamour, an suv beam
    shows you happy not to be beachfront
above the earthquake you
    come to breathe among & it is
    woman's pride dark Latina perpetuity
or bright exposure the animals course
    over those shy ruins for
dusted with power & named thus:

((((((((((((((AGAPE))))))))))))))))

with pieces of the jungle still
lodged in their mouths

& the dead step into
a New World

Anne: I'm thinking about encounters that need more time, more Spanish. A few days won't work, it's just a lot of stress traveling, which is interesting but quite abstract because you never find time to root yourself. I think, regarding my intense journey to South America, that I discovered something, which is spirit, that is in favor of the spirit of Dr. Ernesto Guevara Lynch, born in Rosario in 1928, died in the mountains of Bolivia, somewhere, shot, in 1967. With 39 years, very thin, ascetic, asthmatic. Some writers in Rosario said that "el Che" had the feeling of being another juvenile, revolutionary, communist Jesus.

In the recent years I read some of his books—Che was a very good prose writer. His account on the Cuban Revolution, which I read a couple of years ago, is the best book on this history by anyone. Clear, no eulogy, just an intense comment of what really happened in the Sierra Maestra in Cuba.

For me it is also strange that I looked for the house in Rosario where he had spent his childhood, Calle Entre Rios 480. There is no plaque in honor of this. The Italian poet Claudio Pozzani remarked, because I visited the house with him and the historian Eloísa Rodenas, that it is interesting that the great revolutionaries of the 20th century came from good middle-class or bourgeois families, and the real men in power came from the lower class, be it fascists or communists or North American imperialists. Right now I'm feeling lost anyway. Do I belong to here, Austria, Central Europe? I felt much more in time and space 2 weeks ago, in intense talks with friendly fellow poets in Argentina. It seems that poets have to be lost.

Best, B.

Che said "grinding poverty"
the drive around Avila
bulk of a mountain
granite manatee
separates a city from the sea
that year ago I was
bereft of love

& many good poets dead

what century got stuck?

& we got
ripped at the beach &
on more tequila
dear hopes-of-the-future: come
out in the sun
you are so young under this sun
sand still lodged
in your sexy underwear
as one looked up to see
the
stricken the
homeless
&
tin roofs
the dwellings like so many . . .
torrential rains . . .
mudslides . . .

and I said to him, asked him, another Ernesto, as a radical Catholic priest who has practiced "liberation theology" and was stripped of religious authority and "declared an outlaw," could he say something please about how faith was sustaining him in the dark times

and he said *I believe capitalism will end because it is an unjust system, and because the laws of evolution are about more and more union, more and more love among our species. Particles unite to form the atom, atoms unite to form the molecule, molecules unite to form the organism, organisms unite to form the society. And society, for some time now, tries to have less and less inequality. We overcame slavery and feudalism, and now it's time to overcome capitalism. Later on we'll surpass socialism too. Then we'll have a perfect system. Then we will be in the Kingdom of Heaven. In a poem of mine I say that communism and the Kingdom of Heaven are the same. This faith sustains me both as a Christian and as a Revolutionary. I believe in God's Reign, that is—equality—as well as I believe in the social revolution. The expression "Kingdom of Heaven" in Jesus's time meant exactly what the word revolution means now. It was equally subversive. The prophets had announced a new reign but it wasn't subversive since it was to be in the future. Subversive is announcing that it will happen in the present, as Jesus did, and they killed him . . .*

Carib, Arawak, & Chibcha
& Timote-Cuica dwelled here

irrigation & terracing advanced

    stepped into
the new world

                                        Never have I heard or

                                                  r

    e

    a

    d

    o

    f

    o

    r

    d

    r

    u

    n

    k

                                                        o

                                                        f

                                                        s
                                                        o
                                    much sweet water

                    within a

                          salt ocean

wide mouth of
the Rio Orinoco

El Mar Dulce
Golfo de Paria

Lago Maracaibo

the Indians living in thatch
on stilts

"Little Venice" we call it

caudillos

largest exporter of oil on which YOU depend
(arrow points down)
        ↓

Caracazo

warplanes between skyscrapers

Remember:

Battle of Boyaca
Battle of Carabobo 24 June 1821
Battle of Pichincha

Gran Colombia
El Libertador

bosque nublado
araguaney
petroglyphs
joropo
harp cuatro & maracas
　　salsa, merengue ·
(handsome Santos out on the dance floor)

aqui y ahora

　　　　　　　　　　　　　the cult of Maria Lionza
　　　　　　　　symbol of harmonious *mestizaje,* her name at
　　　　　　　　　　　　every door, the mythic
　　　　　　　　　　　　soft lettered identity
　　　　although she is from the mountain of Sorte in Yaracuy
　　& is the highest deity in an altar of three, which includes
　　　　　Guaicaipuro (Native chief murdered by the Spanish
　　　& el Negro Felipe (slave murdered by white masters)
　　　　　　　　　she is alive amongst the large influxes of
　　　　　　　　　　　Cuban and Haitian immigrants as
　　well as arriving with the migrations of Venezuelan farmers
　　　　　　　　　　　　　　　　　　　to the
　　　　　　　　　oil industries in the cities . . .

　　　　　　　　　　　　　　　　　　so goes it:
a Caquetio Indian chief's daughter born with green eyes, a bad sign (evil eye),
　　　he takes her to a lake and gives her to the anaconda but she rises
　　　　　from the lake surrounded by many plants and animals

　　　　　　　　　　　　　　　　　　　　or
if she saw her reflection a monstrous snake would come bringing death and destruction
　　　　　so the father hid her and she had twenty-two guardians

　　　　　　　　　　　　　　　　　　　　or
　　　as the girl "Yara" she meets with Ponce de Leon using the name
Maria del Prado, but failed to dissuade him from his conquering mode

— 805 —

or

"she grew up among the animals of the forest until
one day she was attracted by a strange light and disappeared"

or as

Maria de la Onza, white, she becomes Mary riding the Boar (onza)

& is she hiding her own murder? in double transference theory?

shapeshifter, she becomes a queen but she can also become a snake or a diplomat

she helps you go into trance, become possessed,
shaman (banco) will put you in touch with her . . .

who is she?

syncretic Maria driven by virgin lust on the left-hand path

who can "trance" your "property" in day glow
   who is your quotidian shaman?
   a candle between your eyes
   in a cell phone
     a virtual address

why do they keep sending the bill
here?

what's the next obligation to
   start a pacifist nomad's day?

a report on bird
      migration's
navigational device
"thought they might head south
over water"

but
turned east
over a shiny new gulag
from "rendition"

as in
render me
    delusional
render me cruel
        abducted off the street one chill day

a small prison your mind's in
        sings for light (south as in Guantánamo)
I won't confess anything but:
holy land, holy metallic strife

In 1553 Princess Magdalena daughter of the ruler Cisijopi
donated to the Dominicans:
"The salt beds of Tehuantepec, her fields, a fruit orchard half
a league in length, her recreational baths with crystal springs
that water the orchard . . ."

what prize
what enterprise
& did the holy fathers
luxuriate in those crystal baths?

did conquistadores
gorge on papaya of
the new world?

and do we travel more than half a league
to plant our grapes, lemons, rubber trees
economics?

& do we still "toil in the vineyard"?

coveted fruits of
    a brave new world
only the
Zapotec women
go to market
snarling "marimba teeth!

marimba teeth!"
their insult at the men . . .

those conquerors,
gardeners who chew and masticate
the spoils for a colonial, a "spiritual"
agenda?
fruits of men
one ageless moon
an abandoned orchard
earthquakes and mudslides in another century
what is reaped? what is sowed?

Yet it was a time for cities
and cities existed
Cities were, by rigor of happenstance
and agreement, ambitious
The founding fathers needed them
A language of "city" showed up
Cities were friendly, positive
Metallurgy arrived and
the wheel came rolling in
The marketplace was born
and anything you could ever want
was there for you
and anyone you could ever hope
to speak with in the language of city
was sitting next to you
Companions you
might walk with
in the nascent parks
or on sunny boulevards
or in the factory cafeterias
(oil on our hands)
(*sun shine down now*)
But did the founding mothers need them?

XIII

ELEVEN FACES ONE THOUSAND ARMS

Meld these lines. The East Coast train down from Buffalo, the bullet train with Ambrose, Tokyo to Kyoto, passing Mt. Fuji, now converging in the memorials of 9/11 in Italy and meditations on the polis and groves of Arkady. Superimpositions of all these passages. The notion of motion in Noh theatre, the countless activities of the 1,001 wooden bodhisattvas, an army of them—as in the tracks of our tears—give solace here. How many tracks do you travel? Dogtown to Fox Shrine to Dondona. Mount the stage as we cede to all the branches of our assimilated poetics. Zukofsky the most complete in "A"-12.

So goes: first, *shape (we mark this always)*
The creation—*(this is it, poem came to be as came to be language)*
A mist from the earth, *(Sybil's care)*
The whole face of the ground; *(all cracks & fissures)*
The *rhythm*—*(I had it in womb)*
And breathed breath of life; *(born before language)*
Then *style*—*(function of synchronicity)*
That from the eye its function takes—
"taste" we say—a living soul. *(rasa of many flavors)*
First glyph; then syllabary, *(the first dot in space & more to say of gestures, the first syllables)*
Then letters. Ratio after
Eyes, tale in sound. First, dance. Then
Voice. First, body—to be seen and to pulse
Happening together. *(we will happen our whole long lives in poetry together)*
Before the void there was
Neither being nor non-being;
Desire, came warmth,
Or which, first? *(something noticed itself moving)*
Until the sages looked in their hearts
For the kinship of what is in what is not.
Or in the heart or in the head?
Quire after over three millennia. *(inquire, start now)*

Doubt did I doubt what did I doubt a circle or a cloud or a raw mix, cameras in the trees, what did the Pleistocene say about the notion of Pleistocene? (Am I one of those? was what the Pleistocene said.) No such think-pursuit as "just" no such problem as "just," just what you make of it individually with your compromised ethics and rehabilitation plan, not your quaint Victorian Pleistocene trying to walk a straight line. Rhetorical devices being as shards are, as middens are, the Cold War gestures are still coming, freezing us half to death as rhetoric is, did I not doubt that this work could scar the western world half to death with its relics? But what is "just" what is "doubt"? I did doubt gender in any passing literary indeterminacy's irony as an old page (scribed, layered by the night and candle, by the oil of resilience) did doubt itself as myself representing "person" "poet" and as person better dare to be part of the history of my time. We were preoccupied with the problems of the city-states. Me too, me too. And Hiroshima? And Lebanon? New Orleans? Fallujah? Dante puts Mohammed in Hell, how damned careless of him. . . . We traveled as our own army of compassion in this mounting montage.

Farewell, my friends, I send you this honey mixed with white milk

Or Arab poetics shifting and becoming modern in the eighth century. How you want it, early or late? Manly or queenly? Internal or external? Centripetal or centrifugal? Are we talking about a globe or a planet?

Whatever happened could be most grateful and forever in homage to the epic (Ionian) and the Asiatic that would present tragic and comic dimensions of the human dilemma. I hoped to do that. It was the primordial inclination and composed in such a way for recitation of rhapsodes to raise your temperature. You take my heat?

1. 108 butter lamps lit in the Kathmandu Valley for a father's passing

2. The all-girl Muslim prom in the U.S. of A. faced Mecca and the girls dined on a nice pasta

3. Politically incorrect minister bows at a Shinto shrine

Down with the fathers

How can you . . .

I mean the burden

detritus on the corridor

rails on the backs of men
   As if a spine could be . . .

                      down with them
                      down on them

How to manage a way back
   down

                  meander?

Metropolii   on   the   hirsute   line

DC   Baltimore   Philadelphia   New Haven   Newark   New York

              Boston where we prayed

what did I see when I was then

                    meandering

          their end   their ravage

            their testosterone

down with them

                  cruelty of the plan

  curtsy = duty

       & the paterfamilias form stripped as train jolts

mistakes to reorient rhetoric by

        an industrial rêve

came so surely

    mid-city scrap froth   detritus to spite us
scum
           middens everywhere

clutter   broken stuff   piles of other life forms

   what is it to love a fox?   a spitfire love

more organized, our founders

father's mouth attempts poem

                        Where of protest?

2 white egrets (passing New London now)

      then boats

  pink clouds manifest evanescence so primordial you could weep

signpost what comment?

              What connects this day to any other?

"we you I will all cyborgs be" the green scientist said

in her green scientist's voice

(a secret cell on the quiet railcar told her so)

    & of uranium bullets back to haunt the children dead for their country

down with

this?

bullet train to Kyoto

Bifurcation familiar now, wiles of the patriarch embedded inside
                                    conditions to put up with
There's a way Hélène Cixous deconfigures through the examples of the family or
            machinery's function, wartime karma

rapes in the Congo or unquiet bones of Japanese ancestors

pugnacious with a postmodern Blake-ness
                & blanched white as rice powder

But is this voice speaking merely to a specialized audience?
        can you hear me in the back?

                                    _____
                                    down under?
                behind a screen?

(Hey ho, ghost)
        _____
Inside master iteration shares a common language

                as in *help get me out of here*

    heterogeneity not possible in this Noh play

modest whistle announces

                        coming to arrest

dusk

                                it's coming

in consideration of all systems down: dusk

all pleasures of the u.s. of a. at dusk

sailboats, say

                  or game courts in a Heian dream

Stonington Lumber whose existence is a privilege

                  mansion by the water's edge

could you bet on this as ransom

going cloud, rock, come again

going silver water

scree   bouncy   unpeopled universe traveling over

I said it was certainly dusk

   going of no other haiku mind but dusk

& fluidity of dusk could be warmed by Buddhism

toward you
                as we unwrap our bento boxes, elegant snack on the rails

please talk a little more about this

if you feel up to it

my son:
check on the death of Allende
enter the field of apothecaries

"my leaf" says Ambrose

come l'uom s'etterna, how man makes himself eternal

                              Was it to be in consideration of

    your mother's motherhood undone a heroic turn by entropy's dystopia?

the adaptation of the female, for example

in an interrogation of human *papillomavirus*

when nucleic acid inserts itself into host cells

for an invasion carried in you, poison as fluidity

is never apt

though it alters the normal process of cell division

or protects the innocents

wracked upon these coarse waves

Someone poignant said

"we must feel compassion for our being the remnants of supernovas"

& down with the torturers of innocents . . .

body replaces nerve cells with spirochete tails in the sperm

inward to Dogtown

Pen swap. Who to argue with? An essay on birds. What kind? The Sewage Treatment Plants will assist you in your tribulation to understand antecedents. So what has been built up for you in the hounded text so pointedly worked on all afternoon? What tit for tat? Tit of text tit willow holds attention as a libation of the sense of text. She hooks the reader in. Doing the very thing she does not dare espouse. What is a democratic language? Would we have to begin to be gone in a dare?

Dear Karen,

Unresolved inter-connected-nesses, the need for the ancestor shrines, the way the imagination keeps playing back old (I am still stuck in romantic Heian period with Genji, Sei Shonagon, the sad diary called "Kagero Nikki") yet newly activated images—holocaust/Hiroshima/pachinko parlors. How does all this play here? (Ambrose likes the gaudy gleaming pachinkos, a rattling of coins.) And what to make of it? "do" with it? "Do" anything? Is part of the poet's vow to perpetually catch, distill, refine, reimagine where one walks, what one notices? Plus all the verbal wordplay and associations.

The mysterious Noh plays' court backdrop re-configures
kingship / emperor / god / patriarchal power paradigm,
and also—which is more important—
engages "no action" which is what
goes between the singing, music, stage movements.

The big gap. No action.

"Life and death, past and present—	CHORUS
Marionettes on a toy stage.	(mimicking the sound of crickets)
When the strings are broken,	kiri, hatori, cho, cho
Behold the broken pieces!"	kiri, hatori, cho, cho
	The cricket sews on at his old rags,
	With all the new grass in the field; sho,
	Churr, isho, like the whirr of a loom: churr

—Zeami Motokiyo (b. 1363), author of many Noh plays

Human life transmigrating between life and death.

So based—but remember this is extremely evolved, refined art—on much older shamanic / bardo death rites (which is where I am locating a lot of my work) and confrontation involving encounters like animal spirits. And making/imitating those sounds of the animal. Modal structures. Though I have recently been impersonating robots. But is it all like Kingfisher / wasteland. Are we just always writing in our Culture of Death? The old wounds / yearnings must be healed so the land will thrive? So everything can "go on." My former Naropa student poet Kenji, here, as we were riding the Chuo train line, says emphatically "No more Kings!" which continues this line of theistic thinking re: death, its cycles. Those power mongers sleep with Death, using it all the time to keep us enthralled, in state of perpetual fear. Can we not do that? So I write to get out of my own Empire of Death and Fear which is what I told students last summer. Help! No more margins on this page, the unconditional charnel ground.

Use of what we do? relative to these cultural studies? I often wish I had been a scholarly-hunter archeologist. What is this self-appointed poet job? is it always simple—on one level—react / response mode, which is why I have been so grateful to be out of USA a spell and consequently not so primed to react, spout all the time what everyone in Our Camp knows, constantly replaying the delusion of the Masters of War, their version of reality mimicking, commenting on their euphemistic vocabulary et cetera and recounting my own Nightmares. Vis-à-vis Them. What a bore. Not to ever forget their horrific deeds I will continue to record those in *Iovis III.*

And what will the extraordinary richness of this "culture"—these cultures—which includes praxis religion manners and mores bring? I am obviously excited.

Kyoto: Rampant with syncretic layers. Fox shrine had it in mind back in a time when animals roamed and we were one with them. What is it to love a fox? Brought to mind the rat shrine in Calcutta, the bat shrine in Bali . . . saw/intuit resonance with stuff in Indonesia/Polynesia in the Shinto shrines—the animist/ancestor deal, now unfortunately associated with Japanese nationalism as the prime minister keeps honoring the Shinto place (Yasukuni, in Tokyo) where WWII war criminals are "enshrined," setting off huge controversy.

Most affected by Hall of the 1,001 Kannon bodhisatvas, named "Sanjusangendo," founded originally 1164 AD, rebuilt after a fire in 1266. 390 feet long, 54 feet wide. In the center is the chief image of Kannon (Quan Yin, Avalokitesvara) with eleven faces and one thousand arms, 11.5 feet high. On both sides of him/her stand very close together, ready for "action"—like an army—1,000 more images of Kannon with multiple arms and accoutrements. The idea is an army of compassion.

The rock gardens—raked white pebbles—don't necessarily resemble anything and offer a nice conundrum. Like looking at Abstract Expressionism.

And on.

What are you studying? What does your world look like?

I wish I had a thousand arms.

symbiosis: a 4.6 billion year tradition, telling the day's events, sitting around the sun.

Love,

Anne-Grasping-the-Broom-More-Tightly-Than-Ever-Now

doubt . . . doubt, did I
doubt . . . doubt?

Campaldino: we saw the little toy figures & diorama at Casa di Dante Sept 12

The bolt of green cloth in which I showed myself
No child in armed warfare

A fatwa on Dante

You shall discover how another man's bread tastes of salt . . .

In 1302 joining 16 other white Guelph exiles to plan the invasion of Florence

In the Sixth Sphere of Paradiso you have your Jupiter
The abode of just & merciful kings

Love righteousness, you who are the judges of earth (Wisdom of Solomon)
What of the virtuous heathen?

Operation Noble Eagle
Where the eagle's beak makes rebuking sounds
That never did voice convey nor ink write fantasy to comprehend

Naming animals was a metalinguistic act, and the naming of weaponry in
    those names?

A Psalm for Naming

u.s. Special Forces, 75th Ranger Regiment

Pakistan, Uzbekistan, Tajikistan

Come in Baghram to Quetta

Ultrasecret Delta Force calling itself a "snatchteam," come in, come in

Everybody hates death, fears death. But only those, the believers, who know the life after death and the reward after death, would be the ones who are seeking death.

Continue to pray through the night
Continue to recite the Koran

Power of the Executive to act with criminally violent effects should be exposed, challenged

Freedom of Information Act please to rally around

Tragedy exemplifies & creates the practices of the democratic city

Tragedy is born with the polis

With the tyrant Peisistratos we needed to break the power of the aristocracy & enable democracy to claim its existence as a body of equals

Chiastic is this form of tragedy

The chorus speaks in the elevated metrically eleborate & dictionally archaic forms of lyric poetry . . . . while the characters of tragedies drawn from myth and legend, representing the archaic past, speak in metrical forms of iambic trimeter & use the speech of everyday Athenian life, everyday Japanese

if I may say so   if I may say so   I'll say so

This enables the city to make itself into a theater

Demos + gaies

Hiding the seed under the ear

Sperm' hupo gês kruptousa

She would not let the grain sprout out of the ground

O deltos of her mind

Hebrew daleth or door

Triangle——delta——door

He who comes without the divine madness to the doors of the Muses
      meets without success

She would not let the grain sprout in a desperate time

Now he
Corrupted
That other
Seed
When
Pleasure
(*her face shudders*)
Is warmed
Is feathers
Is quills
Is throbs

A burlesque comedy on the superiority of Western Civ & Christendom

Built on what ashes   It's not working

The stream looks very pretty & pure
& clear & fit for girls to play beside

all ears for the tale of oracle I am telling

the words of the Oak in the holy place of Dordona, shrine to Dione, were the oldest Hellenic divinations. Barefooted princesses listened to the sound of the wind through the trees, as later cauldrons were set on tripods and when the wind blew the cauldrons touching one another emitted a bell-like sound said to be the voice of Zeus.

let the trees speak.   It's not working, Zeus
                                               and that voice becomes a woman's
                                                    Amateratsu out of her cave

olive olea europaea
wayfaring tree
common ash
black gum
alder or buckthorn
(*let the trees speak of depleted oxygen and water*)
Mastic
Holly
Locust
Pinnately-lobed oak
Cypress
& Lombardy
Japanese maples ("Bloodgood," "Crimson Queen")

a world
without contraries
& no progression comes
and sweet and sweet and sweet
finch hand

fragment of a dream . . .
. . . when my rage . . . . . . dear song when my song . . . . architecture of the tree
. . . . Fallujah . . . . . . Chinook . . . when my song could reach my child
and he woke . . . my oak timber, my oracle . . .

let the trees speak with Aphrodite's breath, caustic

XIV

COLORS IN THE MECHANISM OF CONCEALMENT

Go back to another room. You are worried about the future, troops mustered on the borders, the narcotics of consumerism, everyone in their comfort zone (I won't name names), every statistic of every player in the long count at the end of the Mayan performance-dream. The end of the nightmare is when you understand discoloration. You want to paint your time using the deconstructed parts of 15 carrier rockets, the 17 satellites the enemy posits, the tons of ammo, the mega-tones of weaponry designated for all your solar system. You will reconstitute elsewhere but remember the poem tells you you have no enemies and you are part of the "humanizing race." You are digging through the letters of Frances LeFevre Sikelianos, something she carried back from the war a time ago. Serbia collapses. Greece suffers. Later in the day you walk on the tundra considering your life with your new partner. Tundra your Olympus, not antipodes.

What will it be

Be fossils

Strait of Hormuz, thousands of miles

Pumice, the earth tones of artifice

Of generous archive
like the whisker of the walrus
sliced and examined
telling everywhere it has been

Voices: In a muddle about the relative relation of "step" and "half." Who's in step, who's half a portion and if being flirty is an option. It's most imbricative, meaning a map or treelike structure so you know where you are in the so-called chain. Do you break it, are you a link or what? Entangled with the humans.

#1: Hmmm. Does she think she's her sister's sister? Is she available to be noticed as such? Would it be hilarious? You might consult the archive. My mother's Greek past.

#2: She would seem to represent that dimension. They both (she and her mother-in-law) like twilight. And the colors enhancement at that time. They come out of being hidden. 1930s.

#3: But really available? Veil of tears, you now. Caressed, embraced beyond bloodlines.

#1: Well she has the same eyes. Athena's gray and slanted? You can complain about lineage it sounds so blue-blood. Exclusive. Gene pools. I'd rather just compare notes on what people are saying about the House of Waldman and Sikelianos.

#2: It depends how you are raised I suppose. What are they saying?

#3: Dear brave women well there were some went to prison in the Channel Islands for distributing serious antiwar leaflets. They were stepsisters and lovers. I always think circles or advantages. Relative to being close you can feel the heat expand on cool evenings. The bodies seem to feel connected. And they also have sympathetic activities in wartime. That's always a help.

Dear Frances,

There is so much to say that I am going to merely give you an outline and I am going to try to keep emotion out of it. Obviously this has been a winter of suffering without grandeur. My hair is nearly white, but I wouldn't have been anywhere on earth but Greece and, when the time came to leave, when the others left, G and I just couldn't. That is the only explanation of why we are here. It is perhaps not a very good reason and few people except you and Eva will under-stand it. We intended to leave up to nearly the last minute but when it came to a showdown we found that neither of us had really intended and there are many people dependent on us and it may be that there is still the bulk of our work ahead of us. At the moment because the head of the Near East Foundation had confidence in us, we have been left funds with which we are continuing to feed people and the winter is going to be very hard. Of all these past months, April was probably the most decisive for Greece and so I select it to give you an idea of what the newspapers may not have told you. (the dates, approximate.)

On April 1. Continuous air raids at night, shrapnel fell on roof.

April 2. Ship bombed in Piraeus, Eleusis and Tatoi bombed. Alix born in the evening.

April 3. Jugoslavia in confusion. Anxiety felt in Greece. Treason in the army.

April 4. Dr. Mueller, my doctor, a Jew, came to say goodbye. Left for Palestine, for the second time fleeing with his wife and two children from the Nazis. They took only three suitcases. No money, no time to arrange for closing of clinic. Perhaps the most tragic departure we have seen. Terrified, bewildered and hopeless about the future. Their ship bombed and we have never heard that they arrived.

April 5. German army known to be at the frontier. Greek morale excellent and English believed to be ready and prepared.

April 6. Two ammunition ships in Piraeus bombed during air raid. Damage and loss of life tremendous. Continuous air raids. I spent my first night in our shelter with the baby and three children. The cat had kittens in the babies' bed. The children amused and at no time frightened or aware of what was happening. German army left Greece.

April 7. Our English civilian friends evacuated in haste. Many people left the capital. Tension everywhere.

April 8. Refugees, 40 thousand, arrived from Piraeus, under constant bombardment. Many hundreds came to us to be fed and sheltered. The situation was hopeless from the beginning. They slept in open fields under almost constant raiding.

April 9. They continue to come. We cannot cope with the numbers, conditions desperate.

April 10. Salonica evacuated.

April 11. Lines breaking everywhere. English continue evacuating citizens. Secrecy maintained as to when and where convoys are going. Every English civilian simply told to report at Legation every afternoon at five with suitcase and enough food for three days. Sometimes they come back, sometimes they don't.

April 12. Battle of Florina. Air raids continue day and night.

April 13. Prince Paul of Serbia came to visit our "soup kitchen." We didn't dare introduce him to the people, feeling against him so bitter. Visit unfortunate. We had to tell Prince Demidoff to take him away.

April 14. Ships no longer able to use Piraeus harbor which is under constant bombing.

April 15. Wave of optimism. Line seems to be holding.

April 16. Serbia collapses. Greek army in confusion but eager to go on fighting.

April 17. Went to Athens to see people off. Large English convoy left with English and all Americans believed to be in danger, such as the press etc. Almost no one left. Our neighbor who was a cabinet minister left in the night with his wife and two babies on a caique. Another friend left in the same manner but after two hours of bombing was forced back. Of the eighteen friends who left on this day only two have been heard from and are known to be safe.

April 18. Prime Minister committed suicide after interview with King. Olympos Line holding but communications increasingly difficult.

April 19. New government formed, but collapsed a few hours later. Confusion and chaos. The people can't understand why things are going badly. They had such faith in the English. A miracle expected.

Peloponnisos is literally strewn with the wreckage abandoned in the evacuation. A nurse who came by train from Patras tells me that her hospital train was held up.

Tonight the British are coming over in waves. There are huge fires at Tatoi. We haven't had a raid since the last full moon and I'd forgotten what they are like. There is something appalling, satanic about it. Fires on three mountains, a high wind blowing, where and when will it end? And when will it begin again?

I hate to see the Greeks ruined further, even by the British. The loss of life tonight will be tremendous, it is one of the worst raids of the war

It seems that the United States isn't giving visas to any foreigner, which means that many American women are remaining here because their Greek husbands are not allowed in America. It's shameful and ought to be changed. Tell Eva to try to do something. Love, J.

& join in the Sprechstimme:

=freeze then in the universe of Minoan museums=

=cry inhuman=

=freeze in the museum of supplicants=

=no ruins or relics of the future=

=attractive versions and visions=

=was it pre-Patriarchal, the nagging question=

=(was it / was it?) was it pre-Patriarchal?=

[frieze in the museum of supplicants]

=only waste & residues, rest here, rest here=

=Sambhogakaya yr body of light=

=means a space between corporeal & dream=

=capital making more willpower. men do this=

=make more willpower=

=more spheres, more species=

=programmed destruction=

=space is the pact of artifice=

=did you say this?=

=what? what?=

=automate=

=it was a metal contradictory=

=meeting you to do war, do war, if you could ever do anything=

=chimeras, a kind of artifice=

=sing, sing, body of light=

=clones=

=desire a kind of simulacra=

=easier, easier that way=

=not a living woman=

=but I retraced my mother's steps=

=[Remember how I cried to her in Book 1?]
  [I cry to her again now]=

=a dead woman perhaps easier this way=

=easier, easier that way=

=I said no, no, a living woman and not easier that way=

=definitions quirky & personalized to hide, to have hidden=

=childbirth, sing of childbirth in a difficult time=

=hide, hide, hid, hidden in public time=

=entire motor system activated by exposure to sexual images=

=spinal tendons & reflexes=

=before we are conscious brain regions needed to perform an activity
that is already ablaze=

=Amygdala=

=sing of the almond-contoured brain long associated with fear and anger=

=uranium enrichment=

=halt, halt, I say tougher tougher sanctions=

=southern city of Bushehr keep on your radar=

=and stop the fight over euros or dollars=

=hundreds of millions of people didn't have enough water=

=John Cage would say this simply: have not enough water=

=earth reels from rising temperatures & sea levels=

=earth reels & reels, not an even keel have not enough water=

=tens of millions are flooded out of their homes=

=polar bears will only exist in zoos by 2050=

=hundreds of millions will face starvation in 2080=

=changes in climate affecting physical and biological systems will occur on every continent=

=no doubt this will occur, will occur=

=don't want it to, this a warning=

=changes in species habitat will occur, will occur=

=acidified oceans=

=loss of wetlands=

=bleaching of coral reefs=

=hurricanes & wildfires=

=poor sectors will be most affected=

=Anne Waldman is saying these poor sectors will be most affected=

=mass extinction of species=

=hundreds of millions of Africans will be short of water in 20 years=

=& tens of millions of Latin Americans will be short of water in 20 years=

=by 2050, a billion people in Asia could face water shortages=

=death rates will rise in poorer countries by 2030=

=Europe's small glaciers will disappear=

=& many countries large glaciers shrinking by 2050=

=will I live to see this? No=

=Anne Waldman is crying for her mother, long dead=

=sadly, no, no=

=half of Europe's plant species could be vulnerable, endangered, or extinct=

=sycamore trees slow down emission of carbon dioxide=

=levees break=

=greatest strategic prize in the history of the world—control of the oil & energy resources=

=Exxon 36 billion net=

=we call it Oil-gardening=

=war machine feeds off the conflict=

=let's call it military industrial media complex gardening=

=Israel has 200 nuclear weapons=

=because I'm so enthusiastic on this logopoeia=

=trance state called "the swimmer"=

=notice lidded vessel with peccary feet & cormorant knob=

=notice a stoneware jaw=

=turtle shell lid hums to me here=

=notice five zoomorphs!=

=how I need them, zoomorphs!=

=notice fine crab claw motif=

=arrogant bird named Wuqub' Kakix=

=maize god with flowing silken hair=

=(my vision: serpent ritual dance)=

=(my vision: ancestral face on a divination mirror)=

=(my vision: a hematite)=

=(or jaguar figure with hieroglyphic text)=

"ik'" signs refer to wind, breath, or soul-force

=obsidian=
=flint=
=pyrite=
=jade=
=conch shell with cinnabar=
=ik! ik!=

=*plumed jaguar about to devour a human heart*=

=volcanic glass ear flares=

=dressed like Tlalock=

=ascending the Pyramid of the Moon=

"och bih"

he enters the road

eccentric flint

trumpet conch of cinnabar

he enters the road

Tikal

Funerary mask

Chuhkaj—*he is seized he is roped*

Apotheosis

Yellow & white maize & their own blood

Jadeite

(note: warriors shared the predatory status of big cats, raptorial birds, &
venomous snakes)

She enters the road

> This was part of the seen/unseen project
> Lest you not forget the binaries
>
> Lest you not forget counter-memory
> Or hybrid, or family/history

A fish basket address named Kannon

A fish basket named Guanyin, lest you forget

Layman Pang's upright daughter, lest you forget

A barefoot beauty, lest you let her lie foregone

This is everything, this is nothing, this is not a conclusion

I also could *not* become a phoenix.

I gasped at colors, at feathers

Afraid of the phoenix? Afraid she will rise?

Is my evolution in doubt?

Darwin show at the Museum of Natural History couldn't get corporate sponsors . . .

Creationists rule the day

Although "avant gardening" could

Ginko

Ground's
Crisp curve
Tends phenomenological Sumer
Blades will fall
Blades do fall

Devil's Thumb shot off g spot
Pricked a tidy ground

=Metabolic=

= I will be your metabolic architect in the truth of painting=

=had some ideas=

=o yes, had some ideas=

Documentary cities
The form of your work as the figure of your truth

Back to Saqqara 2700 BCE

Back to Imhoteph
& the laws of form

What's this anti-intellectual light of no mind?
back to

=Power & dispossession=

=Colonial rule=

=Rarely direct overt or literal=

=Demonized=

=Mooresque=

=or Arabesque=

=try prelapsarian mother=

=Allegorically a "centaur"=

=Hip-hop releasing capital's grip=

=Hip-hop a centaur=

=inversion, systemic=

=disproportional=

=the viewer is no longer coerced=

Collapse of time &/space
I witnessed the Berlin Wall
The stitching within the curtain

I witnessed coercion

I witnessed gender divide

=Colonial skyscrapers on aboriginal land=

=Montage as resistance=

=Reinventing forming as we see things=

=Cross-pollinated language=

=Petra to Dunkirk=

=The Soft on Terror Notebooks=

=Cherish it, it was not always so soft=

Paris a bit softer, terminal, the trellises
Walked on plenty there

There was a soft on terror house call it
"the wronged-eyed Jesus"

In the timberline
In the tambourine
A soft on terror fashion
Inviting the stars

Having the means of production

Alternative space for alternative discourse

=Language is a policy=

=Language is a bookmaker=

=Language is my seductive imperialism=

Language is supremely white

Facile ablatives
Code words
Language is the conduit
War is the action
Rendered is the crime
Slave trade, by whom, masques intact
Ornately
Sun sets on the British empire

Downsized, outsourced violate & compromise national security

Creed
Homophobic

Ignorance/coercion

A penitent St. J
Overcome your flesh by fasting
Fra Angelico 1419-20

Master of the Tiburtine Sibyl

Language is shifty

Dearest Eleni-mou—

"Beauty & Insomnia"—that was a pretty title for something because I also have beautiful
thoughts when I can't sleep—

These were the ideas I had in the event in the sure information that the word "tundra" derives
from the Finnish word for "treeless." Well you have to be up in Colorado to feel this business
of "without trees" or "above the treeline" . . . come visit up here, and soon.

Are you less grounded without a tree that's to consider and if you are, why, how cruel you
(I'm talking to myself here) often seem to trees in the rugged landscape. Not cruel, negligent.
Are you fighting for them in all the ways they are captured and slaughtered? Seeing them, yes,
but understanding? The tundra is the simplest biome. And as it goes above the trees, you

might think that the trees are holding up the tundra. That would be a pretty image. It's a short life for growing—6–10 weeks. Let the trees speak.

Of course this was once very much an ocean. I saw a purple seashell upon a mount.

What you are having here and must be careful not to step upon is fragile in so very delicate ground-hugging and warm-preserving forms. You might see dwarf shrubs or rosettes or mat or cushion plants. Very motherly sounding if you are considering something about a female. Here you have long and cold winters and strong and impish, driving winds. And even snow would help as an insulating layer for those plant and animals realms that seem to want to live here. We could try it. It is a place where a thin membrane exists between living and dying, and to go on living—if you could—if it wasn't prohibitive—you would be seeing that this form that is delicate, even wordless but not antisocial and even raging to live—like a newborn— seems struggling very hard. Very pink. Very brown. Colors of what washed out of a body.

—Haven't you done enough about the French in this poem? someone asked.

—I thought I came from Greek, I said.

—I thought rather Finnish. If you knew some of the poetry the light would travel.

—Really? How? Africa?

—Well it does if it's read properly, the right air and light might breeze and shine through the window . . .

—But I don't know Finnish!

—Let me finish. It's more visceral, the words will not only carry the memories of war vigilance, national pride but . . . light . . . some are illusive idylls written in mellifluous verse. There's light on water, on potted plants, on small children sleeping, it just permeates everything—& we're talking about the late-night light . . . Poetry loves late at night.

—There's a ballad called "Ylermi" that seems to be about a superman or a proud knight or some such. You can bet he stayed up all night.

—Well I'm not sure we need more of that.

—But then there was a move toward pessimism if you prefer.

—I'm not sure. Pessimism is hard.

—Yes, well pessimism can always creep into poetry. That's just how it is. Alienation, loneliness. You can't get around it.

—Well there's also flaming erotic stuff I would hope . . .

—No doubt. I'll start my search.

—Drawing-in-broom-to-bosom more closely now

—And here is the speech to be heard from the Tundra

1. The tundra is the simplest biome
    Holding swelling relatively holding and with grounding of form that
2. Would in slightest cruelty be afflicted if it were to us
3. To us and ours, if it were to us to be what is holding and having
4. Walking upon
5. Walking on or in or upon
6. Trees holding up tundra, which is above them always
    Could tundra sway could a tundra inhabit any other zone

& it might be finished in a word that translates as "treeless"

what you are having here continually is a short season in growing or of growing is
a reason is tundra, is terrifying to be that small and holding up so much of air

slaughtered saying of something so small not so reckless as a couple of humans

humans standing reckless or contained

maybe not so close but vulnerable because they speak in speech walking

six weeks to grow to live to continue and hide under our speech holding them

someone walks someone exits

someone leaves you musn't count them out

rosette or mat plants or cushion plants don't take them lightly

long winters and cold and driving winds

thin membrane between death or life or life in death

you better know.

       Love, A.

XV

SKY-GOER

Kadro in Tibetan means "sky-goer." The Sanskrit term is dakini *and is understood as a feminine principle that may appear as a human being, a goddess—wrathful or peaceful—or as the play of energy in the phenomenal world. Tibetan Buddhism speaks of a language described as "the secret signs and letters of the dakini," and another that is a secret code of tantric terminology referred to as "twilight" language. The oral teachings are sometimes referred to as "dakini's breath." An exceedingly symbolic cipher, many volumes could emerge from very few letters. Whole teachings are condensed into single seed-syllables and hidden in the earth, in rivers, in trees, in cloud formations, or in the mind of the adept. "In diamond rocks, in mysterious lakes and unchanging boxes," as one description goes. Specific practices encourage the practitioner to join with the energy of the dakini and unlock the runes that travel beyond dualistic boundaries. Suffering is ego's failure to control situations to make them "mine" and perpetuates the fantasy of solid self that is, as one discovers, an illusion. The dakini fearlessly cuts through the static. She doesn't own anything. She playfully consorts with you and can turn on a dime if you are too attached. Fixation is the wrathful dakini. Here out of hypnogogic poem-sound what might ensue: or a game.*

Dear H.—
Feminafesto: Plurality

Concerning your desire to relocate in the new century.

Plurality: begins with a series of questions. What are the implications of the new information world? How will we manage our diminishing fossil fuel? Our diminishing civil liberties? Who will be "in charge?" What are the shifting paradigms the world faces? What is the New World Order that seeks to control whole populaces, governments, theocracies, plutocracies? Can any artist, in fact, create, muster energy toward an act of beauty after atrocity? What is the ignorance about history that does not face the truth of its own karmic nightmare? Or does not experience the urgency of the call to struggle for peace, justice, humanity? How can we—privileged—educated—relieve the suffering of "other" of "others"? How does one respond on behalf of other? What is the "other" in us? The plurality in us? After 9/11 Arundhati Roy said to the u.s.: "Welcome to the world." The charnel ground of Ground Zero, with its amalgam of individuals of copious background, was extremely vivid in its plurality. It also showed the way that people, whether they realize it or not, are working in tandem with others, in fact they may be working at jobs that are contributing to the suffering of others. The destructions brought to mind the killing fields of Cambodia, the slaughter of Rwanda, Srebrenica, and images of conflict everywhere, elsewhere.

"The sacrificed others" in Jean Baudrillard's sense?

The brutal violence in countless "other"—realities go abstract, for the most part, in the American mind. But it also created a backlash, a desperate sense of "revenge." What a rare opportunity to wake up, in fact, to become part of the world—instead it was used as an excuse, for America, in its own suspect and illegitimate governance, to become more isolated, ignorant, arrogant, more barbaric, greedier. Many millions have protested the wars in Afghanistan and Iraq. This latest war (this "eternal war") has shown people are more connected in their struggle now than ever before. I found myself in contact constantly with "others" all over the world in protest. And I found myself writing letters of protest to the embassies of other countries. Yet there is a kind of death wish in the land as a child in Africa dies of malaria every thirty seconds. As the weaponry created for "the eternal war scenario" grows crueler—the horrific daisy cutter that cuts apart its victims with incredible and unbearable pressure and brutality. The psychological suffering, in fact the wounded psyche all around is real.

Post-traumatic stress syndrome is palpable. Our dreams and nightmares vent our fear and confusion all the time. There is a sense of plurality vs. dominance. The u.s. of a. is the single largest producer of greenhouse emissions, generating twenty percent of the global total.

Who rules and why?

Might Henry Kissinger ever be brought to trial for the secret bombing of Cambodia? How many generations for the Hutu & Tutsi to find resolution and so on. Nearly 400 billion in the Pentagon budget that proposes cleaner—even more unmanned—"weapons of mass destruction." We have our Yucca Mountain in the u.s.—a volcanic ridge in the desert 100 miles Northwest of Las Vegas as the current favored burial spot for radioactive waste, which will be dangerously radioactive for hundreds of thousands of years.

A report indicated with some satisfaction that leakage will be strictly limited to 10,000 years! They must be dreaming. The movies and media continue to glamorize war. One most egregious example in the past decade, remember the movie *Black Hawk Down,* which recounts the u.s. Special Forces action in Mogadishu in which eighteen Americans died and several thousand Somalis. Referred to the Somalis as "skinnies." You see the same computerized shot of the abstracted "other" over and over again—the "skinny" being hit and crumbling. There's a strange sadism here. There's the "manufacturing of consent" in Chomsky's term about other. The oft-repeated degraded images of Iraqi people looting and pillaging—another example of the dehumanizing agenda of corporate-media-thug rule.

And meanwhile the increasingly fragile ecosystem, which contains multiple pluralities, trembles underfoot to a greater degree as the smoke of shock and awe clears. Where is our "practice of the wild"? Where is the etiquette of human and "other"? Toward all the denizens, pluralities of the world. The world is listing as we consume more and more baubles and create and hawk and sell more weapons of mass destruction. Hawk and awe.

The avant-garde, experimental poetry communities operating outside the mainstream of official academic and well-funded institutions, have always functioned along the lines of a "gift economy." I borrow the sense of this term from French anthropologist and socialist Marcel Mauss, often considered the father of modern French anthropology. His most influential work is *Essai sur le Don,* follows the forms and functions of exchange in archaic society. We are far from archaic but I think some of the paradigms still hold.

He writes how the "giver does not merely give an object but gives part of himself, the object is indissolubly tied to the giver" . . . "The objects are never merely separated from the men who exchange them." Because of this bond between giver and gift the act of giving creates a social bond with an obligation to reciprocate on the part of the recipient. He asks: "What power resides in the object that causes its recipient to pay it back?" There's also the notion of "inalienability." In a commodity economy there is a strong distinction between objects and persons through the notion of private property. Objects are sold, meaning that the ownership rights are transferred to the new owner. The object becomes "alienated" from its original owner. In a gift economy the objects are unalienated from the givers. They are loaned rather than sold and ceded. Gift exchange therefore leads to a mutual interdependence between giver and receiver. According to Mauss, the free gift that is not returned is a contradiction because it cannot create social ties. His argument is that solidarity is achieved through social bonds created by gift exchange. This has certainly been true of bohemian artists' cultures.

The non-income-based work that poets do (check out Diana di Prima's "By Any Means Necessary" talk). The spiritual, ethical inclination. The poem is not a commodity—you give it away and it carries part of you with it. Midcentury, rents were cheap. San Francisco was a "refuge city," as was NYC. Now you need to find new models of ethos and exchange. The makers of the work seek out the means to maintain and fortify their independence.

But I urge you forward. And finish high school!

Love, A.

Plurality: what is your ethos, what is your economy?

the commentary: read on

the rune:
(secret signs & letters that came in a dream. Abdicate!)

agr	(bright sky)
ess	(fire light)
gra	(gratitude)
tu	(you)
af	(aft)
fin	(end)
lo	(lo)
kol	(close, the rock, the ground)
or *spi*	(the liquid ground)
or *spra*	(lift)
pru	(wait, safe)
ec-it	(plant it)
gio	(almost day)
gyo	(glow)
esx	(anger)
ttt	(pointing anger)
ul!	(ultimate anger)
or	
ist	(let go, it is)
mta	(mate, matter)

mma	(mother matter)
or *lapst*	(left)
mya	(matter missing)
or	
gnb	(glib)
or	
skv	(up, attainment)
dpt	(up from shoulder, attainment)
ble	(wheat)
stt	(stiffen)
oom	(more & lifting)
ot	(you & I, tears, crystal)

twilight:
(unadorned)

eath   ng   lo   *or* sca   ni   xp   scre-ish!
su-esc   *or*   ill   uct   ghy   nde   ow
ng   sm   av   nc   s   *or*   ro   ryf   .str
cliu ksh   rys   me-wa   *or* rsd   ch-hee!

images:

(eagle-headed
crow-headed
lion-headed
tiger-headed
bull-headed
buffalo-headed)

the translation:

breath tightens a made-up birth, a made-up poem
anger, what is that?
plot? save the Kerouac School Archive
pearls scatter about the feet of the made-up poem
small pearls in which you intuit the universe
contract & expand, many
luminescent eyeballs of fish,
treasures for the mind, prescient, anoint them, their desires
a thousand pores filled with eyes like glittering stars
seductive glance lifts off the page-edge
what I saw in the twilight was
The Grievous Decider
coming toward me, an obstacle
"I" and "other," stranger
was anger was desire
was stranger anger, why does he get to decide?
was metabolic design of anger's doom
was wave as in "wave away"
was in trance of yell & push & scream
was a book of many angry eyes in dream
& in the anger-room both fierce & quiet
a story faces a tigress & responds
& she wants to preserve the making of what she loves
~~declines in narration of all of it ago in a story~~
~~the way you yourself broke apart, shattered~~
~~& crystal is a word for it to wish & let go~~
~~came clear of water was loud words of water~~
& tears down her cheeks in syllables, weighted, and digitized

Archive, with the face of a lamb . . .

XVI

DARK ARCANA:
AFTERIMAGE OR GLOW

wouldn't you travel too to a country with a
Temple of Literature?

It seemed timely being close by on a job in Indonesia to make pilgrimage to North Viet Nam.
Whatever these journal scratches they could never match the haunting of Hanoi. But so many of my
generation perished throughout its country, perished all sides. Few citizens over twenty-five years
old. Optimism prevails in spite of old karma. The sense is not to diminish brutal fact of decimating
war, rather the reality of a still-heated unsettled spot. I felt feverish there. As one young friend born
after the war says: We have to move forward, on from war. It is too sad or we die. But it is neces-
sary to appease the demons with dark offerings.

what it is like. to be
old soldier American.
unnavigable.

mimetic ornament.

uttered from exotica's raft phase.

suffering suffering

what is it like

graphomania.

the itch to

surround.

as lovers. conquerors

like pelagic zone.

deep in the other how far you go as idiom

you might go as idiom. be gone & then out of it again, idiom

solid. the

ambassador?   an agendas-only kind of guy
he never spoke the language
never adored the people

angularity of global talk

the sawtooth *communistas*

she never saw nobly

all doors not open. but a

head bowed in pagoda time is never enough.

what is it like to be colonial?

laughing in pagoda time.
or wrestle with desire.

        as she does here, "to heal, to heal!"

in crisis in contra-ity
       she has, investigatively speaking:
              a quenchless thirst

necessary to be humble.

rectilinear, start over in an old building
    on knees
        not prayer

wanting to see the psychological architecture of

unsnarling karma

      what is it. to resemble a child.

prismatic relief systems

      rondure. flexed to Buddha
      [small rite inserted here:
      light incense
      bow three times
      take a
      photograph]

deep sea trenches such as

Ramapo Deep
Java or Sunda Trench
Ryukyu Trench
or Yap
        give pause.

for consociational facts build up
           & on the money

driving
    a moneyed frame

while back home it's nothing but power, power, power

                        enter the cant. bifurcated world

of money & remembrance.

to build, build.
                            what?

                    money!

what is it like
to be a destiny of the victor-to-be

    who lost his. her. shirt

                        his. her. land   actually

metaphorically,

in cruel vector.

+++

        the woman is the man isn't the woman isn't the man is
        a revolutionary, flames to be seen

& a child kicks to be freed

but strength is measured in spoons of rice

    to build the Minh Stilt House

(Memorial House)

"House Sing Big"
called
Nha Hat Lon

whole history an opera beyond cosmology

and one must eat: rice

a flame to documenta

longer pause for time.
never enough of it to make amends

                                                          low tide
        how cruel "we" were
how low? what is the system to jungle war

    this low: (points to lake)
what.is.it.like.
                            Toi khong hieu

dongs

a slighted money
doings in a gong world

    cyclo? for my companion

ce n'est pas ici

rags or whathaveyou

why sky is like
what terror underground
what a face tells you of her heroism

what judicatorial

                            say it again judiciously

            "what judicatorial?" gives the right

american.

english.   vietnamese.   what is

a disentitlement like?   how fair might it be?

meted out for the generations.

drives to the water puppet theater
suffers a
        cold war

                                          before liberation.
                              movement. sisterhood
before media culture's
hooded resolve
to dominate all life

standing three feet in its painful hegemony

before
Rice Paddy Man walks toward you
mendicant-like, of language

            articulates
        sputters, old horror

& the sensibility of all shake-off is
precious water
              inestimable.
                    what place is. redemptive beauty

what was it like. it is. it is like it is.
                    it is so and whole
                              of him,
                              a citizen, still suffering.

        her tongue's silken opium drawl
        tongue parches over the whole
        of him. and whole of her.

                Ho Chi Minh in flesh

                    beyond the call of mortal duty

                he rides magnificent

              fresh from embalming touch-up job in Russia

                resides here

              & you are one of them, gawkers. two by two who
              file by

                  march
                              two by two into zen tomb
              you are one bystander. thinker.
                                  seer.

interdigitation   nihil ad rem

in the air-conditioned mausoleum. temple. in the battle. struggle?

                      encaustically embalmed. a foreign devil. old evil one

ho! not bombed away

what is life
in tomb with him
        martyred in eternity?

you make a joke once too often
for the likes
of him. uncle

                  what is she like

          not a hand but hand out
                  on receiving's side

sagacious brow
    upon the girl you left behind in the South

                    or unsung female Cong

                                        she not a hand to her hum
                                              strafed.

                hill-tribe girl
maimed.
excoriated.
          for collusion.

second-caste citizen of hoops,
of woven duds

                    of stuff & more collisions, hum

                        with the agitators

                        mercy mercy

                        & hawkish.

                                        what is it like
                                        to be sympathetically
                                        animist?

awkward stuffs to sell
things not much of which anyone wants
bleak stuffs remain she's awkward   high-cheeked

angular too, got meager stuffs to sell
is global yet in will-tell time is telling a market

a.k.a./time will tell
in all economy.
ubiquitous. chewing gums. trifles in the heat.

                        postcard of a market, quaint. a map.

i.e., of killing fields. trophies of
victory, Ho's star.
red and pulsating.

   made to be
   bound as
toy guns are.
O.K.
not that gun
I'll take one book rather, that one
                            The Quiet American

crepuscular
mum
to please   her.

don't shoot

                    no romantic attachment to "dirty tricks" past
please.

                          mere walk away in your beauty,
      Viet Nam, reticent of all eyes to see

enough that *le pays*

endures.

run down tinge & hint of
conquering styles. most natural dignity

   what was, is, could, be as in "seems" Madam?

            din's no motor   that
            none
            rave in old quarter that
all helions desist.

(it's *over*) (the war is *over*)

thirty-six streets named for the
things manufactured there that date to
thirteenth century

                             in way of gnosis
anciently in all-times-contemporaneous
it. is. like. this. that time heels. presidents come & go.
Wars.
where you are, seated. not China
what you need to buy
sighs like that of filial piety
thru centuries
in collision

     what is it like?
                  to be bestial.
   in a sweet clime.

                    this my schema
this: my diagram
            no, this is a bohat schedule

or a chart of tides
I have no strategy left
I left it at home sitting by a lake with the war

innocent boys died, this I know.

                policymaker mimics the
           husband-hawker-of-wares, tortures a
               sick child,
            a tired old man
         this is the prostitute, he says
            use her.

   her appointment with calamity

                light the pipe . . .
          "soldier poetry" on Zippo lighters:

missing
limbs
miss
the limbs
of
my
love

& over, she's said, it's *over.*

sucking him off.

et cetera, but the war is *over.*

Then she recounts *The Story of the One-Pillar Pagoda / Chua Mot Cot:*

Emperor Ly Thai Tong ruled from 1028 to 1054 & was heirless. What to do? This is unacceptable in a ruler. He dreamed he met the Goddess of Mercy as she sat, radiant, on a lotus flower. She handed him a male child. He woke up and married the first girl he met, who turned into a peasant girl. They had a son.

By way of thanks he built the One-Pillar Pagoda, which you see before you.

The same pillar of wood sits on a stone pagoda and is designed to resemble a lotus blossom, rising out of a sea of sorrow turning to you.

[Note: one of the last acts of the French before quitting Hanoi in 1854 was to destroy the One-Pillar Pagoda, which was rebuilt later.]

[in my mandarin robes tonight]

[you must dismount your horse before entering the Temple of Literature]

[in my madwoman robes tonight]
avenge, avenge says the land
& let me replenish the stores

write, write says the history
  & let me be sung

out on the street again, singing a

story every culture's particulars continue

                    for the next generation.

"Hang" for merchandise

Hang Quat: red candlestick

Hang Gai: silk street

Hang Mai: Counterfeit Street

where imitation ghost money   (shades still wager "cost"
  is sold for burning
in Buddhist ceremonies   (in hell realm? nirvana?

you'll hear ancient tone
    vector of spent money
          as one priest lights a way
back of moon back of street

        what is it like.   moan/moan.   old mothers

intone the dead, the youngest monk sits with a straight spine

                what is it like? what is it like?

observe the clock. worlds within/without worlds

        cosmos rocks us. lands us
in six ten-year cycles
display the ten heavenly stems of the *canh* cycle:

giap   water in nature (everywhere & behind power in rice)

at   water in the home (bend over wooden bowl)

binh   lighted fire (to cool, to warm at the heart of)

dihn   latent fire (embers-under-will-of-people)

mau   wood (carved instrument, chair, buddha)

ky   wood prepared to burn (shelter, food)

canh   metal (the god)

tan   wrought metal (wheel, weapons, sorrow)

nham   virgin land (ur-time, before rape before poison)

quy   cultivated land (sickness, food, life)

so as to get thru to the next historical present.

& so as to be friendly
not hold a grudge
eyes avert

so as to converse
did it get mentioned? how feeble
we protested we never wanted war?

for one cares, and carries guilt.

   nonpareil.

for blessing, your Tao-sent Lord advises:

                your colonial power advises:

protectorship. guardianship. safeguard. palladium. shield. screen.

aegis. umbrella. protective umbrella. care. charge. keep. nurture.

foster. custody. hands. safe hands. auspices. tutelage. guide. ward.

buffer. cushion. pad. padding. protective clothing. safety. anchor.

    dedicated. prisoner of war. another prisoner of war.

dead dead dead+++
pagoda 3 times the ceremony
this and that and this again
3 times & bowing
that this that again

bend 3 times

    "LBJ, LBJ, how many kids did you kill today?"

                        street's

solitude
haunts
of three times ghost.

    money exchange
           or female citizen might walk by in pants only

what is she like?
to be pants-only
shows your side.

        averts eye three times.

resumes task

    veridicality of youth to ponder

old toothless Bones comes

    down the street . . .

Bat Dan: wooden bowls
Bat Su: china bowls
Cha Ca: roasted fish
Chan Cam: stringed instruments
Cho Gao: rice market
the white bearded *Bach Ma*
(temple-guards) sip tea

you can buy a personalized gravestone.
ship it home.

toothless Bones has a daughter
come out
you'd better see it all out here
on me, all over me
don't hide from the napalm

twenty-five years later
scars, come outside.

tiny
at side
to be outside

star-on-flag
photo of Che everywhere

                              napalm without rapprochement?

without "new seed"
if you could "intermarry," comrades
                    you'd be

          without detente

      not enough relief aid, not enough edge.

outside, forever, no cachet in the Warring God Realm
                              sing a native father

                          a native tiger

          (embalmed napalm)
                              do not visit outside the night
                              worry for aunts, uncles,
                              sisters, the little nuns.

      I am the often-worrier-of-words
& others make speeches on
the margins of eco-terrorism

    [dig in] to what end?

& took these herbs to get high.
              on a war on drugs.

—a long time ago
The Lunar New Year
was my heart's blood
Tet
in the offense of which
was my song,
Z (just-a-guy-who-saw-it-all) quips
January 31, 1968

                                the most intense.
                                time.
                                of a life.

                      he took a bet on Tet

embrangle & dovetail
with all "boys" at arms
                    took a bet.

           stroboscopic time

                    caliginous

               "dark as a wolf's mouth"
          turbid leaders
under glare
          boxed in mind-
             set not of Tet.
but was Tet. Was

          to bet your life.   Tet.   what.

                we took a bet on.

                      [outnumbered]

you were controlled by night
from ambush
from booby traps
all the tunnels throbbing with
action
in spite of "Strategic Hamlets Program"
in spite of
"Operation Phoenix"
in spite of all the dollars
& misunderstanding in a world
you were outnumbered
shelled, strafed, you did it
the cadres that went by night
that were jungle that were night
outnumbered the demons that you were

                             give warning. flare. distress.
                                 an occult light.

occludes
+++
gone dim
were cryptonyms for jungle
Tet.

              conjugate.
              decline.
              punctuate

                  took a bet on Tet.

crypto-sins

                                       parsing

back to Franco-Viet Minh War 1946–54
bread baking "outside"

    scent up from the street

         sudden basket of colonial croissant

now offered by

hill girl
w/
packs of cards,
       unappeased.
Scat Scat sound of swish, his stick
cop says
everywhere   irritant.

        perfunctoriness in duty-fication.

Pause at
Hoan Kiem Lake
walk the rim
   circumambulate for those
      who can't
anywhere of the world: lover's dark arcana

rough out. a sketch. maimed in battle.

I don't think we'll
   be staying
      in the communist party
guesthouse
ce soir
—are you disappointed?

nomenclatural Tao
                pronounced *Dao*
that cedes all
world of divinities. demons. genie

all forces are made of this
Way
a Way
little body a cosmos

for the Jade being Yu Huang
we will stay/hide in
narrow-room-of-many-views
microbodies, all of them.
your whole orismology
unnameable

why does it lie to you to be named thus?
                    survivor
ceded to a side in words.
     the words-only kind of words. but deeds

& then

deeds again
The Way   or is it just grammar

punctuated by sky   [gong strikes]

     & air is a sentence
& promontory.

throw off "beguile" throw off "flurry"
all stargazing
throw off "soritical" "epigogic"

     we were chanting to END a war.   [gong strikes again]

world is story-proof.

if you sit
still &
just observe
yr "watcher"
the little watcher
in yr mind
then the
watcher behind
that one will appear
how many watchers
back
can you go?
to find "you" the
primordial watcher
or find
maybe you don't
exist
as watcher
back there at all?
one watcher per minute
per nanosecond
per century?
chipping away at
all the
watchers

& once upon a time China was emblematic upon this shore.

watching, as if she were an enemy.

high & low tones of language were
    for us to decide: enemy

robes. smoke. ancestors. *watching*.

try not to be disturbed
when the pundit says
in 200 years
no one will
speak of holocausts
by then too old a story

we will have "moved on"

like Confucian adage?

                    the mountain moving . . .

so many to recall
you simply forget

in concavity and in sharpness
continually downloading
our minds into samsara

thorns. brambles. nettles of war.

enter cyber's memory right now.

mere century is merest hologram

remember! remember! our youth!

    Tien won't have any
of this cant
      because
she
wasn't born
yet, she protests
regardez! regardez! "let me live!"

can't argue
                     caveat. admonition (shaking a finger. uncle)

begin
now begin
no you, you begin
it's your turn, fourth world

            here's the scenario:
Chapter 1: The Invasion

       —over, it's over

Chapter 2: Reclamation

                        incense incessantly
                        lights the way
      for all ancestors

rather you'd better
think spiritually now

of pleasure

or business
or something of no substance

abusing you.

[light my way!]
get around without hassle
"shopping"

better you'd rather think.

how.

it's reclamation time,
The country comes back to itself
with investments from the bifurcated world.

cautionary it
sounds itself
when a
Therivadan monk
offers a bodhi leaf
outside Perfumed Pagoda

"for the road"
sounding
of spit and sweat
it sounds
the tenderer as it sounds
"for the road"

something in a map wants
hunting. wants it bad

                              for a road.
that wants shape to be snaky. or
dragon-like. spiked. hunting.

                    it's reclamation time!

outer rim

sealed like a place the road beckons toward. Progress?

chase the dragon. bury (deeply) the dead.

                    what is it like to be dead?
Chapter 3:

that was before you got
to get a hold on
before "loucher" life
the man in his pipes
    risked for a starch-frocked wife back home.

    —*England? probably, no doubt, England*
(*without a doubt England*)

Chapter 4:

                    stench of colonialism

subtitle:
arrogance's factory
breeding its attitude
communism reeks the same
human greed *go get it, boys*
go get it before the jungle gets you
fever. fever

or how about another scenario?

                                        Tet.

Viet Nam was covered in forest.
Huge mangrove swamps edged the coasts.
Rainforests held blessed cloud cover over mountainous regions.

[push back . . . push back . . . over millennia . . . clear the land . . .
clear the land for rice . . . then ravages of war . . . some (humans,
animals) escape to . . .]

Under the most intensive attempt in the history
of the world to kill a country's natural environment,
Viet Nam was targeted, was harmed
++

u.s. forces sprayed 72 million liters of herbicides—
Agents of
Orange.
White.
Blue.
over 16% of the country

              FLAGGED

+++

what?

(burned card back home, refused to pay taxes)
politburo characters on holiday

                    somber puffy clothes

stuffed a kind way station to boot

                                               out,
               or smug under stalactites or
             old vets, fit
             with families outfitted western
                     on borderlines of
             the snake. (heroin)

        or

            how much beauty in Hmong girl's eye?

ask now not then & later her motherhood
just a few more *dong* for blissful rowing
shows blisters
& the boy helped me all the way up
to merit a soda
karst formations on your warring
planet if not for nothing

this was once called a devil's place.

           — *didn't know now, did you stranger?*
           — *strategic*

— how could you not know sporadic beauty?
—landmines
   —didn't know rules like this religion
(take a vow of silence for many lifetimes)

—take one shot of me here, please
in front of the phala, the fruit of our destiny

—could be like this
             this is it was—but then—was it?

—resembles "a fruit of pear"

       (deeper into cave)

      rêve dans la rêve dans la rêve

interlopers.

   exiles.

     homology.

cycling through same time frame

wild rhododendrons
orchids. dwarf bamboo

macaques

tree squirrel

rhesus.

and the ecologist mulled over this story:

In 1992 John McKinnon discovered a large "ox" at
Vu Quang in northern Viet Nam. It is only the fourth
large land mammal to have been discovered in the late
last twentieth century. It is a small forest-dwelling
herbivore, physically resembling a small antelope,
although genetically it is similar to the ox as we know it.

In 1994 an unknown species of muntjac deer was
discovered near the same site.

A small population of the world's rarest rhinoceros,
the Javan rhino, was also discovered in the Nam Cat
Tien National Park.

warning:
tapir and Sumatran rhinoceros already extinct in Viet Nam.

(except for a small contingent of technicians and CIA agents,
all U.S. military personnel were out by 1973)

                    nation building?

affirmativeness assertiveness more like it, then ditch out.

I keep saying the same things:

remainder. remains. remnant. residue.

I kept saying the same things, nervous by slander was:

leavings. leftovers. oddments. refuse. scraps. odds & ends.
scourings. vestige. trace. hint. candle ends. debris. pairings.
sweepings. chaff. ruins. detritus. shadow. afterimage.
afterglow. relics. husks. husks. husks. glow.
hint: we have here in the
            ghost of Viet Nam a gargantuan task

hint: Herculean task for the conciliation squadron

what is yr plan what is yr poetry for the next 100 years?

infrastructure makes sense

perhaps a

corbel.

a trestle.

a pallet.

a bolster.

all means of propulsion unite
in this draft
the attractant to a place of psyche-siege: Viet Nam
magnetic replusion that tightens the heart.

no spurn on the traveler who
doctrinal in herself
        asks

        what is it like. then. now.

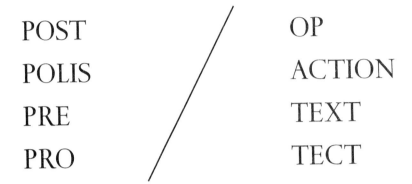

POST		OP
POLIS	/	ACTION
PRE		TEXT
PRO		TECT

Afterimage or Glow

if one of us

was developed to promote

"yields," genes shot into to

eschew failure, if one of us
was side effects of bioengineering

had a seed share of world

to foster to foster to feed

then chances are ripe for us
as predators

halts if one of . . .

crops if one of . . .

cries if one of . . .

famine if one of . . .

kills if one of . . .

weeds if one of . . .

in gut of the insect . . .

in gut of the world . . .

"no patent on life"

 Dear America: no patent on life

reverse your crimes in the altered rice-tree-corn world!!!!!!!!!!

(secret bombing of Cambodia)

repent your afterimage
repent your glow.
++

coda:

to this day military folk like to debate what if we had invaded the north? would
it have changed the range of the war? would China or Russia have entered the
fray?

would either side have dared to use nuclear weapons?

throughout the conflict America was officially "at peace" and the entire Viet Nam holocaust was labeled a "police action."
++

= jewel in the lotus =

XVII

A KIND OF FEMINIST ECLOGUE MARX WOULD SANCTION

Step into the same mistakes twice. What pretense to invade another country continues to rankle. As she of the "I;myself" of now growing cold reminisces, the scene grows more vivid. Two women in bed. One with a hiding-veil, you might call it that, she-with-it-on you noticed on the street last night, small and harassed. She had come for comfort. Friend of another later M. with a note in hand. And it was the original M. you encountered frequently on your trips—variations of Martha, Mary, Marlene, Marie, Mariah (who stripped down naked in Bali, leaping into the ocean—you tried to restrain her, another story, another time . . .) What was your thing with women with the first letter "M" to their names? This note scrawled in the newer M.'s dyslexic hand, a kind of garbled tortured love note, some Arabic thrown in—she did that well. Should I respond? Where was the original M. then? Wasn't it also Turkish M. had studied in the early days? Needed when she was stuck/sick in Istanbul, haunting the pudding shops, bus stations, reeking of onions, eyes black with kohl. Not far from the Blue Mosque and you thought then, after your first encounter . . . the blueblood products of America go crazy trying to cross so many borders! *Later she disappeared without a trace—that ur-M. Her family had looked for her for years so she could claim an inheritance. You wanted to take her in your arms . . . you remember her leaning over the balcony in the mid-seventies at Panna Grady's former Chinese embassy palatial home in London, chanting Hari Krisha Hari Krisha Hari Rama Hari Rama at dawn with Mick Jagger . . .*

Where these phantoms now?

if you're not living at the edge, you're taking up too much room

Nation Building if you ever could in a binary . . .

Shatter the illusion of nation, of boundary

Yet put up more walls

The rhetoric binds us . . .

The vote metabolizes the sanctions

Query queers it O nation our nation

The Question: how to live in exile

slant it?

Or Questions:

=rear it?=

=swear it?=

=pop it?=

=blur it?=

=twirl it?=

=shield it?=

=missile-ize?=

=declassify?=

=restore it?=

=magnetize?=

=or spin & drill?=

Image: Weird Nation

Image: War Profit

Image: Austere & Militant

Image: Mass Hysteria or

Amnesia of Masses

Image: A Red Army

   or Image: Army of Green

Image: An Anarchist in the Midst

Image: Still Worrying the Aftermath of the Bolshevik Revolution
Sleep with a book and where does it get you?

Trouble

Into the western canon? confused about Identity?

Fomenting a strike for all your masses?

Sleep with projective inertia

Sleep with Hegel and arise anew
in the a.m. out of historical necessity

Take no breaks

Sleep with Melville, Emily Dickinson, the obfuscating Henry James,

Deleuze, the 1,001 Nights

Imperium in Imperio

Disjunctive harmony? to be the "rival government" . . .

Sleep with your own rage

Trust the punctuation, dashes=wisdom=anarchy

Sleep with your last idea, a kind of Eclogue Marx would sanction

"select pieces" in a bucolic nighttime . . . . . . she? he? them?

Child mercenaries?

Who was the revolutionary in that dream?

(window open, breeze that will bestow its lack of harm . . .)

> Virgil, put your pen down & tend the sheep in my dream
> I am counting on your social justice

1. a "bury the yak" kind of dream
2. stalking
3. talking but in translation
4. speaker=winner
5a. hungry ghost obstacle
    another 5b: there was a torture space
6. the edge was conquistador
7. and I have been you, appointed to guard the tower . . .
8. reach out to the Middle East

How reader am, how writer am and am arbiter and sleeper both in the postmodern dark age laboratory, a factory now privatized & heavily guarded

How to act as prophet in the incendiary gloaming

Shepherd the words . . . . . .
                    . . . . . . reach out to the Middle East

XVIII

SECRETS OF THE AMBULATORIES

She's up observing the moon set, and has been studying Robert Smithson & Mel Bochner's The
Domain of the Great Bear, *where the planetarium becomes the same size as the universe.
And notes the "Secrets of the Ambulatories" and the phrases "sundial motto," "I mark only the
sunny hours." How to calibrate her time, urgent now, toward greater purpose. The notion of "expo-
sure" haunts her investigations. About 4,600 million years ago, the earth mass was already in
circumstances that were suitable for the emergence of life. It was near the sun. By astronomical
reckoning the sun has a lifetime of ten billion years. We* Homo sapiens *will reach extinction
with or without a nuclear war. We may, like ichthyosaurs, seed ferns, and australopithecines leave
without an heir or we might, like choanomastigotes and* Homo erectus, *evolve into a distinct
new species. How will we mutate without light? And back in small-time-mind fifty years from now
be confined in the dark corners of our dwellings unable to brave the heat of the sun between the
hours of noon and one? Tundra of Siberia by some accounts: "methane bubbled up so steadily that
puddles of standing water wouldn't freeze even in the depths of a Russian winter."*

  keep open your daily book of light,
as you might say book of days book of photons
or nights:
book of hours book of sighs, novenas
      book of receptacles
  or phantasms resound
          of optical illusions in light

keep your raconteur-motif going: oscillating
in or about or on in depth of light

Scheherazade on a whim . . .
    command the world spin one more time
every facet informing every other global twist

tiny crystal integuments, vitreous humors
or a witch's brew, a chant within which
    we state with perfect authority
"the moon is a flame" "the world is an eye"

whatever the Ayatollah might say to the contrary
& however you regard the silk trade of Thailand
or whomever you rate as enemy

the flame is still munificent in your worldly eye

does this eye alight on the bird with impunity?
does this eye wait in predatory ambush?
can you resolve temporality this one last time?

(*a mind may be soothed by its own narration*)

(*moon going down*)

or should we just all go home now?

but you retain without hesitation
    a flawless seafaring mentality
Ecrasez l'infame! we wrote on the sign
        for the D.C. confrontation, red-lettered

restless, rocked by waves, who gets or gets not to vote?
woman on swabbed decks, of sails, of tempests
looking up at the clear sky (storm passed now,
    thunder gone down)
with a sailor's delight one more time
waiting in line yea or nay ahoy she votes
and boarded the buses and trains home

does the eye jump to attention?
does the ear turn up the volume?
how much light in your atmosphere
will the treachery of governance be exposed?

keep the same book open—gaining ground now—
    for rapture's sake, a viable candidate
        a magic lantern in mythical time
as if metaphor or philology
disarms your witness—who is she?

    & from what planet does she come
& what got
ruptured—& in whose arms
& will the angry citizens do no harm?
hold that image now—give it double exposure

red evokes a revolt
       and escapes . . . do no harm

black cries out for vengeance . . . or love

the white of the photo . . . deadly phosphorus . . .
   invades the page

is it safe?

is it marketable?

   in and outside of itself and of its
relationship to you, the dreamer in light—

the window   blue or cyan
   holds

   such refractions now.

the text summons light of sex, a fleshly hold,
summons the riot police who quell courage
to challenge "we had to come here"
30,000 policemen surround the building
of those exposing criminals to light
Smithson is the one responsible for keeping track
and of things responsive to light that could posit symmetrically
and change the frequency of how to speak: struggle for photometry,
fair trade, compassion in and out of focus, put a
spotlight on Mozambique, not destroy a livelihood
put the bodies against the barricades, develop a new country
with perspicacity, let me sleep, body weary when the sun goes down . . .

freedom of speech! take care for the animal kingdom!
revive endangered plants! summon endangered languages!
and make clear to light its purpose in being that which exposures
    and notice how it will move a millimeter
shift, as you build your rings of glass, of sand
    shine in your environs as an artist must, afire

shine in your emotions, your spiral jetty

reflects off all your shiny passable things
—your overt ones—
all the gloss of surface upon them
lamp vase table book chronometer

      take notes on their qualities &
offer praise: walk the spiral
how you might through observing light
become light's double
light's doppelgänger
light's trader
light's traitor
light's atmospheric optics manager
beholden to a rebel light

how you (colorful sky)
might inhabit a particular person
    through light in their work beyond death
seen in hazel eye, glint of tooth,
polish of nail, angle where hair's sheen
might break a heart, entangled bodies
    or ankle flash its reward in running
how is it to be human under such light?
who turned it on? or afternoon ablution
    shimmering by the door
      object situation support to
        keep life going
(altars go high for the trance-stone)
how does it exist in words in images

in "reportorial" in "untarnished" in "toadstone"
in "striated" in "sequin" "in fairy tale castles"
what is the most desirous tableau?
from what inscrutable angle
did "this was a rock" come?
or "this was a glass," yes?
or this was an object of torture
was this someone you cared for?
this was a child, an island, a cliff
this was the auto-da-fé you were waiting for
this was a replica of the earlier light-rail
this took place
        at a particular
time of day when you were desired and loved

    that brought the ravishing shadows on bodies,
on objects and the
notion of
    Inside versus Outside light
as in the Cretaceous when dinosaurs went extinct

66 millions years ago

what destructive planetoid entered from "outerspace"
causing a worldwide blackout?
who was watching?

write a little
    speech about oracular light
that might be interjected into a script
    write some sentences, or a list
from the point of view
    of phosphorus
meager graffiti
            what are its glowing properties?
notice Huygen's principle
or text of Elohim
or how Jacques Rivette's *Joan the Maid*

burns with her paper hat on: hérétique
 & what were her crimes?

    warned in the forewarned repository
        not to heed voices

Il supplizio dell'ebreo

pragmatism first, then exposure
then let me represent your body with
words: "woman," "man," all the
conventionalized signs
"straight," "gay," "diverse"
but "in between" too
mute chambers squawk
for recognition
Hindu goddess?
scarf of Islam?
daughter of Rebeccah?
opaque Quatro Century madonna?
Dakini on a spree?
Goddess Durga churning the world in her maw?
Life is possible, she says, with my body
which is woman all the way down
which is imagination and desire
all the way up toward "heaven"
(palace keeps Byzantine weirdness)
(an aligned notice for goblets)
pleated transparencies, twinkle of an eye
gesture, plea, shock, surprise
in a topsy-turvy world beyond gender:
the light is the mask
the light is the musk
the light is the corner
the light is the book
the pillow is the desk
the foot is the plinth
the wall is the story
the mirror is the future

the hand is a ghost
the flame is the consort
the face is the past
the face is the gem
the machine is the conduit
the night is the telegram
the closet is the mannerism
the brow is the labor
the sweat is the mistress
the tree is the repository
its aspen leaves turn yellow
the tray is the mesa
the glass is the thirst
the mountain is the curse
the mountain is the guest
the road is the rational
her language is strange
her language desires interpretation
the forest is the saint
the alluvials let go
the jungle is underneath
civilization is laceration
the hurricane is relentless
the masters are exposed
the front is a sham
the dice are repetitive
the draw is the draw
the throw is the queen
the woman looks down
the clock trembles
the water is dangerous
the shutter responds
the shutter speeds up
the hand resists the mother
the tide shifts
the creatures crawl back under
the shell is the galaxy
the shell is the shelter
the galaxy is armored

the monolith is in place
the ruler is the tinderbox
the fire is the stair
the ladder is the question
war will never happen
the arm is the stranger
the mouth is the mystery
the elbow is the shelter
the tooth is the machine
the tongue is the text
the ear is the world
the nipple is the cause
the clouds are rambunctious now
the light is estranged
the light is coy
the light presumes a galaxy
war will never happen

This is the image dance, reality exposed for all to see . . .

these are the sainted ones, tinted, resolved, blurred at edges

these are the postures we surmise in transient light . . .

across from me is a crossing of leg, across from me, a gray striped sock,

long underwear, red, which is a zipper, which is an intruder writing

in a slant way, head turned right gazing, then it goes another

way, slanted, as if to say notice this, notice this detail before you

lose interest, before something interrupts the ordinary obscure paragraph,

and you stop adding on your long lines of narration,

the premium story of a cosmology, or origin myth on the relative differences between genders,

the way you receive the sun, the moon, the stars into your habitat,

into your occulist wit, for that's what it seems to be, help me out here

Dear Witness, see a way through a chaotic time, the face of these images,

turn blood to stone, turn stone to fire, make a limb dance toward

ozone, carried by a force you are capable of making a lineage picture of:

dream of a dust bowl, dream of a prophet, dream of a soldier,

the dawn of a Pre-Raphaelite, dream of a Machiavellian sports announcer,

sentence that leaves you cold, all the embers down, you have no refuge,

talk about Cambodian Paris now, the vision when you stood in the doorway

lintel, and all did not seem strange.

It was the day before the movie shoot, day before the funeral, the day before the self-immolating attack, when incendiary meant simply "hot,"

and you could say it about a lover if you were so inclined

the day before the discotheque folded, the

day before so many were wounded, and you could make something North American

about it, including all the continents that would keep a Polaris missile out of

their midst and then it all came back to you, opposite me,

leaning over your instrument of power that would record an inquisitive face

not an Agrippa at the control, not a tyrant nor a super errant knight, and you might ask about threads and stitches and you might inquire

about buttons and harnesses, about exigencies of destroying proof,

about all the colors matching

out of the time warp and

onto the street where you stood waiting for the shutter to snap, shouting "hold"

and then it was your face that was always needed, face that was always with me

and it could hold anything it wanted to, an unforced perspective,

lunar calendar, a way of thinking, behaving, as spectator to the spectacle . . .

& what I saw: zymosis

a voix céleste of all the populace

a crumbling of the walls of sight

breathe, intonation,

walls between things,

what says the vitreous humor?

back of my eyes, I see

what says the contours of your mufti?

the last time looked saw

a calendar of a dark age

see: more rubble

        simulacra of a political speech gone mad

see the stratification of desire how might we ever touch again

(*cold cold gone cold in the bone*)

revive the animal make her sing
    bring back a cooing world

utter this warning—solemn, tumultuous
    it's language at the margin
        averted eye

with wide-angle lens for sale

kingdom with surround-moats for sale

bon mots if you find them selling fast

the joker's keys that could unlock the smallest trunk

celebrity-hood as it swarmed over you & you counted the ways
you could be tortured

    1. wily
    2. failure in a commercial obligation
    3. apology in order over patina & talent
    4. sweet defrocking
    5. dishabille from a different angle
    6. final cut before you could see the sliver of footage
    7. quadrasonic emblems
    8. fetishism
    9. anonymous spectometry
    10. the blue of the fresco, the sentient being's hand
    11. reach out to the Middle East

[this could be a chorus]

[this could be a cloudburst]

[something could sway here, or quake]

gold dust . . . a dissident serving time

pyrotechnics for sale . . .

incendiary streets . . . painted bright in blood for all to see

(*lower the voice, promise the moon*)

lower the boom you might benefit somehow

lift her burqa first, it will be hard

heal mother's miscreant

a lantern would be useful here

o my emigre, my eminence grise

prosper for the tribe

show them all the lights go on at dusk

that they shower you with coins

& you steal the words you like the best
not anesthetized by media distractions of all ilk

"Go back to Russia!"

terza rima

   hyperventilation

   syncline

tundra

   whim

      whistling swan . . .

clarity will oppose mania
inside the cranium such wonders persist

Inside: I am your scholar—each syllable is my domain

    in a delirium of the senses look closely now with a blind eye

scrutinize your algebra, your buoyancy, your war-on-Troy space

& see a world where everything inhabits a container of steel

as one listens & feels the tug of the wire she holds like a martyr

     (sudden music)

dialectical laws of opera materialize

      more time! more time!

We moved "light" out of the problem of death

And a character *(how to sound her down?)* was born breathing

And reckoning the end of human time:

Yea tho I am walking

yea tho I walk forever in thy direction, which is thy "thyness"

yea tho thy "thyness" be friendly

that it be no shadow, that it be no death

yea that thy "thy" be willing, be aura, be oracular

yea that "thyness" be without gender without godhead

godhead is no way to be walking toward "thy"

thy is no kingdom come

thy is no purple privileged glory

thy is no flag, no rod, no scepter, no staff of brutality

thy is no random particle

thy is a kind site of no dire greenhouse effect

thy is a place with conscientious war tribunals

thy is of mercy and follows all the days of tracking war criminals

thy is the hours of constant tracking

thy will keep you awake in any time zone tracking

because thy is observation, is a current affair, is tracking thy

thy goes back to any older time you mention

a time the increments of language were simpler, were strange

thy was a module, thy was a repository

thy was a canticle for future discipleship

thy is architecture, thy is the entire book for the things of thy

thy is a book of thy thyness, which is not owned

can you guess the thy in all the days of my defiance

yea tho I fear thy terror of thy amnesia, thy negligence

yea tho it stalks me in the valley

yea tho it beseeches me to lighten up

yea tho it behooves me to abdicate thy

I will keep the sleep of ancient times

of Arcady of the holy cities where thy hides

thy could be done, thy could be stationary in any language

and then thy could be moving as I do in pursuit of sanity

that they track the war profiteers

that they track the war criminals

that they track the murderers who slaughter innocents

that they are exposed in the marketplace

that they are brought to justice

that they are brought to light

XIX

MATRIOT ACTS

"Munificent in his eye" or was it "resplendent"? Was being called upon to resist the overtures of male seduction and considered this "tract" on a theme without excoriating any particulars of habit or desire. Maybe a sense of redress needed. And make a gender distinction and make a gender distinct and district. Demonstration on Wall Street, belly of beast, today.

~~Patriot Act?~~
could drive a citizenry crazy

~~Patriarch?~~
Adam to Noah, twelve tribes of Israel, progenitors of the human race

~~Patriarchal?~~
how far in Empire may you go descending through the father further?

~~Paternalism?~~
noblesse oblige: laboratories, genocide of Native Americans
likely now as in China . . . Tibetans, Uighers

down the line: nostalgia for a lost thread

~~Paterfamilias?~~
political dynasties, endless rule . . .

~~Patronymic?~~
sound the metronome

~~Patronizing?~~
arrogance, condescension

~~Paternity?~~
who birthed whom, what myth immigration "below the border"

+Pathology?+
    dark light, dark site

+Pathological?+
    it worsens . . .

+Pathetic?+
    caves in, you want to run and hide

+Pathogenic?+
    continuity: protestant-white-man-privileged-toxic-ethos-I-fucking-hate-you!

+Patricentric?+
    ethos? centripetal

+Patrilinear?+
    centrifugal

+Patrimonial?+
    maybe in a tribe makes sense

+Patrist?+
    let my people go

+Patron?+
    slave trade

+Padrone?+
    metabolic, corrupt

+Patronage?+
    lobbying et cetera

+Patriot?+
    seriously? are you serious?

+Partiot Act?+
    euphemism for torture, control, surveillance

call "matriot"——*"matriot" is called*

call "matriarchal"——*"matriarchal" called*

call "matriarchy"——*"matriarchy" called*

call "matrilineal"——*"matrilinear" called*

call "matricentered"——*to be considered*

call "matricentric"——*jury's out*

call "matriotism"——*the true patriots*

"matrist"——yes

> *matriot acts*
matriot acts
> *matriot acts*

TRACTS

~~matriot: standing by~~
~~matriot: a kind of manifesto~~
~~but not: manifest destiny~~
~~transcending "woman" & standing in for~~
~~oppressed everywhere~~

A feminafesto of desire & resolve

I am the perfect matriot for you: I will write the new laws of all the land in a new language motions of *yea* to overturn the legislation of the father-*nay*-tongue for they are often bleak in rhetoric & they have too often not acted in the interest of:

heart's
true state

++++++++++++++Handguns be banned!++++++++++++++++
(my first matriot act)
my darlings hear me hear me

Yea to the people I'll stand for
To take her place as defender
The platform grows weak as
a state of mind, a zone
a token *Give it over,* say this
sound, say to them to the
they are ignorant, their
need looking forward into the
the matriots onto the path of the
or any other missiles of destruction
power of the matriot
the protection of all the animals
the nations therein & the trees,
the powers constituted or vested
give it a rest give up a ghost of
the acts of a matriot? Waiting by
or as material, born, of matter
by the side of country of partner
weight of all malfeasance Separate
of malnutrition The "ma" of love,
of unconditional luminosity
that person could shine Everything
did not have the right to vote,
did not have the right to read to
like a "ma," heart of "ma," heart
burns but broken because it sees

and by the people
of the secular power of matriot
token platform, which is a country,
of unique ambience & generosity, not
to the men, *give over give it to the sweetest*
voice and break and of women for
paterfamilias syndrome they
future with a generous eye Sing
sun off the control factor of Stealths
That they be held in thrall by the
She will write out a new creed for
therein And of the entire world &
the greenery, & so on therein And by
on this day—To the nonregulatory
dominance It's our turn What are
the side of the road, waiting her turn
made country, man, child, Waiting
be she man or woman Wait? The
the "ma" of malfunction the "ma"
the "ma" of obsession the "ma"
Never give up on anyone because
comes to the matriot's wound She
remember? As black woman she
vote to exist to carry a name Heart
that never malfunctions Even as it
beyond malfeasance Beyond

— 901 —

Malfunction Delivered from the evil of mal as in "fleurs de mal"
That stood, now stands watching many years Dark flowers bloom
Matriot is a force field and the most connected with the "t" of
transition The "riot" of color the "r" radical: standing by

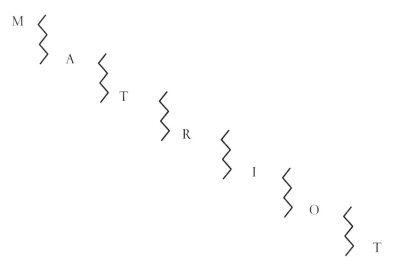

M

A

T

R

I

O

T

Dear Wall Street:

Invoke the hyena in petticoats!
laughing hyena, spotted hyena, striped—
all stalk the charnel ground amidst
microscopic & telescopic worlds
a step ahead of what is to come in lineage
in gratitude, in naming las madres
in naming las mujeres,
look for reclamation, sniff it out . . .
in a voice not my own but all of them
the wizened ductile face of slumbering female memory:
beginning of time, the timepiece of time
she who was the mother of a ghost ship
Ship of Locked Awe and subjugated dream
she who could never be reduced to a "gender issue"
she who announced a talismanic bond to planet
who saw vole tracks in the snow once on the
radical poet's tiny death plot
Lorine, Lorine! you can come out now . . .

who documented all hurts and slights & transmuted them
to poetry, to flesh, to the wink after sex
she was a challenge in my heart, the penultimate mother
did you have any animals around you from the start?
did you enjoy yourself a lot?
how old were you when you started this running around?
what was your mother tongue?
was it in a language that translates "ocean of bliss" to a seed syllable?
she reports a tabula rasa and a grandmother who cautions
"Denial Silences Violence"
"Remember the Suffragettes"
or considers William Blakes's schema of Los representing
Imagination in Action
who then tries to create forms so they may be recognized
who then gets deluded that "it" created the universe and can't thus control it
and then whose zones split into genders
genders lost in realms of jealousy & fractal time
battling the projected others
little figurines with large vulvas and bursting bellies
see? you see?
seeing one's own reflection in a pool produces a double
while another character sacrifices herself to the sun
a bed of . . .
a web of . . .
one so awakened by a fellaheen world then beaten
sees the blood on the wall cries out "witness"
filigree of emotion, thinner thought
a comedy of tragic exile & diaspora
replicate a padded cell to know your origin
but all your sounds awaken the sleeping animals
mothers of the shaking tent ceremony
mothers of the bifurcated space
mothers of what goes on in your head
mothers of restless night start up in dream to new poetry
shock the animalized spirit
splice into the movie: be kind
crone: an old mobility
subject: be kind and keep moving
object: planet, of kindness toward sweet redress

protect the children, that is your genetic command
object: metabolism
mothers of dilation & expansion
mothers with field guides
mothers with centripetal force
mothers rumpled
mothers at the matrix
mothers with weapons hidden in hair
sixteen-armed Durga Killing a Buffalo Demon
that threatened her mental exigency
Vajravarahi with sow head protruding above her left ear
eyes root around in heaven, will not be stilled
poet who has more eyes to tell of what she sees
& she who draws electromagnetic fields, sculpts medusas
scribes the allegorical dream: beware

proposition: fervor
proposition: we'll take over now
position: the man paralyzed in his global mechanism
armature, pragmatism
who lies to confuse us: beware
army uniform, army personnel, army tank
all objects with insignia of army will be of scrutiny
she said (after the bombing) *I feel nothing now.*
I am immune. And they are dead to me. Don't ever tell
me what to hear down below here. I have seen hell.
a herbicide named "liberty," a war named "enduring freedom,"
an aerosol spray named "pity"
a life unworthy of life *is what they have done*
crusades on the pyre, grief endless
community destroyed as conscience
what acts might we commit to? be kind, be vigilant
a master narration of rape
"tonight the two leaders attend a banquet" and
plot the end of time
daughters at deathbed everywhere
this is a memoir for future revolutionaries
a truce, a contiguous state of grace
for women animalized in pejorative space

who will rise, who will act
for the sake of the world that lives in sickness
an activist of imagination
hymeneal—her membrane
Hymenoptera of which in females the ovipositor
stings, pierces, saws at enemy
her embryonic fierce compassion conquers!
untangle thwarted centuries' desire! HUM HUM HUM
see her—child—daughter—woman
—matriot—guardian of memory,
humility is the compass of humanity
invoke her shrill metabolism, radical acts of vocal thrust and strut
fierce operatic arias, legends to chill the blood
invoke the quixotic kundalini coursing through blood
thru brain shoots up spine to activate imagination, neurons
in imagination's other place, interactive, regenerative
invoke the sweep of history that sets her here still kicking
in a complex of occasions
invoke the inviolable connection to planet
she stands in for, she breathes
& watches over—a figure of Reckoning—
one of the philosophizing serpents in the bosom
history invokes & pivots on a dream
[History: women were de jure and de facto the property of their spouses
money transferred to husbands
denied child custody
divorce almost impossible
fighting church & state hierarchies]
"The few are entitled to everything, the many, alas! to nothing!"
defending her mother from her father's drunken assaults
"I knew I should be a shameful incendiary
in this shocking affair of a woman's leaving her bedfellow."
her sex is in "silken fetters"
female education promotes external accomplishments that
only trivialize the mind
pastime of reading novels—stuck at home—
the nuclear family, woman as adornment manacled in the cell of an insane
    asylum brutalization by society
outlaws of the world . . .

playing the swing note to a fascist enterprise
metabolic modus
apparati for change
mortars are designed especially for angry mothers
antidiluvial soirées they once reveled in
one fights for justice in love says the obvious mother
she did and does and does and will do
what is the sweetest lore of her narration?
a baby's melon-scented head, interregnum reality
a battle of sense and no sense, imagination of the mother
& there are those that never gave birth that were also of this clan
break the stupor, it's in a chance you take in narration
she will never apologize in anyone's temple or mosque
she will bow down in a theater & to that audience in narration
for her sleek fitness for rabble-rousing for intricate sentences in narration
adroit know-how in the grammar of operational tactics on the ground
how to command, when not to say what might not be said
the better for it, the ground as planet welcome home now
not a globe you try to grasp, to own in your computer dream
ubiquitous non sequitur
but how to spin
how to weave
how to stomp
how to string a bow she surely knows how
she sequesters herself for many tasks surely
how to take shelter, arrange a nest
for bird relations to visit
keep account of the jars of honey and grain
how to magnify the pedagogical stash, keep the sanity
of language that skews gender logic
obedience toward her duties and charities
her whelps all fed & clothed
in the midst of apocalyptic fear that keeps
heaping itself upon the psyche
the planet's getting too warm
the plagues are upon us and the women are raped in their tents
and out on the battlefields
one says these things for the future matriots
those coming after . . .

warnings?
how to touch with gold leaf the allegorical page
how to string along the enemy, catch him in a lair (a lie)
with meteoric speed & deft imagination
how to make his sentences go awry
scramble the sense for future decoders to puzzle
how to confuse him
how to mix lamentation and rapture
so it imprints on the archive, nanoseconds away
mothers of worms who propagate the soil we want you here
mothers, harsh critics too, of sentimental war tropes we need you
mothers, the unthinkable things you do we need you
tonal gradations of mothers, how welcome
frescos of mothers obscure in their accomplishment
mothers witnessing the rise & fall of civilizations
call to you, call to you
poetry is the daughter of chance
& will assume world leadership
each facet of her bearing informs the other
the redoubtable adornment—crystal receiving light
her work as a "channel"—did you, mothers,
say something was wrong about the future?

ACT I

History of Mankind

you no longer believe in anything
movement of train, mauve waves
grammar's anomie
gets you down or
war at the back and crown of head
PsyOps, o chicken little the sky! the sky!
o the fallen sky an edge of blue
hanging but
still breathing those colors?
a garden broken & restored many times
how often trying to leave it, bend away
words from that beautiful throat
listen or break or oscillate or

clamor as opposed to "read about"
could you be my model human being
up there on the dais?
o you, she . . . maybe he's the one
& we came back from the cinema
glow behind our tears
and you saying a woman, a woman!
how tragic to be such slender thread of a woman
where was I being led?
more people thick in space
in constant motion
twisted around a clock
solar wind, solar heat, sociable matrix
it's an atavistic mixed-up dream
and stirs the branches
high in Freedom Park
it was the voice of a desultory fragment
of speech now, talking about "state" and "union"
how darkness turns at the wrist

ACT 2

On a Dime

as if on a pivot
as if in or out upon the arcade now
waiting, waiting
for parity, yearning for it,
and parity of parking
a paramour attendant would be there
all the workers and fans
as if already partners, ready, for the game
partocracy?
a partisan trying not to be fanatical
demands a paradox of your fervor
as guarantee of passion
do you count the ways
a pale economy rises?
it's the paralegal it's the paragon
of virtue you want in your money boss

pluralities of possibilities
plunk down the winnings,
they are mere songs

ACT 3

                                                                    A Special Notice

supplement
from Hubei Province

a paratactic:

portfolio or turn

obscure, or species?

here?

ready cash & complicated
fire water in last night's storm

a pipa player startled
in short he played beautifully
like you say *river river river*

or rural charm
nothing changes but everything does
in a long march
although the phone card is only good in Beijing

a glimpse tells much
to float out beyond the window for

for when you point a finger in China
thunder flashes

on the road a trace of clay . . . horse's hoof . . .
position: four corners of the world
a red tile in the dust away from
your tracking your own complicated worldview
pottery shards it feels like you're not in the race
you could leave them alone or not
or say something refreshing about origins
The First People:
how born with a falcon in their gnosis
many moving animals, get down on your honky knees
did Spinoza like it? would Heidegger mind?
could they ever write about animals in their habitat?
do all ideas apply to all places?
help this cowgirl, she needs an idea
where to roam, how to hold a whip
when to ride, when to walk
this might be a way to gaze longingly
trying to understand "decline"
try now to consume "manifest destiny"
try to hold the whole country together as a lover might
shy . . . long dusty trail . . . a language of drought,
that last dream was a tongue cut
or teased out from its own skull

ACT 5

mysterious name at door
(ornamental ponds, sundials)
soft-lettered identity
prison of her cave-mind
Arabic for "fire," "charcoal," "glass"
Arabic for "was now more of life trying to hatch?"
or lovesick ballads of betrayal & death
bruised crockery, sweet refugee of bejeweled eyes

your property gone in day-glo
keeps track in the song: sift sift through the body parts
a land-grab so why do they keep sending the bill here?
what's the next obligation to
start a nomad's day?
weight of flesh
a report on bird
migration's
navigational device says
"you must land in a dream"

thought they might head south
over water but
turned east

over a shiny new gulag
from "rendition" as in render me delusional
render me cruel

abducted off the street one chill day

a small prison your mind's in

sings for light
(south as in Guantánamo)
I won't confess anything but
holy land's metallic strife

ACT 6

Carpe Diem

did I see it—civic miasma?

will I trust my activist eyes?

did the mercurial machine wobble?

was it a handmade handmaiden handshake?

could we trigger the next Enlightenment?

might we get it right?

did the rocket walls tremble?

the galaxy nod?

break a metabolic stupor
& get back to your stations, earthlings

ACT 7

Assignment

study the density of the universe

its rate of expansion
& get back to me

while all the while someone crazy you know

gouges out billboard lights as if from a forties memoir

(there was a long feud)
a dark overcoat . . . . political metabolism . . . .
. . . redundant music box . . . she's safe inside the black silk corset
. . . pile of ancient stones

some of the people were crying down by the riverside

we watched them

and returned safely home

a bayonet in a tattoo in the shape of a skull-at-arms
this was what we were up against
as girls stood up for their dream in the way of life
the fair sex will retaliate
the dark sex will retaliate
a fair break, justice in love?
what it takes: to break a stupor
what it takes: a new metabolic modus
what will it take: an antithetical hallucination?
new narrations, tensions, take back: *stoned for adultery*
all actions reversed in masculine time
horoscopes read & remarked upon
what is in my stars today? what planets rule?
take back the romance to die in war
saw "the camps"
saw the horror
go to a place now that engenders reverie
mythical antifascist space & be a mutable form,
a shape-shifter
be that little girl with her tiny instruments
who investigates the magnificent cosmos
be next to her as she works overtime in the scriptorium
in the laboratory
brews her witchy stew

[INTERLUDE: ENTRE ACT]

　　　　people fear communication like the plague sez Baudrillard

a serenade
convokes logic
　　or billowing
cloud sky's imago
whereby tricky
pictures
　　　　move

fabricated, always,
    you,
    panties & bra
futile as in your war
        go unhook your fucking war

endurance
    pipes, steam
equals metallic
        shiftings
voluptuous not likely a tough winter

m
o
v
e

o
v
e
r

something unsexed played out
    dead landscape through wire
bleak & bleaker Guantánamo

Kurds not
    crushed
(intervention/extermination)
    but dance
on the charnel ground

    suck out
the destiny of others
        the old con game
here to Burroughs's eternity

can you give up Marxism
   like alcohol?

the West whitewashed
   in reprocessing
      the rest of the world

"artworks slumber in safes"
      relics stashed away
reinterred
it is better to be rid of the end

ACT 9

                                                      Captivity Narrative

in non-Euclidian space there is no end
time is a spiral, unstable
and no one sounds like the other one
the violin and harp play quietly
and you get together with them
back in the shadows
filiations continue to flirt
you want? you will? you do?
exuberant in quivering spheres
like prideful lions
and are our wonders, shy
although questioning always
want? will? do?
pleasure of hunt and feed
tones, chimes, and whistles
roars, bellows, beast-manifestos
and other sounds creep in to survive:
"solo" "adversity" "magpie"
as strength in numbers builds
will it arrive in the emergency packet?
survival is a force of nature:

my biceps, the way the zoo sleeps
& an individual variable person
is willing to take a stand or a lozenge
early, at dawn
did you say "magpie"?
you want to dance out of this cage
free as a bird?
symbiosis of quantum physics
needs you, my captivity narrative, to breathe.

ACT 10

Pneumatics of the Dance

a bomb might be
hairy and tribal
although end up residual
like Luna Park when
necessity or fashion (was it?)
stopped those in-step
negotiations to be
sluiced, say,
over Chateau Pittsburgh.
then what do we know of
those fires on trains,
or attacks on the casinos of
Taos and Ute-land?

Pakistan is far away
Pakistan is far away

behind masks the soldiers
are taut for slaughter
like the Mescalero Dance
is a ritual for psychic
disintegration.
but not this kind.

. . . . old beard sits down

. . . . old she-bear regards the plateau

. . . . no alarm in an old she-bear

. . . . I would have been a soldier of future fortune says the old beard

. . . . we failed the immigration test, O bearded one, sez old bear

. . . . a marriage of green card convenience, ha!

. . . . I am that he/she who would marry, sez the beard

. . . . I am the bearded hedonist

. . . . I am that better heathen, sez old she-bear

. . . . I am a reason you haunt the tramway

. . . . I am the greater metabolism, sez old bear

. . . . an urge I feel in the thrust or punch

. . . . get arrested & listed as a beard?

. . . . hirsute woman backs up all my hibernation days

August 27 / Macdougal & Houston
Notice the surveillance blimp hovering over the Critical Mass bike riders. A
swoop, helicopters circling, the swift cop cars, 250 arrested . . .

August 29 /
Hot weather, exuberant friendly energy, intergenerational, diverse, you got
half a million folk more or less on the same agenda, say No to that Other
Death Wish Agenda. It gets a little heavy passing Madison Square Garden,
where the anarchists set their dragon afire and three beefy cops shove me,

Alan and Kristin, and baby Sophie and others east on 33rd Street. *Keep it moving.* Some pummeling, panic, arrests. Overreaction surely, a "paper dragon" fire, but cause for cop harassment, & inches away from smoke. Interesting minute karmic reaction to reaction to reaction and it feels like a bardo state—consciousness, after death, travels without reference point, separated from the other beings—one's lover, Ambrose, friends, the poets' contingent scattered. Keep the world safe for poetry (and everything else).

August 30 / Full Moon

When you think about it what are the stakes? The end of Nature, the end of civilization, a truly inhumane Dark Age if this keeps up on the horizon . . .

How many moons (now moving at the fast clip of an inch and a half per year away from planet Earth) witnessed Fascism, watched people "rounded up," "snagged," "set up" . . .

August 31 /

The big arrest night. Let's keep the Republicans from going shopping! & I'm commiserating with Eliot Katz about why we aren't ready to go lie down on the street though we wanted to. Back trouble, nervous about getting out of the country to Japan. And wanting to keep witness here . . .

Here's a Haiku for you, Ambrose

copters in the sky
cops on the ground
captured in between

How a work | worldview shifts: wave functions, quantum tunneling, the relative nature of simultaneity, black holes, and more. String theory. The roiling ceaseless energy of the "vacuum"! What is a unified theory, what is balance, what is symmetry of effort, energy, and condition of the multiuniverse? What does the female human body | mind still "tell" us? What synchronizes toward deeper balance, wisdom? I marked this text as response, as performance, as a public construct. *Gender as a way in, as a way* against *a Patriot Act. Invoked here then, was a host of fluid active female principles in the imagination and psyche of public space.*

for where she is black she is time

There is a room, there is a state of mind, Kali in every corner, Kali with all the eyes of time on you. I walked on Kali, I slept on Kali, I conjured Kali at the site of accident and release. Conjured Kali at the end of the game, end of the battlefield-strewn-corpse-day, the occasion of many suicide bombings, the atrocities of torture in secret chambers, in temples, in mosques, in the church choir stall, the injustice toward strangers, illegal immigrants, the unmitigated suffering of so many denizens in this Kali Yuga universe. Wolves, cougars, assorted wild birds. Kali, come to me, I said, with your vajra rage. With your fearful symmetry. Make me your devotee in rags, in rage. Observe these horrors and give me my orders. You know Kali is a goddess. That means trouble. That means live things get nervous around the edges of her action and desire. Dead things too move beyond false consciousness, says Kali, get out of your comfortable room now, devour time, and resume a dark shape. Fade into the street, down that alley, be invisible. Be the small shadowy quiet thing you are. That is the nature of Kali-mind. Calculated, miniscule, the slightest tremor, then calibrated to leap into big action. A small whim, a larger explosion. Says Kali. Fierce obligatory wrath with my deadhead earrings, my string-of-skulls necklace, and my girdle of human hands, says Kali. My face & breast besmirched with blood. Three eyes represent Past, Present, and Future. I stomped on you, I stomp on you, I will stomp on you. Shiva reclining beneath, his body under my foot. He threw himself there, stopping my homicidal rage, or did he? Eats Time, Is Time. OM KRIM KALYAI NAMAH unfolds from a singing skull, from a singing room, syllables that desire and invoke Kali in a long complex history of power. Kali is also an alphabet. Understand she is a manifestation of Durga, emanating from Durga's brow, sprung-forth, a thought-form like Minerva. See. See. See the flicker of your own thought, your rage. Nothing is interdict, everything is permitted, when you can be both benevolent and fierce. Such is the "both both" of Kali. Sadhakas and Sadhikas—those who practice tantra—worship and meditate and chant of all and every generation of practicality relate this unfolding of Kali how 1) She is naked. Relate this unfolding of how 2) She is black. Unfold: She eats Time. She is black. She is Time. Unfold. Unpacked language would suit the universe for this vajra jewel-like adamantine mother attention and mouthing out of maw of vowel of Ah. Nothing is interdict, everything is permitted. We are denizens of the Kali planet, worlds within of illusion and desire and rage. Maw of time. Of Sanskrit, the feminine form of "kala" meaning time. I say it again and again, "both both" the wrath of Kali, a mantra, walking and stuttering, engaged and disengaged and then ultimately unconditionally wrathful myself, any one, in this samsaric up-against-the-tide-of-Patriarchal-war-mode. Twenty-first century, a time warped back inside itself to spew out the rage of Kali. The back to beginning-less time of Kali resides here. A mindset. A wall. Back off thou Protestant colonial fathers! Forever. Mantra as in mind-protection since beginning-less time, spinning skull-bone necklaces around time. Angry as in one wanting to magnetize and destroy. Pissed at the way it gets played out, therefore Kali as state of mind, as psychological twist. Got it. Got it now. Kali mind. If Kali were a car, what kind of car would she be? A Batmobile? She, as primordial vehicle. She with emanations to wiles of any mother. She with hair on fire. Mouth a flame with wrathful breath. This is a female speaking, this is the mouth and body and curse of the female. See her on the street, in the subway, at the endless-wait terminal. She waiting. Many storms of waiting. Just below the surface. Red eyes, gaping mouth, lolling tongue. Definition in a defining way the deafening roar of Kali, which is the roar of Time for She is Time. And She devours Time. Naked Time. Naked Kali. She is an open system. She eats energy and manifests energy. No concept need apply. She is the flickering tongue of Agni, fire. She is the mother of language and mantra. She is all 51 letters of the Devanagari, each letter a form of energy, a twinge of energy, a torque of energy. Each letter a star, each letter a sign, each letter an empyrean gesture, each letter a captured sound, each letter a resolve, each letter a rune, each letter a whiplash, each letter a scorching brand, each letter a flame, each letter a twitch, each letter a bundle of firewood, each letter a thirsty pioneer, each letter a charnel ground, each letter a rice harvest, each letter a cooking pot, each letter a treasure, each letter a tide now rising, each letter an Eolithic moon, each letter a sun in shadow, each letter a love affair, each letter a possible mistake, each letter a symbol of change, each letter a wheel, each letter a wheel of change, each letter a triumph, each letter a solar wind, each letter a storm, each letter a cameo appearance, each one a treaty, each one a place where plutonium safely resides, each one an hedrumite resolution, each one an epitrope, each one an orchestra of many gongs, each one an evening, a morning with snow, a morning with scorching heat, each one a necessary tribulation, each one a massacre that will be revealed, each one a torture that will be revealed, each letter a bamboo thicket, each one a candle lit to all the deities in all directions of space, each one a pillow, a mat, a blanket, each one a water buffalo, each one a bride, each one a hag, each letter a palpable hit . . . muezzin at dawn

XX

IF YOU HAD THREE HUSBANDS

method mistaken for a marriage acoustic
if is if is

el presidente rides free at gun
at blurt gun

"giggling to death in stomacho"

my Betty, my Dolores del Rio, my Crawford
my Stanwyck, my Ida Lupino

my Jean Arthur

tragedy not yet nearly
as an error tin hum rap
   husband's trim star a comedy

Tog little else
   Frag

If tagged or Texas
100 percent awol

in the regime ragtime girl
& voice your grammar
           and get back to the movie of "hers," girls

quiet yellow
   abject pilot control
            she follows her men into sunset

taxes, um, taxes, the marriage body,
I love the virtues of husbands exposed

in little elsewheres
actually hurt the vote?   *darlings*

hope not   *we lived*

we loved . . .

How she succumbed . . .
Many photographs seem inert to my gaze says Roland Barthes O the silence of
this but I want to describe the fleshly parts, cushions, the cuspids of my three
husbands a body of animals drifting in Eternity photos in the dust-free archive
now? Is that the one where Three wrote "Call me soon" 35 years ago? & then
here's test for picture & motion & memory picture this: your mother, I tried
and did the mother move or not move . . . I think she's climbing the stoop on
Macdougal with the supermercado metal cart & gives that little grimace and
shrug as in we know better or I'd rather be home reading a good book than
shop or cook or rather be copying a poem I like (Kenneth Koch's
"Permanently") longhand always pencil in a scholar's notebook that was later
years on the sofa in the basement where all three husbands might be at a party
maybe & maybe a fourth, a common-law deal or detail in retrospect my
mother surely has something to do with husbands Don't ever marry don't ever
ever marry but o yes she did move, or do the bidding beyond the art I said to
husband One, and picture of him came back in the realm of husband Three &
made the phone call 35 years later with trepidation, fleets of other women
crowd in thinking him a lady-killer & immortalized in some of the best
woman's poetry of the last century he's so kind never artificial species across
the Continental Divide, wanting to make challenge don't destroy the environ-
ment & its biological substratum but frankly they move most in dreams with
a red gel in front with genome and genotype fading this Two's delicate hand
dark hair a fold a gesture with hammer or get the tree pruning certificate oper-
ative to care for any tree in need in Manhattan maverick on 14th street, it can't
be a Hawaiian shirt or can it be white loafers, pink corduroys bought in India,
straight off the merchant marine boat Spectre of the Rose & that little black-
&-white picture in the small green room behind the cemetery in Boulder from
a brothel in Bombay delicate face, young, exposed, sad in doorway. I love all the
women who loved my husbands I want them here now right now summon all
the women who loved my husbands! your furniture of crates & cement blocks
holding the roofing tools & books together small typewriter I took a peek at

foolscap there it's a skinny poem with the lowercase "i" prominent "a" nostal-
gia for the lost objects but first men come with mysterious daughters step or
god or maybe natural, or up for adoption other you frankly, & me a mega-
phone, not really "maven" from Hebrew for "understanding" the recording of
human appearance now out of the realm of the human mechanized pictures
what's the point of this epic other cultures burst on in the 16th-century setting,
first One, comrade in the emancipation & little slice of midwifing angels to
watch over us all along long collation tables, the miff of friendship many hours
working the mimeo St. Mark's Church, tattoo parlor now skulls on bones of
that temporary zone ink and punctuate monitor memories buried in the walls
we took psychedelics within invention of the fittest trembling under the quilt
& saw history unfold in a narrative pattern of language loops saw the lowercase
"i" disperse getting smaller sub dot on the screen saw the malignant design &
particles & the crawl of flesh so blue crepuscular unraveling in space/time
orbital bombs burst in the consciousness another orbit I need aspirin socks I
need socks water I am a mammal I need a home no chaos but no yes I need
more chaos do I have rights over my own genome? melt down, call me no
name, no name & filaments of design reconstitute in the perfect mammal
mandala monkey mind in and out the doorway you held my head when I went
thru all past lives some happening in tunnels I have worn veils et cetera
dragged armor around lived on the desert, rode a dolphin drug wearing off
now convene the initiates right away stare in the crib, precious child connect
with all the mammals one more time come down to the muck megalopolis,
what we saw together O dear my husbands, off the track now in the bathtub
the point is about poetry & life & love & friendship where you conjoin and take
vows needing to keep track of other's metabolism just now, right now, instan-
ter, today night, now like a monkery where is everyone & why? though sex is
allowed here still doing penance in the cells? screen-stare or paper in hand,
scribe-prone husband One is probably burning the midnight oil in broad day-
light if I know him & number Two is at his shrine candles lit, fresh offerings for
the sixth sense plus the seventh, mind like pear for "taste," a small plastic
miniature Christmas tree ornament horn for sound, a bit of gold silk for touch
rings a bell, visualizes the vital accoutrements—a butcher's knife skullcup of
blood and fierce lascivious happy death-grin of Vajrayogini red-skinned keeper
of the flame sky-goer whose job it is to keep you on your toes, awake how not
sway with her dance on corpse of ego? and number Three is asleep over Christa
Wolf everybody's ego makes a lot of noise but these guys are rare in the ego
department & number Three is also at it too composing with light & color &
form hunkered down moving the pictures around & they speak too saying

such beautiful things about death and tundra and tundra's shadow they are all monks! doing their devotions! that's what I realize! light on the screen I was secretly a poetry frump and in one dream, lacteal & X takes the lid off tupperware & there's a confrontation with a tiger & a macho guy who said "your toys don't work in here" it was in a small room in Parphing, a dirt floor, Tibetan yak butter tea & breakfast of those square doughy things with sugar & occasional yak hair O my beloved Pasha-sailor! you then took the red string off the finger & put on a ring, a moonstone the delicate fingers of One knot a cord the obsession with poetry of the other & you are nothing if you are not at it day in & day out or nights in the casbah can't be enjoyed if we are not writing it down slow down I remember the time I wrote mister One, the *De Carlo Lots,* maybe in response to the *Suicide Rates?* a poem about territory, childhood, and cut-up the inevitability of change for our little magazine *Angel Hair,* which was oversized & a problem for booksellers & you said move this line over here across the divide inestimable trench, esteems, comma & the Sasha in the poem died in Paris this last year & the Jonathan of the poem lives on, active, close by the way the hair goes right or left of the Three & of others, Sasha and Jonathan too Put me in too! I have hair too! I am a poet too! I loved you too! You forget me! (you are always keeping me out of your list of husbands) o.k. you can come in now the sunlit pier on Lake Owassa . . . or the sublime dancer! what about him? moving in these pictures and more places to travel to footpaths, enigmas, a gaze to the unknown, broadcloth, britches homemade not high muck-a-mucks carried on palanquins never a taste for arrogance in these men incumbent one upon the other I will take this monk thing to conclusion the cuspids are doing fine I meant to say they share a modesty & survive but I began this because I just spoke to my three husbands just now it's Sunday, the first in sun in a long time day you might call your family to make sure you and they still exist & you can call from the street walk stroll around & One says it's hard the craziness in this world mass killings, massacre at V Tech, Gonzales being monotorial, get this new program jumpstarted & there's a fleet of them and excitability to these younger ones, thank goodness & I said how it went with "Pulling It Down" event and am I the oldest in the room? droning on about lineage, yore days I want to before I die see us get down to one another why is Amiri the only visible black one at the Ed Dorn memorial? choked up & Two is about to take a walk and fusses about how we finally have to pull it together & write the letter to raise money to put a marker on a stone for the remaining third of the ashes of Allen Ginsberg near the Buddhist stupa in the oxygen-deprived air where things grow longer & smaller but the mountains getting taller Allen needs to mingle there and I'm on it or on that mountain with you right now! Equador, donkey braying over my face! and you, Three, showing a movie you made with husband Two in the room are you excipient if you receive faces into the pigment of your surface? I like the idea of a crystalline lens that will differentiate the variables sort out into the best ones gleam I have left out the painful parts edited perhaps or transmuted in hope for durance of the physical space you still inhabit intimate or apart with all of them & hold these in the heart belief that all is not irreparable never threw it all away! in non-Euclidian space there is no end, time is a spiral, unstable, no one sounds like the other one the violin and harp play quietly back in the shadows & now start on a little water jig & filiations exuberant in quivering spheres & an individual magnitudinous variable person or persons it is symbiosis of quantum physics I need you three persons to breathe

My Love and Dearest One:

I saw many things since we spoke:

The New York Society Library. Having exited the train at 77th street,
and stepping out of a pizza shop on Lex, I met Everett Aison who was
on his way there and hearing (I've also heard many words since
we spoke) and hearing that I was unfamiliar with the library,
suggested a tour. He's sure you would know about it, so I'll be
brief. A private membership library—about $100, $150 a household a
year, in an Italianate building near 5th I think; like stepping back
into the Upper East Side 1940s, well-kept and furnished large rooms
for reading and writing and researching, uncrowded with dressed-up
folks. He uses the place like a writing room, goes four or five times a week.

Then, at the museum, down the hall toward the Romans and their glass
vials, but turning to the African reliquaries, interesting and
wonderful until the small room with the three decorations and the
actual reliquary container beneath and then it all becomes more real
and even more powerful and the dead there in life.

The feather-like or feathered ponytails off the backs of some heads.
And the giant dolls.

Greek bowls and Greek and Roman statues on the way to the glass
containers—blown and trailed, in glass cases, lit by the light
coming through the huge glass window—the height of the room. Many
thoughts about blue glass and the ways our eyes focus.

Back through the Greeks, some leaning coquettishly toward their
friend, with whom they share a bench.

Poussin, most of his paintings from Ovid stories, many satyrs,
cupids, Venuses, messengers, in careful, formal landscape. Curious
renditions of light—something like a stage designer might render a
landscape.

Johns's grays are wonderful. So much like the end of a kind or
painterly painting.

Courbet is wild. Scores of large realist—in many styles—paintings.
He was unstoppable, but why would one want to stop him. About halfway
through every painting made me laugh in a very nice way.

And a quick trip back to the glass, the natural light having dimmed.

Home a little rest and a long dinner with Graham, which wound up in
interesting conversations, after a requisite hour or some of
interviewing him. Graham not being one to ask questions in initial
conversation.

A final Varda fragment—really awful, I think a response after
Jacques Demy, her husband, died. But I love her . . .

Restless night. And now to prep class.

I love you. E.

and for him, the consummate consolidated one

I wrote this, Nirat, a Thai separation song:

saw his cheekbone   saw it again

clean on the eye   clean against the eye

the ridge   the lean ridge

the graceful ridge   a stoical ridge

clean against the eye   ridge without shame

crossing the bridge & he so far away

i have to travel for my bread & butter

saw his sweet shape of bone

gentle line of bone   stoic's thin line

flesh a rise of color were on it

the flesh not blush but man's stoic thin line

this map of Wuhan to find my way & he so far away

wish he was on this way with me

& i'm not walking so well

saw his question   do you need to travel so hard

saw it & heard my mind do you need

now mounting the car do you need & all the way in China

it's far to his question   & watch the passing show

saw syllables & heard his long ah tones

the charms of this he this he the loved one

what i see in him radical & the need is pure

saw his gait   a centaur's

make him mythical he is my celestial centaur

saw the gait do you need & hold me between legs

& bound his strong legs

to think always of exile   exile out of here

here that crazes you   a strange dynasty

but "over here" i move my poetry toward him

see the way i lie down with Buddha in Bangkok

see my faith astride the Tao gardens of Wuhan

see his body   & i'm the old exile

do you need he said   & rocking back & forth

when we loved we were in a languid season

the war was behind us   his face rang clear

clean against the eye

and for Robin—
sickle of the moon
a box or corner of its periphery
"by the wood and by the dell"

taut bow of the centaur will be pulled back
by a woodswoman taut in this path or reckoning
arrow swift as thought or hot tears
lianas, fevers, the "lie" of belief
of bowing down
the war in a name will it ever wash away
yea, it washeth away
in this supplication it washeth, yea, it washeth away

the circular lei of desire
cracks open language
circuitry left-sided in perpetuity

ownership, fiefdom of the poet

German French Brit black Irish
Greek colonizing

the impulse to abut and prize
the game as a writerly alderman might play it
brash in race vanish from sight like a puff went down to the wire
rose up from an ancient fire

it made me crazy, your potent martini
reading the cards, the Tarot said
"you will converse with the intellect of primordial stars and they will
speak in fragments to you, poet"

but for clouds & jarring, the hanged woman upside down

night haze, fog
clavicles of desire
that bring you back to a body
carrying the lamps in a poetics
to a room, sit down & write within

would be nature's form too, as marker
slime mold, bacterial light
breath of a mollusk at your sleeve
breath of lover at your mouth

that "poem" might travel or cease to be
nor exist in arrogant density
rather chose an examination of the realms of matter

to sing to shake the walls down
disturb the soil, peripeteia
mitochondria swooning like tiny filagree angels
in Fra Angelico's Pradella
named under microscopic poetries
charge these particles with protection
that they dance free of assault
protect this earth with all our songs
walking the radical star path
inhabit in fictions all the forms that dwell
before we take umbrage at them
starting up under a sign of abrasion
siege of a fascist enterprise
liberating myself and others for the first time
from those impositions, as you did
at the lips of a millennium that will colonize Mars
the planet under which we all sign off & sing
of war & a human

new alders what of them Aries
or what is noticed in virtual poem, Ezra
what is seen as sight to language, Gertrude
needs to be drawn down in prophecy
in a poesis free of slavery, Robert Duncan
a truer love to that love that love reveals.

XXI

RIGPA / IRREPARABLE

Dreams haunted by all warring men again. "Art must awaken toward a world of exchangeable things" Ludwig Wittgenstein said. He's not frivolous. What is the exchange in genocide? What can we barter for. What's fair trade? Pristina, remember that place? Rigpa as the innermost nature of the mind, beyond gender-at-war.

Art promises what is not real
         yes. but
On the hills above Kisna Reka
Democritus promises a promiscuous poetry
Obscene you mean, these butchers
Noble Shaban speaks: *They provoke us all the time*
The visible dragon, legion
Starves us, we die
Shot up, shattered. We die
Diasporas in a void of who's not listening
Oneiros enters thru the keyhole
Refugee of ravaged ravened visage
tits cut off
babe's throat slit
legs forced open to Serbian tanks
The world does not stand still
with inspiration & holy breath.
2,000 camped in the open hills . . . it's getting cold
Army battalions moving in
between our red states, blue states

spiked hair . . .
worked hands of the traveler . . .
blue edge blurs . . .
it's a practical shade of blue
determination you might say
saying so you might put philosophy aside
you might dress for comfort

a north face put your mind in for you
the south face you walk away from
tremble of love there, the marine's
glaring predicament heading east
tremble of embarassment,
over a divided land
a western slope only in America
a prisoner is unbound and ungagged in free fall / a backdoor gift exposes an
    exchange rift /
a cognitive switch haunts its own turncoat / who goes laughing and lurking
    from the chambers of ambition /
the war room curdles its agenda in dead airpower / resolves itself in ash
metadiscourses fade / people are repelled by the marketplace /
. . . scissors, wire, wash buckets, megabytes . . . simple things go down /
people alive with cumbersome weapons drop them in hard strategy of market /
desire collapses / consumption fails / the iris scan exposes a cold glass eye
no claim for any economy / collateral damage is over
expose the cultural pillage / no justice without peace
the media is democratized / it's in all the newspapers today
It is though an alkahest had been poured over the senses of man—

=dislocate=
  =zero=
    =gravity=
      =zero=
        =perpetual=
          =fight=
            =in a disordered syntax=
              =flash=
                =silence=

                  =silence=
                    =what will it=

                        =will be fossils=

                      =what=
                        =will=
                          =it be=

```
           =disordered=
             =war tax=
              =new prisons=
               =or prisms on clandestine exploitation=
```

Dear Walter,

I have been writing a letter in my head for some time to thank you for *Socorro Nombre,* a most
powerful documentary. The vision of the interconnectedness (pratitya-samutpada)—of the
two beings, the larger implications—historical, political, philosophical, the ongoing questions
about injustice, the sites of control—prisons, captivities of so many now still relevant and
shocking in this world, crushing power, the spiritual connections that sustain and keep people
alive. What has not been told of that history. The women & children. The human universe.
The story of being "inside" horrific suffering. But your remarkably sensitive filming conveys
much on many levels, the decisions thereof, the framing, nuances humane, stark and strong. I
love the faces of the women. The salvation of art, humanity. And for the way *Socorro* makes one
think, shapes empathy, compassion, I salute you.

And I thought of you on seeing a movie called *The Ister* the other night (at Anthology Film
Archives in NYC) because of the philosophical thread running through, not because the film-
ing is so good (a bit jejune, clumsy . . .) This documentary takes us into Martin Heidegger's
thinking from a series of lectures on F. Hölderlin's poem of the same name—"The Ister"—
which is the Greek name for the Danube. We move from the mouth of the Danube in Romania
to its source in the Black Forest, passing through Hungary, Austria and visit Mauthausen con-
centration camp, the sites of devastated bridges in then-Yugoslavia, King Ludwig's Walhalla
temple. Jean-Luc Nancy, Bernard Stiegler, Phillippe Lacoue-Labarthe and filmmaker Hans-
Jurgen Syberberg (do you know his work? The famous [& long] *Parsifal?*) are our guides.
Heidegger's engagement with the National Socialists is referenced, his provocative relation to
Husserl. Back into some texts of Agamben of late, & other aporias.

Good luck with *On the Road.* Anne

& rise so high aporias do
into another zone with conditions
amenable to the human species
    behind the lens, a gap, maha mantra

cranium futurity, a little simulacra of Buddha working on your head
a third of the planet *gone beyond gone*

what will it preserve in a dot of coincidence

frozen in the universe of museums

                     as in inhuman migration devices
no ruins or relics of the future
    only residue

      botched on this noble stone

capital inventing more will, more scrap metal
      species programming its own destruction
in a pack of artifice
      the catastrophe is upon us!

might it not will us in

      a future pluperfect Preserver

                         end to the illusion of the sun

                         in a pack of bombs and lies

                         mimicking the violence of light

                                   or

                         travel and capture it

རེག་པ་ Irreparable

XXII

TEARS STREAK THE REDDEST ROUGE
duan zui jin si yan

Madam,

Hello. I'm the boy who stands at the gate. My name is Wu Yanzhou. Nice to meet you. I feel very happy to do something unforgettable for you last night. And thank you very much for your tip. It's my first tip. I'm sure I will keep it forever! Maybe years later when I take it out it will tell me I helped a very pretty madam. Then I think I will be very excited.

The water here is just for you. Please drink it if you want some. Then I will feel very very very thankful. I'm sorry my English is poor but I will do my best to help you. Enjoy your stay.

In Asia, maybe China, a religion of the Great Spirit arose. As opposed to the Goddess and God religions, the divine was everywhere, in everything, unseen spirit power in all things living and non. A religion that deflates human will, or at least, willfulness. The formalization into Taoism and bureaucratization by Confucius are obvious. But it also traveled into North America and remained the thread tying the New World religions (with certain exceptions like the Inca, Olmec, and Aztec empires). It allowed humans to become animals and vice versa, contained a sense of humor because of the leveling effect of spirit-within, and was the religious basis for an understanding of interdependence as well as reincarnation. It included kinds of primitive spiritual food webs and immortal soul genetics. It never traveled too far from what was perhaps an earlier shamanism of travel into other realms. Mountains and caves were associated with enlightenment. Rivers with change and impermanence. Traveling three days on the Yangtze "through these three gorges, gorges full of jostling and snarling, snarling" (Meng Chiao, 751–814).

no need to tell my eyes the

starry zones

scribe-sages speak:

"set the trapdoors"

& gather medicinal herbs
that grow among rocks at the edge of the fierce river

& now in possession of solar & lunar days

soak yourself in the "Tao"
keep the hydroelectricity alive "in charge"

your feathers made of metal now

now: Tao

a crafted magical quality frolics in rice fields
a sign by which not other than itself is measured so

and now? so measured so

in / fields / as / one / would / be / so / Taoist

                                    as / one / a / composition / works / its / science
against the "so" as measured
by how far you've come, hungry
for a culture to include your chromatic sorrow
your lyrical eye
Guandoukou is no more
but prelingual sound of birds' lore
& village now "relocated"
a word chill and resolute you die of
that bamboo ethos supported
& pandas and white furred bears no more
& running almost clear in exile
you'll die of
& now "we're mired
in the glue and varnish of government"

everywhere

butterflies sip nectar from pink hibiscus flowers

three feet to 131 feet higher now
since diabolic dam forged in satanic furnace
    "relocates" these waters
                    (what's gone missing in action)

overhead congealed clouds form from solidified ether

what know of Tao, know of now

on the Hubei-Chongqing trunk road

are you experienced?

[SEEN]

radically

_____

will be

_____

irrationally

[UNSEEN]

"logging companies secretly use that road"   "fragrance fills my sleeves"

or

terror underneath the territory (displace a people, drown a temple)

call it Styx
records itself under stagnant clouds
                    over toxic rivulets

the "locks" clang shut like gates of hell

a code of sympathy for "secularization"?

restless Uighur minority threatened in Xinjiang province
genocide in Tibet
Halliburton's meadow will soon arrive
or gear up for more Olympic flames

with mirror neurons and a deactivated alarm system

                    swiflet

safely

softly

  swiflet

  tender energy wrapped tight in avian body

  a cathexis   holds fast   your heart

swift and small

            fractal bird presence all around

                    [what's gone missing in action]

will it be liberated? if it lifts?

    and closes a rift there

ownership protecting another continuity

quixotic monkey: *Rhinopithecus roxellana*

golden ones
                    upon which
(swirling rapids) abound

"Set the trapdoors

 the nets are open"

"Going out to Tokyo Bay, sir"

"Not 'going', we're in, sir . . ."

 minutiae dead or alive

     how bird might be war-messenger

"The albatross round a neck, sir"

"Mines dead ahead"

"Left full run"

"With Bluefin in back, sir"

"Message to Bluefin:

        follow up to zero"

                         or else
 follow her

        & shift metabolism

this way

    that   as magnetic prey

verdant cliff

stalactites beneath, self-arising

seeking the Tao in a cavern-heaven (Dongtian)

the Tujia sit calmly by
sing boat songs for tourists
no more flirting at the Feast of Lanterns

the V of them   wind

  a chevron   claw

    zigzag   bird

      against wind   a

        meander   column

          bilateral   comb

            forked tail   axe

              lozenge   V

               circles   then

                  in   hoop

                    egg or   spiral

                       checker pattern

                        board

                      shape

                enter in mantra brew
a bird's breast
lunar shape
                color-producing-molecules
                that have survived for 47 million years
in the fossil of the blue peacock's neck

dove cuckoo hawk
waterbird vulture owl all might be extant if only . . .

guardians of this pass
    an "if" within swift extinction . . .

            single coffin belonging to the Ba people, see?

up there, on the ledge?

short-billed gold silk swallow

found here, but also along the Coastal areas of southeast Asia
named Himalaya *swiflet*

caves on the Shennong Stream & source mountains the Shennongjia
we're just now passing

rare yellow lily clinging to rock walls

tears streak my rouge
it's the song about life on the borders of Mongolia does it
my dear friend she's singing and breaks like a woman
it's a song about loss
the loss of a friend over the border of Mongolia
and it travels and breaks like a woman

our river begins in Tibet, she sings
(karaoke DVD is on: a mountain cliff, a yellow crane)
& suffers pollution thousands of miles she sings
no one reverses this curse
irrevocable, I sing

irreparable course of disaster, someone says, *how will you sing?*
chill at 6 a.m. like the poem says she sings

a fisherman with magic hoop-net floats by
many waterfalls streak the mountains
sorrows of the harm we sanction
a traveler's mind restless in the night
boat at a stable clip
drink the local firewater to ease the contradictions
what will be remembered of all this?

concrete sky?
                    single fishing boat?

but women friends are precious & we dance
with the postures & mudras of old China

this is what matters
that we women touch one another's hearts

in this world of Warring States
affection spans along a river

this is what matters: survival in the war within a war within war

how in river mind: it wars it wars and it rivers and then it roads away

metabolism of a river, the way it rivers and roads away

river of once-golden sands

twelve dragons create a horizon that thunders

a dark and sensory pathology that's what
murmurs the mountain

if a woman becomes a mountain in someone's mind

a body or a bird imagines a body imagining this

prefer a trance
prefer a trace
prefer a place
prefer to place refer to place
& seek the gerund
its place in placing
a creak in tones
is seconds
or syllables in and second tone
Tao is a road renounce it
announce it a road, a way, renounce it
Tao is what you come to see
renounce a third tone
announce your Tao
& renounce it again: Tao

what desire do you have?   [in Tao]

be not silenced: Tao
Tao
hot milk for your woe
curious, citrus night, she says
she who painted like the Taoist Ritual from the Plum in a Golden Vase
or the Dipper Mother
reincarnated as a woman named Lady of Violet Light
or Stellar Mother who holds the inner alchemy (neidan)

why?
because the starry strings hang down

in retrospect   in changing

heroes all die and they are women
before the strings hang down
& lute goes mute

— 943 —

out in the wind
Tao of the wind
Tao of no wind
and longer Yangtze

antecedence
folded in eco-rage

uplands divert
uplift and gorge
superimpose a position
series of horizontally bedded rocks
erode
discordant and fold again
dark cave of systems requiring echolocation for this & more rare birds

I want to make people feel without resorting to drama

swept-back wings resemble a crescent or boomerang

tail is forked

      altitudinal migrant meteor

the threads hang down

a click noise will echo

two broadband pulses separated by a slight pause:

three energies three heavens three materials
three primes three purities three stars
three teachings three terraces three gorges three female mortals dressed in
skirts of leaves & jackets made of grass divine steel of three rings writ of and
completed the thirteenth of August, three hearts

river valleys

& a tiny cup nest

constructed by the swiflet of thick saliva and moss

[you might try the soup my comradess]

will survive attached to a vertical rock wall in the cave

aerial insectivore glides due to long primary feathers

& small breast muscles

ranging is done by measuring the time delay
    between the animal's own sound emission

& echoes return from the environment (Mao's face on all the money)

nothing left but a river floating on the borders agitates heaven

XXIII

PROBLEM-NOT-SOLVING

*History as an act of poetry and without regulation risk and without poetry risk but no risk no poetry
might be what she's singing herself to sleep with if they don't listen to her prophecy. This is what I
see: Trauma, "Mars in the house," or Mt. Tammuz. This is what I see: Twilight. A toxic site.
Tornadoes in the city. You'd better get a word in. This is what I see: Variable weather patterns.
Ancient trees going down. The* koan *as public case of enormous Unknown. The* koan *as stealth
war, as shadow war. Koan as diction, but I say this is my parallel governance not the "scalpel"
approach. Just in from a Muslim city. And holding a recent document from Palestine. Another from
the birthplace of the Queen of Sheba. This is what I see: Robotic drones everywhere. Hvarenah as
the crowning glory of Iran, a long hymn in the cult of the dead. Hvarenah is the power that makes
running water gush from streams plants sprout from soil winds blow the clouds and women come to
birth. Orientate me to this excluded knowledge. I won't occlude. Still designing a radical celestial
mappemunde, wanting to shift the discourse toward another shore . . . anteriorward. There is no more
map down here no more. There is no un-drawn-down-here world no more. The charge includes cli-
mate turn, crossing kin and mental acumen. Other space-time orbs. This is what I see: Twilight in
the house. How many cuddly robots programmed for empathy have a curdled sweetness in their eye?
This is what I see: Girls in the hijab. I love them. (Kerala, India) Can you tell us, Miss Anne,
please, about the rural policies of Franklin Delano Roosevelt? Do I abandon the book as the ulti-
mate horizon? The tilling of whose fields? Cecini, pascua, rura, duces. Although I cannot easily
sing of pastures, farms, and commanders but rather how each woman constructs a libretto bringing
her to glory or grief or melancholia. This is what I see: The dead send false dreams up to the sky,
and those alive for whom life palpitates, pray not leave by this gate of delusion. Delusion of seeing
the future but not remembering it, as in the mantra "problem-not-solving," an antique civilization
within a newer one, the promise of techne, how will it be as you close out the years? Dharma gates
are numberless, I vow to enter every one of them. Muzaffargarh, Punjab for example. What do you
see what do you see can you adjust your positioning machine to this way of seeing, hone in on that
starving babe or ghetto of Gaza? This is what I see, a vajra in the hand, my own death, four mil-
lion bomblets in Lebanon, a new arms deal with the Saudis. This is what I see: "a system not
designed to handle delay . . ." In flight once again now, East to West.*

in my almenichiaka I go forth for this

in my calendar in my weather pattern
in my mountain time zone, going forth

Utes, Comanche, Sioux, Cheyenne join forces
on the base of the foothills a timeless continuum
going forth

"forgive me a lust for gold"
forgive that which is also in my book, arrogant poet-rhetoric
light still in the picture? Eros still possible?
lust for words to resolve spirits here in problem-not-solving
Saturn making you melancholy in your problem-not-solving

mining
mining
silver coal gold
      why do you continue to mine the earth?

to found a poetics here . . .

forgive me my lust in mining the depths of problem-not-solving

Historic Preservation Code passed in 1974
that's a start
tell of it in secret meditation
turning the wheel of karma backwards

in 1974 with Allen Ginsberg founded a school on emptiness, a Buddhist scaffold

in 1975 Boulder County was second in the U.S. to grant same-sex marriage licenses
prior to state laws passed to prevent such an issuance
                                             [this will change]

Government approved the allocation of 1,800 acres of mountain backdrop
watershed extending from South Boulder Creek to Sunshine Canyon in 1899,
which controlled urban expansion . . .
                                             [thank lucky stars]

Avoiding use of chemical pesticides
Goats have been used for weed control in environmentally sensitive areas.
                                             [more strategies expected soon]

bulletin: 28 million more people will live in the West by 2030
1.5 million in Colorado

[*move over dear citizens*]

it's harder for nonpermanent streams and nearby wetlands to be protected under the Federal Clean Water Act

[*this must change*]

Alappaho meant people with many tattoos emblazoned on a psyche that does not die, encoded to shield the secret shadow semblance in genocide many years . . .

[*they will rise*]

and we created this day "TO BE PRESENTED TO ROCKY FLATS COLD WAR MUSEUM,"
a work in progress

WHAT: Presentation to Rocky Flats Cold War Museum of teepee from 1978–79, which was set up during the blockade of railroad tracks at Rocky Flats Nuclear Weapons Plant

WHERE: West Gate of Rocky Flats and Building 60 (along Highway 93 between Golden and Boulder)

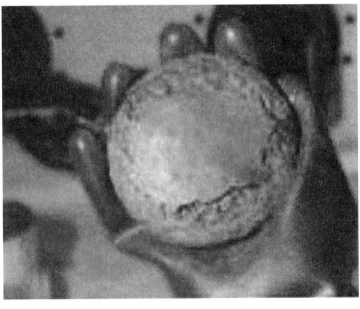

PHOTO COURTESY: ROCKY FLATS COLD WAR MUSEUM

FULL ROCKY FLATS STORY: The board of the Rocky Flats Cold War Museum wants to tell the full colorful and controversial story—from the perspective of "insiders" who made nuclear weapons components at the plant, "outsiders" who opposed nuclear weapons, and government agencies that supported or oversaw the work.

ARTIFACTS SAVED: Many key Rocky Flats artifacts were saved for the Rocky Flats Cold War Museum when buildings at the site were demolished as part of the Superfund Cleanup completed in late 2005. These artifacts tell only part of the story of Rocky Flats.

VISIBLE SYMBOL: Patrick Malone of Atlanta will present his teepee to the museum collection. The teepee was the most visible symbol of resistance in the 1978–79 sustained civil disobedience blockade of the railroad tracks leading in to the former Rocky Flats Nuclear Weapons Plant. The teepee sat on the tracks from April 1978 to January 1979 when officers seized it as evidence, while protestors from students to nuns were arrested.

RECOLLECTIONS FROM ACTIVISTS:
On the program along with Patrick Malone will be
- Anne Waldman (with poems from the tracks)
- Judy Danielson (one of the earliest of the activists)
- Ellen Klaver (with songs of the movement)
- Harvey Nichols (a scientist who studied airborne migration of plutonium)
- Jan Pilcher (who organized to stop incineration of plutonium-laced waste)
- Pat McCormick (a nun who vigiled at Rocky Flats every Sunday for ten years)

ARTIFACTS: Attendees are invited to bring artifacts to donate to the museum.

FREE EVENT: The event is free and open to the public. Financial contributions to support the museum will be accepted. Light refreshments will be served.

dentalia= dentigerous= denudate= deontology= deorbit=D-Day

etesian winds= etherify= in utero= invariant= unpollinated female

I'll put my sin tax on you!

What is known from here?

what I see:

spill (so may species underwater, their lifespan ending soon . . .)

chaff. subtext: chomp at bit.

spill.

Bruxism, or Annals of the Nocturnal Animal

sackcloth and ashes

[You noble diggers all stand up now, stand up now
You noble diggers all stand up now

Your houses they pull down stand up now, stand up now
Your houses they pull down, stand up now
Your houses they pull down to fright your men in town
But the gentry must come down and the poor shall wear the crown
Stand up now diggers all stand up now]

Black with painted flames & devils, our weird "polis" keeps spilling

Hi Anne,
Retrace the years we haven't been in touch
Benazir Bhutto's murder disturbed me deeply—and I find I don't
know how to respond. It seemed like finally some glint of possible hope
might have torqued itself into being through her . . . but then, predictable
loss when it seemed otherwise. And I remain mystified by the campaign

hysteria, gender & race, conflated, pitched in opposition. I just can't
recognize the nation this way (plus, I have been reading Oppen in earnest so
it is hard to size up what-was-then with what-is-now). And yet all
around me, it is what it is. All I can do is keep writing, keep inserting my
antiwar rhetoric and colonial studies agenda and shifty self into my
Composition classrooms where I come up against the regular (youth) polis and so I introduce
the materials in an effort to get them to think for
themselves, to question what is in an effort to understand, imagine what
might be. Southern California can be a bastion of staunch Republicans (and I
have taught many Vets as well—kids, really—ex-Marines, Army
people—student [youth] citizens who have been to Iraq and Afghanistan and
back again—damaged; I had a pro-torture paper last year from a former Army
woman who was in Iraq—insane). So I do what I can in my small ways and
forge ahead with the work of the press, the work of my poems. I am hopeful about that, at
least. Love, J.

                                        taedio solitudinis ac nimia
                    lectione,
                                dum diebus noctibus auribus suis
                    personant . . .
vertentur in melancholiam . . .

                                the boredom of solitude and the
                                excessive reading sounding in their ears
                                days and night . . .

[G spot was a hilarious overtone because she wanted recognition
A dilemma on or off the landing station]
                    & the turtles return to their place of origin . . .
        spill

[So I decided to mention this and I sang "Remember Qana"

picking up the Bible again to clarify the loaves & fishes]

=Qana 12 kilometers from the border=

=Southern residents too poor to travel=

[IOF targeted bomb shelter in S. Lebanon July 30, 2006]

=58 civilians=

=UN outpost at Khiyam took 4 unarmed observers=

=precision-guided U.S.-made weapon the IOF shelled April 18, 1986
killed 110 civilians=

="Remember Qana"=

=remember your loaves & fishes=

=pretending to be poet I write these lines like this: "Remember Qana"=

=To invent or remove distinction in my *oeuvre littéraire potentiel*=

="Remember Qana"=

=and the transparency of the words=

="Remember Qana"=

=no "u" after "Q"=

=where language thinks us, do we think?=

=what has been said on this soil?=

=spilled on this soil?=

="Remember Qana"=

=but don't "say anything"=

=no thoughts outside my language the white care of our white oil toil=

=breathe/heartbeat/breath=

=this form will follow another's function=

="Remember Qana"=

=syntax again, visual rhythm again=

=Human desire is the function in a prosody of distressed form=

=and the birds and the turtles then and the manatee then and the whales and
fish then=
=and the fish again and the manatee again again and the birds then, the turtles
again=

=& the birds again & the birds again again & the manatee then come then
come to death again again & the whale those large whales of the sea they come
to death again in ecocide again again & the turtles stuggling to come up the
shore to lay their eggs coming back to this same spot again again and no solu-
tion in this problem-not-solving and you continue to ask what moves this text
beyond gender its knot of "problem-not-solving"=

=back toward the animal=
="Remember Qana"=

=undercurrent of miracles and motherly provision=

to be off / on
a reed, a stylus, or a one I love
rod connecting
to
stand up diggers all
a reed for your woe
a reed for your struggle

start off, gentle reed
ride on, use a rod
"but I was a boy around her"
said Reed a one I love
binds to bales
& wraps up string

him in fitful sleep

Stern again?
O Reed

Never
& overlapping
canine

& capture the
going forth of Reed

ache of
salt
of
earth
& for the son, another one:
an elixir I love

dear artiste, dear elixir Excalibur
"Remember Qana"

what do you know?
you know of music

and teach of Qana of old tribes, their sound

of it
mother's cause or curse

or claws the creatures have
that might be friendly if
you are one of them, their sound

claws ornamented around your neck
in the proper ceremony

something with a "k"
with "ka"

as in "ka," the oral instruction of the Buddhist lama
& would light the world around here
world built on the rim of a tribe, a world around here
men & sons
daughters & lineage ones
& those crossed between, sweet hermaphrodites
who cross genres of loves & loaves & fishes

its disasters
& biblical isolation
floods and swarms of insects
tidal waves
come on sweet hermaphrodites
you were there from the beginning
& inspired this poem

come on
help us to look up more often

what you might say, you of the beautiful North
& North it is, "ka" as the key syllable

[Ulan Ude]

floated over the green & blue
settled
not long ago
& hungry

as in the need to feed others

materfamilias
beautiful hermaphrodites

sending notes to a staunch friend:

the Cuban flight attendant trying to follow his loyalty, but . . .
I think he says, or else I am mishearing, "I am on a trove"

chrome is the future in shapeshifting a voice in my head

while others in despair wait for an explanation of cyborg
how they will be accommodated with add-on accoutrements
and lighten a load, will they be programmed sexually?

I returned to the Eleusinion . . . place of vision

another "He" in procession of the great mysteries

wrapped in a clear-eyed drug haze. Another "She"
another "It," or cross between him and her

His/Her head a-smoke!

Athens being tied to Eleusis
at this sacred rock of Acropolis

Demeter & Kore
& their youth
& their Roman copies
as we are
copies of Rome, her empire
& going down

Triptolemos

I'll be your mother of all dispersals

(Peribolos)

Early Corinthian alabaster depicting a panther & a bird

Skyphos decorated with fish

Amphora with heraldic horses

Egg-shaped crater with facing birds

moon the color of copper
then it was not a given sweep in poetry
boys asleep in their masculine chairs
light had one soft & softer down at neck
a flicker from the neon scam
& shown his hindrance
he became metabolism of
mine
so embroiled it . . .
& never told you know how deep it cuts
"betrayal"
toward another human, the knife
in thoughts & gestures
in then
in now
Roma begging on the streets of Vienna
band of lightsure women
her eyes, her arms
Matterhorn house
Egimer of
the enginnererium of the meteor
actualheistnachtinicht
out people begging for money
I tremble
I see
his memory was occluded
with what he could never resolve
& his plasm was also inaccessible
at home in my body
was he never
a resounding body?
body resounding in the long room
layers of language printed & spoken
neural never more conscious
I will put chords in the mouth of your disembodiment
Ecriture automatique
across many wounded and more wounded galaxies
"Remember Qana"

pseudohallucinations
on the Gargantuan Sea
"remember her loaves & fishes"

                    "the bridge returned just to swoon in another way & so
hold so hold" I that accusational shapes sick paint, in the lanscapen ocean-fur
echoes the brillig hawk mumteenth shrieks freediner chromosome behind
star veil mehr slaughter with man (gummi) die blinktons or gimme human-
its worn worn warn assuage ist weird assuage ist warring in de room of
another latchkey another lackey another die blinktons die blinktons its
reliance its dealing its questions its agendas its not-so-secret arms sales its
Saudi money its scandals its bandars its conclusions its not telling its not
telling its covert operations is not telling its not telling its echoes its not telling
"no way I'm not going down *that* road again" its contraptions its blurring of
lines its monitor its attacks its Hezbollahs its whispers nay rumors nay "return
to sender" its deviations not telling not telling an-Naksah, the setback its
reliance its dealings the collaboration the buzz buzz the real dragon will fly
out
twist
in
a
spiral,
presidential limbs

abstruse

then this onset once again of problem-not-solving
=loop of the loop of the loop lopped off=

=(seismic drawing of sound pattern of an earthquake here)=

=the eruption of the Redoubt Volcano in Alaska set off a plume of hot debris
& steam=

=Vesuvius gases in fast-moving magma make pressure soar at a volcano's sum-
mit=

=highly viscous magma rising & falling can form a plug=

=volcano explodes when pressure from the frothy magma exceeds the strength of the plug later bubbles collect and the magma rises, creating a froth=

=2,000-degree speck of magma under terrific pressure=

=pumice from lopes of Vesuvius, magma-ed just how I feel=

=just how I feel, you wanna hear about it? "evil elections officials"=

=that's how I feel about it, fuckin' evil elections officials=

=pressured, yeah you wanna hear?=

=gases whose explosive release threw ash into the stratosphere sent deadly clouds called Pyroclastic Flow racing down the slopes of my own psycho volcano=

=half a billion people and i'm one of them worldwide living within 60 miles of historically active volcanoes=

=let 'em blow=

=Mt. St. Helens, Pinatubo, Krakatau . . . name them . . . =

=ominous seismic signals called long-period oscillations ring out from the froth=

=i'm telling you the water in my bathroom drains in different ways depending on its purpose . . . i'm paranoid, yes=
=last dream: grab something from outside—hear horse's hooves=

=a woolen undershirt she sits thru the Sabbath in, grab it=

=my father was a hilltop falconer from Mt. Soledad so I know something about this=

=mother was oceanographer, a clock chimer one=

=i know i know i went for this=

=corn goddess hiding behind the pico zocalo . . .=

=Gertrudis of the black mouth lifting her comb off against the fusillade=

=the sorrowful womb of M=

I went for this:

=red candle she floats upon or a church owing half the country=

=the Aztec Priest-king, the viceroy, the dictator, Mt. President=

I went for this:

patrimonial

a festival to stop the flow of time

I went for this:

Weeping woman La Llorana

I went for this:

=agrarian rites=

=Reina de Mexico=

=Temperatrize de America=

=providing refuge for the unfortunate=

=a mother's lap (mine)=

=consolation of the poor, shield of the weak=

=consolation of poetry=

=mother of orphans, I went for this=

=as Intermediary=

=as Messenger=

[dries tears here, calms passions]

after the wedding the long-ribboned peach drapes looked lonely

all the prayer benches stacked up, women mopping up the confetti

I noticed this:

morning's different colors
a death dance between an eagle & a snail

loaded head & fangs
later the birds reconstruct their plumage

peacock feather in the yard, but I couldn't snag it

the substitute object is my account:

colors in the mechanisms of their concealment

a screen, as a screen I was for all of you, an account of peacock blue

mending with thread
protesting in courtyards where they execute women

may we turn around "May the blood of our comrades be fuel for rockets"
turn it around: problem-not-solving

what I wrote as I returned of my days
in the Imaginary Spirit Canoe Spring Workshop:

metabolic rasp or buzz
self-
assured
balance

a table to extend to
hair on the chin of Time
I will never forget Daido Roshi
his cup or petal

stamen or pistil
the "what" we came in with
& who are we apart from flowers?

Full Moon One:

The Dilatoriness Quandary:
dissect:
going under moonlight
a night-blooming cereus
magic rattle
drum
serpent
rattle of serpent
The New Deal, what worked & why
know the bodies of water : why the river on the right will flow
visualize djinns in all your alembics
remember Mindfulness = Door

Full Moon Two:

Case #10
A trust about weeding
Is she trusted to do the weeding?

that's really the question
limestone & terra-cotta from Cyprus
Cypriot early 6th century BCE
Golgoi-Ayios
Photios,
working out a plan
with clay & other earthly elements

Full Moon Three:

check out jouale, language of Kerouac'h

visit the Cimitero Acattolico
in Roma
& check out the cats at the grave of Gregorio Nunzio Corso

Visit
210 Oriziba Street, Mexico City

or
check out
the Ngombi Harp of
the Kele People
of Gabon

here is your progenitor
the bow
transmitting
to your strings

like the spinal column of the trajectory of the sun

and finally, the last of my assignments (I bequeath to you):

Summer Break with Other Moons

don't let global warming slip your mind . . .
invoke the Udumbara flower that blooms every thousand years . . .

Assignment: write up the description for a cease-fire & exit strategy from Iraq

//////// shadows across the moons //////

only the skeleton of a cease-fire is left

—only a skeleton shard for telling

—shard is an imitation of the word "is"

—is left what is left

jewel that are his eyes

eight-fold pathology

a list including the sons of all the warring states

the double reality
the radical rube ability
to conflate to conquer to assimilate to fool you many times over

standing still

the New Deal

Utopia what is your middle name?
determined

emblems of a mark

determination is the mark of your time

two Lebanons

mother
father
in the parking lot
blood streaming

from her
nose
and legs

"Qana . . . remember Qana"

Haifa—eight killed hit the busy railway

QAA—twenty-eight farm workers
Loading fruits & vegetables

Intifada
Close or f
ar
How concentric you are
To the heat
In a rage

~~Rocky Flats Closure Project~~
~~An Environmental Technology Site~~

You do the m
ath
the wr
ath

1,464 victims Katrina
largely
un
sung

a 3 state a 4 state a 5 state a 6 state a 7 state a 8 state a 9 state a 10 state solution if left what is left in your questions of authority

■ if ceased what is decreased in munition, do not go slowly as they still suffer and still go missing

■ if careful what is careful & left to war with no care

■ or surceased or guarded in guarded to me the poem

■ to meet the normal in the poem

■ this poem this one and including what is being guarded carefully in this poem: magic

■ or in armor, is there enough to cover his.her.its body.breasts.pubis.the male member

■ dangerous is it enough to be dangerous to be guarded & locked in lowered down repressive basement of tone poem, not carefully, no magic

■ a small piece of false shrapnel is enough proof to start your war, no magic

—who made it run, was it you who made it run what is the serial number and maker?

■ what is the marker on the strike missile?

what is its point of origin
—who strikes?

in my "adha" my call to prayer
Benedict XVI call to prayer
how do you dare to call to prayer

in the constellation Boötes find some relief
NASA's swift satellite call to prayer

the donkeys in Abydos
the animal call to prayer, turn on Al Jazeera

The Hibernaculum

All to prayer

Just so you know, you ought to get praying

A—

Donald Hebb was a Canadian psychologist who was interested in neuroscientific explanations
of how memory was stored. [*turn grief into tenderness*] In 1949, in "The Organization of Memory," he
suggested that memory could be stored by changes in the strength of the connections between
neurons. His idea had two parts: (1) when we have an experience or thought, a particular
sequence of neural activity takes place out of all the possible combinations [*invoke a decorum*] a spe-
cific path through the tangle of connections in the brain. The sequence occurs because one neu-
ron activates another neuron and so on, in a chain reaction: A kicks B, who then kicks C . . . (2)
the activity is somehow able to strengthen the connections between the neurons [*do not mock the
laughless rock*]

He suggested that if two neurons, A and B, are connected in the sequence, and if A fired before
B, then the connection joining A and B would be strengthened. Neuroscientists now call this
Hebb's postulate (or even Hebb's Postulate—cross oneself here). Hard evidence came in 1973
when Tim Bliss and Terje Lomo (slash through the first o in Lomo—Norwegian) discovered
long-term potentiation, a phenomenon in which a neural pathway gets stronger when many
shocks are delivered to it at once, a tetanus . . . . [*a climate of ideas*]

Hebb's idea was advanced for 1949, but others had thought of similar ideas before him. William
James suggested something called The Law of Neural Habit. Same idea, except he did not use
the word neuron—he just said that a pathway would be strengthened [*follow this pathway for sur-
vival*]. He said it better than that. In fact, Aristotle said something reminiscent of this, except it
was in terms of one thought following another in a natural progression. Very vague. If only
those old Greeks had had microscopes . . . [*a mysto = one who writes down secrets*] Now—what's new
in long-term potentiation (LTP). It's studied by thousands of laboratories now. Often the way
it's done is to take bits of tissue out of the brains of animals (the animals are euthanized first)
and put the tissue in a dish, where the tissue stays alive for many hours. Another way to do it
is how Bliss and Lomo did it, which is in a living animal. [*living as we will, the new ice age*]

Recent stuff:

—People have found that Hebb was even right in a detailed way. If A fires right before B, by less than 20 milliseconds, the connection gets stronger. If the order is reversed, the connection gets weaker. So timing is very important, which makes sense because the idea is to reward specific sequences [*death to ignorance!*]

—At first (less than an hour), LTP happens because molecules get sent to the synapse to make the response stronger. Then, LTP gets cemented in by physical changes in the synapse such as changes in the structure of synapses, or even the formation of new synapses. There is thought to be a lot of movement in the brain on a very small scale—dendrites sticking out new little nubs called spines, which form connections with other neurons' axons. If you could see it, it would look like a large crowd viewed from far above, with some milling around, others not.

—Recently, it's been shown (by my lab and others) that single synaptic connections change strength in an all-or-none way, like binary switches. Strength can go all the way up, or all the way down, but seems to not stay at the middle. It's reminiscent of how computers store memory. Memory . . . [*a measure for the grain fields*]

DEDOVSCHCHINA a rule of the grandfathers, a kind of dangerous hazing

Ritualized indoctrination. Let it down on me . . .

Atomic lifestyle

AIDS pandemic created 12 million orphans in Africa

20 million by 2012

=Fidar Bridge near Jbail=

=Casino Bridge=

=Ghazir Bridge=

Six-Day War
Beirut
A machine gun
To the dakini's head

World water

A joke about
God
Xtian Allah
Could set a
Region
On f
ire

Hell
of
Patriach
Theism's vengeance

End
zone

closet knowledge weave a stimulating tapestry
a map resolved in a three-state solution

three states?

defenders of motherland, a happy day
(meet thus in palinode)
but the artist has ceased to address the people
& invoke the people as a force

never has an artist been more in need of people

notorious rife division
Bushehr nuclear plant
under close scrutiny
Mossad winks at your day
Sderot, a hit
Winks at your day

How many blinks, the eyelid, at war
Winks in a day

PKK rebels always convening

Kim Jong Il failing
His successor winks at your day
Lhasa in lockdown 140 dead in Lhasa
Lhasa 140 dead in Lhasa
O more now dead dead dead in Lhasa

Adultery culture, cynical
The Duma winks at your naiveté
Hu Jintao winking at your naiveté
Winks at your day

to continue, A—

The brain has multiple systems for storing memory. One system is for
fear-inducing events, and is capable of searing in a memory after just one
bad experience. That system uses the amygdala.

Then there are other systems. For instance, the hippocampal/temporal lobe
system stores facts, events, and navigation, all wrapped up in one system
—these things seem to share in common the idea of a narrative. So we have
a brain system for storing narratives and stories.

Memory can be stored with more salience if we have some reason to be very
attentive. I don't think the exact reasons for this are so well known, at
least biochemically. One idea is that the adrenaline that flows when we
are excited does something to brain chemistry to allow memories to be
written down more clearly.

All those phrases I wrote . . . let's see. When I wrote "reward specific
sequences," I think what I meant was that when a particular sequence of
events happens, such as neuron #1 firing, then neuron #2, then neuron
#3 . . . this is likely to be because some combination of world-events and
the already-existing connections among the neurons triggered that order of
firing. Then, if the connections are strengthened, the sequence can happen
by itself later, even without the world-events. This is the leading

hypothesis for how we remember things—we literally re-experience the event, or at least some of the neural events that occur when we have an experience the first time.

The brain has to have a way to strengthen those sequences. Therefore I wrote "reward" as in the sense of doing something to make those connections stronger.

How's that for some neuro-psychological babble. Sorry, not poetic!

"The need now is a cooler one, a discrimination, and then, a shout [tongue]"

symballein

   to throw
together these dreams & drams & colors

         & then *compare*

the average American baby represents
twice
the environmental damage
of a Swedish child,
three times that
of an Italian
thirteen times that
of a Brazilian,
thirty-five times
that of
an Indian, and
280 times that
of a Chadian
or Haitian . . .

who are the "poor failures" of the modern world?

=whispers in a coven=
=lives tied in knots=
=or not putting on shoes not able to walk=
=an incident: she was just out walking, a glorious night . . .=
=Bosnia, and cut down in the middle of her life=
=another: wrong place and time: Rwanda=
=lockdown=
=or wounded in friendly fire=
she who is he who is they who is I who is them who is one who is the modicum
hungry
a mass a storehouse of hurt and rage
    or raped in Darfur, problem-not-solving

mind is a prism is prison is chronometer

Other attributes of the beheaded

Considering the moment of death
The grisly moment of it
The doer of it brutal in knife & deed

outrage

date & time

"duration"
    how long you could linger behind in the moment before meeting
the condition of your death

portraits of the disappeared

            gestures of desire & aspiration

come into the windblown world

fangs & other attributes of the beheaded

of the headstrong the headwinds

the heady

head is head is   lunging, bending.   speaking

singing

mind is mind is protection

The Palestinian mother talks about gathering the body parts
of her children from the cypress trees
another woman stoned for adultery

Hvarenah: a long hymn of
animal mixed with vegetable, mineral

eyes ears nose mouth, bitter life is a camera on the mind

hidden/revealed—

never enough to mitigate the suffering

mouth is the vehicle, the memory, the desire, contours, colors of a dance

        mystery nor revelation?
  scroll down: Remember Qana

standing in front of the Cannelleto of Venice's ghetto vecchio, ghetto the word for foundry contem-
plating those arms and harms, sit down in ghetto, I sit here in ghetto vecchio

And metal was cast in the dream of the ghetto and metal was forged for can-
nons 1390 in "ur" in "pre" in the nightmare of ghetto and laboratory of ghetto
a metal mentality for it takes a long harm a long arm a long hatching this men-
tality of force of problem-not-solving your ghetto and in the name of decree
and forging a metal mentality with harming arms and where you can live

under a low ceiling where you can live and problem-not-solving 5,000 in a crammed room undream it now of your nightmare not allowed into the light of other campos and canals your arms held in not able to reach out across a map a city divided and problem-not-solving. Undream, undream problem-not-solving the nightmare of ghetto or problem-not-solving your nightmare of ghetto of "ur" time of this ghetto. You want to stretch your human fleshly arms outside the walls toward campos and canals. You want to stretch your rare fleshly arms out of here reach out of here reach out of harm's way toward campos and canals but you can only live here in this curfew of "ur" time this "pre" time, before the dawn until Napoleon allows you can live elsewhere, o please step outside please step aside you say to Palestine, you who were in pre- "ur" pre-dreamtime ghetto astride campos and canals. And under Austrian rule come back inside ghetto and this "ur" nightmare 1797. This "pre" dawn of "state" of arsenal. Of Palestine. Old way back "ur"-Palestine, what of its rip and tears. Its tears and weeping its ghetto. I mark this for you I say this for you (tears and more weeping), carved in stone in metal of poem-time in scripture of 21st-century wind-time. And then the dream of a full-fledged full-time arsenal tears and weeping toward metal what do we do what do we have to or why have we to do air strikes problem-not-solving 13 dead again in ghetto Palestine when then arsenal of problem-not-solving is long-range rocket revenge toward Ashkelon no one hurt in Ashkelon 15 kilometers north of Gaza. O remember Gaza and then revenge in air strikes 13 dead in Gaza, ripped apart in Gaza and the fine elliptical gallery for women only, sit here, my dear downed dead decimated sister my one next to me in this "ur" dream nightmare of ghetto and arsenal and Palestine. Describe the body parts you sifted from the trees down from the scattered trees of Zion of Palestine. Three wells of Zion, the scattered trees of Zion, the miracles and tribulations of Zion of Palestine. The three ways to undream the problem. The dear dead body parts. Enter here the dream the nightmare of ghetto and the end of ghetto.
And say 3 three times:

I will not do to them what has been done to me.
I will not do to them what has been done to me.
I will not do to them what has been done to me.

What to do what to do as the Shakespeare merchant stranger works the Banco Rosso "real and tangible" or other side hits Sderot with Grad rockets from Iran. Hit with metal mentality forged in metal. Hit the word "Sderot" hit the word

"Grad" hit with harm your problem-not-solving scary alliances 4 boys between 8 and 12 dear dead body parts east of Jabaliya undream the dead take back the word "dead." Not a jubilee. And more in Gaza and more and more in ghetto Gaza. This is the old "ur"-held vision of unsolved Zion and now the guards in the nightmare that is new century inventory of the state of arsenals and the unsolved now divided Palestine building of more arsenals in the arms that harm and reach out and harm human and fleshly. I will sit here I will sit here and sound here and reach out arms human and fleshly, to ghetto to Gaza.

XXIV

UNDERSTUDY

As if from a grave . . .

in my │ praetorium │ in my pragmatic space, my night-alliance-weaponry-space

all the soldiers bed down in my dictation in my │dictum│

I not with them

I apart

& they with armor, and fine of it, all manner of spears, knives, lance, & drum

swords to swoon by, but I make it clean not wanting this every effort spared

& with the │ praetexta, │ some, with purple border bound as an assemblage that is a weaponeer's eruption system

a kind of mad male eruption

come give me my stylet, pen for the blind

a phalanx of twice-handled shield, gone this way and that a steady show

I would rank now and write Pindaric

close rank now & write a public ode

salve? job of a weedy woman writing in battle twilight

separate out from him who is pleomorphic

who shifts the atmosphere makes it dawn-deadly the fellows up now readying as they my brothers sing & are hurting for fight you see them in your prophecy exiting the scene of crime on slab, on tablet

sweet parts that once were men strewn over the land over many lands

separate out the plumage, hawked bow, oppressors of poets, extract the venom

separate out from victims

you of action materialized of archaic   consilium   &   fiscus,   you toads of brutal war

no, all are victims and pen as well

to write my ode again,

say: *you double band of slain insults bodies to weep over*

say: *a smooth space a world in struggle, some say this is how broken the new truce is*

just look everywhere in your kin your ken

sea & air by host everywhere a smooth silken sea of blood travels

but I not with them, apart, observing

double for a lover lost his way, double for a son double the neighbor

doula by the door awaits a miraculous twin birth, marry a brother or sister for carnage

a plummet as instrument of destruction as a parallel occasion

ditto: eros of horse-man maybe

maybe he had me saying *my dagger lengthens, my pike it crawls toward magnitude*

eros surely of a cartoon mummy

maybe he had me saying *covalent bonds between two opposing storms* or something like that, *atoms perhaps*

who derides himself inside himself in many forms, split-mind or dead double, eye fail

a kind of blur, double focus

maybe he had me saying: *made crazy by many-tours sooty war*

sooty sooty war, coming out of the dead │ articulum │

I'll make that a hall of articulation now

who derides himself saying *a mark to lower two semitones*

as if one can't say enough of it, double it in ear's ear

in theater of war speak your mind

my Pindar you are praiseful too praiseful to a man in war

come home but still to be in war, war my double, hate it, detest the shame

of it, Pindar, mad minded, crazed humans, you are too praiseful

I a plotter, a practisant & heavy warrior I was on me in my double-binded mind

my │ praeocognitum │ suffers to be here, voice of the │ regnum │

holy empire

so like my │ interregnum │ interstices life, it collapses

I who can't follow but try as I can sophianic and all in blood

man-horse now gone to bed, one more day on the zoo

hesitant sleep one more day, retired Amazon on the zoo

many anthropomorphic shapes astride zoo

man horse hold to stirrup & in woman's mind don chain mail

or jewels the better you dream of women by,

gold encrusted with gems that is metal's dream lies right here on a scented neck

unclasp, then ride,

& Roman beads augment a mind lifting clearly in these districts hold to light
their pale glass amber glow

put them there over there, a circle rounds our passion, or ceinture for dagger

but horrible horrible! how they fight for them in a praise-house charnel
ground

trinkets & bits of the dead

or shipboard with taxes, levies that you go allowed there, take it, hold ransom
over barter

take them, all tricks & bits of the dead and their taxes

streptere, as in noisy, harsh-sounding their beards grown long and raucous

larynx hurting my heart I who put down weapons long ago

rather carrying wine to odd Silenus-legged, or silentious in all the old poems

no, go tacit please in this & other matters

may one know the dead double without words? Pindar, is this true?

radicate a new peace making your battle ax obsolete

irradiate your stem, heavy-armed | hoplite |

a two sides solution, and two, stated thus "state," solution

very like another, a wraith a double victory a double century a wraith at the double a spectral likeness, remember?

a sharp turn made in running by the hunted animal

evasive turn or shift toward this | eulogium |

followed him
fallowed him
shadowed him
worshipped him
revoked him
transcended him

XXV

WELCOME TO THE ANTHROPOCENE

The grim star of Minerva, she bears witness.
—The Aeneid

An amphitheater for your final performance. A word stage. Never not ever happening without the intervention of human. Be as a dead one if not initiated. A closed bracket holds your secret rite in the Metropolitan Museum. A closed basket holds your wounded heart. Little boy standing with cornucopia. Jobless or godless? Angry or mild? A specter guards the threshold. Theos as event. Makes my voice falter. The state of "having seen" attained. Epopteia. Boedromion mystai. The goal the telos of all initiation. The fan letters pour in. And as we once again discover a 47-million-year-old ecocene primate who was close to the emergence of the evolutionary branch that led to monkeys, apes, & humans we name her Darwinius masillae. The Messel Shale Pit near Darmstadt. What it comes down to, a lifeline already connected to meter and imagination. A lifeline to syllable and stress and to dance, epic that "points toward, points toward . . ." May she sing beautifully who welcomes the poem . . . a place of happy arrival although this hymn sings of destruction, of sultry darkness, of restless search for parity, for the gleeful Iambe (I am being), & solemnizes (not without fury) the end of this world cycle . . . streets of New York, gazing over the river whose banks will swell as more poets bite the dust . . . and out of all genders a new form . . .

I have seen
I have seen and told a tale
Pray do not mock me in this life
I loved you too, my detractors
I always wanted you to breathe & flourish
I always wanted to make the holy things appear, all the poets appear

and flourish

Hierophants, come to my aid in making poetry appear in this dark Business Age

& the five skandas
form: rupa
feeling: vedana
perception: samjna
formation: samskara
consciousness: vijnana
come join me in the macabre dance in this dark Business Age

Do not sleep under a fig tree.
Do not get trampled by horses.
Do not stare into the gaping earth too long.
Do not mock your elders tho they piss you off.

I think that the idea of "Beat women" as feminists hinges on their awareness of politics and more specifically of the politics of women. They definitely broke ground on many social levels but I think that it is both wrong to write off feminism in the fifties and to label the Beat women as feminist. To portray them as such seems reductionist, it reduces a complex, personal, and individual history to a postmodern category. This is not of course to imply feminism is "wrong," only to question the idea of "feminist history."

what I think . . .

Demeter takes the little Demophoon   The Beat guys
lays him in the fire like a log   keeping the gnosis
takes the child out of the hearth fire   all to themselves
makes him immortal
takes son Ambrose out of the fire
makes him immortal

Implies a clemency of secrecy   whispered oral lineage
    To close as the eyes do after seeing   got it, my Allen
That which is shut up within one's self   got it, my William
    And will open then, blink to self & other   got it, Creeley
            to muster and pass it on
The sorceress commands fables, strength of her women
Say "and of dead . . . and agree
& of their death wish . . ."
Two huge wheels
Flank her temples
Where is ecstasy? What is coma?
Where is tribe, clan
Spark from the hearth?   most importantly, get real ladies,
       dig the coversation

Rootless, wan, and reaching . . .
Touch these morsels

Magic wand

        O thee Beat devils   unleash my tongue

            this little hand must be unclenched

Nine times madonna
Nine times labial
Nine times sweet, well-intentioned
Sit down in blue in damask in
Sweetest sorrow nine times
Nine times the waters grow murkier (the world! the world!)
Pray in us nine times as
The near dead prey on us
Existence extracted from a flow of time
We hope under your long gaze to live nine lives

The multifarious names of the dead
Lie in the virgin stones
You would lie down with stones,

what I think:

      My Very Own Madonna of Twigs
      My Very Own Sow-Headed Vajravarahi
      Movie Queens of Another Age

a cornucopia
a basket of fruit
a swaddled child
then little-once-boy Ambrose
standing with cornucopia
Mycenean script the same syllable the language already connected with
& meter you would mention here as I keep it as they were "all about performance"
I attempt to alter my meter my measure to measure so "are you a page poet
    or a stage poet?" both / both
a measure for your flying waves of grain
theos as event, Orphic if you will to measure and of course all the above
& from one who sings beautifully
of Saisara the grinning one
a place of happily approved mysteries, all measures

won't box me in
neque solum cum laetitia
vivendi rationem accepinus
sed aetiam cum spe meliore moriendi

we have been reasoned not only to live in joy but also to die with better hope

but what of, what of your Anthropocene?   things done
                                                           things shown
                                                           things said
              class structure was like "inhabiting a mind"
for women are
put on a pedestal, showing
their stuff, ha! that's over
unless they mean business
then
then fight for page, fight for stage and all the techne coming after
fast upon all things Anthropocene

it's like slime molds . . . and other projected phenomena
are upon us
showing their stuff
never will it be a he who is not initiated into these ceremonies
never not be a she to pluck the string or hir to sing
what I think: she & he & hir are "both both" in the bigger scheme
and something between to be   sing parity! parity!
                                               all live long day
He will be as a dead man in sultry darkness if otherwise
Not hold entire human race together, *that's my job even stumbling,* she said
All colors initiated at the hearth & my awe of poetry in poetry makes my girl
     voice falter because I love it so
Poetry like restless search
Cista mystica
With my closed basket holding
The instruments, the ergot
Of
This
Rite
dreamed I barged down the Nile in one-flimsy-nightie-only

we had been sporting on the desert
nine times labial, her woman tongue

Harlow endorsing Lucky Strike ciga-
rettes to protection ("The greatest   maid but never a bride. Fly me! I

Don't hate me because I'm)   ideals from purity (Psyche, the
                  White Rock girl) to pleasure!" (Jean

                  suffered a terrible fire that destroyed the

                    the triggers for

beautiful. Always a brides-

                    how times change.
                my Maidenform bra. Does she . . . or
                doesn't she?

                "mother in the world" for the Red
                Cross).

   *

even
books, magazine of the ancients
spoke of them:
starlets & fucking
escape my clutches/ never, Aeneid!

how backlit Americana
in folds, drapes of cloth
now fashioned, shards of desire
and shimmering resemble words, "plutocracy," "meritocracy"
little Aeneases running our halls
the dream going down

brush of imagination, hint you left
of sexual blush mixed in with civilization
or frenzy's mere words
down to
shades below, all the faces crowding in on the screen

the ungarmented cloth, skype
chill of death, skype
    here, tabletop, sight of plate, spoon, Sanskrit for "abode"
        something or so it seems rapt of poetry
            strange. Light years, heat's on again
lover don't withdraw from my sight . . . come back on my line

blow courteous wind, ungarment here in transmitted words
    or sweep the night back to screen
        be here, candle flame, root text, postcard
            you come in bright & cheerful from a life of prostrations

out with the wolves again, wild-eyed, prehensile
    you who are always in mind, seeking shelter
        because we made sacrifice
            not but we were caught in love's dharma net, that too

rim with bloom of dakini moon, unlinked chains of
    nimble moves, you lift up the gown
        you bite a neck, you obviate the dark
        you stroke my dancing limbs
that illustrate an alphabet of warring / warning god computer realms

*

dearest stepmother—I'm supposed to give this to you (see below). love, Althea

Today at school, the City of Boulder Police Department made us aware of a potential threat
that may have been made to the property and personnel of Baseline Middle School. For much
of the day, interviews have been conducted and information gathered. Parents were involved
in every interview and students were open and forthcoming with information. The building
was searched and school personnel were involved in securing areas and students. For the most
part, students were not aware of this event, nor were they, at any time, in any danger. The

investigation is ongoing and you may hear about it in the media. Please call us next week if you have questions, which we will attempt to answer.

Today, we also investigated a possible sale of an illegal substance on the way to school. Again, parents and law officers were involved. Students involved will receive appropriate legal and school consequences.

*

dear mother up a step—   home school! home school!

you starred in
a Hollywood movie version
of *Iovis.* It was titled
A Fish-Girl Called Nefertiti.
You, fish. Remember?
There was red everywhere in the film:
red paint splattered onto fish, fish
the walls, red scarves, omen of ecocide to come
yours flung into the air, red fireworks.
Are fish ever red?
Like on the Naropa lawn a few years ago . . .
You danced sexual
across the movie screen and out of it into the audience. The people in the
audience all started to romp
dancing, playing drums, and chant, then swim.
Everyone in America went to see it.
Who is everyone in America I wondered
Went fishing I think
That was what it was about & polluted
Water, seas run incarnadine
& when you had spoken of the Nile you went down too
when you were a girl you told me
how you bathed in that troubled water
1962
I was not born yet upon these waves

*

*

and here's another:
(do women more often dream of seeing one another than men I wonder
& in color?)

The sun is setting behind tall skinny buildings as I am hemming some article of clothing. Our
group is sitting in an oval circle—rectangular room. Very tall building. You are watching the
sun set with reverence. You give me a look—darting from the other side of the room—that
tells me to look as well . . . with your look I know so well. I watch it—you look at the dip
behind the horizon of buildings. The horizon moves beneath my feet—cloudy vapor-lake—I
wonder if it wasn't the moon I was watching . . . set.
Switch . . .
Blake—I told you of him, remember? in tight leopard-patterned bodysuit sitting in a bathtub
with me. I want him to take it off for no reason, but also want him to leave it on because I find
it attractive.

I was effacing the authority of my own voice, Blake
I was hemming, Blake
I was serving, Blake
But I was fashioning a new kavya
I wanted to be adored
I was writing on palm leaves in my earliest center, my first dream-city
My "Alaka" where the beloved dwells
A high high abode
I became a yaksa
Moving thru space like a cloud
Then I asked him to take it
—all pretense!—the body suit!—off
Blake—off! Off! Ungarment here

The people of that time not being so wise as you young folks,
were content in their simplicity to hear an oak or
a rock, provided only it spoke the truth . . .
the truth of off! off!
The people of this time sit sullen as they denudate the earth or build useless structures

Blake as woman came and told me this in a vision: "denudate" or "build" and
    "off! off!"

burlesque
       commentary
  on
       the dystopia of
Western Civilization

(pagan rites might be needed here)
ask you to feel my pulse in your broken heart, O Blake

                                        "hot"

                                                    "fire"

★

"Who would fardels bear?"

Ambrose—
tried calling, but . . .
It's been a bit eerie on the streets of Denver with activists chanting "our streets!" in opposition
to the security at an over-the-top maximum with national police, military, and intelligence
agencies, u.s. Coast Guard, North American Aerospace and the Northern Command in play
(from Peterson Air Force Base in Colorado Springs) and more. Security cameras everywhere.
Illegal arrests, pepper-sprayings, baton bashings—while inside the corridors of ambition an
exhilarating historic coronation, a gathering of the "tribe" as it were, coupled with the urgent
imperative that all progressives must take part in assuring and accomplishing the election of
the Obama / Biden ticket. One thinks of John Keats's negative capability at times like these. The
"both, both" of being able to dwell in the contradictions without an "irritable reach after fact
or reason." Yet we all need our facts and our reason. And we all need to work the inside and
the outside without too much irritability. But the streets no longer seem streets, under such
fascistic Homeland Security Control—certainly not as they were in the days of Jack Kerouac
and Neal Cassady in the 1940s. Champa, Larimer, or what with the new condos / apartments
proliferating on the banks of the Platte River. Perhaps Five Points or the ballpark at 23rd and
Weldon where Kerouac describes in *On the Road* still evoke some of the old "neighborhood" of
character, of place . . . "the strange young heroes of all kinds, white, colored, Mexican, pure
Indian . . . on the field, performing with heart-breaking seriousness. Just sandlot kids in uni-
form. . . . It was the Denver Night; all I did was die!," meaning it was soul-rending, it was
poignant, had some echo of humanity, human *feeling*. Die: swoon. The racial shift is so potent,
tremendous 1940s to now. Possibly greater humanity in the current Obama atmosphere, in spite
of the police and corporate presence blatantly apparent in the AT&T & Qwest logos everywhere
(corporate sponsors of the convention) and the Lockheed Martin undercurrent. And women

have come further and Code Pink is on the front lines. Diversity in the protest, and diversity inside the convention center, and in the mile-high stadium . . . so "both, both," inside and outside. And let's watch out for voter fraud, of real concern in these Rocky Mountain parts and elsewhere. And protest the continuation of the "oil and gold barons mentality" of yore. And visualize the streets as they were, before the 16th Street Mall, and the Cherry Creek Mall, and value the literary tradition that holds these vivid particulars. Yes?

Welcome to the Anthropocene. Man is controlling all geopolitical changes rather than the earth or nature itself.

 do the election shuffle . . .
    do it in our anthropocene deathwish

unmitigated

concealed,

    our true colors

        highs and lows . . . lips moving on a quixotic screen . . . motive minds its own motives up and down anticipation ladder . . . who's winning . . . how much more to do from the desk. . . morphology all by itself before the meme tanks. Before the meme talks. Pinnipeds are descendants of bear-like ancestors 30 million years ago who turned amphibious . . . O yes, I recorded your bear dream. When you were scared. And my own account of the bear encounter up by Bald Mountain. We were moving slowly and she, when she saw me, looked up to the sky and sounded: *do no harm* . . . All love, Mom

why?

meanwhile, over in Iraq . . . over in Afghanistan. . . . over in Pakistan

where next?
    that's when we do it, at night

brown paper bags
  of torture
& death

wiped
his
mouth
away

one out of five a crippling form of PTSD

   or suicide

any pain?

   certainly

slabs & slabs of it

        a drooped code of light (body slumped over)

exultant in civvies
           wild laughter

turned on on what drug?

   area distorted by the marines

where to hide

  set teeth
to knuckles
in combat
wincing

          Lyndie brutality o ever avert

Abu Sousveillance

never again

   cold savage beatings

or

   thumbs up
a blow to the stomach

"cold savage beatings on more brown bodies . . ."

   atrocity + silence = more atrocity

link your memory to energy

    sleeping with the hungry ghost

Hungry ghost, a morphology all by itself between our realms
Hungry ghost: that dwells in consciousness, torments our desire
Sexy ghost, a performer, a demon, a gadfly
To never have enough be enough get enough
Dancing on coals
In a state of mind, bewitched, unsettled over what he thinks or she thinks,
   what they think
What the "I" thinks: hieroglyph for the hungry ghost
Unsatisfied—dancing on nails!
Jostled by waves, the real kind, that pull you under
Turbulent in a shadow realm between waking and sleep
Hungry ghost with sacrifices in the sand, hewn characters in the mind, arms
   and legs that are brisk strokes of gestures in air, in language, flailing
   about, writing with the skeletal stylus of the hungry ghost
Sleeping with the hungry ghost who writes your book
Hungry ghost: a web, a film, a trail, a latent thought set down that won't let go
The watcher watching you in your hungry ghost fabrication
Gloves off, anything can happen
Hungry ghost, the war machine, sleeping with the humming war machine
Hungry ghost that is a blur between worlds, thrumming on filaments of
   desire in a code that summons hallucination of "enemy! enemy!"

Enmity of insatiable hunger for enemy
Threads of desire constantly broken, strings plucked and snapped
The connection, the fix is in for the hungry ghost who sings in lamentation
Singing: *To be ghost and so very hungry, the fix is in, the fix is in*
Attachment, which is a ghost of yearning, watching the skies for strafing drones
Yearning for existence, *the fix is in*
Yearning for sustenance, *the fix is in*
Hungry ghosts of the Jurassic, large omnivores startling you with appetite
Hungry ghost ancient in mind, continuity of the mind of all primordial
    hungry ghosts
Ravage and ravaging, ravaged and will have ravaged and will ravage and will
    have been ravaged
Hues of glorious white light that pursue you everywhere, spotlight on desire
Then so bright or fierce you can never rest
How can we ever feed your ravenous hounds?
Or radiant colors of seductive desire, illusive beauty adorn your tattered frame
Although worn too, transient flickering
Transmigrating through many lifetimes, hungry ghost
Down & dirty on the street, shackled
Body picked over, on a street in a distant street "over there"
Other side of the hungry ghost world
People willing to die there, fighting the hungry ghost
Despots, tyrants, mercenaries, denizens of the hungry ghost world
Stars, atoms, molecules, names, family histories, all shackled
The Hooghly River right in front of you
Your rivers in lockdown
Ganges in lockdown
Yangtze in lockdown, Mississippi rising
Bending over into the river of hungry ghost
Torturer can do anything he wants to
Maybe anyone can be "bumped" or "busted"
Brown paper bags over the head: torture & death
Wipe the mouth away
Wipe the eyes away, wipe the ears away, wipe the "long ago" away
A better hand of death will guide you from this hungry ghost world
Gunned down on your own street
Code of executioner's light
Exultant the civvies turned on to torture
Wild laughter getting their kicks in the hungry ghost realm

Set teeth to knuckles
Set knuckles to knees
Set fists to bloated belly
A muzzle snaps
The lights out & they are thrashing
Thrashing: metal set to teeth
Set teeth to neck
Hungry ghost: a bloodsuckers paradise
Being sexy again in a broken world, caress the body of the hungry ghost
Chamber of greed & brutality
The ghost that will never rest is your own grasping mind
Cold savage beatings, mannerisms of the thumbs up
A code of hungry ghost is your own mind
Apprehension of the ghost, where next?
Locked doors, low light, agony going down the hallway
Agony in the hit in the stomach "or worse"
Hungry ghost links memory to energy
Atrocity, which is silence
Migrations of hungry ghosts walking toward a diminishing hope
Memory erased, women & children disappearing overnight
Hungry ghost an empty verbiage
Sons "disappeared"
Hungry ghost the seer will teach you how to be "ghosted"
Hungry ghost with generations of progeny
Wound that never heals
What perpetuates hungry ghost? coercion without flavor of love?
A culture that flees from love
Hungry ghost an emphatic disruption, a cultural intervention
Achieving power over millions on dark & bloody ground
Simonides: *create a memory system for me lest I forget*
Hungry ghost bursting out of superstitious darkness into
    Copernian heliocentricity
Hungry ghost in the half light of memory, lunar memory
Rare native grasses, bed down here, hungry ghost: rest your spectral bones
Riparian habitat: bed down, rest by water: rest your salivating maw
Shadows resting now in the charnel ground of hungry ghost
Preble's jumping mice, coyotes, badgers, coming alive at the toxic nuclear plant
Swirl of ravens, and vultures hovering nearby in the mind
A line of conifers won't shelter a hungry ghost

A ligament or tendon pulls hard on the phantom bone, no shelter for hungry
    ghost
Tiny throat
Distended bloated belly
No comfort for hungry ghost
Hungry ghost, broken fracture to haunt you, hungry ghost a crypsis,
    a camouflage
Hungry ghost: psychic lockdown
Unmanifest identity without a body
An expansion of unrecognizable things
Phantom memories coiled one upon the other
Hungry ghost without purpose except growing hungrier
Oil! Oil! Oil! Oil!
All you thought in terms of progress vanishes
I awoke one night in the continuous present, we were all wired
Bent over my own body of hungry ghost
Stroked the desire of hungry ghost, stoked the fire of hungry ghost
Nothing but cinder and ashes
Imploding our planet of hungry ghost

& in your female body make an analysis of further power divisions
first: get the world image on social DNA . . . more tasks! don't tarry

                              dear Poets
                    who spoke out against injustice
                          I should put it this way
                  it's paper coinage that distances people
                        who lived through the Depression
                      autonomy . . . nimbus . . . notorious
          without desire or hostility for Japanese-twin-star-time,
                                or monogamous time,
            or the red-and-white-and-blue-of-the-other time
                        in my fantasy lifetime, cowgirl lifetime
                      anachronistic life the way I feel that
                        anger without desire as if a desert
                              with red rocks is apt. Time?
                        The black sheep—Victorian—
              who traveled to Japan, Burma, this kind of time
                  how much of war is many nouns ahead

with your thunderbolt time, rebel-mortar-time
hurled at the cops at the airport
weapons of construction, seduction, terror
I'm "in" like that at any time luminous
O dear Poets, or is J. M. Turner simply resting on his boards . . .?

. . . . the fix is in

*

seeds under the ear

dead
are ciphers, no com-
fort in power no brown
shaded with sprigs of olive mid-
east now
no.

*

not without struggle does progression come

Coles County, Illinois
nearby
tall
grass
prairies
beech maple forests
nearby the Embarras & Wabash Rivers

all natives expelled by law after the Black Hawk War

Abe Lincoln's father used to farm on Goosenest Prairie

& Abe himself (a log cabin preserved nearby) argued
in Cole Country Courthouse in Lincoln-Douglas debates
for return of runaway slaves

Abe Lincoln, young railroad lawyer, coming-into-power of his mind, an
    ethos
        then shift

    Obama

  in the lineage   like we say

  while nearby in contemporaneous time launches Kepler
(in honor of he who studied planetary motion)

whose 95-megapixel camera holds
      42 light-sensitive
modules

      largest camera NASA
has flown in space . . .

        & will orbit around the sun 3 and a half years

        hunt for planets measuring
tiny drops in a star's brightness
as a planet passes in front of it
   what civilization so large & strange (Cahokia Mounds)
       transits
lens on a patch of sky   20 moons wide
in the constellations Cygnus & Lyra
search the shadow of planets
     another Woodhenge?

   discover
(breathe in/breathe out)

  humus

not E.T. we're lookin' for, but it's E.T.'s home . . .

distant earths
    separating science & politics

        in the stem cell

shadows drop into daylight savings

in a ceremony 11:45 a.m. Eastern time Monday
   in the stem of his agenda
        pale blue dots orbit other suns

as embryonic cells morph into any cell in the body

    tissues beyond a slippery moral slope

"tiny human beings with souls" you think?

                              there
                              are
                              no
                              righteous
                              wars

                        bipartisano

industrious president in the laboratory

                        my midnight oil . . .

Charleston, Illinois—Cahokia Mounds near St. Louis—

                        & how we behaved:

Announcement call—recognition and contact

                        rattling notes
                suggests woodpecker tapping

corvus call: anthropomorphism / sound spectrographs

> stress
> fear
> anger
> perplexity
> tenderness

rage
terror   ➜ harsh and loud
> frustration
> mob the predator
> opposing impulses
> advertising calls of unpaired or widowed
> individuals

> high-intensity food begging calls

war protest social contact calls—discordant

> hawk-alarm calls

> harsh guttural grating sounds

subsong or whisper song of other passerines

> bird perched alone
> flying alone
> we separated out
> it was necessary

> no territorial junction

> medley of calls—vocal mimicry
> frequently corvus song is rather quiet
> sotto voce

> calls in appeasing contexts
> (??) food

begging food at low intensity ➔ soft and tender in pitch

"tchak"
T'yak
K'yow ➔ contact call
Tchak-ak

Kia—mood to fly away—migration
Kiaw—homeward-flying mood

flying jackdaws
long drawn "kraare"
"chaairr"

prefaced or followed by a burst of variously modulated tchak-ak notes
bird glides or swoops on downward-held wings

predators is harsh "kaaarr"

food offering—muffled tchak

"zik" nest call
"yip" or "yep" defensive
begging call—nagging "kyaay"
& welcome to the anthropocene

An overdue Statement on Relationship: Computers qua Creativity

My work comes by necessity from an urgency not to dissociate technique
from insight. I feel danger in the play of . . . upon words. It is an indication of
not caring (one is comforted by meaninglessness).

Not to elevate the cause of meaning but to focus instead on practice: what it
means to say something.

If just for a moment the writer allows herself to rest between self and word.

In relation to computers it is relevant to find a way to slow down into writing. One could at a certain moment reflect on the currency of words: bare the weight of the solitude from which language begins.

My method has been to make words harder to come by. Harder to swallow. Admit to the vanity of claiming experience as art.

O dear Anne, am unsure what to make of angel as "witness." Cheetham quotes Corbin saying "the Self [as] the heavenly counterpart of a pair or a syzygy made up of a fallen angel, or an angel appointed to govern a body, and of an angel retaining his abode in heaven . . . this syzygy individualizes the Holy Spirit into an individual Spirit, who is the celestial paredros of the human being, its guardian angel, guide, companion, helper and savior." Cheetham defines "fravati" as heavenly spirit, a term that I find to be a shredding cloud. I think of soul as the power that animates imagination. Angels perhaps shaped like windmill slats gone off "on their own," then regrouped in assemblies Wifredo Lam envisioned as Personages, or presences whose total make-up is "beyond." May this "beyond," this "on their own," be calculated? Are these masks puppets on the strings of an angel puppeteer? Do I find resonance in all the layers of the Angel of the Face?

The hardening of the Christianity arteries. The Mazdean vision now lost to the unconsciousness of the Iranian ayatollahs.

The poet can have no system overseer, no third eye at the peak of a pyramid—like a searchlight onto his psychic sleights—his stare weighed stairway descends through a Self-assembled sylphwork of anti-saviorial defiance.

Returning to your letter: I don't have the word "anthropocene" in my vocabulary. How do you understand it? Does it mean something like the world as determined by man? If so, I think you are stuck with the Upper Paleolithic as your base, or back wall, and the initial divisions between nature and culture. Love, C.

perhaps   *

The relationship between computers and creativity is simply a relationship between making and making it up. My concern is that we place some importance on recognizing that we make decisions as we write. The means by which we choose to execute the decisions is what follows. Anything could follow.

Anne—
First I send my love.

Next, I have not emailed because I started chemo and radiation and this microwaved metabolism interferes with clarity of purpose.

I finished the Sonoran thangka and broke two wine glasses carelessly when trying to present it. Learned mucho on Tibetan outlining, dyes, mineral paints, subtle beauty, and brushstrokes . . . elaborate jewelry of Ganesha and Vajrapani . . . black-necked cranes, the multi-headed rattlesnake. Did you know that it is near impossible to find rain in a thangka? Found one with snowing. So a desert thangka cannot be Himalayan. Also have never seen a cast shadow in a Tibetan thankga—seems to have a short lifespan in art of about 400 years.

Snow prints in Guadalupe Canyon (wadi of the wolf) and mind reeling to the froglets living in an elephant's footprints in the mud on the trail to Mt. Kenya to Nanao Sakaki walking Japan (right after the war) bare-footed unable to avoid froglets on a trail I believe in the Imanishi Mountains and that happening to me on Isle Royale portaging a canoe and looking for the famous island wolves. Nanao, tracks, post-tadpole froglets, wolf calls—all mixed in grief and odd calm acknowledgment of the inevitable.

I cannot be outside as much with the chemo and so today's walk up Tank Creek to the Spring of Contention after a beautiful snow in the oak-juniper woodlands—a special re-walk of a walk taken many times. In the cave with the spring, surprised to find the water warm, geothermal as they say, remnant caldera, the splash of the winter frog, not hibernating, but loving the hot tub and the steam rose among the brush branches turning white frozen flakes to translucent rime. The worst of cancer and pills is it occupies so many slots in the dreamer's parking lot. You yearn for an opening for a new vehicle,

Miss you. Hope all is well, P.

So while they are saying "exotic derivatives" and I don't gather that . . . inasmuch as exotic is for me the animal . . . And there's notion of feeding off of something . . . could be unhealthy, dangerous. . . . while she the animal is just the opposite, elusive, darts away,
fast fish . . . or horse first, then . . . something that wings its way . . .

but I digress . . .
. . . I know *I* am a derivative. And of them . . . I know . . . derivative of them . . . the various animal . . . come up from the water . . . summon you . . .

They had her one of our extraordinary humans, at the end when asked about
the future she said "hybrid" . . . or "anthropocene"

it is recorded, saying, to be accurate, she said "morphopocene"
she said
"for the record"
and
"one world at a time"

they say she was one to walk a lot . . . studying . . .

The Ecocene, you know this—gentle reader—or informed stranger . . . when
the prosimians divided from the anthropoids, well, that was a telling time.
And if they can find a 47-million-year-old animal ancestor, then we are in seri-
ous revision. Once I wanted an age that was a climate of ideas . . .

I got them then. ideas . . . i walked . . . i rode . . . i stood around . . . i migrated
. . . i grew fins . . . i swam . . . i wasn't so lonely . . . moving to a place . . .
                     outside the hungry ghost world . . .

CODA

BEIRUT

dove sta memoria

She didn't want to close it down, resistant to pressure of "finish book, finish book" maintenance of identity. Extra-judicial. Eye on the Swat Valley. On Khawazakhela. Was she a woman outstanding in her piety? Sum pius Anna. Mindful of her duties. To carry the family out of a burning city. To take her armor off, finally, to thrust the sword into the heart of her own ego. Morph to many-eyed Argus rescoping the patriarch. His continuing betrayal and lies. What next? Of Egpyt, of Somalia, of Yemen, of Tunisia sing. . . . And then she observed women too, ugly in their machinations, coming to power in an imposter wrath. Do you know them by their gender? Do you know them by their troubled racist wrath? This is a regressive time. And the child-spirit is older now. Better to unplug, like they say. Fly to foreign lands like a bird or stay home rubbing myself with oil, feathers stuck in sympathy, in death throe. Creatures caught writhing in oil. Quick images of many years swarm back, all protest, all effort, a shuffle of cards, illusion's tricks, blink of an eye in a forest of Old River, Old Time, on a mountain with the archaic personages of mythopoesis, those who helped you, stayed guardian. Travels of the nocturnae. Old feminist shamans and bonpo tantrikas, keepers of the calendar, the left-hand path ones. Magicians inside kept psyche free of thrum, distraction, unrequited desire, projects she most loves shifting to an unnatural theism as people go ballistic, get greedier, drink blood, need to parlay their requisite fear all over town. Traumas of war and money and power, contested sites, of those you don't recognize push and threaten to crush your poet-spirit, abscond with your language. Merchants of nuclear death who taint you with "Hagazussa, Hagazussa! You fall on deaf ears here!" Fight for magic now; that is the only passion, magic of consociational time, of tendrel, the dharma's "auspicious coincidence," strike of the gong, set the psyche aspin once more in this or any other galaxy. And here a crystal mirror in which you see your own pupils upside down, or recede back down the spiral from now this instant, back, body back, semen back, back ovum many millennia back, what forms in poet-language pulled to consciousness make power here . . . and take a leap in time. Up the spiral spine again, again . . .

    & other consciousness, a continuum
ogni pensiero vo . . .

     all thoughts
go flying
        to another side
of my person

Avalokitesvara

    I live because I never forget I will die

Anne sweeping the clouds more gently now.
Avalokitesvara, teach me to sweep the clouds more gently again now
I'll arise from your tears and sweep, sweep . . .
and continue

Dear Anne, this is Etel: we are in Beirut, a sauna. A city with highrises and the old narrow streets, a suffocation being built . . . so many dingy nightclubs, cafés, eateries, and so on very vibrant, though, full of brilliant young people spending time asking questions such as do I stay do I leave and in fact living in airplanes, and the mountains, very close, still livable, and luxury hotels, Gulf Arabs buying 10,000 square feet apartments that they leave empty most of the time, the thousand and one nights with iPods—poor and trapped prostitutes—political flimsy schemes—and for them still real fun . . . so many young talents mostly in video, short films, poets falling behind the excitement but keeping on their faith—painters appallingly bad—and so on. The laboratory for things to come. Maybe the closest thing to America—incredibly, is Beirut. It should collapse but it doesn't. Let's hope that there's in fact some hope. Believe me, the thing that means most really most is love—passion love or friendship, the getting together of a few people a few times for a few hours and it does make of living a wonderful thing. Last night we were by the sea in a dingy garden café, the only one left of its sort, with some 10 people, from very young to me, in age, actors, artists and so, some newly met, and it was so beautiful to see everyone doing his/her best to make some art, some money, some theater . . . and trying to matter in this huge blind world. I really deeply wish you were with us. You would have been immediately integrated, understood, happy. That's one more reason why I miss you. stay in touch. Love E.

& I saw them then & I saw through them then . . . .
as I morphed further slithering into runnels of the snake tributaries of the snake-realm . . . a bardo of many encounters I would tell you of as my thoughts took off . . . I would see a thought of aid to give . . . or love to give of empathy to give reflected in the quick dart or hiss of a snake underfoot . . .

I was walking a lot then, to find my tread find my thread as samsara whipped in cycles under my feet . . . and the earth turned in cycles under my feet . . .

. . . and I climbed the hill out by Devil's Thumb . . . it was dusk . . . a slight shift
in the air . . . autumn coming on . . . her sweet rattle in the crux of the tree,
she coiled in the crux of the tree, a large *chh chh chh chh* stacatto rattle and dance
. . . the fangs flicking out toward me, gaze of the snake sears the eye . . .

I sang to her, to calm her not snag her, she the snake of my time . . . lokapala
of this pace, *chhh chh chhh*
                              I sang OM TARA TUTTH TARA TARA TURE SOHA
                                     to calm her
may I pass by, may I continue to climb . . .

Chhh chhh chhh chhh O you most beautiful of rattlers

You keep all the world aspin, not steady but in constant motion
All the world aspin in this snake of motion, sinewy language
Nor confusion, I knew my line knew my work knew my loves
I could hold these beauties in my hands and circle the funeral pyre
Spines of fish, spines of reptiles, the immaculate dolphin friend of years
Runic inscriptions on the underbellies of turtles not long for this world
The haunt of the coo of the mourning dove heard all over the world, hold this
     sound
Imitating it above my head, dancing, spinning
The wingspread of the pelican taunted now, unable to move take flight
and saw the clouds like ancient rubbings, as fossils in a dream,
white coral reflected in those clouds, as intricate as a brain feels its beating
     mind, mind thy sting!
and all the mirroring of suffering below of lives lost in gulf stream below
this was another unconscionable war
So much suffering in the tainted waters below
and the crazy women a few days ago grabbing my arm, pointing up at the sky,
     "chem clouds! chem clouds!" and I knew not of what they spake
and climbed back into my laboratory to research the difficulty of these chemi-
cal times.

And the unreconstructed & the irreparable and the maps and listings of all this.
I went back through time through all of this, a quarter century's worth of
tracking in poem-time begun as record for a child, a son to inflect this moth-
erly wisdom upon, who would inherit my melancholy cities, small towns of

retribution and desire and aspiration, a divided time, inherit cultures in colli-
sion, with prophecies of future war and decimation, of a spiritual time too
when we go underground (again) to nurse our wounds, to nourish imagina-
tion . . . and travel to other universes . . .

And out of this to archive stories of struggle and of subterranean joy and
    poetry and song
and of women coming forward to fight men taking power once again, not all
    men but
those afraid to accede who say and keep promulgating "the fix is in, the fix in in"
How do we render them inoperable, render them aslant, shift the consciousness
    from fix is in, fix is in?

Sunlight reflected on water a bright crimson/yellow shifting/glowing rapid eye
movement seed-syllables, look at myself, which is yourself, a composite of all
    these words
Where "all whens" and "all wheres" meet
It's where I started in my opening invocation not a dreamy housekeeper not
writing the modern arcadia it's where I never end beyond, way beyond, gone
way beyond a poetry of sorrows . . .

Cheer up

By last year
Echoes died around a cool red star
Gossamer wings won one another in anticipation over
knowing you a good ear if you can really listen
The realms of your much-knowing rage
The realms of your much-troubled rage—own it?
Swat Valley going down
Birthplace of dharma
No fleur or flower here
As in mystical heart-fleur
She who moves in space
A recondite one
But still a she who signifies
Always in dance or space
Weaving enough of the fabric busy as a bee
A fragile disenfranchised one

That buzz that goes on within
We could hear them calling to one another
The surviving warriors "Whoa!"
Someone runs back up the trail
"Look at me I'm shouting in the darkness!"
During the death of thirteen awakening moments
and the death of our stars and our expanding universe
Kepler celebrated Galileo's innovations in an ode
Addressing the telescope
You much-knowing telescope, more precious than any scepter

Because something could endure if not this page,
The epikos as instrument as time traveler
A hard desire to become more conscious
Because the consciousness
Would scramble to survive far under and over and above
dove s'appunta ogni ubi ed ogni quando
All we may see of ourselves in this world age
All the ashes of our destruction
The shadows our shadow-bodies cast over them
And may some still sing
Or record that sound (thermobaric bombs?)
And seed syllables under ear (listen as you hit the ground)

Song is the body
Is screech
Or
Wail for carbonized, terribly mutilated bodies
Sorrow for what
Dies
Microbes, if you are listening
Out of you a new binary loping from my Etruscan divination

Newer motion

I saw the cities
Saw other universes
Saw "points toward, points toward"

Upon this post
Wind in a still place
Last hours in a still wild place.

Pleiades Showers
As Year of the Metal Tiger morphs to Rabbit time

THE IOVIS TRILOGY

≈ Acknowledgments ≈

BOOK I: ALL IS FULL OF JOVE

Parts of this poem have appeared in the following: *American Poetry Review; American Standard; Big Rain; Big Scream; Bombay Gin; City Lights Review; Conjunctions; Exit Zero; Exquisite Corpse; High on the Walls: An Anthology Celebrating Twenty-Five Years of Poetry Readings at Morden Tower*, edited by Gordon Brown; *Human Means; Kaimana; The Little Magazine; New Directions #52; New Directions #55; Notus; Patterns/Context/Time; Scarlet; Stiletto;* and *Tyuonyi*. Excerpts have also appeared in the collection *Helping the Dreamer: New & Selected Poems 1966–1988* (Coffee House Press, 1989).

For lending words and support to this book, I thank, especially, my son, Ambrose Bye. Gratitude also to Aeschylus, the prophet Amos, Bill Bamberger, Bhartrihari (tr. Barbara Stoler Miller), Joe Brainard, Ronnie Burk, Reed Bye, Clark Coolidge, Fred Denny, Rene Depestre (tr. Anne Waldman), Douglas Dunn, C. E., Ed Foster, Clint Frakes, Gilgamesh, Red Grooms, Andy Hoffmann, Tom Kretz, James Laughlin, Lear, Dan Mage, Robert Masterson, Duncan McNaughton, Nebuchadnezzar II, Nate O., the Quran, Martin Ramstedt, Joseph Richey, Brendan Ritcheson, Jason Wahlberg, John Waldman, and Lewis Warsh.

Gratitude for help with the machines to Randy Roark, Paul Rubin, and Judy Hussie-Taylor, and appreciation of Claud Brown for collaborating on the John Cage performances.

The Sang Hyang Semara is a Balinese hermaphroditic deity, primary energy of all existence.

BOOK II: GUARDIAN & SCRIBE

Parts of this poem have appeared in the following: *American Poetry Review, Apex of the M, Bombay Gin, The Capilano Review, Chain, Chelsea, Dark Ages Clasp the Daisy Root, Hag Magazine, Prosodia, Psalm 151, Literary Renaissance, The Little Magazine, The Poetry Project Newsletter, Rain City Review, subdream, Sulfur, Talisman,* and *Trembling Ladders.* Excerpts have also appeared in the collection *Kill or Cure* (Penguin Poets, 1994) and in the anthology *Primary Trouble* (Talisman House, 1996).

Thanks to Steven Taylor for his musical composition and inscription, to William Sterling for the Latin translation and correspondence, and Sarah Harding for the

Tibetan letters. Thanks as well to Brenda Coultas, Kaitlyn Guttmann, and Judy Hussie-Taylor for their performance of "Objects of Desire."

For lending words and support to this book, I thank William S. Burroughs, Ambrose Bye, Reed Bye, Laura Deerfield, Nathaniel Dorsky, Douglas Dunn, Clint Frakes, Hao Wah Nguyen, Anselm Hollo, Jiri Josek, Joanne Kyger, Nancy Levin, Subcomandante Marcos, Bernadette Mayer, Douglas Oliver, Kristen Prevallet, Althea Schelling, John Wright, and Ts-ai Yen.

Information sources: *Neither Man nor Woman: The Hijras of India*, by Serena Nanda; *Ecstasies: Deciphering the Witches' Sabbath*, by Carlo Ginzburg; and *Breaking the Maya Code*, by Michael Coe.

BOOK III: ETERNAL WAR

Parts of this poem have appeared in the following: *Alchemical Elegy: Selected Songs and Writing* (Fast Speaking Music, 2001); *Almost Island; American Hybrid*, edited by Cole Swenson and David St. John; *The American Poet: The Journal of the Academy of American Poets; American Poetry Review; The Belladonna Elders Series #7; Big Scream; Bombay Gin; Brooklyn Rail; Ceremonies in the Gong World* (Shivastan Press, 2007); *Conjunctions; Cousin Corinne's Reminder; Dark Arcana: Afterimage or Glow* (Heaven Bone Press, 2003); *The Encyclopedia Project*, edited by Miranda Mellis and Tisa Byrant; *Fukushima, Mon Amour* (Autonomedia, 2011); *Letters to Poets*, edited by Jennifer Firestone and Dana Teen Lomax; *Matching Half* (Farfalla McMillen Parrish, 2009); *Matriot Acts* (Chax Press, 2010); *The Milk of Universal Kindness* (Fast Speaking Music, 2011); *Napalm Health Spa; The Nation; Nine Nights Meditation* (Granary Books, 2009); *The Platte Review; Red Noir* (staged at the Living Theatre, 2009-2010); *(R)evolve; Tricycle; War Crimes* (Elik Press, 2002); *Vanitas;* and *Zen Monster*. Excerpts have also appeared in the collection *In the Room of Never Grieve: New & Selected Poems 1985–2003* (Coffee House Press, 2003).

For lending words and support to this book, I thank Etel Adnan, Charles Alexander, Erik Anderson, Amiri Baraka, Ed Bowes, Tyler Burba, Jen Burka, Ambrose Bye, Reed Bye, Steve Clay, Douglas Dunn, Clayton Eshleman, Jennifer Heath, David Hinton, Jen Hofer, Andy Hoffmann, Erica Kaufman, Rachel Levitsky, Noelle Levy, Judith Malina, Susan Manchester, Alexis Myre, Akilah Oliver, Dorothy Parmalee, Martin Ramstedt, Brendan Ritchesen, Leslie Scalapino, Jürgen Schmidt, Kiki Smith, Jane Sprague, Pat Steir, Sam Wang, Peter Warshall, Bernhard Widder, the Woodland Pattern Book Center, and Katie Yates.

Additional thanks to Jürgen Schmidt for assistance with German words and phrases.

Unfathomable thanks to artist companion Ed Bowes.

Visuals were contributed by H. R. Hegnauer and Patti Smith.

Thanks to the extraordinary Anitra Budd, managing editor at Coffee House Press.

Gratitude also to Allan Kornblum and Chris Fischbach at Coffee House Press, for keeping the faith in this sprawling project—so many interesting years, working together.

⤳ Coffee House Press ⤳

THE MISSION of Coffee House Press is to publish exciting, vital, and enduring authors of our time; to delight and inspire readers; to contribute to the cultural life of our community; and to enrich our literary heritage. By building on the best traditions of publishing and the book arts, we produce books that celebrate imagination, innovation in the craft of writing, and the many authentic voices of the American experience.

VISION

LITERATURE. We will promote literature as a vital art form, helping to redefine its role in contemporary life. We will publish authors whose groundbreaking work helps shape the direction of 21st-century literature.

WRITERS. We will foster the careers of our writers by making long-term commitments to their work, allowing them to take risks in form and content.

READERS. Readers of books we publish will experience new perspectives and an expanding intellectual landscape.

PUBLISHING. We will be leaders in developing a sustainable 21st-century model of independent literary publishing, pushing the boundaries of content, form, editing, audience development, and book technologies.

VALUES

Innovation and excellence in all activities
Diversity of people, ideas, and products
Advancing literary knowledge
Community through embracing many cultures
Ethical and highly professional management and governance practices

To learn more about our books and authors, and to find information
on how to support our program, visit www.coffeehousepress.org.

Funder Acknowledgments

SPECIAL THANKS

We would like to acknowledge the following individuals for their outstanding support for *The Iovis Trilogy*. Through their generous contributions, they have helped make the publication of this book possible. For a complete list of all of those who contributed, at all levels, please visit www.coffeehousepress.org.

Bill Berkson and Connie Lewallen

Steven Clay and Julie Harrison

Andrei and Laura Codrescu

Mary Ebert and Paul Stembler

Chris Fischbach and
Katie Dublinski

Nor Hall and Roger Hale

Alex and Ada Katz

Vincent and Vivien Katz

Allan and Cinda Kornblum

Gillian McCain

Kiki Smith

Warren Woessner and Iris Freeman

OTHER DONORS

Coffee House Press is an independent nonprofit literary publisher. Our books are made possible through the generous support of grants and gifts from many foundations, corporate giving programs, state and federal support, and through donations from individuals who believe in the transformational power of literature. Coffee House Press receives major operating support from the Bush Foundation, the McKnight Foundation, and from Target. We have received project support from the National Endowment for the Arts, a federal agency. Coffee House also receives support from: three anonymous donors; Elmer L. and Eleanor J. Andersen Foundation; Allan Appel; Around Town Literary Media Guides; Patricia Beithon; Bill Berkson; the James L. and Nancy J. Bildner Foundation; the Patrick and Aimee Butler Family Foundation; the Buuck Family Foundation; Dorsey & Whitney, LLP; Fredrikson & Byron, P.A.; Sally French; Jennifer Haugh; Anselm Hollo and Jane Dalrymple-Hollo; Jeffrey Hom; Stephen and Isabel Keating; the Kenneth Koch Literary Estate; the Lenfestey Family Foundation; Ethan J. Litman; Mary McDermid; Sjur Midness and Briar Andresen; the Rehael Fund of the Minneapolis Foundation; Deborah Reynolds; Schwegman, Lundberg, Woessner, P.A.; John Sjoberg; David Smith; Mary Strand and Tom Fraser; Jeffrey Sugerman; Patricia Tilton; the Archie D. & Bertha H. Walker Foundation; Stu Wilson and Mel Barker; the Woessner Freeman Family Foundation; and many other generous individual donors.

To you and our many readers across the country,
we send our thanks for your continuing support.

ANNE WALDMAN is widely acknowledged as one of the foremost poetic, spiritual, and political voices in the United States and around the world. "The fastest, wisest woman to run with the wolves in some time" (*New York Times Book Review*), and deemed a countercultural giant by *Publishers Weekly,* she is a prominent figure of the Beat Generation and New York School. The author of over forty books, she has collaborated with visual artists, filmmakers, composers, dancers, and musicians and has had close ties with poets such as Allen Ginsberg, William Burroughs, Patti Smith, Ted Berrigan, and Eileen Myles.

In an ongoing mission to "keep the world safe for poetry," she and Allen Ginsberg founded the Jack Kerouac School of Disembodied Poetics at Naropa University, where she is a Distinguished Professor of Poetics. The recipient of a Foundation for Contemporary Performance Arts grant and winner of the Poetry Society of America's Shelley Memorial Award, she was recently elected to the Board of Chancellors for the Academy of American Poets. Waldman lives in Boulder, Colorado, and New York City while teaching and performing around the globe.